D1524409

# The Economics of Innovation

# The International Library of Critical Writings in Economics

*Series Editor:* Mark Blaug

Professor Emeritus, University of London
Consultant Professor, University of Buckingham
Visiting Professor, University of Exeter

# The Economics
# of Innovation

*Edited by*

# Christopher Freeman

*Emeritus Professor of Science Policy*
*Science Policy Research Unit*
*University of Sussex*

*Visiting Professor*
*Maastricht Economic Research Institute*
*on Innovation and Technology*
*University of Limburg*

An Elgar Reference Collection

Published by
Edward Elgar Publishing Limited
Gower House
Croft Road
Aldershot
Hants GU11 3HR
England


Edward Elgar Publishing Company
Old Post Road
Brookfield
Vermont 05036
USA



**British Library Cataloguing in Publication Data**

The Economics of innovation. - (The International library of
    Critical writings in Economics)
    1. Technological innovation. Economic aspects
    I. Freeman, Christopher, *1921*- II. Series
    338.064


ISBN 1 85278 171 8


Printed in Great Britain by Galliard (Printers) Ltd, Great Yarmouth

# Contents

# Acknowledgements

The editor and publishers wish to thank the following who have kindly given permission for the use of copyright material.

Academic Press Inc. for article: D. Mowery (1983), 'The Relationship between Intrafirm and Contractual Forms of Industrial Research in American Manufacturing, 1900-1940', *Explorations in Economic History*, **20**, 351-74.

American Economic Association for articles: P.A. David (1985), 'Clio and the Economics of QWERTY', *American Economic Review*, 75, 332-7; G. Dosi (1988), 'Sources, Procedures and Microeconomic Effects of Innovation', *Journal of Economic Literature*, **XXVI**, 1120-71.

Basil Blackwell for articles: R.R. Nelson and S.G. Winter (1974), 'Neoclassical vs Evolutionary Theories of Economic Growth: Critique and Prospectus', *Economic Journal*, December, 886-905; N. Rosenberg (1976), 'On Technological Expectations', *Economic Journal*, **86**, 523-35; E. Mansfield, M. Schwartz and S. Wagner (1981) 'Imitation Costs and Patents: An Empirical Study', *Economic Journal*, **91**, 907-18; W.B. Arthur (1989), 'Competing Technologies, Increasing Returns and Lock-In by Historical Events', *Economic Journal*, **99**, 116-31; G. Silverberg, G. Dosi and L. Orsenigo (1988), 'Innovation, Diversity and Diffusion: A Self-Organisation Model', *Economic Journal*; R. Kaplinsky (1983), 'Firm Size and Technical Change in a Dynamic Context', *Journal of Industrial Economics*, **XXXII**(1), 39-59; E. Mansfield (1985), 'How Rapidly does New Industrial Technology Leak Out?', *Journal of Industrial Economics*, **XXXIV**(2), 217-23.

Beech Tree Publishing for article: F. Kodama (1986), 'Japanese Innovation in Mechatronics Technology', *Science and Public Policy*, **13**(1), 44-51.

Butterworth Scientific Ltd for articles: J.S. Metcalfe (1981), 'Impulse and Diffusion in the Study of Technical Change', *Futures*, **13**(5), 347-59; C. Freeman (1984), 'Prometheus Unbound', *Futures*, **16**(5), 494-507.

Elsevier Science Publishers B V for articles: L.L.G. Soete (1979), 'Firm Size and Inventive Activity: The Evidence Reconsidered', *European Economic Review*, **12**, 319-40; E. von Hippel (1982), 'Appropriability of Innovation Benefit as a Predictor of the Source of Innovation', *Research Policy*, **11**(2), 95-115; K. Pavitt (1984), 'Sectoral Patterns of Technical Change: Towards a Taxonomy and a Theory', *Research Policy*, **13**(6), 343-73; M.A. Maidique and B.J. Zirger (1985), 'The New Product Learning Cycle', *Research Policy*, **14**, 299-313; D. Sahal (1985), 'Technological Guideposts and Innovation Avenues', *Research Policy*, **14**(2), 61-82; D. Teece (1986) 'Profiting from Technological Innovation: Implications for Integration, Collaboration, Licensing and Public Policy', *Research Policy*, **15**(6), 285-305; J. Fagerberg

(1987), 'A Technology Gap Approach to Why Growth Rates Differ', *Research Policy*, **16**(2-4), 87-99.

John Wiley & Sons Inc. for article: J.E. Elliott (1980), 'Marx and Schumpeter on Capitalism's Creative Destruction: A Comparative Restatement', *Quarterly Journal of Economics*, August, 45-68.

Pergamon Press plc for articles: J.M. Utterback and W.J. Abernathy (1975), 'A Dynamic Model of Process and Product Innovation', *Omega*, **3**(6), 639-56; B. Gold (1980), 'On the Adoption of Technological Innovations in Industry: Superficial Models and Complex Decision Processes', *Omega*, **8**(5), 505-16; C. Perez (1985), 'Microelectronics, Long Waves and World Structural Change: New Perspectives for Developing Countries', *World Development*, **13**(3), 441-63.

University of Chicago Press for article: S. Winter (1986), 'Comments on Arrow and on Lucas', *Journal of Business*, **59**(4) part 2, 427-34.

Westburn Publishers Limited for article: R. Rothwell and P. Gardiner (1988), 'Re-Innovation and Robust Designs: Producer and User Benefits', *Journal of Marketing Management*, **3**(3), 372-87.

Every effort has been made to trace all the copyright holders but if any have been inadvertently overlooked the publishers will be pleased to make the necessary arrangement at the first opportunity.

In addition the publishers wish to thank the Library of the London School of Economics and Political Science for their assistance in obtaining these articles.

# Summary

Interest in the economics of innovation has been growing very rapidly in the 1980s. Whereas Schumpeter stood almost alone in the first half of the century, there has been a renewed burst of empirical and theoretical analysis in the most recent period. This selection of the seminal papers published in the 1980s starts with Schumpeterian theory but goes beyond his pioneering formulations. About half of the papers were originally published in leading journals of economics but the other half were published in journals dealing with policies for science and technology as this is an area where technology and economics meet. Whereas in the 1960s most of the literature was published in the United States, in the most recent period European economists have made a major contribution. This is reflected in the selection of papers which cover all the recent major developments including evolutionary theory, strategies of firms, path dependency, diffusion of innovations and paradigm change.

# Introduction

All schools of thought in economics have always recognized the central importance of technical innovations and of organizational innovations for the competitive performance of firms and of nations and for the long-term growth of the world economy. However, in spite of this consensus, in the first half of this century the vast majority of economists devoted little or no attention to the study of technical change and were content to leave this to historians or to technologists. Schumpeter was almost alone among leading economists in placing innovation at the centre of his theoretical system from his first classic work on the *Theory of Economic Development* (1912) until his death in 1950.

In the second half of this century the climate has changed. At first in the 1950s the change was slow and almost imperceptible but it has been gathering force in the past thirty years. There are many indications of this. One example is in relation to the *diffusion* of innovations through the economic system. When he made his pioneering study of research on diffusion in the early 1960s Rogers (1962) could find only one example of empirical research by economists on the diffusion of innovations in manufacturing industry. A quarter of a century later in his paper on diffusion at the DAEST Conference in Venice he reported on the explosion of research publications in this area (Rogers, 1986). A similar story could be told in relation to the study of research and development activities within enterprises, the origins of innovations, the role of patents, the influence of innovation on competitive trade performance and on productivity growth.

In all these areas and in others too there has been an upsurge of empirical research and of more fundamental theoretical analysis. This growth of interest was clearly apparent already in the 1960s, especially in the United States, when the pioneering work of Mansfield, Nelson, Rosenberg and Scherer in particular stimulated a whole generation of post-graduate students. The Conference on the *Rate and Direction of Inventive Activity* (Nelson (ed.), 1962) convened by the National Bureau of Economic Research was a major landmark in this upsurge. But it was notable that even as late as 1971 in an earlier volume of 'Readings' on *The Economics of Technological Change* (Rosenberg (ed.), 1971) not a single paper came from an economist working outside the United States. This situation has now changed dramatically and in the 1970s and 1980s European economists have contributed substantially to the research in this field. This is now becoming increasingly true of economists from Japan and other countries too.

Because of the huge increase in publications relating to the economics of innovation the task of selection has been extremely difficult. It proved necessary to exclude certain topics almost entirely. The economics of innovation as it relates to international trade, under-development, financial institutions, agriculture, employment, regional development and project evaluations are among the important areas which receive all too little attention. Most of these topics are however the subject of other volumes in this series of 'Critical Writings'.

It was essential to concentrate attention on the 'heartland' areas of the economics of innovation in order to keep the selection within manageable proportions and to focus attention on the most significant advances both in theoretical and empirical work. Moreover because the field is moving so fast the selection has been made almost entirely from the publications of the most recent period i.e. the last dozen years or so. This has meant the exclusion of much material relating to the period, already referred to, which was published in the 1960s and early 1970s; for example, the work of Nelson on the economics of basic research; of Scherer on firm size, oligopoly and research; of Mansfield on diffusion of innovations; or of Schmookler and others on the role of 'demand-pull' and 'supply-push' in generating innovations. Fortunately this stream of early United States literature has already been amply represented in earlier anthologies on innovation (for example Rosenberg (ed.), 1971) and in major review articles (for example, Kamien and Schwartz, 1975; Kennedy and Thirlwall, 1972; Mowery and Rosenberg, 1979). However, this selection does include one major paper by Dosi which is both a recent and original synthesis of innovation theory and a summary of much of the post-war literature relating both to the origin of innovations (including the R. and D. system) and the diffusion of innovations.

The Dosi paper constitutes the whole of Part II of the book and serves also as an introduction to the main themes discussed in Parts III, IV and V. However, since it concentrates on the *micro*-economics of innovation, it is preceded by a first section devoted to the basic theme of Schumpeterian economics - the evolution of the economic system as a whole. Part III deals with the innovative behaviour of firms and with the diversity of this behaviour in various industrial sectors. Part IV deals with the selection environment confronting entrepreneurs in their efforts to launch innovations. This selection environment consists not only of markets and competitive firms but also a wider institutional framework which includes an 'appropriability regime', industrial standards and other structures which may penalize some and encourage other types of innovation. The patterns of innovation which emerge from this interaction of firm-level activities and strategies and the selection environment are the subject of the final section of the book - Part V. The wheel has then come full circle to the evolution of the macro-system discussed in Part I.

The agenda for much of the research on innovation in the late 1970s and 1980s was set out by Nelson and Winter (1977) in their seminal paper entitled 'In Search of Useful Theory of Innovation'. In this paper they pointed to certain fundamental characteristics of innovation which present a challenge to mainstream economic theory as well as to economists working on a more Schumpeterian approach. The uncertainty inevitably associated with innovation means that some of the central assumptions of neo-classical theory relating to rational profit-maximizing behaviour are untenable. Moreover, disequilibria or multiple equilibria are more characteristic of the system's evolution than the general equilibrium postulated in mainstream theory.

This fundamental challenge to orthodoxy is the subject of the five papers included in the first part of this volume. It starts with Nelson and Winter's own statement of the problem in 1974 which foreshadowed their major contribution to 'An evolutionary theory of economic change' (1982). As they are the first to acknowledge, the attempt to develop an evolutionary theory owes a great deal to Schumpeter (1942) who insisted that the first thing to understand about capitalism is that it is an 'evolutionary process'. Elliott's paper, which follows that of Nelson and Winter, compares Schumpeter's evolutionary theory with that of Marx. Although this is an exploration in the history of economic thought it is essential to a proper understanding of the fundamental issues involved in the contemporary debate. Evolutionary theory necessarily implies the restoration of *history* to a central place in economic thought. This is apparent above all in the current recognition of the crucial importance of path-dependency in the decision-making of the firm, recognized alike by leading neo-classical theorists such as Hahn (1987) and Schumpeterian economists such as Arthur (see his paper in this volume). As Elliott points out both Marx and Schumpeter were distinguished by their Herculean efforts to integrate economics with sociology and economic history.

This emphasis of evolutionary economics on the importance of history has much in common with some trends in the new institutional economics. They could both be described as attempts to interpret economics as if technical change and institutional change really mattered.

The brief paper by Winter ('Comments on Arrow and Lucas') is a small gem, which is included in order to point out the contrast between the evolutionary approach and the sustained attempts to rescue orthodox theory (described by Winter, following Blaug, as the 'Classic Defence' of the rationality-optimization paradigm). Winter highlights the growing difficulties of the advocates of the 'Classic Defence' in the face of the massive empirical evidence on the *actual* decision-making process within firms, above all in relation to innovation. They now almost all concede that the rationality theory is 'not descriptive of the actual process by which decisions are reached' and that most decisions emerge from adaptive learning processes. They have had to retreat into the increasingly esoteric realms of 'as if' theorizing – firms cannot actually make rational optimizing decisions in the real world because of uncertainty about the future but they nevertheless supposedly behave 'as if' they were managed by super-optimizing, all-knowing agents, as otherwise they would not survive. Winter, like most of the economists represented in this volume finds it hard to understand why so many economists continue their work *as if* Ecclesiastes was right and there is nothing new under the sun. Evolutionary economists take the proposition of Heraclites as self-evident: that you cannot bathe in the same river twice. 'We Heraclitean types find it difficult to understand what the Ecclesiastes types are talking about, what with the universe expanding, the continents drifting, the arms race racing, and the kids growing up.'

However, it is not sufficient in the development of any discipline for the defects of an established theory to be pointed out or its main tenets to be refuted by the empirical evidence and by theoretical arguments. It is also necessary for better models and theories to be developed. No-one would claim that the evolutionary economists have been completely successful in the 1980s in this endeavour. But they have certainly made some significant progress with the agenda set out by Nelson and Winter in 1977. They themselves set the wheels in motion and the 1980s ended with an attempt to synthesize the work of a large group of evolutionary economists in a major book (Dosi, Freeman, Nelson, Silverberg and Soete (eds), 1988). This stream of work is represented here by the two concluding papers in this section by Fagerberg on the one hand and by Silverberg, Dosi and Orsenigo on the other.

Fagerberg's paper offers a 'Technology Gap' explanation of why growth rates differ. It analyses the evidence for 25 countries for the period from 1960 to 1983 and demonstrates a close correlation between the level of economic development and the level of technological development. Finally, the paper by Silverberg *et al* describes an original evolutionary model of the diffusion of innovations, which attempts to take into account the main findings of empirical research on technological and behavioural diversity, uncertainty, learning processes and disequilibrium dynamics.

These empirical research findings are the subject of the next three sections of this volume. In their agenda-setting paper Nelson and Winter (1977) put the main emphasis on the *diversity* of innovation in various industrial sectors and within industrial firms. They pointed to the need to explain this diversity in any satisfactory theory and (an even more difficult task) to explain how ordered patterns of innovation could emerge despite this diversity and the uncertainty inevitably associated with innovation. How can structure, conformity and order emerge from this chaotic variety?

Dosi's paper in Part II, although a long one, actually condenses the results of an enormous amount of empirical research on the sources of innovation, the search procedures developed by firms in various industrial sectors, the nature of technological trajectories and paradigms, the characteristics of the 'technology accumulation' process within firms and its relationship to publicly available results of basic research, incentives to innovation including appropriability and inducement mechanisms, sectoral patterns of innovation, industrial structures, and patterns of diffusion. Most of the work which follows in Parts III, IV and V is referred to in Dosi's paper. It thus forms both an admirable summary of three decades of research findings and a useful introduction to the papers which follow.

In keeping with the historical approach which has been stressed, the first paper in Part III by Mowery deals with the early history of industrial R. and D. in the United States. The industrial R. and D. laboratory was itself an institutional innovation and its establishment and diffusion raises numerous interesting issues. Among the most important are that raised by Mowery: why did firms prefer to do their own R. and D. rather than sub-contract it to the numerous independent specialized contract research institutes and cooperative associations which were growing up in parallel with the in-house facilities? Mowery's explanation, based on the historical evidence, is that the market mechanism could not work in this area because of the unique characteristics of technology accumulation, the complementarity between research and production activities (especially of course in the case of process innovation), and the need to combine a variety of heterogeneous inputs in the innovative process.

Mowery rejects alternative explanations based on the appropriability of research results and the lack of protection afforded by research contracts. That some of these explanations may be regarded as complementary rather than alternatives is suggested by some of the later papers in this section and in Part IV. In particular the paper by Teece develops the theory of 'complementary' assets in the explanation of strategic innovative behaviour of firms. This highlights the firm-specific advantages of knowledge accummulation within firms especially in relation to production and marketing.

The paper by Gold which follows that of Teece is based on in-depth studies of the actual decision-making processes of firms in adopting innovations. It serves to re-emphasize the importance of 'bounded rationality' – the severe limitations on the capacity of firms to make ex-ante assessment of future changes in the environment, future modifications to innovations which are diffusing and the future streams of costs and benefits. The paper also provides an incisive critique of much of the earlier research on diffusion, in particular the implicit or explicit assumption in many models of an unchanging product diffusing to a stable number of potential adopters in an unchanging environment.

Both this paper and the later paper on diffusion by Metcalfe (Part IV) point to the necessity for diffusion research to take into account the *systems* aspects of innovation and the behaviour of *producers* as well as *users* of innovations. The systemic and cumulative aspects of innovation are also central features of the paper by Rothwell and Gardiner on 'Re-Innovation and Robust Designs' and the paper by Maidique and Zirger on 'The new product learning cycle'. Just as much research on diffusion in the 1960s and 1970s tended to concentrate on the individual product, so also much research on success and failure of original innovations tended to concentrate on the individual innovation project, rather than families of innovations or a stream of attempted innovations by successful (or unsuccessful) firms.

The original model for much of this research on success and failure was the SAPPHO project at the Science Policy Research Unit designed by Curnow and Freeman in the late 1960s (SPRU, 1972; Freeman, 1982) and continued by Rothwell *et. al.* during the 1970s (Rothwell *et. al.* 1974). But just as it was necessary to exclude the early work of Mansfield and his colleagues in relation to diffusion, so it was possible in this case to include only the more recent critical re-appraisal of this stream of research. The paper by Maidique and Zirger both presents such a critique and also the results of their own SIPRO project at Stanford. While using the original SAPPHO technique of paired comparisons this attempts to cover not just individual projects but a succession of attempted innovations within firms. The authors point out that this has the advantage of taking into account the cumulative learning process within firms and between firms, and in particular learning from *failure* as well as from success. Rothwell and his colleagues had already in the 1970s in the course of their own work in the SAPPHO project moved on from the study of the successful individual innovation to the study of the successful innovating firm and the paper included in this volume takes this approach one stage further by analysing the concept of 'robust designs' – projects which provide the bases for successive profitable generations of a product, 'stretching' its capacity with each 're-innovation'.

The emphasis from empirical research results on knowledge accumulation within firms as the source of innovation success was accompanied by recognition of the diversity of this learning process within different industries and sectors. Both the original SAPPHO project and its various successors were careful to stress that the results applied to particular sectors under investigation, such as chemical processes, scientific instruments or textile machinery. None were so large in scope as to make it possible to generalize about innovations across the entire economy. The paper by Maidique and Zirger is also specific to one industry – electronics – although the results are of wider significance because of the diffusion of micro-electronic technology through the entire system. However, the development of a data bank on innovations at SPRU covering a very wide range of industrial sectors made it possible for Pavitt to develop an original taxonomy of sectors in terms of their characteristic styles of innovative activities. His much-cited paper made use not only of the SPRU data bank but the cumulative results of much other research on individual sectors and firms. His paper not only synthesized the results of this research but contributed substantially to one of the main demands made by Nelson and Winter in their research agenda – the analysis and explanation of diversity in a way which would aid policy formulation. Pavitt's taxonomy points to the need for sector-specific technology policies which however must take into account the inter-sectoral flows between industries. Scherer's (1982) input-output matrix of technology flows makes essentially the same point. Pavitt distinguished three major categories of industry:

1. 'science-based', for example, electronics and chemicals
2. 'production-intensive', for example, steel, automobiles
3. 'supplier-dominated', for example, agriculture, services

As he would be the first to agree, the actual mix of industries in each category changes historically over time with the rise of new industries and the transformation or decline of old ones. It is possible, for example, that a number of service industries and even agriculture may not be so 'supplier-dominated' in terms of their innovative inputs in the 21st century as they have been in the 20th. This point is important in relation to the final paper in this section by Kodama. His analysis of 'technology fusion' was facilitated by the nature of the Japanese R. and D. statistics, which make it easier than in most other countries to analyse those R. and D. activities which cross sectoral boundaries. Diversification into new sectors appears to be particularly important in the Japanese context. As Maidique and Zirger suggest in concluding their paper this may be one of several features distinguishing a Japanese model of strategic innovation behaviour (Imai *et. al.* 1982; Freeman, 1987).

The innovations which emerge and survive in a capitalist economy are shaped of course not only by the searching, re-searching and learning activities of firms and a network of supporting scientific institutions and universities, but also by a selective environment. The interplay between the innovative efforts of firms and this environment is the subject of the papers grouped in Part IV. It is not possible for reasons of space to consider more than a few aspects of this complex environment. Those which have been chosen are however characteristic of the main thrusts of innovation research in the past quarter century. The first topic is the Schumpeterian market structure debate which has continued ever since Schumpeter (1928) first suggested that monopoly and oligopoly provided a more favourable environment to nurture innovations than small firm competition. The second related topic is the appropriation regime which has already been introduced in Part III and in particular the role of patents in this regime. The third topic has also been introduced with Gold's paper and relates to other institutional aspects of the environment on *diffusion* of innovations.

In relation to the first of these topics the papers by Soete and Kaplinsky illustrate the changing nature of the debate on market structure and innovations which has rumbled on for over half a century. In the 1960s there was a strong tendency to question the validity of the Schumpeterian hypothesis on the basis of empirical data relating mainly to patents, and to argue that in the larger firms in particular, R. and D. and inventive activity did not increase in proportion to size. Soete on the other hand claims that better and more recent data for the United States in the 1970s tended to validate the original Schumpeterian position for most industries. In the 1980s, however, the role of new small firms in making innovations was increasingly apparent in such areas as electronic instruments, CAD and software. This led a number of researchers not so much to disagree with Soete's vindication of Schumpeter but to emphasize the changing historical context. Phillips (1971) had already pointed to the contrast between the 'young' Schumpeter with his emphasis on the individual innovative entrepreneur and the 'mature' Schumpeter (1942) extolling the virtues of oligopoly and insisting that 'perfect competition is not only impossible but inferior'. But this contrast could be explained as much by changes in the external environment as by changes in Schumpeter's theory. It would be astonishing if his work has not reflected the increased concentration of industrial R. and D. in the 1920s and 1930s.

Equally, the new wave of small firm innovations in the 1970s and 1980s demands investigation and analysis. As Pavitt, Robson and Townsend (1987) have conclusively shown, this does not mean that large oligopolistic firms have been displaced as the main focus of innovative activities in advanced capitalist societies. What it does mean, as the Kaplinsky paper demonstrates, is that with the emergence of revolutionary new technologies, a wave of entirely new opportunities opens up for small firms, which are sometimes able to exploit such new opportunities more rapidly. These highly innovative small firms are a very small proportion of the total universe of small firms, but they play an exceptionally important role in the early periods of 'paradigm' change in technology. As Kaplinsky's analysis already demonstrated in the case of CAD, the processes of concentration identified by Marx and Schumpeter have not ceased to operate. The debate on innovation and market structure, therefore, points to the importance both of a long-run historical approach and to the importance of cyclical phenomena of birth, growth and maturity in relation both to technologies and industries.

Schumpeter emphasized that the dynamism of a capitalist economy was due to the profits to be made by innovators and, following Marx, he stressed the tendency for these profit margins to be eroded as a result of the diffusion process. How large their profits are, however, and how rapidly they are eroded will depend partly upon the 'appropriability' of the returns from innovation and this in turn is related to such institutional factors as the patent system, industry standards and the taxation regime as well as the costs of imitation and other barriers to entry.

Mansfield, like Rosenberg, Nelson and Winter, has been so prolific in his contributions to innovation research and has pioneered in so many fields that the problem of editing a volume such as this one is to decide what to leave out rather than what to put in. However, the two papers included here are among the more recent contributions and break entirely new ground. His work and that of his colleagues on imitation costs and patents and his later work on 'How rapidly does new industrial technology leak out?' both illuminate important aspects of the diffusion process, hitherto neglected by most empirical research. They complement the work of von Hippel and taken together these three papers and that of Teece go a long way to explaining some of the variations in innovative behaviour in different sectors of the economy recorded by Pavitt. Von Hippel's combination of theoretical reasoning with analyses of the empirical evidence on appropriability offers the basis for a general theory in this area based on the feasibility (or otherwise) of capturing significant benefit from output-embodied knowledge.

Finally, Metcalfe's paper restores the balance in diffusion research between the factors affecting the potential *adopters* and their behaviour and the hitherto relatively neglected *suppliers* of innovation. Taken together with the Mansfield and von Hippel papers we have some of the main elements of a complete diffusion theory. However, our understanding of the selective environment would still be incomplete if it did not take account of the topics discussed in the last two papers by Paul David and by Arthur. Both of these papers demonstrate that any diffusion is a path-dependent process. In general theoretical terms they show that random fluctuations may determine which of several possible alternatives is 'selected', for example, from competing technological systems. Once the selection has identified the leading candidates, there are then very powerful self-reinforcing mechanisms which serve to 'lock out' the alternatives and strengthen the position of the leading contenders. These mechanisms include scale economies of various kinds, increasing returns from learning by users and producers and their inter-action, availability of skills, components, materials and sub-systems.

Contrary to the assumptions of the 'Classical Defence' of optimizing rationality, the system which is 'selected' is not necessarily the 'best' or most efficient system. 'Events early on can lock the system into an inferior technological path'. That this is indeed the case is beautifully demonstrated by Paul David in the case of QWERTY. Other examples are the US colour TV system and FORTRAN as a programming language. Clearly, standards, whether set *de facto* by leading suppliers or *de jure* by national and international authorities can have a powerful influence on the diffusion path of any product, or process. Clearly, also, a satisfactory approach to diffusion must take into account the inter-action between competing technologies and the inter-action between the various elements of technological *systems*. As both Gold and Metcalfe have argued and as almost all the papers in Parts III and IV have shown, the study of the *individual* innovation, the diffusion of *individual* products or processes, although an essential starting point, is an inadequate basis for the understanding even of those specific innovations. They have to be located in a wider *systems* context. For this reason innovation research has moved increasingly in the 1970s and 1980s in the direction of analysing *patterns* of innovations, *trajectories* of technology and *paradigms* in the development of technological systems. This stream of research is the subject of the final set of papers in Part V.

Again the historical approach is preferred and the section is introduced by Rosenberg's paper 'On technological expectations'. It recalls Gold's analysis of the problems confronting decision-makers *ex ante* when considering whether to adopt a new process. Rosenberg argues that *expectations* about the future direction and pace of technical change play an important part in such decisions. This could lead in some cases to the paradoxical result that the expectations of a major improvement in an innovation could lead to a *delay* in the diffusion process, rather than an acceleration. Waiting may sometimes be the most sensible decision as during the diffusion process it may often happen that modifications are made which better suit the needs of specific groups of users. Rosenberg quotes numerous examples from the history of technology which confirm and illustrate these points, especially in times of radical change from one major technological system to another, as for example from steam to electric power.

Both the papers which follow – by Sahal and by Utterback and Abernathy – represent attempts to identify characteristic patterns of the evolution of technology. Sahal starts from the rejection of either exclusively demand-pull theories of technological development or of pure supply-push theories, maintaining that 'technology both shapes its socioeconomic environment and is in turn shaped by it. Neither is a sole determinant of the other, the two co-determine each other'. He stresses in particular the influence of scale and size on the evolution of technology: 'one of the most important clues to understanding the process of innovation is to be found in the web of links between the functional performance of a technology and its size and structure'. Ultimately, Sahal argues that the process of scaling up (or of miniaturization) reaches limits and that at this time radical innovations are needed to open up new 'avenues of innovation'. Some of those avenues may be so broad that they afford new opportunities in many sectors – recalling Nelson and Winter's 'generalized natural trajectories'.

Sahal's approach, like that of Metcalfe, points to the importance of cyclical phenomena in the growth of industries and technologies and to the importance of *timing* in relation to public policy. Utterback and Abernathy also stress the cyclical path of evolution of technology and their work is of particular interest in relation to the issue of *process* innovations associated with scaling up. It also indicates an important link between theories of evolution of technology and the problems of firm strategies discussed by Teece and others in Part III.

The last two papers in the book are attempts to place the whole discussion of technological trajectories, patterns of innovation, and the selection environment in the wider context of the evolution of the economic system as a whole. Thus the wheel turns full circle to the discussion in Part I on evolutionary theories of economic change. Many authors (for example, Dosi, 1982) have drawn a parallel between Kuhn's idea of 'paradigms' in the development of science and the evolution of technology. But the notion of a 'techno-economic paradigm', as put forward by Carlota Perez in her paper on micro-electronics and world structural change, has several original distinguishing features.

In the first place her concept of a change in 'techno-economic paradigm' is one of a change in the basic approach of designers, engineers and managers which is so pervasive that it affects almost all industries and sectors of the economy. Secondly, she argues that the *economic* motivation for such a change of paradigm lies not only in the availability of a cluster of radical innovations offering numerous new potential applications, but also in the *universal* and *low cost* availability of a key factor or combination of factor inputs. She suggests that this key factor was cheap *steel* from the 1880s to the 1930s, cheap *oil* from the 1930s to the 1980s, and cheap micro-electronics (chips) at the present time. Finally, she argues that before a new techno-economic paradigm can generate a new wave of world-wide economic growth, there is a period of adaptation of the socio-institutional framework, corresponding to the recession and depression phases of Schumpeter's 'long waves' of economic development. The old institutions were adapted to a now increasingly obsolete technological style. They tend to 'lock out' alternative systems. There is therefore a period of 'mis-match' between the new technology and the old framework. The need for new institutions is perhaps most obvious in relation to education and training, but if affects almost all institutions, including the capital market, standards, proprietary aspects of technology, government regulation of various sectors of the economy, industrial relations, trade union structure and so forth.

The Perez paper therefore offers a link between the cyclical theories of technological evolution advanced by Sahal, Utterback, Abernathy and others and the theories of path-dependency, structural change and 'lock-out' of alternatives put forward by Arthur, David, Dosi and others in earlier sections of the book. My own paper, which concludes this selection, is again an attempt to place the whole debate on change of paradigm in the wider historical context of the evolution of the capitalist system as a whole. It also addresses the fundamental question of the environmental hazards confronting the global economic systems and argues (perhaps over-optimistically) that it is possible to adapt the specific forms of growth to minimize these hazards. This puts the emphasis, as in the Perez papers, on the social and political choices which are made in the regulatory regime governing the use and abuse of technology. It is these choices, together with the continuing advances in fundamental science and technology which will co-determine the future rate and direction of invention and innovation.

## References

G. Dosi, (1982), 'Technological paradigms and technological trajectories', *Research Policy*, **II**(2), 147-162.

G. Dosi, D. Freeman, R. Nelson, G. Silverberg, L. Soete, (eds) (1988), *Technical Change and Economic Theory*, Pinter Publishers, London and Columbia University Press, New York.

C. Freeman, (1982), *The economics of industrial innovation*, Francis Pinter, London and MIT Press, Boston.

C. Freeman, (1987), *Technology Policy and economic performance: Lessons from Japan*, Pinter Publishers, London.

F. Hahn, (1987), *Scottish Journal of Political Economy*.

K. Imai, *et. al.* (1982), 'Managing the new product development process', Institute of Business Research, Hitotsubashi University, Tokyo.

M. Kamien, and N. Schwartz, (1975), 'Market Structure and Innovation: a Survey', *Journal of Economic Literature*, **13** (1).

C. Kennedy, and A.P. Thirlwall (1972), 'Technical Progress', in *Surveys of Applied Economics*, **1**, 115-77.

D. Mowery, and N. Rosenberg, (1979), 'The influence of market demand upon innovation', *Research Policy*, **8**, 102-53.

R.R. Nelson, (ed) (1962), *The Rate and Direction of Inventive Activity*, National Bureau of Economic Research, Princeton.

R.R. Nelson, and S.G. Winter, (1977), 'In Search of useful theory of innovation', *Research Policy*, **6**, 37-76.

R.R. Nelson, and S.G. Winter, (1982), *An evolutionary theory of economic change*, Harvard University Press, Cambridge.

A. Phillips, (1971), *Technology and Market Structure*, Lexington.

K. Pavitt, M. Robson, and J. Townsend, (1987), 'The size distribution of innovative firms in the UK; 1945 - 1983', *Journal of Industrial Economics*, **35**(3), 297-319.

E.M. Rogers, (1962), *Diffusion of Innovations*, Free Press, New York.

E.M. Rogers, (1986), Diffusion of Innovation: three decades of research, paper delivered to the DAEST (Venice) Conference, to be published in (Eds) F. Arcangeli, *et. al.*, Oxford (forthcoming).

N. Rosenberg, (ed.) (1971), *The economics of technological change*, Penguin Modern Economics Readings, Harmondsworth.

R. Rothwell, *et. al.* (1974), SAPPHO updated - Project SAPPHO, Phase 2, *Research Policy*, **3**(3), papers 258-91.

F.M. Scherer, (1982), 'Inter-industry technology flows in the US', *Research Policy*, **11**(4), papers 227-45.

J.A. Schumpeter, (1912), *The Theory of Economic Development*, Duncker und Humblot, Leipzig (English translation, Harvard University Press 1934).

J.A. Schumpeter, (1928), 'The instability of capitalism', *Economic Journal*, 361-86.

J.A. Schumpeter, (1942), *Capitalism, Socialism and Democracy*, McGraw Hill, New York.

SPRU, (1972), *Success and failure in industrial innovation*, Centre for the Study of Industrial Innovation, London.

# Part I
# Innovation and Evolutionary Models of Economic Growth and Development

# [1]

## NEOCLASSICAL *vs.* EVOLUTIONARY THEORIES OF ECONOMIC GROWTH: CRITIQUE AND PROSPECTUS[1]

THE relationship between technical change and economic growth has recently been reviewed in four major articles: by Nadiri in the *Journal of Economic Literature* (Nadiri, 1970), Pavitt for OECD (1971), Mansfield in *Science* (1972) and Kennedy and Thirlwall in the ECONOMIC JOURNAL (1972). It is our contention in this paper that there is a sharp inconsistency between the two bodies of research surveyed in these articles—the macro growth literature and the micro literature on technological change *per se*—that calls into question the basic tenets of neoclassical theory. In Section I we discuss neoclassical growth theory, and the nature of its inconsistency with the micro studies of technological change. We also consider the apparent attractiveness of the Schumpeterian alternative to neoclassical theory.

The basic elements of an evolutionary growth theory are discussed in Section II. It is proposed that this theory provides the framework for a rigorous and rich analysis of the processes of technical change and dynamic competition, encompassing several of the Schumpeterian ideas. Section III describes a particular evolutionary model and discusses some simulation results. Acceptance of the view that growth is an evolutionary, not a neoclassical, process involves a number of important changes in perspective and interpretation, and these are discussed in Section IV.

### I. ECONOMIC GROWTH THEORY: THE NEOCLASSICAL STRUCTURE AND THE SCHUMPETERIAN ALTERNATIVE

In economics (as in physics) what we refer to as a theory is more a set of basic premises—a point of view that delineates the phenomena to be explained and modes of acceptable explanation—than a set of testable propositions. The theory points to certain phenomena and key explanatory variables and mechanisms, but generally is quite flexible about the expected conclusions of empirical research, and a wide class of models is consistent with it. Inadequate or incomplete explanations or even contradictions with the data, generally are interpreted as puzzles and problems to be worked on within the broad framework proposed by the theory, rather than grounds for its rejection. Thus it clearly is a delicate business to "evaluate" a particular

[1] The authors are professors of economics at Yale University and The University of Michigan respectively. We are indebted to Carlos Diaz-Alejandro and Robert Evanson for useful comments on an earlier draft, and to the editors and two anonymous referees for comments which led to a significant improvement of the version first submitted to the ECONOMIC JOURNAL. Herbert L. Schuette figured importantly in the development of the simulation model to which we make frequent reference. Financial support for this research was provided by the Institute of Public Policy Studies at Michigan, and by the National Science Foundation under Grant GS-35659; this support is gratefully acknowledged.

theory or, even, to state precisely what the theory is, and what it is to "explain".

We take it that there is at least rough agreement among economists on what growth theory is to explain. The minimal set of phenomena to be explained are the time paths of output, input and prices. Nations have grown at various rates over time, and in given eros nations have grown at different rates. Once we disaggregate the growth experience of particular countries it is apparent that certain sectors have developed much more rapidly than others, and that the sectoral pattern of growth has varied over time. While different theories may define and delineate these central phenomena somewhat differently, and may also divide on questions of the relevance of data of other types (*e.g.* productivity differences among firms), almost all economists would agree that a satisfactory growth theory must be able to explain the above phenomena.

We also take it that most economists would agree that the following are essential elements of the neoclassical explanation. The dominant theme derives from the theory of the firm and production in a competitive industry. At any time firms are viewed as facing a set of alternatives regarding the inputs and outputs they will procure and produce. Firms choose so as to maximise profit or present value, given external conditions facing the firm. The sector is assumed to be in equilibrium in the sense that demand and supply are balanced on all relevant markets and no firm can improve its position given what other firms are doing. If we think of a "macro" economy with one sector and with no Keynesian difficulties, growth occurs in the system because over time factors of production expand in supply and production sets are augmented; in an "industry" growth model, changes in demand must be considered as well. The time paths of output, input, and prices are interpreted as the paths generated by maximising firms in a moving equilibrium driven by changes in product demand, factor supply, and technological conditions.

As a glance at the recent survey articles (or at Solow's recent (1970) volume) testifies, the theory comprises a variegated family of specific models. The empirical work generated by the theory is similarly diverse. Various neoclassical econometric models have "explained" growth reasonably well on the basis of input growth and technical change, if the criterion is a high $R^2$. Growth accounting has proceeded apace and has provided an intellectual format for enriching our understanding of the factors which have influenced growth.[1] Thus the theory has been robust in the sense that it continues to survive and to spawn a considerable amount of research which has enhanced our understanding of economic growth. This is a strong plus for neoclassical theory.

However, neoclassical explanations have run into difficulties. To a considerable degree the success of the calibration and testing work alluded to

---

[1] For a critique of the growth accounting literature, see Nelson (1973).

above has been due to the *ad hoc* flexibility of the theory. Thus in the early days of growth accounting, the "residual"—which was as large as the portion of growth explained by increases in the factors of production then considered— was simply labelled technical change, and the theory thereby preserved. We are still doing roughly the same thing when we try to explain growth by improvement in the quality of different factors (however measured) without giving an explicit account of how these quality improvements came about or explaining in a persuasive way how these factors affect growth. In our view, and that of the authors of the survey articles, research of this type has served principally to establish the need for a richer analysis of the sources and effects of technical advance and of factor quality improvements.

In fact, such an analysis is to some extent available in the body of research on technological change done by economic historians, researchers within the industrial organisation tradition, and scholars interested in invention and innovation *per se*. Studies by historians like Usher, Landes, Habakkuk, David, Temin, Rosenberg, and by students of industrial organisation and technical change like Schmookler, Jewkes, Sawers and Stillerman, MacLaurin, Peck, Griliches, Mansfield, and Freeman have revealed extremely interesting facts about the technological change process.[1] However, while some of these are in harmony with neoclassical themes, others are quite discordant. We have, for example, much evidence of the role of insight in the major invention process, and of significant differences in ability of inventors to "see things" that are not obvious to all who are looking. The same pattern apparently obtains in innovation. Relatedly, there are considerable differences among firms at any time in terms of the technology used, productivity and profitability. While these studies show clearly that purpose and calculation play an important role, the observed differences among persons and firms are hard to reconcile with simple notions of maximisation, unless some explicit account is taken of differences in knowledge, maximising capabilities, or luck. The role of competition seems better characterised in the Schumpeterian terms of competitive advantages gained through innovation, or early adoption of a new product or process, than in the equilibrium language of neoclassical theory.

The difficulties can be seen most sharply by considering the major role of the concepts of innovation and imitation in the literature on technical change referred to above, and the awkwardness of these concepts within neoclassical theory. The concept of innovation carries the connotation of something novel, and clearly is not adequately characterised in terms of an induced change in choice within a given and constant choice set. Nor does a more or less mechanical treatment of the expansion of the choice set, whether spontaneously or as a result of R and D, capture the nature of

[1] Rather than providing specific references to the illustrative sample of works, it seems appropriate to refer to the broad bibliographies in the aforementioned survey articles. See also the bibliography in R. Nelson, M. J. Peck and E. D. Kalachek (1967).

innovation, as it has been analysed in the literature not bound by neoclassical terms. Similar difficulties affect the concept of imitation. It is apparent that the fact that one firm imitates another often reflects a tacit admission that the other firm was doing a better thing. The fact that lagging firms often fail suggests the futility of dealing with this challenge to the assumptions of neoclassical theory by arguing that the lagging firm may have been optimising because it saved on R and D costs.

The problem here is more than inability of the theory, at least in simple form, to be useful to certain kinds of research, and goes beyond the fact that there are some interesting data that are difficult for the theory to digest. Research within the neoclassical theory now acknowledges the centrality of technical change in the growth process. The "indigestible" phenomena appear—the minute the neoclassical blinkers are removed—to be basic characteristics of the technical change process.

The recent survey articles do not confront this problem squarely. Nadiri sidesteps it largely by ignoring the micro literature on technological advance, despite the importance he attributes to technical change. Pavitt ignores the macro literature. Mansfield leaves the tension between the two literatures unanalysed. However, the organisation of the recent article by Kennedy and Thirlwall does make the division explicit. The analytic structure used in the first part of the survey, on the effect of technical change, is predominantly neoclassical growth theory. There is an explicit or implicit commitment to the assumptions of faultless maximisation and equilibrium. Very few of the studies of the second part of the review, concerned with the processes of technical change, employ these assumptions. Several of these studies (for example, the models of diffusion) implicitly deny them.

In another recent article appraising the state of growth theory there is sharper awareness of the problems. Nordhaus and Tobin remark:

> "The (neoclassical) theory conceals, either in aggregation or in the abstract generality of multi-sector models, all the drama of the events— the rise and fall of products, technologies, and industries, and the accompanying transformation of the spatial and occupational distributions of the population. Many economists agree with the broad outlines of Schumpeter's vision of capitalist development, which is a far cry from growth models made nowadays in either Cambridge, Mass. or Cambridge, England. But visions of that kind have yet to be transformed into theory that can be applied to everyday analytic and empirical work." (1972, p. 2.)

But much of the research within the economic history and industrial organisation traditions has been concerned with just that drama.

We would concede, of course, that recent theoretical developments have considerably broadened the scope of neoclassical theory. Various models have been proposed that explicitly dispense with the perfect information assumption. Some of these view the firm as searching for the best alternative, balancing the costs of search against the expected benefits. Models of invest-ment and employment expansion incorporate distributed lag and other adaptive behaviour structures. These developments are steps in the direction of a richer theory that can encompass some of the phenomena currently proving indigestible. However, they pose the question of what remains of the theory if they are accepted. They drastically alter the characterisation of the choice set over which the firms are supposed to maximise and raise some questions regarding the very meaning of maximisation.[1] Equilibrium tends to be preserved as a characterisation only of steady state conditions which are not assumed generally to obtain.

It seems obvious that research on economic growth within the neoclassical theory is creating new intellectual problems more rapidly than it is solving them. One can continue to search for solutions to these problems guided by the assumptions of neoclassical theory. Or, one can try a new tack.[2]

As the Nordhaus–Tobin quote remarks, it is apparent that many econo-mists studying growth are much attracted to the perspective sketched out by Schumpeter 60 years ago in Chapter 2 of his *Theory of Economic Development* (1934, original publication 1911).

The core ideas of Schumpeterian theory are of course quite different from those of neoclassical theory. For Schumpeter the most important firms are those that serve as the vehicles for action of the real drivers of the system— the innovating entrepreneurs. Firms (and entrepreneurs) may seek profit, and may innovate or imitate to achieve higher profit. However, the emphasis on careful calculation over well-defined choice sets is absent. The competi-tive environment within which firms operate is one of struggle and motion. It is a dynamic selection environment, not an equilibrium one. The essential forces of growth are innovation and selection, with augmentation of capital stocks more or less tied to these processes.

What accounts for the fact that this highly plausible interpretation has been relatively neglected in theoretical discussion? As Nordhaus and Tobin suggest, the likely explanation is that the neoclassical approach has held sway because of its apparently greater susceptibility to *formal* modelling. Fuller assimilation of the Schumpeterian contribution may be achieved if an appro-priate formal framework for it can be developed.

---

[1] In particular, there is a serious question whether it is possible to construct an internally consistent theory involving optimising actors for whom *all* information and computation is costly—as opposed to theories in which the perfect information assumption is merely shifted back a stage or two in the logic. See the discussion of this point in S. Winter (1964).

[2] The Keynesian revolution is the obvious example of a crisis in economics which led to such a "new tack". Perhaps another crisis is building now; there has occurred in the last few years a remark-able surge of authoritative grumbling about the state of the discipline, particularly in presidential addresses. See Phelps Brown (1972); Hahn (1970); Leontief (1971); Worswick (1972).

## II. Elements of an Evolutionary Theory of Economic Growth

In this section we introduce the elements of an evolutionary theory of
the behaviour of firms and economic sectors.[1] Many of the specific concepts
and orientations presented are, we believe, of broad applicability. They are
relevant not only to the problems of economic growth and technical change
but also, for example, to the dynamics of inflation and the control of monopolies. Indeed, we consider them applicable to some systems in which government bureaucracies replace business firms as key actors. However, since our
present focus is on growth, and technical change, we will present the ideas in
a manner appropriate to that area of inquiry, and draw illustrative examples
from it. In the following section, we reduce the scope of the discussion still
further. The simulation model discussed there represents a particular case
within the evolutionary theory in the same sense that a model with a Cobb-
Douglas production function, neutral technical change, exogenous labour
force growth, and savings proportional to income represents a particular
member of the class of neoclassical models.

The first major commitment of the evolutionary theory is to a "behavioural" approach to individual firms. The basic behavioural premise
is that a firm at any time operates largely according to a set of decision rules
that link a domain of environmental stimuli to a range of responses on
the part of firms. While neoclassical theory would attempt to deduce these
decision rules from maximisation on the part of the firm, the behavioural
theory simply takes them as given and observable. The plausibility of this
approach has, we think, been adequately established by previous work on the
behavioural theory of the firm.[2] For purposes of theoretical analysis, we deal
with abstract decision rules stated in the language of mathematics or a
computer programme.

The particular rules considered, and the manner of their description, will
vary from case to case depending on the purpose of the inquiry. If the focus
is on the decisions of a single large firm, the descriptions may be quite
detailed. If it is on the historical development of a sector or an entire economy,
considerations of tractability and information availability will dictate a very

---

[1] Space limitations prevent us from exploring here the parallels and divergences between our
proposal and theories of biological evolution; we also omit a full discussion of the relationship of
our work to the many previous uses of biological analogies in the economic literature. However, some
brief references to the latter are in order. A particularly influential article was Alchian's "Uncertainty,
Evolution and Economic Theory" (1950). It should be noted that Alchian comes much closer to
treating the evolutionary approach as a serious alternative theory than does Friedman in his famous
methodological essay (1953). For a critique of use of evolutionary arguments as a crutch for orthodoxy, see Winter (1964). Still more recently, M. Farrell has taken the evolutionary approach seriously
in "Some Elementary Selection Processes in Economics" (1970); his purposes are, however, somewhat narrower than our own, and he makes more direct use of the available mathematical models
in biological theory.

[2] The basic reference is Cyert and March (1963). In an interesting recent paper, Baumol and
Stewart attempt a replication of a portion of the empirical work reported in the Cyert and March
volume, with reasonably satisfactory results (1971).

simple and stylised characterisation of individual firm rules. For example, in our simulation study and in other work we have identified the "production decision rule" of the individual firm with a list of coefficients characterising the unit level of operation of a single productive technique. This treatment reflects, but in a highly stylised way, what we believe to be a fact about firm behaviour, namely, that commitments to routinised production methods are maintained for fairly long periods and adjustment to changing conditions is sporadic rather than continuous.

The assumption of short-run stability in the decision rules provides an essential element of continuity on which to base an evolutionary analysis. Firm decision rules are not immutable, however, and the processes of change are as basic to the evolutionary story as the sources of continuity. While an assumption of constancy in decision rules may be a good approximation for purposes of relatively short-range predictions, understanding of longer-term trends must be based on analysis of the mechanisms that operate to modify both the rules applied in individual firms and the relative importance of different rules in determining economic outcomes at a more aggregate level.

Prominent among the processes of rule change in the individual firm are those that involve deliberate, goal-oriented "search" or "problem-solving" activity. Such activity takes a wide variety of forms and can occur at different "levels" in a hierarchical structure of decision rules. For example, a firm's R and D policy may commit it to a certain level and pattern of search for new products and productive techniques, but also the R and D policy itself may be regarded as a decision rule subject to change by higher-order search processes. Regardless of the particular rule involved, however, a theoretical model of the search process must comprise answers to the following questions: (i) What goals of the firm are operative in the search process, and how do they affect it? (ii) What determines the intensity, direction and strategy of search activity? (iii) What is the field of search, *i.e.* the set from which possible rules are drawn, and how are the likely search outcomes distributed in it?

Our general answers to these questions do not represent irrevocable commitments; neither are they as complete as we would like. Tentatively, we adhere to the orthodox view that some form of the profit motive is the dominant motivational consideration; however, the logic of the evolutionary approach is equally consistent with a "managerialist" emphasis on growth or "the quiet life". On the question of the intensity of search, one appealing hypothesis is that search is stimulated by adversity, or by perceived "problems" or "exceptions" arising with the existing decision rules. On the other hand, it is clear that firms institutionalise at least some forms of search activity, *e.g.* in R and D or operations research programmes, and thus continue searching even when things are going well. The influences on the direction and strategy of search are obviously complex, but among the major considerations which one would certainly want to include are market prices, information concerning the decision rules of other firms (the basis for imitative behaviour), and exogenous changes in relevant knowledge. Finally, the modelling of the set of possible decision rules will be specific to the purposes of the inquiry. When the concern is with the evolution of productive technique, we may, as noted above, identify rules with vectors of technical coefficients. The set of possible rules then bears a superficial resemblance to a production set—superficial because the production set characterises *known* techniques whereas we are concerned with the set of (physically) *possible* techniques.

Evolutionary theory involves, finally, explicit analysis of the economic selection mechanism—the change in the weighting of different decision rules that comes about through the expansion of firms using profitable rules and the contraction of firms using unprofitable ones. The first step in such analysis is to delineate the set of actual and potential firms whose behaviour is to be studied; depending on the purpose of the inquiry this set may include the firms of an entire economy, of a large sector, or of a narrowly defined industry. The nature of the decision rules that determine entry or exit, expansion or contraction, must be specified. Next, the "selection environment" must be characterised. This involves specification of, at a minimum, the following: (i) the conditions of supply and demand for current inputs and outputs, (ii) the functioning of the financial and capital goods markets facing the firms of the sector. Thus, the selection environment is at once the medium through which exogenous influences (*e.g.* shifts in input supply curves) are transmitted to the firms in the sector; and the medium through which the firms of the sector influence each other (*e.g.* the expansion of one firm resulting in higher input prices to the others as well as to itself). And, of particular importance to an evolutionary analysis, the selection environment determines the way in which these influences impinge on the investment decisions of firms.

The general logic of the selection mechanism may now be described. The current decision rules of firms determine their input and output decisions, and hence, collectively, the prevailing market prices. Prices determine profitability and in conjunction with firm investment rules and capital market rules, the rates of expansion or contraction of individual firms. With the sizes of the firms thus altered, the firm decision rules yield different input and output decisions, hence different price and profitability signals, and so on. By this process, clearly, aggregate input and output and price levels for the sector would undergo dynamic change, even if search processes did not modify the individual firm decision rules.

But individual firm rules *do* change, and the phenomena of search and selection are simultaneous, interacting aspects of the evolutionary process. The same prices that provide selective feedback also influence the directions of search. Through the joint action of search and selection, the firms evolve over time, with the condition of the industry on each day bearing the seeds of its condition on the day following.

The conceptual scheme just set forth has distinct advantages over neo-classical theory as a basis for interpreting the phenomena of economic growth. First of all, it offers a natural definition of innovation—change of existing decision rules. It is far easier to make use of a term that has the connotation "new" or "novel" in a theory that explicitly relies on notions of routine behaviour than in one that presumes flexible maximising behaviour always. Secondly, and relatedly, explicit introduction of the concepts of profit-motivated search and problem-solving behaviour provides a basis for the discussion of a distinctive entrepreneurial function. By contrast, the neo-classical over-emphasis on consistent maximising behaviour by one and all renders entrepreneurship otiose (a point well made by Baumol, 1968). Thus the proposal offers a systematic framework for a Schumpeterian analysis of the competitive process. However, acceptance of the evolutionary point of view need not imply a complete loss of contact with orthodox conclusions—the equilibrium theorem of Winter (1971) shows, for example, how the two may be reconciled in the (hypothetical) long run.

### III. A SIMULATION STUDY

The theoretical structure just set forth is obviously very roomy; a large family of specific models could be established within it. As yet, we have been able to familiarise ourselves with only a few of those models, and these few are far from ideal representatives. They do not, for example, draw on specific descriptive information of firm decision processes to the extent that we consider desirable. Both the decision rules imputed to firms and the characterisa-tions of rule-change processes are extremely simple and must be considered to be in the nature of temporary expedients. In spite of these deficiencies, and the attendant danger that the flaws of the exemplars may be (wrongly) imputed to the general approach, we describe one of these primitive models here. This should serve to establish that there is at least some reasonable prospect of developing a formal counterpart for our appreciative theory.

The model we use for illustrative purposes here is described in much greater detail in another paper (Nelson, Winter and Schuette, 1973).[1] In its quantitative, empirical aspects it is based on the data employed by Solow in his classic 1957 article "Technical Change and the Aggregate Production Function" (1957); it provides an evolutionary parable as an alternative to Solow's neoclassical one. In its formal, mathematical aspects the model is a

[1] This report is available from the Institute of Public Policy Studies, The University of Michigan, Ann Arbor, Michigan 48104, USA, at a price of $1.00 per copy. A detailed documentation of the computer programme is also available at the same price. We would be happy to arrange to transfer the programme itself to anyone who wished to experiment with it and had access to appropriate equipment for doing so. Winter (1971) and Nelson (1974) contain mathematical analyses of closely related models.

Markov process in a set of "industry states"; this seems to be a highly convenient framework for evolutionary analysis and one that we are continuing to employ, although in more complex formulations, in our current work. In various aspects of its structure and operation, the model illustrates the possibility of developing precise analytical counterparts for some of the concepts introduced in the preceding section of this paper.

The model involves a number of firms, all producing the same homogeneous product by employing two factors—labour and physical capital. In a particular time period a firm is characterised by its production technique—described by a pair of input coefficients, $(a_L, a_K)$—and its capital stock, $K$. A firm's production decision rule is simply to use all its capacity to produce output, using its current technique—no slowdown or shutdown decision is allowed for. A *firm state* is a triple $(a_L, a_K, K)$, indexed by time and the identification number for a particular firm. The *industry state* at time $t$ is the (finite) list of firm states at time $t$. Given the basic behavioural assumption, aggregate output and labour demand are directly determined by the industry state. The cost of capital (required dividend payout) is taken to be exogenous and constant. The wage rate is endogenous, and is determined in each time period by reference to a labour supply curve. Thus, given these factor price determination mechanisms, the industry state also implies aggregate and firm values of profits, labour share, *etc.*

Changes in the industry state are generated by applying probabilistic transition rules, independently, to the individual firm states. Technique changes by individual firms are governed, first of all, by a satisficing mechanism. If the firm's rate of return on capital exceeds a target level, the firm retains its current technique with probability one. Otherwise a probabilistic search process generates a possible alternative technique. The probability distribution governing search outcomes is constructed in a manner that reflects the influence of "closeness" and of "imitation". The alternatives turned up are likely to be characterised by input coefficients close to those currently in use by the firm, or to be techniques that currently account for a large proportion of output by other firms in the industry. Finally, a test is applied to determine if the technique turned up by the search process is actually less costly, at the prevailing wage rate, than the one the firm currently uses. If the answer is yes, the firm changes technique.

A simpler rule governs the change in the individual firm's capital stock. The capital stock is first reduced by a random depreciation process, and then augmented by "gross profit"—defined as the excess of revenue over the sum of the wage bill and the required dividend payout. This assumption is the most direct way possible of introducing the selection mechanism into the picture. Apart from the randomness in depreciation, the growth rate of a firm is made to conform to its rate of excess return on capital. Clearly, this assumption cannot be regarded as a serious theory of the financing of aggregate investment. The model involves no personal saving, no taxation of corporate profits or personal incomes, no government surplus or deficit, and no financial intermediation. It is immune to Keynesian difficulties, since gross saving and gross investment are both equal to gross profit, firm by firm. Thus, following the dubious tradition of neoclassical growth theory, the model ignores the problems of short-run adjustment. The implicit *long-run* theory of the level of aggregate investment is that it accommodates population growth and the labour-saving bias of technical change.

The simulation model is linked to Solow's data, and to United States economic growth, in the following ways. First, the set of one hundred techniques used in the simulations was chosen, randomly, from a region that brackets the values in Solow's time series for the period 1909–49. A simulated time period corresponds to a year, and wage rates are quoted in 1929 dollars per man-hour. The model's labour supply curve shifts to the right at 1·25 % per year, a rate roughly comparable to the rate of labour force growth in the United States. The depreciation rate in the model is 0·04, and critical rate of return in the satisficing mechanism is 0·16. Initial conditions for the simulations were established by giving the firm's initial techniques in the vicinity of the 1909 aggregate input coefficient values, and capital stocks of a convenient size from a computational point of view. The labour supply curve was positioned so as to yield, at the initial level of aggregate labour demand, approximately the 1909 wage rate.

The model has a number of other features, which we will mention only in passing. There are special assumptions governing "entry", *i.e.* firms making transitions from zero to positive capital stocks. The general rate of technical change in the model is controllable by a programme parameter that determines how local the local search is, *i.e.* how tightly the search outcome distribution is concentrated around current technique. It is also possible to introduce factor-saving bias into the local search mechanism, and to alter the relative weights of imitation and local search.

In summary, then, the model comprises a number of very simple firms interacting in an equally simple selection environment. Technically advanced firms reinvest their profits and expand, thereby driving up the wage rate facing other firms. Firms with low rates of return look for better techniques, sometimes finding them and sometimes not: but since they reject technical regress in favour of the *status quo*, progress is achieved on the average. Imitation helps to keep the technical race fairly close, but at any given time there is considerable cross-sectional dispersion in factor ratios, efficiency and rates of return.

How do the quantitative results look? In a word, the answer is: plausible. In Table I the Solow data, and the results of a simulation run, are displayed side by side. There is, of course, no reason to expect agreement between the real and simulated data on a year to year basis. The simulation run necessarily reflects non-historical random influences. But more than that, and of particular importance to this comparison, the simulation model (unlike

TABLE I

*Selected Time Series from Simulation Run 0001, Compared with Solow Data, 1909–49*

| Year | $Q/L$ Sim. | $Q/L$ Solow | $K/L$ Sim. | $K/L$ Solow | $W$ Sim. | $W$ Solow | $S_K$ Sim. | $S_K$ Solow | $A$ Sim. | $A$ Solow |
|---|---|---|---|---|---|---|---|---|---|---|
| 1909 | 0·66 | 0·73 | 1·85 | 2·06 | 0·51 | 0·49 | 0·23 | 0·34 | 1·000 | 1·000 |
| 1910 | 0·68 | 0·72 | 1·84 | 2·10 | 0·54 | 0·48 | 0·21 | 0·33 | 1·020 | 0·983 |
| 1911 | 0·69 | 0·76 | 1·83 | 2·17 | 0·52 | 0·50 | 0·25 | 0·34 | 1·040 | 1·021 |
| 1912 | 0·71 | 0·76 | 1·91 | 2·21 | 0·50 | 0·51 | 0·30 | 0·33 | 1·059 | 1·023 |
| 1913 | 0·74 | 0·80 | 1·94 | 2·23 | 0·51 | 0·53 | 0·31 | 0·33 | 1·096 | 1·064 |
| 1914 | 0·72 | 0·80 | 1·86 | 2·20 | 0·61 | 0·54 | 0·15 | 0·33 | 1·087 | 1·071 |
| 1915 | 0·74 | 0·78 | 1·89 | 2·26 | 0·56 | 0·51 | 0·24 | 0·34 | 1·108 | 1·041 |
| 1916 | 0·76 | 0·82 | 1·89 | 2·34 | 0·60 | 0·53 | 0·21 | 0·36 | 1·136 | 1·076 |
| 1917 | 0·78 | 0·80 | 1·93 | 2·21 | 0·59 | 0·50 | 0·23 | 0·37 | 1·159 | 1·065 |
| 1918 | 0·78 | 0·85 | 1·90 | 2·22 | 0·62 | 0·56 | 0·21 | 0·34 | 1·169 | 1·142 |
| 1919 | 0·80 | 0·90 | 1·96 | 2·47 | 0·57 | 0·58 | 0·29 | 0·35 | 1·190 | 1·157 |
| 1920 | 0·80 | 0·84 | 1·94 | 2·58 | 0·64 | 0·58 | 0·19 | 0·32 | 1·192 | 1·069 |
| 1921 | 0·81 | 0·90 | 2·00 | 2·55 | 0·61 | 0·57 | 0·25 | 0·37 | 1·208 | 1·146 |
| 1922 | 0·83 | 0·92 | 2·02 | 2·49 | 0·65 | 0·61 | 0·21 | 0·34 | 1·225 | 1·183 |
| 1923 | 0·83 | 0·95 | 1·97 | 2·61 | 0·70 | 0·63 | 0·17 | 0·34 | 1·243 | 1·196 |
| 1924 | 0·86 | 0·98 | 2·06 | 2·74 | 0·64 | 0·66 | 0·26 | 0·33 | 1·274 | 1·215 |
| 1925 | 0·89 | 1·02 | 2·19 | 2·81 | 0·59 | 0·68 | 0·33 | 0·34 | 1·293 | 1·254 |
| 1926 | 0·87 | 1·02 | 2·07 | 2·87 | 0·74 | 0·68 | 0·15 | 0·33 | 1·288 | 1·241 |
| 1927 | 0·90 | 1·02 | 2·16 | 2·93 | 0·67 | 0·69 | 0·25 | 0·32 | 1·324 | 1·235 |
| 1928 | 0·91 | 1·02 | 2·18 | 3·02 | 0·70 | 0·68 | 0·23 | 0·34 | 1·336 | 1·226 |
| 1929 | 0·94 | 1·05 | 2·27 | 3·06 | 0·68 | 0·70 | 0·28 | 0·33 | 1·370 | 1·251 |
| 1930 | 0·98 | 1·03 | 2·47 | 3·30 | 0·62 | 0·67 | 0·37 | 0·35 | 1·394 | 1·197 |
| 1931 | 0·99 | 1·06 | 2·46 | 3·33 | 0·70 | 0·71 | 0·29 | 0·33 | 1·408 | 1·226 |
| 1932 | 1·02 | 1·03 | 2·57 | 3·28 | 0·69 | 0·62 | 0·32 | 0·40 | 1·435 | 1·198 |
| 1933 | 1·02 | 1·02 | 2·46 | 3·10 | 0·85 | 0·65 | 0·16 | 0·36 | 1·452 | 1·211 |
| 1934 | 1·04 | 1·08 | 2·45 | 3·00 | 0·85 | 0·70 | 0·19 | 0·36 | 1·488 | 1·298 |
| 1935 | 1·05 | 1·10 | 2·44 | 2·87 | 0·87 | 0·72 | 0·17 | 0·35 | 1·500 | 1·349 |
| 1936 | 1·06 | 1·15 | 2·51 | 2·72 | 0·82 | 0·74 | 0·22 | 0·36 | 1·499 | 1·429 |
| 1937 | 1·06 | 1·14 | 2·55 | 2·71 | 0·83 | 0·75 | 0·22 | 0·34 | 1·500 | 1·415 |
| 1938 | 1·11 | 1·17 | 2·74 | 2·78 | 0·76 | 0·78 | 0·32 | 0·33 | 1·543 | 1·445 |
| 1939 | 1·10 | 1·21 | 2·66 | 2·66 | 0·88 | 0·79 | 0·20 | 0·35 | 1·540 | 1·514 |
| 1940 | 1·13 | 1·27 | 2·75 | 2·63 | 0·84 | 0·82 | 0·25 | 0·36 | 1·576 | 1·590 |
| 1941 | 1·16 | 1·31 | 2·77 | 2·58 | 0·90 | 0·82 | 0·23 | 0·38 | 1·618 | 1·660 |
| 1942 | 1·18 | 1·33 | 2·78 | 2·64 | 0·95 | 0·86 | 0·20 | 0·36 | 1·641 | 1·665 |
| 1943 | 1·19 | 1·38 | 2·79 | 2·62 | 0·93 | 0·91 | 0·22 | 0·34 | 1·652 | 1·733 |
| 1944 | 1·20 | 1·48 | 2·80 | 2·63 | 0·97 | 0·99 | 0·20 | 0·33 | 1·672 | 1·856 |
| 1945 | 1·21 | 1·52 | 2·82 | 2·66 | 0·97 | 1·04 | 0·20 | 0·31 | 1·683 | 1·895 |
| 1946 | 1·23 | 1·42 | 2·88 | 2·50 | 0·96 | 0·98 | 0·22 | 0·31 | 1·694 | 1·812 |
| 1947 | 1·23 | 1·40 | 2·89 | 2·50 | 0·98 | 0·94 | 0·21 | 0·33 | 1·701 | 1·781 |
| 1948 | 1·23 | 1·43 | 2·87 | 2·55 | 1·01 | 0·96 | 0·18 | 0·33 | 1·698 | 1·809 |
| 1949 | 1·23 | 1·49 | 2·82 | 2·70 | 1·04 | 1·01 | 0·15 | 0·33 | 1·703 | 1·852 |

$Q/L$   Output (1929 dollars per man-hour; Solow data adjusted from 1939 to 1929 dollars by multiplying by 1·171 = ratio of implicit price deflators for GNP).

$K/L$   Capital (1929 dollars per man-hour).

$W$   Wage rate (1929 dollars per man-hour; Solow data adjusted from 1939 to 1929 dollars).

$S_K$   Capital share (= 1 — labour share).

$A$   Solow technology index. (Recalculation on the basis of figures in other columns will not check exactly, because of rounding of those figures. Solow figures shown for 1944–49 are correct; the values originally published were in error.)

Solow's analysis) generates its own input history on the basis of very simple assumptions about behaviour and institutional structure. The period in question involved episodes of depression and war, and while these episodes might be considered as historical random events, the simulation model is not prepared to deal with them realistically. The same trend in the labour force, the same Say's Law assumption, the same link of investment to retained earnings, persists year by year. Since the model's historical accuracy is so sharply limited by these considerations we have not attempted to locate parameter settings that would, in any sense, maximise similarity to the real time series. For example, it would have been easy to assure better match of initial conditions. A less obvious case is this. In the run shown we assumed no factor-saving bias in the search process and a "required dividend" of 2 % of capital; for reasons we shall discuss shortly, it seems likely that we could have matched better certain aspects of the real data if we had modified these assumptions somewhat. Thus, the history generated by the simulation model reflects the workings of long-run mechanisms built into the model, without any contact with the reality of particular years, and with simplifying assumptions that in any case would preclude mimicking reality in detail. Comparisons of actual and simulated data must therefore focus on general patterns.

So considered, the simulation is quite succesful. The historically observed trends in the output–labour ratio, capital–labour ratio and the wage rate are all visible in the simulated data; as in the historical data the movements are far from monotone. The column headed A in the table shows the Solow-type index of technology, computed data on the neoclassical hypotheses of constant returns to scale, marginal productivity pricing, and Hicks-neutral technical change.[1] The simulated average rate of change in this measure is about the same as in the Solow data (indicating, essentially, that we have chosen an appropriate value for our localness-of-search parameter). It is interesting to note, however, that our relatively "chaotic" world of simple-minded firms generates somewhat *smoother* technical progress than Solow found in the real data for the United States. For example, our series shows only five instances of negative technical progress, whereas Solow's series shows eleven—and the run shown is typical in this respect.

Pursuing further the neoclassical analysis of our simulated data, we have estimated production functions from the aggregate time series produced by the simulation model. The fits are typically excellent, with $R^2$ usually exceeding 0·99; the parameter estimates are typically, though not consistently, satisfactory. When a Cobb-Douglas function is fitted to the Table I data[2] by regressing log $Q$ on log $K$, log $L$ and $T$(ime), it yields an $R^2$ of 0·999 and the three coefficients are respectively, 0·34, 0·65, and 0·012. If this is the sort

[1] The $A$ values shown are the rounded results of computations involving more decimal places than are displayed in Table I. Hence an attempt to replicate the calculation using the data shown will lead to $A$ values slightly different from those shown.

[2] The data used in the regression were more exact than those shown.

of result that represents "success" for neoclassical theory, then the world clearly does not have to be very neoclassical for such success to occur.

Perhaps the most noticeable discrepancy between Table I and the historical data is that our series for non-wage income $(s_K)$ runs lower and is more volatile than the historical series; also, the capital–labour ratio grows somewhat too fast. Both the $s_K$ problem and the $K/L$ problem are a reflection of the fact that our required dividend rate of 2 % is too low. This diagnosis is confirmed by our other experiments with the model. However, it is still not clear whether, without assuming labour-saving bias in local search, one can generate both a plausible share series and plausible behaviour of the capital–labour ratio in the same run (see Nelson, Winter and Schuette (1973) for more extensive discussion).

The excessive volatility of the capital share series is quite typical of our experimental results. In part, this is probably an artifact—though it is not clear whether the most important artifacts are in our simulations or in the firm accounting procedures and statistical estimation methods that underlie the "real" data. We conjecture, however, that much of the volatility problem may be traceable to one highly unrealistic assumption of the model: the labour market always clears. If it did not, period-to-period changes in the demand for labour would be reflected more in the unemployment rate and less in the wage rate; very likely the result would be smaller fluctuation in the non-wage share. To explore this conjecture properly one would have to build a model not only with a more realistic labour market, but also with more realistic treatment of aggregate demand and of short-term capacity utilisation decisions. (We do not, of course, have to apologise to neoclassicists for our failure properly to integrate these considerations into our growth model.)

## IV. Changes in Perspective

The results of the simulation study described above indicate that a model within an evolutionary theory is quite capable of generating aggregate time series with characteristics corresponding to those of economic growth in the United States. One does not have to extrapolate the performance of evolutionary theory very far beyond the present primitive level in order to conclude that neoclassical models are unlikely to be decisively superior in this area. Nor is it reasonable to dismiss the evolutionary theory on the grounds that it fails to provide a coherent explanation of these macro phenomena. Indeed, many of the familiar mechanisms have a place in the evolutionary framework, and their specific characterisation in that framework may be more persuasive to many people than the neoclassical formalisation.

Consider, for example, the empirically observed nexus of rising wage rates, rising capital intensity and increasing output per worker. Our simulation model generated data of this sort. In that model, as in the typical neoclassical one, rising wage rates move firms in a capital intensive direction.

When firms check the profitability of alternative techniques that their search processes uncover, a higher wage rate will cause certain techniques to fail the "more profitable" test that would have "passed" at a lower wage rate, and enable others to pass the test that would have failed at a lower wage rate. The former will be capital intensive relative to the latter. Thus a higher wage rate nudges firms to move in a capital-intensive direction compared with that in which they would have gone. Also, the effect of a higher wage rate is to make all technologies less profitable (assuming, as in our model, a constant cost of capital) but the cost increase is proportionately greatest for those that involve a low capital–labour ratio. Since firms with high capital–labour ratios are less adversely affected by high wage rates than those with low capital–labour ratios, capital-intensive firms will tend to expand relatively to labour intensive ones. For both of these reasons a higher wage rate will tend to increase capital-intensity relatively to what would have been obtained: and output per worker will be increased; a more capital-intensive technology cannot be more profitable than a less capital-intensive one unless output per worker is higher.

Perhaps it is the familiar sound of accounts like the foregoing that provokes a reaction we have frequently encountered, namely that our "story" is really just what sophisticated neoclassicists have believed all along. Or, alternatively, it is a neoclassical model with unusually strong assumptions concerning the costs of information and adjustment. We do not think, however, that a devout neoclassicist should insert our model into his book of acceptable scripture until he has scrutinised it very closely for signs of heresy.

Although the firms in our simulation model respond to profitability signals in making technique changes and investment decisions, they are not maximising profits in any fundamental sense. Their behaviour could be rationalised equally well (or poorly) as pursuit of the quiet life—since they relax when they are doing well, and typically make only small changes of technique when they do change—or of corporate growth—since they maximise investment subject to a payout constraint. Neither does our model portray the economy as being in equilibrium. At any given time, there exists considerable diversity in techniques used, and in realised rates of return. The observed constellations of inputs and outputs cannot be regarded as optimal in any Paretian sense—there are always better techniques not being used because they have not yet been found, and laggard firms using technologies less economic than current best practice. And, of course, there is no reason to suppose that rates of discovery and diffusion of new techniques in our model world could not be favourably influenced by policy tools.

It is our position that these differences (and others yet to be mentioned) are essential. And while we can applaud the ecumenical spirit that leads people to nod their agreement to these doctrines, such tolerance tends to deepen the mystery of where the basic neoclassical commitments are to be found.

On our reading, at least, the neoclassical interpretation of long-run productivity change is sharply different from our own. It is based on a clean distinction between "moving along" an existing production function and shifting to a new one. In the evolutionary theory, substitution of the "search and selection" metaphor for the maximisation metaphor, plus the assumption of the basic improvability of procedures, blurs the notion of a production function. In the simulation model discussed above there was no production function—only a set of physically possible activities. The production function did not emerge from that set because no assumption was made that firms used the most efficient activities. The exploration of the set was treated as an historical, incremental process in which non-market information flows among firms played a major role.

We argue—as others have before us—that the sharp "growth accounting" split made within the neoclassical paradigm is bothersome empirically and conceptually. Consider, for example, whether it is meaningful to assess the relative contribution of greater mechanisation versus new technology in increasing productivity in the textile industries during the Industrial Revolution, scale economies versus technical change in enhancing productivity in generation of electrical power, or of greater fertiliser usage versus new seed varieties in the increased yields associated with the Green Revolution.[1] In the Textile Revolution the major inventions were ways of substituting capital for labour, induced by a situation of growing labour scarcity. It could plausibly be argued that in the electric power case, various well-known physical laws implied that the larger the scale for which a plant was designed, the lower the cost per unit of output it should have. However, to exploit these latent possibilities required a considerable amount of engineering and design work, which became profitable only when the constellation of demand made large-scale units plausible. Plant biologists had long known that certain kinds of seed varieties were able to thrive with large quantities of fertilisers, and that others were not. However, until fertiliser prices fell, it was not worth while to invest significant resources in trying to find these varieties. In all of these cases patterns of demand and supply were evolving to make profitable different factor proportions or scales. But the production set was not well defined in the appropriate direction from existing practice. It had to be explored and created.[2]

---

[1] There obviously are many references on each of these developments. The ones that bring out our point most nicely are, on textile mechanisation, D. Landes (1970), on electrical power, W. Hughes (1971), on the fertiliser-seed interaction, Hayami and Ruttan (1971).

[2] We are simply elaborating here our earlier point that a theory of induced innovation blurs the distinction between moving along a production function and a "technological advance". For an earlier discussion of this point see Nelson, Peck and Kalachek (1967, Chapter 2). There is clearly some resemblance between our approach to technical change and the "technical progress function" employed by Kaldor (1957) and Kaldor–Mirrlees (1962). More generally, there is a substantial overlap between our concerns and those involved in the "Cambridge controversies". Within that area of overlap, our position seems to be closer to the English Cambridge than the American one. Nevertheless, there are pronounced differences between our complaints about the neoclassical theory and the complaints made in the English Cambridge, and even more pronounced differences in

The question of the nature of "search" processes would appear to be among the most important for those trying to understand economic growth, and the evolutionary theory has the advantage of posing the question explicitly. In the simulation model we assumed technical progress was the result strictly of the behaviour of firms in the "sector" and that discovery was relatively even over time. However, it is apparent that the invention possibilities, and search costs, for firms in particular sectors change as a result of forces exogenous to the sector. Academic and governmental research certainly changed the search prospects for firms in the electronics and drug industries, and for aircraft and seed producers. In the simulation, the "topography" of new technologies was relatively even over time. However, various studies have shown that often new opportunities open up in clusters. A basic new kind of technology becomes possible as a result often of research outside the sector. After a firm finds, develops, and adopts a version of the new technology, a follow-on round of marginal improvements becomes possible. This appears to be the pattern, for example, in petroleum refining equipment and aircraft. However, this pattern does not show up in cotton textiles, after the industrial revolution, or in automobiles, where technical advance seems to have been less discrete. The search and problem-solving orientation of an evolutionary theory naturally leads the analyst to be aware of these differences and to try somehow to explain or at least characterise them.

The perspective on the role of the "competitive environment" is also radically different in the evolutionary theory, and leads one to focus on a set of questions concerning the intertwining of competition, profit, and investment within a dynamic context.[1] Is the investment of a particular firm strictly bounded by its own current profits? Can firms borrow for expansion? Are there limits on firm size, or costs associated with the speed of expansion? Can new firms enter? How responsive are "consumers" to a better or cheaper product? How long can a firm preserve a technically based monopoly? What kind of institutional barriers or encouragements are there to imitation? The answers to these questions are fundamental to understanding the workings of the market environment. The dynamics of their treatment, like that of the nature and topology of "search", is an empirical issue within our theory.

Sectors clearly differ sharply. Consider Phillips' (1971) description of competition in the industry that produces aircraft for commercial airlines. This is a sector in which firms are able to borrow money from the outside and are not limited to their own financial resources. It also is an industry in which firms are able to expand capacity rapidly but in which it is costly and

---

the theoretical prescriptions offered. In particular, we are much more concerned about the neglect of the details of technical advance, adjustment and firm decision making. It would take us much too far afield to try to sort these issues out completely—judging by experience in the Cambridge controversies, it may be impossible to do so..

[1] Our intellectual debts to F. Knight (1921), as well as to Schumpeter (1934, 1950) should be obvious.

time-consuming to imitate another company's successful product. In this institutional regime a company that comes up with a superior product has a great advantage over its competitors. Because of the lags and costs of imitation, other firms may simply be out of luck. The selection environment here is obviously vastly different from that in agriculture. In agriculture it is very difficult for a successful firm to expand rapidly, because of the costs and complexity of purchasing particular pieces of adjacent land. Conversely, an elaborate subsidised mechanism has been established to disseminate widely among farmers information regarding the best new techniques; imitation is easy. Thus one farmer is unable to inflict serious hardship on others because of a technological advantage, and new technological departures are easy to mimic.

## V. SUMMARY AND CONCLUSIONS

We return now to our opening theme—the tension between the micro and macro literatures concerned with technical change and economic growth. It is obvious that a great deal of diversity and change is hidden by the neoclassical macro approach based on aggregation, maximisation and equilibrium. Indeed, the principal virtue of those tools is the gain in analytic tractability and logical coherence that has been obtained precisely by abstracting from all that diversity and change. No one would claim that this gain has been costless.

The question is, how high is the price? For us, the evidence is compelling on a number of points that are either denied or obscured by neoclassical orthodoxy. Firms pursue profits (and perhaps other goals), but their choice sets are not sufficiently static and well defined to make profit *maximisation* descriptively plausible. For the individual firm, technical change is an aspect of the pursuit of profits. There are significant rewards for solving problems, or for guesses made early and correctly. Corresponding penalties exist for being wrong or late. These rewards and penalties are not mere conjectural possibilities, they actually occur, and the occurence helps to shape the future course of events. This is because the firms are *not* all alike, and the situation is *not* one of moving equilibrium. The extent of the rewards and penalties, and the rates of introduction and diffusion of new techniques, depends on a complex of environmental and institutional considerations that differs sharply from sector to sector, country to country, and period to period. And the aggregates are what you get by adding up.

In short, the diversity and change that are suppressed by aggregation, maximisation and equilibrium are not the epiphenomena of technical advance. They are the central phenomena.

Still, if facing up to that diversity and change meant turning one's back on analytic tractability and logical coherence, it might be a hard choice. This, we have argued, is not the case. Theorists can work analytically with dynamic systems in which the abstract individual firms differ significantly from one another. The choice of assumptions can be informed by what is known of actual firm behaviour, the micro processes of technical change, and the characteristics of selection environments. This solves at a stroke the problem of squaring the theory with the known micro details. And if we want to discuss aggregates, we can—as in our simulation study—obtain them by adding up. An evolutionary theory is a real alternative.

RICHARD R. NELSON
SIDNEY G. WINTER

*Yale University*
*University of Michigan*
*Date of receipt of final typescript*: *July 1974.*

REFERENCES

Alchian, A. A. (1950). "Uncertainty, Evolution and Economic Theory," *Journal of Political Economy*, Vol. 58 (June).
Baumol, W. J. (1968). "Entrepreneurship in Economic Theory," *American Economic Review*, Vol. 58 (May).
—— and Stewart, M. (1971). "On the Behavioural Theory of the Firm," in R. Marris and A. Wood (eds.), *The Corporate Economy: Growth, Competition and Innovative Potential*, Cambridge: Harvard University Press.
Cyert, R. & March, J. (1963). *A Behavioural Theory of the Firm*, Prentice Hall, Inc., Englewood Cliffs, N.J.
Farrell, M. J. (1970). "Some Elementary Selection Processes in Economics," *Review of Economic Studies*, Vol. 37.
Friedman, M. (1953). "The Methodology of Positive Economics," chap. 1 in *Essays in Positive Economics*, University of Chicago Press.
Hahn, F. H. (1970). "Some Adjustment Problems," *Econometrica*, Vol. 38 (January).
Hayami, Y. & Ruttan, V. (1971). *Agricultural Development, An International Perspective*, Johns Hopkins Press, Baltimore.
Hughes, W. R. (1971). "Scale Frontiers in Electric Power", chap. 4 in W. Capron (ed.), *Technological Change in Regulated Industries*, Brookings Institution, Washington.
Ijiri, Y. & Simon, H. A. (1971). "The Relative Strength of Middle-Sized Firms and the Curvature in Firm-Size Distributions," paper presented to the Econometric Society, December.
Kaldor, N. (1957) "A Model of Economic Growth", ECONOMIC JOURNAL, Vol. 87 (December).
—— and Mirrlees, J. A. (1962). "A New Model of Economic Growth," *Review of Economic Studies*, Vol. 29 (June).
Kennedy, C. & Thirlwall, A. P. (1972). "Surveys in Applied Economics: Technical Progress," ECONOMIC JOURNAL, Vol. 82 (March).
Knight, F. (1921). *Risk, Uncertainty and Profit*, Houghton Mifflin Company, New York.
Landes, D. (1970). *The Unbound Prometheus*, Cambridge University Press.
Leontief, W. (1971). "Theoretical Assumptions and Non-observed Facts," *American Economic Review*, Vol. 61 (March).
Mansfield, E. (1972). "Contribution of R and D to Economic Growth in the United States," *Science*, Vol. 175 (February).
—— (1962). "Entry, Gilbrat's Law, Innovation, and the Growth of Firms," *American Economic Review*, Vol. 53 (December).
Meyer, J. & Kuh, E. (1957). *The Investment Decision*, Harvard University Press.
Nadiri, M. I. (1970). "Some Approaches to the Theory of Total Factor Productivity: A Survey," *Journal of Economic Literature*, Vol. 8 (December).
Nelson, R. (1972). "Issues and Suggestions for the Study of Industrial Organization in a Regime of Rapid Technical Change," in V. R. Fuchs (ed.), *Policy Issues and Research Opportunities in Industrial Organization*, National Bureau of Economic Research, New York.
—— (1973). "Recent Exercises in Growth Accounting: New Understanding or Dead End?" *American Economic Review*, Vol. 63 (June).
—— (1974). "The Effects of Factor Price Changes in an Evolutionary Model," Mimeo. (March).
—— Peck, M. and Kalachek, E. (1967). *Technology, Economic Growth and Public Policy*, Brookings Institution, Washington, D.C.

Nelson, R., Winter, S. and Schuette, H. (1973). "Technical Change in an Evolutionary Model," University of Michigan Institute of Public Policy Studies, Discussion Paper No. 45.

Nordhaus, W. and Tobin, J. (1972). "Is Growth Obsolete?" in R. Gordon (ed.), *Economic Research: Retrospect and Prospect, Economic Growth*, National Bureau of Economic Research, New York.

Pavitt, K. (1971). "Conditions of Success in Technological Innovation," OECD, Paris.

Phelps Brown, E. H. (1972). "The Underdevelopment of Economics," ECONOMIC JOURNAL, Vol. 82 (March).

Phillips, A. (1971). *Technology and Market Structure: A Study of the Aircraft Industry*, D. C. Heath and Co., Lexington, Mass.

Schumpeter, J. A. (1934). *The Theory of Economic Development*, Harvard University Press.

—— (1950). *Capitalism, Socialism and Democracy*, 3rd ed., Harper and Brothers, New York.

Solow, R. (1957). "Technical Change and the Aggregate Production Function," *Review of Economics and Statistics*, Vol. 39 (August).

—— (1970). *Growth Theory*, Oxford University Press.

Winter, S. G. (1964). "Economic 'Natural Selection' and the Theory of the Firm," *Yale Economic Essays*, Vol. 4 (Spring).

Winter, S. G. (1971). "Satisficing, Selection and the Innovating Remnant," *Quarterly Journal of Economics*, Vol. 85 (May).

Winter, S. G. (no date). "An SSIR Model of Markup Pricing" (mimeo.).

Worswick, G. D. N. (1972). "Is Progress in Economic Science Possible?" ECONOMIC JOURNAL, Vol. 82 (March).

# [2]

## MARX AND SCHUMPETER ON CAPITALISM'S CREATIVE DESTRUCTION: A COMPARATIVE RESTATEMENT*

### JOHN E. ELLIOTT

Despite well-known differences, the respective visions of capitalism's future by Marx and Schumpeter show striking and neglected similarities. This is illustrated, first, by their strong focus upon capitalism's progressive and creative properties; second, by their analyses of capitalism's dysfunctional properties; and third, by their respective analyses of the creatively destructive character of institutional and attitudinal change in advanced capitalism.

It is well-known that Schumpeter postulated an "inevitable decomposition of capitalist society" [1950, p. xiii]. "Can capitalism survive?" he asked pointedly. "No, I do not think it can" [1950, p. 61]. Capitalism's prospective demise is not perceived to emanate from "its breaking down under the weight of economic failure. . . ." Instead, "its very success undermines the social institutions which protect it, and 'inevitably' creates conditions in which it will not be able to live and which strongly point to socialism as the heir apparent" [1950, p. 61]. In short, the "paradoxical conclusion" is not the result, but the process: "capitalism is being killed by its achievements" [1950, p. xiv].

How does Schumpeter's vision of capitalism's future prospects compare and contrast with that of Marx who, by fascinating coincidence, died during the year of Schumpeter's birth (1883)? Since Schumpeter's *Capitalism, Socialism and Democracy*, greater emphasis has been placed on the contrasts than on the parallels. Popular expositions generally present a sharp dichotomy between the themes of Marxian contradiction ("capitalism cannot survive because of economic failure") and Schumpeterian paradox ("capitalism is being destroyed because of its very creative success").

No doubt there are differences between the two men, some quite striking, in ideological commitment, economic analysis, and social vision. But there are important parallels as well. A comparative restatement of these two perspectives, focusing on important similarities, is overdue. There is more "Schumpeter" in Marx's writings than

* The author would like to thank Professors Horst Betz and Richard Schenning, and two anonymous referees for helpful comments on an earlier draft on this paper.

many Marxists are willing to accept,[1] and more "Marx" in Schumpeter's analysis than even Schumpeter was willing to recognize.[2] On the specific subject of "capitalism's creative destruction," the two respective theories seem closer to each other than either is to any other prominent vision of capitalism's future. At the very least, they are much closer than has been popularly supposed. The prima facie evidence supporting this interpretation is reinforced by Marx's recently published *Grundrisse,* which also incorporates a process of creative destruction and supercession. As the present author has noted elsewhere: "Socialism is conceived and nurtured in capitalism's womb, and is its product, not merely its heir apparent. It emerges on the basis of capitalism's development and creativity as well as emanates from its conflicts and contradictions. Capitalism's very success stimulates changes which both portend and facilitate the process of movement toward socialism" [Elliott, 1978–79].

This paper compares the Marx-Schumpeter visions of capitalism's creative destruction, with emphasis on three major themes: (i) capitalism as a revolutionary economic system; (ii) capitalism's economic dysfunctioning from a creative destruction perspective; and (iii) capitalism's transformation and socialization.

## CREATIVE DESTRUCTION I: CAPITALISM AS A REVOLUTIONARY ECONOMIC SYSTEM

The "essential point to grasp" about capitalism, according to Schumpeter, is that it is an "evolutionary process," as "was long ago emphasized by Karl Marx." Capitalism is "by nature a form or method of economic change and not only never is but never can be stationary" [1950, p. 82]. This evolutionary dynamic of capitalist development has three salient characteristics: It comes from *within* the economic system and is not merely an adaptation to exogenous changes. It occurs *discontinuously* rather than smoothly. It brings *qualitative* changes or "revolutions," which fundamentally displace old equilibria and create radically new conditions. Economic development is accompanied by growth, i.e., sustained increases in national income. But

1. Schumpeter described the *Communist Manifesto* as "an account nothing short of glowing of achievements of capitalism; and even in pronouncing *pro futuro* death sentence on it, he never failed to recognize its historical necessity. This attitude, of course, *implies quite a lot of things Marx himself would have been unwilling to accept"* [1950, p. 7, italics added].

2. Schumpeter frequently cited "similarities in results" between his analysis of capitalism and that of Marx, but felt that they were "not only obliterated by a very wide difference in general outlook, but also reached by such different methods, that stressing parallelisms would be highly unsatisfactory to Marxians" [1951, p. 161].

mere quantitative growth does not constitute development per se. "Add successively as many mail coaches as you please, you will never get a railway thereby" [1961, p. 64n]. The immediate stimulus to development emanating "in the sphere of industrial and commercial life, not in the sphere of the wants of the consumers of final products," is "innovation," i.e., the new product, method of production, market, source of supply, or form of industrial organization [1961, pp. 65–66]. The innovational process "incessantly revolutionizes the economic structure *from within,* incessantly destroying the old one, incessantly creating a new one. This process of Creative Destruction is the essential fact about capitalism" [1950, p. 83].

Interestingly, Schumpeter virtually identified his own position on creative destruction *in this sense* with that of Marx. As Marx expressed it in the *Communist Manifesto,* the bourgeoisie "has played a most revolutionary role in history." Inter alia,

> It cannot exist without constantly revolutionising the instrument of production, and thereby the relations of production, and with them the whole relations of society. The need of a constantly expanding market for its product chases the bourgeoisie over the whole surface of the globe. The bourgeoisie, by the rapid improvement of all instruments of production, by the immensely facilitated means of communication, draws all nations, even the most barbarian, into civilisation. The bourgeoisie, during its rule of scarce one hundred years, has created more massive and more colossal productive forces than have all preceding generations together [Marx and Engels, 1976, pp. 487–89].

The key point of Schumpeter's commentary on these famous passages is not their description as a "panegyric upon bourgeois achievement that has no equal in economic literature" [1949, in Hamilton *et al.,* 1962, p. 354], or even his observation that "all of the achievements referred to are attributed *to the bourgeoisie alone* which is more than many thoroughly bourgeois economists would claim" [1950, p. 7n]. What is noteworthy is the strong Schumpeterian cast given to his description of Marx's analysis of capitalism's revolutionary role as

> "constant revolutionizing of production," creation that spells the obsolescence and consequent destruction of any industrial structure of production that exists at any moment: capitalism is a process, stationary capitalism would be a *contradictio in adjecto.* But this process does not simply consist in increase of capital by saving—as the classics had it. It does not consist in adding mailcoaches to the existing stock of mailcoaches, but in their elimination by railroads. Increase of physical capital is an incident in this process, but it is not its propeller [1949, in Hamilton *et al.,* 1962, p. 355].

Finally, Schumpeter concludes, "not more than that (i.e., Marx's analysis in the *Manifesto*) is implied in anything I shall say about the performance of capitalism" [1950, p. 7n].

Marx's emphasis on capitalism's creative propensities is reinforced by the *Grundrisse*. Capitalism, Marx argues in this work, destroys the old pre-capitalist economy "and constantly revolutionizes it, tearing down all the barriers which hem in the development of the forces of production, the expansion of needs, the all-sided development of production, and the exploitation and exchange of natural and mental forces" [1973, p. 410]. Capitalism's "universalizing tendency," both technologically and geographically, radically distinguishes it from all previous societies. Capitalism contains an "endless and limitless drive to go beyond its limiting barrier. Every limit appears as a barrier to be overcome" [1973, pp. 334, 408]. The extended analysis of the *Grundrisse,* combined with the earlier commentary in the *Manifesto* and the brief, but pointed, designations in *Capital* of development of technological and economic preconditions for socialism as the "historical mission" of capitalism, undergirds the conclusion that Marx's descriptions of capitalism's creatively destructive proclivities were not mere verbal fluff, but were instead a strategic component of his analytic program.

Beyond the general theme of capitalism's revolutionizing propensities are other parallels between the two. Marx, no less than Schumpeter, perceived capital accumulation to occur irregularly, in bursts, with cyclical consequences [Marx, 1906, pp. 672, 693–94]. Similarly, the perception of change as emanating from within the economic system, notably from the sphere of production rather than consumption, mentioned above as one of several prominent elements in Schumpeter's definition of economic development, is of course vintage Marx. Even their respective analyses of the process of innovation-competition-reduction of innovative profits contain similar elements.[3]

Turning from similarities to differences, it has often and appropriately been observed that Marx's discussions of capitalism's creative properties are usually accompanied by identification of its

3. "The capitalist continually tries to get the better of competition by incessantly introducing new machines, . . . producing more cheaply, and new division of labour in place of the old. . . . If, now, by a greater division of labor, by the utilisation of new machines and their improvement, by more profitable and extensive exploitation of natural forces, one capitalist [increases productivity and creates extraordinary profits], [his] *privileged position. . .* is not of long duration; other competing capitalists introduce the same machines, the same division of labor. . . . On the basis of [the] new [lower] cost of production [and associated lower prices], the same game begins again. . . . We see how in this way the mode of production and the means of production are continually transformed, revolutionised. . ." [Marx, *Wage Labor and Capital,* in Elliott, 1980, Ch. 2].

contradictory features and prognoses of its future demise.[4] This is certainly true, although whether this sharply separates the analyses of Marx and Schumpeter is open to question. for economic contradictions take on a different cast when examined from a creative destruction perspective (see the following section).

More important here than differing perspectives on capitalism's performance are alternative perceptions of its social relations. The difference is not primarily that of the classificatory schema itself, i.e., that Schumpeter writes of "entrepreneurs," while Marx writes about "capitalists." A resurrected Marx could easily agree that not all capitalists are equally adept in the exercise of the entrepreneurial-innovative function and that "a man without wealth, but with energy, solidity, ability and business sense" *may* become a capitalist, bringing "an unwelcome number of new soldiers of fortune into the field and into competition with the already existing individual capitalists," expanding capitalism's social base, and enabling it to "recruit ever new forces for itself out of the lower layers of society," thereby solidifying its rule [cited in Balinky, 1970, p. 89, italics added]. On his part, Schumpeter made it clear that successful entrepreneurs *become* capitalists (or landowners), while unsuccessful ones presumably become workers or managers [Schumpeter, 1961, pp. 78–79]. Similarly, Marxian capitalists and Schumpeterian entrepreneurs share important elements of conduct and motive. The successful Marxian capitalist, like his Schumpeterian entrepreneurial counterpart, presumably embodies a significant "will to found a private kingdom," a "will to conquer," and a "joy of creating" [Schumpeter, 1961, p. 93]. The Schumpeterian entrepreneur presumably embodies a passionate drive for enlargement of profits and power that closely rivals that of the Marxian capitalist. Certainly, *neither* is perceived as a hedonistic maximizer of utility from consumption goods.[5]

---

4. Marx and Engels "sang a veritable hymn of praise to the glory of capitalism in their *Communist Manifesto,* which nevertheless sounded its knell. . . . [Their] poetic description of the achievements of the capitalist mode of production serves only to underline still more strikingly the contradictions which it at the same time engenders. . . . Marx sees no contradiction between acknowledging and emphasizing this 'historically necessary mission' of capitalism and constantly pillorying whatever is exploitative, inhuman, and oppressive in it. Marx keeps in view all the time the[se] two *contradictory aspects* of capitalist historical reality. . ." [Mandel, 1971, pp. 56–57, 110].

5. Schumpeter: "[I]n no sense is his characteristic motivation of the hedonist kind [i.e.,] capable of being satisfied by the consumption of goods. . . . Hedonistically, . . . the conduct which we usually observe in [entrepreneurs] would be irrational" [1961, p. 92]. Marx: "Use-values must therefore never be looked upon as the real aim of the capitalist. . . . The restless never-ending process of profit-making alone is what he aims at . . . [the] boundless greed after riches, [the] passionate chase after exchange value . . ." [1906, pp. 170–71].

The key difference between Schumpeter and Marx may best be described as follows:[6] Each begins with a simple model of exchange economy. Although the institutional details are different, each is characterized by private property, market exchange, and competition, but in each the perceived *essential properties of capitalism are missing.*[7] The first stage of the analysis specifies the economic behavior of such a simple exchange economy. The second stage incorporates the perceived essential properties of capitalism and inquires into the prospective effects on economic behavior of this capitalist modification of the institutional structure. (A third stage, examined below, analyzes the transformation and socialization of capitalism's institutions, e.g., from competition to monopoly.)

In Marx's version of the (pre-capitalist) exchange economy, there are no separate classes of capitalists and landowners. Work and ownership coalesce. The artisans, merchants, and independent peasants, who own their own means of production and work for themselves, exchange their commodities, but do not employ the labor power of a separate, propertyless proletariat. The absence of a capital-labor class division precludes the creation of surplus values from the employment of labor power in production, while competitive pressures conduce to the elimination of pure economic profits in exchange. In Schumpeter's simple model of exchange economy, broadly similar conclusions are reached, but through a different institutional structure. A capital-labor relation exists, but the capitalist-employer is "capitalist" in name only, for he is devoid of or precluded from exercising crucial capitalist-entrepreneurial functions. Pure competition distributes wages and rents to workers and landowners on the basis of the value of the marginal product of labor and land, respectively. Perfect competition operates with a vengeance. "Everyone has equal access to 'capital.' Under these circumstances, clearly, no surpluses can accrue to employers of labor; for if they did, the laborers would themselves turn employers and compete the surplus away" [Sweezy,

6. Succeeding discussion extends and applies to a comparison of Marx and Schumpeter a mode of exposition developed most effectively by Meek in an earlier discussion of Marx [1967, pp. 99 ff].

7. More precisely, for Marx, "simple commodity production" is perceived as a distinctly different, pre-capitalist mode of production from capitalist economy. Although similar, in embryonic form, to capitalism in certain respects, it is perceived to lack fundamental defining properties of capitalism, as described in the next paragraph [see Elliott, 1978]. Schumpeter's simple model of the exchange economy is nominally capitalist (in Marxist terms) in its institutional structure, but lacks certain properties crucial to its real-world, dynamic character. Although a useful methodological device for each—Meek aptly called it a "mythodology" [1967, p. 98]—the distinction for Marx also held important historical significance.

1953, p. 277; and Schumpeter, 1961, pp. 30 ff.]. The "how" of production is a simple matter of production technology and resource
prices; the "what" follows readily from adaptation to market
demands.

What are the differentiating properties of capitalism, and how
is the model of the behavior of the exchange economy modified by
incorporating those properties? For Schumpeter, the *"differentia
specifica"* of capitalist economy is provision of credit by banker
capitalists to entrepreneurs to finance innovative investment [1961,
pp. 69–70]. This enables entrepreneurs to bid resources away from
other uses to new, innovative activities. By incorporating new technologies, sources of supply, etc., innovations create surpluses of revenues over costs. Competition tends to eliminate these surplus values,
but innovation re-creates them.[8]

For Marx, surplus profits are certainly generated (prior to their
elimination through competition) by the process of innovation, as is
described pointedly in *Wage-Labour and Capital* [see footnote 3].
But capitalism's surplus values are fundamentally created and sustained through the class division between capitalist employers and
workers and the accompanying capitalist "class monopoly" of the
means of production, with the resulting differential, generated within
*production* itself, between the value of labor power and the value of
output [Medio, in Hunt and Schwartz, 1972]. Why doesn't *competitive exchange* eliminate these differentials? First, the real wage is kept
below the level of the value of the output by the pressure of the reserve
army of the unemployment, which alternately rises during cyclical
depressions, falls during cyclical expansions, and rises again with
labor-saving inventions stimulated by rising wages during booms.
Second, competition rages within the capitalist class itself, generating
strong pressure (not merely enticement) to innovate, thereby decreasing costs and raising national income above the value of labor
power. But competition does not extend easily to the process of *becoming* a capitalist. It is easy for capitalists and small businessmen
to become workers. Millions do so through the process of bankruptcy,
especially during depressions. But, because both technology and credit
availability favor the large, established firm, it is difficult for workers
to become businessmen, much less major capitalists. Consequently,

---

8. Thus, Schumpeter defends Marx's conclusion (and his own) under dynamic
conditions: "Surplus values may be impossible in perfect equilibrium but can be ever
present because that equilibrium is never allowed to establish itself. They may always
*tend* to vanish and yet be always there because they are constantly recreated" [1950,
p. 28].

although competition tends to adjust commodity prices (other than labor power) so as to equalize profit rates among different sectors, it is not sufficient to eliminate aggregate surplus values.[9] As was already noted, this would require "equal access to 'capital'" and perfectly free interclass (not merely interindustry) mobility—conditions inconsistent with Marx's perception of capitalism's fundamental institutional structure and behavior.

### CAPITALISM'S ECONOMIC DYSFUNCTIONS FROM A CREATIVE DESTRUCTION PERSPECTIVE

Many who might otherwise accept broad similarities between the Marxian and Schumpeterian visions of capitalism's creatively destructive properties balk at the thought of drawing parallels between their respective analyses of capitalism's dysfunctional properties. After all, did not Marx sharply delineate contradictory and dehumanizing features of the capitalist system, and incorporate these features as strategic elements in the impending drama of capitalism's prospective demise and supercession? And did not Schumpeter, on his part, explicitly reject the hypothesis of capitalism's "breaking down under the weight of economic failure"?

The answer to these questions is, most assuredly, "yes." And yet, the popular conclusion of a virtual Marx-Schumpeter dichotomy is unpersuasive, because it is countervailed by other powerful similarities that emerge more clearly when capitalism's dysfunctional propensities are assessed *from a perspective of creative destruction.* Differences between Marx and Schumpeter concerning capitalism's dysfunctions take on a different hue when "bathed in [creative destruction's] penetrating light." The net conclusion is that differences between the two are substantially less than is popularly supposed. Although by no means identical, their respective views on this subject on balance are closer to one another than that of either was to any other prominent system of socioeconomic thought.

As for Marx, his analyses of capitalism's dysfunctions never blinded him to its "positive" aspects, as summarized tautly in his 1847 draft outline subsequently published as *Wage Labour and Capital*:

9. In the third stage of their analyses, differences between Schumpeter and Marx on the generation of surplus values decrease. For Schumpeter, the shift to "trustified capitalism" makes it increasingly difficult for workers to become capitalists. Thus, competition does not work as smoothly to eliminate surplus values. For Marx, increasing barriers (e.g., factory legislation) are placed on expanding "absolute surplus values" by increasing working hours, stimulating greater emphasis on expanding "relative surplus values" through innovation and technological improvements.

If one says "positive aspect of wage labor" one says "positive aspect of capital," of large-scale industry, of free competition, of the world market... without these production relations neither the means of production—the material means for the emancipation of the proletariat and the foundation of a new society—would have been created, nor would the proletariat itself have taken to the unification and development through which it is really capable of revolutionising the old society and itself [Marx and Engels, 1976, p. 436].

Indeed, capitalism's dysfunctional features themselves serve as cause as well as effect of its development process, and certainly do not repudiate its creative success. Alienation of the worker from his product, the work process, and his tools and means of production, although brought to a peak under capitalist auspices, establishes and reinforces capitalists' dominion over labor and production, and gives them the power and incentives to expand their own wealth and thereby to develop society's productive forces. Exploitation of surplus values from workers, although systemic to capitalism and a "miserable foundation" for wealth [Marx, 1973, p. 705], "is capitalism's means of creating an economic surplus, distributing the surplus to a politico-economic elite, and investing the surplus and generating economic growth" [Elliott, 1978–79, p. 6]. Recurrent capitalist depressions are the "most striking form in which advice is given [capitalism] to be gone and to give room to a higher state of social production." Still, by annihilating a large part of existing capital values, they "violently" lead capitalism back to the point where it is able to go on "fully employing its productive powers without committing suicide" [Marx, 1973, p. 750]. Monopoly and centralization of capital, although reinforcing and intensifying capitalism's proclivities toward alienation, exploitation, and cyclical depression, (i) enable rapid expansion in the scale of operations and, thereby, dramatic large-scale investment projects (e.g., railroadization) which would be impossible through mere growth of existing enterprises; (ii) by "accelerating and intensifying the effects of accumulation" hasten "revolutions in the technical composition of capital" [Marx, 1906, pp. 688–89].

Although capitalism's dysfunctions contribute significantly to its eventual demise, they are insufficient, either as preconditions for or as transition to the new society. Other elements, notably economic development and working class solidarity and resolve to build the new society, are also necessary. Further, Marx's vision of growing economic contradictions should not be characterized as simply another (radical) diagnosis of failure in capitalism's "economic engine." We may agree with Schumpeter that Marx visualized an impending period of system decay, i.e., a "more or less prolonged historical period. . .[in which] capitalism would begin to work with increasing friction and display the symptoms of fatal illness" [1950, p. 41]. Still, Marx did not suggest either secular stagnation or a stationary state. "In a real sense it can be said that Marx's entire theoretical system constitutes a denial of the possibility of indefinite capitalist expansion and an affirmation of the inevitability of the socialist revolution. But nowhere in his work is there to be found a doctrine of the specifically economic breakdown of capitalist production" [Sweezy, 1956, pp. 191–92]. Advanced capitalism à la Marx would certainly be a less creative and more tense society to live in. Still, despite Marx's occasional apocalyptic statements [1906, pp. 534, 836–37; and 1973, pp. 749–50], it is discordant with his overall view to ascribe capitalism's impending demise as emanating uniquely or specifically from some imminent moment of final "economic breakdown" per se. Capitalism's death and socialism's birth, in Marx's perspective, is pushed by the class struggle and pulled by institutional change as well as propelled by more strictly (and increasingly severe) socioeconomic contradictions [Elliott, 1976, 1978–79, and 1980, Chs. 7–8].

Turning to Schumpeter, the most direct starting point is to observe that, although he differed from Marx on details (notably concerning such long-run tendencies as increasing cyclical intensity and increasing "immiserization" of labor), he never denied the existence of any of Marx's *major* dysfunctional features of capitalism. Alienation, class struggle, surplus values, cyclical crises, depressions, unemployment, inequality in wealth, power, and income, and monopoly and centralization of capital are all woven into Schumpeter's analysis. Thus, Schumpeter's rationale for capitalism is not burdened by the need to disprove the broad contours of Marx's critique. Nor is it constrained by a perspective that admits the practical relevance of some dysfunctional properties (e.g., exploitation, unemployment, monopoly), but insists that "in principle" they would not exist in ideally functioning, perfectly competitive markets.

Instead, Schumpeter confronts Marx directly. First, whatever its dysfunctional proclivities, capitalism has been an immense success. Second, dysfunctional propensities actually perform a creative function in industrialization. Third, capitalism shows no likelihood of imminent breakdown "under the weight of economic failure." To illustrate, consider cyclical depressions, inequality and surplus values, and monopoly [1950, pp. 63–106].

In Schumpeter's analysis, cyclical fluctuations are no barrier to economic growth. Indeed, growth results from a cyclical development process, in which depressions are, largely, a "normal" and healthy period of absorption of the bunching of innovations during the preceding prosperity. Further, contractions eliminate inefficient, non-innovating businesses, as new products and methods replace the old in a "perennial gale of creative destruction" [1950, p. 85]. Similarly, surplus values are the normal result of innovations. Because of tremendous uncertainties involved, i.e., the possibility of failure and the likelihood of competitive encroachment in the event of success, the lure and occasional realization of extraordinary profits may well be the price society pays for the evolutionary contributions of its entrepreneurial leaders. Further, in practice capitalism reduces inequality: by increasing opportunities for entry into the ruling strata relative to earlier, more class-bound societies; by the creation of mass-produced products that especially benefit working masses; and by philanthropy and social legislation underwritten by capitalist growth. As for monopoly, innovation does create a monopoly position for the innovating firm. But because of the tendency for innovations to spread, by imitation and extension to allied fields, the industrial pioneer's monopoly position is only temporary. The possibility of temporary retention of above-normal innovative profits may well stimulate greater technological improvement, and practices that protect these temporary monopoly positions may be the price for technological progressivity and higher growth rates. In short, although the content and emphases are different, the analyses of capitalism's dysfunctional properties in Marx and Schumpeter share important common elements. For both, capitalism is tremendously creative and successful. Its dysfunctional propensities actually serve as cause as well as effect of its development process. And whatever its tendencies toward system-decay, it is not in danger of imminent economic collapse.

## CREATIVE DESTRUCTION II:

### CAPITALISM'S TRANSFORMATION AND SOCIALIZATION

Thus far, "creative destruction" has referred to the revolutionizing process whereby the new product or method displaces the old. But Schumpeter describes a broader process for which the expression also seems appropriate, namely one wherein capitalism, through its creative success, leads on to its own destruction and prepares the way for a socialist economic system to supercede it. In this broader sense, "creative destruction" is also common to both Marx and Schumpeter. Differences, as well as similarities, between the two visions may be conveniently summarized by interweaving commentary on Marx into Schumpeter's organizational format.[10]

### Obsolescence of the Entrepreneurial Function

In entrepreneurial capitalism, innovations are embodied in new firms. But in "trustified capitalism," the "competitive economy is broken up by the growth of great combines. . . and the carrying out of new combinations must become in ever greater measure the internal concern of one and the same economic body. The difference so made is great enough to serve as the water-shed between two epochs in the social history of capitalism" [Schumpeter, 1961, p. 67]. The large corporation, with its research departments, automatizes economic progress, making the social function of the entrepreneur, as the innovative outsider, increasingly obsolete. Consequently, the positions and incomes of the active entrepreneurs and those portions of the "entire bourgeois stratum" dependent upon them evaporate. Because capitalist enterprise, "by its very achievements, tends to automatize progress, we conclude that it tends to make itself superfluous—to break to pieces under the pressure of its own success." In the end, the giant corporation "ousts the entrepreneur and expropriates the bourgeoisie as a class. . ." [1950, p. 134].

For Marx, capitalism is characterized by a de facto class monopoly of the means of production even under competitive conditions. It is difficult (though not impossible) for workers to become capitalists, whether infused with heroic entrepreneurial spirit or not. However, as Marx turns to the stage of corporate, big business capitalism, a Marxian counterpart to Schumpeter's point emerges, and the differences between the two perspectives subside. Schumpeter's basic point is not that entrepreneurship becomes obsolete, but that, as innovation becomes increasingly automatized, entry of new blood into the mainstream of business activity, much less circulation into the ruling circles of society, becomes increasingly difficult. Although a resurrected Marx would insist that this is difficult enough to begin with, he would presumably agree that it becomes much more so as production and innovation become more concentrated and centralized. In short, for both Marx and Schumpeter the large corporation, a product of capitalist development and technology, renders the economic and social position of the small-scale, competitive firm and its associated small bourgeoisie increasingly obsolete. Consequently,

---

10. For a fuller examination of Marx's analysis of creative destruction, per se, in contrast to those aspects particularly relevant to comparisons between Marx and Schumpeter, see Elliott [1976, 1978–79].

economic power and social position become more heavily concentrated and centralized in the hands of the established capitalist and corporate elite, and the small capitalist (Marx)-entrepreneurial (Schumpeter) escape routes from working class life are increasingly closed off, reducing the solidity of capitalist rule.

## Destruction of the Institutional Framework

For Schumpeter, capitalism's very economic success undermines its institutions though the development of the large corporation, notably atomistic competition and private property. As for competition, the argument that monopoly power reduces economic performance, quite apart from its accuracy, "misses the salient point." Even if large-scale firms were managed with angelic perfection, the elimination of small-scale producers and consequently their "dependents, henchmen, and connections" profoundly affects the political structure and reduces political support for capitalism [1950, p. 140]. "Here of course," Schumpeter observes, "Marx scores" [1950, p. 140]. "He not only predicted the emergence of big business; he visualized industrial concentration as part of the logic as well as the factual pattern of the accumulation process" [1950, p. 34]. In short, Marx, like Schumpeter, did not perceive the "concentration and centralization of capital" as perversion of an ideally competitive state, but as the logical consequence of competition itself in the industrialization process. Further, for Marx no less than for Schumpeter, some of the most profound consequences of big business, corporate capitalism were socio-political, and monopoly was perceived to play a strategic role in capitalism's creative destruction and prospective demise [Marx, 1906, pp. 836–37].[11]

As for private property, here the intellectual distance between the two is quite small. According to Schumpeter, the "separation of ownership and management" in the large-scale corporation has resulted in the disappearance of the "specifically proprietary interest" and the "evaporation" of the "material substance" of property–its "visible and touchable reality"—and, thereby, the evaporation of "moral allegiance" for industrial private property. Eventually, nobody is left who really supports capitalism as did the small-scale owner-

11. The sociopolitical implications of monopoly are described in even more pointed terms in the writings of the later Engels who argues, for example, in *Socialism: Utopian and Scientific*, that because of trends toward monopoly and the large scale corporation, exploitation is becoming "so palpable that it must break down. No nation will put up with production conducted by trusts, with so barefaced an exploitation of the community by a small band of dividend-managers" [in Elliott, 1980, Ch. 7].

managers of the nineteenth century. "Thus the modern corporation, although the product of the capitalist process, socializes the bourgeois mind. . ." [1950, p. 156]. Moreover, the "bureaucratization of economic life"—an "inevitable complement" to both democracy and modern economic development—is stimulated by and within the large-scale corporation [1950, p. 206]. This immensely simplifies the the transition to a socialist "bureaucratic apparatus" by establishing new modes of managerial responsibility and executive selection that are "not without an appreciable measure of rationality" and that "could no doubt be reproduced in a socialist society" [1950, pp. 206–07].

In Marx's roughly comparable interpretation, the (emerging) industrial corporation is itself a product of capitalist development. Its growing economic role emanates from capitalism's enlarging appetite for investment funds with large-scale production and accumulation. But the corporation has profound effects on the capitalist property system, notably a "transformation of the actually functioning capitalist into a mere manager. . . and of the owners of capital into mere owners. . ." and an "abolition of the capitalist mode of production within capitalist production itself, a self-destructive contradiction, which represents. . . a necessary transition to . . . social property outright. . ." [Marx, 1909, pp. 516–517, 519]. Thus for Marx, like Schumpeter, bureaucratized corporate capitalism is a "phase of transition to a new form of production." It aims at the "expropriation" of small-scale, individual production, although it appears as the centralization of capital and "appropriation of social property by a few. . ." [Marx, 1909, p. 520]. Moreover, it "establishes a monopoly in certain spheres and thereby challenges the interference of the state. It reproduces a new aristocracy of finance, a new sort of parasites in the shape of promoters, speculators and merely nominal directors; a whole system of swindling and cheating by means of corporation juggling, stock jobbing, and stock speculation. It is private production without the control of private property" [Marx, 1909, p. 519].

Marx supplements his analysis of corporations with a parallel description of worker cooperative factories, which are perceived to evolve out of capitalist industrialization, are facilitated by the development of the credit system, and, like corporations, are a form of "transition from the capitalist mode of production to the associated one, . . ." [Marx, 1909, p. 521]. Thus, the credit system, itself effect as well as cause of capital accumulation and capitalist development, generates a transformation and socialization of capitalist property relations eventually "turning over into communism" [cited by Nicolaus in "Introduction" to Marx, 1973, p. 55].

## Destruction of the Protecting Strata

Both Marx and Schumpeter perceive capitalism in the dominant Western European model as emerging out of feudalism, and the surge to dominance of the industrial bourgeoisie as emanating from the creatively destructive impact of an industrializing capitalism on pre-capitalist values, institutions, and class positions. Adapting Marx's classic analysis of the nineteenth century British Constitution,[12] Schumpeter further argues that the industrialist, outside the economic arena, is "rationalist and unheroic." He lacks the "mystic glamour" that "counts in the ruling of men" [1950, p. 137].[13] He requires an aristocratic class to protect him, to manage the affairs of church and state and leave him "unfettered" to carry out his revolutionary economic leadership. For Schumpeter, the landowning aristocrats were "partners of the capitalist stratum, symbiosis with whom was an essential element of the capitalist schema" [1950, p. 139]. Thus, capitalism's very success in removing pre-capitalist institutions and classes leaves the bourgeoisie "politically helpless" and unable "to take care of its particular class interest. . ." [1950, p. 138]. Although Marx would no doubt disagree that capitalists are "politically helpless," he would presumably agree that the "romantic glory" of the aristocracy, which to some degree lingers on as a residual ideological vestige as its economic base is transformed by industrialization, may facilitate capitalism's consolidation, and yet that the "necessary victory of the capitalist. . . [and] the final ruin of the old aristocracy . . ." [Marx, 1964, pp. 113, 143] removes yet another barrier in the historical process of movement toward post-capitalist society. Still, Marx believed that the working class was able to exploit conflicts between capitalists and landlords, as illustrated by developments in the 1840s. Manufacturers had courted working class support for repeal

12. Marx described the British Constitution as "an antiquated and obsolete compromise made between the bourgeoisie, which rules in actual practice, although *not officially,* in all the decisive spheres of bourgeois society, and the landed aristocracy, which forms the *official government.*" Through the Reform Bill of 1831, the bourgeoisie "gained general *political* recognition as the *ruling class,* but only on the condition that "the whole business of government. . . remained the guaranteed domain of the landed aristocracy" [Marx, 1974, p. 282]. The agents of this compromise are the Whigs, who function as the "*aristocratic representatives* of the bourgeoisie. . . ." In exchange for a "monopoly of government and the exclusive possession of office," they assist the industrial and commercial middle class in conquering those concessions to its class interest which have become "*unavoidable* and *undelayable*" [Marx, 1974, p. 250].

13. Marx writes of "the *aristocratic* condition of land-ownership which reflects a romantic glory upon its lord. . . and puts the workers on the estates. . . in directly political. . . relations of respect, subordination and duty" to the lord [1964, pp. 114–15].

of the Corn Laws. With the repeal, the working class "found allies (e.g., for new social and factory legislation) in the Tories panting for revenge" [1906, p. 311].

### Growing Hostility and Social Classes

According to Schumpeter, although Marx analyzed capitalism in economic terms by a "bold stroke of analytic strategy," he defined it sociologically, in terms of the class dominance of capitalists. Thus, by an "ingenious tautology," the full realization of working class interests requires the supercession of capitalism, and socialism in turn is perceived as an economic society dominated by the working class [1950, p. 19]. Schumpeter rejected this interpretation of the relations between social classes and economic systems partly because, like Lenin, he believed that working class interests, *if* left alone to develop spontaneously, tend more to trade unionist and petty bourgeois aspirations. The Schumpeterian worker aspires not to overthrow the capitalist, but to extract more from him through shrewd bargaining or to escape from him through small-scale entrepreneurial or business activity. However, (i) workers are not left alone to develop class interests spontaneously, and (ii) other factors, emanating from the capitalist evolutionary process, stimulate class struggles and growing hostility toward capitalism. As to (i), capitalist evolution "produces a labor movement" and "the rise of the labor interest to a position of political power and sometimes of responsibility" [1950, p. 153; and 1939, II, p. 697]. In conjunction with corporations, labor unions have collectivized the labor market, thus socializing capitalism's institutional structure. Also, intellectuals have often invaded labor organizations and labor politics, providing "theories and slogans" (e.g., class war), and radicalizing the labor movement, "eventually imparting a revolutionary bias to the most bourgeois trade-union practices . . ." [1950, p. 154].

Marx's different but related commentary on these points would be that capitalist development contributes directly to working class organization and solidarity. Capitalist power, cyclical crises, and monopoly stimulate the establishment of labor unions as protective devices in the economic struggle to keep wage rates up, while improvements in transportation and communication centralize the class struggle, making it increasingly political in character. Indeed, the "real fruit" of the class struggle lies in the increasing political unity and organization of the working class rather than in specific wage negotiations [Marx and Engels, 1976, p. 493; and 1974b, pp. 224–29]. The socialist intelligentsia, Marx would presumably agree, thrive on

criticism and are given wide opportunities to "nibble at the foundations of capitalist society" through freedom of public discussion as
well as improved means of communication [Schumpeter, 1950, p. 151],
and play a guiding and educative role in the development of working
class organization. However, Marx was committed to a view of the
working class "as the decisive force charged with the social transformation of society" [Leonhard, 1974, p. 87]. For Marx, no amount of
theorizing or organizing by an intelligentsia (or body of professional
revolutionaries) can substitute for working class solidarity and resolve
to "effect its interests in a general form" [Marx to Bolte, cited in
Padover, 1971, p. 61].

As to (ii), Schumpeter's basic point is that capitalism, by its own
evolution, stimulates hostility and class struggles beyond those emanating from capital-labor relations. Some examples are capitalism's
self-destruction, noted earlier, of its own institutional framework; the
fact that although capitalism's basic rationale (economic progress)
rests on long-run considerations, "[f]or the masses, it is the short-run
view that counts," and in the short run, inequalities, surplus values,
and unemployment "dominate the picture" [1950, p. 145]; and capitalism's creation of a "New Middle Class," which, together with
farmers and small businessmen, may constitute a majority of the
population, and whose interests and attitudes, though often different
from those of the working class more narrowly conceived, are generally
just "as hostile to the interests of the bigger and big bourgeoisie" [1939,
pp. 697–99].

For Marx, the *basic* class struggle of advanced capitalism is, of
course, that between the large bourgeoisie and the working class.
Given this fundamental conflict, there are related conflicts, problems,
or sources of disenchantment, several already enumerated. As for
short-run problems versus long-run rationale, one suspects that if
Marx could directly confront Schumpeter, he would contend that the
cat had been let out of the bag, for what is the long-run rationale if it
is not capitalism's "positive" or creative properties, and what are
short-run problems of depression, etc., if not capitalism's dysfunctional properties?

### Public Policy and Social Change

When Marx and Schumpeter turn to public policy and social
change their respective arguments show striking parallels, despite
important differences of emphasis and perspective. First, each believed that the capitalist state, under the pressure of "social reform-
ers" (Schumpeter) or the class struggle (Marx), may engage in social

legislation and reform, provided that such policies do not constitute *"significant interference with the capitalist process"* [Schumpeter, 1950, p. 69], or, phrased negatively, that the consequences of not providing concessions to the working class "are sufficiently dangerous to the stability and functioning of the system as a whole" [Sweezy, 1956, p. 249].

For Marx, the best single example was a bundle of reforms comprised of "factory legislation," i.e., restriction of working hours, sanitation regulation, child labor laws, and education. These reforms, which were as much the product of nineteenth century capitalist development as its technology and industry,[14] constitute genuine concessions to working class interests; departures from a laissez-faire, market-oriented economy and movements toward as well as portents of the socialist society to come; and a practical school for the political education of the working class [Marx, 1906, Ch. 10]. To this list Schumpeter added ample unemployment compensation, care for the aged and the sick, public health, collective goods of various kinds, and limited public ownership. In the United States, Schumpeter observed, the "better part of the task could even now be accomplished *without undue strain on the system"* [1950, p. 70, italics added].

Second, however, none of these reforms constitutes a social revolution or radical transformation of the capitalist system. Both Marx and Schumpeter expected this to happen. For Schumpeter the transformation of, plus hostility toward, "trustified" capitalism combine to give birth to public policies incompatible with it, "policies which do not allow it to function" [1939, p. 1038], either through the imposition of injurious financial burdens on the capitalist-enterprneurial sector or the alteration of the institutional environment so as to excessively constrain industrialists' power and autonomy. As illustrations, Schumpeter cited developments during the New Deal, notably burdensome income, corporation and estate taxes, labor legislation, public utility regulation, and anti-monopoly policies. The injurious effects of these programs on private investment and innovation were heightened by the rapidity, hostility, and anti-business spirit with which they were enacted, and the overzealous, tactless

14. According to Marx, factory legislation partly constituted concessions to curb social tensions and working class fervor "that daily grew more threatening. . ." [1906, p. 263]. More significantly, they represented increasing recognition by capitalists of a class interest in collective action to sustain the labor force and its capacity to produce and reproduce itself, that is, to prevent intensity of unregulated exploitation by individual capitalist employers, the collective effect of which could potentially unduly sap the health and life of workers and thereby threaten the viability and continuity of the capitalist system itself [Marx, 1906, Ch. X, esp. pp. 310–30].

manner in which they were administered [1939, pp. 1038 ff.]. "Faced by the increasing hostility of the environment and by the legislative, administrative and judicial practice born of that hostility, entrepreneurs and capitalists—in fact the whole stratum that accepts the bourgeois scheme of life—will eventually cease to function" [1950, p. 156].

Although from a Marxian perspective the reference to the New Deal would appear premature and misplaced, the *general character* of the Schumpeterian vision of the role of public action under late-stage capitalism has a strong counterpart in the *Communist Manifesto*. There, Marx and Engels present a three-stage model for social revolution and transition to socialism. The first step is for the proletariat to "win the battle of democracy" and achieve political supremacy. In advanced democracies such as the United Kingdom and the United States, this follows essentially, though not automatically, from genuine universal suffrage. The second step is to engage in measures that in themselves appear "economically insufficient and untenable" (most of which, indeed, have been implemented in modern industrial societies) but that make "despotic inroads on the rights of property," and that, "in the course of the movement, outstrip themselves, necessitate further inroads upon the old social order, and are unavoidable as a means of entirely revolutionising the mode of production" [Marx and Engels, 1976, p. 504].[15] The third is to transfer the physical means of production, by degrees, to worker-state control.

Although brief, this strategy is sophisticated. It satisfies Schumpeter's interpretation of Marx's revolution as differing "entirely, in nature and in function, from the revolutions both of the bourgeois radical and of the socialist conspirator. It is essentially "revolution in the fullness of time" [1950, p. 58]. It also bears a striking resemblance to Schumpeter's vision of capitalism's final death-knell. The "moment" of the revolution is a dynamic *period* of transition in which socialization of the means of production occurs fairly late in the process. "Private industry will be allowed to continue to exist surrounded by such a climate of economic and political arrangements that it will slowly. . . have to transform itself." Public measures which challenge capitalist-corporate autonomy and wealth "will slowly ease private industry out. . . by gradually creating the economic conditions

---

15. For a contemporary application of this kind of strategy, see Gorz's distinction between "reformist" and "nonreformist" reforms [1967].

which will make the further existence of private industry economically unviable" [Avineri, 1968, p. 206].

## Capitalist Transformation and Socialization

Capitalism's "tendency toward self-destruction" [Schumpeter, 1950, p. 162], which, for Marx, is associated with tendencies toward system-decay and, for Schumpeter, "may well assert itself in the form of a tendency toward retardation of progress" [1950, p. 162], embodies for both a process of transformation and socialization. For Schumpeter, the various factors discussed earlier—"objective and subjective, economic and extra-economic. . . reinforcing each other in imposing accord. . . [—] make not only for the destruction of the capitalist but for the emergence of a socialist civilization. . . . The capitalist process not only destroys its own institutional framework but it also creates the conditions for another" [1950, p. 162].

But "transformation," Schumpeter adds, may be a better word than "destruction." Capitalism, he suggests in a 1928 article, is "in so obvious a process of transformation into something else, that it is not the fact, but only the interpretation of this fact, about which it is possible to disagree. . . . Capitalism. . . creates, by rationalizing the human mind, a mentality and a style of life. . ." which is not only "incompatible with its own fundamental conditions, motives and social institutions," but which provides the preconditions for a socialist future [1951, pp. 71–72]. Capitalism's self-destruction does not simply provide a "void" in which virtually anything might happen. Instead, "things and souls are transformed in such a way as to become increasingly amenable to the socialist form of life." In short, the capitalist "economic process tends to socialize *itself*—and also the human soul" in that "the technological, organizational, commercial, administrative, and psychological prerequisites of socialism tend to be fulfilled more and more" [1950, pp. 168, 219]. The same factors that explain capitalism's coming demise also "strongly point to socialism as the heir apparent" [1950, p. 61].

On this overall theme of capitalism's transformation and socialization, there are strong parallels in Marx's writings. Beyond specific examples already cited, notably corporations, workers' cooperatives, labor unions and labor politics, and factory legislation, the following passages from the *Grundrisse* are illustrative:

[T]he *material and mental conditions* of the negation of wage labour and of capital, themselves already the negation of earlier forms of unfree social production, *are themselves results of its [capitalism's] productive process* [p. 749]. [The capitalist

MARX AND SCHUMPETER                    65

mode of production] is itself fleeting, and *produces the real conditions of its own suspension* [pp. 541–42]. [Capitalism's "historic destiny" is fulfilled] when the severe *discipline of capital*, acting on succeeding generations, has *developed general industriousness* as the general property of the new species—and, finally, when the development of the productive powers of labour, which capital incessantly whips onward with its unlimited mania for wealth, . . . have flourished to the stage where. . . wealth require[s] a lesser labour time of society as a whole, and where the labouring society relates scientifically to the process of its progressive reproduction. . . [p. 325]. [The] universalist tendency of capital [will, at a] certain stage of its development, *allow itself to be recognized* as being itself the greatest barrier to this tendency and hence will drive towards its own suspension [p. 410]. (Italics and material in brackets added.)

Similarly, in the often-cited "expropriators are expropriated" passage of *Capital,* socioeconomic dysfunction and system-decay provide the rhetoric and revolutionary class struggle the drama, but the bulk of the analytic thrust of the argument is comprised of a twofold model of capitalist transformation and socialization. First centralization of capital, "accomplished by the action of the imminent laws of capitalistic production itself," stimulates technological, social, organizational, and administrative preconditions of socialism, notably:

The co-operative form of the labour-process, the conscious technical application of science, the methodical cultivation of the soil, the transformation of the instruments of labour into instruments of labour only usable in common, the economising of all means of production by their use as the means of production of combined, socialised labour, the entanglement of all peoples in the net of the world-market, and this, the international character of the capitalistic regime [1906, p. 836].

Second, along with monopoly, misery, and exploitation "grows the revolt of the working-class, a class always increasing in numbers, and disciplined, united, organised by the *very mechanism of the process of capitalist production itself"* [1906, pp. 836–37, italics added], thus providing organizational and psychological bases for working class solidarity and action in making the transition to and building the new society.

Certainly, there are important specific differences between the two visions, especially concerning this second aspect of Marx's analysis. As noted, Marx makes the working class the agent of social transformation, whereas Schumpeter explicitly disconnects Marx's linkage between socialism and the labor movement.[16] Throughout this section, we have noted other particular differences. In addition,

16. According to Schumpeter, "the labor movement, though often allied with socialism, has remained distinct from it to this day. . . the labor movement is not essentially socialist, just as socialism is not necessarily laborite or proletarian" [1950, p. 310].

Marx, in the *Grundrisse,* delves more deeply and specifically than Schumpeter into the prospective transformative effects of science, technology, and automation upon productivity, leisure, the composition of labor, and the character of work [Marx, 1973, pp. 705 ff.; and Elliott, 1978–79]. On the overall theme of capitalism's future, however, the parallels are again quite striking. Marx's vision is far from one of simple economic failure, while Schumpeter's analysis, no less than Marx's, is one of transformation and socialization as well as destruction based on economic success. At one point, Schumpeter revealingly recognizes the broad similarity with Marx's analysis, indeed minimizes the differences between the two perspectives. "In both these respects [transformation and socialization] Marx's vision was right. We can also agree with him in linking the particular social transformation that goes on under our eyes with an economic process as its prime mover." Further, in the end "there is not so much difference as one might think between saying that the decay of capitalism is due to its success and saying that it is due to its failure" [1950, p. 162]. At the very least, parallels and similarities are sufficient to temper significantly the popular myth of a sharp dichotomy and unbridgeable gulf between these two heroic perspectives on the internal dynamic of modern capitalist society.

In closing, we should note two final overall parallels and one major caveat. First of the overall similarities is that Schumpeter's analysis of capitalism's prospects is "not pure economics, of course," but economics "seen in a wide context and with a broad historical horizon." The combination of economic theory, politics, sociology, and history, which is Schumpeter's "major characteristic" [Stolper, 1979, pp. 69, 64], is strikingly similar to Marx's endeavor "to unite economic history, sociology and economics in a kind of ménage à trois. . ." [Meek, 1967, p. 101]. Second, Schumpeter's vision, like Marx's, contains no timetable. Its constituent elements, "while everywhere discernible, have as yet nowhere fully revealed themselves." Superficial "temporary reverses" on the "surface" may easily mask "the tendency toward another civilization that slowly works deep down below." The Schumpeterian outlook, no less than the Marxian one, is a *long-run* vision in an accounting system in which "a century is a 'short-run' . . ." [1950, p. 163].

The major caveat, of course, is that the comparative commentary in this paper has focused exclusively on the vision(s) of capitalism's creatively destructive properties and preparation for socialism, where parallels between Marx and Schumpeter are strongest. In ideological commitment, in the details of their respective technical analyses of the behavior of the capitalist economy, and in their perceptions of the socialist future, differences in perspective are both clear and significant.[17]

UNIVERSITY OF SOUTHERN CALIFORNIA

17. Brus [1975, p. 17] summarizes this latter point, deserving of a separate paper in its own right, aptly as follows: "Whilst in its understanding of socialism as a product of historical development Schumpeter's conception displays a number of points of resemblance to the Marxist position as most generally understood, in its actual definition of socialism and the problems connected with it there is a clear difference to be seen. . . . The resemblance concerns the aspect of continuity (of socialism in relation to capitalism) whereas the differences relate to the *aspect of negation;* in Schumpeter this aspect barely exists, whereas in the Marxist conception it is at least of equal importance."

# REFERENCES

Avineri, Shlomo, *The Social and Political Thought of Karl Marx* (Cambridge: Cambridge University Press, 1968).
Balinky, Alexander, *Marx's Economics* (Lexington: Heath, 1970).
Brus, Wlodzimierz, *Socialist Ownership and Political Systems,* translated by R. A. Clarke (Boston: Routledge and Kegan Paul, 1975).
Elliott, John E., "Marx Resurrected: The Transformation and Socialization of Capitalism," *Bulletin of the Association for Comparative Economic Studies,* XVIII (Summer 1976), 53–69.
——, "Marx's Socialism in the Context of his Typology of Economic Systems," *Journal of Comparative Economics,* II (March 1978), 25–41.
——, "Marx's *Grundrisse:* Vision of Capitalism's Creative Destruction," *Journal of Post Keynesian Economics,* I (Winter 1978–79), 148–69.
Engels, Frederick, in John E. Elliott, *Marx and Engels on Economy, Society, and Politics* (Santa Monica: Goodyear, 1980).
Gorz, André, *A Strategy for Labor* (Boston: Beacon, 1967).
Leonhard, Wolfgang, *Three Faces of Marxism* (New York: Holt, Rinehart and Winston, 1974).
Mandel, Ernest, *The Formation of the Economic Thought of Karl Marx* (New York: Monthly Review, 1971).
Medio, Alfredo, "Profits and Surplus-Value: Appearance and Reality in Capitalist Production," in *A Critique of Economic Theory,* E. K. Hunt and Jesse G. Schwartz, eds. (London: Penguin, 1972).
Meek, Ronald L., *Economics and Ideology and Other Essays* (London: Chapman and Hall, 1967).
Marx, Karl, *Capital,* Vol. I (New York: Modern Library, n.d. Originally published by Charles H. Kerr, Chicago, 1906).
——, *Capital,* Vol. III (Chicago: Kerr, 1909).
——, *Early Writings,* translated by T. B. Bottomore, ed. (New York: McGraw-Hill, 1964).
——, *Letter to Friedrich Bolte,* in Saul K. Padover, ed., *Karl Marx on Revolution* (New York: McGraw-Hill, 1971).
——, *Grundrisse (Introduction to the Critique of Political Economy),* translated, with a Foreward by Martin Nicolaus (New York: Vintage, 1973).
——, *Surveys from Exile: Political Writings,* Volume II, introduced by David Fernback, ed. (New York: Random House, 1974a).

——, *Wages, Prices and Profit,* in *Karl Marx—Frederick Engels, Selected Works* (New York: International Publishers, 1974b).
——, *Wages,* in *Karl Marx–Frederick Engels, Collected Works,* Vol. 6 (New York: International Publishers, 1976).
——, *Wage Labour and Capital,* in John E. Elliott, *Marx and Engels on Economy, Society, and Politics* (Santa Monica: Goodyear, 1980).
——, and Frederick Engels, *The Communist Manifesto,* in *Karl Marx—Frederick Engels, Collected Works,* Vol. 6 (New York: International Publishers, 1976).
Schumpeter, Joseph A., *Business Cycles,* Vol. II (New York: McGraw-Hill, 1939).
——, *Capitalism, Socialism and Democracy* (New York: Harper, 1950).
——, *Essays,* Richard V. Clemence, ed. (Cambridge: Addison-Wesley, 1951).
——, *The Theory of Economic Development* (New York: Oxford, 1961).
——, "The Communist Manifesto in Sociology and Economics," *Journal of Political Economy,* LVII (June 1949), 199–212; in Earl Hamilton, Albert Rees, and Harry Johnson, *Landmarks in Political Economy,* Vol. 2 (Chicago: University of Chicago Press, 1962).
Stolper, Wolfgang, "Joseph Alois Schumpeter—A Personal Memoir," *Challenge,* XXI (Jan./Feb. 1979), 64–69.
Sweezy, Paul M., *The Present as History* (New York: Monthly Review, 1953).
——, *The Theory of Capitalist Development* (New York: Monthly Review, 1956).

# [3]

**Sidney G. Winter**
*Yale University*

## Comments on Arrow and on Lucas*

Such a number of interesting and provocative things are put forward in Lucas and in Arrow (in this issue) that I would like to be able to dissect them in detail. For example, Lucas states that "the problem of controlling inflation has been 'successfully solved' in a scientific sense" (p. S405). I am tempted to explore the limits of the set of problems that might be said to be scientifically "solved" in the Lucas sense, but I fear that this would take up a good deal of space. Arrow deplores the use of homogeneity assumptions as a device for adding content to otherwise inconclusive economic theories, but presumably he does not believe that the Sonnenschien-Mantel-Debreu theorem is the ultimate conclusion regarding the useful content of the propositions of general equilibrium theory. Some restrictions of intermediate strength are presumably called for, and I would like to make the case that strong empirical generalizations about the nature of human actors—such as those describing the biological requirements for survival—are available and relevant in this connection. This too would take some space to develop in detail, though not as much as the first subject.

Given the constraints, I must choose a focus. I will focus on what I take to be the main message that Lucas has put forward regarding the relationship between "adaptive behavior" and the rationality assumptions employed in standard economic theory. This message is recognizable as the intellectual descendant of similar discussions by Friedman and Machlup in the 1940s and 1950s, and the ideas involved remain extremely influential in the discipline today. I will present and comment on my own statement of this position, which I (following Blaug [1980]) will call the "Classic Defense" of the rationality-as-

* Helpful comments on an earlier draft were received from R. Antle, J. Demski, and O. Williamson. Errors that I have persisted in, willfully or otherwise, are definitely not their responsibility. Research support from the Sloan Foundation is also gratefully acknowledged.

(*Journal of Business*, 1986, vol. 59, no. 4, pt. 2)

S428                                                    Journal of Business

optimization paradigm in economic theory. This discussion will provide a framework for occasional more detailed comments on both Lucas and Arrow.

Although there are significant distinctions to be made among the various views put forward by Friedman, Machlup, Lucas, and others, there is a major common theme that is the characteristic feature of the Classic Defense. This is the willingness to concede that the rationality assumptions of economic theory are not descriptive of the process by which decisions are reached and, further, that most decisions actually emerge from response repertoires developed over a period of time by what may broadly be termed "adaptive" or learning processes.

Lucas is unusually explicit in his acknowledgment of these points; in my view, this explicitness represents progress in the statement of the Classic Defense: "We use economic theory to calculate how certain variations in the situation are predicted to affect behavior, but these calculations obviously do not reflect or usefully model the adaptive process by which subjects have themselves arrived at the decision rules they use. Technically, I think of economics as studying decision rules that are steady states of some adaptive process, decision rules that are found to work over a range of situations and hence are no longer revised appreciably as more experience accumulates" (Lucas, in this issue, p. S402). This statement may be compared with Friedman's use (1953, p. 22) of the analogy between the behavior of a businessman and that of a skilled billiards player, and Machlup's discussion of the routine decisions of a driver overtaking a truck (1946, pp. 534–35).

I have argued elsewhere (Winter, 1975 pp. 89–95) that the willingness not only to limit the scope of theoretical propositions by the "as-if" principle but also to concede in general terms the character of the underlying reality is an important and underemphasized aspect of the long-standing "realism of assumptions" controversy (see also Nelson and Winter 1982, pp. 91–95). It leaves the door open (at least a crack) for those of us who advocate more explicit reliance on empirically grounded behavioral generalizations at the foundations of economic theory. Lucas's statements in his paper here open the door wider and might even be read as proposing the terms of a possible modus vivendi between standard theory and a more empirically based behavioralism. But they leave me even more puzzled than ever as to how the proponents of as-if optimization manage to derive their familiar bottom-line endorsement of "business as usual" in economic theorizing from the premises of their argument. As I read Lucas's firm repudiation of (unidentified) "attempts to reconstruct economics from the ground up in the image of some other science" (p. S402), I am led once again to suspect that the premise from which this methodological conservatism derives is conservatism itself, otherwise known as behavioral inertia (cf. Winter 1975, pp. 111–13).

Both the strengths and the limitations of the Classic Defense seem to me to have been left somewhat obscure by the long discussion of economic methodology.[1] That discussion has tended to focus on matters of high principle that transcend disciplinary boundaries, rather than on the more specific issues surrounding the concept of rational economic behavior. What follows is an attempt to restate the Classic Defense in what is intended to be a sympathetic fashion—but since my reserves of sympathy are limited, I cannot fairly attribute this viewpoint to Lucas or other proponents of the position I seek to characterize. It is a view that I am at least tempted to agree with—but it may not be what they believe.

The argument is in seven steps. (1) The economic world as a whole, or some identifiable sector thereof, is reasonably viewed as being in proximate equilibrium. (2) Individual economic actors repeatedly face the same choice situation or a sequence of highly similar choice situations. (3) Actors have stable preferences and thus evaluate the outcomes of individual choices made according to stable criteria. (4) Given repeated exposure, any individual actor could identify and would seize any available opportunity for improving outcomes (and, in the case of business firms, would do so on pain of being eliminated by the competition of others who would identify and seize such opportunities). (5) Hence, no equilibrium can arise in which individual actors fail to maximize their preferences—any superficially stationary position involving nonmaximization would be altered according to the logic of the previous point. (6) Since the world is, as noted, in proximate equilibrium, it must exhibit, at least approximately, the patterns implied by the assumption that actors are maximizing. (7) The details of the adaptive processes referred to in point 4 are complex and probably actor and situation specific; by contrast, the regularities associated with optimization and equilibrium are comparatively simple. Considerations of parsimony therefore indicate that the way to progress in economic understanding is to explore these regularities theoretically and to compare the results with observation.

Although I concede some force to this argument, I have reservations about every step. Some of these are beyond the limited scope of the present discussion; others are at least briefly noted below. The first point of the argument deserves special attention, however, for it marks a psychological divide that is fundamental to one's outlook on economics. To be willing to limit the aspirations of economic science to the study of the steady states of adaptive processes is presumably to view vast realms of apparent rapid change as either unimportant or illusory; it is to join with the writer of Ecclesiastes in maintaining that "there is no new thing under the sun." I, on the other hand, side with Hera-

---

1. For an excellent overview of the discussion as it relates to the theory of the firm, see Blaug (1980, ch. 7).

S430                                                        Journal of Business

cleitus in arguing that "you could not step twice into the same river, for new waters are ever flowing on to you." It is the appearance of stability that is illusory; just look a little closer or wait a little longer.[2] We Heraclitean types find it difficult to understand what the Ecclesiastes types are talking about, what with the universe expanding, the continents drifting, the arms race racing, and the kids growing up. The observed predictive performance of economic models also seems to us to be considerably more consonant with the Heraclitean view than with the alternative. Still, it is ultimately a question of philosophical outlook, and *de gustibus non disputandum* (except among philosophers, of course).

The Classic Defense provides, nevertheless, an important perspective on where economic science stands today. To the extent that our science does have empirical successes to its credit that are theoretically explained by the rationality-as-optimization paradigm, I believe it is largely because the various conditions set forth in the Classic Defense are approximately satisfied in some particular segment of economic reality over an extended period of time: approximate equilibrium prevails, similar choices are faced repetitively, a stable set of preferences roughly separable from other domains of preference is applied, and so forth. To cite an important example, I believe that the efficient markets hypothesis must be scored as an empirical success for the standard approach and that the Classic Defense provides the meta-explanation for this feat of successful (but partial) explanation of the functioning of financial markets. Any effort to "reconstruct economics from the ground up" should be one that preserves the discipline's major empirical successes, and the Classic Defense provides useful guidance as to where these successes are to be found and how they might be explained in a theory with quite different foundations.

My objections to the Classic Defense pale into insignificance compared with my objections to an alternative image of economic rationality that seems to have ever-increasing influence among theorists. This is the image of the economic actor as superoptimizer.[3] When the question is raised, as it often is, whether a particular choice problem is not just a subproblem of some higher-level optimization problem, the answer for the superoptimizer is always yes—and he or she has that one correctly solved too. Thus, the superoptimizer never makes an ordi-

2. For thoughtful essays from the Heraclitean viewpoint, see Day (1984) and Solow (1985).
3. I first encountered this useful term in Mirrlees and Stern (1972). Various authors have discussed the possibility that paradox or contradiction may arise when the attempt is made to apply the notion of full "superoptimizing" rationality in a world in which all information processing is costly (though the term itself is not used in most of these discussions). (See Winter 1964, 1975; Savage 1967; Radner 1968; Day 1971; Nozick 1981.)

nary human mistake, whether in making the first transaction in one of Plott's (in this issue) experimental games or in choosing the consumption level in the first instant of a program calculated to maximize an integral of discounted utility over a lifetime. Superoptimizer never departs from the rules of Bayesian inference, applied within the framework of the prior distribution with which he or she is somehow endowed at "birth." Subtle inferences from observations to underlying conditions are always correctly made, as in models of fully revealing rational expectations equilibrium or in recent models of reputation effects (Kreps et al. 1982).

Above all, the superoptimizer has unlimited access to free information-processing capacity. Were it not so deeply ingrained in the intellectual routines of the discipline, this characterization of human capability would be recognized as being totally inappropriate in a science concerned with the social implications of resource scarcity. Even to minds inured by disciplinary tradition to the violence that this assumption suffers from common sense and everyday observation, Tversky and Kahneman's results (in this issue) on "framing effects" should be profoundly disturbing. These results refute, as squarely as an empirical result ever can, the assumption that human beings have effectively unlimited information-processing capacity. Superoptimizers cannot display framing effects because, to them, no logical problem is "opaque."

Lucas makes passing, and possibly whimsical, reference to superoptimization in footnote 2 of his paper. He suggests that the pigeons in the experiments of Batallio et al. (1981) might be modeled as superoptimizers who are making fully rational choices from the very first peck of a control key. To his credit, he appears to deprecate the usefulness of this sort of approach and returns to his endorsement of the Classic Defense. Arrow appears to be concerned that recent theorizing under the rubric of "common knowledge"—the latest example of the trend toward ever more subtle conceptions of economic rationality—may be pressing beyond the limits of what is sensible. Of course, if the evidence on framing effects is taken seriously—and it seems that Arrow (1982) does take it seriously—then it should be apparent that those limits were breached some time ago.

But if economic man is not a superoptimizer, what sort of optimizer can he be? There is no logically defensible stopping point in the hierarchy of *N*-meta rationalities since the behavior characterized at any particular level is always subject to rational critique and elaboration at the next higher level. This is the conundrum that has driven theory down the path it has taken; the disciplinary rituals that are believed to mandate this theoretical odyssey have been performed by the discussants and referees of thousands of papers. They are right; there is no logical reason to limit the process, and the race to be the first to explore the next level drives the climbers on.

S432                                                    Journal of Business

There are, however, empirical reasons for limiting the process and closely related reasons involving the requirements for a fruitful relationship between theory and empiricism in economics. The great virtue of the Classic Defense is that it does not represent human beings as superoptimizers, and it offers, albeit implicitly, an empirical basis for deciding when the impulse to impute more rationality should be checked. The suggestion is that the experience of the actor with the situation envisaged has a lot to do with the level of rationality the actor should be expected to display in that situation—provided that by "rationality" one means nothing more than the sorts of consistency properties that are the core of the economist's notion of rationality.

As a forceful and elegant elaboration of this same idea, let me submit my favorite quotation from the writings of Joseph Schumpeter, originally published in 1911.

> The assumption that conduct is prompt and rational is in all cases a fiction. But it proves to be sufficiently near to reality, if things have had time to hammer logic into men. Where this has happened, *and within the limits in which it has happened,* one may rest content with this fiction and build theories upon it. . . . Outside of these limits our fiction loses its closeness to reality. To cling to it there also, as the traditional theory does, is to hide an essential thing and to ignore a fact which, in contrast with other deviations of our assumptions from reality, is theoretically important and the source of phenomena which would not exist without it. [1934, p. 80; emphasis added]

The problem with the notion of the economic actor as superoptimizer is it denies that any such limits exist. The problem with the Classic Defense is that its proponents, while they acknowledge the reality of the limits, do little to help define them and nothing to explore the important phenomena that lie beyond them.

From Schumpeter's basic question whether things have had time to hammer logic into men, some more specific observations about the scope of the Classic Defense may be derived. (1) It is the actions actually taken in a steady-state situation that are subject to repeated testing, not the decision rules that underlie those actions. For this reason, the support that the Classic Defense provides for standard comparative statics results is much weaker than is commonly supposed (Winter 1964; Nelson and Winter 1982, ch. 7). (2) Since the defense by itself provides no indication as to how long it takes for adaptive processes to reach something like steady-state conditions, it provides no guidance regarding the quality of the predictions that standard economic models may be expected to provide in particular cases. (3) Since sophisticated learning requires sophisticated arrangements for the collection, storage, and analysis of information, it may be expected in general to be more characteristic of firms than of consumers—a distinction the defense does not make explicit. (4) The Classic Defense offers no support when the decision under consideration is unique (such as the choice of a lifetime policy) or irreversible.[4] (5) Finally, if taken seriously, the Classic Defense would condemn economists to silence on major policy questions in a world undergoing path-dependent historical change, since change is continually presenting economic actors with truly novel choice situations (or so it appears to a Heraclitean type).

From my own historically unique vantage point and subject to the qualifications inherent in my own bounded rationality, the following conclusions seem to emerge. Although the Classic Defense applies to a domain of inquiry that is significant, that domain is far too small to be acceptable as a definition of the limits and ambitions of the discipline. There is an important role for inquiry into the learning and adaptive processes of boundedly rational economic actors who are forced to act in a changing world that they do not understand. What economics needs is to hold on to the empirical successes it has achieved within the scope of the Classic Defense, recognize that that scope is drastically narrower than the allocation of theoretical effort would imply, and get on with the important business of building a successful empirical science that extends beyond the scope of the Classic Defense.

## References

Arrow, K. J. 1982. Risk perception in psychology and economics. *Economic Inquiry* 20 (January): 1–9.

Arrow, K. J. In this issue. Rationality of self and others in an economic system.

Battalio, R. C.; Kagel, J. H.; Rachlin, H.; and Green, L. 1981. Commodity choice behavior with pigeons as subjects. *Journal of Political Economy* 89 (February): 67–91.

Blaug, M. 1980. *The Methodology of Economics.* Cambridge: Cambridge University Press.

Day, R. H. 1971. Rational choice and economic behavior. *Theory and Decision* 1:229–51.

Day, R. H. 1984. Disequilibrium economic dynamics: A post-Schumpeterian contribution. *Journal of Economic Behavior and Organization* 5 (March): 57–76.

Friedman, M. 1953. The methodology of positive economics. In *Essays in Positive Economics.* Chicago: Chicago University Press.

Kreps, D. M., et al. 1982. Rational cooperation in finitely repeated Prisoner's Dilemma. *Journal of Economic Theory* 27 (August): 245–52.

Lucas, R. E., Jr. In this issue. Adaptive behavior and economic theory.

---

4. Consider, e.g., the sort of rational expectations model with overlapping generations studied in Lucas's paper. He suggests that results from experimental economics might be used to sharpen the predictions of such models by offering an empirically based choice among the many theoretically possible equilibria. His proposal, however, involves the giant step of substituting a repetitive choice situation where learning is possible for a choice situation that is unique for the actors in the underlying model. Since real actors "only go around once in life," it is not clear that the experimental results would warrant any confidence in the corresponding predictions about reality—even assuming the results to be supportive in the fashion Lucas expects.

S434 Journal of Business

Machlup, F. 1946. Marginal analysis and empirical research. *American Economic Review* 36 (September): 519–54.

Mirrlees, J. A., and Stern, N. H. 1972. Fairly good plans. *Journal of Economic Theory* 4 (April): 268–88.

Nelson, R. R., and Winter, S. G. 1982. *An Evolutionary Theory of Economic Change.* Cambridge, Mass.: Harvard University Press.

Nozick, R. 1981. *Philosophical Explanations.* Cambridge, Mass.: Harvard University Press.

Plott, C. R. In this issue. Rational choice in experimental markets.

Radner, R. 1968. Competitive equilibrium under uncertainty. *Econometrica* 36 (January): 31–58.

Savage, L. J. 1967. Difficulties in the theory of personal probability. *Philosophy of Science* 43 (December): 305–10.

Schumpeter, J. A. 1934. *The Theory of Economic Development.* Cambridge, Mass.: Harvard University Press.

Solow, R. M. 1985. Economic history and economics. *American Economic Review* 75 (May): 328–31.

Tversky, A., and Kahneman, D. In this issue. Rational choice and the framing of decisions.

Winter, S. G. 1964. Economic "natural selection" and the theory of the firm. *Yale Economic Essays* 4 (Spring): 225–72.

Winter, S. G. 1975. Optimization and evolution in the theory of the firm. In R. H. Day and T. Groves (eds.), *Adaptive Economic Models.* New York: Academic Press.

# [4]

# A technology gap approach to why growth rates differ *

Jan FAGERBERG

*Economics Department, Norwegian Institute of International Affairs, P.O. Box 8159, 0033 Oslo 1, Norway*

This paper contains a discussion and test of the technology gap approach to development and growth. The basic hypotheses of the theory are tested on pooled cross-sectional and time-series data for 25 industrial countries for the period 1960–1983. The sample includes, in addition to 19 OECD countries, 6 of the most important industrial economies from the non-OECD area. The findings of the paper confirm that there exists a close correlation between the level of economic development, measured as GDP per capita, and the level of technological development, measured through R&D or patent statistics. Furthermore, for the group of 25 countries as a whole, technology gap models of economic growth are found to explain a large part of the actual differences in growth rates, both between countries and periods. As expected, both the scope for imitation, growth in innovative activity and "efforts" to narrow the gap (investment) appear as powerful explanatory factors of economic growth. However, when the non-OECD countries, and later USA and Japan, are removed from the sample, the explanatory power of the technology variables, especially growth in innovative activity, diminishes.

## 1. Introduction

Why do growth rates differ? When students of economic growth nearly thirty years ago started to study this question, they expected differences in the supply of capital and labour to be of utmost importance. Much to their surprise, differences in the growth of capital and labour explained [1] only a small part of the actual differences in growth between nations (Abramowitz [1], Solow [32], Denison [9]). One of the consequences of these paradoxical findings was to put technology in the forefront of theoretical and empirical studies of growth. Solow [32] and others extended the neoclassical theory of growth by including technology as a third factor of production in addition to capital and labour. According to this approach, technology should be regarded as a free good, growing at a constant, exponential rate.

The technology gap approach, developed by Posner [24], Gomulka [11], Cornwall [7,8] and others, also emphasizes the crucial role of technology in the process of economic growth, but from a radically different perspective. According to this approach, the international economic system is characterized by marked differences in technological levels and trends, differences which can only

* This is a revised version of a paper presented at a Seminar at Science Policy Research Unit, University of Sussex, on 17 October 1985. The research presented in the paper has been supported financially by the Norwegian Institute of International Affairs (NUPI) and the Norwegian Research Council for Social Sciences and the Humanities. Andreas Lindner at the Science, Technology and Industry Indicators Unit, OECD, and Paul Claus at World Intellectual Property Organisation have both been very helpful in furnishing me with unpublished data on patent activities. Furthermore, I want to thank the participants at the seminar and colleagues at NUPI for comments and proposals for improvements, retaining, of course, sole responsibility for the final version.

Research Policy 16 (1987) 87–99
North-Holland

[1] The term "explain" in the present context refers primarily to the fit of a regression. Obviously, neither the models in "the growth accounting" literature, nor "the technology gap" models to be developed later, can claim to be "explanations" in the sense that all relevant functional relationships and variables are included. While economic development is shaped by a large number of interrelated factors, of which many cannot be easily quantified, the models discussed and developed in this paper include only a few variables, all on a very high level of aggregation. Therefore, the tests presented in this paper cannot be expected to explain all the observed differences in growth between countries. What they can do is to test the explanatory power of a few vital variables and in this way increase our understanding of economic processes and give directions for future research. The "growth accounting" debate is in my view an excellent example of this.

be overcome through radical changes in technological, economic and social structures. The main hypotheses of the technology gap approach to economic growth may be summarized as follows:

(1) There is a close relation between a country's economic and technological level of development.
(2) The rate of economic growth of a country is positively influenced by the rate of growth in the technological level of the country.
(3) It is possible for a country facing a technological gap, i.e. a country on a lower technological level than the countries on "the world innovation frontier", to increase its rate of economic growth through imitation ("catching up").
(4) The rate at which a country exploits the possibilities offered by the technological gap depends on its ability to mobilize resources for transforming social, institutional and economic structures.

Hypotheses 1 and 2, laid down in the seminal contributions by Posner [24] and Gomulka [11], may be regarded as the basic hypotheses of the technology gap theory. Curiously enough, with one notable exception (Pavitt and Soete [23]), very little empirical research has been done in order to test these hypotheses. In contrast to this, the "catching up" hypothesis (3) has been tested extensively, using the level of economic development as a proxy for technological development (Gomulka [11], Singer and Reynolds [30], Cornwall [7,8] and others). [2] The results seem generally to support this hypothesis. Regarding the last hypothesis, the research process is still in an early phase, but the results so far seem to support this hypothesis also (Parvin [21], Cornwall [7,8], Abramowitz [2]).

The purpose of this paper is to test the basic hypotheses of the technology gap theory and analyse the differing growth performance of the industrial countries during the last twenty years. For this purpose it was found necessary to include in the sample, in addition to 19 OECD countries, 6 of the most important industrial economies from the non-OECD area: Brazil, Argentina, Mexico, Korea (South), Hong Kong and Taiwan. In the next section the relation between levels of eco-

nomic and technological development is discussed and tested. With the results in mind, the third section presents a test of a technology gap approach to "why growth rates differ".

## 2. Economic and technological levels of development

Most people, economists or not, would probably agree with the proposition that economic and technological levels of development are closely related. But they would probably disagree on how levels of technological development should be defined and measured. Following traditional neoclassical theory, the level of technological development of a country depends primarily on the relation between capital and labour. The technology gap theorists on the other hand relate the technological level of a country to its *level of innovative activity*. A high level of innovative activity means a high share of "new" goods in output and an extensive use of "new" techniques in production. Since "new" goods command high prices and "new" techniques imply high productivity, it follows that countries with a comparatively higher level of innovative activities also tend to have a higher level of value-added per worker, or GDP per capita, than other countries. [3] Of course, a country may increase its level of economic development by mainly imitating activities, but it cannot, according to the way of reasoning sketched above, surpass the most advanced countries economically without passing them in innovative activities as well.

Measures of technological level and/or innovative activity may be divided into "technology input" measures and "technology output" measures (Soete [31]). Of the former type, expenditures on education, research and development and employment of scientists and engineers may be mentioned, of the latter, patenting activity. Regarding the former type, these measures may be said to be related to the innovative capacity of a country as well as its capacity for imitation, since a certain scientific base is a precondition for successful

---

[2] For an overview, see Choi [6].

[3] This is the argument with runs through the whole "neotechnological" tradition, from Kravis [14] to Posner [24], Vernon [33] and Hirsch [13]. For a more recent formulation, see Krugman [15].

*J. Fagerberg / A technology gap approach*                                          89

imitation in most areas. [4] This study confines itself to one "technology input" measure, R & D. Patenting activity, on the other hand, is more directly related to inventive activity and process and product innovation than to imitation.

The main problem concerning R & D as an indicator of technological level is that the data generally are of poor quality, especially for years earlier than 1970, and for non-OECD countries. Yearly time-series dating back to the early 1960s exist for a few countries only. Another problem is whether or not military R & D should be included. [5] Patent statistics, on the other hand, are available for a lot of countries and for long time-spans. Furthermore, studies on the relation between patenting activity and R & D on the firm or industry level seem to indicate a close relation between patenting activity and R & D. [6] Differences in national patenting regulations have made it more difficult to compare patenting activities across countries. [7] But, as pointed out by Soete [31], this problem may be significantly reduced by limiting the analysis to patenting activities of different countries in one common (foreign) market. Contrary to Soete who used foreign patenting in USA as indicator, this paper uses foreign patenting on the world market. [8] This has several ad-

vantages. [9] First, it gives data for USA, which is of great importance in an analysis of technological gaps and trends. Second, the propensity to patent in the US market probably varies more than the propensity to patent in foreign markets in general.

Figure 1 compares the development of average civil R & D as percentage of GDP, patenting activity (less domestic patents) and average GDP per capita in constant 1980 prices for the OECD countries between 1963 and 1982. [10] All variables are expressed relative to average 1963–82 to facilitate comparison. Before 1973, the R & D and patent indicators show a relatively similar pattern. During the 1960s both show a strong upward trend, strongest for patents, with peaks in 1968/69, followed by a slowdown in the early/mid 1970s. It is an interesting fact that both indicators peak several years before GDP per capita, indicating that innovative activity cannot be seen as a mere reflection of economic activity. After 1973, however, patenting activity continues to decline, while the growth in R & D picks up again from 1979 onwards. This general slowdown in patenting activity affects most countries except Japan, Finland and the Asian NICs. However, in general the diverging trends in the two technology indicators in the last years (after 1978) should be interpreted with great care because new international patenting channels may have influenced the general pro-

---

[4] The role of R&D as a necessary precondition for imitation is emphasized by, among others, Freeman ([10], p. 185) and Mansfield et al. ([18], p. 209).

[5] I have chosen to exclude military R&D. The main reason for this is that if included, the size of the military sector of a country, relative to the military sectors of other countries, would have influenced the rank of the country relative to other countries in terms of technological level. For instance, a country like Japan, which for political reasons does not have a military sector, would have obtained a lower rank in terms of technological level if military R&D had been included.

[6] This was pointed out already by Schmookler ([26], pp. 44–55) in a case study of USA for the year 1953. More recent evidence pointing in the same direction may be found in Griliches ([12], especially ch. 1 and 3).

[7] Nevertheless Soete [31] found a quite close correlation between levels of domestic patenting and R&D expenses in a cross-country study covering the business enterprise sector in 19 OECD countries.

[8] That is: Total patent applications of residents in country x in all countries which report patent applications to WIPO (World Intellectual Property Organisation) less patent applications by residents of x in country x.

[9] A possible disadvantage is that since patent regulations differ between countries, and several studies show that the level of external patent applications of a country is correlated with the level of its exports, external patent applications of a country may be influenced by the geographical breakdown of its export. However, case studies show that external patenting is not significantly affected by differences in patent regulations between countries. Thus, this problem is probably not of major importance. Differences in "attractiveness" between countries in relation to patenting from abroad seem mainly to depend on the size and level of economic development in the recipient country. Also the level of exports and subsidiaries of MNEs of the patenting country in the recipient country seem to be of importance, but here the direction of causation is not at all clear. For discussion and tests of the relation between external patenting and characteristics of the patenting and the recipient country the reader is referred to Schiffel and Kitti [25], Bosworth [4,5] and Basberg [3].

[10] The reader is referred to the appendix for further information regarding sources and methods.

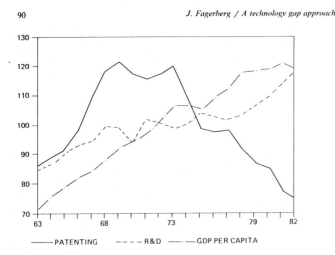

Fig. 1. Technology indicators 1963–82 (OECD).

pensity to patent through the established national channels. [11]

Tables 1 and 2 present indexes of technological level for 25 countries in the periods 1960/63–68, 1969–73, 1974–79 and 1980–82/83. The first index is based on patent statistics, while the second is based on R&D data. In both cases the sources and methods are the same as in fig. 1 above. Both indexes are expressed relative to average in the period (average level = 1). To construct an index of technological development based on patent statistics, it was necessary to normalize the levels of patenting activity according to the size of the country and the propensity to patent in foreign markets. This was done by dividing the number of patent applications filed by residents of a country in foreign markets by the number of inhabitants and the share of exports in GDP in the country. The reason for including the degree of openness of the economy in the index is that the propensity to patent in foreign markets is assumed to be dependent on the importance of the

[11] Since 1 June 1978 national channels for filing applications for patents have been supplemented by a European channel (EPC) and an international channel (PCT). If the applications filed through these channels are added to the data supplied through the WIPO member countries, the measure of patenting activity would show an upward trend (OECD [20]).

Table 1
Index of technological level (patent data) [a]

|             | 1960–68 | 1969–73 | 1974–79 | 1980–83 |
|-------------|---------|---------|---------|---------|
| USA         | 5.091   | 4.701   | 3.342   | 3.391   |
| Japan       | 0.509   | 1.113   | 1.430   | 2.053   |
| FRG         | 2.561   | 2.502   | 2.542   | 2.228   |
| France      | 1.527   | 1.459   | 1.347   | 1.276   |
| UK          | 1.460   | 1.218   | 0.987   | 1.081   |
| Italy       | 0.534   | 0.502   | 0.486   | 0.593   |
| Canada      | 0.536   | 0.486   | 0.545   | 0.561   |
| Austria     | 0.765   | 0.769   | 0.844   | 0.802   |
| Belgium     | 0.477   | 0.379   | 0.351   | 0.285   |
| Denmark     | 0.734   | 0.853   | 1.037   | 0.837   |
| Netherlands | 1.045   | 0.952   | 0.956   | 0.850   |
| Norway      | 0.305   | 0.326   | 0.463   | 0.396   |
| Sweden      | 2.517   | 2.216   | 2.457   | 2.222   |
| Switzerland | 5.601   | 5.820   | 5.796   | 5.152   |
| Finland     | 0.313   | 0.500   | 0.786   | 1.178   |
| Ireland     | 0.090   | 0.110   | 0.118   | 0.143   |
| Australia   | 0.403   | 0.516   | 0.691   | 0.925   |
| New Zealand | 0.251   | 0.284   | 0.440   | 0.563   |
| Spain       | 0.172   | 0.158   | 0.200   | 0.184   |
| Brazil      | 0.011   | 0.013   | 0.022   | 0.026   |
| Argentina   | 0.045   | 0.070   | 0.068   | 0.068   |
| Hong Kong   | 0.015   | 0.015   | 0.036   | 0.067   |
| Taiwan      | 0.011   | 0.010   | 0.028   | 0.075   |
| Korea       | 0.001   | 0.003   | 0.007   | 0.016   |
| Mexico      | 0.025   | 0.027   | 0.031   | 0.027   |
| Standard dev. | 1.461 | 1.423   | 1.296   | 1.193   |

[a] The index is defined as follows: Index = [PAT/ (POP∗X/GDP)], relative to average of the sample, where PAT = Patent applications filed in other countries; POP = Population; X = Exports in constant prices; GDP = Gross national product in constant prices.

Table 2
Index of technological level (R&D data) [a]

|           | 1963–68 | 1969–73 | 1974–79 | 1980–82 |
|-----------|---------|---------|---------|---------|
| USA       | 1.821   | 1.558   | 1.413   | 1.407   |
| Japan     | 1.636   | 1.576   | 1.584   | 1.711   |
| FRG       | 1.581   | 1.681   | 1.689   | 1.740   |
| France    | 1.690   | 1.338   | 1.218   | 1.211   |
| UK        | 1.745   | 1.505   | 1.340   | 1.400   |
| Italy     | 0.774   | 0.775   | 0.707   | 0.703   |
| Canada    | 1.254   | 1.004   | 0.869   | 0.914   |
| Austria   | 0.436   | 0.537   | 0.747   | 0.841   |
| Belgium   | 1.200   | 1.206   | 1.113   |         |
| Denmark   | 0.654   | 0.836   | 0.788   | 0.776   |
| Netherlands | 1.963 | 1.840   | 1.624   | 1.363   |
| Norway    | 0.818   | 1.030   | 1.096   | 0.928   |
| Sweden    | 0.971   | 1.100   | 1.316   | 1.472   |
| Switzerland | 2.595 | 2.025   | 1.933   | 1.661   |
| Finland   | 0.414   | 0.740   | 0.820   | 0.885   |
| Ireland   | 0.589   | 0.651   | 0.658   | 0.573   |
| Australia | 1.091   | 1.056   | 0.812   | 0.725   |
| New Zealand | 0.523 | 0.669   | 0.682   |         |
| Spain     | 0.174   | 0.229   | 0.284   | 0.290   |
| Brazil    |         |         | 0.528   | 0.435   |
| Argentina | 0.218   | 0.176   | 0.284   | 0.363   |
| Hong Kong |         |         |         |         |
| Taiwan    | 0.425   |         |         |         |
| Korea     | 0.305   | 0.291   | 0.495   | 0.602   |
| Mexico    | 0.120   | 0.176   |         |         |
| Standard dev. | 0.665 | 0.537  | 0.454   | 0.450   |

[a] Civil R&D in percentage of GDP relative to average in the sample.

home market relative to export markets.

The indexes of technological level reveal several interesting facts. Firstly, as can be seen from the standard deviations, the absolute differences in technological levels between countries are greater on the patent-based index than on the index based on R&D data. This is consistent with the assumption that patent statistics measure innovative activities, while R&D data measure both innovative

and imitating activities. Secondly, the ranking of the countries is very similar on the two indexes. For instance, the seven technologically most advanced countries in the early 1960s, according to patent statistics, were Switzerland, USA, FRG, Sweden, France, UK and the Netherlands. With one exception these countries also were the technologically most advanced according to R&D statistics. A similar relation holds for later periods. Thirdly, the two indexes give broadly the same picture of the changes in relative technological position through time. Both indexes show an increase in the technological levels relative to other countries for countries like Japan, Finland, and Korea, and a similar decrease for "old superpowers" like US, UK and the Netherlands. Furthermore, it may be noted that both indexes show a decreasing technological gap (measured in terms of standard deviation) from the early 1960s to the early 1980s. But this process seems to have slowed down in the late 1970s.

Table 3 presents a formal test of the relation between the two measures of technological level. Since the relation between them is non-linear, and the ranking is what interests most, the test is performed by calculating the Spearman rank correlation separately for each period. The test shows a strong positive correlation between the two rankings, significant at a 1 percent level at a one-tailed test. Table 3 also presents similar tests of the relation between the technological level on the one hand, and the level of economic development measured as GDP per capita in fixed prices on the other hand. In both cases a positive correlation existed between the two rankings, significant at a 1 percent level at a one-tailed test.

In summary, the results of this section support the general hypothesis of the technology gap theory of a strong positive relation between the level

Table 3
Rank correlations – economic and technological level

|                              | 1960/63–68 | 1969–73 | 1974–79 | 1980–82/83 |
|------------------------------|------------|---------|---------|------------|
| R&D index/ Patent index [a]  | 0.784      | 0.829   | 0.839   | 0.827      |
| R&D index/ GDP per capita [a,b] | 0.642   | 0.677   | 0.709   | 0.701      |
| Patent index/ GDP per capita [b,c] | 0.837 | 0.826   | 0.838   | 0.795      |

[a] Sample = 20.
[b] Fixed prices, at the price levels and exchange rates of 1980.
[c] Sample = 25.

of technological and economic development. [12] However, this is only a first step in testing the theory. Of particular interest is whether or not the technology gap theory may explain the differing growth performance of industrial countries in the post-war period. This will be discussed in the next section.

### 3. Technology gaps, innovation and economic growth

The technology gap approach, following Schumpeter [27–29], analyses economic growth as the combined result of two conflicting forces; innovation which tends to increase technological gaps, and imitation or diffusion which tends to reduce them. Countries on a comparatively low economic and technological level may realize higher growth rates than other countries by exploiting the potential for imitation. But this is certainly no "law". It depends both on their own efforts and the innovative efforts of the more advanced countries in increasing the "gap".

Attempts to test models which explain economic growth (or productivity growth) as a function of both technology gaps and efforts or "capacity" for exploiting the gap, have been made by Parvin [21], Cornwall [7,8], Marris [19] and Lindbeck [16]. In general, these studies show that both technology gaps, measured (in different ways) by GDP per capita, and efforts in exploiting it, measured by investment ratios, have significant influences on growth. however, a common omission in all these models and tests is that they do not include any variable measuring differing trends in innovativeness between countries, as pointed out by Pavitt [22]. According to Pavitt, this is a major weakness, because innovation plays an increasingly important role in the process of growth.

Pavitt and Soete [23] have tried to extend the models developed by Cornwall [7,8] and others by including US patents per capita and growth in US patents. The model was tested for seven different time periods using cross-sectional data for the period 1890–77 covering 14 OECD countries. The results do not seem to indicate any stable relations between the variables involved for the period as a whole. Surprisingly, the "gap" variable (relative GDP per capita) does not seem to influence economic growth, except for the period 1970–77, and then with an opposite sign of what could be expected. A significant positive effect of patent growth on economic growth between 1950 and 1970 turns to a significant negative effect in the period 1970–77. The level of patents does not seem to matter much, except for the last period and then with a negative sign. Pavitt and Soete also tested alternative models, replacing either economic growth with productivity growth as the dependent variable, or patent statistics with R&D statistics as independent variables. The results were not qualitatively different, with the exception that the "gap" variable performed better when productivity growth was taken as the dependent variable.

Generally, the results obtained by Pavitt and Soete cannot be interpreted as fully supporting the technology gap approach. Pavitt's assumption of the increasing importance of innovativeness for growth does not seem to get any support at all. One possible reason for this somewhat disappointing result may be the inclusion of both a technological level variable and an economic level variable in the same model. These variables reflect to a high degree the same basic relationship, and are – as shown by Pavitt and Soete themselves – closely correlated. By including both types of variables in the same model, and by estimating on cross-sectional data only, a problem of multicollinearity appears.

Although the general approach of this paper is quite close to that of Pavitt and Soete, the test presented in the following differs from their test in several respects. Firstly, in terms of model specification, the model does not include more than one "gap" variable; GDP per capita. This variable was preferred for two reasons: (1) As shown in the previous section, the ranking according to GDP per capita and patent- or R&D-based indexes of technological development was quite close. (2) The other two indexes have some disadvantages compared with the GDP index. The patent index clearly overestimates the absolute differences in technological level between countries, and R&D data do not exist for several countries and periods.

---

[12] This confirms the results obtained earlier by Pavitt and Soete [23]. They tested the correlation between GDP per capita, US patents per capita and R&D expenditure per capita in selected years up to 1977 for a sample of 14–15 OECD countries. The results indicated a positive and significant correlation between economic and technological level, especially after 1963.

A second difference between this test and that of Pavitt and Soete is that the sample in this test is not limited to OECD countries, but includes some of the more important industrial countries of the non-OECD area as well. The importance of including these countries in testing a technology gap theory can hardly be questioned. Thirdly, the present test differs from that of Pavitt and Soete in the method of estimation. While Pavitt and Soete estimated on cross-country data from different periods, this test uses a pooled time-series cross-country data set. Both methods, of course, have their advantages and problems, but in the present context the latter method should be more efficient because it uses more information. [13]

In general, the model tested contains three variables; the potential for imitation, the efforts mobilized in exploiting this potential and the growth of innovating activity. For reasons mentioned above, GDP per capita (TG) was chosen as a measure of the potential for imitation. As in most other studies the investment share (INV) was chosen as an indicator of the efforts in exploiting the potential for imitation. This is, of course, a simplification since institutional factors obviously are very important for imitation and the associated structural changes to take place. But the share of investment may also be seen as the outcome of a process in which institutional factors take part; i.e. differences in the size of the investment share reflect differences in institutional systems as well. To measure growth in innovative activity, growth in patent applications abroad (PAT) was chosen. In theory, growth in R&D could have been used instead, but since R&D data are lacking for several countries and periods, this was not possible.

The following variables were used:

$GDP_i$ = growth of gross domestic product in country $i$ in constant prices

$TG_i$ = gross domestic product per capita in country $i$ in constant 1980 market prices (1000 US $)

$PAT_i$ = growth of patent applications from residents of country $i$ in other countries

$INV_i$ = gross fixed investment in country $i$ as percentage of GDP in constant prices

$W$ = growth of world trade in constant prices

Since annual observations are heavily affected by short-run fluctuations, average values of the variables covering whole business cycles were calculated, using the "peak" years 1968, 1973, 1979 and 1983 (final year) to separate one cycle from the next. As mentioned above, this gives a pooled cross-country time-series data set with a maximum of 100 observations for each variable. Further information regarding the data is given in a separate appendix to this paper.

Two different versions of the model were tested:

(1) GDP = $f$(TG, PAT, INV),
(2) GDP = $f$(TGa, PATa, INVa, W).

The first model may be regarded as a pure "supply-side" model where economic growth is supposed to be a function of the level of economic development TG (negative), the growth of patenting activity PAT (positive) and the investment share INV (positive). However, it can be argued that this model overlooks that differences in the overall growth rate between periods also are heavily affected by other factors, especially differences in economic policies. According to Maddison [17], who generally favours a technology gap approach to economic growth, the economic slowdown in the 1970s could partly be explained by too "cautious" economic policies. The second model takes this into account by assuming that the average growth rate of all countries is determined by the growth of world demand, but that the deviations from this average growth rate are determined by the three technology gap variables mentioned above. It may be regarded, then, as an extreme "Keynesian" version of the general technology gap model. In this version, all variables (except the growth rates of GDP and world demand) are expressed as the difference between the value of the variable for country $i$ and the average value of the variable for all countries in the sample. [14]

---

[13] Cross-country estimates are confined to the relation between variables at a specific point of time. Pooled data sets combine this information with information on the overall changes in, for instance, growth, technology gaps and growth of innovative activity through time.

[14] This implies that the average value of each of the variables TGa, PATa, INVa in each period in this transformed data set is defined as zero. Thus, the growth rate (GDP) of an "average" country, defined as having average values of these three variables, would be determined exclusively by the growth in world demand (W) (and the constant term).

To test the sensitivity of the results for changes in sample and periods, each model was tested for three different samples: (1) all countries, (2) OECD countries and (3) small and medium-sized OECD countries (SMD = OECD countries less USA and Japan), and three periods: (a) 1960–83, (b) 1960–73 and (c) 1974–83. To test for serial correlation in the residuals of the cross-sectional units, we used the Durbin–Watson statistics adjusted for gaps (DW(g)). [15] The results are given in table 4.

For the period as a whole, the technology gap models explain a large part of the actual differences in growth rates, both between countries and between periods. As expected, both GDP per capita, patent growth and the investment ratio appear as powerful explanatory factors of economic growth, even if the effect of GDP per capita decreases somewhat when the non-OECD countries are removed from the sample. Both models give essentially the same picture, but the effect of growth in patenting activity is somewhat smaller in the "Keynesian" model than in the "supply-side" model. This is not surprising since in the "Keynesian" model the general slowdown in economic growth in the 1970s is explained by the slowdown in world demand, while in the "supply-side" model this is taken care of mainly (but not exclusively) by the slowdown in patenting activity. Both models go a long way in explaining the differences in economic growth, both between countries and periods, but in terms of fit the "Keynesian" is in general the most successful one. [16]

When the models are estimated on data before and after 1973, some interesting results emerge. Notably, for all three groups of countries, the effect of GDP per capita decreases from 1960–73 to 1974–83, while the effect of the investment ratio increases. Keeping in mind that the technology gaps were significantly reduced from the 1960s to the 1970s, one possible explanation is that the cost of imitation has increased as the distance to the world innovation frontier has decreased. Another interesting result is that when the non-OECD countries, and later USA and Japan, are removed from the sample, the "technology variables" become gradually less important, even if the signs of the coefficients do not change. For the group of OECD countries, patent growth ceases to influence growth after 1973, and for the group of small and medium-sized developed countries this variable does not seem to have significant effects on economic growth, neither before, nor after 1973. In general, for this group of countries, the patent growth variable may explain some of the slowdown in the 1970s, but it does not explain "why growth rates *differ*" between countries.

The last result calls for some reflection. Obviously, it is not very surprising that technology gap models are better suited for a sample of industrial countries on different levels of development than for a sample of countries on approximately the same level of development. But it is surprising to find that differences in the growth of innovative activities seem to have strong effects on the differing growth performance of industrial countries in general, but much less so for the developed countries, especially the small and medium-sized ones. In terms of data, it is not difficult to see why. For the period as a whole, only a few countries have trends in innovative activities that differ much from other countries; Japan, Finland, Korea, Taiwan, Hong Kong and to some extent Brazil. When the majority of these countries is excluded from the sample, it is not surprising that the importance of the variable is reduced.

To test the sensitivity of this result for the way data were handled, two additional tests were carried out. First, for the OECD countries as well as the SMD countries, a three-year lag was introduced for the patent growth variable. This did not alter the result significantly. Second, a cross-country regression was carried out for the period 1979–83, replacing the patent growth variable based on WIPO statistics with the growth of total external patent applications *including patent applications through international channels (EPC / PCT)*. Because of data limitations, only 11 countries were included in the regression. The result was

---

[15] This test was suggested to me by Professor Ron Smith of Birkbeck College, London. What it implies is that we leave out the differences between the residuals of different cross-sectional units, and the corresponding residuals, from both the numerator and the denominator, thereby reducing the number of observations by one per cross-sectional unit. Given the short time series, this test was applicable to the 1960–83 period only.

[16] This may be interpreted in support of Maddison's view, i.e. that differences in demand policies between periods have significant effects for economic growth, and that a large part of the economic slowdown in the 1970s may be explained in this way.

Table 4
The technology gap approach tested

---

*All countries, 1960–83 ( N = 99)*
GDP = 2.04 − 0.19TG + 0.18PAT + 0.13INV,
(1.99) (− 3.90) (7.79)      (3.21)
     **   *     *      *

$R^2$ = 0.67
SER = 1.56,   DW(g) = 1.56

GDP = 0.29 − 0.19TGa + 0.13PATa + 0.14INVa + 0.55W,
(0.97) (− 4.64)   (5.47)      (3.70)      (12.62)
       *       *       *       *

$R^2$ = 0.75
SER = 1.35,   DW(g) = 1.56

*OECD countries, 1960–83 ( N = 76)*
GDP = 1.02 − 0.14TG + 0.18PAT + 0.16INV,
(1.03) (− 2.46) (6.62)      (4.07)
      *     *     *

$R^2$ = 0.68
SER = 1.21,   DW(g) = 1.81

GDP = 0.51 − 0.13TGa + 0.09PATa + 0.16INVa + 0.51W,
(2.20) (− 2.72)   (2.86)      (4.87)      (14.35)
 **   *      *      *      *

$R^2$ = 0.79
SER = 0.98,   DW(g) = 2.36

*SMD countries, 1960–83 ( N = 68)*
GDP = 0.44 − 0.17TG + 0.16PAT + 0.19INV,
(0.38) (− 2.74) (5.26)      (3.82)
      *     *     *

$R^2$ = 0.60
SER = 1.22,   DW(g) = 1.81

GDP = 0.46 − 0.14TGa + 0.03PATa + 0.15INVa + 0.50W,
(2.04) (− 3.04)   (1.02)      (3.76)      (14.55)
 **   *          *      *

$R^2$ = 0.78
SER = 0.90,   DW(g) = 2.26

*All countries, 1960–73 ( N = 49)*
GDP = 3.02 − 0.32TG + 0.10PAT + 0.17INV,
(2.26) (− 4.00) (2.41)      (2.80)
  **   *     *     *

$R^2$ = 0.54
SER = 1.47

GDP = 5.78 − 0.31TGa + 0.13PATa + 0.14INVa − 0.09W
(2.10) (− 4.11)   (3.09)      (2.43)      (− 0.30)
 **   *      *      *

$R^2$ = 0.60
SER = 1.39

*OECD countries, 1960–1973 ( N = 38)*
GDP = 1.91 − 0.18TG + 0.09PAT + 0.17INV,
(1.54) (− 2.17) (2.06)      (3.16)
 ***  **     **      *

$R^2$ = 0.50
SER = 1.10

GDP = 5.10 − 0.21TGa + 0.12PATa + 0.15INVa − 0.02W,
(2.20) (− 2.62) + (2.95)      (2.91)      (− 0.07)
 ***   *      *

$R^2$ = 0.59
SER = 1.02

*SMD countries, 1960–73 ( N = 34)*
GDP = 4.01 − 0.14TG + 0.02PAT + 0.08INV,
(2.72) (− 1.61) (0.46)      (1.07)
 *    ***         ****

$R^2$ = 0.12
SER = 1.00

GDP = 3.01 − 0.18TGa + 0.05PATa + 0.08INVa + 0.21W,
(1.33) (− 2.13)   (1.16)      (1.25)      (0.80)
 ***   *      ****     ****

$R^2$ = 0.26
SER = 0.94

*All countries, 1974–83 ( N = 50)*
GDP = − 1.82 − 0.10TG + 0.12PAT + 0.24INV,
(− 1.27) (− 2.01) (4.13)      (4.48)
 ****  **     *     *

$R^2$ = 0.70
SER = 1.29

GDP = 0.32 − 0.11TGa + 0.11PATa + 0.22INVa + 0.59W,
(0.81) (− 2.22)   (4.26)      (4.43)      (4.63)
  **      *      *

$R^2$ = 0.75
SER = 1.19

*OECD countries, 1974–83 ( N = 38)*
GDP = − 1.74 − 0.08TG + 0.03PAT + 0.21INV,
(− 1.51) (− 1.43) (0.65)      (5.01)
 ***   ***        *

$R^2$ = 0.51
SER = 0.91

Table 4 (continued)

| | |
|---|---|
| GDP = 0.72 − 0.07TGa + 0.03PATa + 0.19INVa + 0.43W, | $R^2$ = 0.59 |
| (2.35) (−1.29)   (0.62)     (4.76)      (4.18) | SER = 0.84 |
|      **     ****                *            * | |

*SMD countries, 1974–83 (N = 34)*

| | |
|---|---|
| GDP = −2.34 − 0.10TG + 0.03PAT + 0.24INV, | $R^2$ = 0.51 |
|   (−1.90) (−1.72)  (0.71)      (4.93) | SER = 0.89 |
|      **      **                  * | |
| GDP = 0.64 − 0.09TGa + 0.02PATa + 0.21INVa + 0.44W, | $R^2$ = 0.58 |
|   (1.94) (−1.60)   (0.55)      (4.44)      (4.07) | SER = 0.84 |
|      **     ***                 *            * | |

Method of estimation: Ordinary least squares
* = significant at a 1% level (one-tailed test); ** = significant at a 5% level (one tailed test); *** = significant at a 10% level (one-tailed test); **** = significant at a 15% level (one-tailed test).
SER = Standard error of regression; DW(g) = Durbin–Watson statistics adjusted for gaps.

that when USA and Japan were included, the patent growth variable was significant, otherwise not.

Many of the countries included in the test, among them the non-OECD countries, had a very low level of patenting activity in the early 1960s (and still have) compared to other countries. It may be dangerous to draw conclusions from high growth rates when the initial levels were very low. However, in terms of R&D, where the initial levels were higher, the tendencies seem to be the same for countries where data exist. Japan had a very high share of civil R&D in GDP in the early 1960s compared to other countries. Nevertheless, its share has grown very rapidly and currently enjoys the highest level in the world. Finland and Korea both had rather low shares compared to other countries in the 1960s, but they grew very rapidly throughout the 1970s, and both countries have now (1982/83) shares close to the average of the sample. Thus, the available evidence seems to support that these countries have followed a separate way of development characterized by rapid imitation, high growth in innovative activities and rapid economic growth.

## 4. Conclusions

The main findings of this paper are the following:

(1) There exists a close correlation between the level of economic development, measured as GDP per capita, and the level of technological development, measured through R&D or patent statistics.

(2) Technology gap models of economic growth explain rather well the differences in growth between the industrialized countries as a whole in the post-war period. Both the scope for imitation, growth in innovative activity and "efforts" to narrow the "gap" (investment) seem to be powerful explanatory factors of economic growth. This has not changed qualitatively after 1973, but the scope for imitation seems to have decreased and the costs of imitation increased, compared with the 1960s.

(3) The models are less well suited in explaining the (much smaller) differences in growth between developed countries, especially the small and medium-sized ones, most of which are on approximately the same level of development.

The findings of this paper confirm that many of the small and medium-sized European countries have attained very high levels of GDP per capita with moderate levels of innovative activity. Thus, to explain the differences in growth between these countries in the post-war period, a much more detailed analysis of economic, social and institutional structures should be carried out. The prospects for this group of countries will partly depend on whether or not competition through innovation will be the dominant form of competition in international markets in the future. The decreased scope for imitation which is revealed in this study and the general upturn in R&D efforts during the last years may be taken as an indication of a growing importance of technological competition on the international level. If correct, this implies that the future growth of the small and medium-sized European countries in part depends on their ability to change the trend towards a stagnating innovative level compared to other countries.

## Appendix

### Methods

Growth rates are calculated as geometric averages for the periods 1960-68, 1968-73, 1973-79 and 1979-83, or the nearest period for which data exist. Levels and shares are calculated as arithmetic averages for the periods 1960-67, 1968-73, 1974-79 and 1980-83, or the nearest period for which data exist.

### Sources

*Real GDP per capita, 1980 market prices in US $:*
Taiwan: *Statistical Yearbook of the Republic of China 1984*
Other countries: *IMF Supplement on Output Statistics*

*Growth of gross domestic product in constant prices:*
OECD countries: *OECD Historical Statistics 1960-1983*
Hong Kong, Taiwan and Korea 1960-73: E.K. Chen, *Hyper-growth in Asian Economies* (MacMillan, London, 1979)
Taiwan 1973-83: *Statistical Yearbook of the Republic of China 1984*
Hong Kong and Korea 1973-83 and Mexico, Argentina and Brazil: *IMF Supplement on Output Statistics*

*Gross fixed capital formation as percentage of GDP:*
OECD countries: *OECD Historical Statistics 1960-1983*
Taiwan: *Statistical Yearbook of the Republic of China 1984*
Other countries: *IMF Supplement on Output Statistics*

*External patent applications:*
OECD countries: *OECD/STIIU DATA BANK*
Other countries: World International Property Organisation (WIPO): *Industrial Property Statistics*, various editions and unpublished data.

Table A1
Growth of real GDP

|  | 1960-68 | 1968-73 | 1973-79 | 1979-83 |
|---|---|---|---|---|
| USA | 4.5 | 3.3 | 2.6 | 0.7 |
| Japan | 10.5 | 8.8 | 3.6 | 3.9 |
| FRG | 4.2 | 4.9 | 2.4 | 0.5 |
| France | 5.4 | 5.9 | 3.1 | 1.1 |
| UK | 3.1 | 3.2 | 1.4 | 0.4 |
| Italy | 5.7 | 4.6 | 2.6 | 0.6 |
| Canada | 5.6 | 5.6 | 3.4 | 0.8 |
| Austria | 4.2 | 5.9 | 2.9 | 1.5 |
| Belgium | 4.5 | 5.6 | 2.2 | 0.9 |
| Denmark | 4.6 | 4.0 | 1.9 | 0.9 |
| Netherlands | 4.8 | 5.3 | 2.6 | -0.3 |
| Norway | 4.4 | 4.1 | 4.9 | 2.3 |
| Sweden | 4.4 | 3.7 | 1.8 | 1.2 |
| Switzerland | 4.4 | 4.5 | -0.4 | 1.4 |
| Finland | 3.9 | 6.7 | 2.4 | 3.3 |
| Ireland | 4.2 | 4.8 | 4.6 | 2.2 |
| Australia | 5.0 | 5.5 | 2.6 | 1.7 |
| New Zealand | 3.1 | 5.1 | 0.6 | 2.1 |
| Spain | 7.5 | 6.8 | 2.5 | 1.2 |
| Brazil | 8.5 [a] | 9.3 | 6.8 | 0.8 |
| Argentina | 2.8 | 3.2 | 2.3 | -1.9 |
| Hong Kong | 8.5 | 8.4 | 8:3 | 6.7 |
| Taiwan | 9.0 | 10.6 | 8.0 | 5.6 |
| Korea | 7.6 | 10.7 | 9.0 | 4.5 |
| Mexico | 6.7 | 6.6 | 5.9 | 2.6 |

[a] 1962-82.

Table A2
Real GDP per capita, 1980 market prices in US $

|  | 1962-67 | 1968-73 | 1974-79 | 1980-82 |
|---|---|---|---|---|
| USA | 9,419 | 10,746 | 11,905 | 12,706 |
| Japan | 4,018 | 6,365 | 7,827 | 9,063 |
| FRG | 7,374 | 9,132 | 10,618 | 11,806 |
| France | 6,530 | 8,311 | 10,004 | 11,000 |
| UK | 6,836 | 7,788 | 8,726 | 9,054 |
| Italy | 3,972 | 5,075 | 5,864 | 6,486 |
| Canada | 7,310 | 8,961 | 10,624 | 11,157 |
| Austria | 5,139 | 6,624 | 8,180 | 9,198 |
| Belgium | 6,133 | 7,823 | 9,516 | 10,186 |
| Denmark | 8,264 | 9,889 | 10,975 | 11,571 |
| Netherlands | 7,070 | 8,857 | 10,214 | 10,586 |
| Norway | 7,993 | 9,550 | 11,668 | 13,385 |
| Sweden | 9,638 | 11,399 | 12,797 | 13,368 |
| Switzerland | 12,177 | 14,317 | 15,010 | 15,855 |
| Finland | 5,848 | 7,485 | 8,891 | 10,004 |
| Ireland | 3,285 | 4,059 | 4,718 | 5,024 |
| Australia | 7,796 | 9,429 | 10,262 | 10,775 |
| New Zealand | 6,135 | 6,890 | 7,495 | 7,249 |
| Spain | 3,056 | 4,047 | 4,935 | 5,054 |
| Brazil | 1,024 | 1,366 | 1,954 | 2,217 |
| Argentina | 2,166 | 2,583 | 2,786 | 2,652 |
| Hong Kong | 1,676 | 2,389 | 3,436 | 4,710 |
| Taiwan | 490 | 780 | 1,448 | 2,037 |
| Korea | 592 | 871 | 1,337 | 1,613 |
| Mexico | 1,227 | 1,546 | 1,844 | 2,133 |

The OECD data are adjusted WIPO data. Data for the non-OECD countries are compiled from published WIPO statistics except for Hong Kong, Korea and Taiwan 1975–83 where data are compiled by WIPO from unpublished sources. Unfortunately, the quality of the data for some of the non-OECD countries prior to 1975 is far from perfect. To avoid year-to-year fluctuations, caused mainly by bad statistics, from influencing the calculated growth rates, some efforts were made to adjust the growth rates accordingly (see table A3 for details).

*R & D as percentage of GDP:*
The R & D data are estimates based on the following sources:
OECD countries: *OECD Science and Technology Indicators, Basic Statistical Series (vol B (1982) and Recent Results (1984))*
Other countries: *UNESCO Statistical Yearbook* (various editions) and various *UNESCO surveys on resources devoted to R & D*

Military R & D expenditures were, following OECD, assumed to be negligible in all countries except US, France, FRG, Sweden and UK. The R & D data for these countries were adjusted downward according to OECD estimates. The estimates were taken from OECD, Directorate for Science, Technology and Industry: *The problems of estimating defence and civil GERD in selected OECD member countries* (unpublished). For other countries, civil and total R & D as percentage of GDP were assumed to be identical.

*Population and export shares in GDP:*
Data on population and export shares in GDP were taken from: *OECD Historical Statistics 1960–83, OECD National Accounts* (various editions), *IMF Supplement on Output Statistics, UN Monthly Bulletin of Statistics* (various editions) and *Statistical Yearbook of the Republic of China 1984*

*Growth of world trade at constant prices:*
The growth of total OECD imports was used as

Table A3
Growth in external patent applications

|            | 1960–68 | 1968–73 | 1973–79 | 1979–83 |
|------------|---------|---------|---------|---------|
| USA        | 6.7     | −1.7    | −6.1    | −4.3    |
| Japan      | 22.8    | 10.9    | 0.9     | 1.0     |
| FRG        | 5.2     | 0.7     | −6.7    | −8.7    |
| France     | 6.3     | 0.5     | −6.1    | −4.8    |
| UK         | 3.1     | −2.4    | −9.5    | −2.2    |
| Italy      | 5.9     | 0.6     | −0.3    | −8.7    |
| Canada     | 5.7     | 2.9     | −5.7    | −3.2    |
| Austria    | 4.5     | 3.0     | −5.0    | −6.5    |
| Belgium    | 5.9     | −5.8    | −8.7    | −4.4    |
| Denmark    | 8.6     | −3.0    | −5.8    | −2.9    |
| Netherlands| 2.2     | −1.4    | −4.6    | −9.2    |
| Norway     | 1.2     | 5.9     | −6.2    | −7.3    |
| Sweden     | 5.3     | 0       | −4.5    | −4.9    |
| Switzerland| 5.2     | 0.6     | −7.3    | −9.1    |
| Finland    | 10.0    | 8.1     | 4.0     | 4.2     |
| Ireland    | 10.4 [a]| 7.9     | −2.7    | −6.6    |
| Australia  | 5.1     | 9.4     | −1.7    | −2.7    |
| New Zealand| −0.7    | 10.3    | 1.7     | −2.4    |
| Spain      | 8.8 [a] | 2.0     | −2.7    | −9.0    |
| Brazil     | 7.5 [a] | 16.0    | 3.4     | −19.2   |
| Argentina  | 16.3 [a]| 1.4     | −3.8    | −15.9   |
| Hong Kong  | 8.8 [a] | 4.2     | 14.8    | 0       |
| Taiwan     | 22.2 [a]| 17.9 [b]| 21.0 [d]| 12.7    |
| Korea      | n.a.    | 13.5 [c]| 16.3 [d]| 18.9    |
| Mexico     | −0.6 [a]| 4.8     | −9.5    | 1.1     |

[a] 1969/70–1964/65.
[b] 1968–75.
[c] 1969–75.
[d] 1975–79.

Table A4
Gross fixed capital formation as percentage of GDP

|            | 1960–67  | 1968–73 | 1974–79 | 1980–83  |
|------------|----------|---------|---------|----------|
| USA        | 18.0     | 18.3    | 18.3    | 17.4     |
| Japan      | 31.3     | 34.7    | 32.0    | 30.4     |
| FRG        | 25.2     | 24.4    | 20.9    | 21.5     |
| France     | 22.3     | 23.3    | 22.7    | 20.9     |
| UK         | 17.8     | 19.2    | 19.4    | 16.9     |
| Italy      | 21.7     | 20.6    | 20.0    | 19.2     |
| Canada     | 22.1     | 21.6    | 22.9    | 21.8     |
| Austria    | 26.4     | 27.2    | 26.4    | 24.0     |
| Belgium    | 21.6     | 21.7    | 21.9    | 18.3     |
| Denmark    | 23.4     | 24.4    | 22.1    | 16.7     |
| Netherlands| 25.0     | 25.0    | 20.9    | 19.2     |
| Norway     | 29.0     | 27.4    | 32.9    | 25.8     |
| Sweden     | 23.9     | 22.6    | 20.6    | 19.2     |
| Switzerland| 28.0     | 27.9    | 22.7    | 23.6     |
| Finland    | 26.6     | 26.2    | 27.2    | 24.9     |
| Ireland    | 18.7     | 23.3    | 26.1    | 26.7     |
| Australia  | 25.8     | 25.3    | 22.7    | 23.1     |
| New Zealand| 21.1     | 20.8    | 23.2    | 21.4     |
| Spain      | 20.2     | 22.7    | 21.6    | 19.5     |
| Brazil     | 18.6 [a] | 25.3    | 27.2    | 21.7 [b] |
| Argentina  | 18.6 [a] | 24.6    | 25.1    | 19.5 [b] |
| Hong Kong  | 26.7 [a] | 21.7    | 28.1    | 32.8     |
| Taiwan     | 15.4     | 23.1    | 27.8    | 28.3     |
| Korea      | 17.4 [a] | 25.6    | 30.3    | 28.2     |
| Mexico     | 18.5 [a] | 21.1    | 23.6    | 26.1 [b] |

[a] 1962–67.
[b] 1980–82.

proxy (8.1, 9.4, 4.0, 1.3). The data were taken from: *OECD Historical Statistics 1960–1983*.

## References

[1] M. Abramowitz, Resources and Output Trends in the United States since 1870, *Am. Econ. Rev.* 46 (1956) 5–23.

[2] M. Abramowitz, Rapid Growth Potential and its Realisation: The Experience of Capitalist Economies in the Postwar Period, in: E. Malinvaud (ed.), *Economic Growth and Resources* (London, 1979).

[3] L. Basberg, Foreign Patenting in the U.S. as a Technology Indicator, *Research Policy* 12 (1983) 227–237.

[4] D. Bosworth, The Transfer of U.S. Technology Abroad, *Research Policy* 9 (1980) 378–388.

[5] D. Bosworth, Foreign Patent Flows to and from the United Kingdom, *Research Policy* 13 (1984) 115–124.

[6] K. Choi, *Theories of Comparative Economic Growth* (Iowa State University Press, Ames, 1983).

[7] J. Cornwall, Diffusion, Convergence and Kaldor's Law, *Econ. J.* 85 (1976) 307–314.

[8] J. Cornwall, *Modern Capitalism. Its Growth and Transformation* (Martin Robertson, London, 1977).

[9] E.F. Denison, *Why Growth Rates Differ: Post-War Experience in Nine Western Countries* (Brookings Institute, Washington D.C., 1967).

[10] C. Freeman, *The Economics of Industrial Innovation*, 2nd edn (Frances Pinter, London, 1982).

[11] S. Gomulka, *Inventive Activity, Diffusion and Stages of Economic Growth*, Skrifter fra Aarhus universitets økonomiske institut nr. 24, Aarhus (1971).

[12] Z. Griliches (ed.), *R&D, Patents and Productivity* (Chicago University Press, Chicago, 1984).

[13] S. Hirsch, *Location of Industry and International Competitiveness* (Clarendon Press, Oxford, 1967).

[14] I. Kravis, "Availability" and Other Influences on the Commodity Composition of Trade, *Journal of Political Economy* LXIV (1956) 143–155.

[15] P. Krugman, A Model of Innovation, Technology Transfer and the World Distribution of Income, *Journal of Political Economy* 87 (1979) 253–266.

[16] A. Lindbeck, The Recent Slowdown of Productivity Growth, *Econ. J.* 93 (1983) 13–34.

[17] A. Maddison, *Phases of Capitalist Development* (Oxford University Press, New York, 1982).

[18] E. Mansfield, A. Romeo, M. Schwartz, D. Teece, S. Wagner and P. Brach, *Technology Transfer, Productivity and Economic Policy* (Norton, New York, 1982).

[19] R. Marris, How Much of the Slow-down was Catch-up?, in: R.C.O. Matthews, *Slower Growth in the Western World* (London, 1982).

[20] OECD, *Indicators of the Technological Position and Performance in OECD Member Countries during the Seventies*, Directorate for Science, Technology and Industry, Science and Technology Indicators, Working Paper No. 2 (1984).

[21] M. Parvin, Technological Adaptation, Optimum Level of Backwardness and the Rate of per Capita Income Growth: An Econometric Approach, *American Economist* 19 (1975) 23–31.

[22] K. Pavitt, Technical Innovation and Industrial Development, *Futures* (Dec. 1979) 458–470, (Febr. 1980) 35–44.

[23] K. Pavitt and L.G. Soete, International Differences in Economic Growth and the International Location of Innovation, in: H. Giersch (ed.), *Emerging Technologies: Consequences for Economic Growth, Structural Change, and Employment* (J.C.B. Mohr (Paul Siebeck), Tübingen, 1982).

[24] M.V. Posner, International Trade and Technical Change, *Oxf. Econ. Pap.* 13 (1961) 323–341.

[25] D. Schiffel and C. Kitti, Rates of Invention: International Patent Comparisons, *Research Policy* 7 (1978) 324–340.

[26] J. Schmookler, *Invention and Economic Growth* (Harvard University Press, Cambridge, MA, 1966).

[27] J. Schumpeter, *The Theory of Economic Development* (Oxford, 1934).

[28] J. Schumpeter, *Business Cycles I–II* (Mc Graw-Hill, New York, 1939).

[29] J. Schumpeter, *Capitalism, Socialism and Democracy* (London, 1947).

[30] H. Singer and L. Reynolds, Technological Backwardness and Productivity Growth, *Econ. J.* 85 (1975) 873–876.

[31] L. Soete, A General Test of Technological Gap Trade Theory, *Weltwirtschaftliches Archiv* 117 (1981) 639–659.

[32] R. Solow, Technical Change and the Aggregate Production Function, *Rev. Econ. Stat.* 39 (1957) 312–320.

[33] R. Vernon, International Investment and International Trade in the Product Cycle, *Quarterly Journal of Economics* (1966) 191–207.

# [5]

## INNOVATION, DIVERSITY AND DIFFUSION: A SELF-ORGANISATION MODEL

Gerald Silverberg*

Giovanni Dosi**

Luigi Orsenigo***

May 1988
Fifth draft

forthcoming in The Economic Journal

\* Institute for Social Research, University of Stuttgart, W. Germany; from January 1988: MERIT, University of Limburg, Maastricht, The Netherlands

\*\* DAEST, Venice, Italy and SPRU, University of Sussex, Brighton, UK; from December 1987: Dept. of Economics, Faculty of Statistics, University of Rome "La Sapienza", Italy

\*\*\* Bocconi University, Milan, Italy and SPRU, University of Sussex, Brighton, UK

We gratefully acknowledge comments on an earlier paper on which this work is partly based by several participants at the International Conference on Innovation Diffusion, Venice, 17-21 March 1986, and in particular those of Richard Nelson, as well as comments on earlier drafts by two anonymous referees and an Associate Editor. The work of one of us (G.S.) was partially supported by a grant from the Deutsche Forschungsgemeinschaft, while the research of another one of us (G.D.) has been part of the activities of the Designated Research Center, sponsored by the E.S.R.C. at the Science Policy Research Unit (SPRU), University of Sussex.

## 1. Introduction

The diffusion of new products and new processes of production within and between business enterprises is clearly one of the fundamental aspects of the process of growth and transformation of contemporary economies.

It is well known that the diffusion of new products and pro- cesses takes varying lengths of time: some economic agents adopt very early after the development of an innovation while others sometimes do it only after decades. Moreover, during the dif- fusion process the competitive positions of the various agents (adopters and non-adopters) change. So do the economic incentives to adopt and the capabilities of the agents to make efficient use of the innovation. Finally, the innovation being adopted also changes over time, due to more or less incremental improvements in its performance characteristics which result in part from its more widespread use.

Contemporary analysis of diffusion has been essentially con- cerned with the following questions: (a) why isn't a new technol- ogy instantaneously adopted by all potential users? (i.e. what are the "retardation factors" preventing instantaneous dif- fusion?), (b) how can the dynamic paths of diffusion be represen- ted? and (c) what are the relevant variables driving the process?

However, innovation diffusion has rarely been formally treated as part of a more general theory of economic dynamics in which diversity of technological capabilities, business strategies, and expectations contribute to shape the evolutionary patterns of industries and countries (a remarkable exception is the evolu- tionary approach developed in particular by Nelson and Winter (1982) who, however, are more concerned with the general features of industrial dynamics than with the specific characteristics and

1

implications of the diffusion process).

In this work, we shall analyse the nature of diffusion processes in evolutionary environments characterised by technological and behavioural diversity amongst the economic agents,
basic uncertainty about the future, learning and disequilibrium
dynamics.

First, we shall identify some fundamental characteristics of
technology, innovation and diffusion which, we suggest, must be
accounted for in theoretical models. Second, against this background, we shall briefly review what we consider the major
achievements and shortcomings of the current models of innovation
diffusion. Third, we shall present what we call a "self-organisation" model of innovation diffusion, that is, a model whereby
relatively ordered paths of change emerge as the (partly) unintentional outcome of the dynamic interactions between individual
agents and the changing characteristics of the technology.
Fourth, the main properties and simulation results of the model
will be discussed.

## 2. Characteristics of Technology and Dynamic Industrial Envir-
   onments

A renewed interest in the economics of innovation over the last
two decades has brought considerable progress in the empirical
description and theoretical conceptualisation of the sources,
characteristics, directions and effects of technical change. We
review these topics in Dosi (1986) . Here it suffices to summarise some of the major findings directly relevant to the diffusion
of innovations concerning the nature of technology and the characteristics of firms and innovative environments.

(a) Technology - far from being a free good - is character-

2

ised by varying degrees of <u>appropriability</u>, of <u>uncertainty</u> about the technical and, a fortiori, commercial outcomes of innovative efforts, of <u>opportunity</u> for achieving technical advance, of <u>cumulativeness</u> in the patterns of innovation and exploitation of technological knowhow and hardware, and of <u>tacitness</u> of the knowledge and expertise on which innovative activities are based. Particular search and learning processes draw on technology-specific knowledge bases, related to both freely available information (e.g. scientific results) and more "local" and tacit skills, experience and problem-solving heuristics embodied in people and organizations.

(b) Technologies develop along relatively ordered paths (or "trajectories") shaped by specific technical properties, search rules, "technical imperatives" and cumulative expertise embodied in each "technological paradigm" (cf. Dosi (1984); for similar arguments see Nelson and Winter (1977), Sahal (1981) and (1985), Arthur (1985), Metcalfe (1985) and within somewhat different perspectives, Atkinson and Stiglitz (1969) and David (1975)). Relatedly, Winter (1984) defines different "technological regimes" according to whether the knowledge base underpinning innovative search is primarly "universal", and thus external to individual firms, or, alternatively, is primarily "local" and firm-specific.

(c) As a consequence of (a) and (b), diversity between firms is a fundamental and permanent characteristic of industrial environments undergoing technical change (see also Metcalfe (1985) on this point). Inter-firm diversity (even <u>within</u> an industry) can fall into three major categories.

First, there are technological gaps related to different technological capabilities to innovate, different degrees of

3

success in adopting and efficiently using product and process
innovations developed elsewhere, and different costs of production of output. In Dosi (1984) we define these forms of diversity as <u>technological asymmetries</u>, meaning unequivocal gaps
between firms which can be ranked as "better" and "worse" in
terms of costs of production and product characteristics.

Second, diversity relates to differences between firms in
their search procedures, input combinations and products, even
with roughly similar production costs (on this point, see Nelson
(1985)). Similarly, firms often search for their product innovations in different product-spaces and concentrate their effort on
different sections of the market. Let us call this second set of
sources of diversity <u>technological variety</u>, meaning all those
technological differences which do not correspond to unequivocal
hierarchies ("better" and "worse" technologies and products).

Third, one generally observes within an industry (and even
more so between industries) significant differences in the strategies of individual firms with respect to the level and composition of investment, scrapping, pricing, R & D, etc. Let us call
these differences <u>behavioural diversity</u>.

Evolutionary processes in economic environments involving
innovation and diffusion are governed to different degress by
<u>selection</u> mechanisms and <u>learning</u> mechanisms. Selection mech-
anisms tend to increase the economic dominance (e.g. profitability, market shares) of some firms with particular innovation
characteristics at the expense of others. Learning mechanisms, on
the other hand, may both spread innovative/imitative capabilities
throughout the (possibly changing) set of potential adopters and
reinforce existing disparities via cumulative mechanisms internal
to the firm.

Learning processes generally occur via (a) the development

4

of intra-and inter-industry "externalities" (which include the diffusion of information and expertise, interfirm mobility of manpower, and growth of specialised services); (b) informal processes of technological accumulation within firms (of which learning-by-doing and learning-by-using are the best known examples of such "internalised externalities") and (c) processes of economically expensive search (R & D being, of course, the best example).

After a brief survey of the current state-of-the-art in the theory of innovation diffusion, we shall present a model which, in our view, makes a serious attempt to incorporate some of these features of innovative environments in a novel, yet consistent and realistic way.


## 3. Diffusion Models: Results and Limitations


Three basic approaches dominate current economic thought on innovation diffusion (cf. Stoneman (1983) and (1986), Arcangeli (1986)). First, the line of enquiry pioneered by the seminal work of Mansfield (1961) and (1968), and Griliches (1957) tries to identify the empirical regularities in diffusion paths, typically represented by S-shaped curves. In Mansfield's "epidemic" approach, diffusion is generally found to be pushed by the expected profitability of the innovation and driven by the progressive dissemination of information about its technical and economic characteristics. Thus, diffusion is interpreted as a process of adjustment to some long term equilibrium contingent upon learning by potential adopters.[1]

Empirical work on diffusion, however, whilst confirming the role of profitability in adoption decisions, has shown that differences in the characteristics of innovations, of product mixes, and of the potential adopters are also key factors in the diffusion process (see, for example, Nabseth and Ray (1974), Gold (1981), Davies (1979), David (1975)).

These findings, together with theoretical considerations about the crudely mechanical nature of epidemic diffusion models, lend support to a second approach, namely one based on "equilibrium diffusion models". Here, diffusion is seen as a sequence of equilibria determined by changes in the economic attributes of the innovation and the environment (see David (1969), Davies (1979), Stoneman and Ireland (1983), Ireland and Stoneman (1983), David and Olsen (1984), Reinganum (1981)). This approach has undoubtedly provided important insights into diffusion processes. Amongst other things, it has shown the importance of (i) differences (such as size) between potential adopters; (ii) the interactions between the supply decisions of the firms producing innovations and the pace of their adoption; (iii) the technological expectations of suppliers and adopters; (iv) the patterns of strategic interactions amongst both suppliers and adopters; (v) the market structure in both the supplying and using industries. However, these results are generally achieved at a high theoretical price. Radical uncertainty is de facto eliminated and maximising behaviour is assumed.[2] The analysis is often undertaken in terms of the existence and the properties of equilibria, while nothing is generally said about adjustment processes. Information about the techno-economic characteristics of the technologies is generally assumed to be freely available to all agents. The nature of "technology" is radically simplified and assumed to be embodied in given technical features of production inputs.

A third approach is explicitly evolutionary and represents

the diffusion of new techniques and new products under conditions
of uncertainty, bounded rationality and endogeneity of market
structures as a disequilibrium process (Nelson (1968), Nelson
and Winter (1982), Metcalfe (1985), Silverberg (1984), Iwai
(1984a) and (1984b)).[3]

The model that follows is in this evolutionary tradition, and
thus allows for disequilibrium processes, endogeneity of market
structures, etc. It also explicitly incorporates those assumptions of "equilibrium" diffusion models which capture important empirical characteristics of innovative environments
mentioned earier, such as the relevance of expectations and
differences between agents, as well as some features implicit in
Mansfield-type models, such as imperfect information and asymmetric technological knowledge.[4]

## 4. A Self-Organisation Model of the Diffusion of Innovations and the Transition Between Technological Trajectories

In two previous papers, one of the present authors (Silverberg
(1984) and (1987)) attempted to demonstrate the relevance to
economic theory of the self-organizational approach to dynamic
modelling pioneered by Eigen, Haken, Prigogine and others[5]. In
essence the argument proceeds from the observation that in complex interdependent dynamical systems unfolding in historical,
i.e., irreversible time, economic agents, who have to make decisions today the correctness of which will only be revealed considerably later, are confronted with irreducible uncertainty and
holistic interactions between each other and with aggregate variables. The a priori assumption of an "equilibrium" solution to
this problem to which all agents ex ante can subscribe and which
makes their actions consistent and in some sense dynamically

7

stable is a leap of methodological faith. Instead we proposed employing some of the recently developed methods of evolutionary modelling to show how the interaction of diverse capabilities, expectations and strategies with the thereby emerging selective pressures can drive a capitalistic economy along certain definite patterns of development.

Drawing on a dynamic model of market competition with embodied technical progress investigated in Silverberg (1987), we embed the question of diffusion into the larger one of the transition of an industry between two "technological trajectories". Choice of technique is no longer a choice between two pieces of equipment with given (but perhaps imperfectly known) characteristics, but now involves skills in using them which can be endogenously built up by learning by doing or by profiting from the experience of others, as well as expectations about future developments along the various competing trajectories. As we shall see, the diversity in firms' capabilities and expectations is an irreducible element driving the diffusion process.

In the sectoral approach taken here industry-level demand is taken as given and growing at some exponential rate. Firms command some market share of this demand at any given time, but market shares may change over time as a dynamic response with a characteristic time constant (reflecting the "freeness" of competition and such factors as brand loyalty, information processing and search delays and costs, etc.) to disparities in the relative competitiveness of firms. This concept, so dear to close observers of the business scene, has to our knowledge evaded incorporation into a systematic economic theory until now. The evolution of market structure is governed in our approach by an equation relating the rate of change of a firm's market share to the

difference between its competitiveness (defined below) and average industry competitiveness (averaged over all competing firms
in an industry, weighted by their market shares). This equation
is formally identical to the equation first introduced into
mathematical biology by R. A. Fisher in 1930 and more recently
applied in a variety of contexts and studied in considerable
mathematical detail by Eigen (1971), Eigen and Schuster (1979),
Ebeling and Feistel (1982), Hofbauer and Sigmund (1985), and
Sigmund (1986). Our use of this equation differs from most biological applications, however, in that the competitiveness parameters, rather than being constants or simple functions of the
other variables, themselves change over time in complex ways in
response to the strategies pursued by firms and feedbacks from
the rest of the system. In a systems theoretic sense this equation may be regarded as the fundamental mathematical description
of competitive processes. It is worth emphasizing the difference
between our approach and standard theoretical conceptualisations
of competition. The latter generally identify the circumstances
under which no relative competitive shifts or profits can be
realised (impossibility of arbitrage, uniform rate of profit,
etc.) and then assume that the system must always be in or near
this state.

If we denote by $f_i$ the market share in percent of real orders
of the ith firm, by $E_i$ its competitiveness and by $\langle E \rangle$ the average
competitiveness of all firms in the industry (= $\Sigma f_i E_i$), then the
evolution of market shares is governed by the following equation:

(1)   $f_i = A_9 (E_i - \langle E \rangle) f_i$ .

We define the competitiveness parameter as a linear combination
of terms reflecting relative price and delivery delay differentials:

9

(2)   $E_i = -\ln p_i - A_{10} dd_i$ ,

where $p_i$ is the market price of the ith firm and $dd_i$ its current
delivery delay.[6]

   Silverberg (1987) presents a basic dynamic structure for dealing with strategic investment in the face of uncertainty with
respect to the future course of embodied technical progress,
overall demand and changes in relative competitiveness. In this
framework, entrepreneurs are seen as being fully conscious of the
ongoing, process nature of economic growth and technological
change, so that their decisions, particularly concerning fixed
investment, take account of and try to anticipate these developments. Decision-making is incorporated on the one hand in certain
robust rules of thumb (for the most part feedback rules dealing
with oligopolistic pricing and production policies) and "animal
spirits" in the form of decision rules governing replacement
policy (the payback period method) and expansion of capacity
("estimates" or "guesses" of future demand growth corrected by
experience). Technical change is embodied in vintages, and the
resulting capital stocks are not assumed to start in, and in
general need not converge to steady-state distributions.

   The capital stock (measured in units of productive capacity)
of each firm is represented as an aggregation over nondecaying
vintages between the current period t and the scapping date
$T_i(t)$:

(3)   $K_i(t) = \int_{T_i}^{t} K_i(t,t')dt'$ ,

where $K_i(t,t)$ is gross investment at time t (in capacity units),
$K_i(t,t') = K_i(t',t')$ if $T_i(t) < t' < t$ and

          $= 0$ otherwise.

10

This aggregate capital stock may be a composite of different technologies as well as different vintages of a single technological trajectory. A payback calculation is performed by each firm with its desired payback period (which may differ between firms) to determine a desired scrapping date for its capital stock $T_{di}(t)$ by solving:

(4)  $P(t)/(c(T_{di}) - c(t)) = b_i$,

where $P(t)$ is the price of new capital equipment per unit capacity, $c(..)$ is the unit operating cost at time $t$ of the vintage in question, and $b_i$ is the target payback period of the ith firm.[7]

The actual scrapping date adjusts to this desired date via a first-order catch up procedure:

(5)  $\dot{T_i} = z_i \max[A_{1i}(T_{di} - T_i), 0]$

where $z_i$ is a rationing parameter between 0 and 1 (the ratio of current cash flow to desired gross investment) which may arise if the ith firm, due to financial constraints, is not able to fully finance its desired investment program (otherwise it is 1). The amount of capacity scrapped as a result of this decision (as well as a possible desire to reduce overall capacity) is

(6)  $S_i = K_i(t,T) \dot{T}$.

Net expansion (or contraction) of capacity is governed by a desired expansion rate $r_i$ for each firm:

(7)  $N_i = r_i K_i$.

The capital stock changes over time due to additions from gross investment and removals due to scrapping:

(8)  $\dot{K_i} = N_i = K_i(t,t) - S_i$.

11

The desired rate of capacity expansion may be set initially at any level ("animal spirits") but is revised over time using first-order feedback from the deviation of the rate of capacity utilisation u from its desired level $u_0$:

(9)   $\dot{r}_1 = A_{13} (u_1 - u_0)$.

Labour is assumed to be the only current cost of production and can be decomposed into prime and overhead components.[8] The prime unit labour coefficient is an average over the historical technological labour/output coefficients $a(t)$ weighted by vintage (in the following the firm subscript i has been suppressed for simplicity):

(10)   $\langle a \rangle = \int_T^t a(t') K(t,t') dt' / K(t)$.

It changes over time due to additions of more productive new equipment through investment and removal of marginal equipment through scrapping according to the following equation derived from (10) by differentiation:

(11)   $\langle \dot{a} \rangle = [K(t,t)(a(t)-\langle a \rangle) + S(\langle a \rangle - a(T))] / K$.

If net investment is taking place, i.e., $N > 0$, then all scrapping serves the purpose of replacement investment R, so that $K(t,t) = N+R$, $S = R$ and

(12)   $\langle \dot{a} \rangle = [N(a(t)-\langle a \rangle) + R(a(t)-a(T))] / K$,

which shows that replacement investment contributes more to lowering unit costs per unit of investment outlay than does expansion investment. Thus unit costs are determined by the age structure of the capital stock and the history of technological change it represents. They will vary over time as a result of the

12

scrapping and expansion strategies of the firm under the constraint of its ability to finance its investment plans, itself a
function of cost and profitability.[9]

Overhead labour per unit output at full operating capacity is
assumed proportional to prime unit labour. Total overhead labour
is then this value multiplied by total productive capacity K (and
thus is independent of the rate of capacity utilisation, contrary
to total prime labour, which is directly proportional to it).

The level of production is set such as to compensate for
deviations of the current delivery delay (dd) from some industrywide standard level ($dd_0$):

(13) $\dot{u} = A_5 (dd-dd_0) u (1.1 - u^2)$, $u < 1$,

$\qquad = 0$, $u = 1$ and rhs above $> 0$.

The quadratic saturation term is introduced to represent bottlenecks in the production process near the full capacity limit.
Delivery delay dd is the ratio of order backlog L to current
production y (= uK), and the order backlog is governed by the
rate equation

(14) $\dot{L} = d - y$,

where d is incoming orders (= $f_i$ x total market demand).

Firms' prices are determined as a dynamic compromise between
the desired markup on unit costs and relative competitiveness.
Since only relative prices are of importance here, we take the
logarithm of price variables throughout. Let $p_i$ be the log of the
ith firm's market price and $p_{ci}$ its desired markup price based on
its unit prime costs. Then

(15) $\dot{p}_i = A_7 (p_{ci} - p_i) + A_8 (E_i - \langle E \rangle)$.

Pricing policy is regarded as a compromise (depending on the

13

"degree of monopoly" characteristic of an industry) between
strict cost-plus pricing and a concession to the "prevailing"
market price (the geometric mean of all prices weighted by market
shares) via relative competitiveness. This structure of pricing
allows the changing relative cost structure of firms to be transmitted through the market and makes intelligible such phenomena
as price leadership or being under price pressure . Firms at a
competitive (in general mostly cost) disadvantage are thus forced
to lower their prices somewhat to prevent excessive losses of
market share, while firms enjoying a competitive advantage are
free to realise short-term profits by raising their prices. The
ratio of $A_8$ to $A_7$ determines to what extent competitive pressures
overrule the markup principle (which remains valid however at the
aggregate level) and enables the model to span the entire range
of market structures between pure monopoly and pure competition.[10]

As the model now stands, with a single vintage structure for
each firm, it already accounts for the diffusion of new technology in the case in which a unique best practice technology is
apparent to all agents (this perspective on diffusion was first
introduced by Salter, 1962). The process of investment under the
assumption of some long term rate of technical progress implicit
in the payback method ensures that advances in productivity will
be continually incorporated into the capital stock, even if
entrepreneurs differ in their assessment of the appropriate payback to use. Thus diffusion of technical progress is already
guaranteed by the standard methods of investment policy at this
first level of analysis.

However, in order to capture the collective dynamic of advance
along different technological trajectories we propose the following additional structure. We compare two technological trajec-

14

tories representing at any time the maximum productivities attainable in best practice vintages of the respective technologies. We assume that these are both changing at some rate, and
that the second technology is always absolutely superior in
productivity. Moreover, the relative price/capacity unit of the
two technologies may also be changing. The actual productivities
realised by firms are a product of this underlying value and the
specific efficiency or skill with which firms master each technology (between 0 and 100%). For simplicity we assume all firms
begin with technology 1, and technology 2 first becomes available
at time t*. Furthermore, technology 1 is already mature, i.e.
skill levels are saturated at 100%. The firms initially possess
lower (and possibly varying) efficiencies with technology 2, but
the margin for further development is not knowable with any
precision. Firms only know the product of this efficiency and the
underlying potential. They may (and in fact must) make guesses
about the rate at which further improvements in efficiency
(equally applicable to previously installed vintages) and further
embodied technical progress (only applicable to current investment) will be achieved. This formulation reflects the fact that
the productivity of a technology realised in practice is not just
a function of the presence of the requisite machines, but con-
jointly requires certain levels of specific expertise and experience (from specialized scientific and engineering training to
shop floor apprenticeship and work discipline) both internal and
external to the firm. Hence investment decisions are not merely a
question of determining the best practice technology at a given
time, but one of weighing the propects for further development
either by acquiring experience with it now to gain a jump on
competitors or waiting for a more opportune moment and avoiding

15

possible development costs.[11]

We identify the evolution of the efficiency parameter with movement down the well-known learning or experience curve using a logistic dynamic and a variable rate of change equal to the rate of growth of cumulative production with the technology (this corresponds to the classic power law learning curves on cumulative production reported in the literature for values well below saturation). This represents internal learning and is only achieved if the firm actually produces with the new technology. Writing $s_i$ for the internal skill level of the ith firm using the new technology, $P_i$ for its current production and $CP_i$ for its cumulated production with the new technology, we have

$$(16) \quad \dot{s}_i = A_{15} (P_i / (CP_i + C)) s_i (1 - s_i), \quad \text{if } s_i > s_p,$$

where C is a constant proportional to the capital stock and $s_p$ is the level of skill generally available in the industry even to those firms not yet producing on the new technological trajectory.

In addition, the experience acquired by individual firms can "leak" out and become available to the rest of the industry. In practice this can take the form of skilled labour and management moving between firms (or setting up their own companies), manufacturers diffusing the results of experience gained with their equipment to other users in the form of operating instructions and the like, trade organisations and publications, educational institutions, or even industrial espionage. We represent this by having the level of generally available skill (public skill) lag behind the average of internal skill levels with an exponential delay:

$$(17) \quad \dot{s}_p = A_4 (\langle s \rangle - s_p),$$

16

where $\langle s \rangle = \Sigma\, f_i s_i$ .

Firms profit from this learning externality because they "float" on the rising general skill level even if they are not yet employing the new technology:

(18) $s_i = s_P$ if $s_i = s_P$ .

In deciding on whether to switch to the new technology firms may want to abandon their normal investment criteria to take into consideration the gains in productivity they may be able to realise even after new equipment is installed as well their desire to attain early proficiency in it use and thereby get on a possible virtuous circle. These will depend on how optimistic they are about the future development potential of the new trajectory and the extent to which temporary advantages can be appropriated (which is related to the relative rates of internal and external learning) as well as what their competitors are planning. To this end firms select an "anticipation bonus" they award to the new technology in making their choice of technique. They multiply the current realisable productivity by their bonus for the new technology and compare it with the best practice productivity of the old in a payback calculation. This means that the new technology is preferred if its adjusted productivity is higher than that of the old and 1) it is cheaper per unit of capacity at the time of comparison or 2) it is more expensive but the difference in price can be recouped within the desired payback period by the savings in labour cost. If $c_1$, $P_1$ and $c_2$, $P_2$ are the unit cost and price per efficiency unit of the old and the new technique, respectively, then the calculation is

(19) $(P_2 - P_1)/(c_1 - c_2/s_i X_i) \leq b_i$ ,

17

where $X_i$ is the anticipation bonus of the ith firm (cf. eq. 4). The last case in which its (adjusted) productivity is lower but its price is also lower is excluded here as being of limited empirical interest.

It remains to decide what changes this introduces into the replacement rule. The reference value entering into the payback calculation for replacement uses the maximum of the old best practice productivity and the currently realisable new best practice productivity. This ensures that scrapping does not fall below the rate that would have prevailed if investment had continued in the old technology, and that it only accelerates when the new technology actually proves its superior performance on the shop floor.

The above model represents a dynamical system which, due to the vintage structure, should be categorised as a set of differential-difference equations with age-dependent effects. This is a class of systems whose mathematical properties, even in the most simple cases, are still only poorly understood. Many of the mathematical elements going into the model, however, have a well-known pedigree, such as the replicator dynamics governing market shares (see e.g. Sigmund, 1986). Consequently, we are forced to resort to "experimental mathematics" in the form of a computer implementation to uncover some of the economic properties of the model.

## 5. Market Dynamics, Diffusion, and the Collective Rationality of the Adoption Decision

The system as described above admits several dimensions of structural and behavioural variability over time: firms can be of different sizes, characterised by different unit costs, delivery

delays, rates of capacity utilization, skill levels, age profiles
of capital stock, etc. Of course, in this model as in a large
part of the diffusion literature (e.g. David, 1969, Stoneman and
Ireland, 1984), a distribution of initial characteristics of
firms, with uniform expectations across firms, other things being
equal, will lead to a distribution of adoption dates. In the
general case of diverse firm characteristics and diverse technological expectations, the distribution of adoption decisions will
both result from these initial distributions and contribute to
their endogenous transformation. Thus firms' sizes, skill levels,
and the like cannot be regarded as fixed characteristics to which
the diffusion process can be referred, but rather must be seen
themselves as in part products of that process. However, to focus
more clearly on the strategic aspects of the diffusion process
and the problem of the interdependence of behaviour even in the
absence of diverse firm characteristics, we will neglect this
dimension of the problem. Instead, we will single out the role of
the anticipation bonus (reflecting expectations about the future
course of the new trajectory) in relation to what we term dynamic
appropriability and set all other characteristics identical
across firms.

In the three runs we will now consider, technology 2 is potentially 100% more productive than technology 1 and both are advancing in the embodied sense at 4% p.a., as are nominal wages.
Overall demand is growing at 5%. Technology 2 starts out being
priced higher per capacity unit but this price declines at the
rate of 1% p.a. All 10 firms employed in the first case (Figures
1-4) start out identical in every respect except in their propensity to innovate, i.e. their innovation bonuses. The initial
efficiency level on technology 2 is 30% for all firms. The anti-

cipation bonuses range from 3.33 to 1.0 with a clustering around
1.33 (i.e. the firm evaluates the productivity of technology 2
in its choice of technique decision 33% higher than its actual
present value). The vertical dotted lines indicate the date of
adoption of the firm with the corresponding number.

Figure 1 graphs three measures of diffusion. The curve marked
with squares shows the classic measure of inter-firm diffusion
discussed in the literature: the percentage of potential adopters
already employing some quantity of the new technology. It shows
the typical S-shape familiar to students of diffusion. Just near
it (marked with a diamond) is a curve depicting the current
market share of adopters. If this curve lies above/below the
previous one, adopters as a whole have gained/lost market shares
over time. The aggregation hides the fact that the vicissitudes
of individual adopters can vary quite widely. The last curve
represents the percentage of overall productive capacity embodied
in the new technology. This results from both inter and intra-
firm diffusion as well as shifts in the relative sizes of firms
and is the key variable in analysing the impact of the innovation
at the industry and the economy-wide levels. It displays the
classic smooth S-shaped form Fisher and Pry (1971) found in
measuring diffusion in capacity terms.

Figure 2 plots market shares and reveals the microeconomic
drama going on beneath the aggregation surface. Firms 1 and 2,
which adopt as soon as the innovation appears on the market (year
10), just manage to maintain respectable market shares. Firm 3
innovates 2 1/2 years later and does around 2 percentage points
better in holding on to market share. Firm 4 is the clear winner
in this saga, benefitting from the mistakes of firms 1-3 but
still getting in on the ground floor to increase its market share
by over 50%. Firms 5-8 are also net profiters from the market

20

reshuffle to a small extent. Even firm 9, one of the laggards, manages to recover its initial market share after taking something of a beating. Firms 10 demonstrates the pitfalls of missing the boat by not providing for an anticipation bonus. It has evidently been pushed into a vicious downward spiral which completely eliminates it from the market.

Figure 3 depicts the realised productivity of the entire capital stock of each firm, corrected for the rate of capacity utilization, and divided by the old best practice productivity to eliminate the underlying exponential trend. The early adopters suffer a loss as they first go down the learning curve and then pull ahead. The middle adopters suffer only minor losses and soon overtake the early group, while the late adopters manage to get on the "track" but consistently remain below the industry average (the dashed curve).[12] Firm 10, finally, is thrown completely off the track and never comes close to closing the gap.

The evolution of the firm-specific and external skill levels is shown in Figure 4. The early adopters do indeed build up a lead in their internal efficiency, but the middle and late adopters start from a higher initial level due to external learning and eventually overtake them. Even firm 10 manages to rise above the public skill level for a while after it adopts.

If we now naively rerun history (in a run there is no point in plotting) by giving all 10 firms the anticipation bonus used by the winner of the first round (firm 4), something surprising occurs. The new technology is not adopted at all because no firm is willing to incur the development costs associated with bringing it to commercial maturity. This makes it clear that technological innovation and diffusion are characterised by collective effects and an inextricable tension between private and social

21

gain.

This is further brought out in the third run (Figures 5-8), which is an example of "early adopters receive their just deserts". All parameters of this run are identical to those of the first one except for a doubling of coefficient $A_{15}$ in eq. (14). This accelerates the rate of internal learning and thereby raises the dynamic appropriability of the innovation for the early adopters. Although the actual times of adoption have hardly changed, the relative fortunes of the competing firms change considerably. The first adopters (firms 1 and 2) are clear net beneficiaries, followed by firm 3. All of the middle adopters are huddled closely together with little change in their market shares, while the straggler firm 10 is once again catapulted from the market.

What story does this one sequence of runs out of many possible ones have to tell us about strategic behaviour in innovative environments? In some respects the prospective shift of technological paradigm creates a Prisoner's Dilemma situation: conservative entrepreneurs would all prefer to avoid accelerated capital replacement and costly development expenditures. Yet profits may eventually be reaped and irreversible market share gains realised by adopting early. This threat thus forces entrepreneurs to take an anticipatory position and can be ultimately self-justifying, if the innovation is indeed potentially superior. This latter fact, of course, remains uncertain until the diffusion process is well underway. Moreover, the adoption decision is complicated by the learning externality. The dynamic appropriability of the new trajectory, as we have seen, serves as a bifurcation parameter. For high enough values a first-in strategy is preferable, for lower values a second-in one is. But a second-in strategy is only possible if there is a sacrificial lamb in the form of a first adopter. And first adopters exist because the precise value of the dynamic appropriability is unknown.

One might inquire whether some distribution of adoption times may not exist satisfying a Nash equilibrium, i.e., given that it is clear that adoption will actually take place in a certain sequence, no single entrepreneur has an incentive to locally deviate from his adoption decision. This is precisely what Reinganum (1981) has studied in a static context. In comparison with our model, however, it should first be noted that the payoffs to adoption cannot simply be expressed as a function of the percentage of the industry already adopting. This is because nonlinear cumulative causation a) makes the form of the interaction between agents exceedingly complex and subject to bifurcations, and b) in evolutionary games such as our own, outcomes are in terms of expansion, survival or extinction and not of one-time monetary payments.

In the biological literature the evolutionary stable strategy (ESS) concept corresponds to that of a Nash equilibrium.[13] Instead of the rationality postulate, the concept of noninvadability is used. The justification for this procedure is that interactions between strategies are microevents repeated sufficiently often against unchanging boundary conditions to ensure convergence. To what extent can such an argument be invoked to explain market dynamics? Routine rules such as the payback period investment criterion may become established historically through some such process, as is argued in Silverberg (1987). A shift between technological paradigms confronts us with an altogether different situation which is in some ways comparable to the lockin and standards phenomena discussed by Arthur (1985, 1988), David (1985), and Katz and Shapiro (1985 and 1986). Because major

innovations entailing a new endogenous skill regime occur infre-
quently, there can be no "learning" process to ensure a convergence of strategies before the strategies have been irreversibly
implemented. It is the diversity of positions adopted by firms
that allows the potential superiority of a new technological
regime to be developed and exploited. In that process losses and
gains will almost invariably be made before routine procedures
can reassert themselves. Rationality cannot be invoked to guarantee equilibrium because the system is not sufficiently transparent and their is no ex ante coordination mechanism. But if diversity may have inevitably negative consequences for some participants, at the system-level it is necessary to probe the development potential and trigger the collective development process.
Lockin to an inferior technology of course is an associated
danger. By the time another such decision arises, crucial parameters such as the dynamic appropriability will have almost
certainly changed, so that the successful strategies of the last
round may no longer be valid. Or they invalidate themselves
because now they are being copied.

Figures 9 and 10 and Tables 1 to 3 summarise the results of 35
runs conducted for the same distribution of anticipation bonuses
as in Figures 1 - 8 but for a range of values of the internal and
public learning rates ($A_{13}$ and $A_4$). Figure 1 plots the time for
the new technology to increase its share in total capacity from
10 to 90% and is a measure of the speed of diffusion. A very
regular pattern emerges, with the speed of diffusion increasing,
but at a declining rate, as a function of both parameters. A
threshold can be discerned in the region of low learning rates.
Below it only a few pioneer firms adopt the new technology, but
are then driven off the market. Non-adopters manage to dominate
the industry, the diffusion process reverses, and the technology

24

ultimately disappears, even though it is potentially superior.

In Figure 10 the bifurcations in the qualitative nature of the market reshuffle become visible. As we have seen, for low values of the learning parameters, non-adopters eventually increase their market shares at the expense of adopters (the peak of the cliff). For a middle range of values some (but of course not all) of the later adopters profit most in terms of markets share gains from introducing the new technology (the plateau). As we suspected, a threshold exists in the $A_4$-$A_{15}$ plane beyond which first adopters emerge with the largest gains in market share (the foot of the hill). This threshold is primarily a function of the internal learning rate but, surprisingly, declines somewhat with higher public learning rates. Tables 1 and 2 summarise the original data.

## 6. Conclusions

In the first part of this paper we underscored the role of technological expectations, cumulativeness, internal and public knowledge, and strategic competition in any discussion of the dynamics of innovation-induced technological change. We then went on to formulate a model based on a number of behavioural assumptions on the one hand, and a structure of feedback loops on the other. This removed the question of diffusion from the largely static framework in which it has traditionally been placed and led to a dynamic coupling between the behaviour of individual agents and the environment in which they are operating. Although, as we have argued, a considerable range of microeconomic diversity and disequilibrium must remain an irreducible feature of such a system, the diffusion process itself shows a rather stable and invariant structure. Thus our simulations show that while some firms may be incurring short-term losses for long-term gains in market share, and others are driven onto a vicious spiral towards bankruptcy, nevertheless the S-shaped form of the diffusion curve (which however is not necessarily a logistic and may even decline during the early phases) stands out. It is this superposition of micro-economic drama and system-level logic which makes the Schumpeter-ian entrepreneur a crucial element in the innovation process.

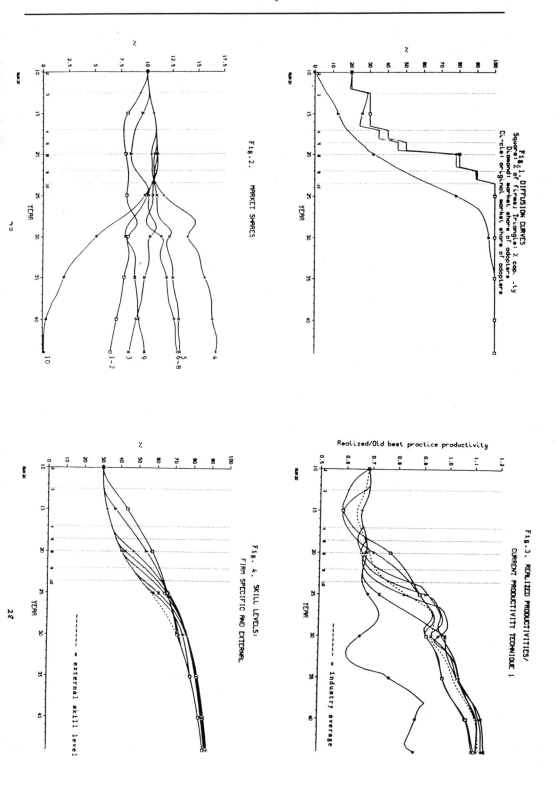

Fig. 1. DIFFUSION CURVES
Square: % of firms; Triangle: % capacity
Diamond: market share of adopters
Circle: original market share of adopters

Fig. 2.    MARKET SHARES

Fig. 3.    REALIZED PRODUCTIVITIES/
CURRENT PRODUCTIVITY TECHNIQUE 1

------- = industry average

Fig. 4.    SKILL LEVELS:
FIRM SPECIFIC AND EXTERNAL

------- = external skill level

Realized/Old best practice productivity

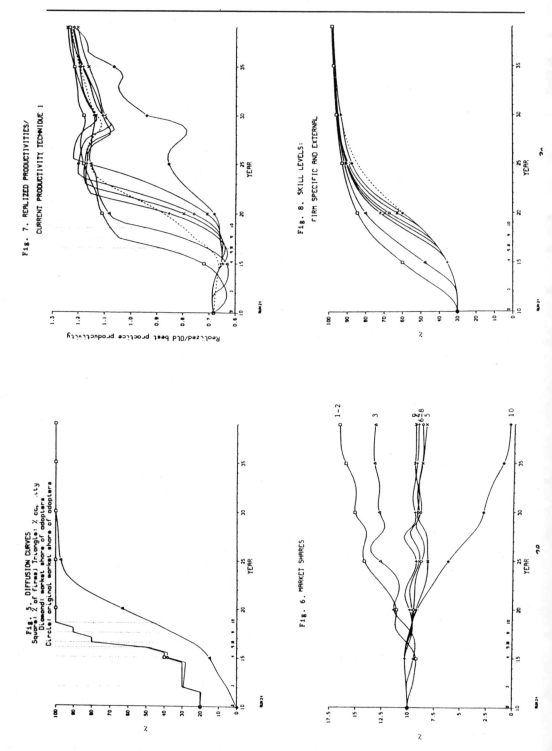

Fig. 7. REALIZED PRODUCTIVITIES/
CURRENT PRODUCTIVITY TECHNIQUE 1

Realized/Old best practice productivity

Fig. 8. SKILL LEVELS:
FIRM SPECIFIC AND EXTERNAL

Fig. 5. DIFFUSION CURVES
Square: % of firms; Triangle: % capacity
Diamond: market share of adopters
Circle: original market share of adopters

Fig. 6. MARKET SHARES

FIG. 9. TIME TO DIFFUSE FROM 10% TO 90%

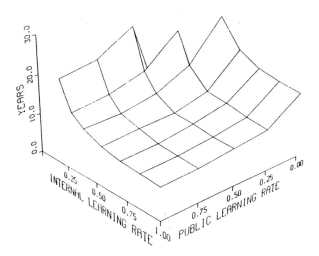

FIG. 10. DIFFUSION WINNER: FIRST VS LATER ADOPTERS

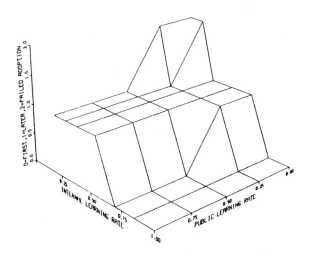

Table 1. Time for capacity share of new technology to diffuse from 10% to 90% for different values of parameters $a_4$ and $a_{15}$ (fd = failed diffusion).

| $a_{15}$ \ $a_4$ | .1 | .325 | .55 | .775 | 1.00 |
|---|---|---|---|---|---|
| .2 | fd | fd | 29.51 | 23.53 | 21.50 |
| .3 | fd | 27.02 | 19.01 | 16.02 | 14.52 |
| .4 | 29.52 | 19.03 | 14.51 | 12.54 | 12.04 |
| .55 | 22.04 | 14.04 | 11.54 | 10.99 | 10.01 |
| .7 | 19.00 | 13.03 | 10.99 | 9.52 | 9.01 |
| .85 | 17.53 | 11.53 | 10.01 | 9.02 | 8.53 |
| 1.0 | 16.50 | 10.56 | 9.52 | 8.53 | 8.04 |

Table 2. Asymptotic results of diffusion process in terms of relative market shares. fd = failed diffusion and relative decline of adopting firms
1 = later adopters attain largest market shares
f = first adopters attain largest market shares

| $a_{15}$ \ $a_4$ | .1 | .325 | .55 | .775 | 1.00 |
|---|---|---|---|---|---|
| .2 | fd | fd | 1 | 1 | 1 |
| .3 | fd | 1 | 1 | 1 | 1 |
| .4 | 1 | 1 | 1 | 1 | 1 |
| .55 | 1 | 1 | 1 | 1 | 1 |
| .7 | 1 | 1 | f | f | f |
| .85 | f | f | f | f | f |
| 1.0 | f | f | f | f | f |

**Notes**

1. One may for example represent this diffusion process as the transition between two "classical" long term equilibium positions: see Metcalfe and Gibbons (1983).

2. To be precise, in Davies' original model adoption decisions are based on rules of thumb explicitly justified in terms of "bounded rationality". Yet, subsequent developments within this approach have been explicitly based on maximising behaviour of the agents.

3. See also Eliasson (1982) and (1986). On the connection to empirical analysis see Gort and Klepper (1982), Gort and Konakayma (1982) and Levin et. al. (1985).

4. A more detailed discussion of the empirical basis of the hypotheses entering into the model presented below can be found in Dosi, Orsenigo and Silverberg (1988).

5. For a multidisciplinary overview of self-organisational modelling and its methodological philosophy see Haken (1983), Nicolis and Prigogine (1977) and Prigogine (1976).

6. Product quality factors could also be included in this expression, but for simplicity we restrict the analysis here to markets with fully standardised commodities.

7. In the economics literature a number of seemingly "self-evident" rules have been applied to decide when technologically obsolete equipment should be replaced by new equipment. One calls for an old vintage to be replaced when its unit variable costs exceed total unit costs of current best practice. Another indicates replacement when unit variable costs exceed the price attained per unit of output. A substantial specialised literature exists, however, dealing with optimal replacement beginning with Terborgh (Terborgh, 1949; see also Smith, 1961). Under suitable assumptions about the rate of future technical progress this leads to the so-called square root rule.
    Terborgh shows that the payback criterion is a reasonable approximation to the square root rule. Given that uncertain technological expectations (which are an extrapolation from past experience in this rule) play a major role, and that surveys of industrial practice consistently reveal rate of return or payback period calculations to be widely entrenched, we have opted for this simple criterion in our treatment of replacement. For a discussion of optimal replacement in the evolutionary framework employed here see Silverberg (1987).

8. Other current costs of production could be incorporated by making the prime unit labour coefficient and nominal wage rate vectors.

9. The exact functional relationship is reminiscent of Kaldor's technical progress function, but shows that the rate of change of *average* productivity is a function of the gaps between best practice, average and marginal vintage productivities *and* the

division of gross investment between modernization and expansion.

10. For a more detailed discussion of the price interactions to which this system leads see Silverberg (1987).

11. Thus in a very suggestive study of the diffusion of numerically controlled machine tools in German industry, Kleine (1983) reports that some firms invested in the new technology even though it did not yet satisfy their normal investment criteria because they hoped to build up superior skills specific to a technology which they anticipated would play a decisive role in the future. Others took a more conservative attitude, by no means irrational prima facie, and waited for the smoke to clear before buying into a more mature technology. The spread of knowledge about the availability and purported superiority of NC equipment played almost no role since the firms surveyed were well informed from the start by suppliers and trade publications. Similar observations on computer adoption decisions have been made by Stoneman (1976).

12. It should be borne in mind that productivity is only part of competitiveness. The response of delivery delays to production and capacity expansion decisions also contributes to changes in market shares and realised price margins.

13. For a discussion of the specific features of evolutionary games in various contexts see Axelrod (1984), Hofbauer and Sigmund (1984), Thomas (1984), and Zeeman (1979 and 1981).

References

F. Arcangeli (1986), "Innovation Diffusion: A Cross-traditions State of the Art", SPRU, University of Sussex, Brighton

W.B. Arthur (1985), "On Competing Technologies and Historical Small Events. The Dynamics of Choice Under Increasing Returns", Technological Innovation Programme Workshop Paper, Department of Economics, Stanford University

W.B. Arthur (1988), "Competing Technologies: An Overview", in G. Dosi, C. Freeman, R. Nelson, G. Silverberg, and L. Soete, (eds.), **Technical Change and Economic Theory**, London, Francis Pinter, forthcoming.

A.B. Atkinson and J.E. Stiglitz (1969), "A New View of Technological Change", **Economic Journal**, 79, 573-578

R. Axelrod (1984), **The Evolution of Cooperation**, New York, Basic Books

P. David (1969), "A Contribution to the Theory of Diffusion", Stanford, Stanford Center for Research in Economic Growth, Paper No. 71

P. David (1975), **Technical Choice, Innovation and Economic Growth**, Cambridge, Cambridge University Press

P. David (1985), "Clio and The Economics of QWERTY", **American Economic Review, Papers and Proceedings**, 75, pp. 332-337

P. David and T. E. Olsen (1984), "Anticipated Automation: a Rational Expectations Model of Technological Diffusion", Stanford, Center for Economic Policy Research

S. Davies (1979), **The Diffusion of Process Innovations**, Cambridge, Cambridge University Press

G. Dosi (1984), **Technical Change and Industrial Transformation**, London, Macmillan

G. Dosi (1986), "The Microeconomic Sources and Effects of Innovation. An Assessment of Some Recent Findings", Brighton, SPRU, University of Sussex, DRC Discussion Paper

G. Dosi, L. Orsenigo and G. Silverberg (1988), "Innovation Diffusion as a Self-Organizational Process", in F. Arcangeli, P. David and G. Dosi (eds.), **Innovation Diffusion**, Oxford, Oxford University Press, forthcoming.

W. Ebeling and R. Feistel (1982), **Physik der Selbstorganisation und Evolution**, East Berlin, Akademie Verlag

M. Eigen (1971), "Selforganization of matter and the evolution of biological macromolecules", **Die Naturwissenschaften**, 58, pp. 465-523

M. Eigen and P. Schuster (1979), **The hypercycle: A principle of natural selforganization**, Berlin-Heidelberg-New York, Springer-Verlag

G. Eliasson (1982), "On the Optimal Rate of Structural Adjustment", Stockholm, Industrial Institute for Economic and Social Research, Working Paper No. 74

G. Eliasson (1986), "Micro Heterogeneity of Firms and Stability of Industrial Growth", in R. Day and G. Eliasson (eds.), The **Dynamics of Market Economies**, Amsterdam, North-Holland

J.C. Fisher and R.H. Pry (1971), "A Simple Substitution Model of Technological Change", Technological **Forecasting** and Social Change, 3, pp. 75-88

B. Gold (1981), "Technological Diffusion in Industry: Research Needs and Shortcomings", Journal of Industrial Economics, 29, pp. 247-269

M. Gort and S. Klepper (1982), "Time Paths in the Diffusion of Product Innovation", Economic Journal, 92, pp. 630-653

M. Gort and A. Konakayama (1982), "A Model of Diffusion in the Production of an Innovation", **American Economic Review**, 72, pp. 1111-1120

Z. Griliches (1957) "Hybrid Corn: An Exploration in the Economics of Technological Change", Econometrica, 25, pp. 501-522

H. Haken (1983), **Synergetics: An Introduction**, 3rd ed., Berlin-Heidelberg-New York, Springer Verlag

J. Hofbauer and K. Sigmund (1984), **Evolutionstheorie und Dynamische Systeme**, Berlin and Hamburg, Verlag Paul Pavey

K. Iwai (1984a), "Schumpeterian Dynamics. An Evolutionary Model of Innovation and Imitation", Journal of Economic Behavior and **Organization**, 5, pp. 159-190

K. Iwai (1984b), "Schumpeterian Dynamics. II: Technological Progress, Firm Growth and "Economic Selection", Journal of Economic **Behavior and Organization**, 5, pp. 321-351

N. J. Ireland and P. Stoneman (1983), "Technological diffusion, Expectations and Welfare", Warwick, Warwick University

M. L. Katz and C. Shapiro (1985), "Network Externalities, Competition and Compatibility", **American Economic Review**, 75, 424-440.

------------------------- (1986), "Technology Adoption in the Presence of Network Externalities", **Journal of Political Economy**, 94, 822-841.

J. Kleine (1983), **Investitionsverhalten bei Prozessinnovationen**, Frankfurt/New York, Campus Verlag

R. C. Levin, W. M. Cohen and D. C. Mowery (1985), "R & D Appropriability, Opportunity and Market Structure: New Evidence on some Schumpeterian Hypotheses", **American Economic Review. Papers and Proceedings**, 75, pp. 20-24

E. Mansfield (1961), "Technical Change and the Rate of Imitation", **Econometrica**, 29, pp. 741-766

E. Mansfield (1968), **Industrial Research and Technological Innovation**, New York, W. W. Norton

J. S. Metcalfe and M. Gibbons (1983), "On the Economics of Structural Change and the Evolution of Technology", Manchester, Manchester University, paper presented at the 7th World Congress of the International Economics Association, Madrid, September 1983

J. S. Metcalfe (1985), "On Technological Competition", Manchester, Manchester University

L. Nabseth and G. Ray (1974), **The Diffusion of New Industrial Proceses: An International Study**, London, Cambridge University Press

R. Nelson (1968), "A 'Diffusion' Model of International Productivity Differences in Manufacturing Industry", **American Economic Review**, 58, 1218-1248

R. Nelson (1985), "Industry Growth Accounts and Cost Functions when Techniques are Proprietary", New Haven, Yale University, Institution for Social and Policy Studies Discussion Paper

R. Nelson and S. Winter (1977), "In Search of a Useful Theory of Innovation", **Research Policy**, 6, pp. 36-76

R. Nelson and S. Winter (1982), **An Evolutionary Theory of Economic Change**, Cambridge (Mass.), The Belknap Press of Harvard University Press

G. Nicolis and I. Prigogoine (1977), **Self-Organization in Non-Equilibrium Systems**, New York, Wiley

I. Prigogine (1976), "Order through Fluctuation: Self-Organization and Social System", in E. Jantsch and C.H. Waddington (eds.), **Evolution and Consciousness**, Reading (Mass.), Addison-Wesley

J. Reinganum (1981), "Market Structure and the Diffusion of New Technology", **Bell Journal of Economics**, 12, pp. 618-624

D. Sahal (1981), **Patterns of Technological Innovation**, New York, Addison Wesley

D. Sahal (1985), "Technology Guide-Posts and Innovation Avenues", **Research Policy**, 14, pp. 61-82

W. Salter (1962), **Productivity and Technical Change**, Cambridge, Cambridge University Press

K. Sigmund (1986), "A Survey of Replicator Equations", in J.L. Casti and A. Karlqvist (eds.), **Complexity, Language and Life: Mathematical Approaches**, Berlin-Heidelberg-New York-Tokyo, Springer-Verlag

G. Silverberg (1984), "Embodied Technical Progress in a Dynamic Economic Model: the Self-Organization Paradigm", in R. Goodwin, M. Krüger and A. Vercelli (eds.), **Nonlinear Models of Fluctuating Growth**, Berlin-Heidelberg-New York, Springer Verlag

G. Silverberg (1987), "Technical Progress, Capital Accumulation and Effective Demand: A Self-Organization Model", in D. Batten, J. Casti, and B. Johansson (eds.), **Economic Evolution and Structural Adjustment**, Berlin-Heidelberg-New York-Tokyo, Springer-Verlag

V. Smith (1961), **Investment and Production**, Cambridge, Harvard University Press

P. Stoneman (1976), **Technological Diffusion and the** Computer **Revolution**, Oxford, Clarendon Press

P. Stoneman (1983), **The Economic Analysis of Technological Change**, Oxford, Oxford University Press

P. Stoneman (1986), "Technological Diffusion: The Viewpoint of Economic Theory", paper presented at the Conference on Innovation Diffusion, Venice, 17-21 March 1986

P. Stoneman and N. J. Ireland (1983), "The Role of Supply Factors in the Diffusion of New Process Technology", **Economic Journal, Conference Papers**, 93, pp. 65-77

G. Terborgh (1949), **Dynamic Equipment Policy**, New York, McGraw-Hill

L.C. Thomas (1984), **Games. Theory and Applications**, Chichester, Ellis Harwood

S. Winter (1984), "Schumpeterian Competition in Alternative Technological Regimes", **Journal of Economic Behavior and Organization**, 5, pp. 137-158

E.C. Zeeman (1979), "Population Dynamics from Game Theory", in Z. Neticki and C. Robinson (eds.), **Global Theory of Dynamical Systems**, Berlin-Heidelberg-New York, Springer Verlag

E.C. Zeeman (1981), "Dynamics of the evolution of animal conflicts", **Journal of Theoretical Biology**, 89, pp. 249-270

# Part II
# Sources and Effects of Innovation

# [6]

*Journal of Economic Literature*
*Vol. XXVI (September 1988), pp. 1120–1171*

# Sources, Procedures, and Microeconomic Effects of Innovation

*By* Giovanni Dosi

*University of Sussex and University of Rome*

*Fabio Arcangeli, Paul David, Frank Engelman, Christopher Freeman, Massimo Moggi, Richard Nelson, Luigi Orsenigo, Nathan Rosenberg, Michele Salvati, G. N. von Tunzelman, two anonymous referees, and the participants at the meeting of the Committee on Distribution, Growth, and Technical Progress of the Italian National Research Council (CNR), Rome, November 16, 1985, have helped with various redraftings. A particularly grateful acknowledgment is for the insightful and patient help of Moses Abramovitz.*

*This work has been undertaken at the Science Policy Research Unit (SPRU), University of Sussex, as part of the research program of the Designated Research Centre, sponsored by the Economic and Social Research Council (ESRC). Earlier support to the research that led to this paper by the Italian National Research Council (CNR) is also gratefully acknowledged. The statistical research has been undertaken with the assistance of Stephano Brioschi, Ilaria Fornari, and Giovannu Prennushi.*

## I. Introduction

THIS ESSAY concerns the determinants and effects of innovative activities in contemporary market economies. In the most general terms, private profit-seeking agents will plausibly allocate resources to the exploration and development of new products and new techniques of production if they know, or believe in, the existence of some sort of yet unexploited scientific and technical opportunities; if they expect that there will be a market for their new products and processes; and, finally, if they expect some economic benefit, net of the incurred costs, deriving from the innovations. In turn, the success of some agents in introducing or imitating new products and production processes changes their production costs, their market competitiveness and, ultimately, is part of the evolution of the industries affected by the innovations.

It is the purpose of this essay to analyze the processes leading from notional technological opportunities to actual innovative efforts and, finally, to changes in the structures and performance of industries.

Thus, I shall discuss the sources of innovation opportunities, the role of markets in allocating resources to the exploration of these opportunities and in determining the rates and directions of technological advances, the characteristics of the processes of innovative search, and the nature of the incentives driving private agents to commit themselves to innovation.

It is not my purpose to review the whole body of innovation-related literature.[1] Rather I limit my discussion to a selected group of (mostly empirical) contributions and focus on the microeconomic nature of innovative activities and the effects of innovation upon techniques of production, product characteristics, and patterns of change of industrial structures. The discussion will aim to identify (a) the main characteristics of the innovative process, (b) the factors that are conducive to or hinder the development of new processes of production and new products, and (c) the processes that determine the selection of particular innovations and their effects on industrial structures.

There are two major sets of issues here: first, the characterization, *in general*, of the innovative process, and, second, the interpretation of the factors that account for observed differences in the modes of innovative search and in the rates of innovation between different sectors and firms and over time.

Typically, the search, development, and adoption of new processes and products in noncentrally planned economies

are the outcome of the interaction between (a) capabilities and stimuli generated within each firm and within industries and (b) broader causes external to the individual industries, such as the state of science in different branches; the facilities for the communication of knowledge; the supply of technical capabilities, skills, engineers, and so on; the conditions controlling occupational and geographical mobility and/or consumer promptness/resistance to change; market conditions, particularly in their bearing on interfirm competition and on demand growth; financial facilities and patterns and criteria of allocation of funds to the industrial firms; macroeconomic trends, especially in their effects on changes in relative prices of inputs and outputs; public policies (e.g., tax codes, patent laws, industrial policies, public procurement). It is impossible to consider here each of these factors in detail and the survey will focus upon the procedures, determinants, and effects of the innovative efforts of business firms; however, at each step of the analysis, I will try to show how those broader factors affect the opportunities, incentives, and capabilities of innovating in different firms and industries.

The empirical evidence rests on studies of several industries and technologies; however, particular attention is devoted to the characteristics and effects of microelectronics-based innovations. The obvious reason is the pervasiveness of these technologies and the scope of the transformations that-they are inducing in the contemporary economic system.

Various forms of innovations affect all sectors of economic activity. The present discussion, however, concentrates on the production of goods (in primis, manufacturing) and it emphasizes the efforts concerned with the improvements of the techniques of production and the search for new products.

---

[1] An extensive survey of the literature on innovation and technical change can be found in Freeman (1982). See also National Science Foundation (1983). A more specific survey on technical change and productivity growth is in Nelson (1981a). Other surveys of the economics of technological change, oriented more to the theoretical literature, include Charles Kennedy and Anthony Thirlwall (1981), and Paul Stoneman (1983).

TABLE 1

R & D EXPENDITURE BY COUNTRY AND BY SOURCE OF FINANCE, R & D REAL GROWTH AND R & D EMPLOYMENT

| Country: | USA | Japan | West Germany | United Kingdom | France | Italy |
|---|---|---|---|---|---|---|
| Yearly Percentage Growth of Total National (R & D) Expenditures (at Constant Prices) | | | | | | |
| 1969–75 | −0.6 | 8.3 | 6.2 | 1.3 | 2.3 | 4.9 |
| 1975–81 | 4.2 | 7.9 | 4.7 | 3.1 | 4.2 | 4.6 |
| 1981–83 | 3.8 | 8.2 | 1.9 | −0.7 | 4.7 | 4.9 |
| Total R & D as Percentage of GDP: | | | | | | |
| 1983 | 2.7 | 2.8 | 2.8 | 2.8 | 2.5 | 1.6 |
| Total R & D Employment per Thousand of Total Labor Force: | | | | | | |
| 1983 | 6.6 | 5.8 | 4.7[a] | 3.6[a] | 3.9 | 2.3 |
| Business-financed R & D as a Percentage of Total R & D: 1983 | 49.0 | 65.3 | 58.1 | 42.1 | 42.0 | 45.5 |
| Business-performed R & D as a Percentage of Total R &D: 1983 | 71.1 | 63.5 | 69.8 | 61.0 | 56.8 | 57.0 |
| Military R & D as Percentage of Total R &D: 1983[b] | 27.8 | 0.6 | 13.5[c] | | | |

*Sources:* National Science Foundation (1986), OECD (1986), Peri Patel and Keith Pavitt (1986) and elaborations by the author (in terms of ratios to GDP and total labor force).

*Note:* i) Unless otherwise specified, the data of rows 4 to 8 refer to 1983; ii) despite normalization efforts, stimulated in particular by the OECD, some discrepancies are still likely to appear among the various countries in coverage and definitions; iii) some caution should be used in comparing rows 4 and 5: the differences are the likely result of both statistical discrepancies and different relative wages of research workers to average workers in each country.

[a] 1981 (Source for R & D employment: National Science Foundation).

[b] Calculated by Patel and Pavitt (1986).

[c] All Western Europe.

In Part II I recall some stylized evidence on the allocation of resources to research and on the patterns of innovation across countries and sectors. The interpretation of these observed patterns will begin in Part III with an analysis of the characteristics of the search process aimed at the discovery and development of innovations. Part IV discusses the nature of the opportunities and knowledge on which innovations draw and the incentives leading profit-motivated actors to innovate and/or imitate other people's innovations. I argue that the suggested interpretation of the innovation process helps to explain why sectors differ in their modes and rates of innovation. Moreover, firms within each industry differ,

too, in their propensity to innovate. Part V discusses this phenomenon. Finally, Part VI considers the relationship between innovative activities and the dynamics of industrial structures and performances.

## II. Searching for Innovations—The General Patterns

Modern industrial countries devote a significant share of their income and labor force to formalized activities of pure and applied research and technological development, within both nonprofit institutions (universities, government laboratories, etc.) and business enterprises. Table 1 provides an overview of employ-

*The Economics of Innovation*

TABLE 2

UNITED STATES R & D EXPENDITURES BY TYPE AND BY SOURCES OF FINANCE, VARIOUS YEARS (PERCENTAGES)

|  | 1960 | 1970 | 1980 | 1983 |
|---|---|---|---|---|
| Total R & D | 100 | 100 | 100 | 100 |
| *Basic research* financed by | 8.9 (100) | 13.6 (100) | 12.9 (100) | 12.6 (100) |
| Federal government | 5.3 (59.7) | 9.5 (70.1) | 8.9 (68.8) | 8.4 (66.4) |
| Industry | 2.5 (28.6) | 2.0 (14.9) | 2.0 (15.7) | 2.3 (18.4) |
| University and colleges[b] | 0.5 ( 6.0) | 1.3 (10.0) | 1.3 (10.0) | 1.3 (10.0) |
| Other nonprofit institutions | 0.5 ( 5.7) | 0.7 ( 5.1) | 0.7 ( 5.6) | 0.7 ( 5.3) |
| *Applied research* financed by | 22.3 (100) | 21.9 (100) | 22.4 (100) | 23.4 (100) |
| Federal government | 12.5 (55.9) | 11.8 (53.8) | 10.5 (47.0) | 10.6 (45.4) |
| Industry | 9.1 (40.6) | 9.3 (42.4) | 10.7 (47.7) | 11.6 (49.6) |
| University and colleges[b] | 0.5 ( 2.1) | 0.4 ( 1.7) | 0.7 ( 3.0) | 0.7 ( 2.0) |
| Other nonprofit institutions | 0.3 ( 1.3) | 0.3 ( 2.0) | 0.5 ( 2.3) | 0.5 ( 2.0) |
| *Development* financed by | 68.9 (100) | 64.5 (100) | 64.6 (100) | 64.0 (100) |
| Federal government | 46.8 (68.1) | 35.7 (55.3) | 27.6 (42.7) | 27.6 (43.1) |
| Industry | 21.8 (31.7) | 28.6 (44.4) | 36.7 (56.7) | 36.0 (56.3) |
| University and colleges[b] | 0.01 ( 0.1) | 0.0 ( 0.1) | 0.1 ( 0.2) | 0.02 ( 0.2) |
| Other nonprofit institutions | 0.01 ( 0.1) | 0.2 ( 0.2) | 0.2 ( 0.3) | 0.02 ( 0.3) |

*Source:* National Science Foundation (1986).

*Note:* i) Data in parentheses are percentages of each research category subtotal; ii) Subdivisions between "pure" research, "applied" research, and "development," are taken from NSF classifications.

[a] Based on preliminary estimates.

[b] Federally funded university-based research is included in the "federal government" source.

ment and expenditures on R & D by country, shares of business-performed research, and sources of finance.[2]

As regards the composition of R & D

[2] In an effort to standardize definitions and data collection on research expenditures, the Organization of Economic Cooperation and Development (OECD) has proposed, in the so-called "Frascati Manual," that "Research and Experimental Development comprise creative work undertaken on a systematic basis in order to increase the stock of knowledge . . . and the use of this stock of knowledge to devise new applications" (OECD 1981, p. 25). Within that general definition, "pure" research broadly corresponds to activities aimed at knowledge growth, "applied" research involves the search for "applications," and "development" concerns the activities of design, implementation, and prototype manufacturing of the "new applications" themselves. Still the details of the activities actually surveyed in different countries—in terms of both expenditures and employment—are often not strictly homogeneous and some caution should be used in comparing the investment figures on R & D among different countries. For an in-depth discussion of R & D measurement problems, see Freeman (1982).

expenditures (see Table 2 for evidence on the USA), about one-tenth is devoted to pure research, more than one-fourth to applied research, and the rest to development. Not surprisingly, pure research, with its character of relative publicness, is financed mainly by the federal government, universities, and other nonprofit institutions, while industry meets about one-half the cost of applied research and development; however, private industry also devotes roughly 20 percent of its total R & D expenditures to pure research.

Moreover, within the broad picture of national R & D investments, one observes marked intersectoral differences in the allocation of resources to research (see Table 3). As regards the sources of these investments and their institutional location, in contemporary market economies roughly half of the total investment in R & D is, as said, financed by business

1124    *Journal of Economic Literature, Vol. XXVI (September 1988)*

TABLE 3
EXPENDITURES ON RESEARCH AND DEVELOPMENT AS A PERCENTAGE OF VALUE ADDED BY SECTOR AND BY COUNTRY
AND SECTORAL RATIOS OF R & D USE TO EXPENDITURE

| Sector | USA | Japan | West Germany | France | United Kingdom | Italy | Estimated USA Ratio of Use to Generation of R & D[a] |
|---|---|---|---|---|---|---|---|
| Electric and electronics industries | 12.7 | 8.5 | 8.8 | 13.7 | 16.2 | 5.7 | 0.34 |
| Chemicals | 6.5 | 7.7 | 5.8 | 7.0 | 6.8 | 5.5 | |
| Organic and inorganic chemicals | 4.3 | 8.0 | } 8.4 | } 7.6 | 5.3 | } 6.0 | 0.50 |
| Drugs | 12.1 | 10.0 | | | 17.8 | | 0.17 |
| Petroleum refineries | 6.4 | 3.0 | 0.6 | 3.4 | 2.0 | 4.6 | 1.31 |
| Instruments | 20.5 | (8.6)[b] | 8.3 | (5.4)[b] | 8.5 | (1.2)[b] | 0.14 |
| Office machinery and computers | 21.7 | 7.5 | } 4.2 | } 2.4 | 19.8 | } 2.7 | 0.11 |
| Industrial nonelectrical machinery | 2.5 | 2.9 | | | 2.5 | | 0.17 |
| Aerospace | 32.6 | } 7.2 | 30.8 | } 10.0 | 30.9 | } 6.6 | 0.37 |
| Transport equipment | 10.0 | | 5.5 | | 3.1 | | |
| Motor vehicles | 12.6 | 6.5 | 5.9 | n.a. | 4.2 | n.a. | 0.20 |
| Ships | n.a. | 7.8 | 1.2 | n.a. | 0.8 | n.a. | } 0.32 |
| Other transport equipment | n.a. | n.a. | 1.6 | n.a. | 0.0 | n.a. | |
| Food, drink, and tobacco | 0.7 | 1.3 | 0.5 | 0.3 | 0.8 | 2.4 | 1.18 |
| Textile and clothing | 2.7 | 1.3 | 0.5 | 0.5 | 0.3 | 0.3 | 1.31 |
| Rubber and plastic products | 2.5 | 2.8 | 1.9 | 4.4 | 1.1 | 1.8 | 1.12 |
| Ferrous metals | 1.6 | 2.9 | 1.6 | 1.1 | 1.1 | 0.5 | 1.63 |
| Nonferrous metals | 2.4 | 4.3 | 1.8 | 2.4 | 2.1 | 3.2 | 1.06 |
| Fabricated metal products | 1.1 | 1.2 | 1.4 | 1.0 | 0.8 | 0.0 | 0.49 |
| Lumber, wood products, and furniture | .7 | —[c] | —[c] | —[c] | —[c] | —[c] | 1.33 |
| Paper and printing | .7 | —[c] | —[c] | —[c] | —[c] | —[c] | 1.31 |
| Stone, clay, and glass | 1.9 | —[c] | —[c] | —[c] | —[c] | —[c] | 0.86 |
| Total manufacturing | 8.1 | 4.9 | 5.4 | (4.6)[d] | 6.6 | (2.9)[d] (1.7)[e] | 0.42 |

*Sources:* OECD (1986), National Science Foundation (1986), OECD, *Industrial Structures Statistics,* various years, and Scherer (1982); data of R & D expenditures and value added have been aggregated, whenever necessary, by the author for comparability purposes.

*Notes:* The sectoral R & D intensities are calculated as the ratio of business-performed R & D to sectoral value added.

Special caution must be taken in comparing the data along any one row: The coverage of value-added data differ among countries (e.g., for Italy, it includes only firms with more than 20 employees).

[a] Ratio of the total R & D used to the R & D performed by the sector as estimated by Frederick M. Scherer (1982).

[b] Professional instruments include photographic equipment.

[c] No comparable data available.

[d] Estimates based on the subset of manufacturing for which sectoral data are available.

[e] Based on aggregate OECD data on the Italian economy.

and roughly between half and two-thirds of R & D is carried out by business firms (cf. Table 1).

Of course, Tables 1 through 3 show only the commitment of resources to innovation that fund formalized research activities, typically in R & D laboratories; however, in addition to formalized R & D, and in many ways complementary to it, a significant amount of innovation and improvements is originated through design improvements, "learning by doing," and "learning by using" (see, for example, Kenneth Arrow 1962a; Rosenberg 1982; David 1975; Samuel Hollander 1965; Louis Yelle 1979). Such informal effort is generally embodied in people and organizations (primarily firms) (David Teece 1977, 1986; Keith Pavitt 1986a), and its cost is hard to trace. Again, sectors differ in the relative importance of the four basic modes of technological advance, namely (a) economically expensive and formalized processes of search whose costs are measured in the tables; (b) informal processes of diffusion of information and of technological capabilities (e.g., via publications, technical associations, watch-and-learn processes, personnel transfers); (c) those particular forms of "externalities," internalized within each firm, associated with learning by doing and learning by using; and (d) the adoption of innovation developed by other industries and embodied in capital equipment and intermediate inputs (cf. Pavitt 1984).

In the interpretation of the evidence on innovative activities in contemporary economies, one faces, first, the question of the nature of the process leading from a perception of an economically exploitable opportunity to its actual development: That is, what do people actually do? How do they search? Why do sectors differ in their search procedures?

Second, one should account for the observed directions of technological change: To what extent do such observed patterns represent reactions to market signals? Are there other factors that influence the patterns of technological change?

Third, one should explain why sectors differ in their commitment of resources to search activities and in the rates at which they generate new products and processes of production. In short, I call "propensity to innovate" the empirical outcome of both sets of phenomena

and try to disentangle its determinants.

In the following, I deal, in turn, with these questions.

## III. *Innovation: The Characteristics of the Search Process*

Over the past 20 years, various analyses have been made of the process of innovation, concerned with both the relationship between inputs and outputs of innovative activities (that is, the relationship between the resources devoted to innovative search and rates of generation of innovations, however measured) and the nature of the innovation process itself. In this section I focus first on the second issue.

These analyses, which can be classified under the broad heading of "innovation studies" (Zvi Griliches 1984b), include those of William Abernathy and James Utterback (1975, 1978), E. W. Constant (1980), David (1975), Freeman (1982), Burton Klein (1977), Nelson and Sidney Winter (1977, and 1982), Rosenberg (1976, 1982), Devandra Sahal (1979, 1981, 1985), Pavitt (1979, 1984), Eric von Hippel (1979, and 1982), and Dosi (1982, 1984). The analytical aims of these studies are different and their contributions quite heterogeneous. Nonetheless, most of them point toward some common characteristics of innovation which, in my view, are of crucial importance in the economics of technological change.

### A. *Innovation as Problem-solving: Technological Paradigms*

In very general terms, technological innovation involves *the solution of problems*—for example, on transformation of heat into movement, shaping materials in certain ways, producing compounds with certain properties—meeting at the same time some cost and marketability requirements. Typically, the problems are "ill structured," in that the available information (e.g., on the limits in the cutting speed of a certain machine, the physical reasons it breaks at higher speed) does not provide by itself a solution to the problem (relevant discussions of this class of problems are in Herbert Simon 1973, 1979; and Nelson and Winter 1982; see also Massimo Egidi 1986 and Dosi and Egidi 1987). In other words, an "innovative solution" to a certain problem involves "discovery" and "creation," since no general algorithm can be derived from the information about the problem that generates its solution "automatically" (more on this in Dosi and Egidi 1987). Certainly, the "solution" of technological problems involves the use of information drawn from previous experience and formal knowledge (e.g., from the natural sciences); however, it also involves specific and *uncodified* capabilities on the part of the inventors. Following Nelson and Winter (1982) and Winter (1984), I use the term *knowledge base* for the set of information inputs, knowledge, and capabilities that inventors draw on when looking for innovative solutions. A first characterization that can be made of different technologies is in terms of the degrees of "publicness" and universality versus tacitness and specificity of their knowledge bases (Winter 1984). Following Michael Polanyi (1967), *tacitness* refers to those elements of knowledge, insight, and so on that individuals have which are ill defined, uncodified, unpublished, which they themselves cannot fully express and which differ from person to person, but which may to some significant degree be shared by collaborators and colleagues who have a common experience. Conversely, scientific inputs are typically universal and public. Nelson (1986) cites the results of the Yale questionnaire, showing that in 30 sectors out of 130, university research—especially in chemistry, materials science, computer science, and

metallurgy—is considered to be very important for sectoral innovativeness; in the cases of biotechnologies François Chesnais (1986) analyzes a complex thread of joint ventures between university and industry. Also the knowledge base in several chemical sectors is directly linked to scientific knowledge on chemical/physical properties of complex organic molecules.

However, even in these rather science-based activities and, more so, in other technologies, public knowledge is complementary to more specific and tacit forms of knowledge generated within the innovating units (for evidence, see Freeman 1982; SPRU 1972; J. Langrish 1972; Michael Gibbons and Ron Johnston 1974; and Pavitt 1984). For example, in mechanical engineering (e.g., machine tools) an important part of the knowledge base consists of tacit knowledge about the performance of previous generations of machines, their typical conditions of use, the productive requirements of the users, and so on. In the case of microelectronics, one finds three major and complementary forms of knowledge, namely (a) advances in solid-state physics (e.g., electrical properties of semiconductors at the micron/submicron level) (b) knowledge related to the construction of semiconductor manufacturing and testing equipment, and (c) programming logics. As regards the applications of microelectronics, embodied in components and equipment, the fundamental forms of knowledge consist of (a) systems architectures and systems engineering; (b) programming logics (ranging from the logics embodied in the "firmware" of computers, to the proper applicative software), (c) the interfaces between information processing and the mechanical or chemical processes to which it is applied (e.g., the interfaces between an electronic control and the mechanical movements of a machine tool or the flows in a chemical plant), and (*d*) the interacting devices (e.g., sensors).

The crucial point is that this (technology-specific and sector-specific) variety in the knowledge base of innovative search implies also different degrees of *tacitness* of the knowledge underlying innovative success and, as will be discussed below, also helps explain the differences across sectors in the typical organization of research activities. Whatever the knowledge base on which innovation draws, each problem-solving activity implies the development and refinement of "models" and specific procedures.

Elsewhere (Dosi 1982, 1984), I suggest a broad similarity, in terms of definition and procedures, between *science* and *technology*. More precisely, as modern philosophy of science suggests the existence of scientific paradigms (or scientific research programs), so there are *technological paradigms*. Both scientific and technological paradigms embody an *outlook*, a definition of the relevant problems, a pattern of enquiry. A "technological paradigm" defines contextually the needs that are meant to be fulfilled, the scientific principles utilized for the task, the material technology to be used. In other words, a technological paradigm can be defined as a "pattern" of solution of selected technoeconomic problems based on highly selected principles derived from the natural sciences, jointly with specific rules aimed to acquire new knowledge and safeguard it, whenever possible, against rapid diffusion to the competitors. Examples of such technological paradigms include the internal combustion engine, oil-based synthetic chemistry, and semiconductors. A closer look at the patterns of technical change, however, suggests the existence of "paradigms" with different levels of generality, in several industrial sectors.

A technological paradigm is both an *exemplar*—an artifact that is to be devel-

oped and improved (such as a car, an integrated circuit, a lathe, each with its particular technoeconomic characteristics)—and a *set of heuristics* (e.g., Where do we go from here? Where should we search? What sort of knowledge should we draw on?).

These aspects of technological change which relate to the improvement of some typical performance attributes of exemplars (e.g., four-wheeled internal-combustion cars, jet aircraft) underlie Sahal's idea of "technological guide posts" (Sahal 1981, 1985), a guidepost being the basic artifact whose technoeconomic characteristics are progressively improved. Basic artifacts (such as car) are also functionally specified (e.g., a car's locomotive attributes) in relation to some use in the socioeconomic system (a car is used jointly with human time for household mobility and also in market production activities). (For an attempt to map characteristics of technological paradigms and socioeconomic uses or "needs," see Paolo Saviotti and J. Stanley Metcalfe 1984.) In this respect, technological paradigms define "bundles" of characteristics of the various commodities. If, following Kevin Lancaster (1971), the latter are defined in terms of combination of hedonic attributes, technological paradigms restrict the actual combinations in a notional characteristics space to a certain number of prototypical bundles.

On the other hand, the development and improvement of these basic "exemplars" involve the development of specific competences and "rules." Rosenberg (1976) highlights the importance of "focusing devices," that is, typical problems, opportunities, and targets that tend to focus the search process in particular directions.

Of course, the procedures, competences, and heuristics involved in the search process are, to varying degrees, specific to each technology. In other

1128     *Journal of Economic Literature, Vol. XXVI (September 1988)*

words, each technological paradigm involves a specific "technology of technical change."[3] For example, in some sectors (such as organic chemicals), these procedures relate to the ability of coupling basic scientific knowledge with the development of new molecules that present the required characteristics. Thus, one often searches around the existing compounds, helped by the scientific knowledge of the relationship between chemical structures and physical properties, by previous experience, and by chance. In other sectors (such as microelectronics devices) the methods of innovative search involve scientific advances on submicron electrical flows in semiconductors, the development of more sophisticated hardware capable of "writing" the chips at the desired level of miniaturization, and advances in the programming logic to be built into the chips. In mechanical engineering, the search process is generally "focused" by trade-offs involved in the use of machines (e.g., between speed, flexibility to different uses, and cutting precision). The skills required by this search process typically involve also unwritten and relatively tacit experience in design and use of mechanical equipment, and more recently, in the interface between electronic controls and mechanical movements. Yet in other sectors (e.g., the top end of textile, clothing, leather, and shoemaking) fundamental "search skills" are the capabilities of understanding/anticipating/influencing the trends in tastes and fashion.

It quite often happens that prototypical problem-solving models, rules on how to search and on what targets to focus, and beliefs as to "what the market wants" become the shared view of the engineering community. A paradigm is economically

exploited and reproduced over time also through the development of institutions that train the would-be practitioners in methods for the improvement of basic exemplars, and peers' judgments are also based on the success achieved in the refinement and use of these methods (in this respect, Noble's history of the development of American engineering schools and their relationship with industry and Hughes' history of electrification are vivid illustrations of the institutional process that goes together with the establishment of "technological paradigms;" see David Noble 1987, and Thomas Hughes 1982).

### B. Technological Paradigms and Patterns of Innovation: Technological Trajectories

A crucial implication of the general paradigmatic form of technological knowledge is that innovative activities are strongly *selective, finalized* in quite precise directions, *cumulative* in the acquisition of problem-solving capabilities. This accounts also for the relatively ordered patterns of innovation that one tends to observe at the level of single technologies, as shown by several studies of "technological forecasting" (for a comprehensive review and discussion, see Joseph Martino 1976). Let us define as a *technological trajectory* (Nelson and Winter 1977; Sahal 1981, Dosi 1982, Theodore Gordon and Thomas Munson 1981; Saviotti and Metcalfe 1984) the activity of technological process along the economic and technological trade-offs defined by a paradigm.

Thus, for example, technological progress in aircraft technology has followed two quite precise trajectories (one civilian and one military) characterized by log-linear improvements in the trade-offs between horsepower, gross takeoff weight, cruise speed, wing loading, and cruise range (Sahal 1985 and an oral com-

---

[3] This was also the title of an important conference, coordinated by R. Nelson at the Royal College of Arts, London, July 1985. See also Nelson (1981b).

munication of P. Saviotti on ongoing research at Manchester University). In microelectronics, technical change is accurately represented by an exponential trajectory of improvement in the relationship between density of the electronic chips, speed of computation, and cost per bit of information (Dosi 1984). More generally, there is growing evidence that specific "innovation avenues" are a widespread feature of the observed patterns of technical change (Sahal 1985). Of course, there is no a priori economic reason why one should observe limited clusters of technological characteristics at any one time and ordered trajectories over time. Indeed, given consumers with different preferences and equipment users with different technical requirements, if technology had the malleable attributes of information and if the innovative search were a purely random process, one would tend to observe sorts of "technological indifference curves" at any one time, and, over time, random search all over the n-dimension characteristics space. Of course, "how different" are consumers and users of goods, pieces of equipment, intermediate components, is, in principle, an empirical question. However, relatively wide differences (given the high dimensionality of the space of characteristics/technical requirements demanded by consumers/users of commodities) cannot be ruled out by either casual empiricism or general theoretical arguments. Moreover, for whatever distribution of characteristics at any arbitrary time *t*, one should expect that income growth and division of labor among different productive activities would increase such diversity of micro demands. Were technologies simply pieces of information (or "recipes") that could be added, convexly combined, etc., one would also tend to observe an increasingly dispersed variety of technical and performance combinations in ac-

tual products and production inputs. Over time, this would lead toward the exploration of the entire characteristics space of final products, machine tools, components, etc. Indeed, the evidence surveyed suggests that one still observes "explorations" limited to some, much smaller, subsets of the notional characteristics space. It is precisely the paradigmatic cumulative nature of technological knowledge that accounts for the relatively ordered nature of the observed patterns of technological change.

Engineers typically try to improve the desirable characteristics that are specific to a certain product, tool, or device, keeping in mind the trade-offs among them. Relatedly, historical evidence strongly suggests that a major impulse to innovation has derived from *imbalances* between the technical dimensions that characterize a "trajectory" (or "avenue") e.g., between cutting speed and tool resistance in machine tools or shuttle speed in eighteenth century looms and spinning speed in spindles. For a discussion of several examples of this process of solution of technical imbalances, which Hughes (1987) calls "adverse salients" and "critical problems," see Rosenberg (1976, especially chapter 6). Arguments broadening the scope of "imbalances" to the relationships between technical change and social roles and behaviors of different groups of workers are in William Lazonick (1979, 1987), and von Tunzelmann (1982). Other examples can be drawn from David Landes (1969).

Conversely, a change in the paradigm generally implies a change in the trajectories: Together with different knowledge bases and different prototypes of artifacts, the technoeconomic dimensions of innovation also vary. Some characteristics may become easier to achieve, new desirable characteristics may emerge, some others may lose importance. Relatedly, the engineers' vision of future technological advances changes, together with a changing emphasis on the various trade-offs that characterize the new artifacts. Thus, for example, the technological trajectory in active electrical components based on thermionic valves had, as fundamental dimensions, heat-loss parameters, miniaturization, and reliability over time. With the appearance of solid-state components, heat loss became much less relevant, while miniaturization increased enormously in importance and also the rates at which progress could be achieved shot up. More generally, it has also been suggested that major clusters of prevailing technological paradigms (e.g., those related to oil-based synthetic chemistry, to electromechanical production, or, more recently, to microelectronics) involve the intensive utilization of some crucial input abundantly available at low cost (e.g., energy in the former two examples, and information-processing in the latter; Carlota Perez 1987).

### C. *Technology: Freely Available Information or Specific Knowledge?*[4]

The view of technology just presented is very different from the concept of technology as information that is generally applicable, and easy to reproduce and reuse (Arrow 1962b), one where firms can produce and use innovations by dipping freely into a general "stock" or "pool" of technological knowledge. It implies that firms produce things in ways that are differentiated technically from the products and methods of other firms and that they make innovations largely on the basis of in-house technology, but with some contributions from other firms, and from public knowledge. In such circumstances, the search process of industrial firms to improve their tech-

nology is *not* likely to be one where they survey the whole stock of notional technological knowledge before making their technical choices (see Nelson and Winter 1982). Given its highly differentiated nature, firms will instead seek to improve and to diversify their technology by searching in zones that enable them to use and to build on their existing technological base and also on their existing markets, distribution arrangements, and so on (Teece 1982, 1986). In other words, technological search processes in each firm are cumulative processes too. What the firm can hope to do technologically in the future is narrowly constrained by what it has been capable of doing in the past.

The distinction between *technology* and *information*—with the latter being only a subset of the former—entails important analytical consequences for the theory of production. To illustrate that distinction let us take a scientific analogy (note also that *science* is somewhat closer to *information* in that the ethos of the scientific community is to disclose results, while in privately generated technology it is to withhold and appropriate them, see Partha Dasgupta and David 1985). Certainly, a good part of "science" can be embodied in "information." There are freely available journals, textbooks, and university lectures that disseminate this information. Moreover, there are market conditions of access to it; for example, there is a market for textbooks and economic conditions of access to higher education (e.g., the level of registration fees, the availability or scarcity of grants for students unable to support themselves); however, in any proper sense of the word, getting a PhD is not simply acquiring information, and it is even less true to say that there is a market for PhDs. In this analogy, "information" stands vis-à-vis innovative technological capabilities as a subscription to the *American Economic Review* stands vis-à-vis

---

[4] This paragraph is partly based on Dosi, Pavitt, and Soete (1988), which in turn draws from Pavitt (1984d).

winning the Nobel Prize in economics: In both cases there is an irreducible element that is not information and cannot be bought and sold, but rather depends on cumulatively augmented abilities and skills. In each technology there are elements of *tacit and specific* knowledge that are not and *cannot* be written down in a "blueprint" form, and cannot, therefore, be entirely diffused either in the form of public or proprietary information (see Polanyi 1967 and the discussion of this same issue in Nelson and Winter 1982).[5] Of course, this does not imply that such skills and forms of tacit knowledge are entirely immobile: People can be hired away from one firm to another or can start their own firms (and sometimes supply goods and knowledge to competitors of their own original firm), learning procedures of one firm may be imitated by other firms, and so on. It still holds, however, that the innovative activities present—to different degrees—firm-specific, local, and cumulative features. This is borne out by empirical studies.

It has been found that *information* about what other firms are doing spreads quite quickly (Edwin Mansfield 1985); however, the ability to produce or replicate innovative results is much more sticky. Successful innovations are more

---

[5] Egidi (1986) develops an analogy between "technology" and linguistic structures: As the semantics and syntax of natural languages shapes what is said and how it is said, so technology involves coherent chains of routines (". . . first take a piece of iron and the hammer, then do so and so, then place it under the lathe, . . ." etc.). In turn, these routines involve abilities that cannot be deduced either from the nature of the inputs (the piece of iron, the hammer, the lathe, etc.) nor by the sequence of operations. This is obviously the case also of linguistic production: the knowledge of the Oxford Dictionary (the semantics) and of English grammar (the syntax) constrains and shapes what can be said but is by no means sufficient to generate the ability to write *Hamlet*. In a different perspective, changes in technologies as a creative process of generation of new skills are discussed in Mario Amendola (1983) and Amendola and Jean-Luc Gaffard (1986).

closely related to firms' existing ranges of technological and marketing skills than unsuccessful ones (Robert Cooper 1983; Modesto Maidique 1983); they tend to occur in product fields proximate to firms' current fields; the activities that firms undertake entail initial learning costs that are recovered later as a consequence of cumulative improvements in product performance and in wider market applications (John Enos 1962; David 1975; Rosenberg 1976, 1982; Sahal 1981; Morris Teubal 1982; Paul Gardiner 1984; Roy Rothwell and Gardiner 1984).

Once the cumulative and firm-specific nature of technology is recognized, its development over time ceases to be random, but is constrained to zones closely related technologically and economically (e.g., related markets and distribution networks) to existing activities. If those zones can be identified, measured, and explained, it also is possible to predict likely future patterns of innovative activities in firms, industries, and countries (see David 1975; Sahal 1981, 1985; Pavitt 1984; Dosi, Pavitt, and Luc Soete 1988).

Each technological paradigm, I suggest, entails a specific balance between exogenous determinants of innovation (e.g., university-based advances in pure science) and determinants that are endogenous to the process of competition and technological accumulation of particular firms and industries. Moreover, each paradigm involves specific *search modes, knowledge bases, and combinations between proprietary and public forms of technological knowledge.*

Given these features of technology and technological innovation, how are search processes organized? Who are the actors that undertake them? How do they relate to the rest of the economic system?

### D. *How Organizations Build Knowledge Bases*

The increasing complexity of technologies and research activities in this cen-

1132     *Journal of Economic Literature, Vol. XXVI (September 1988)*

tury militates in favor of formal organizations (R & D laboratories of big firms, government and university labs, etc.) as opposed to individual innovators, as the most conducive environments to the production of innovations. This is also shown by the secular growth in the share of corporate as opposed to individual patents registered in the USA as well as other western economies.

David Mowery (1980, 1983) has reconstructed the growth of research and development activities in American industry from the beginning of this century. Notably, he finds that industry-performed R & D—which grows at a much higher rate than industrial output or employment—also tends to be internalized within manufacturing companies. In other words, contrary to Stigler's hypothesis (George Stigler 1956), R & D growth has not led to a comparable process of market-based division of labor and the emergence of specialized "innovation suppliers." Inhouse R & D is the dominant form of organization for corporate technological search (on this point, see also Leonard Reich 1985; Rosenberg 1985; and Nelson 1986). As Richard Nelson puts it, "the modern industrial R & D laboratory, linked within the firm with production and often marketing, had a number of advantages over reliance on outside research and development laboratories, particularly when aspects of the relevant technologies were somewhat idiosyncratic and tacit, and R & D needed to be tailored to those idiosyncracies and to particular firm strategies. In addition to the general advantage of integration in such circumstances stressed by Oliver Williamson (1985), here, as Mowery has stressed, integration had the additional advantages of facilitating better information flow from the R & D laboratory to those who would have to implement the new technology, and from the latter to the former. It also served to limit cross-

organization information leaks" (Nelson 1986, p. 10). Of course, one often observes also market transfers of innovations and technical competences—such as licensing and consultancy deals; however, "the predominant mode of industrial research in the private sector, at least in the United States, is the integrated research organization, part of a business enterprise which engages in at least one other activity vertically related to research and development such as manufacturing, marketing, distribution, sales and service" (Teece 1986, p. 1). Moreover, even when licensing and other forms of interfirm transfer of technology occur, they do not stand as an all-or-nothing substitute for in-house search: One needs to have substantial in-house capacity in order to recognize, evaluate, negotiate, and finally adapt the technology potentially available from others.

Williamson's analysis (1975, 1985) of the costs of transactions involving informational asymmetries, monitoring problems, and possibilities of opportunistic behavior is clearly part of the interpretation of this phenomenon: Market transactions involving research activities generally imply (a) incomplete specifications of contracts, given the uncertainty about the research outcomes; (b) lack of adequate protection of proprietary information; (c) possibilities of "lock-in" phenomena with research suppliers, who can subsequently earn rents from that asymmetric advantage; (d) weak incentives to least cost performance; (e) monitoring costs (on all these points, see Teece 1988).

In addition (and complementary) to these transaction-related factors, however, the foregoing discussion of the nature of technology and innovative search suggests another set of factors related to the characteristics of knowledge and problem solving. Indeed, the heuristics on "how to do things" and "how to improve them" are often embodied in *organizational routines*, which, through practice, repetition, and more or less incremental improvements make certain firms "good" at exploring certain technical opportunities and translating them into specific marketable products. In such matters, there is a significant amount of organizational indivisibility, because organizational learning may well not be additive in the learning of individuals or groups who compose the organization: indeed, it was Adam Smith who first emphasized the possible dichotomy between "system learning" (e.g., the beneficial effects on economic efficiency of the division of labor), on the one hand, and the degrading brutality which repetitive and mindless tasks could imply for some groups of workers, on the other. Intrafirm processes of specialization and division of labor are good examples of this possibility. Individuals and groups may well decrease the scope of knowledge and competences that they are required to put into production or innovative search (in a sense, they may be required to "forget"), while at the same time these same individuals and groups become linked through routines that increase organizational efficiency (on whatever criterion the latter is evaluated). For example, the emergence of the modern factory has also implied "deskilling" of particular categories of craftsmen; the abilities of several groups of artisan-like workers became redundant, the skills of *making* particular machines became increasingly separated from the skills involved in *using* them; the introduction of electromechanical techniques of automated mass production in big plants has further reduced the knowledge required of significant portions of the work force. These same processes, however, have been associated with major increases in the abilities of (more and more complex) business orga-

nizations to learn, that is to "store" and develop internally, procedures for a growing production efficiency.

The exploration of the characteristics of the organizational competences with specific reference to research an innovation is still at an early stage (see Pavitt 1986a; Teece 1986, 1988; Winter 1987a, 1987b Neil Kay 1979, 1982); however, in my view, they are a fundamental ingredient (together with transaction costs and monitoring factors emphasized by Williamson 1985) of the explanation of both the integration of research within production/marketing units and, more generally, of the *boundaries of the firms* in contemporary market economies. More precisely, Teece (1986) and Pavitt, Mike Robson and Joe Townsend (1987) have independently put forward the conjecture that these boundaries are defined by the scope of their "core competences," that is, loosely speaking, by the scope of what "they are good at" and the relevance of this specific knowledge to the activities of innovation, production, and marketing of a certain commodity. This—it is suggested—affects also the scope of efficient vertical integration and diversification of any one firm (more on this in Dosi, Teece, and Winter 1987).

Organizational routines and higher-level procedures to alter them in response to environmental changes and/or to failures in performance embody a continuous tension between efforts to improve the capabilities of doing *existing* things, monitor *existing* contracts, allocate *given* resources, on the one hand, and the development of capabilities for doing new things or old things in new ways. This tension is complicated by the intrinsically uncertain nature of innovative activities, notwithstanding their increasing institutionalization within business firms. The technical (and, even more so, the commercial) outcome of research activities can hardly be known ex ante (for empirical evidence on individual research projects, see Mansfield 1968 and Mansfield et al. 1977). In general, the uncertainty associated with innovative activities is much stronger than that with which familiar economic model deals. It involves not only lack of knowledge of the precise cost and outcomes of different alternatives, but often also lack of knowledge of what the alternatives are (see Freeman 1982; Nelson 1981a; Nelson and Winter 1982). In fact, let us distinguish between (*a*) the notion of uncertainty familiar to economic analysis defined in terms of imperfect information about the occurrence of a *known list of events* and (*b*) what we could call *strong uncertainty* whereby the list of possible events is unknown and one does not know either the consequences of particular actions for any given event (more on this in Dosi and Egidi 1987). I suggest that, in general, innovative search is characterized by strong uncertainty. This applies, in primis to those phases of technical change that could be called *preparadigmatic:* During these highly exploratory periods one faces a double uncertainty regarding both the practical outcomes of the innovative search and also the scientific and technological principles and the problem-solving procedures on which technological advances could be based. When a technological paradigm is established, it brings with it a reduction of uncertainty, in the sense that it focuses the directions of search and forms the grounds for formating technological and market expectations more surely. (In this respect, technological trajectories are not only the ex post description of the patterns of technical change, but also, as mentioned, the basis of heuristics asking "where do we go from here?") However, even in the case of "normal" technical search (as opposed to the "extraordinary" exploration associated with the quest for new paradigms)

strong uncertainty is present. Even when the fundamental knowledge base and the expected directions of advance are fairly well known, it is still often the case that one must first engage in exploratory research, development, and design before knowing what the outcome will be (what the properties of a new chemical compound will be, what an effective design will look like, etc.) and what some manageable results will cost, or, indeed, whether very useful results will emerge (Mansfield et al. 1977).

As a result, firms tend to work with relatively general and event-independent routines (with rules of the kind "... spend x% of sales on R & D," "... distribute your research activity between basic research, risky projects, incremental innovations according to some routine shares ..." and sometimes metarules of the kind "with high interest rates or low profits cut basic research," etc.). This finding is corroborated by ample managerial evidence and also by recent more rigorous econometric tests; see Griliches and Ariel Pakes (1986) who find that "the pattern of R & D investment within a firm is essentially a random walk with a relatively low error variance" (pp. 10–11). In this sense, Schumpeter's hypothesis about the routinization of innovation (Joseph Schumpeter 1942) and the persistence of innovation-related uncertainty must not be in conflict but may well complement each other. As suggested by the "late" Schumpeter, one may conjecture that large-scale corporate research has become the prevailing form of organization of innovation because it is most effective in exploiting and internalizing the tacit and cumulative features of technological knowledge (Mowery 1980; Pavitt 1986). Moreover, companies tend to adopt steady policies (rules), because they face complex and unpredictable environments where they cannot forecast future states of the world, or even "map" notional events into actions, and outcomes (Dosi and Orsenigo 1986; Heiner 1983, 1988). Internalized corporate search exploits the cumulativeness and complexity of technological knowledge. Together with steady rules, firms try to reduce the uncertainty of innovative search, without, however, eliminating it.

Internalization and routinization in the face of the uncertainty and complexity of the innovative process also point to the importance of particular organizational arrangements for the success or failure of individual innovative attempts. This is what was found by the SAPPHO Project (cf. Science Policy Research Unit 1972 and Rothwell et al. 1974), possibly the most extensive investigation of the sources of *commercial* success or failure of innovations: Institutional traits, both internal to the firm—such as the nature of the organizational arrangements between technical and commercial people, or the hierarchical authority within the innovating firm—and between a firm and its external environment—such as good communication channels with users, universities, and so on—turn out to be very important. Moreover, it has been argued (Pavitt 1986; Robert Wilson, Peter Ashton, and P. Thomas Egan 1984) that, for given incentives and innovative opportunities, the various forms of internal corporate organization (U form versus M form, centralized versus decentralized, etc.) affect innovation and commercial success positively or negatively, according to the particular nature of each technological paradigm and its stage of development.

In general, each organizational arrangement of a firm embodies procedures for resource allocation to particular activities (in our case, innovative activities), and for the efficient use of these resources in the search for new products, new processes, and procedures for im-

provements in existing routines; however, the specific nature of these procedures differs across firms and sectors. For example, the typical degrees of commitment of resources vary by industry and so do the rates at which learning occurs. I now turn to the interpretation of these phenomena.

## IV. *Opportunities, Incentives, and the Intersectoral Patterns of Innovation*

Clearly, the commitment of resources by profit-motivated agents must involve both the perception of some sort of opportunity and an effective set of incentives. Are the observed intersectoral differences in innovative investment the outcome of different incentive structures, different opportunities, or both? Jacob Schmookler, in his classic work, argued that the serendipity and universality of modern science provide a wide and *intersectorally indifferent* pool of opportunities that are exploited to different degrees in each economic activity according to differential economic incentives, and, in particular, to different patterns of demand growth (Schmookler 1966). (In fact, he was not so much concerned with innovative investments as with innovative outputs, which he measured by patents. However, the same argument applies: For identical opportunities, the elasticity of innovative outputs to R & D inputs should be the same.) Schmookler's thesis has been criticized on both theoretical and empirical grounds (see Rosenberg 1976, chapter 15, and Freeman 1982). The foregoing analysis of the innovation process supports these criticisms and helps to clarify the merits and limitations of Schmookler's hypothesis.

### A. *Technological Opportunities: Exogenous Science and Specific Learning*

I first discuss the role of science-related opportunities for innovation and, then, the importance of other sources of opportunities.

Scientific knowledge plays a crucial role in opening up new possibilities of major technological advances. In this century, the emergence of major new technological paradigms has frequently been directly dependent and *directly linked* with major scientific breakthroughs; see, for example, the origin of synthetic chemistry (John Beer 1959; Freeman 1982), the transistor (Nelson 1962; H. S. Kleiman 1977; Dosi 1984), and bioengineering (Orsenigo 1988). Certainly, in western civilization there is a long history of linkages between science and technology, hinting at rather close feedbacks, at least since Leonardo da Vinci and Galileo. What is new and increasingly important in this century is that the generation and utilization of part of the scientific knowledge is internal to, and often a necessary condition of, the development of new technological paradigms. Until the end of the nineteenth century, technological innovations were typically introduced by imaginative craftsmen; for example, engines were developed by practical-minded inventors well before the works of Carnot on thermodynamics. In this century, as far as major innovations are concerned, one moves somewhat closer to the "transistor archetype," whereby the discovery of certain quantum mechanics properties of semiconductors, yielding a Nobel Prize for physics, and the technological development of the first microelectronics device have been one and the same thing (Nelson 1962; Ernest Braun and Stuart MacDonald 1978; Dosi 1984).

Prima facie, the increasing role of scientific inputs in the innovative process can be taken as evidence of the importance of factors exogenous to competitive processes among private economically motivated actors. This is true, subject, however, to two qualifications.

First, the link between science and technology runs also from the latter to the former. It has been noted, for example, that the development of scientific instruments has exerted a major impact on subsequent scientific progress. In general, however, the scope, timing, and channels of influence of technological advances on science have a different nature from the more direct influence of scientific discoveries on technological opportunities. A detailed discussion is beyond the limits of this survey. (On these topics, see John Bernal 1939; Rosenberg 1982; and Derek de Solla Price 1984.) Second, scientific advances play a major *direct* role, especially at an early phase of development of new technological paradigms. It is often the case that the establishment of a major new paradigm involves also the solution of problems of a theoretical nature and/or the development of devices, compounds, molecules, and so on which are themselves challenging tests for the scientists (the transistor, polypropylene, and genetic engineering are obvious examples).

In a sense, progress in general scientific knowledge yields a widening pool of *potential* technological paradigms. In another work (Dosi 1984), I analyze the specific mechanisms through which a few of these potential paradigms are actually developed, economically applied, and often become dominant. Here, suffice it to say that this process of selection depends, in general, on (*a*) the nature and the interests of the "bridging institutions" (Freeman 1982) between pure research and economic applications (these institutions, which can be private establishments, such as Bell Labs, or public organizations, are instrumental in applying theoretical advances to the development of practical devices even under remote or nonexistent direct economic incentives); (*b*) quite often, especially in this century, strictly institutional factors, such as public agencies (e.g., the military); (c) the trial-and-error mechanisms of exploration of the new technologies, often associated with "Schumpeterian" enterpreneurship; (d) the selection criteria of markets and/or the technoeconomic requirements of early users (e.g., the technical specification of NASA and the Pentagon in the early days of integrated circuits, FDA requirements in the case of bioengineering, and the technical needs of the American navy in the case of nuclear reactors).

Once a technological paradigm becomes established, the objectives and heuristics of technological search often tend to diverge from those of scientific inquiry. This is partly due to the different ethos of the technological and scientific communities. (For example, the development of a first transistor had a deep scientific interest; a "better" transistor might have had a great interest for the engineer, but very little for the scientist); however, particular scientific activities (especially of an applied nature) often become part of the technological search along the "trajectories" defined by a particular paradigm. In other words, part of the scientific activity becomes "endogenized" within the activities of technological accumulation and search of profit-motivated firms (consider, for example, the applied scientific research of drug and chemical companies; for an analysis of the relationship between "endogenous" and "exogenous" research with regard to this case, see Chesnais 1986 and Orsenigo 1988).

All this has to do with the science-related opportunities of innovative activity; however, it has already been mentioned that, even in technologies that draw more directly on scientific advances, the knowledge base underlying innovative search also includes more specific forms of technical knowledge. A fortiori, this applies to technologies less directly dependent on science. These considerations have important implications for technological opportunities.

First, the specificity, cumulativeness, and tacitness of part of the technological knowledge imply that both the realized opportunities of innovation and the capabilities for pursuing them are to a good extent *local* and firm-specific. Second, the opportunity for technological advances in any one economic activity (and, thus, also the "innovative productivity" —were we able to measure it—of a dollar investment in R & D) can also be expected to be specific to and constrained by the characteristics of each technological paradigm and its degree of maturity. Moreover, the innovative opportunities in each economic sector will be influenced by the degree to which it can draw from the knowledge base and the technological advances of its suppliers and customers. The sectoral specificity of technological opportunities is also consistent with Scherer's findings that in econometric cross-firm, cross-industry estimates of rates of innovation—approximated by patenting—42.5 percent of the total variance must be attributed to the interindustry component: Frederick Scherer suggests that a good part of such variance is likely to relate to interindustry differences in opportunity (admittedly, despite the lack of any quantitative measure of it; Scherer 1986, ch. 9) other analyses confirm such sectoral specificities (e.g., Pakes and Mark Schankerman 1984).

In many respects, the idea that technological opportunities are *paradigm-bound* is also consistent with the historical evidence and interpretive conjectures put forward earlier by Simon Kuznets (1930) and Arthur Burns (1934) about a "secular retardation" in the growth of output and productivity, by commodity and industry, stemming—in the terminology suggested here—from the gradual

1138    *Journal of Economic Literature, Vol. XXVI (September 1988)*

exhaustion of technological opportunities along particular trajectories.

New paradigms reshape the patterns of opportunities of technical progress in terms of both the *scope* of potential innovations and the *ease* with which they are achieved. Moreover, they generally spread their effect well beyond their sector of origin and provide new sources of opportunity, via input-output flows and technological complementaries, to otherwise stagnant activities. The emergence of new paradigms and the diffusion of their effects throughout the economy are possibly the main reasons why in modern economies we have not seen an approach to a "stationary state." More precisely, one tends to observe two broad phenomena which reinforce each other. First, new technological paradigms have continuously brought forward new opportunities for product developments and productivity increases. Second, a rather uniform characteristic of the observed technological trajectories is their wide scope for mechanization, specialization, and division of labor within and among plants and industries (Nelson and Winter 1977). Contrary to the pessimistic expectations of classical economists and contrary also to many prevailing contemporary formalizations of problems of allocation of resources in decentralized markets, decreasing returns historically did not emerge even in those activities involving a given and "natural" factor such as agriculture or mining: Mechanization, chemical fertilizers and pesticides, new breeds of plants and animals and improved techniques of mineral extraction and purification prevented "scarcity" from becoming the dominant functional feature of these activities. A fortiori, this applies to manufacturing. Similarly, new technological paradigms, directly and indirectly—via their effects on "old" ones—generally prevent the establishment of decreasing returns in the

*search process* for innovations. Think of the effects of biotechnology on the search efficiency for new drugs or the effects of electronics controls and computers on the innovative opportunities in machine building.

Contemporary studies of technological effort and progress, indeed support the conjecture that (*a*) at any point in time, technological opportunities vary according to the sectors and the degrees of development of the various paradigms under which they work, and (*b*) this is an important part of the explanation of why the commitment to innovative investment varies across sectors. (These hypotheses are supported on both empirical and theoretical grounds by Michael Gort and Richard Wall 1986.) Another—complementary—reason for interindustry differences in R & D investment relates to the different *modes of innovative search* that each paradigm entails. For example, in some technologies (e.g., electronics, organic chemicals, drugs, aerospace) innovation involves laboratory research and/or complex development and testing of prototypes. In other technologies (e.g., several kinds of nonelectrical machinery) innovation is much more "informal," often embodied in incremental improvement in design, and as such neither recorded nor, often, perceived as the result of an "investment" in R & D.

As argued by Rosenberg (1976, pp. 277–79), differentiated scientific and technological opportunities determine different cost structures of technological advance (for example, the cost of a *x* percent improvement in the trade-offs implied by a particular technological trajectory). The cross-sectoral distribution of technological opportunities is far from homogeneous (Scherer 1982, republished in 1986; Pavitt 1984; Louise Dulude 1983). The appearance of new paradigms is unevenly distributed across sectors and so are (a) the degrees of technical difficulties in advancing production efficiency and product performance, and (b) the technological competence to innovate, embodied in people and firms. These distributions of opportunities and competence, in turn are not random, but depend on (a) the nature of the sectoral production activities, (b) their technological distance from the "revolutionary core" where new paradigms are originated, and (c) the knowledge base that underpins innovation in any one sector. As regards the effects of demand levels and changes upon sectoral rates of innovation (Schmookler's "demand pull" hypothesis, whose discussion introduced this section), all the foregoing considerations need not conflict with the hypothesis that, *other things being equal*, market size and market growth may exert a positive influence on the propensity to innovate. However, the ceteris paribus clause is indeed a crucial one, since—it has been argued in this section—technological opportunities may vary widely across sectors and also over the history of individual technologies.

Given any one level of notional opportunities for innovation, the incentive to commit resources to their discovery and development will depend, of course, on the incentives that interest-motivated agents perceive in terms of expected economic returns. Let us consider the nature of these incentives.

## B. *Appropriability of Technological Innovations*

As suggested by the classical and—even more so—Schumpeterian traditions, varying degrees of private appropriation of the benefits of innovation are both the incentive to and the outcome of the innovative process. To put it another way, each technology embodies a specific balance between public-good aspects and private (i.e., economically appropriable) features (see Arrow 1962b; Nelson 1984; and for an empirical analysis, Richard Levin et al. 1984 and Chesnais 1986). Call *appropriability* those properties of technological knowledge and technical artifacts, of markets, and of the legal environment that permit innovations and protect them, to varying degrees, as rent-yielding assets against competitors' imitation.

Appropriability conditions differ among industries and among technologies: Levin et al. (1984) study the varying empirical significance as appropriability devices of (a) patents, (b) secrecy, (c) lead times, (d) costs and time required for duplication, (e) learning-curve effects, (f) superior sales and service efforts. To these one should add more obvious forms of appropriation of differential technical efficiency related to scale economies. In an extreme synthesis, Levin et al. (1984) find that for most industries, "lead times and learning curve advantages, combined with complementary marketing efforts, appear to be the principle mechanisms of appropriating returns for product innovations" (p. 33). Learning curves, secrecy and lead times are also the major appropriation mechanisms for process innovations. Patenting often appears to be a *complementary* mechanism which, however, does not seem to be the central one, with some exceptions (e.g., chemicals and pharmaceutical products). Moreover, by comparing the protection of processes and products, one tends to observe that lead times and learning curves are relatively more effective ways of protecting process innovations, while patents are a relatively better protection for product innovations. Finally, there appears to be quite significant interindustrial variance in the importance of the various ways of protecting innovations and in the overall degrees of appropriability: Some three-quarters of the industries surveyed by the study reported the existence of at least one effective means of protecting process innovation, and more than 90 percent of the industries reported the same regarding product innovations (Levin et al. 1984, p. 20).[6]

Take, as an example, the case of microelectronics. Here one should distinguish between patterns of appropriability in the "core" technologies (semiconductors, computers, telecommunications, industrial controls) and in the technologies where it is applied (e.g., machine tools, consumer durables, cars). In the former, appropriability is a function of cumulative R & D (Franco Momigliano 1985); lead times; quite often, economies of scale in production (e.g., semiconductors and computers) and in R & D (minimum thresholds are sometimes very high, as in telecommunications); marketing and servicing networks (as in mainframe computers). Conversely, in the sectors where microelectronics is introduced as part of processes and products, the patterns of appropriability continue to correspond broadly to the "traditional" sector-specific features (see below for a more detailed taxonomy). An additional source of appropriability, however, relates to the capability of internalizing and/or efficiently exploiting the interfaces and synergies between microelectronics and applicative processes, for example, the capability of mastering both innovation in electronic equipment and the design of mechanical machinery. In fact, the latter is an example of a more general phenomenon, discussed by Teece (1986), whereby the control of complementary

technologies becomes a rent-earning firm-specific asset.

In general, it must be noticed that the partly tacit nature of innovative knowledge and its characteristics of partial private appropriability makes imitation, as well as innovation, a creative process, which involves search, which is not wholly distinct from the search for "new" development, and which is economically expensive—sometimes even more expensive than the original innovation (for evidence on the cost of imitation relative to innovation, see Mansfield, Mark Schwartz, and Samuel Wagner 1981; Mansfield 1984; and Levin et al. 1984). This applies to both patented and non-patented innovations.

C. *The Driving Forces of Technical Change*

I have argued that opportunities—stemming partly from "exogenous" scientific advances and partly from the knowledge endogenously accumulated by the firms—and appropriability conditions account for the varying degrees of commitment of business enterprises to innovation. It is important to remark that what has just been said does *not* imply that market-determined inducement mechanisms are irrelevant to the propensity to search for new products and new techniques. The levels and changes in demand (market size and growth, income elasticities of the various products), and the levels and changes in relative prices, in particular the price of labor to the price of machines[7] and also to the price of energy are influential factors. Indeed, they are likely to be fundamental ones, influencing (a) the rate and also the direction of technical progress, particularly within the boundaries defined by the nature of each technological paradigm, and (b) the selection of potential paradigms

---

[6] For detailed discussions of appropriability mechanisms, see also Christopher Taylor and Aubrey Silberston (1973), von Hippel (1978, 1980, 1982) and Terje Christian Buer (1982). The relative costs of innovation versus imitation—which is clearly a good proxy for appropriability—are studied by Levin et al. (1984) and Edwin Mansfield (1984). A detailed company-level study of patenting strategies is presented in Sally Wyatt and Gille Bertin (1985).

[7] On this point compare Paolo Sylos Labini (1984).

for exploration and thus for eventual appearance and dominance. My general point, however, is that the observed sectoral patterns of technical change are the result of the interplay between various sorts of market-inducements, on the one hand, and opportunity and appropriability combinations, on the other.

As an illustration of these points take, first, the case of automobiles. Throughout the seventies there was a clear inducement to produce energy-saving cars. Moreover, the more general demand conditions appear to be supportive (a very large market, although not growing very fast in advanced countries). Finally the appropriability conditions seemed favorable (relatively few producers with extensive distribution networks, marketing a complex product that is not so easy to copy). However, despite these favoring conditions, and leaving aside a significant change in the composition of output and demand (from big to smaller cars) progress in energy saving was rather modest: The technical opportunities on the internal combustion engine trajectory were certainly the major limiting factor. (Energy saving in U.S.-manufactured cars was, indeed, quite substantial, but this was due to the fact that American products were behind the "best-practice frontier" already reached by European and Japanese producers.)

Conversely, one can cite examples of a relatively low commitment to research and innovation, despite significant scientific and technological opportunities, due to the lack of satisfactory appropriability conditions. A case in point is part of agricultural research (until the advent of bioengineering) (Nelson 1986). There, the atomistic structure of production did not provide any incentive to research on seed variety, and so on, for individual farmers and lack of sufficient appropriability hindered industry-based research. Thus, most of the research in these fields

has been publicly sponsored (e.g., in the USA, by the Department of Agriculture): the exceptions are hybrid sterile varieties, in addition, of course, to most industrial inputs to agriculture—pesticides, fertilizers, machinery—whose appropriability conditions have been broadly similar to the rest of manufacturing industry.

Finally, one can find examples of industries where both opportunities and notionally adequate appropriability conditions are there, but the firms generally lack the appropriate skills and technical competence to undertake research and innovation (to my knowledge, this is, for example, the case of Italian ceramic producers with respect to advanced ceramic materials or, more generally, of most firms in developing countries).

The conceptualization of technology and technical change based on "paradigms," "guideposts" or whatever name is chosen, also helps in resolving the long debate in the innovation literature about the relative importance of "market pull" (cf., again, Schmookler 1966) versus "technology push" (for critical review, see Mowery and Rosenberg 1979). As known, in the former approach innovation is represented as a choice/allocation process on some sort of metaproduction function (the innovation possibility frontier) driven by market signals. In the latter, innovation drops from an exogenous domain (typically, it is a freely available by-product of scientific advances) and thus can be treated parametrically; however, the evidence from diverse technologies, such as aircraft (Constant 1980; Sahal 1981), agricultural technology and farm equipment (David 1975; Sahal 1981), synthetic chemicals (Freeman 1982), and semiconductors (Dosi 1984) is at odds with both accounts.

It is often the case that environment-related factors (such as demand and relative prices) are instrumental in shaping (*a*) the selection criteria among new po-

1142    *Journal of Economic Literature, Vol. XXVI (September 1988)*

tential technological paradigms; (*b*) the rates of technical progress; (*c*) the precise trajectory of advance, within the set allowed by any given paradigm. However, it is useful to distinguish between what I call "normal" technical progress (i.e., those processes of innovation within the bounds of a *given* technological paradigm) and "extraordinary" technical progress (associated with the development of new paradigms). As regards the former, I suggest, unlike market-pull accounts, the set of possible trajectories is quite limited, bounded by the rules, technical imperatives, and specific scope of advance of each technology (Mowery and Rosenberg 1979)—which in the short term are to a good extent invariant to market conditions.

On a generally broader time horizon, market conditions exert a powerful influence on the conduct of technological search, but they do so primarily by stimulating, hindering, and focusing the search for new technological paradigms. When established, however, each paradigm—even when at the origin of its selection there were direct market stimuli—remains quite "sticky" in its basic technical imperatives, rules of search, and input combinations. For example, the number of ways of making polymers from fossil fuels is far from unlimited and so are the input intensities, irrespective of input prices. Even the substitution among different fuels (e.g., oil versus coal) often present major technical problems. Certainly, market changes may stimulate the search for new products and new "ways of doing things." I suggest, however, that environmental factors are going to succeed in radically changing the directions and procedures of technical progress only *if* and *when* they are able to foster the emergence of new paradigms (for example, in the earlier example, new materials that substitute for plastics, bioengineering pro-

cesses to produce inputs that are alternative to fossil hydrocarbons).

Moreover, unlike both market-pull and "exogenous" accounts of technical progress, it appears misleading to consider innovation simply as a *reactive* process (to relative prices and demand, in one case, to new exogenous opportunities, in the other). On the contrary, technical progress is largely endogenously driven by a competitive process whereby firms continously try to improve on their basic technologies and artifacts. Whether market signals change or not, firms try to perfect their products and processes, by trial-and-error mechanisms of search and imitations of the results already achieved by other firms, motivated by the competitive edge that innovations are expected to offer. Thus, according to this interpretation, each body of knowledge, expertise, selected physical and chemical principles, and so on (that is, each paradigm) constrains both the opportunities of technical progress and the boundaries within which "inducement effects" can be exerted by the market, while appropriability conditions motivate the economic agents to explore these technological opportunities as a rent-yielding competitive device. Finally, the evolution of the economic environment, in the longer term, is instrumental in the selection of new technological paradigms, and, thus, in the long-term selection of the fundamental directions and procedures of innovative search.

### D. *Inducement Factors, Patterns of Technical Change, and Irreversibility*

Whatever the nature of the stimuli to change products and production processes exerted by an economic environment on microeconomic agents, ". . . they are naturally led to search the technological horizon . . . within the framework of [their] current activities and to attack the most restrictive constraint . . ." (Rosenberg 1976, p. 11). "Most mechanical productive processes throw off signals of a sort which are both compelling and fairly obvious; indeed, these processes when sufficiently complex and interdependent, involve an almost compulsive formulation of problems" (Rosenberg 1976, p. 11). The foregoing discussion on the general "paradigm-bound" nature of technical change allows the extension of Rosenberg's thesis to most contemporary innovative processes and also reconciles it with those historical interpretations of different national/sectoral patterns of innovation that trace a cause of different rates of technical progress down to different environmental inducements, especially relative prices, availability or scarcity of natural resources (a *locus classicus* is the debate on the relative degrees of mechanization in the United States and England in the nineteenth century; see Erwin Rothbarth 1946; Hrothgar Habakkuk 1962; Peter Temin 1966; David 1975; Rosenberg 1976, especially chapters 3, 4, and 6).

As known, if one sticks to a general equilibrium framework and a representation of technology based on well-behaved production functions or convex production possibility sets, it is very difficult and often logically incoherent to attribute any observed bias in the rates and direction of technical change to particular biases in relative input prices (see David 1975 for a critical overview of a long debate). In the last instance, "economic incentives to reduce costs always exist in business operations, and precisely because such incentives are so diffuse and general, they do not explain very much in terms of the *particular sequence and timing of innovative activity*" (Rosenberg 1976, p. 110); however, specific incentives, *coupled with the paradigm-bound, cumulative, and local nature of technological learning can* explain particular

rates and directions of technological advance (David 1975, 1986a and 1986b; Nelson and Winter 1982; Anthony Atkinson and Joseph Stiglitz 1969; W. Brian Arthur 1983, 1988).

To illustrate this point, consider the following story. Suppose that, once upon a time, when an imaginary technological history began, there were production possibility sets with all the right properties of continuity, convexity, and so on. Then, people started learning in a particular direction (to make it easy, suppose that this particular direction was triggered by an exogenous relative-price shock). With the help of some cumulativeness in technological knowledge and in search skills, *local* technological capabilities (that is, capabilities associated with the neighborhood of particular input combinations and output characteristics) developed more than proportionally to the "general" growth of knowledge on other notional portions of the production possibility set. Thus, other things being equal, technological progress became easier in this direction than in others. Then, with or without further shocks, people proceeded in this direction of search, which, in turn, further increased specific knowledge and skills. It is easy to see the moral of the story: One ends up with dynamic increasing returns along specific trajectories that channel also the response to particular environmental incentives to innovate. (A formal equivalent of this story is told in Arthur 1983, 1988).

A fundamental implication of this view is that, even when technical change is "triggered," say, by relative price changes, the new techniques developed as a result are likely to be or become superior to the old ones irrespective of relative prices—immediately, as in the case of several microelectronics-based innovations (Soete and Dosi 1983), or after some learning time as in agricultural machinery (David 1975). In other words, if they had existed before, they would also have often been adopted at the "old" relative prices. That is to say, technical progress generally exhibits strong *irreversibility features*.[8]

Let us consider in greater detail the example of microelectronics. As discussed at greater length in Freeman and Soete (1985), Momigliano (1985), Soete and Dosi (1983), and Benjamin Coriat (1983, 1984), electronics-based production technologies are (a) labor-saving; (b) fixed-capital saving (i.e., they often induce a fall in the capital/output ratio; for sectoral evidence in the U.K., see Soete and Dosi 1983); (c) circulating-capital saving (i.e., the optimization of production flows allows a fall in the stocks of intermediate inputs per unit of output); (d) quality improving (i.e., they increase the accuracy of production processes, allow quality testing, etc.); (e) energy saving (in so far as the energy use generally is also a function of mechanical movements of the various machineries, the substitution of information-processing equipment for electromechanical parts reduces the use of energy). Taking all these characteristics together, it is clear that electronics-based production techniques are generally unequivocally superior to electromechanical ones irrespective of relative prices. That is, the new wage/profit frontiers associated with the new techniques do not generally intersect the "old" ones for any positive value (see Dosi, Pavitt, and Soete 1988). Remarkably, this example illustrates also the complex intersectoral linkages in the innovative process and their bearing on the "exogeneity versus endogeneity" issue in technical change. In the example of electronics technologies, unequivocally "superior" techniques and pieces of equipment appear, for several users' sectors, as "dropping from an exogenous domain" (see Section IV C concerning "technology-push" accounts of technical change). In actual fact, they are generated through processes of exploration of technological opportunities *endogenous to some other industrial sectors* (in the example here, semiconductors, computers, industrial controls, etc.). Moreover, even in these cases, the full and efficient utilization of these potentially superior technologies (e.g., electronics-based automation as compared to electromechanical automation) relies on a painstaking process of learning on the side of the users, which is favored/hindered by the technological capabilities of the users themselves and the market conditions in which they operate. (It is an issue that relates also to the economics of innovation diffusion and that is impossible to discuss length in this work: For more historical evidence see Rosenberg 1975, 1982; a highly stylized attempt to model these learning processes is in Dosi, Orsenigo and Gerald Silverberg 1986.)

In other cases, the irreversibility properties of innovation emerge more slowly. At the start, the process of development/diffusion of new technologies may indeed involve choice-of-technique issues (see David 1975 on agricultural machinery). In the long term, the outcome of the rivalry between old and new technologies clearly depends also on the "latent opportunities" in the background, implicit in the two alternative paradigms; however, the degrees to which these opportunities are perceived, exploited, and expanded is likely to show path-dependent, cumulative, and irreversible features (for discussions and examples, see again David 1975, 1986b; Arthur 1983). Learning-by-

---

[8] For microeconomic accounts of the local and irreversible features of technological learning, see David (1975, 1986b). On more general grounds, the study by Anne Carter (1970) on the technological coefficients of the American economy shows (a) the unequivocal superiority of the 1958 coefficients with respect to 1947 coefficients and (b) the dominance of a labor-saving trend on other variations of input coefficients. My informed guess is that this continues to remain true today.

doing and by-using, incremental improvements on the new technologies, and economies of scale in their production tend to improve their performance and lower their cost. Moreover, if adopted, a new product or process then attracts R & D efforts to itself, which, in turn, tend to improve costs and performance further. As a result, whenever the new technological trajectory is established, it is likely *to dominate* the old one (in the sense that, to repeat, it is economically superior, irrespective of relative prices).

Whatever the case, it is important to distinguish between the factors that *induce, stimulate, or constrain* technical change from the *outcomes* of the changes themselves. As analyzed in Dosi, Pavitt, and Soete (1988), drawing upon Rosenberg (1976), inducement mechanisms relate to a broad set of factors, including (*a*) technological bottlenecks in interrelated activities; (*b*) scarcities of critical inputs; or, conversely, (*c*) abundance of particular inputs (e.g., energy, raw materials); (*d*) major shocks in prices/supplies; (*e*) composition, changes, and rate of growth of demands; (*f*) levels and changes in relative prices (first of all, as mentioned, the relative price of machines to labor); (*g*) patterns of industrial conflict. Where the critical stimuli come from depends on the nature of the technologies and on the economic and institutional context of each country: One can find plenty of evidence on the role of each of these factors (for evidence and references on different technologies and countries, see Rosenberg 1976, 1982; Dosi, Pavitt, and Soete 1988; Ergas 1984). However, irrespective of the immediate triggering factor, I suggest that the patterns of innovation tend to follow rather irreversible "trajectories" defined by specific sets of knowledge and expertise. Moreover, irreversibility in the technological advances also means that, using neoclassical language, the changes

*of* the production possibility sets are likely to *dominate* changes *within* any given set. More precisely, at any given time, instead of a well-behaved set we are likely to observe only one (or very few) points corresponding to the best-practice techniques, while, over time, the dominant process of change will imply improvements in these (very few) best-practice techniques, rather than processes of "static" interfactoral substitution. Admittedly, this interpretative conjecture is going to require more evidence and tests (which will not be easy) in order to corroborate its levels of empirical generality. (And there are also more subtle but normatively crucial issues: For example, in the historical evidence, how irreversible and local are learning processes? How powerful are "dynamic increasing return" phenomena? How can we measure, for normative purposes, the likely emergence of nonconvexities, despite the obvious impossibility of making counterfactual historical experiments?) In any case, my assessment of the state of the art in innovation studies suggests, at the very least, that significant path dependencies, nonlinearities, and processes of specific, cumulative learning should be taken very seriously also at the level of the general, theoretical representations.

Finally, the irreversibility features of technical progress tend to be reinforced by the likely emergence of various sorts of externalities and specific infrastructures and institutions associated with the generation and/or exploitation of specific skills. I will now consider these latter aspects of innovation.

### E. *The Externalities of the Innovation Process*

It has already been mentioned above that technology typically involves "public" aspects and "private" ones. The appropriability of the economic returns from innovation clearly relates to the lat-

1146     *Journal of Economic Literature, Vol. XXVI (September 1988)*

ter. Conversely, the "public" aspects essentially take two forms.

First, there are certainly "free-good" elements, in technological progress, essentially stemming from the free flow of information, readily available publications, and so on. As mentioned earlier, economic theory tends to assume this to be the dominant feature of technology (save for institutionally granted rights to appropriation, such as patent rights). Of course, I do not suggest that models such as Arrow's (Arrow 1962a) hinted at such a narrow equivalence of technology and information; however, it is fair to say that it provided some legitimacy for several contemporary formulations that have assumed it as least as a "workable hypothesis". The foregoing survey of the characteristics of technology and technical progress implies a rejection of such a view as, at best, incomplete.

Moreover, the "public" characteristics of technology relates to the information flows and the *untraded interdependencies* among sectors, technologies, and firms and takes the form of technological complementarities, "synergies," flows of stimuli, and constraints that do not entirely correspond to commodity flows. For example, knowledge and expertise about continuous chemical processing may allow technological innovations in food processing even when the latter do not involve any chemical inputs; "arms-length" relationships between producers and users of industrial equipment (such as informal exchanges of information, exchanges of technical specifications, and manpower mobility) are often a fundamental element in the innovation process even if sometimes no economic transaction is involved; at its origins the production of bicycles drew technological knowledge from the production of shotguns, even if obviously neither product is an output or an input in the other activity. All these phenomena represent a

structured set of technological externalities that can sometimes be a *collective asset* of groups of firms/industries within countries or regions (see Bengt-Ake Lundvall 1984 and 1988) or else, tend to be internalized within individual companies (e.g., Teece 1982 and Pavitt 1986a). By a "structured set" of externalities, I mean some sort of consistent, and sometimes hierarchical, pattern linking different industries and technologies (such as different kinds of machinery production and users and producers of particular types of equipment). In other words, technological bottlenecks and opportunities (Rosenberg 1976) and experiences and skills embodied in people and organizations, capabilities, and "memories" overflowing from one economic activity to another tend to organize *context conditions* that (a) are country-specific, region-specific, or even company-specific and (b) as such, determine different incentives/stimuli/constraints to innovation, for any given set of strictly economic signals.

Relatedly, technological progress along any one trajectory is linked with (a) the development of *specific infrastructures;* (b) *system scale economies; (c) complementary technologies;* and (d) *particular technical standards* that positively feed upon specific patterns of innovation David (1986) and Hughes (1982), for example, discuss the interrelation between the development of the electricity-grid infrastructure and what, in the terminology suggested here, are electricity-based technological trajectories. Other obvious examples of "infrastructure technologies" that perform as an externality to a wide range of innovative activities are transport systems and telecommunications. Arthur (1983) and David (1985) illustrate the latter two points in the case of the development of the QWERTY keyboard in typewriters (QWERTY refers to the first top letters in the standard American keyboard). Although it was designed to meet problems which subsequent developments have overcome, and though it is no longer the optimal keyboard, the QWERTY standard has remained dominant as a result of cumulative development on an early lead: The specific skill of typists in QWERTY fostered QWERTY standards on the manufacturing side, which in turn increased the incentive to acquire QWERTY typing skills. Moreover, the interrelatedness between different technologies that compose a technological system or a complex product helps us understand why companies and countries may be "locked" into technologies—see the classic work by incumbent Marvin Frankel (1956) linking this point to development topics. Finally, Teece (1982, 1986) discusses a somewhat similar issue from the point of view of firms' structures and strategic management, identifying the crucial role of internalized complementary technologies in firms' competitive performances.

Untraded interdependences and context conditions are, to different degrees, the *unintentional* outcome of decentralized, but irreversible, processes of environmental organization (one obvious example is Silicon Valley) and/or the result of explicit strategies of public and private institutions.

The evolution over time and the spatial differences in these untraded interdependences also represent an important link between innovation studies and the regional economics of technical change (see Edward Malecki 1983 and Morgan Thomas 1985). Whenever these technological externalities—in the form of specific infrastructures, skill availability, competences embodied in local firms, easier information about new production inputs—reproduce through time as a sort of dynamic increasing returns (Arthur 1986), they also help explain the differentiation in the technological capabilities,

rates of innovation, and rates of diffusion among regions and countries (see Alfred Thwaites and Ray Oakey 1985). In this field, an original tradition of studies has developed particularly in France: the analysis of "filieres" (literally "webs"), linking groups of industries and technologies via input-output flows and technological complementarities, is a promising way of relating the microeconomic process of innovation with the evolution of the wider economic environments (on "filieres," see Joel Toledano 1978; Alexis Jacquemin and Michael Rainelli 1984; Richard Arena, Michael Rainelli, and Andre Torre 1984; Ehud Zuscovitch 1984; Patrick Cohendet, Regis Larue de Tournemine, and Zuscovitch 1982; Jean-Louis Truel 1980).[9]

### F. Determinants and Patterns of Investment in Innovation: Toward a Sectoral Taxonomy

Let me summarize the discussion of the foregoing five subsections. As analyzed in detail by Nelson (1986, 1988), the process of innovation in Western economies embodies complex and varying balances between public and proprietary forms of knowledge, and different combinations between notional opportunities of innovation, firm-based capabilities to reap these opportunities, and economic incentives to do so (related to appropriability mechanisms, market conditions, relative prices, broader socioeconomic conditions such as industrial relations). Moreover, the specific opportunities that are seized, the appropriability mechanisms that are developed, and the actual capabilities that are used tend to grow with each other. Phenomena of hysteresis are likely to emerge:

---

[9] The concept of "filieres" partly overlaps with Hirschman's insights on "backward" and "forward" linkages (Albert Hirschman 1958).

1148     *Journal of Economic Literature, Vol. XXVI (September 1988)*

The exploration of particular technologies and the development of particular problem-solving methods increase the capabilities of firms and industries in these specific directions and thus increase the incentive to do so also in the future. These technology-specific forms of dynamic increasing returns tend to "lock in" the processes of technical change into particular trajectories, entailing a mutual reinforcement (a positive feedback) between a certain pattern of learning and a pattern of allocation of resources into innovative activities where learning has already occurred in the past (for general discussions of these path-dependent processes, see David 1975, 1986a; and Arthur 1983, 1988).

In line with Nelson (1986), I suggest that the different combinations among these factors explain the "rich and variegated institutional structures supporting technical advance that have grown up in capitalist countries" (p. 1). They also constitute the rather complicated constellation of factors by which a significant group of contemporary economists seek to explain the pace and characteristics of technological progress, and its international, interindustry, and intertemporal changes. Certainly, while this outlook appears to be the most promising approach we have, and while it appears to be consistent with some blocks of experience, far more empirical and historical work will be needed to establish its validity and the manner in which the different elements of the new outlook operate. A first step is to generalize on some common empirical characteristics of technologies and sectors (which I do below) and, then, try tentatively to "map" these characteristics into the features of technologies and innovative processes discussed so far (see Section VI).

Scherer, as mentioned, has recently developed an intersectoral matrix of the origin and use of R & D in the U.S. economy, based on the intersectoral generation and use of a large sample of patents (Scherer 1982). The sectoral ratios of (direct plus indirect) use of R & D to performed R & D are shown in the last column of Table 3. On the grounds of a data base on innovations in the U.K. from 1945 to 1979 collected at the Science Policy Research Unit of the University of Sussex, Pavitt (1984) has developed a sectoral taxonomy of sectors of production/use of innovation. The two data sets appear to be in many ways complementary and provide interesting insights into the "anatomy" of contemporary economic systems and their major inner *loci* of innovation generation (the Yale questionnaire—partly discussed in Levin et al. (1984) and summarized in Nelson (1986)—adds further, and broadly consistent, evidence). Pavitt (1984) identified four major groups of manufacturing industries, namely:

1. *"Supplier-dominated" Sectors.* Innovations are mainly process innovations, embodied in capital equipment and intermediate inputs and originated by firms whose principal activity is outside these sectors proper. Supplier-dominated industries include agriculture, textiles, clothing, leather, printing and publishing, wood products, and the simplest metal products. In these sectors the process of innovation is primarily a process of diffusion of best-practice capital goods and of innovative intermediate inputs (such as synthetic fibers) while endogenously generated opportunities are rather limited and so are R & D expenditures. The knowledge base of these technologies tends to relate to incremental improvements in the equipment produced elsewhere and/or to its efficient use, and to organizational innovations. Cumulativeness and appropriability of technological capabilities are relatively restricted and firms are typically not very big (with some exceptions in those activi-

ties characterized by some significant economies of scale in production, such as part of textiles, or in marketing and distribution networks, such as in clothing).

2. *"Specialized Suppliers."* Innovative activities relate primarily to product innovations that enter most other sectors as capital inputs. Firms tend to be relatively small, operate in close contact with their users and embody a specialized and partly tacit knowledge in design and equipment building. Typically, this group includes mechanical and instruments engineering. Opportunities for innovation are generally abundant, but are often exploited through "informal" activities of design improvement (thus, formal R & D is often rather low). Idiosyncratic and cumulative skills make for a relatively high appropriability of innovation (think of the secular advantage of German machine-tool makers).

3. *"Scale-intensive"* Sectors. Innovation relates to both processes and products, and production activities generally involve mastering complex systems (and, often, manufacturing complex products); economies of scale of various sorts (in production and/or design, R & D, distribution networks) are significant; firms tend to be big, produce a relatively high proportion of their own process technologies, often devote a relatively high proportion of resources to innovation, and tend to integrate vertically into manufacturing their own equipment. This group includes transport equipment, several electric consumer durables, metal manufacturing, food products, glass, and cement.

4. *"Science-based"* Sectors. Innovation is directly linked to new technological paradigms made possible by scientific advances; technological opportunity is very high; innovative activities are formalized in R & D laboratories; investments in innovative search are quite high; a high proportion of their product innovation enters a wide number of sectors as capital or intermediate inputs; firms tend to be big (with the exception of new "Schumpetarian" ventures and highly specialized producers). This group includes the electronics industries, most of the organic chemical industries, drugs, and bioengineering. (Aerospace and some military-related activities share with science-based sectors the importance of inputs from scientific advances and of formalized research, while sharing with the production-intensive sectors the importance of economies of scale and of an efficient organization of complex production systems.)

Taxonomic exercises on the intersectoral differences in the sources, procedures, and intensity of innovative search are rather new and a lot of comparative work is still to be done; however, let me briefly mention the importance of these analyses on both positive and normative grounds. As regards the former, the fact that innovations are located at different places within the "capitalist engine" (Nelson 1986, p. 20) demands a better understanding of the factors that tend to concentrate innovative opportunities and investments in some activities more than in others. Taxonomic efforts help in this understanding and also in answering puzzling comparative questions such as, How did Germany and Sweden become so good in mechanical engineering? How does this relate to their productive structure and international competitiveness? Why is the United States relatively strong in science-based industries? (some tentative answers to these comparative questions are attempted in Pavitt 1988; Pavitt, Dosi, and Soete 1988; Ergas 1984). On normative grounds, a more detailed understanding of the intersectoral patterns of innovation directs attention to questions of importance for industrial and development policies. Given the objective of an acceleration of the rate of technical progress, would R & D incentives be well suited for science-based industries but not for "supplier-dominated" industries? Would the development of a large internal market be important for scale-intensive industries but not so much for "specialized suppliers"?

### G. *Some Conclusions*

In this section, I have focused on the broad differences in opportunities, incentives, R & D investments, and innovative procedures among industries. The thrust of the argument has been that these differences exist, are important, and help explain the internal structure of the complex engine which in modern noncentrally planned economies continuously generates new products and production processes. Moreover, intertechnological differences in opportunity, appropriability conditions, knowledge bases, and search procedures help explain what Nelson (1986) calls the "problem of institutional assignment," that is, the location within the socioeconomic system of specific search and development activities to particular actors, for example, why certain activities are undertaken by non-profit institutions and others by business firms, why some sectors produce their own process innovations and others buy them from the market (more on the latter in Williamson 1985; Buer 1982), and why some economic activities contribute a disproportionate share of innovations while others are mainly recipients. Relatedly, the input-output structure of the economy, together with information flows and intersectoral flows of knowledge embodied in people and organizations, diffuses through the system the economic effects of particular innovations, thus amplifying the opportunities for productivity growth and new product development.

There is a yet finer level of analysis, however. After all, industry-specific characteristics are averages of cross-firm distributions. The fact that these averages show recognizable patterns that are relatively stable over time and across countries entails the relative stability of the industry-specific and technology-specific factors analyzed above. Still, one must explain also the intra-industry variance in innovative investments and degrees of innovative success. Moreover, innovation and imitation continuously modify the relative performance and competitiveness of firms and thus affect also the dynamics of industrial structures. Parts V and VI will discuss these topics.

### V. *Intrasectoral Differences in Innovativeness and Economic Performance*

One of the most common features of industrial case studies is the description of significant differences among firms not only in terms of size, but also in terms of technological capabilities, product-market strategies, degrees of innovativeness and competitive success, costs of productions, and profitability. Putting it another way, nothing similar to the "representative firm" stylized by economic theory seems to emerge from the empirical accounts (to see this, consult a random sample of articles in, say, the *Harvard Business Review* and the *California Management Review*, or, for more detail of industrial histories, Alan Altshuler et al. 1984 on automobiles, Dosi 1984 and Franco Malerba 1985 on semiconductors, and Enos 1962 on petroleum refining). With reference to the foregoing discussion, one is led to ask what are the relationships between the characteristics of innovation analyzed earlier, on the one hand, and the intrasectoral differences in firm structures (e.g., in size) and performance (e.g., rates of innovation and production costs), on the other. In this section I focus mainly on the general features of *interfirm, intrasectoral* differences in innovativeness, and, more generally, economic performance, leaving to Section VI a more detailed account of the *processes* that generate them. The empirical reference upon which this section is based is rather commonsensical, for example, the fact that firms can be generally found to be widely different, in terms of various performance indicators and also of behaviors, structures, and strategies. However, these simple ideas might be usefully conceptualized in the sense that meaningful classifications might help, first, in providing empirically sound hypotheses for theoretical modeling and, second, in moderating the innocent acceptance—widespread in the economic literature—of "representative firms," "equilibrium conditions of production," "technological identity of producers," and so on. Thus, in the following, I attempt a classification of the factors that account for *intrasectoral* differences in both structures (e.g., size) and performances (e.g., degrees of innovativeness).

I start from the intrasectoral, interfirm differences in innovative investment as shown by their R & D expenditures.

## A. *Interfirm Differences in R & D*

A long debate has taken place in industrial economics on the relationship between size of firm and innovation (both R & D investments and innovative output, typically patents). I shall not enter the details of the discussion that concern both the meaning of particular measures (it has been argued that patenting underestimates the innovation output of big firms—which appear to show a lower propensity to patent; the R & D expenditures are likely to underestimate innovative contributions of small firms—which

sometimes innovate on an "informal" basis, etc.) and the degrees of empirical corroboration of the improperly termed *Schumpeterian hypothesis* (i.e., that bigness is relatively more conducive to innovation, that concentration and market power affect the propensity to innovate). For reviews and (partly conflicting) findings, see Scherer (1988), Soete (1979), Griliches (1984a), Griliches and Pakes (1986), Morton Kamien and Nancy Schwartz (1982), Wesley Cohen and Levin (1988), and Pavitt, Robson, and Townsend (1987). For the purposes of the present work, it is enough to mention three major regularities that come out of empirical studies.

First, there appears to be a *roughly* log-linear relation within industries between firm size and R & D expenditures (or patenting). This is, however, a rather crude approximation. On closer inspection, subject to industry differences and different measures of innovativeness, one finds better fits of quadratic and cubic relationships between size (i.e., sales or employment) and innovativeness (R & D expenditure, R & D employment, number of patents, or number of innovations); however, irrespective of the form of the econometric model, the estimates show *roughly* nondecreasing returns of innovative proxies to firm size (Scherer 1986 argues in favor of a lower degree of innovativeness for the greatest size classes; Soete 1979, using partly different data, shows the opposite for about a third of his industry sample).

Second, the size distribution of innovating firms *within sectors* depends on the technological characteristics of the sectors themselves. Pavitt, Robson, and Townsend (1987), using the SPRU sample of innovation mentioned earlier, conclude that in sectors with high technological opportunities (chemicals, electrical/electronics) the innovating firms "can be found heavily represented among those that are very large and those that are small" (p. 16). Conversely, in machinery and mechanical engineering (approximately those "specialized suppliers" with the characteristics identified earlier) a relatively greater proportion of innovation is undertaken by small firms (which, however, are "small" in comparison with the size of distribution of the manufacturing firms' universe, but not necessarily in relation to the specific national or world market in which they operate).

Third, irrespective of the statistical proxy for innovativeness (and in particular, irrespective of the choice between an investment measure or an output measure), after allowing for the effect of firm size, one still generally observes a substantial unexplained interfirm, intrasectoral variance, in terms of both R & D investments and, even more so, innovative output. (Moreover, note that a significant proportion of firms in each industry do *not* patent and do *not* produce significant innovations; for evidence, see John Bound et al. 1984.)

There are three obvious caveats for the interpretation of these results. The first relates to the fact that the statistical proxies for innovativeness cannot capture those aspects of technical change, discussed above, based on "informal" learning (thus, independent of measured R & D investments) and/or yielding incremental innovations (hence, unrecorded in patents or discrete innovation counts). The second is that some (generally undetermined) part of the *intra*sectoral variance in innovative performance must be attributed to differences in the actual lines of business (and, thus, in opportunity, appropriability) which are, nevertheless, statistically classified within the "same" industry. Third, some firms may not patent or innovate but still engage in substantial R & D which is simply devoted to keeping up and adapting to what other competitors are doing.

Despite such limitations, however, these empirical regularities tell a story that, in my view, is consistent with the characteristics of the innovative process discussed earlier. More precisely, the intra- and intersectoral differences in the size distribution of firms in general and in particular of innovating firms are linked with the characteristics of different technological paradigms and the ways innovative capabilities develop and can be competitively exploited by individual firms. After all, any particular distribution of firms' characteristics (e.g., size, R & D propensities, unit costs) at any one time is itself the result of processes of corporate learning and market competition whereby certain corporate features turned out to yield a competitive advantage. The general interpretations suggested here are that (*a*) the sectoral distributions of characteristics such as firms' sizes are affected by the specific characteristics of the technological paradigms on which the production of that sector is based, in terms of appropriability, technological opportunities, scope for automation, and economies of scale; however, (*b*) any observed bias in the size distribution of firms in a particular sector is not sufficient evidence to make inferences on the "true" effect of size upon innovativeness. For example, an industry may show a relative bias toward "bigness" even if the latter does not confer particular innovative advantages (or disadvantages); it may be due simply to technical requirements on the production side (such as economies of scale in production and marketing). Alternatively, size may actually be conducive to innovation (because of indivisibilities of R & D projects, high R & D minimum thresholds) or detrimental to it (e.g., if it induces organizational inflexibilities). Finally, there may be cases in which the correlation between size and innovativeness reflects a causal process in the reverse direction: Big firms happened to grow big because they innovated successfully in the past and continue to do so in the present without, however, finding a differential advantage in "bigness" as such. In general, the relationship between industrial structures and degrees of innovativeness runs both ways and the understanding of particular intrasectoral distributions of firms' structural and performance characteristics implies the understanding of the (technology-specific) effects of innovation on firms' economic performance and competitiveness. Some of these effects obviously relate to the scope for economies of scale that each technological paradigm entails. Others relate to the impact that the differential innovative capabilities of certain firms exert on their ability to acquire a lead in efficiency and/or product quality vis-à-vis other firms. Let me start with the former.

B. *Flexibility and Economies of Scale*

Most technological trajectories since the Industrial Revolution involved increasing mechanization of production and increasing exploitation of economies of scale (see Nelson and Winter 1977 and the works cited therein); however, each technological paradigm is characterized by different trade-offs between flexibility (with respect to production runs and variety of outputs, for a given equipment) and economies of scale. Thus, a first determinant of any observed sectoral distribution of firms (and/or plants), by size, relates to the degrees to which individual firms have explored and possibly improved along a particular technological trajectory. Take the contemporary example of the transition from electromechanical patterns of automation to electronics-based ones. As compared to "classical" (electromechanical) automation of mass production, numerically controlled machine tools, flexible manufacturing systems, and robots allow a much greater

flexibility of production in terms of (*a*) acceptable variance of throughputs (defined in terms of number of cost-effectively produced homogeneous items per unit of time), (*b*) acceptable variances in output varieties, and (*c*) minimum scale of production (see Coriat 1983, 1984; Michael Piore and Charles Sabel 1984).

This has two consequences. First, it increases the efficiency of small-scale productions. Second, it is likely to decrease the importance of plant-related economies of scale that were one of the main sources of both productivity growth and production rigidity in "classical" Fordist automation.

Within the electromechanical paradigm, higher efficiency of production (stemming from standardization, economies of scale, etc.), generally associated with "Taylorist" and "Fordist" principles of organization and production, is also correlated with very high degrees of inflexibility—in terms of acceptable variance in production runs and mixes. Figure 1 illustrates such a case. Suppose that, in the "old" technology, the line $AA$ represents the technical relationship between "normal" average total unit costs (*c*) and rates of throughput (*q*), while the line $FF$ represents the corresponding relationship between unit costs and degrees of flexibility (*F*), say, approximated by the standard deviation in the rate and mixes of throughput that does not significantly increase "normal" unit costs. Fundamental dimensions of technical progress along the old technological trajectory are the increasing exploitation of economies of scale and economies of standardization. Thus, any increase of the flexibility requirements (due, for example, to increasing uncertainty about the levels and composition of demand) indirectly represents a retardation factor of technological innovation/diffusion within the electromechanical paradigm, insofar as technical advances are also

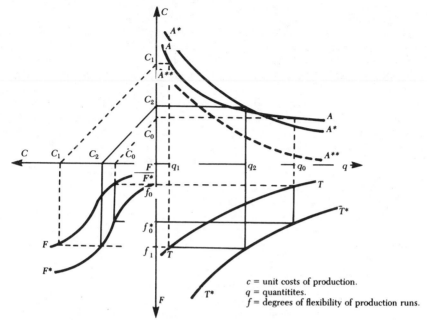

*Figure* 1. The Trade-off Between Flexibility and Economies of Scale

scale biased; however, different technological paradigms embody different trade-offs between flexibility and scale. Suppose for example that, in Figure 1, the line $A^*A^*$ represents the relationship costs/quantities for a new electronics-based paradigm, while the line $F^*F^*$ is the corresponding relationship flexibility costs. Thus, the trade-off quantity/flexibility is $TT$ for the old technology and $T^*T^*$ for the new one.[10] Now, consider again an increase in the desired flexibility. Remarkably, this is likely to have two effects: First, it is likely to hinder "normal" technical progress/diffusion along the "old" technological trajectory while, second, fostering innovation/diffusion in the new technological paradigm. Suppose we start from production runs equal to $q_0$, normal total costs at $c_0$ and a degree

[10] This example owes a lot to the discussions with B. Coriat on automation in general and, in particular, on the car industry.

of flexibility $f_0$. Now, say, an increasing instability of economic growth, an increasing uncertainty about consumers' demand and rivals' strategies increases the required flexibility of production from $f_0$ to $f_1$. On the grounds of the "old" technological paradigm, this would mean very short production runs ($q_1$) and very high costs ($c_1$). The new paradigm (e.g., electronics-based automation) changes the nature of the trade-offs, allowing, for example, the required flexibility to be achieved at throughput $q_2$ and unit costs $c_2$. Moreover, I suggest, the higher technological opportunities of the new paradigm (with its scope for learning, decreasing costs of capital equipment, etc.) in the long term will shift the technoeconomic relation between costs and quantities, say, down to $A^{**}A^{**}$.

In contemporary economies one often observes a fall in plant sizes (see, for example, Fabrizio Barca 1984 on Italy), somewhat analogous to the change in the scale of production from $q_0$ to $q_2$ in Figure 1; however, this empirical observation per se does not allow any conclusion on either the "optimal" or "equilibrium" relationship between characteristics of the technology and size, or on the long-term trends in technical opportunities for economies of scale. As illustrated above, the actual change in production scale is the joint outcome of (a) differences in the scope for economies of scale of the two technological paradigms, (b) (sector-specific) differences in the trade-offs between flexibility and scale economies that they imply, and (c) different degrees of technical progress along the two trajectories defined by the two paradigms.

One can see here a first link going *from* the characteristics of each technology *to* industrial structure (and its changes): The observed intra-industry distributions of firms by size are obviously affected by the sector-specific opportunities for various kinds of economies of scale and the trade-offs between the latter and production flexibility. If different firms position themselves differently on the notional trade-offs between flexibility and scale economies and/or explore and exploit the opportunities of automation at different paces, one should observe a distribution of varying plant sizes and firm sizes even when the propensity to innovate is neutral with respect to size. As an historical example, I suggest we are currently observing, at least in the industralized countries, a process of change in the size distribution of plants and firms that is significantly influenced by (a) the new flexibility-scale trade-offs associated with electronic production technologies, and (b) the painstaking attempts to learn how to use them efficiently and slowly explore the (still largely unknown) potential for economies of scale that they entail (for some highly preliminary and impressionistic evidence, see Mehmet Gonenc 1984; Fabio Arcangeli, Dosi and Moggi

1986 and Giancarlo Cainarca, Massimo Colombo, and Sergio Mariotti 1987); and, possibly (c) an increasing variety of demanded characteristics of products, greater refinement and tolerance for (or desire for) novelty, associated with market segmentation and higher consumers' income. As general outcome of all these factors, in line with Pavitt (1986b), I conjecture that changes in the size distribution (by plant and especially by firm) in the "specialized supplier" industries—machine making, etc.—will tend to be biased toward the bigger size classes, because of R & D indivisibilities, economies of scope based on electronics flexible manufacturing systems, and so on. Conversely, in mass-production industries the higher flexibility of the new forms of automation is likely to allow the efficient survival also of relatively smaller firms (as compared to the past).

More generally, on the grounds of sectoral, and still scattered, evidence, it is plausible to conjecture that, at any one time, there may be a certain number of (technology-specific) size distributions (by plant and by firm), that represent, so to speak, notional "evolutionary equilibria," in the sense that a variety of firms and plants coexist at roughly similar levels of economic performance, by exploiting more economies of scale with less flexibility, more economies of scope and lesser economies of scale, and so on.

This is not the only source of difference among firms. Other differentiating mechanisms relate even more directly to innovation and innovative strategies.

### C. *Innovation, Variety, and Asymmetries Among Firms*

A major implication of the characteristics of cumulativeness, tacitness, and partial appropriability of innovation is the permanent existence of *asymmetries* among firms, in terms of their process technologies and quality of output. That is, firms can be ranked as "better" or "worse" according to their distance from the technological frontier. As discussed in another work (Dosi, Pavitt, and Soete 1988), one can see here an interesting convergence between the findings from international trade analyses suggesting widespread technology gaps between countries (see Freeman 1963; Freeman, C. J. Harlow, and J. K. Fuller 1965; Gary C. Hufbauer 1966; Dosi and Soete 1983; OECD 1968; Soete 1981; and Mario Cimoli 1988) and the evidence from industrial economics within each country on similarly wide gaps in technology among firms as measured by their costs of production (see, for example, Tsung-Yuen Shen 1968; Nelson 1968, 1981a; Bela Gold 1969; and Dosi 1984. This confirms earlier findings by the U.S. Bureau of Labor Statistics, cited in Nelson 1981a). Moreover, some recent studies in industrial economics have begun to explore the existence and intertemporal persistence of above- or below-average profitabilities of individual firms (see Paul Geroski and Alexis Jacquemin 1986; Bruno Contini 1986; Dennis Mueller 1977; and Yiroyoki Odogiri and Hideki Yamawaki 1986); incidentally, note that interfirm profitability differences are likely to underestimate the differences in production efficiency and product technology insofar as their "quasi-rents" are distributed as differential wages and salaries.

Call *degrees of asymmetry* of an industry its dispersions of (*a*) input efficiencies for a given (homogeneous) output and (*b*) price-weighted performance characteristics of firms' (differentiated) outputs— were we able to measure them with precision. Certainly, part of these interfirm asymmetries in production efficiency are due to (*a*) economies of scale in production (see Cliff Pratten 1971; Aubrey Silberston 1972; and Donald Hay and Derek Morris 1979), and (*b*) different vintage distributions of the equipment of each firm (Wilfred Salter 1969); how-

ever—perhaps more important—these asymmetries are also the effect of different innovative capabilities, that is, different degrees of technological accumulation and different efficiencies in the innovative search processes. Other things being equal, one would expect that the higher the potential that a technological paradigm entails for creating asymmetries in product quality and production efficiency (that is, the higher are, *jointly,* technological opportunities *and* appropriability of innovative advantages), the higher the scope for the "best" firms to enjoy a competitive advantage and grow bigger, irrespective of any possible bias in the "returns" of innovativeness to size (I come back to this issue in Section VI). Of course, any observed pattern of asymmetry among firms depends also on many other features of the markets in which firms operate. For example, varying degrees of demand elasticity affect the degrees of protection that any firm enjoys against the greater efficiency of rivals, or conversely, the ease with which technological leaders can grow at the expense of less efficient rivals. In fact, there is here an obvious complementarity between the findings and conceptualizations emerging from innovation studies, on the one hand, and the analyses of entry and mobility barriers in industrial economics, on the other (see, for example, Richard Caves and Michael Porter 1977 and 1978; Scherer 1980; Sylos Labini 1967).

If such asymmetries are a factor of diversity among firms that correspond, in a loose biological analogy, to different degrees of "fitness," there is yet another source of diversity which, in the same analogy, corresponds to roughly equal fitness and "polymorphism." Take, for example, two firms that show identical unit costs and produce the same good. Thus, they do not show any asymmetry, in the sense defined above; however, they might still show differences in their input combinations, which are the particular result of firm-specific histories of technological accumulation (Nelson and Winter 1982; Nelson 1985; Metcalfe 1985; Gibbons and Metcalfe 1986; Dosi, Orsenigo, and Silverberg 1986). Similarly, firms might well search for their product innovations in different product spaces, embodying different characteristics and aimed at different corners of the markets. Call this second set of sources of diversity *technological variety*, to mean all those technological differences that do not correspond to unequivocal hierarchies (i.e., "better" and "worse" technologies and products).

Finally, empirical studies often show the coexistence, within the same industry and for identical environmental incentives, of widely different strategies related to innovation, pricing, R & D, investment and so on. Specifically with regard to innovation one notices a range of strategies concerning whether or not to undertake R & D; being an inventor or an early imitator, or "wait and see"; the amount of investment in R & D; the choice between "incremental" and risky projects, and so on (see Charles Carter and Bruce Williams 1957; Freeman 1982 and the bibliography cited therein). Call these differences *behavioral diversity*.

I suggest that technological asymmetries, varieties, and behavioral diversities manifest themselves also in the "unexplained" variances in R & D, patenting, and a number of discrete innovations cited earlier (Section V A).

To summarize: Each production activity is characterized by a particular distribution of firms according to their R & D investments, innovative output, size, degrees of asymmetries in product quality, and production efficiency. However, the picture of an industry that emerges at any time is itself the result of a competitive process which selected survivors

within the technological variety and behavioral diversity of firms, put a premium or a penalty on early innovators and allowed varying degrees of technological imitation and diffusion. Thus, a satisfactory understanding of the relationship between innovation and distribution of firms' structural and performance characteristics also implies an analysis of the learning and competitive process through which an industry changes. I turn now to these topics.

## VI. *Innovation and Industrial Change: Learning and Selection*

### A. *The Innovative Process and Industrial Structures*

Over time, as innovation proceeds, new products are introduced and later imitated by other firms, better methods of production are developed or adopted in the form of new types of capital equipment, and, relatedly, some firms are able to obtain below-average costs of production and/or a monopolistic/oligopolistic position, in the manufacturing of some new products. In turn, they can exploit these differential advantages by increasing their rates of profit, their market shares, or, of course, a combination of the two. Conversely, some firms find themselves with above-average costs and/or lower-quality products and, through various strategies of imitation, search, and attempts to "leapfrog," must try to catch up in order to improve their profitabilities and market competitiveness. One version or another of this basic process is what determines the sectoral "snapshots" discussed in the previous section and is revealed, over time, also by the changes in the averages and distributions of firms' inputs, productivity, unit costs,. product performances, profit rates, and sizes. Putting it another way, industrial performance and industrial structures are *endogenous* to the process of innovation, imitation, and competition.

Nelson and Winter (1982), Winter (1971), Katsushito Iwai (1981), Gunnar Eliasson (1986a), Gerald Silverberg (1987), Dosi, Orsenigo, and Silverberg (1986), Gibbons and Metcalfe (1986) and Öve Granstrand (1986) have tried to formalize this process in an evolutionary perspective: "Market structure and technological performance are endogenously generated by three underlying sets of determinants: the structure of demand, the nature and strength of opportunities for technological advance and the ability of firms to appropriate the returns from private investment in research and development" (Levin et al. 1984, p. 1). (Treatments of the endogeneity of market structures have been recently developed also within an "equilibrium" framework; see Dasgupta and Stiglitz 1980a, 1980b.) Case studies of individual industries confirm both the endogenous nature of market structures and the causal link going *from* technological success *to* changes in firm size and degree of industrial concentration; in addition to Gort and Steven Klepper (1982) and Gort and Akira Konakayama (1982) who provide comparative intertechnological evidence, see for example, some cross-sectoral evidence in Levin, Cohen and Mowery (1985); and the more qualitative sectoral evidence in Almarin Phillips (1971) on aircraft; Barbara G. Katz and Phillips (1982) on data processing; Wilson, Ashton, and Egan (1980), Dosi (1984), John Tilton (1971), Ed Sciberras (1977), and Malerba (1985) on semiconductors; Altschuler et al. (1984) on automobiles; Chesnais (1986) on drugs and bioengineering; and Momigliano (1983) for a cross-company international econometric analysis of the relationship between levels and changes in various indicators of innovativeness and changes in performance of computer firms.

Broadly speaking, the growing (but still largely inadequate) evidence on the dynamics of industries and technologies highlights complex and varied learning processes whereby firms explore specific domains of perceived technological opportunity, improve their search procedures, and refine their skills in developing and manufacturing new products, drawing partly on their internal accumulated knowledge, partly on artifacts and knowledge developed elsewhere, and partly by copying their competitors. In turn, market interactions select, to different degrees, particular directions of technological development, allowing some firms to grow bigger and penalize others. Note also that in this dynamics, technological asymmetries and technological and behavioral variety *are both the outcome and a driving force* of technological and organizational change. That they are the *outcome* of innovation is straightforward from the earlier discussion: Firms generally learn at different rates, and with modes and behavioral rules specific to their history, internal organization, and institutional context. These interfirm differences are also a major driving force of the process of change in that they underlie the competitive incentive (for the "winners") and the competitive threat (for the "losers") to innovate/imitate products, processes, and organizational arrangements.

Each observed industrial history is, in an essential sense, the outcome of a particular form of this general process; however, in order to account for the specific differences in the patterns shown by individual industries, one should move one step further and, so to speak, "map" the varied characteristics of innovation, as discussed in Sections II to IV, into empirically recognizable classes of evolutionary processes. So, for example, one should be able to link the characteristics of opportunity, appropriability, and so on, of each technological paradigm and the patterns of change in, for example, firms' sizes, market concentration, and degrees of asymmetries. Here the evidence is still highly unsatisfactory and some conjectures can be related only to single case studies and to the plausibility of simulation results; however, the issue is worth pursuing for its analytical (and also normative) relevance.

### B. *Characteristics of Innovation and Patterns of Industrial Change*

In general, the observed changes in industrial structures and the observed dynamics of industrial performance (e.g., rates of introduction of new products and rates of change in sectoral productivities) are the outcome of (*a*) *innovative learning* by single firms (together with that contributed by universities, government agencies, and so on); (*b*) *diffusion* of innovative knowledge and innovative products and processes, and (*c*) *selection* among firms. Relatedly, my general interpretative conjectures are the following. First, the empirical variety in the patterns of industrial change is explained by different combinations of selection, learning, and diffusion and different learning mechanisms (e.g., "informal" learning by doing, learning through formalized R & D, and experience in marketing). Second, the nature of each technological paradigm, with its innovative opportunities, appropriability conditions, and so on (jointly with other economic and institutional factors) helps explain the observed intersectoral differences in the relative importance of the three processes. (Some further discussion of these conjectures can be found in Dosi, Orsenigo, and Silverberg 1986 and Dosi, Winter, and Teece 1987.) I will proceed by making some broad remarks on the nature of the three processes and then highlight the ways in which they are affected by the characteristics of innovation, by means of some "ideal examples," simulation results, and case studies.

To begin, note that each successful innovation—whether related to process technology, products, or organizational arrangements—entails ceteris paribus, an *asymmetry-creating* effect, which allows one or some firm(s) to enjoy some improvement in its competitive position (e.g., lower prices or better products). Of course, changes in the asymmetries among individual firms do not necessarily correspond to changes in the overall degrees of asymmetry in any one industry. For example, a firm that was previously inefficient, or relatively unsuccessful because its product line was unattractive, now succeeds in devising better processes of products. Other things being equal, this might well reduce the dispersion in the general distribution of the industry; however, it still generates an asymmetry between the considered firm and its laggard competitors. Certainly, the possibility of imitation holds out a greater potential for gain (in productivity, etc.) to firms that are relatively laggard than to firms that are relatively advanced. Ceteris paribus, therefore, there is reason to think that the process of imitation and diffusion makes for *convergence*. But asymmetries in the capabilities of firms impose limits on this tendency and its strength remains to be determined. (I am obviously unable to deal here with the vast literature on diffusion which would require a work of its own and I will mention only a few results relevant to the present discussion.) In turn, the higher the asymmetries among firms, the higher also is the possibility for the technological leaders (or, in any case, the most efficient producers) to modify the industrial structure in their favor, and also improve aggregate industrial performance, by eliminating the laggard producers. Vice versa, the lower the degrees of interfirm asymmetries, the more the improvements of whatever indicator of industrial performance have to rely on widespread learning and diffusion processes.

Moreover, note that the concepts of appropriability, cumulativeness, and tacitness of technological capabilities—introduced earlier—bear a direct link with those concepts developed in industrial economics such as entry and mobility barriers in that the former entails forms of competitive differentiation both between incumbents and potential entrants and among incumbents. In this respect, the "degree of asymmetry" of an industry is a synthetic representation of both sets of phenomena.

With these remarks in mind, let me consider in more detail the relationship between features of the innovative process and patterns of industrial dynamics.

Consider, first, differences in technological *opportunity*, holding other characteristics of innovation (such as appropriability) constant. It is straightforward that, ceteris paribus, one would expect the rates of performance improvement over time (e.g., productivity growth) to be positively correlated with the levels of technological opportunities; however, what can one say about the characteristics of the underlying evolutionary process driven by high technological opportunities? Of course, one would expect that, the higher the opportunities are, the higher also will be the innovative learning by some producers and the selective pressures against laggard firms. That is, the higher the opportunities are, the higher also is the probability that some firms will "learn a lot," a lot more than other competitors, and that—on the grounds of their vastly superior performance—they will, so to speak, drive forward the industry by eliminating backward producers. The simulation exercises in Nelson and Winter (1982) broadly

corroborate these conjectures about the relationship between degrees of technological opportunities, possibilities of differential innovative learning, and selection, leading, ceteris paribus, to rather concentrated industrial structures. One must stress, recalling the discussion in Section IV, that "opportunity" is only a necessary but not sufficient condition for its actual exploitation, while the speed of sectoral performance improvements (in productivity and product characteristics) depend on the latter. Given any notional technological opportunity, its effective exploitation by business firms will depend, as mentioned, on factors such as appropriability conditions, and, also on market variables such as the size of the market, the elasticity of demand to price and quality changes, and the degrees of industrial concentration. The rates at which opportunities are actually exploited (in terms of new/better products and more efficient processes of production) by, at least, some firms, and the rates at which these new products and processes diffuse to other firms obviously affect also the rates of change of industrial performance over time—e.g., the rates of productivity growth or the changes in output prices. In this respect, the case studies cited in paragraph V A also present some evidence on the impressive record of productivity growth and real price fall in sectors characterized by promising new paradigms and high technological opportunities, e.g., computers and semiconductors. Moreover, as regards cross-industry analyses, the evidence that one often finds on the statistical link between sectoral R & D intensity and sectoral innovative performance (e.g., sectoral productivity growth) should, in the light of this discussion, be considered as evidence that relatively high technological opportunities tend to be associated with a formalized, R & D–based mode of technological learning (Nelson 1981a).

Second, consider the impact of *cumulativeness* of innovative capabilities. Here, the implications are straightforward. The more technical progress is cumulative at a firm level, the more success breeds success. Firm-level cumulativeness of technological capabilities entails a nonrandom distribution of probabilities of innovative advance and path dependence: Firms that achieve higher levels of innovativeness (competitiveness) increase also their probability of maintaining or increasing their levels of competitiveness (innovativeness). Technological variety and diffusion are then likely to play only minor roles in industrial dynamics, while the rates of innovative learning of the technological leader(s) directly determine rates of change in the aggregate performance of (often highly concentrated) industries. The converse is the case where cumulativeness is relatively low, as has often been true in "supplier-dominated" sectors. Innovations are mainly embodied in equipment and components bought from other sectors, and while technological opportunities might be significant, they are mainly generated *exogenously* to these industrial activities. In fact, they are the result of opportunities of developing, for example, new seeds, fungicides, pesticides, tractors, and textile machinery that can be efficiently adopted in agriculture, textile, clothing, and so on. Under these circumstances, one would expect diffusion of new vintages of equipment to be the main source of industrial dynamics, while selection processes leading to market concentration are likely to be relatively weak. The evidence on the structure of these sectors (for a discussion, see for example Pavitt 1984) is in line with this hypothesis. Suppliers of new types of machinery, components, seeds, and so on have an interest in the most rapid possible diffusion of their outputs, and thus the rates of change in average perfor-

mance (productivity, etc.) in the user sectors depends jointly on (*a*) the pace of innovation in the supplier sectors and (*b*) the variant conditions governing adoption. The former, clearly, puts the upper ceiling to such rates of performance improvement. The latter are especially important in explaining the average gaps between faster- and slower-moving countries (again, for an historical illustration of American versus English agriculture in the nineteenth century, see David 1975).

Third, consider the role of appropriability conditions. Of course, the "ease" of imitation of a certain innovation (and, thus, of its diffusion into the output or the production process of other firms) or the ease with which rival firms may succeed in introducing a competitive product stands, ceteris paribus, in an inverse relationship with its appropriability.

In general, the overall degrees of appropriability, the relative effectiveness of the various sources of appropriability (e.g., patenting, innovative leads, and firm-specific learning by doing), the technological opportunities and their sources (e.g., internally generated by incumbents versus external to the industry and "public"), the size and rates of growth of the market all change significantly over the trajectory of development of a technology (its "life cycle"). These factors, jointly with the conditions governing market competition (e.g., various other sorts of entry barriers, necessary minimum scale, difficulties of breaking into or enlarging markets—both domestic and foreign, price and quality elasticity of demand) govern the evolution of both industrial performances and structures.

Certainly, from an empirical standpoint, the concepts emphasized in this work (such as opportunity and appropriability) do not have obvious and objective counterparts, because they are not directly measurable and empirical studies

Number of
Producers

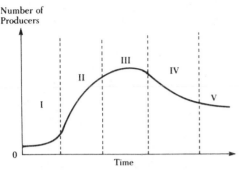

*Figure* 2.  New Products and Number
of Producers

Source: Gort and Klepper (1982), based on a sample of
46 product innovations.

are still difficult and uncertain; however, in my view, statistical difficulties do not detract from their crucial interpretative importance. And, despite all practical drawbacks, it seems to me that the empirical studies now available are quite consistent with this framework of analysis. For example, it has been shown that, along what has been defined here as paradigm-specific "technological trajectories," the net rate of entry of new firms changes. Gort and Klepper (1982) find rather robust cross-innovations evidence (based on 46 innovations) of a five-stage cycle as depicted in Figure 2. It might be worth summarizing their major conclusions: ". . . there is no equilibrium number of firms in an industry"; ". . . [the] ultimate number of producers . . . and the number at each preceding point in time depends upon the sequence of events to that point"; ". . . technical change (innovations) plays a critical role in determining both entry rates and the eventual number of firms in the market"; ". . . the number of firms in product markets technologically adjacent to those of a new product—that is, the number of potential entrants—influence the entry rates"; ". . . the onset of Stage III [flattening net entry rates] and the ensu-

ing net exit in Stage IV is not associated with the maturity of the market as measured by market size or the growth rate in demand"; "rather it corresponds to a decrease in the rate of innovations external to the industry, a compression of profit rates, and the accumulation of valuable experience by incumbent producers" (p. 634). Of course, there is no general necessity for an innovation to pass through all five stages. Whenever radically new (and competing) innovations emerge, one may observe "truncated cycles" (on semiconductors, see Dosi 1984). Still, the major conclusion holds: The net rate of entry and, more generally, the structure of production of any one innovation (the number and size of firms, degrees of industrial concentration, entry barriers, etc.) are endogenous to the technological dynamics, and depend also on rates and modes of innovative learning and on the extent to which this learning is appropriated and internalized within firms as a rent-earning asset.

Empirical and theoretical research on the properties of different modes of industrial evolution is still at a rather early stage; however, the foregoing conjectures and findings highlight the very promising link between the studies of the microeconomic features of the processes through which people and firms search for new products and processes—the domains of the "economics of innovation"— on the one hand, and the analyses of the competitive process, and of the structures, performance, and change of industries—a typical domain of industrial economics—on the other. Innovative learning, of course, is an important competitive weapon. Moreover, the ways economic actors learn also influence the degrees to which they can exploit such a weapon competitively and ultimately change the environment in which they operate. Such a process is inherently "evolutionary," at least in the sense that various economic actors are forced to search for technological changes whose success will only be determined ex post by market selection. Thus, there is inevitably a distribution of "mutations" of which at least some are destined to be "mistakes." In that model, markets select both among firms and among specific technological advances (more on this in Gibbons and Metcalfe 1986); however, such an evolutionary process, unlike a strict biological analogy, is not driven by any purely random change-generating mechanism. Agents learn—from the environment, from their rivals, from their own successes and mistakes—in ways that are specific to the body of knowledge that characterizes each technology, that is, each "technological paradigm." As a consequence, the features of the evolution of each industry are, so to speak, "ordered" by the patterns of learning, and by the ways the latter influence the competitive process; The understanding of the variety of observable industrial structures, performances, and their changes implies, I suggest, a sort of "microfoundation" in the underlying modes by which economic agents accumulate knowledge and competencies on how to solve technological and organizational problems. This, possibly, remains as one of the major fields of analysis of the variegated structures and dynamics by which noncentrally planned economies search for, generate, and select technological innovations. Still, I believe, a fundamental ingredient of the explanation of such variegated industrial structures (and of why in some sectors innovating firms are small and in others large, why some innovating firms diversify beyond the boundaries of their original activities and others do not, why some firms continue to innovate and others slow down, etc.) derives from the equally variegated nature of the evolutionary processes that generated them. Finally, in this perspective, one might

also try to explain (a) the levels and changes of economic performance of different countries as the joint outcome of movements of the "technological frontiers" (that is, unequivocal improvements in best-practice production techniques and production inputs), (b) processes of learning/diffusion to more "backward"/imitative firms (and countries), and (c) processes of selection associated with higher competitiveness or higher international market shares of the most successful innovators (or imitators). Clearly, in considering international differences, factors that go beyond those that differentiate firms within a common national environment need to be considered (e.g., education, financial facilities, legal institutions, cultural traits, forms of social organization). However, it will be interesting to see, first, how far the factors that emerge from the present survey can take us, and, second, how such factors interact with those broader national characteristics which I have just mentioned.

## VII. *Some Conclusions*

The number, variety, and scope of the studies that have been reviewed (albeit a subset of the recent literature on technological change) reveal the progress that has been made over the last 20 years in the conceptualization and, to some extent, in the empirical analysis of the process of generation of innovations and their effects. Some of the themes can be considered as developments on insights and hypotheses already present in the writings of classical economists, and, after them, Schumpeter. Other elements of analysis add novel understanding of the characteristics of technical progress. Certainly, the empirical analysis of the innovative process within and across industries and countries has made a promising beginning and is pursued with vigor. Progress in this area is often constrained by scarcity of the relevant data, but possibly also by the "vision" and approach to empirical analysis of economists who are generally trained to consider technology among the preanalytical data of their models.

In the new view, appropriability; partial tacitness; specificity; uncertainty; variety of knowledge bases, search procedures, and opportunities; cumulativeness; and irreversibility (all concepts defined in Sections II and III) have been recognized as *general features* of technological progress. Relatedly, the endogenous nature of market structures associated with the dynamics of innovation, the asymmetries among firms in technological capabilities, various phenomena of nonconvexity, history dependence, dynamic increasing returns, and the evolutionary nature of innovation/diffusion processes are some of the main elements of the process of technological change.

My impression is that there is a significant gap between the wealth of findings by economic historians, students of technology, applied industrial economists, on the one hand, and the (more limited) conceptualization of these findings in economic theory, on the other. Clearly, there will always be a difference between the "empirical stories" and the "analytical stories" of the theoreticians. The former tend inevitably to focus on the uniqueness of the details while the latter are bound to involve varying degrees of simplification and abstraction.[11] However, the core hypotheses made by the theory should not openly conflict with empirical phenomena that show enough persistence over time and/or across eco-

nomic environments. If one believes this, then some questions immediately come to mind: For example, how does one translate the features of the innovative process, outlined above, into theory-level propositions on microeconomic behaviors, production theory, adjustment processes, and so on? Are these propositions consistent with the corresponding assumptions that one generally makes in economic analysis? Or, putting it another way, can we build incrementally upon standard assumptions in order to account for the foregoing properties of the innovative process? Whatever one's answer to these questions, the field of innovation is, in my view, particularly fascinating and challenging. Innovation and technical change have been a privileged focus of attention also for those who have been trying to model economic dynamics in unorthodox fashion, based on "evolutionary" assumptions, a much looser concept of "equilibria," a characterization of behaviors that leave great room for institutional traits and a big emphasis on competition as a selective mechanism (notably, Nelson and Winter 1982; see also Dosi et al. 1988). However, the challenge that innovative processes pose to this approach is equally formidable. It must show that assumptions which, with little doubt, are empirically more plausible, can also generate models with levels of generality somewhat comparable with those based on a more conventional approach; explore the robustness of results that so far have been obtained mainly through simulations; achieve, despite an admittedly higher complexity, that threshold of elegance that makes models appealing to the professional community.

Almost certainly, competing theories in social sciences are somewhat like competing phenotypes in complex evolutionary environments: There is no way of telling ex ante which one will be "fitter."

[11] This is not the place to engage in a discussion of economic methodology. A rich exchange of views on "theory versus history" which directly touches on many issues involving technical change is in William Parker (1986). A pertinent methodological argument, which, again, is impossible to tackle here, despite several suggestive points and disagreements, is in John Elster (1983).

It is hard to doubt, however, that the domain of innovation, with the characteristics discussed in this review, are a major—and still largely unexplored—frontier of economic analysis.

REFERENCES

ABERNATHY, WILLIAM J. AND UTTERBACK, JAMES M. "A Dynamic Model of Product and Process Innovation," *Omega*, 1975, 3(6), pp. 639–56.
_____. "Patterns of Industrial Innovation," *Tech. Rev.*, June–July 1978, 7, pp. 2–9.
ALTSHULER, ALAN ET AL. *The future of the automobile.* Cambridge: MIT Press, 1984.
AMENDOLA, MARIO. "A Change of Perspective in the Analysis of the Process of Innovation," *Metroecon.*, Oct. 1983, 35(3), pp. 261–74.
AMENDOLA, MARIO AND GAFFARD, JEAN-LUC. "Innovation as Creation of Technology: A Sequential Model"; see Venice 1986.
ANTONELLI, CRISTIANO. "The International Diffusion of New Information Technologies," *Res. Policy*, 1986a, 15, pp. 139–47.
ARCANGELI, FABIO. "Innovation Diffusion: A Cross-Tradition State of the Art." SPRU, U. of Sussex, Brighton, 1958.
ARCANGELI, FABIO; DOSI, GIOVANNI AND MOGGI, MASSIMO. "The Patterns of Diffusion of Microelectronic Technologies." DRC Discussion Paper, SPRU, U. of Sussex, Brighton; presented at the Conference on Programmable Automation, Paris, Apr. 1987.
ARENA, RICHARD; RAINELLI, MICHEL AND TORRE, ANDRE. "Du Concept à l'Analyse de Filière: Une Tentative d'Eclaircissment Theorique." Discussion Paper, LATAPSES, Nice, 1984.
ARROW, KENNETH. "The Economic Implications of Learning by Doing," *Rev. Econ. Stud.*, June 1962a, 29, pp. 155–73.
_____. "Economic Welfare and the Allocation of Resources for Invention," see NBER 1962, pp. 609–25.
ARTHUR, W. BRIAN. "Competing Techniques and Lock-in by Historical Events. The Dynamics of Allocation Under Increasing Returns." IIASA, Laxemburg, 1983; rev. ed. CEPR, Stanford U., 1985.
_____. "Industry Location and the Importance of History." CEPR paper no. 43, Stanford U., 1986.
_____. "Competing Technologies: An Overview," in DOSI ET AL. 1988.
ATKINSON, ANTHONY B. AND STIGLITZ, JOSEPH E. "A New View of Technological Change," *Econ. J.*, Sept. 1969, 79(315), pp. 573–78.
BAILY, MARTIN W. AND CHAKRABARTI, A. K. "Innovation and Productivity in U.S. Industry," *Brookings Pap. Econ. Act.*, Dec. 1985, 2, pp. 609–32.
BAKER, MICHAEL J., ed. *Industrial innovation.* London: Macmillan, 1979.
BARCA, FABRIZIO. "Modello della specializzazione flessibile. Fondamenti teorici ed evidenza empirica," in *Contributi alla ricerca economica.* Rome: Banca d'Italia, 1984.

LE BAS, CHRISTIAN. *Economie des innovations techniques.* Paris: Economica, 1981.
BEER, JOHN J. *The emergence of the German dye-industry.* Champaign-Urbana: U. of Ill. Press, 1959.
BERNAL, JOHN D. *The social function of science.* London: Routledge and Kegan Paul, 1939.
BOUND, JOHN ET AL. "Who Does R&D and Who Patents?" in GRILICHES 1984, pp. 21–45.
BRAUN, ERNEST AND MACDONALD, STUART. *Revolution in miniature: The history and impact of semiconductor electronics.* Cambridge: Cambridge U. Press, 1978.
BURNS, ARTHUR F. *Production trends in the United States since 1870.* NY: NBER, 1934.
BRESNAHAN, TIMOTHY AND DAVID, PAUL A. "The Diffusion of Automatic Teller Machines Across US Banks." CEPR, Stanford U.; see Venice 1986.
BUER, TERJE CHRISTIAN. "Investigation of Consistent Make or Buy Patterns of Selected Process Machinery in Selected US Manufacturing Industry." Sloan School of Management, MIT, PhD diss., 1982.
CAINARCA, GIANCARLO; COLOMBO, MASSIMO AND MARIOTTI, SERGIO. "An Evolutionary Pattern of Innovation Diffusion: The Case of Flexible Automation." Dept. of Electronics Discussion paper; Milan Politecnico; presented at the 14th EARIE Conference, Madrid, Sept. 1987.
CARTER, ANNE. *Structural change in the American economy.* Cambridge: Harvard U. Press, 1970.
CARTER, CHARLES AND WILLIAMS, BRUCE. *Industry and technical progress.* Oxford: Oxford U. Press, 1957.
_____. *Investment in innovation.* Oxford: Oxford U. Press, 1958.
CAVES, RICHARD E. AND PORTER, MICHAEL E. "From Entry Barriers to Mobility Barriers: Conjectural Decisions and Contrived Deterrence to New Competition," *Quart. J. Econ.*, May 1977, 91(2), pp. 241–61.
_____. "Market Structure, Oligopoly, and Stability of Market Shares," *J. Ind. Econ.*, June 1978, 26(4), pp. 289–313.
CHESNAIS, FRANÇOIS. "Some Notes on Technological Cumulativeness, the Appropriation of Technology and Technological Progressiveness in Concentrated Market Structures." OECD, Paris; see Venice 1986.
CIMOLI, MARIO. "Technological Gaps and Institutional Asymmetries in a North-South Model with a Continuum of Goods," *Metroecon.*, June 1988.
CLARK, KIM B. AND GRILICHES, ZVI. "Productivity Growth and R & D at the Business Level: Results from the PIMS Data Base," in GRILICHES 1984, pp. 393–416.
COHEN, STEPHEN ET AL. "Competitiveness." BRIE Working Paper, U. of California, Berkeley, 1984.
COHEN, WESLEY N. AND LEVIN, RICHARD C. "Empirical Studies of Innovation and Market Structure," in *Handbook of industrial organization.* Eds: RICHARD SCHMALENSEE AND ROBERT WILLIG. Amsterdam: North-Holland, 1988.
COHENDET, PATRICK; TOURNEMINE, REGIS LARUE DE AND ZUSCOVITCH, EHUD. "Progrès Technique et

**1166** *Journal of Economic Literature, Vol. XXVI (September 1988)*

Perculation." BETA, U. Louis Pasteur, Strasbourg, 1982.

CONSTANT, EDWARD W. *The origins of the turbojet revolution.* Johns Hopkins U. Press, 1980.

CONTINI, BRUNO. "Organizational Change and Performance in the Italian Industry." Discussion paper, U. of Turin; see Venice 1986.

COOPER, ROBERT. "A Process Model for New Industrial Product Development," *IEE Transaction on Engineering Management*, 1983, 30(1), pp. 2–11.

CORIAT, BENJAMIN. *La robotique.* Paris: La Decourverte/Maspero, 1983.

———. "Crise et Electronisation de la Production: Robitisation d'Atelier et Modele Fordien d'Accumulation du Capital," *Critiques de l'economie politique*, 1984.

CUNEO, PHILLIPPE AND MAIRESSE, JACQUES. "Productivity and R & D at the Firm Level in French Manufacturing Industry," in GRILICHES 1984, pp. 375–92.

CYERT, RICHARD M. AND MARCH, JAMES G. *A behavioral theory of the firm.* Englewood Cliffs, NJ: Prentice-Hall, 1963.

DASGUPTA, PARTHA D. AND DAVID, PAUL A. "Information Disclosure and the Economics of Science and Technology." CEPR Pub. No. 48, Stanford U., 1985.

DASGUPTA, PARTHA D. AND STIGLITZ, JOSEPH E. "Industrial Structure and the Nature of Innovative Activity," *Econ. J.*, June 1980a, 90(358), pp. 266–93.

———. "Uncertainty, Industrial Structure and the Speed of R & D," *Bell J. Econ.*, Spring 1980b, 11(1), pp. 1–28.

DAVID, PAUL A. "A Contribution to the Theory of Diffusion." Center for Research in Economic Growth, Memo No. 71, Stanford U., 1969.

———. *Technical choice, innovation and economic growth.* Cambridge: Cambridge U. Press, 1975.

———. "Clio and the Economics of QWERTY," *Amer. Econ. Rev.*, May 1985, 75(2), pp. 332–37. (An extended version is published in Parker 1986.)

———. "Narrow Windows, Blind Giants and Angry Orphans: The Dynamics of Systems Rivalries and Dilemmas of Technology Policy." CEPR Working Paper No. 10, Stanford U.; see Venice 1986a.

———. "Some New Standards for the Economics of Standardization in the Information Age." CEPR Working Paper No. 11, Stanford U., 1986b.

DAVID, PAUL A. AND OLSEN, TROND E. "Anticipated Automation: A Rational Expectation Model of Technological Diffusion." CEPR Pub. No. 24, Stanford U., 1984.

———. "Equilibrium Dynamics When Incremental Technological Innovations Are Foreseen." CEPR, Stanford U.; see Venice 1986.

DAY, RICHARD AND ELIASSON, GUNNAR, eds. *The dynamics of market economies.* Amsterdam: North-Holland, 1986.

DAVIES, STEPHEN. *The diffusion of process innovations.* Cambridge: Cambridge U. Press, 1979.

DOSI, GIOVANNI. "Technological Paradigms and Technological Trajectories: A Suggested Interpretation of the Determinants and Directions of Technical Change," *Res. Policy*, June 1982, 11(3), pp. 147–62.

———. *Technical change and industrial transformation.* London: Macmillan, 1984.

———. "Institutions and Markets in a Dynamic World," *The Manchester School*, May 1988.

DOSI, GIOVANNI AND EGIDI, MASSIMO. "Substantive and Procedural Uncertainty. An Exploration of Economic Behaviours in Complex and Changing Environments." DRC Discussion paper, SPRU, U. of Sussex, Brighton; presented at the Conference on Programmable Automation, Paris, Apr. 1987.

DOSI, GIOVANNI AND ORSENIGO, LUIGI. "Coordination and Transformation: An Overview of Structure, Performance and Change in Evolutionary Environments," in DOSI ET AL. 1988.

DOSI, GIOVANNI; ORSENIGO, LUIGI AND SILVERBERG, GERALD. "Innovation, Diversity and Diffusion: A Self-Organisation Model." DRC Discussion Paper, SPRU, U. of Sussex, Brighton; see Venice 1986.

DOSI, GIOVANNI; PAVITT, KEITH AND SOETE, LUC. *The economics of technical change and international trade.* Brighton: Wheatsheaf, forthcoming.

DOSI, GIOVANNI AND SOETE, LUC. "Technology Gaps and Cost-based Adjustment: Some Explorations on the Determinants of International Competitiveness," *Metroecon.*, Sept. 1983, 12(3), pp. 357–82.

DOSI, GIOVANNI; TEECE, DAVID AND WINTER, SIDNEY. "Toward a Theory of Corporate Coherence." Presented at the Conference on Technology and the Enterprise in an Historical Perspective, Terni, Italy, Oct. 1987.

DOSI, GIOVANNI; FREEMAN, CHRISTOPHER; NELSON, RICHARD; SILVERBERG, GERALD AND SOETE, LUC, eds. *Technical change and economic theory.* London: Francis Pinter; NY: Columbia U. Press, 1988.

DULUDE, LOUISE S. "Les Flux Technologiques Interindustriels: Une Analyse Exploratoire du Potential Canadien," *L'Actualite Economique*, Sept. 1983, 3, pp. 259–81.

EGIDI, MASSIMO. "The Generation and Diffusion of New Market Routines." Torino, Laboratorio di Economia Politica; paper; see Venice 1986.

ELIASSON, GUNNAR. "Innovative Change Dynamic Market Allocation and Long Term Stability of Economic Growth." Industrial Institute for Economics and Social Research, Stockholm; paper; see Venice 1986.

———. "Micro Heterogeneity of Firms and Stability of Industrial Growth," in DAY AND ELIASSON 1986a.

ELSTER, JOHN. *Explaining technical change: A case study in the philosophy of science.* Cambridge: Cambridge U. Press, 1983.

ENOS, JOHN L. *Petroleum progress and profits: A history of process innovation.* Cambridge: MIT Press, 1962.

ERBER, FABIO. "Microeletronica: Reforma ou Revolucao?" Instituto de Economia Industrial, UFRJ, Rio de Janeiro, 1983.

ERGAS, HENRY. "Why do Some Countries Innovate More Than Others?" Center for European Policy Studies paper no. 5, Bruxelles, 1984.

## Dosi: Microeconomic Effects of Innovation                1167

ERNST, DIETER. *The global race in microelectronics.* Frankfurt and NY: Campus Verlag, 1983.

FARRELL, JOSEPH AND SALONER, GARTH. "Standardization, Compatibility, and Innovation," *Rand J. Econ.*, Spring 1985, *16*(1), pp. 70–83.

FRANKEL, MARVIN. "Obsolescence and Technological Change in a Maturing Economy," *Amer. Econ. Rev.*, May 1956, *45*(3), pp. 94–112.

FREEMAN, CHRISTOPHER. "The Plastics Industry, a Comparative Study on Research and Innovation," *Nat. Inst. Econ. Rev.*, 1963.

———. *The economics of industrial innovation.* 2nd ed. London: Francis Pinter, 1982. (1st ed., Penguin, 1974)

———, ed. *Design, innovation, and long cycles in economic development.* London: Royal College of Arts, 1984. (2nd ed., London: Francis Pinter, 1986).

FREEMAN, CHRISTOPHER; CLARK, JOHN AND SOETE, LUC. *Unemployment and technical innovation.* London: Francis Pinter, 1982.

FREEMAN, CHRISTOPHER; HARLOW, C. J. AND FULLER, J. K. "Research and Development in Electronics Capital Goods," *Nat. Inst. Econ. Rev.*, Nov. 1965, *34*, pp. 40–91.

GARDINER, PAUL. "Design Trajectories for Airplanes and Automobiles During the Past Fifty Years," and "Robust and Lean Designs," in FREEMAN 1984, pp. 121–68.

GEROSKI, PAUL A. AND JACQUEMIN, ALEXIS. "The Persistence of Profits: A European Comparison." Dept. of Economics discussion paper, U. of Southampton, 1986.

GIBBONS, MICHAEL AND JOHNSTON, RON. "The Role of Science in Technological Innovation," *Res. Policy*, 1974, *3*, pp. 220–42.

GIBBONS, MICHAEL AND METCALFE, J. STANLEY. "Technological Variety and the Process of Competition." U. of Manchester paper; see Venice 1986.

GIERSCH, HERBERT, ed. *Emerging technologies.* Tübingen: Mohr, 1982.

GOLD, BELA. *Productivity, technology, and capital.* Lexington, MA: Heath, 1979.

———. "Technological Diffusion in Industry: Research Needs and Shortcomings," *J. Ind. Econ.*, Mar. 1981, *29*(3) pp. 247–69.

GONENC, MEHMET R. "Electronisation et Reorganisation Verticale dans l'Industrie." Thèse de Troisieme Cycle, U. of Paris X, Nanterre, 1984.

GORDON, THEODORE J. AND MUNSON, THOMAS R. "Research into Technology Output Measures." The Future Group, Glanstonbury, CT, 1981.

GORT, MICHAEL AND KLEPPER, STEVEN. "Time Paths in the Diffusion Product Innovations," *Econ. J.*, Sept. 1982, *92*(367), pp. 630–53.

GORT, MICHAEL AND KONAKAYAMA, AKIRA. "A Model of Diffusion in the Production of an Innovation," *Amer. Econ. Rev.*, Dec. 1982, *72*(5), pp. 1111–20.

GORT, MICHAEL AND WALL, RICHARD A. "The Evolution of Technologies and Investment in Innovation," *Econ. J.*, Sept. 1986, *96*(393), pp. 741–57.

GRANSTRAND, OVE. "The Modelling of Buyer/Seller Diffusion Processes. A Novel Approach to Modelling Diffusion and Simple Evolution of Market Structure." Götebord, Chalmers U. of Technology; see Venice 1986.

GRILICHES, ZVI. "Hybrid Corn: An Exploration in the Economics of Technological Change," *Econometrica*, Oct. 1957, *25*(4), pp. 501–22.

———. "Issues in Assessing the Contribution of Research and Development to Productivity Growth," *Bell J. Econ.*, Spring 1979, *10*(1), pp. 92–116.

———, ed. *R & D, patents, and productivity.* Chicago: Chicago U. Press for NBER, 1984.

———. "R & D, Patents, and Productivity, Introduction," in *R & D, patents and productivity.* Chicago: Chicago U. Press, 1984, pp. 1–19.

GRILICHES, ZVI AND LICHTENBERG, F. "R & D and Productivity Growth at the Industry Level: Is There Still a Relationship?" in GRILICHES 1984, pp. 465–96.

GRILICHES, ZVI AND MAIRESSE, JACQUES. "Productivity and R & D at the Firm Level," in GRILICHES 1984, p. 339–74.

GRILICHES, ZVI AND PAKES, ARIEL. "The Value of Patents as Indicators of Inventive Activity." Presented at the Conference on the Economic Theory of Technology Policy, London, Centre for Economic Policy Research, Sept. 1986.

HABAKKUK, HROTHGAR J. *American and British technology in the nineteenth century.* Cambridge: Cambridge U. Press, 1962.

HAY, DONALD A. AND MORRIS, DEREK, J. *Industrial economics: Theory and evidence.* Oxford: Oxford U. Press, 1979.

HEINER, RONALD. "The Origin of Predictable Behavior," *Amer. Econ. Rev.*, Sept. 1983, *73*(4), pp. 560–95.

———. "Imperfect Decisions, Routinized Behaviour and Inertial Technical Change." Provo, Brigham Young U.; in DOSI, ET AL. 1988.

VON HIPPEL, ERIC. "A Customer Active Paradigm for Industrial Product Idea Generation," *Res. Policy*, 1978, *7*, pp. 240–66.

———. "A Customer Active Paradigm for Industrial Product Idea generation," in BAKER 1979.

———. "The User's Role in Industrial Innovation," in *Management of research and innovation.* Eds.: BURTON DEAN AND JOEL GOLDHAR. Amsterdam: North-Holland, 1980.

———. "Appropriability of Innovation Benefit as a Predictor of the Source of Innovation," *Res. Policy*, 1982, *11*(2), pp. 95–115.

HIRSCHMAN, ALBERT O. *The strategy of economic development.* New Haven, CT: Yale U. Press, 1958.

HOLLANDER, SAMUEL. *The source of increased efficiency: A study of Du Pont rayon plants.* Cambridge: MIT Press, 1965.

HUFBAUER, G. C. *Synthetic materials and the theory of international trade.* London: Duckworth, 1966.

HUGHES, THOMAS P. *Networks of power: Electrification in Western society, 1800–1930.* Baltimore, MD: Johns Hopkins U. Press, 1982.

———. "Reverse Salients and Critical Problems: The Dynamics of Technological Change." U. of Pennsylvania paper; presented at the Conference on Technology and the Enterprise in an Historical Perspective, Terni, Italy, Oct. 1987.

1168      Journal of Economic Literature, Vol. XXVI (September 1988)

IRELAND, N. J. AND STONEMAN, PAUL. "Technological Diffusion, Expectations and Welfare," *Oxford Econ. Pap.*, July 1986, 38(2), pp. 283–304.

IWAI, KATSUSHITO. "Schumpeterian Dynamics, Part I: An Evolutionary Mode of Innovation and Imitation and Part II: Technological Progress, Firm Growth and 'Economic Selection.'" Cowles Discussion Papers, Yale U., New Haven, CT, 1981. (rev. ed., *J. Econ. Behav. Organ.*, June 1984, 5(2), pp. 159–90; Sept.-Dec. 1984, 5(3–4), pp. 321–51.)

JACQUEMIN, ALEXIS AND RAINELLI, MICHEL. "Filières de la Nation et Filières de l'Entreprise," *Revue Econ.*, Mar. 1984, 35(2), pp. 379–92.

JENSEN, RICHARD A. "Adoption and Diffusion of an Innovation of Uncertain Profitability," *J. Econ. Theory*, June 1982, 27(1), pp. 182–99.

KAMIEN, MORTON AND SCHWARTZ, NANCY. *Market structure and innovation.* Cambridge: Cambridge U. Press, 1982.

KATZ, BARBARA G. AND PHILLIPS, ALMARIN. "Government, Technological Opportunities and the Emergence of the Computer Industry," in GIERSCH 1982, pp. 419–66.

KATZ, MICHAEL L. AND SHAPIRO, CARL. "Network Externalities, Competition and Compatibility," *Amer. Econ. Rev.*, June 1985, 75(3), pp. 424–40.

KAY, NEIL. *The innovating firm.* London: Macmillan, 1979.

_____. *The evolving firm.* London: Macmillan, 1982.

KENNEDY, CHARLES AND THIRLWALL, ANTHONY P. "Surveys in Applied Economics: Technical Progress," *Econ. J.*, Mar. 1981, 82(1), pp. 11–63.

KLEIMAN, H. S. *The U.S. government role in the integrated circuit innovation.* Paris: OECD, 1977.

KLEIN, BURTON. *Dynamic economics.* Cambridge, MA: Harvard U. Press, 1977.

KUZNETS, SIMON. *Secular movements in production and prices.* Boston: Houghton Mifflin, 1930.

LANCASTER, KEVIN J. *Consumer demand: A new approach.* NY: Columbia U. Press, 1971.

LANDAU, RALPH AND ROSENBERG, NATHAN, eds. *The positive sum society: Harnessing technology for economic growth.* Washington, DC: National Academy Press, 1986.

LANDES, DAVID. *The unbound Prometheus.* Cambridge: Cambridge U. Press, 1969.

LANGRISH, J. *Wealth from knowledge.* London: Macmillan, 1972.

LAZONICK, WILLIAM. "Industrial Relations and Technical Change: The Case of the Self-Acting Mule," *Cambridge J. Econ.*, Sept. 1979, 3(3), pp. 231–62.

_____. "The Social Determinants of Technological Innovation." Presented at the Conference on Technology and the Enterprise in an Historical Perspective, Terni, Italy, Oct. 1987.

LEVIN, RICHARD; COHEN, WESLEY M. AND MOWERY, DAVID C. "R & D Appropriability, Opportunity, and Market Structure: New Evidence on some Schumpeterian Hypotheses," *Amer. Econ., Rev.*, May 1985, 75(2), pp. 20–24.

LEVIN, RICHARD ET AL. *Survey research on R & D appropriability and technological opportunity.*

*Part 1: Appropriability.* New Haven, CT: Yale U. Press, 1984.

LUNDVALL, BENGT-AKE. "User/Producer Interaction and Innovation." TIP Workshop Paper, Stanford U., 1984. (Rev. ed Denmark: Aalborg U. Press, 1985)

_____. "Innovation as an Interactive Process: User-Producer Relations," in DOSI ET AL. 1988.

MAIDIQUE, MODESTO A. "The Stanford Innovation Project," in *Strategic management of technology innovation.* Eds.: ROBERT A. BURGELMAN AND MODESTO A. MAIDIQUE. Worchester Polytechnic Institute, 1983.

MALECKI, EDWARD J. "Technology and Regional Development: A Survey," *Int. Reg. Sci. Rev.*, Oct. 1983, 8(2), pp. 89–125.

MALERBA, FRANCO. *The semiconductor business: The economics of rapid growth and decline.* Madison: U. of Wis. Press, 1985.

MANSFIELD, EDWIN. "Technical Change and the Rate of Imitation," *Econometrica*, Oct. 1961, 29(2), pp. 741–66.

_____. *Industrial research and technological innovation.* NY: Norton, 1968, pp. 127–48.

_____. "R & D and Innovation: Some Empirical Findings," in GRILICHES 1984, pp. 127–48.

_____. "How Rapidly Does New Industrial Technology Leak Out?" *J. Ind. Econ.*, Dec. 1985, 34(2), pp. 217–23.

MANSFIELD, EDWIN ET AL. *Research and innovation in the modern corporation.* NY: Norton, 1971.

_____. *The production and application of new industrial technology.* NY: Norton, 1977.

MANSFIELD, EDWIN; SCHWARTZ, MARK AND WAGNER, SAMUEL. "Imitation Costs and Patents: An Empirical Study," *Econ. J.*, Dec. 1981, 91(364), pp. 907–18.

MARRIS, ROBIN M. AND MUELLER, DENNIS C. "Corporation, Competition and the Invisible Hand," *J. Econ. Lit.*, Mar. 1980, 18, pp. 32–63.

MARTINO, JOSEPH. *Technological forecasting for decision making.* NY: American Elsevier, 1976.

MENSCH, GERHARD. *Das technologische Patt.* [Stalemate in Technology] Frankfurt: Umschau, 1975.

METCALFE, J. STANLEY. "Diffusion of Innovation in the Lancashire Textile Industry," *Manchester Sch. Econ. Soc. Stud.*, June 1970, 38(2) pp. 145–62.

_____. "On Technological Competition," Mimeo. Dept. of Economics, U. of Manchester, 1985.

METCALFE, J. STANLEY AND GIBBONS, MICHAEL. "On the Economics of Structural Change and the Evolution of Technology." Manchester U. Paper presented at the 7th World Congress of the International Economics Assoc., Madrid, Sept. 1983.

MOMIGLIANO, FRANCO. "Determinanti ed Effetti della Ricerca e Sviluppo in una Industria ad Alta Opportunità Tecnologica: una Indagine Econometrica," *L'Industria*, 1983, 4(1), pp. 61–109.

_____. "Le Tecnologie dell'informazione: Effetti Economici e Politiche Pubbliche," in *Tecnologia Domani.* Ed.: A. RUBERTI. Bari: Laterza-Sat, 1985.

MOMIGLIANO, FRANCO AND DOSI, GIOVANNI. *Tecnologia e organizzaione industriale internazionale.* Bologna: Il Mulino, 1983.

MOWERY, DAVID C. "The Emergence and Growth of Industrial Research in American Manufacturing—1899–1946." PhD diss., Stanford U., 1980.

———. "The Relationship Between Intrafirm and Contractual Forms of Industrial Research in American Manufacturing, 1900–1940," *Exploration Econ. Hist.*, Oct. 1983, 20(4), pp. 351–74.

MOWERY, DAVID C. AND ROSENBERG, NATHAN. "The Influence of Market Demand upon Innovation: A Critical Review of Some Recent Empirical Studies," *Res. Policy*, 1979, 8, pp. 102–53.

MUELLER, DENNIS. "The Persistence of Profits above the Norm," *Economica*, Nov. 1977, 44(176), pp. 369–80.

NABSETH, L. AND RAY, G. F. *The diffusion of new industrial processes.* Cambridge: Cambridge: U. Press, 1974.

NATIONAL BUREAU OF ECONOMIC RESEARCH. *The rate and direction of inventive activity.* Princeton: Princeton U. Press, 1962.

NATIONAL SCIENCE FOUNDATION. *The process of technological innovation: Reviewing the literature.* Washington, DC: NSF, 1983.

NATIONAL SCIENCE FOUNDATION. *Science indicators.* Washington, DC: U.S. GPO, 1986.

NELSON, RICHARD R. "The Link Between Science and Invention: The Case of the Transistor," in NBER 1962, pp. 549–83.

———. "A 'Diffusion' Model of International Productivity Differences in Manufacturing Industry," *Amer. Econ. Rev.*, Dec. 1968, 58(5), pp. 1219–48.

———. "Production Sets, Technological Knowledge and R&D: Fragile and Overworked Constructs for Analysis of Productivity Growth?" *Amer. Econ. Rev.*, May 1980, 70(2), pp. 62–67.

———. "Research on Productivity Growth and Productivity Difference: Dead Ends and New Departures," *J. Econ. Lit.*, Sept. 1981a, 19(3), pp. 1029–64.

———. "Assessing Private Enterprise," *Bell J. Econ.*, Spring 1981b, 12(1) pp. 93–111.

———. "The Role of Knowledge in R & D Efficiency," *Quart. J. Econ.*, Aug. 1982, 97(3), pp. 453–70.

———. "Policies in Support of High Technology Industries." Working Paper No. 1011, Institution for Social and Policy Studies, Yale U., 1984.

———. *Industry growth accounts and cost functions when techniques are proprietary.* New Haven: Yale U. Press, 1985.

———. "Institutions Generating and Diffusing New Technology." see Venice 1986.

———. "Capitalism as an Engine of Growth," in DOSI ET AL. 1988.

NELSON, RICHARD R. AND WINTER, SIDNEY G. "In Search of a Useful Theory of Innovations," *Res. Policy*, Jan. 1977, 6(1), p. 36.

———. *An evolutionary theory of economic change.* Cambridge, MA: Belknap Press of Harvard U. Press, 1982.

NOBLE, DAVID. *America by design.* NY: Knopf, 1977.

NORTHCOTT, JIM; KUETSCH, WERNER AND DE LESTAPIS, BERENGERE. "Microelectronics Industry: An International Comparison." Policy Study Institute, London, 1985.

NORTHCOTT, JIM AND ROGERS, PETRA. "Microelectronics in British Industry: Patterns of Change." Policy Study Institute, London, 1984.

ODAGIRI, HIROYUKI AND YAMAWAKI, HIDEKI. "A Study of Company Profit-Rate Time Series: Japan and the United States," *Int. J. Ind. Organ.*, Mar. 1986, 4(1), pp. 1–23.

OECD. *Gaps in technology.* Paris: OECD, 1968.

OECD. *The measurement of scientific and technical activities: Proposed standard practice for surveys of research and experimental developments.* Paris: OECD, 1981.

———. "Committee for Scientific and Technological Policy, Science, Technology and Competitiveness: Analytical Report of the ad hoc Group." Paris: OECD/STP (84) 26, 1984.

———. *Science and technology indicators.* Paris: OECD, 1986.

ORSENIGO, LUIGI. "Institutions and Markets in the Dynamics of Industrial Innovation. The Theory and the Case of Biotechnology." D Phil thesis; SPRU, U. of Sussex, Brighton, 1988.

PAKES, ARIEL AND SCHANKERMAN, MARK. "An Exploration into the Determinants of Research Intensity," in GRILICHES 1984, pp. 209–32.

PARKER, WILLIAM N., ed. *Economic history and the modern economist.* Oxford: Blackwell, 1986.

PATEL, PARI AND PAVITT, KEITH. "Is Western Europe Losing the Technological Race?" *Res. Policy*, 1987, 16(2), pp. 59–85.

PAVITT, KEITH. "Technical Innovation and Industrial Development: The New Causality," *Futures*, Dec. 1979, 11(6), pp. 458–70.

———. "Patterns of Technical Change: Towards a Taxonomy and a Theory," *Res. Policy*, 1984, 13(6), pp. 343–73.

———. "Technology, Innovation and Strategic Management," in *Strategic managment research: A European perspective.* Eds.: J. MCGEE AND H. THOMAS. NY: Wiley, 1986a.

———. "Chips and 'Trajectories': How Will the Semiconductor Influence the Sources and Directions of Technical Change?" in *Technology and the human prospect.* Ed.: R. MACLEOD. London: Francis Pinter, 1986.

———. "Technological Accumulation, Diversification and Organization in UK companies, 1945–83." DRC Discussion Paper, SPRU, U. of Sussex, Brighton, 1988.

PAVITT, KEITH; ROBSON, MICHAEL AND TOWNSEND, JOE. "The Size Distribution of Innovative Firms in the UK: 1945–1983," *J. Ind. Econ.*, Mar. 1987, 35(3), pp. 297–319.

PEREZ, CARLOTA. "Microelectronics, Long Waves and the World Structural Change. New Perspectives for Developing Countries," *World Devel.*, Mar. 13, 1985, 13(3), pp. 441–63.

———. "The New Technologies: An Integrated View." SPRU, U. of Sussex, Brighton English Trans.; originally in *La tercera revolucion industrial.* Ed.: C. OMINAMI. Buenos Aires, Argentina: 1987.

1170     Journal of Economic Literature, Vol. XXVI (September 1988)

PHILLIPS, ALMARIN. Technology and market structure. Lexington, MA: Heath, 1971.
PIORE, MICHAEL AND SABEL, CHARLES F. The second industrial divide. NY: Basic Books, 1984.
POLANYI, MICHAEL. The tacit dimension. Garden City, NY: Doubleday Anchor, 1967.
PRATTEN, CLIFFORD F. Economies of scale in manufacturing industry. Cambridge: Cambridge U. Press, 1971.
PRICE, DEREK DE SOLLA. "The Science/Technology Relationship, the Craft of Experimental Science and Policy for the Improvement of High Technology Innovation," Res. Policy, Feb. 1984, 13(1), pp. 3–20.
RAY, GEORGE. The diffusion of mature technologies. Cambridge: Cambridge U. Press, 1984.
REICH, LEONARD. The making of American industrial research: Science and business at G.E. and Bell, 1876–1926. NY: Cambridge U. Press, 1985.
REINGANUM, JENNIFER F. "On the Diffusion of New Technology: A Game Theoretic Approach," Rev. Econ. Stud., July 1981a, 48, pp. 395–405.
———. "Market Structure and the Diffusion of New Technology," Bell J. Econ., Autumn 1981b, 12(2), pp. 618–24.
ROMEO, ANTHONY A. "Interindustry and Interfirm Differences in the Rate of Diffusion of an Innovation," Rev. Econ. Statist., Aug. 1975, 57(3) pp. 311–19.
RONEN, JOSHUA. "Some Insights into the Entrepreneurial Process," in Entrepreneurship. Ed.: JOSHUA RONEN. Lexington, MA: Heath, 1983, pp. 137–73.
ROSENBERG, NATHAN. Perspectives on technology. Cambridge: Cambridge U. Press, 1976.
———. Inside the black box. Cambridge: Cambridge U. Press, 1982.
———. "The Commercial Exploitation of Science by American Industry," in The uneasy alliance: Managing the productivity-technology dilemma. Ed.: KIM B. CLARK, ROBERT H. HAYES AND CHRISTOPHER LORENZ. Cambridge, MA: Harvard Business School Press, 1985.
ROTHBARTH, ERWIN. "Causes of the Superior Efficiency of USA Industry as Compared with British Industry," Econ. J., Sept. 1946, 56, pp. 383–90.
ROTHWELL, ROY ET AL. "SAPPHO Updated. Project SAPPHO, Phase 2," Res. Policy, Nov. 1946, 3(5), pp. 258–91.
ROTHWELL, ROY AND GARDINER, PAUL. "The Role of Design in Product and Process Change," Design Studies, July 1984, 4(3), pp. 161–70.
SAHAL, DEVENDRA. Recent advances in the theory of technological change. Berlin: International Institute of Management, 1979.
———. Patterns of technological innovation. NY: Addison-Wesley, 1981.
———. The transfer and utilization of technical knowledge, Lexington, MA: Heath, 1982.
———. "Technology Guide-Posts and Innovation Avenues," Res. Policy, 1985, 14(2), pp. 61–82.
SALTER, WILFRED E. G. Productivity and technical change. 2nd ed. Cambridge: Cambridge U. Press, 1969.

SAVIOTTI, PAOLO P. AND METCALFE, J. STANLEY. "A Theoretical Approach to the Construction of Technological Output Indicators," Res. Policy, June 1984, 13(3) pp. 141–51.
SHEN, TSUNG-YUEN. "Competition, Technology and Market Shares," Rev. Econ. Statist., Feb. 1968, 50(1), pp. 96–102.
SCHERER, FREDERICK M. Industrial market structure and economic performance. 2nd ed. Chicago: Rand McNally, 1980.
———. "Inter-Industry Technology Flows in the US," Res. Policy, 1982, 11(4), pp. 227–45.
———. Innovation and growth. Schumpeterian perspectives. Cambridge: MIT Press, 1986.
———. "Inter-industry Technology Flows in the US," Res. Policy. 1982,
SCHMOOKLER, JACOB. Invention and economic growth. Cambridge: Harvard U. Press, 1966.
SCHUMPETER, JOSEPH A. The theory of economic development. Cambridge: Harvard U. Press, 1934 (English translation from 1919 German ed.).
———. Capitalism, socialism and democracy. NY: McGraw-Hill, 1942.
SCIBERRAS, ED. Multinational electronic companies and national economic policies. Greenwich, CT: JAI Press, 1977.
(SPRU) SCIENCE POLICY RESEARCH UNIT. Success and failure in industrial innovation. London: Centre for the Study of Industrial Innovation, 1972.
SIMON, HERBERT. "The Structure of Ill-Structured Problems," Artificial Intelligence, 1973, 4(3), pp. 181–201.
———. "Rational Decision Making in Business Organizations," Amer. Econ. Rev., Sept. 1979, 69(4), pp. 493–513.
SILBERSTON, AUBREY. "Economies of Scale in Theory and Practice," Econ. J., Mar. 1972, 86, pp. 369–91.
SILVERBERG, GERALD. "Technical Progress, Capital Accumulation and Effective Demand: A Self-Organisation Model," in Economic evolution and structural change. Ed.: D. BATTEN. Berlin, Heidelberg, New York: Springer, 1987.
SOETE, LUC. "Firm Size and Innovative Activity: The Evidence Reconsidered," European Econ. Rev., 1979, 12(4), pp. 319–40.
———. "A General Test of Technological Gap Trade Theory," Weltwirtsch. Arch., 1981, 117(4) pp. 638–60.
———. "Firm Size and Innovative Activity: The Evidence Reconsidered," Europ. Econ. Rev., 1982.
SOETE, LUC AND DOSI, GIOVANNI. Technology and employment in the electronics industry. London: Francis Pinter, 1983.
SOETE, LUC AND TURNER, ROY. "Technology Diffusion and the Rate of Technical Change," Econ. J., Sept. 1984, 94(375) pp. 612–23.
STIGLER, GEORGE J. "Industrial Organisation and Economic Progress," in The state of social sciences. Ed.: LEONARD D. WHITE. Chicago: Chicago U. Press, 1956.
STIGLITZ, JOSEPH E. "Information and Economic Analysis: A Perspective," Econ. J. Conference Papers, 1984, 95, pp. 21–41.
STONEMAN, PAUL. Technological diffusion and the

*computer revolution*. Oxford: Clarendon Press, 1976.

――――. *The economic analysis of technological change*. Oxford: Oxford U. Press, 1983.

――――. "Technological Diffusion: The Viewpoint of Economic Theory." see Venice, Mar. 1986.

SYLOS LABINI, PAOLO. *Oligopoly and technical progress*. 2nd ed. Cambridge: Harvard U. Press, 1967.

――――. *Le forze dello sviluppo e del declino*. Bari: Laterza (*The forces of development and decline*. Cambridge: Cambridge U. Press, 1984).

TAYLOR, CHRISTOPHER AND SILBERSTON, AUBREY. *The economic impact of the patent system*. Cambridge: Cambridge U. Press, 1973.

TEECE, DAVID J. "Technology Transfer by Multinational Firms: The Resource Cost of Transferring Technological Know-how," *Econ. J.*, June 1977, 87(346), pp. 242–61.

――――. "Toward an Economic Theory of the Multiproduct Firms," *J. Econ. Behaviour Organ*. 1982a, 3(1), pp. 39–63.

――――. "Profiting from Technological Innovation," *Res. Policy*. 1986, 15(6), pp. 285–306.

TEECE, DAVID J. "The Nature and the Structure of Firms," in DOSI ET AL. 1988.

TEMIN, PETER. "Labor Scarcity and the Problem of American Industrial Efficiency in the 1850's," *J. Econ. Hist.*, Sept. 1966, 26, pp. 277–98.

TERLECKYJ, NESTER E. "R & D and the US Industrial Productivity," in SAHAL 1982.

TEUBAL, MORRIS. "The R & D Performance Through Time of High Technology Firms," *Res. Policy*, 1982.

THOMAS, MORGAN D. "Regional Economic Development and the Role of Innovation and Technological Change," in THWAITES AND OAKEY 1985, pp. 13–35.

THWAITES, ALFRED T. AND OAKEY. RAY P., eds. *The regional economic impact of technological change*. London: Francis Pinter, 1985.

TILTON, JOHN. *International diffusion of technology: The case of semiconductors*. Washington, DC: Brookings Inst., 1971.

TOLEDANO, JOEL. "A Propos des Filières Industrielles," *Revue d'Economie Industrielle*, 1978.

TRUEL, JEAN-LOUIS. "L'Industrie Mondiale de Semi-

Conducteurs." PhD thesis. U. of Paris-Dauphine, 1980.

VON TUNZELMANN, G. N. *Steam power and British industrialisation to 1860*. Oxford: Clarendon Press, 1978.

――――. "Britain 1900–1945: A Survey," in *Economic history of Britain since 1870*. Vol. II. Eds.: RODERICK FLOUD AND DONALD MCCLOSKEY. Cambridge: Cambridge U. Press, 1982.

VENICE, Conference on Innovation Diffusion, 17–21 Mar., 1986. in *Frontiers in innovation diffusion*. Eds.: FABIO ARCANGELI, PAUL DAVID AND GIOVANNI DOSI. Oxford: Oxford U. Press, forthcoming.

WILLIAMSON, OLIVER. *Markets and hierarchies*. NY: Free Press, 1975.

――――. *The economic institutions of capitalism*. NY: Free Press, 1985.

WILSON, ROBERT W.; ASHTON, PETER K. AND EGAN, P. THOMAS *Innovation, competition, and government policy in the semiconductor industry*. Lexington, MA: Heath, 1980.

WINTER, SIDNEY G. "Satisficing, Selection and the Innovating Remnant," *Quart. J. Econ.*, May 1971, 85(2), pp. 237–61.

――――. "An Essay on the Theory of Production," in *Economics and the world around it*. Ed.: S. H. HYMANS. Ann Arbor: U. of Mich. Press, 1982.

――――. "Schumpeterian Competition in Alternative Technological Regimes," *J. Econ. Behav. Organ.*, Sept./Dec. 1984, 5(3–4), pp. 287–320.

――――. "Competition and Selection" in *The New Palgrave: A dictionary of economics*. London: Macmillan, 1987a.

――――. "Natural Selection and Evolution," in *The New Palgrave: A dictionary of economics*. London: Macmillan, 1987b.

WYATT, SALLY AND BERTIN, GILLE. *The role of patents in multinational corporations strategies for growth*. Paris: AREPIT, 1985.

YELLE, LOUIS E. "The Learning Curve: Historical Review and Comprehensive Survey," *Decision Science*, 1979.

ZUSCOVITCH, EHUD. *Une approche meso-economique du progress technique: Diffusion de l'innovation et apprentissage industriel*. Doctoral thesis, Strasbourg, U. Louis Pasteur, 1984.

# Part III
# Innovative Strategies of Firms

# [7]

EXPLORATIONS IN ECONOMIC HISTORY **20**, 351–374 (1983)

## The Relationship Between Intrafirm and Contractual Forms of Industrial Research in American Manufacturing, 1900–1940*

DAVID C. MOWERY

*Carnegie-Mellon University*

During the late 19th and early 20th centuries. American manufacturing firms absorbed a broad range of activities within their boundaries. According to Chandler (1977), this expansion in the firm's boundaries was motivated by the greater efficiency and effectiveness with which specific activities could be carried out on an intrafirm, rather than a contractual, basis. Among the activities absorbed by the firm during this period was research and development. Despite widespread acknowledgment of the importance of R&D for growth, productivity, and output, the basis for the inclusion of this activity within the firm has not received a great deal of attention from Chandler or other scholars.[1] We do not have a good explanation for the fact that in a market economy, an activity of central importance to the growth and development of firms grew most rapidly in the nonmarket sector (i.e., within the firm).

This paper investigates the reasons for the intrafirm location of the industrial research function, by examining the role of independent research organizations and the relationship between in-house and contract research during the early years of industrial research in American manufacturing.

* An earlier version of this paper was presented at the meetings of the Econometric Society, December, 1981. I am grateful to Timothy Bresnahan, Louis Cain, Alfred Chandler, Wesley Cohen, Bernard Elbaum, Stanley Engerman, Alexander Field, Susan Fiske, Therese Flaherty, Steven Klepper, and Nathan Rosenberg for comments and suggestions. This research was supported by the National Science Foundation (PRA 77-21852) and the Division of Research of the Harvard Business School. Address all correspondence to the author at the Social Sciences Dept., Carnegie–Mellon University, Pittsburgh, Pa. 15213.

[1] Total employment of research scientists and engineers within industrial research facilities in manufacturing grew from roughly 3000 in 1921 to over 45,000 by 1946 (Mowery, 1981, Chap. 2). Schmookler (1957) documents the increasing importance during 1900–1950 of corporate research facilities, as contrasted with individual inventors, as sources of patents.

351

352                              DAVID C. MOWERY

A new body of archival data is used in an analysis of the relationship
between contract and in-house research activity during 1900–1940, a
period of rapid growth in industrial research employment. The extent to
which in-house and contract research functioned as complements or
substitutes, the types of research performed on a contractual basis, and
the relationship between firm size and the integration of the research
function into the firm are the central topics of concern.

The issues discussed below clearly touch on a number of important
themes in the development of American industrial research. However,
this investigation also addresses issues of more general theoretical interest.
The paper provides a different perspective on the issues of concern to
Joseph Schumpeter (1934, 1954) and other students of technological change
and industrial organization. Rather than the relationship between market
structure and the levels of research inputs or outputs, this analysis is
concerned with the ways in which the organization of the research function
affects research activity. The findings discussed below suggest that the
importance ascribed by many economic theorists to the appropriability
of the returns from research may be misplaced. In understanding the
organization and evolution of industrial research, the requirements for
knowledge transmission and utilization, as well as the difficulties encountered in the negotiation and enforcement of contracts, acquire an
importance equal to or greater than that of the appropriability of the
returns from research. The results of this inquiry also provide a basis
for an assessment of the degree to which the largest firms in American
manufacturing were the primary beneficiaries of industrial research.

The first section below discusses the historical background and conceptual basis for the hypotheses that are tested empirically. Following
this are a description and analysis of the data on the extent of substitution
or complementarity between contract and in-house research during 1900–
1940. The types of research performed on a contractual basis also are
examined. An examination of the relationship between firm size and the
organization of research is provided next. The final section summarizes
the findings and suggests some implications.[2]

## I. HISTORICAL AND CONCEPTUAL ISSUES

Industrial research in American manufacturing during the 1900–1940
period developed a dualistic structure. Employment of professional scientists and engineers grew rapidly, both in laboratories established within
manufacturing concerns, and in a large number of independent research
firms, not affiliated with a manufacturing enterprise. Between 1900 and

---

[2] The findings of this empirical analysis generally support the theoretical propositions
advanced by Balbien and Wilde (1982). However, the focus of this paper is the reasons
for the existence of parallel research enterprises, i.e., those incorporated within firms and
those acting as independent research performers, rather than the incentives and responses
of the independent research firm, as in Balbien and Wilde.

1940, according to data from the National Research Council,[3] nearly 350 independent laboratories were established. Employment of scientists and engineers within these independent organizations grew rapidly during the period for which data are available. Total employment of scientists and engineers in independent research laboratories was 3300 in 1940, and more than 5000 by 1946.

Despite this rapid growth, economic and business historians have devoted little or no attention to the role of the independent research organization. The limited historical literature on industrial research consists largely of descriptions of the development of the in-house research facilities of a few major corporations (see Mueller, 1956; Jenkins, 1975; Reich, 1977).

This lack of scholarly interest is surprising, in view of the importance ascribed to independent research organizations during 1900–1940 by contemporary observers and practitioners of industrial research. Many of these figures hailed the growth of independent research laboratories as a development that would allow the benefits of industrial research to reach small firms without in-house laboratories. The comments in 1916 of John J. Carty, the first director of the reorganized Bell Telephone Laboratories, are representative:

> Conditions today are such that without cooperation among themselves the small concerns can not have the full benefits of industrial research, for no one among them is sufficiently strong to maintain the necessary staff and laboratories. Once the vital importance of this subject is appreciated by the small manufacturers many solutions of the problem will promptly appear. One of these is for the manufacturer to take his problem to one of the industrial research laboratories already established for the purpose of serving those who cannot afford a laboratory of their own. Other manufacturers doing the same, the financial encouragement received would enable the laboratories to extend and improve their facilities so that each of the small manufacturers who patronized them would in the course of time have the benefit of an institution similar to those maintained by our largest industrial concerns. (Carty, 1916, p. 512)

Such faith in the ability of market mechanisms to handle research is echoed in a more recent statement by George Stigler.[4]

Carty's statement suggests that the primary beneficiaries of the independent research organization were relatively small firms. Such an assertion rests upon two assumptions. Independent research organizations

---

[3] The source and nature of these data are discussed below. For additional analysis, see Mowery (1981, Chap. 2).

[4] ". . . with the growth of research, new firms will emerge to provide specialized facilities for small firms. It is only to be expected that, when a new kind of research develops, at first it will be conducted chiefly as an ancillary activity by existing firms. . . . We may expect the rapid expansion of the specialized research laboratory, selling its services generally. The specialized laboratories need not be in the least inferior to 'captive' laboratories," (Stigler, 1956, p. 281). A more skeptical view of the role of the independent research organization may be found in Baldwin (1962).

354                          DAVID C. MOWERY

are assumed to have provided a full range of services, comparable to
those performed in-house, primarily to firms lacking research facilities.
Second, the ability of a firm to support an in-house laboratory and therefore,
the likelihood that one exists, are assumed to be positively correlated
with increasing firm size; in-house research is observed only among the
largest firms in manufacturing. Both of these assumptions are tested
below. The nature of the relationships among contract research, firm
size, and in-house research has obvious implications for the distribution
of the benefits of industrial research among firms of different size.

Rather than treating contract or in-house research as homogeneous
activities, this analysis focuses on different classes of research activity,
distinguished by the degree of complexity and attendant risk associated
with each. Contractual provision of various classes of research services
is influenced by factors affecting such services' supply and by factors
affecting the demand for them, i.e., the ability of firms to exploit such
contract research services as are available. The supply of contract research
is affected by two factors. The first is the degree to which specialization
in the performance of specific types of research results in declining costs
per unit of research output, i.e., economies of scale. Independent research
organizations would be expected to specialize in research services characterized by such declining unit costs (Stigler's statement cited above
assumes that such scale economies dominate the research process as a
whole). The second factor concerns the degree of interdependence between
specific research activities and other manufacturing and nonmanufacturing
functions within the firm. Where sufficiently strong, such interdependence
allows for greater feasibility or lower unit costs (as compared with
extramural performance of the research task) through the joint performance
of research and other functions within the firm.[5] Scale economies are
likely to be most significant for routinized, relatively simple research
tasks, such as materials testing. Interdependence between research and
other activities within the firm is likely to be important in research
projects requiring knowledge of a highly specialized, idiosyncratic variety,
specific to a given firm, or in research requiring that a wide range of

---

[5] Armour and Teece (1981) discuss "contractual difficulties in the market for technological
know-how" (p. 470), arguing, among other points, that "the transactions costs associated
with buying and selling engineering and scientific manpower are reduced when personnel
can move from R&D to one or several stages of production within an enterprise. Furthermore,
a common coding system, or language, can develop within the vertically integrated enterprise
which facilitates the transfer of technical information. The existence of a common coding
system and the attendant dialogue between departments or divisions facilitates both technology
transfer and the formulation of appropriate research objectives. As a result, the research
activity is likely to be better directed and hence more productive" (p. 471). While these
authors are discussing the effects on R&D of a vertically integrated firm structure, it is
clear that many of the advantages to which they refer result as well from the location of
a industrial research facility within the manufacturing firm.

research and other nonresearch activities be coordinated in the innovation process.[6]

As firms grow in size and structural complexity, the more complex, riskier research project, with severe requirements for interaction and information exchange among various corporate functions, should form the core of their in-house research activities.[7] A great deal of the necessary knowledge for such research and development projects may be highly specific to a given firm or production process, and not amenable to provision by an organization not engaged in both production and research. The specificity of such technical knowledge stems ultimately from the fact that production and the acquisition of detailed technical knowledge, or use and the acquisition of such knowledge, frequently are joint activities. The joint product character of manufacturing output and technical knowledge is the basis for the successful operation of in-house research. The acquisition of such knowledge is a dynamic, cumulative learning process, which relies upon the preservation of continuity in research projects and personnel for its effectiveness.

Independent research organizations are most likely to supply research services characterized broadly by two features. Research supplied via contract will be generic in character, applicable to a relatively wide range of industries and firms, and exploiting little or no firm-specific knowledge. Second, contract research services will deal primarily with isolated or separable aspects of a firm's operations. Improvement of specific production processes employed by many firms, or analyses of input quality, rather than the development of new products, will be supplied by independent research organizations.

The independent research organization thus may be unable to supply certain forms of complex research services. On the demand side, the ability of manufacturing firms to exploit such services as are available may be undercut substantially by problems in two areas. The client firm

---

[6] An idea of the different corporate functions that must be brought together in the innovation process is conveyed by the estimates by the Department of Commerce Panel on Invention and Innovation of the typical distribution of costs in successful product innovations. "Research, Advanced Development, and Basic Invention" accounted for 7.5%, "Engineering and Designing and Product" accounted for 15%, "Tooling and Manufacturing Engineering" accounted for 50%, "Manufacturing Start-up Expenses" accounted for 10%, and "Marketing Start-up Expenses" comprised 17.5% of total costs (1967, p. 9).

[7] Variables measuring the *ex ante* complexity of a specific research project are difficult to devise, even in the absence of data contraints. One broad measure is the extent of technological advance embodied in a given research project; this measure has been employed by Mansfield *et al.* (1971), Summers (1967), and Marshall and Meckling (1962) in studies of R&D project cost overruns. A second measure, drawing on Summers, consists of an estimate of the duration of a research project. Both the degree of technological advance and the duration of a project are expected to be positively correlated with complexity and risk.

356                              DAVID C. MOWERY

requires substantial in-house expertise simply to pose a feasible research problem, or to evaluate and utilize the results.[8] There exist as well difficulties of contractual negotiation and enforcement. The effectiveness of contracts in the provision of research is undermined by the highly uncertain nature of the research enterprise, the imperfect character of knowledge about a given project, and the thin market for specialized research services. These contractual difficulties are likely to be greater, the more technically complex and uncertain is the proposed research. In addition, assessment of the value of the results produced by an independent contractor is difficult without complete revelation of these results.[9] Opportunistic behavior by one or the other party to such a contractual agreement also is likely, due to the small number of alternative suppliers of a highly specialized research service.[10] Finally, the difficulty of specifying all contingencies, and/or the costs of writing such a complete contract, will be very high for complex and highly uncertain research projects.

The range of services supplied by contract research organizations thus is limited, and the ability of firms to utilize these services is enhanced by an in-house research facility.[11] Three hypotheses were tested below,

[8] The argument that an in-house research facility aids greatly in the ability of a firm to exploit extramural research receives support from an examination of industrial research policies in other nations. Writing on the development of cooperative industrial research laboratories in Great Britain, Varcoe (1974) noted that "the relations [of the cooperative research facilities] with the industries and the extent to which the latter availed themselves in practice of the results were not the straightforward matters they were at first imagined to be. Smaller firms frequently had no one capable either of articulating research needs and putting them into scientifically meaningful terms or of understanding the concepts and terminology of technical literature and of relating these ideas to their own problems." (p. 30). Similarly, Caves and Uekusa (1976) note that the Japanese economy invested heavily in research during the postwar period as a means of absorbing and modifying technologies from external sources: "Firms must maintain some research capacity in order to know what technology is available for purchase or copy and they must generally modify and adapt foreign technology in putting it to use—a 1963 survey of Japanese manufacturers showed that on average one-third of the respondents' expenditures on R&D went for this purpose" (p. 126).

[9] This argument was first made by Arrow (1962).

[10] Williamson (1981) argues, "That economic agents are simultaneously subject to bounded rationality and (at least some) are given to opportunism does not by itself, however, vitiate autonomous trading. On the contrary, when effective *ex ante* and *ex post* competition can both be presumed, autonomous contracting will be efficacious" (p. 554).

[11] An alternative to the independent contract research organization is the cooperative or trade association laboratory supported by firms within a single industry to perform research on their behalf. While a number of such research facilities were established during 1900–1940 in American industry, the available evidence on the operation of such cooperative organizations suggests that they played a rather limited role. The 1940 survey by the National Research Council notes the existence of only 28 such research facilities, slightly less than 1.4% of the total number of laboratories reported. Trade association laboratories accounted for 290 research professionals, or 1.04% of total research laboratory employment in 1940. In the U.S., the magnitude of the costs of basic research and the problems of

based upon this view of the role of contract research. Contract research is hypothesized to have functioned as a complement to, rather than a substitute for, in-house research activity for complex research projects during the 1900–1940 period. In other words, the ability of firms during this period to exploit the available contract research services was aided substantially by an in-house research facility. The second hypothesis relates to the supply of research services offered by independent research organizations. Independent research laboratories during 1900–1940 are hypothesized to have provided a limited range of services, avoiding new product development activities and concentrating primarily on such standardized activities as chemical and metallurgical analyses. The third hypothesis focuses on the implications of these aspects of the supply of and demand for contract research for the relationship between firm size and the organization of research. The incorporation within the firm of industrial research is hypothesized to have occurred above relatively low levels of firm size among firms pursuing higher-risk research projects.

## II. DATA AND METHODOLOGY

Data from several sources were utilized in tests of these hypotheses. The National Research Council surveys of industrial research for 1921, 1927, 1933, 1940, and 1946[12] provided a comprehensive tabulation of research facilities within more than 7300 manufacturing firms. The foundation dates for in-house laboratories within these firms also were contained in the 1940 and 1946 editions of the survey. The existence or absence of an in-house research laboratory during the 1900–1940 period thus could be checked systematically. Archival data from three major independent research organizations was used in the construction of a comprehensive list of client firms for each organization, and an assessment of the types

---

utilization of such research results both appear to have worked against such a role for cooperative research organizations. Galambos (1966) described the efforts of the National Association of Cotton Manufacturers (NACM) to undertake cooperative research and advertising programs in the following terms:

> When the American Association and NACM were jointly reorganized in 1916/17, there was considerable enthusiasm for research, especially in New England. Most of this enthusiasm, however, was merely vocal. When the northern association's program got underway, it became obvious that the professional staff were more interested in the work than the members were.
>     The advertising and research ventures foundered for much the same reasons. Management in New England was conservative. It was difficult, furthermore, to see how a particular mill would significantly strengthen its own position through cooperative advertising or research. (p. 77)

Davis and Kevles (1961) discuss industrial opposition to a broader organization for collective funding of basic research in the U.S. during the 1920s.

[12] See National Research Council (1921, 1927, 1933, 1940, 1946).

358                    DAVID C. MOWERY

of research performed for client firms.[13] The three firms are the Mellon Institute in Pittsburgh, Pennsylvania, the Battelle Memorial Institute in Columbus, Ohio, and Arthur D. Little, Inc. of Cambridge, Massachusetts.

The choice of these three firms was based upon several criteria. All three were active during all or a substantial part of the 1900–1940 period. Arthur D. Little was founded in 1896, the Mellon Institute opened in Pittsburgh in 1911, and the Battelle Institute began operations in 1929. The firms also were among the largest independent research organizations in the U.S. during this period. In 1933 (4 years after the foundation of the Battelle Institute), according to data from the National Research Council survey, Arthur D. Little and the Mellon Institute were the two largest independent contract research organizations in the United States, and the three organizations together represented 12.3% of total professional scientific employment in independent research organizations (out of 223 such organizations). In 1940, these three organizations were among the five largest such laboratories, accounting for 13.6% of total scientific employment. By 1946, these firms contained 16% of total scientific employment in all independent research organizations. Inasmuch as these three firms were among the largest of their type, and accounted for a growing share of employment by independent research laboratories during the period, it seems plausible to expect them to have offered the broadest possible range of research facilities and service. While this sample of independent research organizations thus is not necessarily representative of the independent research organizations of this period, the selection bias almost certainly works against, rather than in favor of, the hypotheses discussed above.

Testing these hypotheses required examining the proportion of client firms of the three independent organizations that displayed complementarity between in-house and contract research, and comparing this proportion of complementarity for different types of research projects. The measure of complementarity employed was a "structural" one, in which the existence of an in-house research facility within a client firm was taken as a case in which contract research functioned as a complement, rather than a substitute, for in-house research. Where no in-house laboratory was found within the client firm, the substitute relationship was held to exist. While crude, this measure is the most easily operationalized with the available data (data for expenditures on contract or in-house research by client and other firms were not available).[14]

---

[13] In obtaining these data, I had the invaluable aid of Ms. Rena Zeffer at the Mellon Institute, Ms. Kathy Kelland and Dr. Michael Michaelis at Arthur D. Little, and Dr. George McClure at the Battelle Institute. I am grateful to one and all for their assistance.

[14] No information was available on the characteristics of the research project portfolio of client firms. The implicit assumption in much of the data analysis, therefore, is that industrial research activity is a largely homogeneous undertaking. Obviously, such an

Within this archival dataset, only the Mellon Institute data contained detailed project descriptions that allowed a breakdown of research projects by type. For the Battelle Institute and Arthur D. Little, a division of the project population into "analysis" and "nonanalysis" projects was based largely on the project title. "Analysis" projects were defined to consist of analysis of chemical or materials substances, including coal. Both the Battelle and ADL organizations were heavily involved in performing such routinized analysis projects. In the discussion below, analysis projects are assumed to admit of a lower level of technical complexity. This reflects the fact that the degree of uncertainty about costs, technical feasibility, and outcomes for such tasks is much lower for these types of projects.

Due to inconsistencies in the recording of client data for Arthur D. Little, the most reliable and internally consistent indicators of trends over time in the ADL data are the populations of nonanalysis clients, and the special report clients, a group for which larger and more elaborate projects were performed.[15] The Battelle Institute had among its client firms during its early years a number of mining firms. To preserve the focus of the overall investigation on manufacturing firms, and to minimize industry-mix effects in comparing the data from the three independent research organizations, mining firms were excluded from some of the analyses of Battelle Institute data.

To provide a basis for an assessment of the significance of the results of the structural complementarity analysis, three control populations of manufacturing firms were constructed for comparison with the client firm populations at each of the three independent research organizations during the 1930s. The client firm populations were restricted to clients listed in *Moody's Industrials* during the year in which they first appeared as a client.

Firms in the control samples were also drawn from *Moody's*, by taking firms from pages matching the last four digits of each of a series of random numbers. This generated a large list of candidate firms for the control population, out of which a subset was selected. The control samples were chosen so as to replicate the distribution of the client firm population among years, firm size classes, and across two-digit SIC's.[16] Once constructed, the control populations were examined to determine

---

assumption is open to question. Equally obvious is the fact that this assumption underpins the majority of the empirical work on R&D published by economists.

[15] For the 1918–1928 period, the archives included tabulations of analyses. Prior to this period, analyses were recorded inconsistently, while during 1929–1940, they were consistently excluded.

[16] Where a surplus of candidate firms for a specific year, size class, or SIC was encountered, the firms were ranked by size. Firms whose rank order matched the last two digits of a random number were included in the control sample population.

DAVID C. MOWERY

TABLE 1
Employment of Scientific Professionals in Independent Research Organizations as a Fraction
of Employment of Scientific Professionals in All
In-House and Independent Research Laboratories,
1921–1946

| | |
|---|---|
| 1921 | 15.2% |
| 1927 | 12.9% |
| 1933 | 10.9% |
| 1940 | 8.7% |
| 1946 | 6.9% |

*Source.* Mowery (1981, Chap. 2).

the proportions of firms in each that had in-house laboratories. These proportions were then compared with the level of structural complementarity observed at each independent research facility. This procedure was used in a test of the null hypothesis that the proportion of client firms with in-house laboratories at each independent research organization matched the proportion of firms within the larger population of manufacturing firms with in-house laboratories.[17]

## III. TESTS OF THE COMPLEMENTARITY HYPOTHESIS

An initial assessment of the relative importance of contract and in-house research activity during 1921–46 is provided in Table 1, which displays the proportion of total employment of research professionals in both in-house and independent research organizations accounted for by independent research organizations (excluding the research laboratories of trade associations). Over time, contract research laboratories account for a declining share of total scientific and engineering research employment in manufacturing and independent research laboratories. While employment in both forms of industrial research organization was growing rapidly during this period, employment growth for in-house research substantially outstripped that for the independent research organizations.

Tables 2–4 contain data on the proportion of structural complementarity observed for each independent research organization, while Tables 5–7 classify research projects by type for each organization. It is clear that for a substantial proportion of research clients, the independent research organizations are complements to, rather than substitutes for, in-house research. Such complementarity is most pronounced in the Mellon Institute

[17] The test of the null hypothesis assumed that the difference in the proportions of the firms with research laboratories in the two populations was normally distributed. The use of the normal approximation drew its justification in part from the size of the combined populations (36, 150, and 180 firms), as well as the fact that the control and experimental populations had been constructed to contain equal numbers of firms in various size classes.

and Battelle Institute data (where, respectively, 38 and 47% of the manufacturing client firms during this period have in-house laboratories). However, the results from the ADL data, especially those for the special reports series, where by 1930–1940 over 69% of the client firms have in-house labs, also suggest that contract research was of limited efficacy as a substitute for an in-house research facility.

For both Arthur D. Little and the Battelle Institute, the observed proportion of structural complementarity is higher for the more complex (i.e., nonanalysis) projects than for analysis projects. A much higher proportion of the firms sponsoring special reports at ADL, projects that are more complex and riskier, has in-house laboratories than is true of the firms sponsoring simple chemical analyses. There also is a (less dramatic) difference in the ADL data between the proportion of complementarity observed in the population of chemical analysis clients and that in the population of clients contracting for other technical reports (statistically significant in the 1920–1929 and 1930–1939 periods). The difference in the proportions of structural complementarity for the analysis and special report clients at ADL is significant at the 0.01 level for the entire 1896–1940 period, as well as the 1910–1919, 1920–1929, and 1930–1940 subperiods. At the Battelle Institute, these proportions of complementarity also differ between the population of analysis and nonanalysis projects; one-third of the firms contracting for chemical or metallurgical analysis have in-house laboratories, while among the nonanalysis population of contracts, this proportion rises to 47%. The difference is significant at the 0.10 level, but not at the 0.05 level.

Another interesting aspect of these data is the strong time trend observable in the degree of measured structural complementarity for two of the three independent research firms, ADL and the Mellon Institute. Rather than declining over time, as one would predict if the research

TABLE 2

Structural Complementarity between In-House and Contract Research at the Mellon Institute of Industrial Research

| Years | Total no. of firms sponsoring research at Mellon Institute[a] | No. of sponsoring firms with in-house labs at time of sponsorship[b] |
|---|---|---|
| 1910–1940 | 187 | 71 (38%) |
| 1910–1919 | 73 | 15 (20.5%) |
| 1920–1929 | 60 | 28 (46.7%) |
| 1930–1940 | 54 | 28 (51.8%) |

[a] A number of firms sponsored more than one fellowship, at several different dates. In such a case, the first occurrence is the only one counted, biasing downward the number of firms in the later periods.

[b] "Time of sponsorship" is taken to be the date at which the fellowship began.

362                          DAVID C. MOWERY

TABLE 3

Structural Complementarity between In-House and Contract Research at the Battelle
Memorial Institute

Proportion of client firms at the Battelle Institute with in-house research laboratories (as
recorded in the NRC survey), 1929–1940
   All client firms: 43.6% ($n = 241$)
   Manufacturing firms only: 47.9% ($n = 217$)
   Mining firms: 4.2% ($n = 24$)

Analysis contracts ($n = 60$)
   Percentage sponsored by firms with in-house laboratories: 33.3%

Nonanalysis contracts ($n = 181$)
   Percentage sponsored by firms with in-house laboratories: 47.0%

TABLE 4

Structural Complementarity between In-House and Contract Research at
Arthur D. Little, Inc.

1896–1940
   Technical reports
      All client forms: 5.5% ($n = 5027$)
      Clients for whom analyses were carried out: 3.8% ($n = 2709$)
      Clients for whom other research projects were done: 7.4% ($n = 2318$)
   Special reports: 28.4% ($n = 134$)

1896–1909
   Technical reports
      All client firms: 3.8% ($n = 390$)
      Clients for whom analyses were carried out: 4.1% ($n = 49$)
      Clients for whom other research projects were done: 3.8% ($n = 341$)
   Special reports: 0.0% ($n = 9$)

1910–1919
   Technical reports
      All client firms: 3.6% ($n = 1309$)
      Clients for whom analyses were carried out: 3.4% ($n = 585$)
      Clients for whom other research projects were done: 3.7% ($n = 724$)
   Special reports: 17.4% ($n = 23$)

1920–1929
   Technical reports
      All client firms: 4.9% ($n = 3052$)
      Clients for whom analyses were carried out: 3.9% ($n = 2054$)
      Clients for whom other research projects were done: 7.0% ($n = 998$)
   Special reports: 22.8% ($n = 79$)

1930–1940
   Technical reports
      All client firms: 22.8% ($n = 260$)
      Clients for whom analyses were carried out: 9.5% ($n = 21$)
      Clients for whom other research projects were done: 24.0% ($n = 239$)
   Special reports: 69.6% ($n = 23$)

function were being "spun off" à la Stigler, the proportion of client firms with in-house laboratories is increasing for both of these independent research organizations. The increase in this proportion between the 1910–1919 and 1920–1929 periods is significant at the 0.01 level for the Mellon Institute. Looking at these proportions for the special reports prepared by Arthur D. Little, one observes an increase from 17.4% in 1910–1919 to 22.8% in 1920–1929, and 69.6% in 1930–1940; the increase in this proportion from the 1920–1929 to the 1930–1940 period is statistically significant at the 0.01 level. Consistent with the data in Table 1, there is no evidence of any movement toward increased reliance by manufacturing firms upon independent research organizations for research services.

As in-house research facilities grew in size and number during 1900–1940, contract research institutions increasingly functioned as complements, rather than substitutes (in the "structural" sense defined above). Tests for differences between the proportion of firms in the control and client firm samples with in-house laboratories for each of the three independent research laboratories allowed rejection in each case at the 0.001 level of confidence of the null hypothesis that the proportion of firms with in-house laboratories in the control and client firm populations was identical. The proportion of manufacturing firms utilizing contract research services during the 1930s that had in-house research facilities was significantly greater than the proportion of firms with such research laboratories in a sample of all manufacturing firms.

## IV. CHARACTERISTICS OF CONTRACT RESEARCH PROJECTS

The evidence presented above suggests that in general, firms without in-house research facilities were not the primary clients for independent research organizations. Moreover, firms without in-house laboratories apparently used contract research only for the simplest types of research project. The discussion in Section II concluded that this complementary relationship between in-house and contract research reflected the fact that knowledge and technology transfer are themselves knowledge-intensive processes. Much of the important expertise for innovation also is highly specific to a given firm. Thus, in-house and contract research are complements on the demand side. This section examines characteristics of the supply of research services, focusing on the types of research projects performed on a contract basis.

Were it the case that the central aspect of importance in the relationship between in-house and contract research was the need for in-house expertise to evaluate and exploit the services of an independent contractor, one would observe a wide range of research services offered via contract. In this case, increasing in-house research employment would reflect the growth of a staff within the firm to monitor and evaluate the activities of independent research organizations. The fact that in-house research

364 DAVID C. MOWERY

TABLE 5
Types of Research Sponsored at the Mellon Institute

| New use for materials | Process improvement | Product improvement | By-product utilization |
|---|---|---|---|
| 18 (19.3%) | 75 (38.9%) | 11 (5.7%) | 11 (5.7%) |

employment grew more rapidly than that in contract research organizations during this period suggests that in-house research involved more than such a simple monitoring task. However, a more detailed examination of the characteristics of projects performed on a contract basis is needed. Below, the available data on the types of projects carried out at each of these three independent research organizations are discussed.

*Mellon Institute*

Table 5 contains data on the projects performed for clients of the Mellon Institute. Only those projects whose titles are sufficiently clear were classified; the percentages thus do not sum to 100. The overall tabulation of projects by type reveals that process improvement, e.g., "problems in cement manufacturing processes," is the most important single category of project. With the possible exception of some of the projects dealing with new uses for materials, e.g., "utilization of milk and butter by-products," covering an early phase of product development, new product development activities at the Mellon Institute appear to be minimal. Projects are concerned primarily with improvement of existing processes or the utilization of by-products.

*Battelle Institute*

The Battelle data have descriptions that are less informative than those for the Mellon Institute. Both Arthur D. Little and Battelle, unlike Mellon, did a good deal of work in the provision of analyses of metals and/or chemicals for clients. Battelle was heavily involved in providing such services to the coal industry as well, which involved testing samples of coal for smoke and clinkering characteristics. Nearly 25% of all projects undertaken by the Institute during 1929–1940 were analyses or tests of metals (see Table 6), minerals, or coal, and as such were lower-risk

TABLE 6
Types of Research Sponsored at the Battelle
Institute: Manufacturing Firms Only

| | |
|---|---|
| "Analysis" | 24.9% |
| Other | 75.1% |

undertakings. Among mining firms, few of which had in-house labs, two-thirds of the projects were analyses. Clarence Lorig, who joined the Institute in 1930, noted that during the first decade of Battelle's existence, "problems were clearly defined and had objective solutions" (quoted in Boehm and Groner, 1972, p. 20); these data tend to support his views.

### Arthur D. Little

Chemical analyses were a mainstay of this firm's activities through the 1900–1940 period. Once again, the project descriptions allowed only for classification of the technical reports into analysis or nonanalysis categories. However, the period during which the chemical analyses were recorded, 1918–1928, yields the most complete accounting of the full range of ADL's activities. The "special reports," as noted above, were of a fundamental or long-term nature. Table 7 thus yields a tripartite division of the projects carried out by ADL.

These data indicate the importance of analysis work for the ADL firm, especially during the 1910–1919 and 1920–1929 periods, which are the most complete in their coverage. Once again, the nature of the activities carried out by an independent research organization are concentrated at the low-risk end of the continuum of research projects.

The extent to which independent research organizations may be said to have substituted for in-house research during 1900–1940 appears to

TABLE 7
Types of Research Sponsored at Arthur D. Little (Percentage of Total Clients)

| | |
|---|---|
| **1896–1943** | |
| Analyses | 52.4% |
| Nonanalytic technical reports | 44.9% |
| Special reports | 2.6% |
| **1896–1909** | |
| Analyses | 12.3% |
| Nonanalytic technical reports | 85.5% |
| Special reports | 2.3% |
| **1910–1919** | |
| Analyses | 43.9% |
| Nonanalytic technical reports | 54.3% |
| Special reports | 1.7% |
| **1920–1929** | |
| Analyses | 65.6% |
| Nonanalytic technical reports | 31.9% |
| Special reports | 2.5% |
| **1930–1940** | |
| Analyses | 7.6% |
| Nonanalytic technical reports | 84.0% |
| Special reports | 8.4% |

366                               DAVID C. MOWERY

be limited. The independent research organizations examined here did not offer a full menu of research services for purchase, in particular eschewing new product development activities. Such limitations reflect difficulties of contracting, idiosyncratic knowledge, and the need for the involvement of many components of the firm in such activities as new product development. The firm undertaking particularly complex or risky projects during this period therefore had little choice but to do so in-house. In addition, the ability of firms to exploit even the limited services that were available via contract was affected critically by the presence of an in-house laboratory. Firms lacking such in-house expertise were observed in Section III to utilize contract research primarily for simple analysis projects. The establishment of an in-house laboratory thus was a response to forces affecting both the supply of research services and the characteristics of the demand for contract research.

## V. FIRM SIZE AND THE ORGANIZATION OF RESEARCH

The preceding sections of this paper have argued that the independent research organization did not function effectively as a substitute for in-house research facilities. This section examines one of the empirical implications of this argument. If firms pursuing research were unable to procure a full range of research services via the market, and if an in-house laboratory was critical to the utilization of the research services that were available, research activity should have been incorporated within the firm above low levels of firm size. The magnitude of this threshold firm size also is of importance in any assessment of distributional issues, i.e., the extent to which the growth of organized industrial research primarily benefited larger, rather than smaller, manufacturing firms. The previous sections have argued that firms lacking in-house research facilities were handicapped in pursuing research. If only the very largest firms are observed to have supported in-house laboratories, one may conclude that industrial research during this period primarily benefited large firms, reflecting the limits to contractual provision or purchase of research.

Probit analysis was utilized in an assessment of the relationship between firm size (measured as book value of assets) and the probability that a research laboratory existed within the manufacturing firms in the client populations from these independent research organizations. These data are particularly well suited to an analysis of the influence of firm size upon the organization of research, because the sample populations include a wide range of firm sizes, and contain firms with and without in-house research laboratories. However, all firms in these samples are engaged in research, by virtue of their contract with an independent research organization.[18]

---

[18] The intent of this analysis is less explanatory than descriptive. While the expectation is that firm size will exert a positive influence upon the probability that an in-house

Data on the book value of assets of manufacturing firms sponsoring research projects at the Mellon Institute, Arthur D. Little, and the Battelle Institute were gathered from *Moody's Industrials* for 1930–1940, the only period for which internally consistent data were available for all three independent research organizations. The year of inception of a research contract was utilized as the date for measurement of firm size, and the assets figures were converted into 1933 equivalents with the GNP deflator for private domestic investment. Only firms sponsoring nonanalysis contracts were examined, for two reasons. As was noted above, there are inconsistencies over time in the recording of analysis projects in the Arthur D. Little data, resulting in difficulties in combining observations from the three research organizations. An additional justification derives from the discussion above, where the argument was made that chemical and materials analysis projects were qualitatively different from more complex research projects. The organization of research for these two types of research projects may have responded differently to increasing firm size.

Table 8 displays the results of four probit analyses, one each for the Mellon and Battelle Institutes, and for Arthur D. Little, as well as a combined probit with industry dummies, to control for the effects upon the results of industry mix in the firm sample. One approach to measuring the goodness of fit of these results compares the predicted proportion of in-house laboratories (taking a predicted probability above 0.5 as constituting such a positive prediction) with the actual sample proportion. The "proportion of correct prediction" is fairly high (i.e., in excess of 75%) for all four sets of results. The results for each individual research organization differ significantly (i.e., the assets coefficients are different) in a chi-square test of the significance of the difference between the likelihood functions from probits for individual research organizations and those from probits combining observations from different research organizations.

The probability of existence of an in-house laboratory is roughly 0.5 for 1933 assets of $3.5 million, while this probability approaches 0.9 above $800 million in 1933 assets. The small size of the 0.5 "threshold" is striking, and tends to support the observations set forth above concerning the difficulties of procuring research via contract. Among firms pursuing research, an in-house laboratory appears to be a virtual necessity.

The results for the combined probit with industry dummies in Table 8 indicate that the influence of firm size outweighs any industry-specific differences in the boundary of the firm in the performance of research. None of the industry dummies is significant at the 0.05 level, and only that for chemicals is significantly greater than zero at the 0.10 level. In

---

laboratory exists within a firm, a univariate specification clearly omits other important (and unmeasurable, given data constraints) variables.

TABLE 8

The Influence of Firm Size Upon the Integration of Research, 1930–1940

| | Intercept | $\beta$ (log assets) | Proportion of correct predictions | $n$ |
|---|---|---|---|---|
| Mellon Institute | -4.27 (2.38) | .49[a] (.25) | .95 | 19 |
| Battelle Institute | 5.17[b] (1.0) | .12 (.10) | .76 | 62 |
| Arthur D. Little | -2.02 (1.04) | .22[b] (.11) | .99 | 72 |

| | Intercept | $\beta$ (log assets) | Chemicals dummy | Fabricated metals dummy | Food dummy | Nonelectrical machinery dummy | Primary metals dummy | $n$ |
|---|---|---|---|---|---|---|---|---|
| Combined | -1.91[b] (.07) | .23[b] (.07) | .61 (.39) | .24 (.46) | -.36 (.38) | -.32 (.34) | .11 (.30) | 150 |

[a] Significant at 0.05 level.
[b] Significant at 0.01 level.
Note: Standard errors in parentheses.

a chi-square test of the incremental improvement in the fit of the probit due to the addition of these dummy variables (based on an analysis of changes in the value of the likelihood functions), their effect was not statistically significant.

Among firms actively pursuing research, firm size exerts a significant and positive influence on the probability that such research will be carried out in-house. To assess the implications of the magnitude of the firm size threshold, some sort of benchmark, describing firm size within the overall population of manufacturing firms during this period, is needed. One such measure is found in Kaplan (1964), containing a tabulation of the 100 largest industrial corporations in 1935. The smallest of these has 1935 assets of $73 million, well above the threshold firm size. However, an alternative benchmark, taken from the *Statistics of Income* for 1933,[19] indicates that of 82,836 manufacturing firms filing corporate income tax returns with balance sheet data, only 5063, or 6.1%, had assets in excess of $1 million. The threshold size indicated in these probit results thus is substantially below the size of the largest firms in the economy, but is much larger than that of the median firm in manufacturing.

## VI. CONCLUSION

During the 20th century, industrial research developed within both the nonmarket and market sectors of the American economy. While research employment grew most rapidly in laboratories located within manufacturing firms, a substantial network of independent research organizations also emerged. These independent research organizations were viewed by many important practitioners of industrial research during the 1900–1940 period as possible substitutes for the in-house research facilities believed to be lacking among smaller firms. Such faith in the frictionless performance of market mechanisms in distributing the fruits of industrial research to large and small firms alike appears to have been misplaced. The hypotheses tested above concerned the supply of contract research, focusing upon the types of projects offered via contract, and the demand for contract research, examining the complementarity between in-house research and contract research projects of greater complexity than materials or chemicals analyses. The results suggest that both these demand and supply side forces worked to reduce the effectiveness of contract research as a substitute for in-house research. Firms without in-house research facilities were handicapped in their ability to pursue R&D and innovation.

Rather than functioning as substitutes, the independent and in-house research laboratories were complements during this period, exhibiting a division of labor in the performance of research tasks. The foundation of an in-house laboratory did not result in a "spinning in" of the research

[19] See U.S. Internal Revenue Service (1934, pp. 173–174).

activities previously performed on a contract basis, but a substantial expansion in the range of research possibilities and projects open to the firm.[20]

These results certainly suggest that the benefits of research were restricted to those firms with in-house research laboratories. However the probit analysis does not provide strong support for the contention that only the very largest firms in the economy were able to support such in-house research facilities. Larger firms were more likely to have in-house research laboratories. However, the threshold firm size necessary for support of an in-house research facility, while excluding all but a small segment of the overall manufacturing firm population, is still well below the size of the very largest firms during this period. This finding is consistent with other evidence on the relationship between research employment and firm size during 1921–1946 which suggests that relative to their size, the largest firms in American manufacturing were not disproportionately research-intensive (Mowery, 1983a). The fact that the threshold firm size was not higher may be interpreted as supportive of the arguments emphasizing the difficulties encountered by firms in contracting for research through the market. During this period, such difficulties were sufficiently great to offset the impact of the substantial fixed costs of in-house research.

While these data provide fairly strong support for the three hypotheses set forth above, it is important to consider alternative explanations for the patterns observed. The conceptual basis for the hypotheses discussed above emphasized the unique characteristics of technical knowledge and research as commodities, as well as the importance of the complementary nature of research and production activities, and the need to combine a wide range of heterogeneous inputs within the firm in the innovation process. As a result, the market for many highly specialized forms of research expertise is very thin and the ability to write contracts to cover more complex types of research projects is severely limited. An alternative

---

[20] Balbien and Wilde (1982) suggest that a manufacturing firm is more likely to contract for research with an independent laboratory, the greater is the manufacturing firm's state of technical knowledge (represented in their model as a lower level of initial unit costs). Such a hypothesis suggests a complementary relationship between in-house and contract research; *ceteris paribus*, the presence of an in-house research facility is likely to endow a firm with greater technical expertise, relative to its peers. The authors also suggest that the independent research laboratory will exhibit the greatest veracity in reporting the results of very short-term projects. Such a proposition is consistent with the data presented above concerning the importance of short-term routinized analysis projects in the activities of the independent research laboratories. In reaching these results, the authors rely upon a very strong and somewhat questionable assumption, viz., that the marginal returns to reductions in unit costs reaped by the firm increase as the initial level of unit costs declines. This assumption raises the possibility that, as production costs decline, the firm's research expenditures may increase without limit. Such an assumption is difficult to support with empirical evidence.

explanation for the in-house performance of research emphasizes the importance of the appropriability of the returns from research. The location of research within the firm, in this view, reflects the imperfect protection of research results afforded by contracts. Such an explanation may serve to explain the limited range of research services offered by independent research organizations, the "supply side" hypothesis discussed in Section IV. However, it does not provide an explanation for the higher degree of complementarity between in-house and contract research observed for more complex research projects, the "demand" hypothesis of Section III. Considerations of appropriability do not seem to explain the greater ability of firms with in-house research laboratories to exploit the more sophisticated contract research services that are available.

The differential extent of complementarity observed among projects of varying degrees of complexity or riskiness also is not explained by a hypothesis stating that the observed complementarity reflects partial or "tapered" vertical integration. This refers to an investment by the firm in intrafirm research capacity sufficient to serve a portion, but less than the total amount, of its research needs.[21] Such a strategy would enable in-house capacity to be utilized fully, leaving outside contractors to bear the brunt of market fluctuations. However appropriate for the manufacture of conventional inputs for the firm's production processes, such partial vertical integration involves the loss of the important learning externalities that result from the preservation of an ongoing research operation in areas of major importance.[22] This explanation for the observed complementarity between in-house and contract research also would imply a uniform degree of such complementarity for projects of all degrees of risk. Indeed, if anything, partial vertical integration in research would suggest that the low-risk research project, for which learning externalities are less important, would be the primary locus of complementarity between in-house and contract research. Instead, it is the more complex forms of research that display a greater extent of complementarity between in-house and contract research. The results of the tests of the demand hypothesis in Section III are not compatible with the partial integration explanation.

The data and analysis presented above suggest that the development of industrial research within the manufacturing firm was based on the

[21] For a historical discussion of partial vertical integration by the Du Pont Chemical Company in the manufacture of explosives, see Chandler and Salsbury (1971, Chap. 9).

[22] Grabowski (1968) noted that research professionals "are not perfectly elastic in supply and cannot be alternately fired and rehired in accord once with business conditions" (p. 296), arguing that "there will be significant downward rigidities in this relationship [between R&D expenditures and cash flow] due to the technological necessity of maintaining a reasonably stable staff of researchers" (note, p. 296). See Cohen (1983) for additional discussion.

372 DAVID C. MOWERY

shortcomings of market institutions as mechanisms for the conduct and distribution of research and development. To the extent that industrial research yielded a payoff to firms in terms of performance, then, those firms supporting in-house research facilities may have gained a competitive advantage over firms that relied upon independent research organizations. This evidence does not suggest, however, that this competitive advantage was claimed solely by the largest firms in American manufacturing. While limited in its scope and time coverage, this analysis suggests that research and development is not a commodity like any other, and that the form of organization of research activity interacts in a complex fashion with the content of research and development activity. Comparison of the operation of market and intrafirm models of the organization of other corporate functions during this period may provide useful insights into the basis for the development of the modern corporation in the U.S. and abroad.

## REFERENCES

Alchian, A. A., and Demsetz, H. (1972), "Production, Information Costs, and Economic Organization." *American Economic Review* **62**, 777–795.
Allen, T. J. (1977), *Managing the Flow of Technology*. Cambridge, Mass.: MIT Press.
Armour, H. D., and Teece, D. J. (1980), "Vertical Integration and Technological Innovation." *Review of Economics and Statistics* **62**, 470–474.
Arrow, K. J. (1962), "Economic Welfare and the Allocation of Resources for Invention," In *The Rate and Direction of Inventive Activity*. Princeton, N.J.: Princeton Univ. Press.
Bacon, R. F. (1915), "The Object and Work of the Mellon Institute." *Journal of Industrial and Engineering Chemistry* **7**, 343–347.
Balbien, J., and Wilde, L. L. (1982), "A Dynamic Model of Research Contracting." *Bell Journal of Economics* **13**, 107–119.
Baldwin, W. (1962), "Contract Research and the Case for Big Business." *Journal of Political Economy* **70**, 294–296.
Boehm, G. A. W., and Groner, A. (1972), *The Battelle Story: Science in the Service of Mankind*. Lexington, Mass.: D.C. Heath.
Carty, J. J. (1916), "The Relation of Pure Science to Industrial Research." *Science* **44**, 511–517.
Caves, R. E., and Uekusa, M. (1976), *Industrial Organization in Japan*. Washington, D.C.: Brookings.
Chandler, A. D., Jr. (1977), *The Visible Hand*. Cambridge, Mass.: Harvard Univ. Press.
Chandler, A. D., Jr., and Salsbury, S. (1971), *Pierre S. DuPont and the Making of the Modern Corporation*. New York: Harper & Row.
Cohen, W. M. (1983), "Investment and Industry Expansion: A Corporate Variables Framework." *Journal of Economic Behavior and Organization*, forthcoming.
Committee on Industry and Trade (1929), *Final Report*. London: His Majesty's Stationery Office.
David, P. A., Lewis, J., and Nold, F. (1976), "Multivariate Probit Analysis". Processed: Stanford Center for Information Processing.
Davis, L. E., and Kevles, D. J. (1974), "The National Research Fund: A Case Study in the Industrial Support of Academic Science." *Minerva* **12**, 207–220.

Denison, E. F. (1974), *Accounting for United States Economic Growth, 1929–1969*. Washington, D.C.: Brookings.

Duncan, R. K. (1909), "On Industrial Fellowships." *Journal of Industrial and Engineering Chemistry* **1**, 600–603.

Duncan, R. K. (1911), "On Certain Problems Connected with the Present-Day Relation Between Chemistry and Manufacture in America." *Journal of Industrial and Engineering Chemistry* **2**, 177–186.

Galambos, L. (1966), *Competition and Cooperation*. Baltimore, Md.: Johns Hopkins Univ. Press.

Grabowski, H. D. (1968), "The Determinants of Industrial Research and Development: A Study of the Chemical, Drug and Petroleum Industries." *Journal of Political Economy* **76**, 292–306.

Jenkins, R. V. (1975), *Images and Enterprise*. Baltimore, Md.: Johns Hopkins Univ. Press.

Johnson, P. S. (1973), *Co-operative Research in Industry*. New York: Wiley.

Kamien, M., and Schwartz, N. (1982), *Market Structure and Innovation*. New York: Cambridge Univ. Press.

Kaplan, A. D. H. (1964), *Big Business in a Competitive System*. Washington, D. C.: Brookings Institution.

Kendrick, J. W. (1976), *The Formation and Stocks of Total Capital*. New York: National Bureau of Economic Research.

Klein, R., Crawford, R. G. and Alchian, A. A. (1978), "Vertical Integration, Appropriable Rents, and the Competitive Contracting Process." *Journal of Law and Economics* **21**, 297–326.

Mansfield, E., Rapoport, J., Schnee, J., Wagner, S., and Hamburger, M. (1971), *Research and Innovation in the Modern Corporation*. New York: Norton.

Marshall, A. W., and Meckling, W. H. (1962), "Predictability of the Costs, Time, and Success in Development." In *The Rate and Direction of Inventive Activity*. Princeton, N.J.: Princeton Univ. Press.

Mees, C. E. K. (1920), *The Organization of Industrial Scientific Research*. New York: McGraw–Hill.

Mellon Institute of Industrial Research, *Annual Report*, various issues.

Mowery, D. C. (1981), *The Emergence and Growth of Industrial Research in American Manufacturing, 1899–1945*. Unpublished Ph.D. dissertation, Stanford University.

Mowery, D. C. (1983a), "Industrial Research and Firm Size, Survival, and Growth in American Manufacturing, 1921–46." Presented at the Cliometrics Conference, Iowa City, Iowa, April 29, 1983.

Mowery, D. C. (1983b), "British and American Industrial Research: A Comparison, 1900–1950." Presented at the Conference on the Decline of the British Economy, Boston, September, 1983.

Mueller, W. F. (1955), "Du Pont: A Study in Firm Growth." Unpublished Ph.D. dissertation, Vanderbilt University.

National Research Council (1921), *Bulletin 16*, "Research Laboratories in Industrial Establishments of the United States, Including Consulting Research Laboratories." Washington, D.C.: National Research Council.

National Research Council (1927), *Bulletin 60*, "Industrial Research Laboratories of the United States." Washington, D.C.: National Research Council.

National Research Council (1933), *Bulletin 91*, "Industrial Research Laboratories of the United States." Washington, D.C.: National Research Council.

National Research Council (1940), *Bulletin 104*, "Industrial Research Laboratories of the United States." Washington, D.C.: National Research Council.

National Research Council (1946), *Bulletin 113*, "Industrial Research Laboratories of the United States." Washington, D.C.: National Research Council.

Noble, D. F. (1977), *America by Design*. New York: Knopf.

374                        DAVID C. MOWERY

Peck, M. J., and Scherer, F. M. (1962), *The Weapons Acquisition Process*. Boston: Division of Research of the Harvard Business School.

Reich, L. S. (1977), "Radio Electronics and the Development of Industrial Research in the Bell System." Unpublished Ph.D. dissertation, Johns Hopkins University.

Rosenberg, N. (1982), "How Exogenous Is Science?" In *Inside the Black Box: Technology and Economics*. New York: Cambridge Univ. Press.

Schmookler, J. (1957), "Inventors Past and Present." *Review of Economics and Statistics* **39**, 321–333.

Schumpeter, J. (1934), *The Theory of Economic Development*, translated by R. Opie. Cambridge, Mass.: Harvard Univ. Press.

Schumpeter, J. (1954), *Capitalism, Socialism, and Democracy*, 3rd ed. New York: Harper & Row.

Stigler, G. J. (1956), "Industrial Organization and Economic Progress." In *The State of the Social Sciences* (L. D. White, Ed.). Chicago: Univ. of Chicago Press.

Summers, R. (1967), "Cost Estimates as Predictors of Actual Costs: A Statistical Study of Military Development." In T. Marschak, T. K. Glennan, Jr., and R. Summers, *Strategy for R&D*. New York: Springer-Verlag.

Teece, D. J. (1980), "Economies of Scope and the Scope of the Enterprise." *Journal of Economic Behavior and Organization* **1**, 223–247.

U.S. Department of Commerce Panel on Invention and Innovation (1967), *Technological Innovation: Its Environment and Management*. Washington, D.C., U.S. Govt. Printing Office.

U.S. Internal Revenue Service (1934), *Statistics of Income for 1933*. Washington, D.C.: U.S. Govt. Printing Office.

Varcoe, I. (1974), *Organizing for Science in Britain: A Case-Study*. Oxford: Oxford Univ. Press.

Weidlein, E. R. (1961), "Fifty Years of Science for Human Progress." *50th Annual Report of the Mellon Institute*.

Williamson, O. E. (1975), *Markets and Hierarchies*. New York: Free Press.

Williamson, O. E. (1979), "Transaction-Cost Economics: The Governance of Contractual Relations." *Journal of Law and Economics* **22**, 233–262.

Williamson, O. E. (1981), "The Economics of Organization: The Transaction Cost Approach." *American Journal of Sociology* **87**, 548–577.

# [8]

# Profiting from technological innovation: Implications for integration, collaboration, licensing and public policy

David J. TEECE *

*School of Business Administration, University of California, Berkeley, CA 94720, U.S.A.*

Final version received June 1986

This paper attempts to explain why innovating firms often fail to obtain significant economic returns from an innovation, while customers, imitators and other industry participants benefit. Business strategy – particularly as it relates to the firm's decision to integrate and collaborate – is shown to be an important factor. The paper demonstrates that when imitation is easy, markets don't work well, and the profits from innovation may accrue to the owners of certain complementary assets, rather than to the developers of the intellectual property. This speaks to the need, in certain cases, for the innovating firm to establish a prior position in these complementary assets. The paper also indicates that innovators with new products and processes which provide value to consumers may sometimes be so ill positioned in the market that they necessarily will fail. The analysis provides a theoretical foundation for the proposition that manufacturing often matters, particularly to innovating nations. Innovating firms without the requisite manufacturing and related capacities may die, even though they are the best at innovation. Implications for trade policy and domestic economic policy are examined.

* I thank Raphael Amit, Harvey Brooks, Chris Chapin, Therese Flaherty, Richard Gilbert, Heather Haveman, Mel Horwitch, David Hulbert, Carl Jacobsen, Michael Porter, Gary Pisano, Richard Rumelt, Raymond Vernon and Sidney Winter for helpful discussions relating to the subject matter of this paper. Three anonymous referees also provided valuable criticisms. I gratefully acknowledge the financial support of the National Science Foundation under grant no. SRS-8410556 to the Center for Research in Management, University of California Berkeley. Earlier versions of this paper were presented at a National Academy of Engineering Symposium titled "World Technologies and National Sovereignty," February 1986, and at a conference on innovation at the University of Venice, March 1986.

Research Policy 15 (1986) 285–305
North-Holland

## 1. Introduction

It is quite common for innovators – those firms which are first to commercialize a new product or process in the market – to lament the fact that competitors/imitators have profited more from the innovation than the firm first to commercialize it! Since it is often held that being first to market is a source of strategic advantage, the clear existence and persistence of this phenomenon may appear perplexing if not troubling. The aim of this article is to explain why a fast second or even a slow third might outperform the innovator. The message is particularly pertinent to those science and engineering driven companies that harbor the mistaken illusion that developing new products which meet customer needs will ensure fabulous success. It may possibly do so for the product, but not for the innovator.

In this paper, a framework is offered which identifies the factors which determine who wins from innovation: the firm which is first to market, follower firms, or firms that have related capabilities that the innovator needs. The follower firms may or may not be imitators in the narrow sense of the term, although they sometimes are. The framework appears to have utility for explaining the share of the profits from innovation accruing to the innovator compared to its followers and suppliers (see fig. 1), as well as for explaining a variety of interfirm activities such as joint ventures, coproduction agreements, cross distribution arrangements, and technology licensing. Implications for strategic management, public policy, and international trade and investment are then discussed.

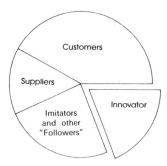

What determines the share of profits captured by the innovator?

Fig. 1. Explaining the distribution of the profits from innovation.

## 2. The phenomenon

Figure 2 presents a simplified taxonomy of the possible outcomes from innovation. Quadrant 1 represents positive outcomes for the innovator. A first-to-market advantage is translated into a sustained competitive advantage which either creates a new earnings stream or enhances an existing one. Quadrant 4 and its corollary quadrant 2 are the ones which are the focus of this paper.

The EMI CAT scanner is a classic case of the phenomenon to be investigated. [1] By the early 1970s, the UK firm Electrical Musical Industries (EMI) Ltd. was in a variety of product lines including phonographic records, movies, and advanced electronics. EMI had developed high resolution TVs in the 1930s, pioneered airborne radar during World War II, and developed the UK's first all solid-state computers in 1952.

In the late 1960s Godfrey Houndsfield, an EMI senior research engineer engaged in pattern recognition research which resulted in his displaying a scan of a pig's brain. Subsequent clinical work established that computerized axial tomography (CAT) was viable for generating cross-sectional "views" of the human body, the greatest advance in radiology since the discovery of X rays in 1895.

While EMI was initially successful with its CAT

[1] The EMI story is summarized in Michael Martin, *Managing Technological Innovation and Entrepreneurship*, (Reston Publishing Company, Reston, VA, 1984).

scanner, within 6 years of its introduction into the US in 1973 the company had lost market leadership, and by the eighth year had dropped out of the CT scanner business. Other companies successfully dominated the market, though they were late entrants, and are still profiting in the business today.

Other examples include RC Cola, a small beverage company that was the first to introduce cola in a can, and the first to introduce diet cola. Both Coca Cola and Pepsi followed almost immediately and deprived RC of any significant advantage from its innovation. Bowmar, which introduced the pocket calculator, was not able to withstand competition from Texas Instruments, Hewlett Packard and others, and went out of business. Xerox failed to succeed with its entry into the office computer business, even though Apple succeeded with the MacIntosh which contained many of Xerox's key product ideas, such as the mouse and icons. The de Havilland Comet saga has some of the same features. The Comet I jet was introduced into the commercial airline business 2 years or so before Boeing introduced the 707, but de Havilland failed to capitalize on its substantial early advantage. MITS introduced the first personal computer, the Altair, experienced a burst of sales, then slid quietly into oblivion.

If there are innovators who lose there must be followers/imitators who win. A classic example is IBM with its PC, a great success since the time it was introduced in 1981. Neither the architecture nor components embedded in the IBM PC were considered advanced when introduced; nor was the way the technology was packaged a significant departure from then-current practice. Yet the IBM PC was fabulously successful and established MS-DOS as the leading operating system for 16-bit PCs. By the end of 1984, IBM has shipped over 500 000 PCs, and many considered that it had irreversibly eclipsed Apple in the PC industry.

## 3. Profiting from innovation: Basic building blocks

In order to develop a coherent framework within which to explain the distribution of outcomes illustrated in fig. 2, three fundamental building blocks must first be put in place: the appropriability regime, complementary assets, and the dominant design paradigm.

D.J. Teece / Profiting from technological innovation     287

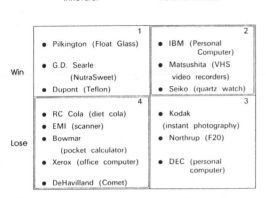

Fig. 2. Taxonomy of outcomes from the innovation process.

## 3.1. Regimes of appropriability

A regime of appropriability refers to the environmental factors, excluding firm and market structure, that govern an innovator's ability to capture the profits generated by an innovation. The most important dimensions of such a regime are the nature of the technology, and the efficacy of legal mechanisms of protection (fig. 3).

It has long been known that patents do not work in practice as they do in theory. Rarely, if ever, do patents confer perfect appropriability, although they do afford considerable protection on new chemical products and rather simple mechanical inventions. Many patents can be "invented around" at modest costs. They are especially ineffective at protecting process innovations. Often patents provide little protection because the legal requirements for upholding their validity or for proving their infringement are high.

In some industries, particularly where the innovation is embedded in processes, trade secrets are a viable alternative to patents. Trade secret protection is possible, however, only if a firm can put its product before the public and still keep the underlying technology secret. Usually only chemical formulas and industrial-commercial processes (e.g., cosmetics and recipes) can be protected as trade secrets after they're "out".

The degree to which knowledge is tacit or codified also affects ease of imitation. Codified knowledge is easier to transmit and receive, and is more

exposed to industrial espionage and the like. Tacit knowledge by definition is difficult to articulate, and so transfer is hard unless those who possess the know how in question can demonstrate it to others (Teece [9]). Survey research indicates that methods of appropriability vary markedly across industries, and probably within industries as well (Levin et al. [5]).

The property rights environment within which a firm operates can thus be classified according to the nature of the technology and the efficacy of the legal system to assign and protect intellectual property. While a gross simplification, a dichotomy can be drawn between environments in which the appropriability regime is "tight" (technology is relatively easy to protect) and "weak" (technology is almost impossible to protect). Examples of the former include the formula for Coca Cola syrup; an example of the latter would be the Simplex algorithm in linear programming.

## 3.2. The dominant design paradigm

It is commonly recognized that there are two stages in the evolutionary development of a given branch of a science: the preparadigmatic stage when there is no single generally accepted conceptual treatment of the phenomenon in a field of study, and the paradigmatic stage which begins when a body of theory appears to have passed the canons of scientific acceptability. The emergence of a dominant paradigm signals scientific maturity and the acceptance of agreed upon "standards" by which what has been referred to as "normal" scientific research can proceed. These "standards" remain in force unless or until the paradigm is overturned. Revolutionary science is what overturns normal science, as when the Copernicus's theories of astronomy overturned Ptolemy's in the seventeenth century.

Abernathy and Utterback [1] and Dosi [3] have provided a treatment of the technological evolution of an industry which appears to parallel

Fig. 3. Appropriability regime: Key dimensions.

Kuhnian notions of scientific evolution. [2] In the early stages of industry development, product designs are fluid, manufacturing processes are loosely and adaptively organized, and generalized capital is used in production. Competition amongst firms manifests itself in competition amongst designs, which are markedly different from each other. This might be called the preparadigmatic stage of an industry.

At some point in time, and after considerable trial and error in the marketplace, one design or a narrow class of designs begins to emerge as the more promising. Such a design must be able to meet a whole set of user needs in a relatively complete fashion. The Model T Ford, the IBM 360, and the Douglas DC-3 are examples of dominant designs in the automobile, computer, and aircraft industry respectively.

Once a dominant design emerges, competition shifts to price and away from design. Competitive success then shifts to a whole new set of variables. Scale and learning become much more important, and specialized capital gets deployed as incumbent's seek to lower unit costs through exploiting economies of scale and learning. Reduced uncertainty over product design provides an opportunity to amortize specialized long-lived investments.

Innovation is not necessarily halted once the dominant design emerges; as Clarke [2] points out, it can occur lower down in the design hierarchy. For instance, a " v" cylinder configuration emerged in automobile engine blocks during the 1930s with the emergence of the Ford V-8 engine. Niches were quickly found for it. Moreover, once the product design stabilizes, there is likely to be a surge of process innovation as producers attempt to lower production costs for the new product (see fig. 4).

The Abernathy–Utterback framework does not characterize all industries. It seems more suited to mass markets where consumer tastes are relatively homogeneous. It would appear to be less characteristic of small niche markets where the absence of scale and learning economies attaches much less of a penalty to multiple designs. In these instances, generalized equipment will be employed in production.

The existence of a dominant design watershed is of great significance to the distribution of profits between innovator and follower. The innovator may have been responsible for the fundamental scientific breakthroughs as well as the basic design of the new product. However, if imitation is relatively easy, imitators may enter the fray, modifying the product in important ways, yet relying on the fundamental designs pioneered by the innovator. When the game of musical chairs stops, and a dominant design emerges, the innovator might well end up positioned disadvantageously relative to a follower. Hence, when imitation is possible and occurs coupled with design modification before the emergence of a dominant design, followers have a good chance of having their modified product annointed as the industry standard, often to the great disadvantage of the innovator.

### 3.3. Complementary assets

Let the unit of analysis be an innovation. An innovation consists of certain technical knowledge about how to do things better than the existing state of the art. Assume that the know-how in question is partly codified and partly tacit. In order for such know-how to generate profits, it must be sold or utilized in some fashion in the market.

In almost all cases, the successful commercialization of an innovation requires that the know-how in question be utilized in conjunction with other capabilities or assets. Services such as marketing, competitive manufacturing, and after-sales support are almost always needed. These services are often obtained from complementary assets which are specialized. For example, the commercialization of a new drug is likely to require the dissemination of information over a specialized information channel. In some cases, as when the innovation is systemic, the complementary assets may be other parts of a system. For instance; computer hardware typically requires specialized software, both for the operating system, as well as for applications. Even when an innovation is autonomous, as with plug compatible components, certain complementary capabilities or assets will be needed for successful commercialization. Figure 5 summarizes this schematically.

Whether the assets required for least cost production and distribution are specialized to the

---

[2] See Kuhn [4].

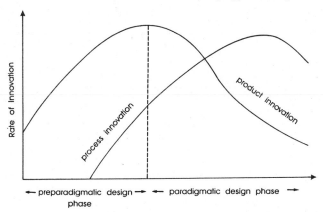

Fig. 4. Innovation over the product/industry life cycle.

innovation turns out to be important in the development presented below. Accordingly, the nature of complementary assets are explained in some detail. Figure 6 differentiates between complementary assets which are generic, specialized, and cospecialized.

Generic assets are general purpose assets which do not need to be tailored to the innovation in question. Specialized assets are those where there is unilateral dependence between the innovation and the complementary asset. Cospecialized assets are those for which there is a bilateral dependence. For instance, specialized repair facilities were needed to support the introduction of the rotary engine by Mazda. These assets are cospecialized because of the mutual dependence of the innovation on the repair facility. Containerization similarly required the deployment of some cospecialized assets in ocean shipping and terminals. However, the dependence of trucking on containerized shipping was less than that of containerized shipping on trucking, as trucks can convert from containers to flat beds at low cost. An example of a generic asset would be the manufacturing facilities needed to make running shoes. Generalized

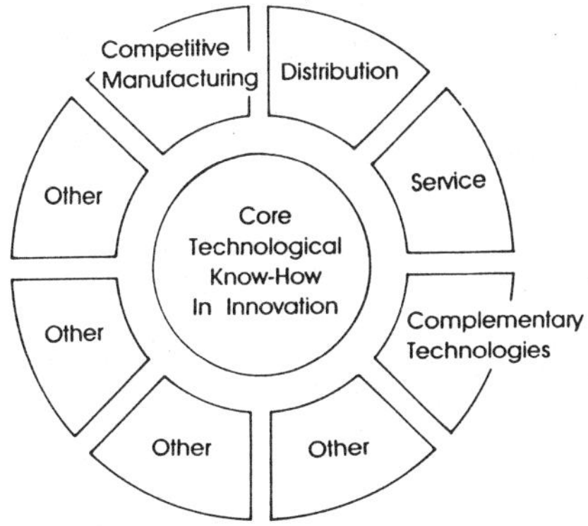

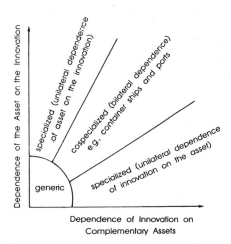

Fig. 5. Complementary assets needed to commercialize an innovation.

Fig. 6. Complementary assets: Generic, specialized, and cospecialized.

equipment can be employed in the main, exceptions being the molds for the soles.

## 4. Implications for profitability

These three concepts can now be related in a way which will shed light on the imitation process, and the distribution of profits between innovator and follower. We begin by examining tight appropriability regimes.

### 4.1. Tight appropriability regimes

In those few instances where the innovator has an iron clad patent or copyright protection, or where the nature of the product is such that trade secrets effectively deny imitators access to the relevant knowledge, the innovator is almost assured of translating its innovation into market value for some period of time. Even if the innovator does not possess the desirable endowment of complementary costs, iron clad protection of intellectual property will afford the innovator the time to access these assets. If these assets are generic, contractual relation may well suffice, and the innovator may simply license its technology. Specialized R&D firms are viable in such an environment. Universal Oil Products, an R&D firm developing refining processes for the petroleum industry was one such case in point. If, however, the complementary assets are specialized or cospecialized, contractual relationships are exposed to hazards, because one or both parties will have to commit capital to certain irreversible investments which will be valueless if the relationship between innovator and licensee breaks down. Accordingly, the innovator may find it prudent to expand its boundaries by integrating into specialized and cospecialized assets. Fortunately, the factors which make for difficult imitation will enable the innovator to build or acquire those complementary assets without competing with innovators for their control.

Competition from imitators is muted in this type of regime, which sometimes characterizes the petrochemical industry. In this industry, the protection offered by patents is fairly easily enforced. One factor assisting the licensee in this regard is that most petrochemical processes are designed around a specific variety of catalysts which can be

kept proprietory. An agreement not to analyze the catalyst can be extracted from licensees, affording extra protection. However, even if such requirements are violated by licensees, the innovator is still well positioned, as the most important properties of a catalyst are related to its physical structure, and the process for generating this structure cannot be deduced from structural analysis alone. Every reaction technology a company acquires is thus accompanied by an ongoing dependence on the innovating company for the catalyst appropriate to the plant design. Failure to comply with various elements of the licensing contract can thus result in a cutoff in the supply of the catalyst, and possibly facility closure.

Similarly, if the innovator comes to market in the preparadigmatic phase with a sound product concept but the wrong design, a tight appropriability regime will afford the innovator the time needed to perform the trials needed to get the design right. As discussed earlier, the best initial design concepts often turn out to be hopelessly wrong, but if the innovator possesses an impenetrable thicket of patents, or has technology which is simply difficult to copy, then the market may well afford the innovator the necessary time to ascertain the right design before being eclipsed by imitators.

### 4.2. Weak appropriability

Tight appropriability is the exception rather than the rule. Accordingly, innovators must turn to business strategy if they are to keep imitators/followers at bay. The nature of the competitive process will vary according to whether the industry is in the paradigmatic or preparadigmatic phase.

#### 4.2.1. Preparadigmatic phase

In the preparadigmatic phase, the innovator must be careful to let the basic design "float" until sufficient evidence has accumulated that a design has been delivered which is likely to become the industry standard. In some industries there may be little opportunity for product modification. In microelectronics, for example, designs become locked in when the circuitry is chosen. Product modification is limited to "debugging" and software modification. An innovator must begin the design process anew if the product doesn't fit the market well. In some respects, however, selecting designs is dictated by the need to meet certain compatibility standards so that new hardware can interface with existing applications software. In one sense, therefore, the design issue for the microprocessor industry today is relatively straightforward: deliver greater power and speed while meeting the the computer industry standards of the existing software base. However, from time to time windows of opportunity emerge for the introduction of entirely new families of microprocessors which will define a new industry and software standard. In these instances, basic design parameters are less well defined, and can be permitted to "float" until market acceptance is apparent.

The early history of the automobile industry exemplifies exceedingly well the importance for subsequent success of selecting the right design in the preparadigmatic stages. None of the early producers of steam cars survived the early shakeout when the closed body internal combusion engine automobile emerged as the dominant design. The steam car, nevertheless, had numerous early virtues, such as reliability, which the internal combustion engine autos could not deliver.

The British fiasco with the Comet I is also instructive. De Havilland had picked an early design with both technical and commercial flaws. By moving into production, significant irreversibilities and loss of reputation hobbled de Havilland to such a degree that it was unable to convert to the Boeing design which subsequently emerged as dominant. It wasn't even able to occupy second place, which went instead to Douglas.

As a general principle, it appears that innovators in weak appropriability regimes need to be intimately coupled to the market so that user needs can fully impact designs. When multiple parallel and sequential prototyping is feasible, it has clear advantages. Generally such an approach is simply prohibitively costly. When development costs for a large commercial aircraft exceed one billion dollars, variations on a theme are all that is possible.

Hence, the probability that an innovator – defined here as a firm that is first to commercialize a new product design concept – will enter the paradigmatic phase possessing the dominant design is problematic. The probabilities will be higher the lower the relative cost of prototyping,

and the more tightly coupled the firm is to the market. The later is a function of organizational design, and can be influenced by managerial choices. The former is embedded in the technology, and cannot be influenced, except in minor ways, by managerial decisions. Hence, in industries with large developmental and prototyping costs – and hence significant irreversibilities – and where innovation of the product concept is easy, then one would expect that the probability that the innovator would emerge as the winner or amongst the winners at the end of the preparadigmatic stage is low.

### 4.2.2. Paradigmatic stage

In the preparadigmatic phase, complementary assets do not loom large. Rivalry is focused on trying to identify the design which will be dominant. Production volumes are low, and there is little to be gained in deploying specialized assets, as scale economies are unavailable, and price is not a principal competitive factor. However, as the leading design or designs begin to be revealed by the market, volumes increase and opportunities for economies of scale will induce firms to begin gearing up for mass production by acquiring specialized tooling and equipment, and possibly specialized distribution as well. Since these investments involve significant irreversibilities, producers are likely to proceed with caution. Islands of specialized capital will begin to appear in an industry, which otherwise features a sea of general purpose manufacturing equipment.

However, as the terms of competition begin to change, and prices become increasingly unimportant, access to complementary assets becomes absolutely critical. Since the core technology is easy to imitate, by assumption, commercial success swings upon the terms and conditions upon which the required complementary assets can be accessed.

It is at this point that specialized and cospecialized assets become critically important. Generalized equipment and skills, almost by definition, are always available in an industry, and even if they are not, they do not involve significant irreversibilities. Accordingly, firms have easy access to this type of capital, and even if there is insufficient capacity available in the relevant assets, it can easily be put in place as it involves few risks. Specialized assets, on the other hand, involve significant irreversibilities and cannot be easily accessed by contract, as the risks are significant for the party making the dedicated investment. The firms which control the cospecialized assets, such as distribution channels, specialized manufacturing capacity, etc. are clearly advantageously positioned relative to an innovator. Indeed, in rare instances where incumbent firms possess an airtight monopoly over specialized assets, and the innovator is in a regime of weak appropriability, all of the profits to the innovation could conceivably inure to the firms possessing the specialized assets who should be able to get the upper hand.

Even when the innovator is not confronted by situations where competitors or potential competitors control key assets, the innovator may still be disadvantaged. For instance, the technology embedded in cardiac pacemakers was easy to imitate, and so competitive outcomes quickly came to be determined by who had easiest access to the complementary assets, in this case specialized marketing. A similar situation has recently arisen in the United States with respect to personal computers. As an industry participant recently observed: "There are a huge numbers of computer manufacturers, companies that make peripherals (e.g. printers, hard disk drives, floppy disk drives), and software companies. They are all trying to get marketing distributors because they cannot afford to call on all of the US companies directly. They need to go through retail distribution channels, such as Businessland, in order to reach the marketplace. The problem today, however, is that many of these companies are not able to get shelf space and thus are having a very difficult time marketing their products. The point of distribution is where the profit and the power are in the marketplace today". (Norman [8, p.438])

## 5. Channel strategy issues

The above analysis indicates how access to complementary assets, such as manufacturing and distribution, on competitive teams is critical if the innovator is to avoid handling over the lion's share of the profits to imitators, and/or to the owners of the complementary assets that are specialized or cospecialized to the innovation. It is now necessary to delve deeper into the appropriate control structure that the innovator ideally ought to establish over these critical assets.

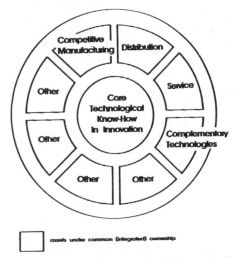

assets under common (integrated) ownership

Fig. 7. Complementary assets internalized for innovation: Hypothetical case #1 (innovator integrated into all complementary assets).

There are a myriad of possible channels which could be employed. At one extreme the innovator could integrate into all of the necessary comple-

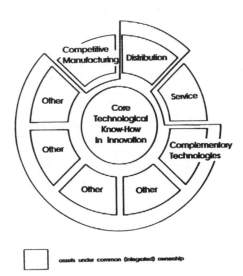

assets under common (integrated) ownership

Fig. 8. Complementary assets internalized for innovation: Hypothetical case #2 (innovator subcontracts for manufacturing and service).

mentary assets, as illustrated in fig. 7, or just a few of them, as illustrated in fig. 8. Complete integration (fig. 7) is likely to be unnecessary as well as prohibitively expensive. It is well to recognize that the variety of assets and competences which need to be accessed is likely to be quite large, even for only modestly complex technologies. To produce a personal computer, for instance, a company needs access to expertise in semiconductor technology, display technology, disk drive technology, networking technology, keyboard technology, and several others. No company can keep pace in all of these areas by itself.

At the other extreme, the innovator could attempt to access these assets through straightforward contractual relationships (e.g. component supply contracts, fabrication contracts, service contracts, etc.). In many instances such contracts may suffice, although it sometimes exposes the innovator to various hazards and dependencies that it may well wish to avoid. In between the fully integrated and full contractual extremes, there are a myriad of intermediate forms and channels available. An analysis of the properties of the two extreme forms is presented below. A brief synopsis of mixed modes then follows.

### 5.1. Contractual modes

The advantages of a contractual solution – whereby the innovator signs a contract, such as a license, with independent suppliers, manufacturers or distributors – are obvious. The innovator will not have to make the upfront capital expenditures needed to build or buy the assets in question. This reduces risks as well as cash requirements.

Contracting rather than integrating is likely to be the optimal strategy when the innovators appropriability regime is tight and the complementary assets are available in competitive supply (i.e. there is adequate capacity and a choice of sources).

Both conditions apply in petrochemicals for instance, so an innovator doesn't need to be integrated to be a successful. Consider, first, the appropriability regime. As discussed earlier, the protection offered by patents is fairly easily enforced, particularly for process technology, in the petrochemical industry. Given the advantageous feedstock prices available in hydrocarbon rich petrochemical exporters, and the appropriability regime characteristic of this industry, there is no

incentive or advantage in owning the complementary assets (production facilities) as they are not typically highly specialized to the innovation. Union Carbide appears to realize this, and has recently adjusted its strategy accordingly. Essentially, Carbide is placing its existing technology into a new subsidiary, Engineering and Hydrocarbons Service. The company is engaging in licensing and offers engineering, construction, and management services to customers who want to take their feedstocks and integrate them forward into petrochemicals. But Carbide itself appears to be backing away from an integration strategy.

Chemical and petrochemical product innovations are not quite so easy to protect, which should raise new challenges to innovating firms in the developed nations as they attempt to shift out of commodity petrochemicals. There are already numerous examples of new products that made it to the marketplace, filled a customer need, but never generated competitive returns to the innovator because of imitation. For example, in the 1960s Dow decided to start manufacturing rigid polyurethene foam. However, it was imitated very quickly by numerous small firms which had lower costs. [3] The absence of low cost manufacturing capability left Dow vulnerable.

Contractual relationships can bring added credibility to the innovator, especially if the innovator is relatively unknown when the contractual partner is established and viable. Indeed, arms-length contracting which embodies more than a simple buy-sell agreement is becoming so common, and is so multifaceted, that the term strategic partnering has been devised to describe it. Even large companies such as IBM are now engaging in it. For IBM, partnering buys access to new technologies enabling the company to "learn things we couldn't have learned without many years of trial and error." [4] IBM's arrangement with Microsoft to use the latter's MS-DOS operating system software on the IBM PC facilitated the timely introduction of IBM's personal computer into the market.

---

[3] Executive V.P. Union Carbide, Robert D. Kennedy, quoted in *Chemical Week*, Nov. 16, 1983, p. 48.
[4] Comment attributed to Peter Olson III, IBM's director of business development, as reported in The Strategy Behind IBM's Strategic Alliances, *Electronic Business*, October 1 (1985) 126.

Smaller less integrated companies are often eager to sign on with established companies because of the name recognition and reputation spillovers. For instance Cipher Data Products, Inc. contracted with IBM to develop a low-priced version of IBM's 3480 0.5 inch streaming cartridge drive, which is likely to become the industry standard. As Cipher management points out, "one of the biggest advantages to dealing with IBM is that, once you've created a product that meets the high quality standards necessary to sell into the IBM world, you can sell into any arena." [5] Similarly, IBM's contract with Microsoft "meant instant credibility" to Microsoft (McKenna, 1985, p. 94).

It is most important to recognize, however, that strategic (contractual) partnering, which is currently very fashionable, is exposed to certain hazards, particularly for the innovator, when the innovator is trying to use contracts to access specialized capabilities. First, it may be difficult to induce suppliers to make costly irreversible commitments which depend for their success on the success of the innovation. To expect suppliers, manufacturers, and distributors to do so is to invite them to take risks along with the innovator. The problem which this poses for the innovator is similar to the problems associated with attracting venture capital. The innovator must persuade its prospective partner that the risk is a good one. The situation is one open to opportunistic abuses on both sides. The innovator has incentives to overstate the value of the innovation, while the supplier has incentives to "run with the technology" should the innovation be a success.

Instances of both parties making irreversible capital commitments nevertheless exist. Apple's Laserwriter – a high resolution laser printer which allows PC users to produce near typeset quality text and art department graphics – is a case in point. Apple persuaded Canon to participate in the development of the Laserwriter by providing subsystems from its copiers – but only after Apple contracted to pay for a certain number of copier engines and cases. In short, Apple accepted a good deal of the financial risk in order to induce Canon to assist in the development and produc-

tion of the Laserwriter. The arrangement appears to have been prudent, yet there were clearly hazards for both sides. It is difficult to write, execute, and enforce complex development contracts, particularly when the design of the new product is still "floating." Apple was exposed to the risk that its co-innovator Canon would fail to deliver, and Canon was exposed to the risk that the Apple design and marketing effort would not succeed. Still, Apple's alternatives may have been rather limited, inasmuch as it didn't command the requisite technology to "go it alone."

In short, the current euphoria over "strategic partnering" may be partially misplaced. The advantages are being stressed (for example, McKenna [6]) without a balanced presentation of costs and risks. Briefly, there is the risk that the partner won't perform according to the innovator's perception of what the contract requires; there is the added danger that the partner may imitate the innovator's technology and attempt to compete with the innovator. This latter possibility is particularly acute if the provider of the complementary asset is uniquely situated with respect to the complementary asset in question and has the capacity to imitate the technology, which the innovator is unable to protect. The innovator will then find that it has created a competitor who is better positioned than the innovator to take advantage of the market opportunity at hand. *Business Week* has expressed concerns along these lines in its discussion of the "Hollow Corporation." [6]

It is important to bear in mind, however, that contractual or partnering strategies in certain cases are ideal. If the innovator's technology is well protected, and if what the partner has to provide is a "generic" capacity available from many potential partners, then the innovator will be able to maintain the upper hand while avoiding the costs of duplicating downstream capacity. Even if the partner fails to perform, adequate alternatives exist (by assumption, the partners' capacities are commonly available) so the innovator's efforts to successfully commercialize its technology ought to proceed profitably.

---

[5] Comment attributed to Norman Farquhar, Cipher's vice president for strategic development, as reported in *Electronic Business*, October 1 (1985) 128.

[6] See *Business Week*, March 3 (1986) 57–59. *Business Week* uses the term to describe a corporation which lacks in-house manufacturing capability.

*5.2. Integration modes*

Integration, which by definition involves ownership, is distinguished from pure contractual modes in that it typically facilitates incentive alignment and control. If an innovator owns rather than rents the complementary assets needed to commercialize, then it is in a position to capture spillover benefits stemming from increased demand for the complementary assets caused by the innovation.

Indeed, an innovator might be in the position, at least before its innovation is announced, to buy up capacity in the complementary assets, possibly to its great subsequent advantage. If futures markets exist, simply taking forward positions in the complementary assets may suffice to capture much of the spillovers.

Even after the innovation is announced, the innovator might still be able to build or buy complementary capacities at competitive prices if the innovation has iron clad legal protection (i.e. if the innovation is in a tight appropriability regime). However, if the innovation is not tightly protected and once "out" is easy to imitate, then securing control of complementary capacities is likely to be the key success factor, particularly if those capacities are in fixed supply – so called "bottlenecks." Distribution and specialized manufacturing competences often become bottlenecks.

As a practical matter, however, an innovator may not have the time to acquire or build the complementary assets that ideally it would like to control. This is particularly true when imitation is easy, so that timing becomes critical. Additionally, the innovator may simply not have the financial resources to proceed. The implications of timing and cash constraints are summarized in fig. 9.

Accordingly, in weak appropriability regimes innovators need to rank complementary assets as to their importance. If the complementary assets are critical, ownership is warranted, although if the firm is cash constrained a minority position may well represent a sensible tradeoff.

Needless to say, when imitation is easy, strategic moves to build or buy complementary assets which are specialized must occur with due reference to the moves of competitors. There is no point moving to build a specialized asset, for instance, if one's imitators can do it faster and cheaper.

It is hopefully self evident that if the innovator is already a large enterprise with many of the relevant complementary assets under its control, integration is not likely to be the issue that it might otherwise be, as the innovating firm will already control many of the relevant specialized and cospecialized assets. However, in industries experiencing rapid technological change, technologies advance so rapidly that it is unlikely that a single company has the full range of expertise needed to bring advanced products to market in a timely and cost effective fashion. Hence, the integration issue is not just a small firm issue.

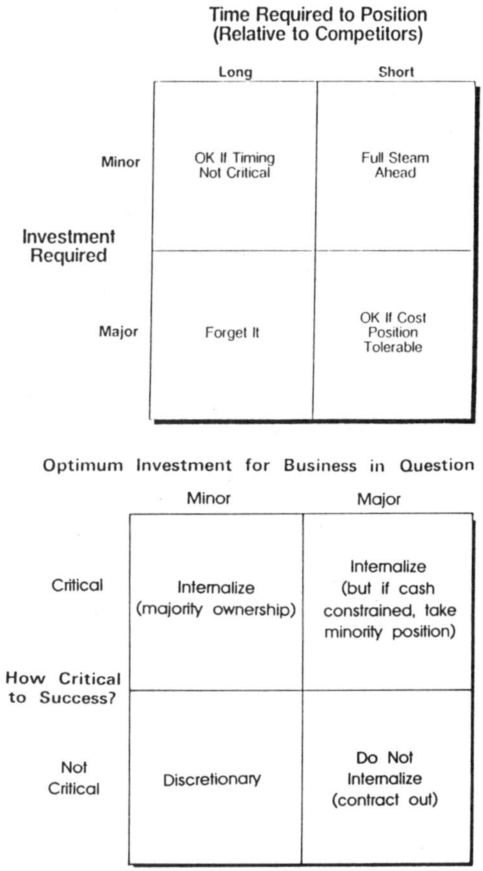
Time Required to Position
(Relative to Competitors)
Long
Short
Minor
OK If Timing Not Critical
Full Steam Ahead
Investment Required
Major
Forget It
OK If Cost Position Tolerable
Optimum Investment for Business in Question
Minor
Major
Critical
Internalize (majority ownership)
Internalize (but if cash constrained, take minority position)
How Critical to Success?
Not Critical
Discretionary
Do Not Internalize (contract out)

Fig. 9. Specialized complementary assets and weak appropriability: Integration calculus.

## 5.3. Integration versus contract strategies: An analytic summary

Figure 10 summarizes some of the relevant considerations in the form of a decision flow chart. It indicates that a profit seeking innovator, confronted by weak intellectual property protection and the need to access specialized complementary assets and/or capabilities, is forced to expand its activities through integration if it is to prevail over imitators. Put differently, innovators who develop new products that possess poor intellectual property protection but which requires specialized complementary capacities are more likely to parlay their technology into a commercial advantage, rather than see it prevail in the hands of imitators.

Figure 10 makes it apparent that the difficult strategic decisions arise in situations where the appropriability regime is weak and where specialized assets are critical to profitable commercialization. These situations, which in reality are very common, require that a fine-grained competitor analysis be part of the innovator's strategic assessment of its opportunities and threats. This is carried a step further in fig. 11, which looks only at situations where commercialization requires certain specialized capabilities. It indicates the appropriate strategies for the innovators and predicts the outcomes to be expected for the various players.

Three classes of players are of interst: innovators, imitators, and the owners of cospecialized assets (e.g. distributors). All three can potentially benefit or lose from the innovation process. The latter can potentially benefit from the additional business which the innovation may direct in the asset owners direction. Should the asset turn out

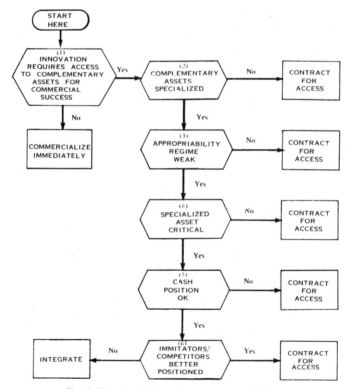

Fig. 10. Flow chart for integration versus contract decision.

D.J. Teece / *Profiting from technological innovation* 297

to be a bottleneck with respect to commercializing the innovation, the owner of the bottleneck facilities is obviously in a position to extract profits from the innovator and/or imitators.

The vertical axis in fig. 11 measures how those who possess the technology (the innovator or possibly its imitators) are positioned vis à vis those firms that possess required specialized assets. The horizontal axis measures the "tightness" of the appropriability regime, tight regimes being evidence by iron clad legal protection coupled with technology that is simply difficult to copy; weak regimes offer little in the way of legal protection and the essence of the technology, once released, is transparent to the imitator. Weak regimes are further subdivided according to how the innovator and imitators are positioned vis à vis each other. This is likely to be a function of factors such as lead time and prior positioning in the requisite complementary assets.

Figure 11 makes it apparent that even when firms pursue the optimal strategy, other industry participants may take the jackpot. This possibility is unlikely when the intellectual property in question is tightly protected. The only serious threat to the innovator is where a specialized complementary asset is completely "locked up," a possibility recognized in cell 4. This can rarely be done without the cooperation of government. But it frequently occurs, as when a foreign government closes off access to a foreign market, forcing the innovators to license to foreign firms, but with the government effectively cartelizing the potential licensees. With weak intellectual property protection, however, it is quite clear that the innovator will often loose out to imitators and/or asset holders, even when the innovator is pursuing the appropriate strategy (cell 6). Clearly, incorrect strategies can compound problems. For instance, if innovators integrate when they should contract,

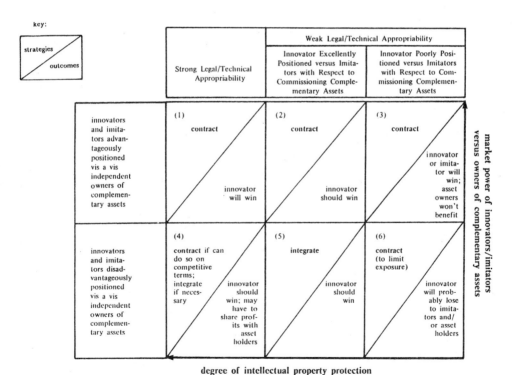

Fig. 11. Contract and integration strategies and outcomes for innovators: Specialized asset case.

a heavy commitment of resources will be incurred for little if any strategic benefit, thereby exposing the innovator to even greater losses than would otherwise be the case. On the other hand, if an innovator tries to contract for the supply of a critical capability when it should build the capability itself, it may well find it has nutured an imitator better able to serve the market than the innovator itself.

## 5.4. Mixed modes

The real world rarely provides extreme or pure cases. Decisions to integrate or license involve tradeoffs, compromises, and mixed approaches. It is not surprising therefore that the real world is characterized by mixed modes of organization, involving judicious blends of integration and contracting. Sometimes mixed modes represent transitional phases. For instance, because of the convergence of computer and telecommunication technology, firms in each industry are discovering that they often lack the requisite technical capabilities in the other. Since the technological interdependence of the two requires collaboration amongst those who design different parts of the system, intense cross-boundary coordination and information flows are required. When separate enterprises are involved, agreement must be reached on complex protocol issues amongst parties who see their interests differently. Contractual difficulties can be anticipated since the selection of common technical protocols amongst the parties will often be followed by transaction-specific investments in hardware and software. There is little doubt that this was the motivation behind IBM's purchase of 15 percent of PBX manufacturer Rolm in 1983, a position that was expanded to 100 percent in 1984. IBM's stake in Intel, which began with a 12 percent purchase in 1982, is most probably not a transitional phase leading to 100 percent purchase, because both companies realized that the two corporate cultures are not very compatible, and IBM may not be as impressed with Intel's technology as it once was.

## 5.5. The CAT scanner, the IBM PC, and Nutra-Sweet: Insights from the framework

EMI's failure to reap significant returns from the CAT scanner can be explained in large mea-

sure by reference to the concepts developed above. The scanner which EMI developed was of a technical sophistication much higher than would normally be found in a hospital, requiring a high level of training, support, and servicing. EMI had none of these capabilities, could not easily contract for them, and was slow to realize their importance. It most probably could have formed a partnership with a company like Siemens to access the requisite capabilities. Its failure to do so was a strategic error compounded by the very limited intellectual property protection which the law afforded the scanner. Although subsequent court decisions have upheld some of EMI's patent claims, once the product was in the market it could be reverse engineered and its essential features copied. Two competitors, GE and Technicare, already possessed the complementary capabilities that the scanner required, and they were also technologically capable. In addition, both were experienced marketers of medical equipment, and had reputations for quality, reliability and service. GE and Technicare were thus able to commit their R & D resources to developing a competitive scanner, borrowing ideas from EMI's scanner, which they undoubtedly had access to through cooperative hospitals, and improving on it where they could while they rushed to market. GE began taking orders in 1976 and soon after made inroads on EMI. In 1977 concern for rising health care costs caused the Carter Administration to introduce "certificate of need' regulation, which required HEW's approval on expenditures on big ticket items like CAT scanners. This severely cut the size of the available market.

By 1978 EMI had lost market share leadership to Technicare, which was in turn quickly overtaken by GE. In October 1979, Godfrey Houndsfield of EMI shared the Nobel prize for invention of the CT scanner. Despite this honor, and the public recognition of its role in bringing this medical breakthrough to the world, the collapse of its scanner business forced EMI in the same year into the arms of a rescuer, Thorn Electrical Industries, Ltd. GE subsequently acquired what was EMI's scanner business from Thorn for what amounted to a pittance. [7] Though royalties continued to flow to EMI, the company had failed to capture the

---

[7] See GE Gobbles a Rival in CT Scanners, *Business Week*, May 19, 1980, issue no. 2637.

lion's share of the profits generated by the innovation it had pioneered and successfully commercialized.

If EMI illustrates how a company with outstanding technology and an excellent product can fail to profit from innovation while the imitators succeeded, the story of the IBM PC indicates how a new product representing a very modest technological advance can yield remarkable returns to the developer.

The IBM PC, introduced in 1981, was a success despite the fact that the architecture was ordinary and the components standard. Philip Estridge's design team in Boca Raton, Florida, decided to use existing technology to produce a solid, reliable micro rather than state of the art. With a one-year mandate to develop a PC, Estridge's team could do little else.

However, the IBM PC did use what at the time was a new 16-bit microprocessor (the Intel 8088) and a new disk operating system (DOS) adapted for IBM by Microsoft. Other than the microprocessor and the operating system, the IBM PC incorporated existing micro "standards" and used off-the-shelf parts from outside vendors. IBM did write its own BIOS (Basic Input/Output System) which is embedded in ROM, but this was a relatively straightforward programming exercise.

The key to the PC's success was not the technology. It was the set of complementary assets which IBM either had or quickly assembled around the PC. In order to expand the market for PCs, there was a clear need for an expandable, flexible microcomputer system with extensive applications software. IBM could have based its PC system on its own patented hardware and copyrighted software. Such an approach would cause complementary products to be cospecialized, forcing IBM to develop peripherals and a comprehensive library of software in a very short time. Instead, IBM adopted what might be called an "induced contractual" approach. By adopting an open system architecture, as Apple had done, and by making the operating system information publicly available, a spectacular output of third part software was induced. IBM estimated that by mid-1983, at least 3000 hardware and software products were available for the PC. [8] Put differently, IBM pulled together the complementary assets, particularly software, which success required, without even using contracts, let alone integration. This was despite the fact that the software developers were creating assets that were in part cospecialized with the IBM PC, at least in the first instance.

A number of special factors made this seem a reasonable risk to the software writers. A critical one was IBM's name and commitment to the project. The reputation behind the letters I.B.M. is perhaps the greatest cospecialized asset the company possesses. The name implied that the product would be marketed and serviced in the IBM tradition. It guaranteed that PC-DOS would become an industry standard, so that the software business would not be solely dependent on IBM, because emulators were sure to enter. It guaranteed access to retail distribution outlets on competitive terms. The consequences was that IBM was able to take a product which represented at best a modest technological accomplishment, and turn into a fabulous commercial success. The case demonstrates the role that complementary assets play in determining outcomes.

The spectacular success and profitability of G.D. Searle's NutraSweet is an uncommon story which is also consistent with the above framework. In 1982, Searle reported combined sales of $74 million for NutraSweet and its table top version, Equal. In 1983, this surged to $336 million. In 1985, NutraSweet sales exceeded $700 million [9] and Equal had captured 50 percent of the U.S. sugar substitute market and was number one in five other countries.

NutraSweet, which is Searle's tradename for aspartame, has achieved rapid acceptance in each of its FDA approved categories because of its good taste and ability to substitute directly for sugar in many applications. However, Searle's earnings from NutraSweet and the absence of a strategic challenge can be traced in part to Searle's clever strategy.

It appears that Searle has managed to establish an exceptionally tight appropriability regime around NutraSweet – one that may well continue for some time after the patent has expired. No competitor appears to have successfully "invented around" the Searle patent and commercialized an alternative, no doubt in part because the FDA

---

[8] F. Gens and C. Christiansen, Could 1,000,000 IBM PC Users Be Wrong, *Byte*, November 1983, 88.

[9] See *Monsanto Annual Report, 1985.*

approval process would have to begin anew for an imitator who was not violating Searle's patents. A competitor who tried to replicate the aspartame molecule with minor modification to circumvent the patent would probably be forced to replicate the hundreds of tests and experiments which proved aspartame's safety. Without patent protection, FDA approval would provide no shield against imitators coming to market with an identical chemical and who could establish to the FDA that it is the same compound that had already been approved. Without FDA approval on the other hand, the patent protection would be worthless for the product would not be sold for human consumption.

Searle has aggressively pushed to strengthen its patent protection. The company was granted U.S. patent protection in 1970. It has also obtained patent protection in Japan, Canada, Australia, U.K., France, Germany, and a number of other countries. However, most of these patents carry a 17-year life. Since the product was only approved for human consumption in 1982, the 17-year patent life was effectively reduced to five. Recognizing the obvious importance of its patent, Searle pressed for and obtained special legislation in November 1984 extending the patent protection on aspartame for another 5 years. The U.K. provided a similar extension. In almost every other nation, however, 1987 will mark the expiration of the patent.

When the patent expires, however, Searle will still have several valuable assets to help keep imitators at bay. Searle has gone to great lengths to create and promulgate the use of its NutraSweet name and a distinctive "Swirl" logo on all goods licensed to use the ingredient. The company has also developed the "Equal" tradename for a table top version of the sweetener. Trademark law in the U.S. provides protection against "unfair" competition in branded products for as long as the owner of the mark continues to use it. Both the NutraSweet and Equal trademarks will become essential assets when the patents on aspartame expire. Searle may well have convinced consumers that the only real form of sweetener is Nutra-Sweet/Equal. Consumers know most other artificial sweeteners by their generic names – saccharin and cyclamates.

Clearly, Searle is trying to build a position in complementary assets to prepare for the competi-

tion which will surely arise. Searle's joint venture with Ajinomoto ensures them access to that company's many years of experience in the production of biochemical agents. Much of this knowledge is associated with techniques for distillation and synthesis of the delicate hydrocarbon compounds that are the ingredients of NutraSweet, and is therefore more tacit than codified. Searle has begun to put these techniques to use in its own $160 million Georgia production facility. It can be expected that Searle will use trade secrets to the maximum to keep this know-how proprietary.

By the time its patent expires, Searle's extensive research into production techniques for L-phenylalanine, and its 8 years of experience in the Georgia plant, should give it a significant cost advantage over potential aspartame competitors. Trade secret protection, unlike patents, has no fixed lifetime and may well sustain Searle's position for years to come.

Moreover, Searle has wisely avoided renewing contracts with suppliers when they have expired. [10] Had Searle subcontracted manufacturing for NutraSweet, it would have created a manufacturer who would then be in a position to enter the aspartame market itself, or to team up with a marketer of artificial sweeteners. But keeping manufacturing inhouse, and by developing a valuable tradename, Searle has a good chance of protecting its market position from dramatic inroads once patents expire. Clearly, Searle seems to be astutely aware of the importance of maintaining a "tight appropriability regime" and using cospecialized assets strategically.

## 6. Implications for R&D strategy, industry structure, and trade policy

### 6.1. Allocating R&D resources

The analysis so far assumes that the firm has developed an innovation for which a market exists. It indicates the strategies which the firm must

---

[10] Purification Engineering, which had spent $5 million to build a phenylalanine production facility, was told in January 1985 that their contract would not be renewed. In May, Genex, which claimed to have invested $25 million, was given the same message, A Bad Aftertaste, *Business Week*, July 15, 1985, issue 2903.

follow to maximize its share of industry profits relative to imitators and other competitors. There is no guarantee of success even if optimal strategies are followed.

The innovator can improve its total return to R & D, however, by adjusting its R & D investment portfolio to maximize the probability that technological discoveries will emerge that are either easy to protect with existing intellectual property law, or which require for commercialization cospecialized assets already within the firm's repertoire of capabilities. Put differently, if an innovating firm does not target its R & D resources towards new products and processes which it can commercialize advantageously relative to potential imitators and/or followers, then it is unlikely to profit from its investment in R & D. In this sense, a firm's history – and the assets it already has in place – ought to condition its R & D investment decisions. Clearly, an innovating firm with considerable assets already in place is free to strike out in new directions, so long as in doing so it is cognizant of the kinds of capabilities required to successfully commercialize the innovation. It is therefore rather clear that the R & D investment decision cannot be divorced from the strategic analysis of markets and industries, and the firm's position within them.

## 6.2. Small firm versus large firm comparisons

Business commentators often remark that many small entrepreneurial firms which generate new, commercially valuable technology fail while large multinational firms, often with a less meritorious record with respect to innovation, survive and prosper. One set of reasons for this phenomenon is now clear. Large firms are more likely to possess the relevant specialized and cospecialized assets within their boundaries at the time of new product introduction. They can therefore do a better job of milking their technology, however meager, to maximum advantage. Small domestic firms are less likely to have the relevant specialized and cospecialized assets within their boundaries and so will either have to incur the expense of trying to build them, or of trying to develop coalitions with competitors/owners of the specialized assets.

## 6.3. Regimes of appropriability and industry structure

In industries where legal methods of protection are effective, or where new products are just hard to copy, the strategic necessity for innovating firms to integrate into cospecialized assets would appear to be less compelling than in industries where legal protection is weak. In cases where legal protection is weak or nonexistent, the control of cospecialized assets will be needed for long-run survival.

In this regard, it is instructive to examine the U.S. drug industry (Temin [10]). Beginning in the 1940s, the U.S. Patent Office began, for the first time, to grant patents on certain natural substances that involved difficult extraction procedures. Thus, in 1948 Merck received a patent on streptomycin, which was a natural substance. However, it was not the extraction process but the drug itself which received the patent. Hence, patents were important to the drug industry in terms of what could be patented (drugs), but they did not prevent imitation [10, p.436]. Sometimes just changing one molecule will enable a company to come up with a different substance which does not violate the patent. Had patents been more all-inclusive – and I am not suggesting they should – licensing would have been an effective mechanism for Merck to extract profits from its innovation. As it turns out, the emergence of close substitutes, coupled with FDA regulation which had the de facto effect of reducing the elasticity of demand for drugs, placed high rewards on a product differentiation strategy. This required extensive marketing, including a sales force that could directly contact doctors, who were the purchasers of drugs through their ability to create prescriptions. [11] The result was exclusive production (i.e., the earlier industry practice of licensing was dropped) and forward integration into marketing (the relevant cospecialized asset).

Generally, if legal protection of the innovator's profits is secure, innovating firms can select their

---

[11] In the period before FDA regulation, all drugs other than narcotics were available over-the-counter. Since the end user could purchase drugs directly, sales were price sensitive. Once prescriptions were required, this price sensitivity collapsed; the doctors not only did not have to pay for the drugs, but in most cases they were unaware of the prices of the drugs they were prescribing.

boundaries based simply on their ability to identify user needs and respond to those through
research and development. The weaker the legal
methods of protection, the greater the incentive to
integrate into the relevant cospecialized assets.
Hence, as industries in which legal protection is
weak begin to mature, integration into innovation-
specific cospecialized assets will occur. Often this
will take the form of backward, forward and lateral
integration. (Conglomerate integration is not part
of this phenomenon.) For example, IBM's purchase of Rolm can be seen as a response to the
impact of technological change on the identity of
the cospecialized assets relevant to IBM's future
growth.

### 6.4. Industry maturity, new entry, and history

As technologically progressive industries mature, and a greater proportion of the relevant
cospecialized assets are brought in under the corporate umbrellas of incumbents, new entry becomes more difficult. Moreover, when it does occur it is more likely to involve coalition formation
very early on. Incumbents will for sure own the
cospecialized assets, and new entrants will find it
necessary to forge links with them. Here lies the
explanation for the sudden surge in "strategic
partnering" now occurring internationally, and
particularly in the computer and telecommunications industry. Note that it should not be interpreted in anti-competitive terms. Given existing industry structure, coalitions ought to be seen not as
attempts to stifle competition, but as mechanisms
for lowering entry requirements for innovators.

In industries in which technological change of a
particular kind has occurred, which required deployment of specialized and/or cospecialized assets at the time, a configuration of firm boundaries
may well have arisen which no longer has compelling efficiencies. Considerations which once dictated integration may no longer hold, yet there
may not be strong forces leading to divestiture.
Hence existing firm boundaries may in some industries – especially those where the technological
trajectory and attendent specialized asset requirements has changed – be rather fragile. In short,
history matters in terms of understanding the
structure of the modern business enterprise. Existing firm boundaries cannot always be assumed
to have obvious rationales in terms of today's
requirements.

### 6.5. The importance of manufacturing to interna-
tional competitiveness

Practically all forms of technological know-how
must be embedded in goods and services to yield
value to the consumer. An important policy for
the innovating nation is whether the identity of
the firms and nations performing this function
matter.

In a world of tight appropriability and zero
transactions cost – the world of neoclassical trade
theory – it is a matter of indifference whether an
innovating firm has an in-house manufacturing
capability, domestic or foreign. It can simply engage in arms-length contracting (patent licensing,
know-how licensing, co-production, etc.) for the
sale of the output of the activity in which it has a
comparative advantage (in this case R & D) and
will maximize returns by specializing in what it
does best.

However, in a regime of weak appropriability,
and especially where the requisite manufacturing
assets are specialized to the innovation, which is
often the case, participation in manufacturing may
be necessary if an innovator is to appropriate the
rents from its innovation. Hence, if an innovator's
manufacturing costs are higher than those of its
imitators, the innovator may well end up ceding
the lion's share of profits to the imitator.

In a weak appropriability regime, low cost im-
itator-manufacturers may end up capturing all of
the profits from innovation. In a weak appropriability regime where specialized manufacturing capabilities are required to produce new products,
an innovator with a manufacturing disadvantage
may find that its advantage at early stage research
and development will have no commercial value.
This will eventually cripple the innovator, unless it
is assisted by governmental processes. For example, it appears that one of the reasons why U.S.
color TV manufacturers did not capture the lion's
share of the profits from the innovation, for which
RCA was primarily responsible, was that RCA
and its American licenses were not competitive at
manufacturing. In this context, concerns that the
decline of manufacturing threatens the entire
economy appear to be well founded.

A related implication is that as the technology
gap closes, the basis of competition in an industry
will shift to the cospecialized assets. This appears
to be what is happening in microprocessors. Intel

is no longer out ahead technologically. As Gordon Moore, CEO of Intel points out, "Take the top 10 [semiconductor] companies in the world...and it is hard to tell at any time who is ahead of whom.... It is clear that we have to be pretty damn close to the Japanese from a manufacturing standpoint to compete." [12] It is not just that strength in one area is necessary to compensate for weakness in another. As technology becomes more public and less proprietary through easier imitation, then strength in manufacturing and other capabilities is necessary to derive advantage from whatever technological advantages an innovator may possess.

Put differently, the notion that the United States can adopt a "designer role" in international commerce, while letting independent firms in other countries such as Japan, Korea, Taiwan, or Mexico do the manufacturing, is unlikely to be viable as a long-run strategy. This is because profits will accrue primarily to the low cost manufacturers (by providing a larger sales base over which they can exploit their special skills). Where imitation is easy, and even where it is not, there are obvious problems in transacting in the market for knowhow, problems which are described in more detail elsewhere [9]. In particular, there are difficulties in pricing an intangible asset whose true performance features are difficult to ascertain ex ante.

The trend in international business towards what Miles and Snow [7] call "dynamic networks" – characterized by vertical disintegration and contracting – ought thus be viewed with concern. (*Business Week*, March 3, 1986, has referred to the same phenomenon as the Hollow Corporation.) "Dynamic networks" may not so much reflect innovative organizational forms, but the disassembly of the modern corporation because of deterioration in national capacities, manufacturing in particular, which are complementary to technological innovation. Dynamic networks may therefore signal not so much the rejuvenation of American enterprise, but its piecemeal demise.

### 6.6. How trade and investment barriers can impact innovators' profits

In regimes of weak appropriability, governments can move to shift the distribution of the

gains from innovation away from foreign innovators and towards domestic firms by denying innovators ownership of specialized assets. The foreign firm, which by assumption is an innovator, will be left with the option of selling its intangible assets in the market for know how if both trade and investment are foreclosed by government policy. This option may appear better than the alternative (no renumeration at all from the market in question). Licensing may then appear profitable, but only because access to the complementary assets is blocked by government.

Thus when an innovating firm generating profits needs to access complementary assets abroad, host governments, by limiting access, can sometimes milk the innovators for a share of the profits, particularly that portion which originates from sales in the host country. However, the ability of host governments to do so depends importantly on the criticality of the host country's assets to the innovator. If the cost and infrastructure characteristics of the host country are such that it is the world's lowest cost manufacturing site, and if domestic industry is competitive, then by acting as a de facto monopsonist the host country government ought to be able to adjust the terms of access to the complementary assets so as to appropriate a greater share of the profits generated by the innovation. [13]

If, on the other hand, the host country offers no unique complementary assets, except access to its own market, restrictive practices by the government will only redistribute profits with respect to domestic rather than worldwide sales.

### 6.7. Implications for the international distribution of the benefits from innovation

The above analysis makes transparent that innovators who do not have access to the relevant specialized and cospecialized assets may end up ceding profits to imitators and other competitors, or simply to the owners of the specialized or cospecialized assets.

Even when the specialized assets are possessed by the innovating firm, they may be located abroad. Foreign factors of production are thus

[12] Institutionalizing the Revolution, *Forbes*, June 16, 1986, 35.

[13] If the host country market structure is monopolistic in the first instance, private actors might be able to achieve the same benefit. What government can do is to force collusion of domestic enterprises to their mutual benefit.

likely to benefit from research and development activities occurring across borders. There is little doubt, for instance, that the inability of many American multinationals to sustain competitive manufacturing in the U.S. is resulting in declining returns to U.S. labor. Stockholders and top management probably do as well if not better when a multinational accesses cospecialized assets in the firm's foreign subsidiaries; however, if there is unemployment in the factors of production supporting the specialized and cospecialized assets in question, then the foreign factors of production will benefit from innovation originating beyond national borders. This speaks to the importance to innovating nations of maintaining competence and competitiveness in the assets which complement technological innovation, manufacturing being a case in point. It also speaks to the importance to innovating nations of enhancing the protection afforded worldwide to intellectual property.

However, it must be recognized that there are inherent limits to the legal protection of intellectual property, and that business and national strategy are therefore likely to the critical factors in determining how the gains from innovation are shared worldwide. By making the correct strategic decision, innovating firms can move to protect the interests of stockholders; however, to ensure that domestic rather than foreign cospecialized assets capture the lion's share of the externalities spilling over to complementary assets, the supporting infrastructure for those complementary assets must not be allowed to decay. In short, if a nation has prowess at innovation, then in the absence of iron clad protection for intellectual property, it must maintain well-developed complementary assets if it is to capture the spillover benefits from innovation

## 7. Conclusion

The above analysis has attempted to synthesize from recent research in industrial organization and strategic management a framework within which to analyze the distribution of the profits from innovation. The framework indicates that the boundaries of the firm are an important strategic variable for innovating firms. The ownership of complementary assets, particularly when they are specialized and/or cospecialized, help estab-

lish who wins and who loses from innovation. Imitators can often outperform innovators if they are better positioned with respect to critical complementary assets. Hence, public policy aimed at promoting innovation must focus not only on R & D, but also on complementary assets, as well as the underlying infrastructure. If government decides to stimulate innovation, it would seem important to clear away barriers which impede the development of complementary assets which tend to be specialized or cospecialized to innovation. To fail to do so will cause an unnecessary large portion of the profits from innovation to flow to imitators and other competitors. If these firms lie beyond one's national borders, there are obvious implications for the internal distribution of income.

When applied to world markets, results similar to those obtained from the "new trade theory" are suggested by the framework. In particular, tariffs and other restrictions on trade can in some cases injure innovating firms while simultaneously benefiting protected firms when they are imitators. However, the propositions suggested by the framework are particularized to appropriability regimes, suggesting that economy-wide conclusions will be illusive. The policy conclusions derivable for commodity petrochemicals, for instance, are likely to be different than those that would be arrived at for semiconductors.

The approach also suggests that the product life cycle model of international trade will play itself out very differently in different industries and markets, in part according to appropriability regimes and the nature of the assets which need to be employed to convert a technological success into a commercial one. Whatever its limitations, the approach establishes that it is not so much the structure of markets but the structure of firms, particularly the scope of their boundaries, coupled with national policies with respect to the development of complementary assets, which determines the distribution of the profits amongst innovators and imitator/followers.

## References

[1] W.J. Abernathy and J.M. Utterback, Patterns of Industrial Innovation, *Technology Review* 80(7) (January/July 1978) 40–47.

[2] Kim B. Clarke, The Interaction of Design Hierarchies and Market Concepts in Technological Evolution, *Research Policy* 14 (1985) 235–251.

[3] G. Dosi, Technological Paradigms and Technological Trajectories, *Research Policy* 11 (1982) 147–162.

[4] Thomas Kuhn, *The Structure of Scientifc Revolutions*, 2nd ed (University of Chicago Press, Chicago, 1970).

[5] R. Levin, A. Klevorick, N. Nelson, and S. Winter, Survey Research on R&D Appropriability and Technological Opportunity, unpublished manuscript, Yale University, 1984.

[6] Regis McKenna, Market Positioning in High Technology, *California Management Review*, XXVII (3) (spring 1985).

[7] R.E. Miles and C.C. Snow, Network Organizations: New Concepts for New Forms, *California Management Review* (spring 1986) 62–73.

[8] David A. Norman, Impact of Entrepreneurship and Innovations on the Distribution of Personal Computers, in: R. Landau and N. Rosenberg (eds.), *The Positive Sum Strategy* (National Academy Press, Washington, DC, 1986).

[9] D.J. Teece, The Market for Know how and the Efficient International Transfer of Technology, *Annals of the American Academy of Political and Social Science*, November 1981.

[10] P. Temin, Technology, Regulation, and Market Structure in the Modern Pharmaceutical Industry, *The Bell Journal of Economics* (autumn 1979) 429–446.

# [9]

OMEGA The Int. Jl of Mgmt Sci. Vol. 8. No. 5. pp. 505 to 516
© Pergamon Press Ltd 1980. Printed in Great Britain

0305-0483 80 0901-0505$02 00 0

# On the Adoption of Technological Innovations in Industry: Superficial Models and Complex Decision Processes

## BELA GOLD

Case Western Reserve University, Ohio, USA

(Received March 1980)

Attention is directed first to the external as well as the internal contexts within which prospective innovations are evaluated. Turning to the actual decision-making processes, a review of the evaluational bases for decision is followed by consideration of how these lead to actual decisions and often to subsequent revisions of the original decisions. The final section is concerned with some common shortcomings of prevailing approaches to evaluating the post-installation effects of technological innovations in industry. It also offers some suggestions for improving such efforts and for using such improvements to enhance the effective appraisal of future innovations.

THE TECHNOLOGICAL competitiveness of firms and industries is determined not by the rate at which significant innovations are developed, but by the extent to which they are applied to commercial operations. The importance of such adoption decisions is further emphasized by the fact that evidence of resistance to the utilization of demonstrably effective technological advances tend to discourage managerial commitments to risky and costly efforts seeking additional advances.

Widespread recognition of the importance of understanding the factors affecting adoption decisions is apparent from the considerable array of publications dealing with them. Unfortunately however, most of these have provided only very limited, and even misleading, insights into the determinants of *actual* decisions about *specific* innovations in *real* firms. Such inadequacies seem to have been due in large measure to an understandable, but nevertheless crippling, premature emphasis on the formulation of broadly applicable generalizations. This has encouraged reliance on relatively superficial concepts and methodologies as well as on highly vulnerable samples both of statistical data and of managerial judgments.

It would appear useful, therefore, to review the key shortcomings of findings published so far and to add the tentative results of an extensive array of empirical studies conducted by our Research Program in Industrial Economics. These may help to highlight the urgent, but still unmet, needs of policymakers in industry and government who are concerned with re-invigorating the technological competitiveness of producers. The related analysis and discussion may also help to meet several other needs, including: the correction of misleading expectations concerning diffusion rates; the displacement of erroneous measures of the 'satisfactoriness' of such rates; the provision of a more systematic framework for managerial evaluations of prospective innovations; and the development of more effective guides for governmental efforts to determine which technological innovations should be encouraged to diffuse more rapidly, or more fully, and also to devise incentives to promote such objectives.

## ON THE DECISION-MAKING CONTEXT OF INNOVATION EVALUATIONS

Most research on innovation–adoption decisions and on diffusion rates has been seriously undermined by overly-restricted as well as unrealistic conceptions of both the external and internal aspects of the decision-making framework that is involved.

### The external context: simplifying assumptions versus realities

Most econometric models of the diffusion of technological innovations are based on the erroneous conception that the diffusion process is like filling a bottle. Thus, it is supposed that a specific innovation is progressively adopted by an unchanging and essentially homogeneous population of potential users. Such prospective users are assumed to have fixed and basically similar objectives, operations, products, decision processes and evaluative criteria; and they are expected to differ significantly only in respect to their respective estimates of the technological risks and profitability of the innovation, the availability to each of the capital required for adopting it, and the attitudes of their managements towards technological and other innovations in general. Accordingly, diffusion rates are expected to change over time as a result of adjustments in the costs of adopting the innovation and in the availability of capital to non-adopters. In addition, the proportion of adopters is expected to increase with evidence of decreasing technological risks and also with growing competitive pressure from earlier adopters.

But each of the fundamental elements of this conception is unrealistic. First, far from being essentially fixed, almost every technological innovation in industry undergoes numerous significant changes in its service capabilities with time. These may affect such factors as reliability, operating flexibility and efficiency, precision and other aspects of the quality of performance, applicability to specialized purposes, and hazards in use. Moreover, these are usually accompanied by changes in investment requirements and operating costs. Hence, 'the innovation' seems to be a fixed entity only to those who are ignorant of its technology and specific applications. To the engineers who seek to increase diffusion of the original innovation by improving and adapting it to the needs of expanding sectors of prospective

---

[1] For a fuller discussion, see Gold [10].

users—and there may be hundreds or even thousands of technical specialists among the domestic and foreign firms involved in relevant development efforts—'the innovation' constitutes a system of continuously changing potentials and limitations.

It should also be noted in this connection that the variety of forms and capabilities and economic effects involved in the metamorphosis of any major technological innovation pales in comparison with the staggering diversity encompassed by the term 'technological innovations'. The fact that these may differ in respect to virtually every characteristic which is likely to have economic effects further undermines the persuasiveness of the numerous studies which have sought to derive general diffusion patterns and general models of adoption decisions on the basis of oddly assorted, as well as miniscule, samples of technological innovations[1].

A second general shortcoming of the traditional approach to the diffusion of technological innovations is the assumption that the population of potential users is readily identifiable and essentially fixed. Actually, most studies have failed even to identify the group of prospective adopters realistically because of an understandable eagerness to utilize the convenient industrial categories offered by available statistical series. But this tends to reflect either a wishful or an ignorant underestimation of the numerous and important differences among the plants included within most of these categories. Among such widely prevailing differences which may affect the potential benefits of particular innovations—or of successive modifications of them—important ones include product designs, product-mixes, the patterns of make-or-buy arrangements, equipment characteristics and modernity, scale of production, quality standards, and various locational advantages and disadvantages involving access to needed inputs and markets. Thus, at any specified time, the current state of development of a particular innovation is unlikely to be directly relevant to the needs of all plants encompassed by the industry categories for which statistical data are readily available.

Moreover, the population of prospective adopters tends to change over time because of changes in the range of sizes in which 'the innovation' becomes available, as well as in its

*Omega, Vol. 8, No. 5*                                             507

service capabilities and limitations. Combined with concomitant adjustments in its investment requirements and operating costs, such innovational modifications may increase its attractiveness to additional groups of firms within, and also beyond, the assumed relevant statistical category. Indeed, the fundamental conceptual inadequacy of the traditional, essentially static, view is the failure to recognize the powerful interacting pressures for continuing change exerted on the *developers* of the innovation to extend its range of applicability in order to expand potential markets and on *prospective adopters* to re-appraise the value of such increasing capabilities.

A third basic weakness of many models of technological diffusion, especially those based on the projection of past statistical data, is their pervasive tendency to ignore significant dissimilarities in the economic conditions which characterized the various periods. A monopolizing concern with the pattern of changes in the quantitative magnitudes constituting the selected statistical series results in overlooking the accompanying changes in business cycles, inflation levels and even such critical changes in the firms and industries involved as are represented by growth rates, profit levels, labor problems, regulatory pressures and input shortages. No effective methods for eliminating the influence of all such factors on diffusion rates have been developed as yet, despite a variety of expedients and much effort; such techniques would be of doubtful value even if successful, for there is little interest in determining what diffusion rates might have been under improbably fixed economic conditions. However, valuable analytical insights might well result from determining the effects of various of these conditions on diffusion rates. For example, one of our studies suggested that, contrary to our expectations, diffusion rates did not increase consistently during periods when new capacity is added[2].

In short, there is ample basis for doubts about the validity and usefulness of the findings of most models of technological diffusion in industry because of their reliance on oversimplified concepts and heterogeneous samples[3]. Hence, the resulting empirical findings should properly be regarded as individual descriptions rather than as broadly applicable analytical generalizations. Moreover, most such findings cannot even be accepted as effective descriptions, except with the explicit understanding that they cover the relationship between a crudely defined cluster of innovations and an even more ambiguous conception of potential adopters.

It would seem to follow, therefore, that the saturation curve so widely used to depict diffusion patterns, or to assess diffusion rates, or to estimate shortcomings in diffusion levels, is misleading. Instead of one fixed estimate of potential users for the entire period of diffusion, with which actual adoption levels are compared, such charts should show the successive increases in the population of potential adopters associated with important changes in the applicability and economic benefits of the original innovation. Thus, Fig. 1b would seem to be more appropriate than the traditional Fig. 1a, and Fig. 1c might be even more accurate in noting that successive stages of innovational developments are associated with changes in potential users as well as actual adopters. The most significant implication of this conceptual re-orientation is that more effective understanding of diffusion patterns and of the factors affecting them requires more knowledgeable estimates of: the population of prospective users in any specified stage of an innovation's development; the number of additional adoptions likely to result from changes in the input and output pressures on prospective users, even without significant improvements in the innovation; and the number and kinds of additional adopters likely to be attracted by alternative further technological improvements in the innovation and by reductions in its investment requirements and operating costs. Incidently, careful research has also led to serious questioning of the traditional use of sigmoid curves to depict diffusion patterns[4].

---

[2] For example, see Gold *et al.* [11].

[3] For example, see the recent compendium by Martino [13].

[4] For example, Ray reported in 1969 that in an international study of the diffusion of various technological innovations in industry, "Neither the curves for individual processes nor their aggregation provided any strong contradictions of this assumption" (i.e. "that the diffusion curves are linear" (Ray [16]). Nor was any support for the general applicability of sigmoid diffusion curves provided by a 1970 publication covering the first 15 years after commercialization of the diffusion of 14 major innovations in steel, coal and iron-mining in the United States (Gold *et al.* [11]).

*The internal context: simplifying assumptions and realities*

The first grossly unrealistic assumption about the intra-firm context of decisions involving the adoption or non-adoption of technological innovations involves the arbitrary foreshortening of needed analytical perspectives. This results from focussing immediately on evaluations of a particular innovation—and how such evaluations might differ among those firms which adopt it and those which do not. But such an approach ignores the frequently dominant, and always important, role of the 'pre-decision environment'. For any period to be covered by current managerial planning and commitments, this covers the specific nature and relative urgency of all of the needs to be dealt with, the availability and relative net advantages of non-technological as well as technological options, and the availability of technical, managerial and financial resources to implement such alternative measures.

Firms within the same general sector of industry may well differ in the relative urgencies of pressures to increase sales, improve product quality, reduce inputs in short supply, lower production costs etc. Because of such divergent needs and disparate resources as well as dissimilarities in managerial strategies, there is no basis for assuming that all firms in an 'industry' are seriously considering the adoption of any specified technological innovations within any given period—much less that they are all considering the same innovation.

A second grossly unrealistic simplifying assumption about the intra-firm context of decisions about adopting technological innova-

tions is that such decisions are based on "expected profitability after adjustments for probable risks and uncertainties". But this is merely a tautology, rather than a useful analytical insight, for it says in effect that a profit-seeking firm makes decisions which seem to favor profits and, hence, that if an innovation is adopted, it is expected to be profitable. As a matter of fact, however, diffusion patterns suggest that numerous firms arrive at quite different evaluations of the same innovation more or less simultaneously. Hence, effective understanding of diffusion patterns requires more thorough study of how expected 'net benefits' are estimated and to what extent such 'evaluations' are really only rationalizations of decisions arrived at on less obvious and less objective grounds.

Despite frequent casual references in capital budgeting discussions to estimating the 'profitability', and even the 'net present value' of technological innovations and other major capital projects, it is extremely difficult to make such estimates within reasonable margins of error. This is due in large measure, of course, to uncertainties about future changes over 5 or 10 years in the level and product composition of market demand, in product and input factor prices, in competitive pressures, and in other important determinants of profitability[5]. But it is even difficult to make such determinations after the innovations have been adopted and put to use because of its many interactions with concomitant changes in other internal operations and management policies as well as in product and factor markets—as will be illustrated by several of the other papers in this volume. It is instructive to note, therefore, that Nabseth and Ray's collection of 8 studies of the diffusion of industrial innovations reports that

---

[5] For a detailed discussion, see Gold [9].

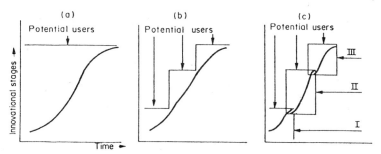

FIG. 1. *Alternative conceptions of innovation diffusion patterns.*

expected profitability was seldom given as a basis for adoption decisions and seldom demonstrated after periods of use [14].

Similar questions can be raised about the frequent casual references in the literature to estimating risk. But how is it done—and how well? One may readily grant that the risk of technological failure tends to decrease with increasing evidences of successful operations. But how effectively can estimates be made of the possibility of further superior improvements after an innovation has been adopted? Even more important, how well can management staffs estimate the wide array of economic risks that may be confronted, such as those cited earlier? At any rate, field research readily demonstrates that many innovations are adopted not in the hope of increasing profitability, but in order to minimize reductions in profitability threatened by competitors' advances, or by prospective special disadvantages facing the given firm.

A third grossly vulnerable basis for studies of decision-making about technological innovations in individual firms is the widespread reliance on *ex post* findings and interpretations. Some well-known studies are even unclear about how long ago the relevant decisions were made (often 10–20 years or more), and about whether the respondents cited were effectively involved in making such decisions (often not). The results of such studies are accordingly open to serious misinterpretations because of the enormous differences between hindsight perspectives and expectations about the unknown future. For example, hindsight judgments tend to stress *ex post* criteria instead of those which loomed largest when the decisions were made; hindsight evaluations are also more likely to rationalize whatever results were actually realized, crediting favorable outcomes to sound decisions while blaming unfavorable outcomes on external developments. Moreover, the judgments of current executives about long past decisions often reflect much unintentional forgetting as well as unacknowledged ignorance. And even the most serious efforts to evaluate the effects of long past decisions can hardly make effective allowances for the effects of interactions with intervening internal and external developments, many of which are likely to have been unexpected.

Finally, attention should also be drawn to the vulnerability of the various studies which have used heterogeneous samples of firms in an effort to identify those characteristics most frequently associated with responsiveness to innovational opportunities. The most effective evaluation of this general approach is Uhlmann's study of 20 characteristics of 126 firms in Germany, Sweden and the United Kingdom covering their responses in a total of 218 cases of innovations representing 18 distinctive types of innovations. Although he found that a number of the individual characteristics were associated with responsiveness to innovations on a statistical basis, no firms represented a substantial combination of such characteristics—indeed their actual patterns were virtually unique, both as among firms in the same sectors of industry and also as among those responding to particular groups of innovations[6].

## ACTUAL DECISION-MAKING PROCESSES

### Evaluational bases for decisions

One of the major gaps in our understanding of decisions affecting the adoption of technological innovations concerns the bases for the evaluations on which such decisions are based. Few studies even bother to cover the expected net results beyond claiming, or merely implying, that improved profitability was expected. But this reveals nothing about the specific arrays of estimated benefits and burdens which underlie such summary evaluations, nor about the bases for such judgements, nor about the margins of uncertainty considered to be associated with each of these estimates. Nor does it provide needed insights into the technological alternatives which were considered and the bases on which they were rejected as less attractive. Even more important, there is seldom any analysis of the changing evaluations over time as a result of which prior decisions to reject a given type of innovation are eventually reversed. Indeed, one cannot avoid suspecting that some (and perhaps most) of the limited number of ostensible analyses of the decisions leading up to the innovations being reported on are *ex post* rationalizations heavily interwoven with hindsight judgements and omissions.

---

[6] For further details see Uhlmann [19].

But efforts to develop sounder diffusion processes—which may increase adoption rates for some innovations while reducing them for others—require fuller awareness of the criteria which are commonly employed, how they are estimated, and how they are weighted in formulating final evaluations. Only by identifying such elements, and then appraising the vulnerability of the means employed to help guide decisions, can attention be drawn to the relative weaknesses of technological as over against economic estimates of prospective results—as a basis for seeking to improve both.

For example, our field research suggests that the most common sources of errors in estimates of the expected technological benefits of innovations center around:

(1) under-estimating the time needed to achieve effective functioning of the innovation, often by a considerable margin;

(2) over-estimating the average utilization rate as a basis for appraising benefits;

(3) under-estimating the need to make adaptive adjustments in the preceding and subsequent operations of an integrated production operation—or in the re-allocation of orders and support resources between a new facility and older facilities devoted to similar operations; and

(4) under-estimating the problems and costs of gaining labor acceptance of associated changes in tasks.

Economic evaluations of the expected effects of technological innovations are frequently based on a wide array of simplifying assumptions, among which the following seem to be the most common and most influential:

(1) that expected reductions in man-hours per unit of output will be accompanied by roughly comparable reductions in unit wage costs;

(2) that expected reductions in material requirements per unit of output will yield parallel reductions in their unit costs;

(3) that resulting cost savings can be carried over into increased profits.

But the first two assumptions ignore the tendency for changes in unit input requirements to *interact* with factor prices. Thus, increases in output per man-hour often engender comparable increases in wages per man-hour, whether through piece rates or through trade union demands, thus tending to minimize expected reductions in unit wage costs. Moreover, trade unions often resist the lay-offs made possible by technological innovations. Indeed, our research reveals that some companies in the US no longer permit the inclusion of expected wage costs savings in justifications for proposed capital projects, on the grounds that these all too frequently prove unrealizable.

In the case of reductions in material requirements per unit of output, the effects on their unit costs seem to be more variable. When such reduced inputs are attributable to tighter specifications of quality or dimensions, price increases may offset the expected cost savings. When such reduced inputs have been made possible by an innovation which is being adopted by competitors as well, the expected cost savings may be accentuated as a result of the depressing effect on the price of such materials due to widespread reductions in demand. But cost savings attributable to shifts to lower-priced materials may shrink in time as competitors also turn to such substitutes and thus increase the demand for them along with attendant prices. Estimates of expected savings in unit material and unit wage costs are also often erroneous because of the tendency to base them on current input prices instead of taking account of recent trends in such prices. Thus, even demonstrable reductions in the quantity of unchanged materials per unit of output may serve only to slow the rate of continuing increases in such unit material costs instead of yielding actual reductions[7].

It is also very important to recognize that the increasing diffusion of cost-saving innovations under competitive conditions tends to generate reductions in product prices as producers struggle to maintain market shares. Thus, the profit margins of early adopters are likely to undergo progressive shrinkage over time. In short, each of the foregoing considerations stresses the importance of seeking to es-

---

For illustrations and further discussion, see Gold [6, pp. 193-197].

*Omega, Vol. 8, No. 5*                                          511

timate the changing pattern of favorable and unfavorable economic effects period by period over the expected life of the innovation instead of simply multiplying current estimates of annual savings by the expected economic life of the undertaking.

In turn, these perspectives necessitate facing up to the serious inadequacies of the long range economic forecasts which are at the core of capital budgeting evaluations of innovational and other major project proposals. Attendant margins of error are likely to be quite large even in forecasts for entire industries, to say nothing of the even greater hazards involved in forecasts for individual firms and even single plants[8]. In view of the extreme difficulties involved, one can readily understand the resulting tendency to project current moods of optimism and pessimism into forecasts of 10 years and longer[9]; and one may even sympathize in some degree with the widespread practice of projecting the trends of the past 10–20 years into the next decade or two, despite the repeated demonstrations of major dissimilarities between the past and the future[10]. But such tolerance should not prevent awareness of the fundamental shortcomings of available forecasting methods and the need, therefore, to avoid placing heavy reliance on them. In particular, it would seem useful to consider minimizing dependence on statistical and econometric forecasting in favor of intensive analysis of the specific pressures and opportunities which lie ahead and to recognize that success is more likely to result from alert recognition of, and effective adjustment to, the inevitable emergence of unexpected developments than on the correctness of the original forecasting[11].

*Decision and revision processes*

It is commonly implied that decisions to adopt innovations somehow emerge automatically whenever continuous evaluations of an array of innovational alternatives finally identify candidates which exceed the current 'hurdle rate' for new undertakings. But there is no basis for this conception of a ceaseless econ-

omic radar scanning of possibilities of all kinds until one or more return a sufficiently profitable echo. Although many firms turn at least a casual eye towards any purportedly exciting new prospects on the horizon, serious evaluative efforts are much too costly to be applied indiscriminately. Hence, although a scanning awareness of current developments represents a minimum requirement for recognizing truly promising targets, most intensive commitments to evaluate particular possibilities tend to be triggered by such circumstances as the following:

(1) a threat to current market share resulting from technological advances by a competitor yielding improvements in product capabilities or prices which are patently attractive to current or prospective customers;

(2) a progressively weakening competive position which requires consideration of developing or adopting risky and costly new technologies as the most promising remaining means of safeguarding survival;

(3) a recent experience involving a technological innovation which yielded substantial competitive advantages as well as increased profitability and thus engendered greater confidence in the practical potentials of additional such undertakings;

(4) persuasive evidence of the imminent commercial applicability of an internally developed technological innovation promising important market benefits.

The point to be emphasized is that, as was suggested above, even the most thorough *ex ante* estimates of the prospective net benefits of adopting innovations tend to be subject to wide margins of error. Whether resulting decisions are favorable or unfavorable to adoption depend, therefore, on the managerial judgments which are invoked as supplements to these ostensibly objective but patently vulnerable estimates. Such judgements seem likely to reflect the value biases derived from the past training, expertise and experiences of various executives[12]. But most executives would nevertheless prefer to defer reliance on such hazardous guides in making major adoption de-

---

* For further discussion and some empirical findings, see Gold [9].
  * For example, see Gold [4].
    * For example see Gold [7].
      * For more detailed discussion, see Gold [9].
        * For a fuller discussion, see Gold [5].

cisions until external pressures threaten rising penalties for continuing delays. As a result, it is not at all uncommon to find that important innovations have been under consideration for several years before being adopted, thereby further emphasizing the importance of learning more about the factors which finally trigger adoption decisions, if our understanding of diffusion patterns is to be significantly improved.

Another over-simplification involves treating adoption decisions as though they were climactic once-for-all actions rather than representing only initial commitments subject to successive modifications on the basis of further information and experience. Of course, innovations differ in the rapidity with which investment decisions are carried out and in the extent to which later adjustments can be made in basic processes, in equipment capabilities, and in product characteristics without forbidding costs[13]. But undertakings that take one or two years to complete are likely to permit repeated modifications or original decisions, and this is even more true of projects taking longer periods.

Recognition of the continuing dynamics of these decision processes has two important implications. It emphasizes the potential errors of inferring the bases for the original decisions from the eventual results—and also of evaluating performance through comparison with the originally defined objectives. In addition, this broader conception highlights the need to study the extent to which later adoptions by firms with multiple operations susceptible to similar applications are based on changing evaluations of the innovation's capabilities as well as of market pressures and of internal urgencies[14].

## APPRAISING INNOVATIONAL EFFECTS

How effectively are the results of technological innovations determined? Such findings would obviously tend to have an important bearing on the rate of diffusion inasmuch as evidences of significant rewards are generally regarded as the most powerful incentive to increasing diffusion. Oddly enough, however,

there is an astonishing paucity of published research evaluating the actual effects of such innovations after they have been installed, in contrast to the considerable literature on estimating the probable effects of technological innovations before decisions are made to adopt or reject them.

Inquiries suggest that the reason for such neglect is the widespread assumption that the purposes, methodologies, applications and interpretations of such undertakings are so obvious as to offer no interesting problems. Our current field research, however, yields the strongly contrasting view that such post-installation evaluations are shot through with difficult problems and dubious bases for many of the results which are reported within firms.

Analysis of the problems and effectiveness of post-installation evaluations of the effects of technological innovations offer several potentially important contributions to the management of innovational processes. To begin with, such appraisals could provide a direct comparison of results with the expectations which led to adoption decisions. Even more important, comprehensive evaluations could explore the specific loci and causes of deviations between expectations and results, thus indicating the relative accuracy of various component estimates and also identifying any variables which were ignored. Moreover, such evaluative efforts may reveal insensitivities in the performance measurement system to innovational impacts, thus counseling changes in order to minimize consistent anti-innovation biases.

### Some shortcomings of current evaluation efforts

Only a limited array of post-installation evaluation methods have been turned up as a by-product of our field research on the effects of technological innovations. Hence, the following judgments must be regarded as preliminary and tentative indications of possible shortcomings.

Most of the 'make good', 'follow-up' and 'post-audit' evaluations examined concentrated primarily on simply measuring actual results, including: the costs of acquisition, construction and installation relative to budget; the acceptability of technical performance; and resulting operating costs. Except for comparisons with allowed budgets and expected total unit costs, few methods were characterized by comprehen-

---

[13] Such possibilities are considered in Eilon *et al.* [2].

[14] For further discussion, see Gold *et al.* [11].

*Omega, Vol. 8, No. 5*                                    513

sive comparisons of actual input requirements, factor prices, product quality and price, output levels and other aspects of performance with the respective estimates which led to the decision. Especially glaring is the common failure to consider the time required to achieve the 'acceptable' levels of performance before evaluation efforts tend to be initiated relative to expectations. Also disappointing is the virtual absence of any systematic efforts to 'learn from results' as a means of improving *ex ante* estimates of the effects of prospective technological innovations in the future.

Our explorations suggest in addition that formal evaluation efforts, except for comparisons of actual expenditures with allowed budgets, seem to be much less common in respect to very large projects and especially when their results seem unfavorable. In explaining such lapses, the two most common reasons given were: that each such project is necessarily unique and hence evaluations would have no feedback value in considering future projects; and that there was no interest in 'spilled milk' or in 'beating dead horses'.

One of the common limitations of post-installation evaluative efforts has been reliance on an overly restricted framework of considerations. Thus, a major part of the decision-making process involves choosing among a variety of available technological and non-technological means of meeting the most urgent needs of the firm at the time of decision. But a comparison of actual results with expectations in respect to the final choice made throws no light on the accuracy of the evaluations which led to the discarding of the other alternatives considered. Nor do such comparisons reveal the effects of having adopted innovations which succeeded in easing what were considered urgent needs at the time of decision at the cost of neglecting other needs which proved more serious. In short, there has been an almost complete failure to evaluate the substructure of evaluations that then determined which of the alternative means of dealing with specified needs should be adopted.

evaluations has been the apparent pressure for biased evaluations. In the case of very large projects, the tendency to seek out and to emphasize favorable aspects of results seems to be attributable to a concern that negative judgments would reflect on high level officials and

be resented by them. Such biases are often built into the evaluation process because allocation of such responsibilities to the officials deemed to have the relevant expertise often involves reliance on those who were also involved in project proposals and decisions. Thus, technical evaluations are usually left to engineers and various cost estimates to the respective specialists—partly because of the absence of effective internal alternatives and partly to protect the confidentiality of findings. Moreover, those assigned to making such evaluations are often led to mute critical judgments lest these inhibit future cooperative relationships with the officials responsible for the project. Indeed, we have not yet encountered any cases of wholly independent evaluations involving technological and economic competence. The seriousness of this problem is indicated by the fact that a senior officer of one of the major steel companies told us that they have abandoned such post-installation evaluations because they were invariably found to be so biased as to render them of dubious value.

A third set of shortcomings of post-installation evaluations arises from the time focus and criteria employed. For example, most cases examined relied on a single, narrowly-focussed evaluation made within 6–12 months of the project's completion. These early estimates tended to yield overly optimistic findings because generous allowances were usually made to offset shortcomings which were *assumed* to be attributable to temporary difficulties in achieving effective operations, to temporarily increased maintenance problems, and to temporary under-utilization. Such early evaluations also tended to be inadequate because it is only after the innovation has achieved effective functioning and reasonably high levels of utilization that efforts to maximize realization of its potentials lead to adaptive adjustments in preceding and subsequent operations, and even to possible modifications in product designs and product-mix. Hence, more effective appraisals would require successive evaluations every 6 months for at least 3 years (or even longer if effective functioning has not yet been achieved—as in some cases of continuous casting, for example) to ensure effective determination of practically sustainable performance levels and to ensure coverage of the wider repercussions of the innovation.

In addition, the actual effects of technological innovations are often measured inadequately because cost accounting categories are not revised to reflect important aspects of the innovation's contributions. These may include changes in the quality of the inputs used, in the nature of the processing or fabrication performed, or in the service capabilities of products. Other significant effects which are commonly disregarded include changes in the flexibility of operations which can be performed and changes in the precision with which processes can be controlled.

Moreover, concentration on the comparison of results with expectations tends to result in inadequate probing of the specific causes of shortfalls. As a result, observed deficiences are all too readily ascribed to unpredictable or external actors. Such minimizing of internal shortcomings obviously prevents identification of needed targets for improvement efforts.

Finally, attention should be directed to the seemingly universal avoidance of estimates of the innovation's incremental contribution to profitability. This implied recognition of the difficulties in attempting such evaluations, even on the basis of actual *ex post* data, raises even more serious doubts about the usefulness of *ex ante* estimates of such profitability effects as a basis for adoption decisions.

*installation evaluations*

Efforts to improve evaluation of the post-installation effects of technological innovations are confronted by a variety of questions concerned with how to reduce biases engendered by common production, costing and other practices. For example, means need to be considered for reducing the favorable biases associated with at least five common production practices encountered in our research. One of these involves shifting the most advantageous orders and the best operators to the new facilities, along with granting them top priority in access to ancillary facilities and to repair and maintenance services. Another such practice involves maximizing the utilization rate of the new facilities at the expense of the oider facilities. Such biases also result from motivating greater labor efforts and care through providing improved pay incentives and working con-

ditions. Still another source of differential advantage frequently involves improving the quality of work inputs from preceding operations and increasing the standardization of the tasks to be performed by the new facilities. And the question must also be faced of how long additional improvements to the initial installation are to be attributed to the original innovation instead of to subsequent innovations.

Parallel problems are also confronted in seeking to minimize unfavorable biases in evaluating the effects of innovational decisions attributable to production conditions. One of these involves under-utilization due to a recession. Another involves the effects of unexpected deficiencies in the quality of the materials to be processed. And a third may be caused by the necessity of modifying product specifications to adjust to changing customer preferences.

An important group of problems relating to proper evaluation of the cost effects of technological innovations concerns whether the following should be treated as increases in the investment embodied in the innovation or as current additions to operating costs:

a. additional outlays in order to improve the effectiveness with which the new facility functions;

b. the cost of interruptions to production caused by introduction of the innovation;

c. the cost of delays before achieving effective functioning of the innovation, including the cost of modifications, 'debugging', training operators and trial runs; and

d. the costs and outlays involved in readjusting preceding and subsequent operations in order to achieve effective integration with the capabilites of the innovation.

A related problem concerns whether to credit the innovation with cost reductions only in its own operations, or to also credit it with all cost benefits resulting from the adaptive improvements made in other operations, including procurement and engineering. Still another problem concerns how to evaluate the contributions of the innovation to changes in revenues apparently associated with innovation-induced adjustments in product quality and in the flexibility of product-mix.

*Omega, Vol. 8, No. 5*                                                                            515

Perhaps the most difficult problems of all involve seeking to disentangle the effects of the innovation from those of a wide array of concomitant developments. Among these, internal developments might include the introduction of other technological and non-technological innovations, as well as changes in management policies relating to prices, marketing, labor relations and other factors affecting competitive position. External developments might include changes in industry supply–demand relationships, changes in the availability and prices of input factors, technological and other innovations by competitors, and modifications in government regulations affecting the industry.

Finally, because many technological innovations require investments which are likely to be embodied in them for 10–20 years or longer, some attention must be given to the problem of longer term evaluations. Because relevant costs, revenues and net investment tend to change from year to year, evaluations of an innovation's effects would also yield changing results over time, quite possibly involving substantial changes in their favorableness[15]. Does this mean that all project evaluations should be repeated annually? For how long can their effects be differentiated from the combined impacts of all other developments? Three other questions seem to be even more fundamental:

a. What would be the significance for current decision-making of learning that some past decisions yielded favorable results in the short-run, but unfavorable results after 5 years whereas others yielded the reverse pattern of results?

b. What margins of error are likely to be associated with the 10–20 year estimates of output, costs, prices, interest rates and profits used in capital budgeting models—and should estimates subject to wide margins of error be used as the basis for decisions to adopt or to reject technological innovations?

c. And if the preceding question is answered in the negative, what alternatives are available to management?

---

For example, see the far-reaching changes in the results of the first float glass plant in the U.S. reported by Steddle later in this volume.

*Strengthening* ex post *evaluations to help improve future decisions*

The actual results of post-installation evaluations of technological innovations are likely to have little effect on current decisions concerning the adoption of new innovations. This absence of a feedback effect is likely to be true in part because *ex post* evaluations tend to vary significantly during the early years after installation, and because there is considerable awareness of the biases commonly reflected by initial evaluations. But the influence of later evaluations also tends to be minimized for two other reasons. Eventual determinations of the actual effects of long past innovational decisions are regarded as increasingly irrelevant to the different innovations and altered urgencies faced in later years. Even more important and instructive, however, is the tendency to view most such eventual results as attributable in larger measure to the effectiveness of management policies during the years in which the innovation was utilized than to the carryover effects of the original decision. In short, the limited usefulness of the kinds of *ex post* evaluations which have been encountered helps to explain the essentially peripheral interest of many managements in such exercises.

Such past shortcomings, however, have prevented realization of the valuable potentials of revised approaches to post-installation evaluations. Needed revisions should include comparisons of the actual results with estimates of: the probable results of having rejected the innovation, or of having delayed its adoption by 1, 2 or 3 years; the expected results at the time of the original decision; the apparent results of the technological and other innovational decisions made by competitors at the time when this firm made its original adoption decision. Revised approaches should then seek to explore the causes of the differences revealed by the preceding comparisons. In particular, it would be instructive to identify which differences were attributable to technological, economic or market factors; which of these represented internal as over against external developments; and, finally, which might reasonably have been predicted at the time of the decision and which were clearly unpredictable.

As a result of such more comprehensive insights into the complex patterns and multiple determinants of the actual effects of technological innovations, consideration might be given to enriching the past objectives, coverage and methods of *ex ante* evaluations. For example, in defining the objectives on the basis of which choices are to be made among alternative innovations, the need might well be recognized to dig beneath the generalized objective of improving profitability and to concentrate more sharply on the specific product, process, cost and other adjustment targets involved in bettering past performance—thereby providing more precise criteria both for choosing among the options being considered and also for evaluating post-installation results. Moreover, instead of merely comparing the relative net benefits of alternative innovations, efforts should be made to clarify the technological and economic assumptions underlying them, and also to indicate the margins of error likely to be involved—including any relevant references to the results of *ex post* evaluations. More particularly, evaluations of prospective technological innovations should seek to specify: the sources and expected magnitudes of the estimated superiority of recommended innovations over current facilities (whether introduced as replacements within present plants, or, if relevant, as parts of new plants); the factor price and other assumptions involved in converting expected technological improvements into economic benefits; and estimated advantages and disadvantages of adoption now versus deferring adoption, including specification of associated assumptions concerning the concurrent behavior of competitors.

Another by-product of attempts to determine the *ex post* effects of technological innovations more effectively may be recognition of the need to change some of the categories commonly used to assess the productivity and cost effects of prospective innovations. Specifically, measures must be designed to take account of changes in input qualities, the nature of processing requirements, the shifting of processing tasks to other operating units, improvements in process flexibility and alterations in product quality. These tend to alter both the physical magnitudes and economic value of productive contributions and yet have been largely or wholly ignored by prevailing measures, which

focus solely on changes in input and output quantities, assuming no significant changes in their qualitative attributes.

## REFERENCES

1. BAIER K & RESCHER N (Eds) (1969) *Values and the Future.* Free Press, New York, USA.
2. EILON S, GOLD B & TILLEY RPR (1973) Measuring the quality of economic forecasts. *Omega* 1(2), 217–227.
3. EILON S, GOLD B & SOESAN J (1976) *Applied Productivity Analysis for Industry.* Pergamon Press, Oxford, UK.
4. GOLD B (1964) Industry growth patterns: theory and empirical findings. *J. Ind. Econ.* XIII(1), 53–73. Reprinted in [6].
5. GOLD B (1969) The decision framework for major technological innovations. In [1].
6. GOLD B (1971) *Explorations in Managerial Economics: Productivity, Costs, Technology and Growth.* Macmillan, London, UK; Basic Books, New York, USA.
7. GOLD B (1974) From backcasting towards forecasting. *Omega* 2(2), 209–223.
8. GOLD B (Ed.) (1975) *Technological Change: Economics, Management and Environment.* Pergamon Press, Oxford, UK.
9. GOLD B (1977) On the shaky foundations of capital budgeting. *California Mgmt Rev.* XIX(2), 51–60. Reprinted in [12].
10. GOLD B (1978) Some shortcomings of research on the diffusion of industrial technology. In [15]; reprinted in [12].
11. GOLD B, ROSEGGER G & PEIRCE WS (1970) Diffusion of major technological innovations in US iron and steel manufacturing. *Jl Ind. Econ.* XVIII(3), 218–224. Reprinted in [8].
12. GOLD B, ROSEGGER G & BOYLAN JR MG (1980) *Evaluating Technological Innovations: Methods, Expectations and Findings.* Lexington Books, Lexington, Massachusetts, USA.
13. MARTINO JP (1979) Development of Predictive Models of the Diffusion of Innovations in Industry. *Report to the National Science foundation,* University of Dayton, USA.
14. NABSETH L & RAY GF (Eds) (1974) *The Diffusion of New Industrial Processes: an International Study.* Cambridge University Press, London, UK.
15. RADNOR M., FELLER I & ROGERS E (Eds) (1978) The Diffusion of Innovations: an Assessment. Report to the National Science Foundation. Northwestern University, Evanston, Illinois, USA.
16. RAY GF (1969) The diffusion of new technology. *Nat. Inst. Econ. Rev.* 48, 40–83. Reprinted in [14].
17. RAY GF & UHLMANN L (1979) *The Innovation Process in the Energy Industries.* Cambridge, University Press, London, UK.
18. SKEDDLE RW (1980) Empirical perspectives on major capital decisions. *Omega* 8(5), 553–567.
19. UHLMANN L (1979) The innovation process: empirical results. In [17].

ADDRESS FOR CORRESPONDENCE: *Professor Bela Gold, Department of Economics, Case Western Reserve University, Cleveland, Ohio OH 44106, USA.*

# [10]

*Journal of Marketing Management*, 1988, **3**, No. 3, 372–387

## Re-Innovation and Robust Designs: Producer and User Benefits

### Roy Rothwell and Paul Gardiner

*New waves of technologies have been sweeping through all industrial sectors in the 1980s. Increasingly, corporate managers have begun to use technology strategies as a major competitive tool. Within these strategies, there are at least a dozen different patterns of redesign and re-innovation. Overall, one of the most important philosophies has been development of robust design configurations. These robust designs have a product family of variants which meet changing market needs with benefits for both producers and users.*

## INTRODUCTION

With the emergence of new clusters of technologies during the 1980s, the ability to generate new product and process innovations has become an increasingly important concern for corporate management. During recent years the term "technology strategy" has appeared with increasing frequency in the management literature, and technology strategies are becoming an essential and core component in overall corporate strategies.

Following the pioneering work of the Boston Consulting Group (1972), many companies during the 1970s adopted so-called "learning curve" strategies, seeking aggressively to gain market share in order to increase accumulated "experience", thereby pushing down production costs. With high rates of product technological change associated with the newly emerging technology clusters, scale and experience effects are likely to be more difficult to achieve as product cycles shorten and product characteristics alter rapidly. Even where products are changing rapidly, however, and market requirements are heterogeneous, firms might, through adopting the appropriate design strategies, achieve both effective scale economies and "shared experience" benefits.

Even during periods in which overall rates of technological change are high, there will be relatively few radical innovations occurring in each sector of industry. Once a new "type" of product has been introduced, e.g. the jet engine or the personal micro computer, subsequent "new" products in the line will be major or minor re-design variations on the original theme. While the original landmark innovations, and the powerful intellectual ideas embodied in them, are unquestionably extremely

372

important, arguably, the greater volume of all product process-embodied technological change consists of a myriad of relatively small design modifications which are part of the extremely important re-design process (see Figure 1).

The point is, what the innovation and marketing literature refer to as a "new product" often is not new in all of its aspects; rather it is a re-design of an existing product containing only limited additional technical novelty. The re-design process (see Figure 2) can be strategically managed to confer considerable benefits on both the producer and the user of the emerging series of products, and it is a process in which the user can himself play a significant role (Rothwell 1986).

Research by the authors has identified a number of characteristic patterns of re-design (see Table 1), and below we will give several examples of how firms have re-designed products by "combining the existing with the new". We will then introduce the concept of the robust design, which is a special type of design capable of evolving into a design family of variants which meet a variety of changing market requirements.

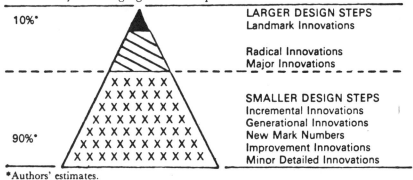

*Authors' estimates.

FIGURE 1 Technical change

## RE-DESIGN COMBINING THE EXISTING WITH THE NEW

The Black and Decker heatgun is an example of a design that initially employed largely existing technology, but which opened up a new and fast growing user segment for the firm. For both amateur and professional decorators, paintstripping using chemical treatments is unpleasant and potentially hazardous. The various types of radiant heater and flame-type strippers also have a variety of operational and safety drawbacks. At the beginning of the 1980s, Black and Decker conceived the idea of a new type of heatgun for paintstripping; however, tradition is strong in the decorating business and there was considerable uncertainty over whether or not the consumer would adopt a new tool. The design of a wholly new tool would have carried with it high development, testing and production costs, and market failure would have resulted in an unwelcome financial loss to the firm.

374                    ROY ROTHWELL AND PAUL GARDINER

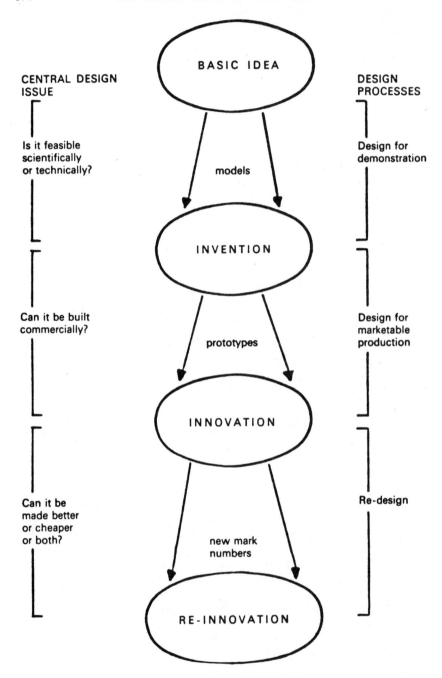

FIGURE 2    States of technical change.

## RE-INNOVATION AND ROBUST DESIGNS 375

TABLE 1 Twelve patterns of re-design.

| | |
|---|---|
| Re-design at | *Conceptualisation State* (e.g. the planned permanently manned US space station was first based on a single power tower concept, next around a dual keel design, and more recently on a somewhat simplified and reduced version of that previous configuration). |
| Re-design at | *Prototype State* (e.g. BMX bikes developed out of small wheeled "shopper" type bicycle designs by Alex Moulton. Originally the small wheeled prototype bikes had a monocoque or unitised metal body structure. They worked alright except it was like riding on a tin drum, and so it had to be replaced by the more traditional tubular steel frames). |
| Re-design with a | *"Leading Edge" Supplier* (e.g. Rediffusion has been one of the world leaders in flight simulators. Part of the reason for this has been the advanced "leading edge" computers supplied by Gould to Rediffusion. Each new generation of computer allows for a new re-design of flight simulators with increased sophistication). |
| Re-design by | *Technical Diffusion* (e.g. the innovative wide chord fan blade design for Rolls-Royce's RB211-535E4 is now being scaled up and scaled down to be diffused into the re-design of bigger and smaller engines). |
| Re-design using a | *Succession of Minor Details* (e.g. following the fuel crisis of the early seventies, locomotive diesel engine designers were able to improve fuel efficiencies by about 2 per cent per year over a sustained period of years). |
| Re-design with | *Incremental Subassembly Changes* (e.g. compared to Boeing's 747-300, the new 747-400 will have an increased wing span of more than 18 ft. due to extensions and the addition of winglets, additional variable camber leading edge flaps, a new 3,000 US gallon tail fuel tank to increase the range by 320 nautical miles, and a regaged wingbox to increase the maximum brake release gross weight to 850,000 lb. Also there is a new, two man, digital cockpit pioneered in Boeing's 757/767s). |
| Re-design using | *New Materials* (e.g. automotive bumpers are frequently now just one large ABS moulding which combines structural, styling, aerodynamic qualities and mounting points for accessories—formerly these features could only be obtained using a mix of different materials and sub-assemblies). |
| Re-design for | *Retrofitting* (e.g. the Didcot electric power station needed to be refurbished. With new computer-aided-designed turbine blades, and instrumentation and control systems overall thermal efficiency has improved and millions of pounds are being saved annually). |
| Re-design of a | *New Generation* (e.g. British Hovercraft's AP1-88 is a total re-design with a simpler welded aluminium structure, separate lift and propulsion systems with industrial diesel power units, rubber belt drives and shrouded fixed pitch propellers). |
| Re-design using | *Hybrid Technologies* (e.g. fully digitalised watches appeared some time ago, but more recently there have appeared watches that have a traditional face and hands but with a digital drive thus combining old and new technologies). |
| Re-design using | *Radical Technologies* (e.g. conventional inertial navigational systems based on gyroscopes are being replaced by new ones using ring laser technologies, and shortly new fibre-optic based gyros will be introduced). |
| Re-design a | *New Integrated package/System* (e.g. Rediffusion's very advanced flight simulator for Boeing's 747-300 combines enhanced visual displays, computing and instructional systems based on sophisticated Gould computers using the latest reflective memory techniques). |

Black and Decker's solution to this high-risk situation was to adopt a deliberate strategy of "designing something new from something old", i.e. a heatgun derived from an electric drill. As things transpired, this represented an extremely shrewd piece of strategic design management. In order to transform the drill into a heatgun, Black and Decker simply replaced the transmission and chuck sub-assemblies with a new heater element and nozzle. This meant that the new tool contained a motor, fan, case and switch which were all reliable and well-proven electric drill components. Because of this, the heatgun was a marginal cost design since two-thirds of it derived from existing drill production lines operating with high economies of scale and (shared) learning curve economies. In addition, two-thirds of the parts for servicing and repairs were already inventoried and only a few new parts for the heater sub-assembly needed to be added, and development and safety testing requirements could be met by concentrating only on the few new additional components. From the point of view of the user, the heatgun was cheaper than might have otherwise been the case, and the majority of its components were tried and tested, thus reducing the reliability problems that often occur with totally new devices.

As things turned out, the heatgun rapidly gained acceptance in the marketplace, but Black and Decker resisted the temptation to rest on its laurels. The firm did not attempt to maximise short-terms profits on its inexpensive, low entry risk design, but quickly embarked on a vigorous programme of re-design. Two years after the introduction of the first hybrid model, a second generation model was introduced. A custom-designed smaller, lighter and cheaper motor was employee because the heatgun required a less powerful and simpler motor than the drill. In turn the balance and ergonomics of the tool could be re-optimised with a new design for the case. This re-design was so complete that the new model contained virtually no parts in common with the drill-derived version and, more importantly from the point of view of commercial manufacturing, the number of component parts was halved. The heatgun, now in its third generation via a process of continued re-design, has evolved into a comprehensive design family of variants, ranging from a basic single temperature/air flow version to a top line version with five electronically controlled heat settings and two airflow rates. In both consumer and industrial versions, a wide range of user price and non-price requirements are being met. The heatgun family has grown into one of the most rapidly established power tool segments that Black and Decker has ever been instrumental in creating.

A second example of a design combining the existing with the new to produce, in this case, something containing radically new features, is the Canon laser photocopier. The laser photocopier produces a digital signal which, unlike the analogue system of its conventional predecessors, can be electronically digitally processed or stored, or transmitted simultaneously to a number of distant slave printers. This means that photocopiers can now become an integral part of office information technology systems.

RE-INNOVATION AND ROBUST DESIGNS                    377

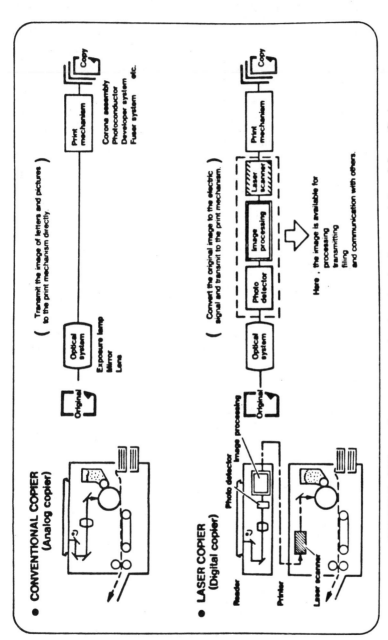

FIGURE 3   Difference between conventional copier (analogue copier) and Laser Copier (digital copier).
*Source:* Canon Laser Copier, 1986 unpaged.

The differences between Canon's conventional (analogue) copier and its recently introduced laser (digital) copier are shown in Figure 3. It can be seen that the laser copier retains the well proven paper handling and optical systems, and the developing, transfer and fixing corona assemblies of the print mechanism, of Canon's conventional copiers. For signal digitalisation, an innovative laser and electronic information processing step has been inserted between the original optical and print systems.

There are severe requirements of the electro-mechanical components of conventional copiers. Having a working lifetime from hundreds of thousands up to millions of copies, and having to handle dusty toners and papers, the engineering design specifications must be stringent. Given the existence of a tried, tested and reliable electro-mechanical copier subsystems, Canon saw no need to design a completely new system around its digital processing sub-assembly. Instead, Canon capitalised on the advantages of the existing subsystems (scale economies, experience curve economies, familiarity to service engineers, distributed inventories of spare parts, proven reliability, customer familiarity, etc.) and combined them with the new electronic subsystem to produce the radically new laser digital copier.

## ROBUST DESIGNS AND DESIGN FAMILIES

In ordinary terms, design robustness implies reliability in use and the ability to handle harsh treatment. Here the term "robust design" has a different and rather special meaning: a robust design is one that has sufficient inherent design flexibility or "technological slack" to enable it to evolve into a significant "design family" of variants. Essentially, a robust design is one that can satisfy the evolving needs of a "set" of user segments. For the manufacturer it offers shared experience benefits and economies of scale combined with economies of scope; for the user it offers maximum choice from among a set of well-proven products. Our model for the robust design is given in Figure 4 and it can, perhaps, be best illustrated with a number of practical examples.

Figure 5 shows the evolution of the original Rolls-Royce RB211 aeroengine into a design family of up-rated, re-rated and de-rated variants. For production and servicing reasons, the original RB211 configuration was a "simplified" design consisting of seven basic modules. This modular configuration inherently allows for different modifications to meet a variety of user thrust and performance requirements. Thus, by removing the large, front, low pressure fan module and replacing it with a scaled-down fan, it was possible to produce the highly successful de-rated (i.e. lower thrust) 535C engine. At the same time, the well proven intermediate and high pressure stages of the original RB211 were retained in the 535C engine design. By running them more easily, their service and performance specifications were substantially improved. This was a user orientated improvement for the airline operators which was highly valued since airlines

# RE-INNOVATION AND ROBUST DESIGNS 379

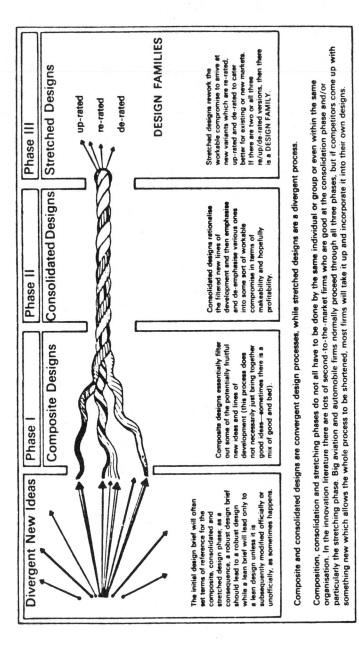

**Divergent New Ideas**

The initial design brief will often set terms of reference for the composite, consolidated and stretched design phase; as a consequence, a robust design brief should lead to a robust design while a lean brief will lead only to a lean design unless it is subsequently modified officially or unofficially, as sometimes happens.

**Phase I**

**Composite Designs**

Composite designs essentially filter out some of the potentially fruitful new ideas and lines of development (this process does not necessarily just bring together good ideas—sometimes there is a mix of good and bad).

**Phase II**

**Consolidated Designs**

Consolidated designs rationalise the filtered new lines of development and then emphasise and de-emphasise various ones into some sort of workable compromise in terms of makeability and hopefully profitability.

**Phase III**

**Stretched Designs**

up-rated
re-rated
de-rated

**DESIGN FAMILIES**

Stretched designs rework the workable compromise to arrive at new variants which are re-rated, up-rated and de-rated to cater better for existing or new markets. If there are two or all three re/up/de-rated versions, then there is a DESIGN FAMILY.

Composite and consolidated designs are convergent design processes, while stretched designs are a divergent process.

Composition, consolidation and stretching phases do not all have to be done by the same individual or group or even within the same organisation. In the innovation literature there are lots of second-to-the-market firms who are good at the consolidation phase and/or particularly the stretching phase. Big aviation and automobile firms normally proceed through all three phases, but if competitors come up with something new which allows the whole process to be shortened, most firms will take it up and incorporate it into their own designs.

FIGURE 4   The evolution of robust designs.

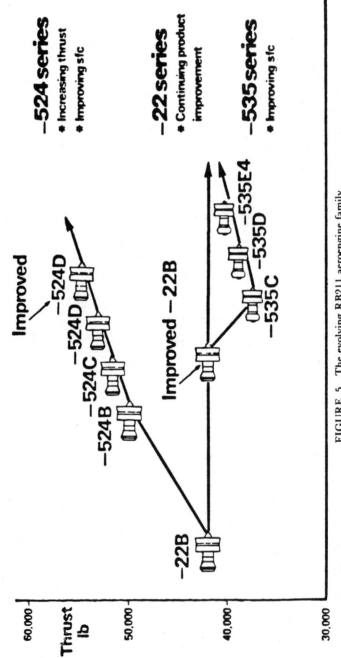

FIGURE 5   The evolving RB211 aeroengine family.

*Source:* RB211–22B Technology and description, Rolls-Royce Limited, TS2100, Issue 20, July 1980. Updated and revised by authors to 1987 figures.

## RE-INNOVATION AND ROBUST DESIGNS                          381

are concerned about not just initial performance and cost characteristics, but those over the whole life cycle of an engine's use. The subsequent re-design and introduction of a new innovative wide chord fan blade design in the front low pressure compressor module resulted in the improved 535E4 engine. This innovative wide chord blade design is currently being diffused back into the RB211 family to improve further the fuel and thrust ratings of the up-rated variants. The designed-in modular based robustness of the initial RB211 was crucial in enabling these major modifications to be undertaken. The family concept has clear advantages for Rolls-Royce in terms of R&D economies, production economies, spares supply, customer credibility (design familiarity), customer support services and general learning economies. The customer gains the advantages of a wider model choice, faster producer response to satisfy evolving requirements, parts commonality and cumulative learning effects in both the use and servicing of the engines. Even now the story has not yet ended. The RB211–524D4D engine with a thrust of 58,000 lb. is to be certified in 1988, and there is now a distinct possibility of evolving the –524D4D into the RB211–700 in the 65,000 lb. thrust class. Lower thrust versions are also likely to be stretched further.

While so far we have described robust designs and design families for physically fairly large and complex technological objects, our same arguments remain valid at the micro level—in this case microelectronics. The chip or microelectronic revolution began with Jack Killby's demonstration of the first integrated circuit to senior staff members of Texas Instruments in September of 1958. Within just three years, the commercial production of integrated circuits had begun. Significantly, even then, these first generation integrated circuits were not just a collection of one-off type devices, but rather they constituted a whole family of devices. Towards the end of 1961, Texas Instruments instituted a six month "crash programme" to design, produce and to begin delivery of a family of new integrated circuits to meet the requirements of the US Air Force's Minuteman II procurement programme. To this end, Texas Instruments had acquired from Fairchild Electronics the new planar processing technology which was given a robust manufacturing configuration such that a family of devices could be produced. Having begun the microelectronics revolution this way, the pattern has subsequently been repeated, first with small scale integrated devices, then medium scale, then large and very large scale integrated devices.

In the 1970s, one of the most dynamic new areas in microelectronics was the development of micro processing units (mpu's) for personal computers. Motorola has been one of the industry's leaders in supplying advanced mpu's. Towards the end of the 1970s, the technology shifted from 8-bit to 16-bit processors. At that time Motorola, while supplying these new chips, was looking forward to the next generation of 32-bit chips for the 1980s. Significantly, Motorola made the strategic decision to not just produce one new 32-bit processor, but rather a family of products that has become known as the 68000 series. This new 68000 series has been a related family of devices that all have the same basic underlying architecture, such that each successive processor will do all that the previous one in the series could do, but with further enhanced capabilities. For instance, the more powerful 68030 processor, which is now being launched on to the market, is fully downward compatible with the previous 68020 processor. This design family philosophy has two important consequences. Firstly, software companies do not have to re-write completely all their programmes for each of Motorola's new and more powerful processors. Secondly, the personal computer users, who have Motorola processors in their machines, can easily transfer over software and data from the earlier to the later and more powerful pc's. This ability to upgrade and to transfer over information and programmes is very attractive to both software writers and pc users.

Often in the past, design stretching was achieved more or less on an ad hoc basis when the original product had been over-engineered. Today, an increasing number of companies are deliberately designing "stretch" into their products. The IBM PC personal computer, for example, is in reality a family of products; because of the deliberate adoption of an "open architecture" it has proved possible to expand and modify the original model and there are now six main variants on the market. IBM's most recent generation of computers, the Personal System/2, is again a family of machines designed to meet a wide range of user requirements.

Other robust designs are the Boeing 707 and 747; the Ford Cortina; Canon photocopiers; and Redifussion's BAe 146 flight simulator. A number of "lean" designs, i.e. designs that lack built-in stretch, have also been identified, examples being the Comet aircraft and the British Leyland 1100 car (Rothwell and Gardiner 1984). Clearly the notion of design robustness, yielding an extended design family of variants, is a powerful concept that has important implications for companies' long-term design and development strategies. While the (short-term) entry costs for a robust design might be higher, the (long-term) strategic benefits can be very considerable indeed.

Boeings' 757 and 767 are each design families in their own right. That is, for each family there is a base series, and then there are derived series with more seats, or extended range versions, or both. Interestingly, Boeings' 757 and 767 also constitute a Super Family.

Development costs of modern commercial aircraft are now so high that they have to be spread over production runs of hundreds of aircraft. The projected sales for a 757 type aircraft (i.e. short/medium range, narrow body) and a 767 type aircraft (i.e. medium range, wide body) were not high enough to justify two completely different and expensive development programmes. Under these circumstances, the problem faced by Boeing was how to achieve economies in technology at both the development and the production stages—particularly given that they are quite different aircraft. As a rule of thumb, the cost profile for modern commercial jets is approximately one-third airframe, one-third engines and one-third avionics.

Given the considerable difference in airframes, the one area in which design commonality could be achieved was on the avionics side. Both the 757 and 767 have very similar advanced electronic screen-based two-man cockpits. Moreover, the majority of avionics system cost is incurred in writing software, which could again be shared across the two aircraft. These new digital electronic screen-based systems represent a major new generational step in the evolution of the design trajectory for commercial aircraft cockpit technology.

For the producer, Boeing, this commonality of avionics offers economies of scale in the technical development programmes and on the production, ordering and assembly side. For the users, the airlines, it meant flight crews for one aircraft could be more quickly qualified for other aircraft in the super family. In addition, servicing and maintenance are considerably facilitated since the 757 and 767 avionics systems have similar servicing menus, diagnostics and electronic fault memory systems.

Since the commercial introduction of the 757 and 767 models during the past few years, Boeing has announced a further addition to the 747 family. With around ten main variants already in the 747 family, the newest and largest—the 747–400 series—is due to enter service in 1988. With advanced aluminium alloys, new winglets, improved engines and more fuel tanks, this newest number of the 747 family will fly further and with more passengers than ever before. In addition, many of the features of the advanced two-man digital cockpit of 757/767 family have been carried over into the design of the flight deck for the 747–400 models, with the result that the number of gauges and instruments have been reduced by 50 per cent and the flight engineer, as the third member of the crew, is no longer needed. For airline operators this will reduce the flight crew salary budget by almost one-third. Furthermore, the cockpit bulkhead could be moved forward, which meant that an extra row of four 38 inch pitch business class seats could be added to the forward compartment. Finally, the possible upgrading of 757/767 flight crew could be done more easily for the new 747–400 models. Families and super families clearly promise many benefits to both producers and users.

## THE HOVERCRAFT: A LEAN TO ROBUST TRANSITION

From its invention in 1954 and the first practical demonstration using a coffee can test rig and balsa wood model in 1955, it was ten years before the world's first commercial hovercraft—the SR N6—was introduced in 1965. This model weighed 10 tons and had a seating capacity of 38. This was followed in 1968 by the 165 ton Mountbatten Class with 254 seats and 30 car spaces. The Mountbatten Class was subsequently "stretched", leading eventually to the Super-4 version in 1978. This had a retro-fitted centre section which lengthened the craft by 55 feet allowing passenger accommodation to be increased to 416 seats and car spaces to 55.

While the "SR N6" series of hovercraft clearly contained a degree of "stretch" it was, for a variety of reasons, difficult and expensive to extend into a design family of variants having a variety of options available simultaneously. The main reason for this was its complicated and rather finely balanced design which, for historical reasons, owed much to aircraft construction techniques. In contrast, the AP1–88 class, first introduced in 1982, allowed for its evolution into a design family of variants.

A number of the main technical differences between the SR N6-type hovercraft and the AP1–88-type are summarised in Table 2. Essentially, the AP1–88 is a simpler, less finely balanced craft in which a number of crucial operating features (e.g. lift and propulsion) were de-coupled, thus enabling various operating parameters to be altered without unacceptably degrading the others. When combined, these changes permitted simplified ordering of off-the-shelf components, easier construction and the enhanced ability to be able to produce simultaneously a number of variants. Thus, the AP1–88 is available in three versions with either a short cab, a half-cabin or a full cabin, depending on the mix of passengers, freight and light vehicles required by the operator. In other words, the AP1–88 has the characteristics of an early-stage design family.

The hovercraft example is interesting for a number of reasons. In the first place, it gives some idea of the basis for design robustness; a degree of design flexibility that enables changes to be made in various operating characteristics without unacceptably degrading other desired operating characteristics. Robust designs are often design compromises, providing a practical "package" of operating features with built-in design flexibility; they are rarely optimised along one specific performance specification, e.g. miles per gallon or speed. Secondly, the hovercraft story suggests that it is not always the most sophisticated or "high tech" design that is the most appropriate; compared to the SR N6, the AP1–88 was a much simpler, "lower tech" design. Thirdly, the AP1–88 was the result of close collaboration between the producer and a main user, which illustrates the importance of strong producer-user linkages during innovation and re-innovation (Rothwell and Gardiner 1985).

TABLE 2

Hovercraft: Lean and robust design characteristics.

| *Lean: SR N6 craft* | *Robust: AP1–88 craft* |
|---|---|
| Gas turbine drive | Standard, air-cooled diesel drive |
| Rivetted aircraft construction | Welded marine type construction |
| Complex linked lift and propulsion system | Split lift and propulsion systems |
| Complex geared transmissions | Toothed belt drives |
| Variable-pitch pylon mounted propellors | Ducted, body-mounted, fixed-pitch propellors |

RE-INNOVATION AND ROBUST DESIGNS                385

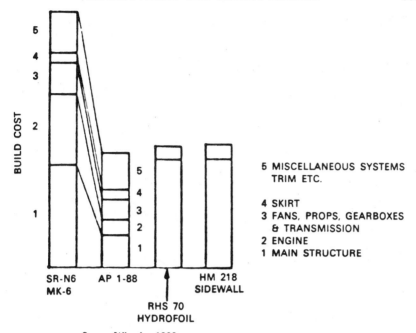

Source: Wheeler 1983.
FIGURE 6   Comparison of build costs.

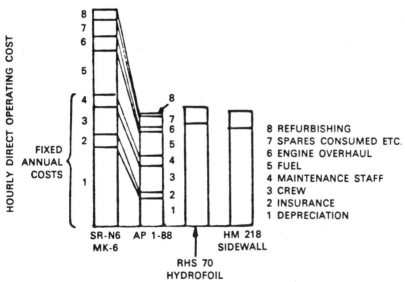

Source: Wheeler, 1983.
FIGURE 7   Comparison of hourly direct operating costs.

Figures 6 and 7 illustrate the cost advantages to the producer and the user respectively in shifting to the simplified AP1–88 design. On both the construction and operating sides, costs were significantly reduced when compared to the earlier SR N6 type of hovercraft and the AP1–88 was cost competitive with both hydrofoil and sidewall type craft. With up-rated, de-rated and re-rated versions available, the AP1–88 design family is able to cater for a wider range of user specifications.

## CONCLUSIONS

Theories of innovation based on "technology push" or "market pull" have proved to be overly simplistic. Producers and users of innovations need to interact during the designed development process, a technology/market coupling which generally yields significant benefits to both—especially in the area of re-innovation which dominates much of the contemporary "real" industrial world. Producers who have developed robust designs are able to manufacture a family of up-rated, re-rated and de-rated products which can meet evolving and changing user requirements. Product families, with "variations on a theme", for the producer, economies of scale in research and development, manufacturing, marketing, sales and servicing; and, for the user, they offer learning from experience, the enhanced possibility of user-inspired modifications, a wider range of alternative price-performance packages, and rapid adaptations to changing environments. In an ever changing world, robust designs and product families are strategically more flexible and economic than leanly configured designs which only satisfy transient producer or user requirements. Strategically, robust designs reduce uncertainties and minimise risks for producers and users. Of course, in a perfect and stable world, with perfect knowledge, producers and users could establish optimum designs for all their individual product and process requirements. Unfortunately, this situation rarely obtains in practice, and, strategically, it is frequently better to opt for a robust (compromise) design configuration rather than for a lean (optimum) one in order better to cope with uncertainty in the marketplace. And, if it can be seen that a product or a process already has a lean design, then at the re-innovation stage it should be more robustly re-configured. Having said all this, there is still considerable scope for managerial judgement in arriving at the relative priorities and significance of the various elements in the package of price and non-price specifications that can make up a robust design with its benefits for producers and users. We have indicated that there are at least twelve patterns of re-design and re-innovation, and there is certainly room for more. The important point is that product and process technologies can and should be strategically managed—with robust designs and product families being one of the ways to achieve this aim.

# References

The Boston Consulting Group (1972), *Perspectives on Experience*, Boston, USA.

Rothwell, R. (1986), "Innovation and re-innovation: a role for the user", *Journal of Marketing Management*, 2(2), Winter.

Rothwell, R. and Gardiner, P. (1984), "Design and competition in engineering", *Long Range Planning*, 17(3), pp. 78–91.

Rothwell, R. and Gardiner, P. (1985), "Innovation, re-innovation and the role of the user: a case study of British hovercraft development", *Technovation*, 4(4).

Canon Laser Copier (1986), In-house publication.

Wheeler, R. L. (1983), *The British Hovercraft Corporation's AP1–88 Hovercraft AIAA–83–0634*, AIAA/SNAME/ASNE, 7th Marine Systems Conference, New Orleans.

# [11]

# The new product learning cycle *

Modesto A. MAIDIQUE

*Department of Management, University of Miami, Coral Gables, FL 33124, USA, and Stanford University, Stanford, CA 94305, USA*

Billie Jo ZIRGER

*Department of Industrial Engineering and Engineering Management, Stanford University, Stanford, CA 94305, USA*

Final version received August 1985

This paper summarizes our extensive study ( $n = 158$ ) of new product success and failure in the electronics industry. Conventional "external factor" explanations of commercial product failure based on the state of the economy, foreign competition and lack of funding, were found not to be major contributors to product failure in this industry. On the other hand, factors that can be strongly influenced by management such as coordination of the create, make and market functions, the quality and frequency of customers' communications, value of the product to the customer, and the quality and efficiency of technical management explained the majority of the variance between successful and unsuccessful products. From these findings a framework for understanding and managing the new product development process that places learning and communication in the center stage was developed.

Successes and failures in our sample were strongly interrelated. The knowledge gained from failures was often instrumental in achieving subsequent successes, while success in turn often resulted in unlearning the very process that led to the original success. This observation has led us to postulate a new product "learning cycle model" in which commercial successes and failures alternate in an irregular pattern of learning and unlearning.

* This research was funded by the Department of Industrial Engineering and Engineering Management at Stanford University. The authors wish to thank Professor Warren Hausman, Department Chairman, for his encouragement and support during this investigation. The authors have benefited from discussions of an early draft of this paper with Mel Horwitch, Nathan Rosenberg, and with members of the Stanford Economics Department TIP Seminar and from the suggestion of an anonymous *Research Policy* reviewer.

Research Policy 14 (1985) 299–313
North-Holland

## 1. Introduction

Many factors influence product success. That much is generally agreed upon by researchers in the field. The product, the firm's organizational linkages, the competitive environment, and the market can all play important roles. On the other hand, the results of research on new product success and failure [1] is reminiscent of George Orwell's *Animal Farm* in that some factors seem to be "more equal than others." But, exactly which set of factors predominates seems to be, at least in part, a function of both the methodology and the specific population studied by the researcher [2].

*The Standford Innovation Project (SINPRO)*

In a survey of 158 products in the electronics industry, half successes and half failures [2], we developed our own list of major determinants of new product success. The eight principal factors we identified are listed below roughly in the order of their statistical significance. Products are likely to be successful if:

(1) The developing organization, through in-depth understanding of the customers and the marketplace, introduces a product with a high performance to cost ratio.
(2) The create, make, and market functions are well coordinated and interfaced.
(3) The product provides a high contribution margin to the firm.
(4) The new product benefits significantly from the existing technological and marketing strengths of the developing business units.

300                          *M.A. Maidique and B.J. Zirger / New product learning cycle*

(5) The developing organization is proficient in marketing and commits a significant amount of its resources to selling and promoting the product.

(6) The R&D process is well-planned and coordinated.

(7) There is a high level of management support for the product from the product conception stage stage to its launch into the market.

(8) The product is an early market entrant.

The study that led to these conclusions consisted of two exploratory surveys described in detail elsewhere [2]. The first survey was open ended and was divided into two sections. In the first part we asked the respondent to select a pair of innovations, one success and one failure. Successes and failures were differentiated by financial criteria. The second section of the original survey asked each respondent to list in his own words the factors which he believed contributed to the product's outcome. Seventy-nine senior managers of high technology companies completed this questionnaire.

The follow-up survey was structured into 60 variables derived from three sources: (1) analysis of the results of the first survey, (2) review of the open literature and; (3) the authors' own extensive experience in high technology product development. Each respondent, on the basis of the original two innovations identified in survey 1, was asked to determine for each variable whether it impacted the outcome of the success, failure, neither or both. Survey 2 was completed by 59 of the original 79 managers.

The results from these two initial surveys were reported earlier [2]. To summarize, we conducted several statistical analyses for each variable and innovation type including determination of means and standard deviations, binomial significance, and clustering. Table 1 shows the binomial significance for the 37 variables which differentiated between success and failure. Combining our statistical results with the content analysis of the initial survey, we derived the eight propositions listed earlier.

Using these eight factors as a starting point, we then developed a block diagram of the new product development process that focuses on the product characteristics and the functional interrelationships and competences that are most influential in determining new product success or failure (fig. 1). In our view the innovation process is a constant

struggle between the forces of change and the status quo. Differences in perceptions between the innovator and the customer and also between the groups that make the building blocks of the innovation process – engineering, marketing and manufacturing – all conspire to shunt new product development or to deflect it from the path of success. Effective management attempts to integrate these constituencies and to allocate resources in a way that makes the new possible. These ideas are the basis of a model of the new product development process that we describe more fully and validate empirically in a forthcoming paper [3].

The eight propositions resulting from our analysis were the objective "truths" that resulted from statistical analysis of our large sample of new product successes and failures. Though coincident in their salient aspects with the work of others [1], these results, however, did not fully satisfy us. Had we missed important variables in our structured surveys? Had our respondents understood our questions? Had we failed to detect significant relations between some of the variables we identified – or between these and some yet undiscovered factors? How valid were our final generalizations?

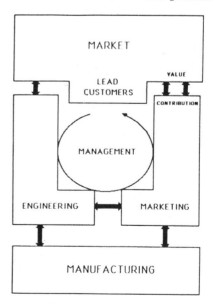

Figure 1. Diagram of the critical elements of the new product development process.

*The Economics of Innovation*

Table 1

Significant variables from survey 2 grouped by index variable

| Successful innovations were: | No. of observations | Cumulative binomial | Significance rating |
|---|---|---|---|
| (1) Better matched with user needs | | | |
| better matched to customer needs | 44 | 8.53 E-09 | + + + |
| developed by teams which more fully understood user needs | 44 | 1.27 E-05 | + + + |
| accepted more quickly by users | 49 | 7.01 E-04 | – – – |
| (2) Planned more effectively and efficiently | | | |
| forecast more accurately (market) | 43 | 1.25 E-07 | + + + |
| developed with a clearer market strategy | 45 | 1.24 E-04 | + + + |
| formalized on paper sooner | 45 | 3.30 E-03 | + + + |
| developed with less variance between actual and budgeted expenses | 46 | 2.70 E-02 | – – |
| expected initially to be more commercially successful | 42 | 8.21 E-02 | + |
| (3) Higher in benefit-to-cost | | | |
| priced with higher profit margins | 51 | 6.06 E-08 | + + + |
| allowed greater pricing flexibility | 52 | 1.02 E-06 | + + + |
| more significant with respect to benefit-to-cost ratio | 43 | 6.86 E-03 | + + + |
| (4) Developed by better-coupled organizations | | | |
| developed by better-coupled functional divisions | 39 | 1.68 E-07 | + + + |
| (5) More efficiently developed | | | |
| less plagued by after-sales problems | 35 | 5.84 E-05 | – – – |
| developed with fewer personnel changes on the project team | 28 | 6.27 E-03 | – – – |
| impacted by fewer changes during production | 41 | 1.38 E-02 | – – |
| developed with a more experienced project team | 39 | 2.66 E-02 | + + |
| changed less after production commenced | 47 | 7.19 E-02 | – |
| developed on a more compressed time schedule | 39 | 9.98 E-02 | + |
| (6) More actively marketed and sold | | | |
| more actively publicized and advertised | 39 | 4.74 E-03 | + + + |
| promoted by a larger sales force | 28 | 6.27 E-03 | + + + |
| coupled with a marketing effort to educate users | 37 | 1.00 E-02 | + + |
| (7) Closer to the firm's areas of expertise | | | |
| aided more by in-house basic research | 25 | 7.32 E-03 | + + + |
| required fewer new marketing channels | 25 | 7.32 E-03 | – – – |
| closer to the main business area of firm | 30 | 8.06 E-03 | + + + |
| more influenced by corporate reputation | 29 | 3.07 E-02 | + + |
| less dependent on existing products in the market | 36 | 6.62 E-02 | – |
| required less diversification from traditional markets | 24 | 7.58 E-02 | – |
| (8) Introduced to the market earlier than competition | | | |
| in the market longer before competing products introduced | 44 | 1.13 E-02 | + + |
| first-to-the-market type products | 39 | 1.19 E-02 | + + |
| more offensive innovations | 46 | 5.19 E-02 | + |
| generally not second-to-the-market | 36 | 6.62 E-02 | – |
| (9) Supported more by management | | | |
| supported more by senior management potentially more impactful on the careers of | 31 | 1.66 E-03 | + + + |
| the project team members | 32 | 5.51 E-02 | + |
| developed with a more senior project leader | 39 | 9.98 E-02 | + |
| (10) Technically superior | | | |
| closer to the state-of-the-art technology | 36 | 3.26 E-02 | + + |
| more difficult for competition to copy | 45 | 3.62 E-02 | + + |
| more radical with respect to world technology | 42 | 8.21 E-02 | + |

And most important, what were the underlying conceptual messages in this list of factors? In short, we were concerned that perhaps our statistical analysis might have blurred important ideas.

Reflecting on his research on the individual psyche, Carl Jung once put it this way [4]:

> The statistical method shows the facts in the light of the average, but does not give a picture of their empirical reality. While reflecting an indisputable aspect of reality, it can falsify the actual truth in a most misleading way.... The distinctive thing about real facts, however, is their individuality. Not to put too fine a point on it, one could say that the real picture consists of nothing but exceptions to the rule, and that, in consequence, reality has predominately the characteristic of irregularity.

Such irregularities have caused one of the most experienced researchers in the field to wonder out loud if any fundamental commonalities exist at all in new product successes. "Perhaps," Cooper observed [5], "the problem is so complex, and each case so unique, that attempts to develop generalized solutions are in vain."

## 2. Methodology

To address the concerns noted above, we prepared individual in-depth case studies for 40 of the original 158 products to search for methodological flaws or significant irregularities that might challenge the results of our statistical analysis (table 1). The case studies were prepared under the supervision of the authors by 45 graduate assistants [6]. Seventeen West Coast electronics firms which had participated in the 1982 Standford-AEA Executive Institute and in our original two surveys served as sites for the 20 case studies. This subset of the original product pairs served as the subject of analysis for the case studies. Two or more project assistants interviewed managers and technologists and prepared written reports that included interview transcripts or summaries, background information on the firm, the competitive environment, the product development process, the characteristics of each of the two products, validation of the original survey 2 and a critical review of the factors that contributed to success or failure in each

case. Overall, 101 managers and technologists were interviewed in 148 hours of interviews.

Most of the companies supplied the research teams with detailed financial, marketing and design information regarding each one of the products, including in some cases internal memoranda that traced the products' development histories. Because of the confidentiality of this data, we must not identify any of the firms, much as we would like to thank them for their contributions to the project. In some cases, to illustrate a point, we have chosen to use examples from the public domain, or from published cases we or others have written about, and we may mention a company by name; however, the companies that collaborated with the project are either left anonymous or given fictitious names which, when first introduced, are placed in quotation marks.

This paper reports how these case studies and the associated interview transcripts enriched our earlier conclusions. In section 3 we begin to clarify the terms that we had employed in our survey, specifically "user needs" and "product value". In section 4 we explore the meaning of success. The case studies led us to expand our concept of success and failure beyond the one-dimensional confines of financial return. Indeed, success and failure often appear to be close partners, not adversaries, in organizational and business development. Finally in section 5 we postulate an evolutionary model of new product development, which we believe leads to a better understanding of the relationship between success and failure. For many of the propositions we present here, we lack the analytical support that underlies the eight factors identified in our original research. Nonetheless, we feel that these findings, which we hope will help to illuminate further research – including our own – are as important as our statistical results.

## 3. Defining "user needs" and "product value"

The detailed case studies largely reinforced the principal findings of the overall study [2]. But the case studies also enriched some of the findings from structured questionnaires by providing fresh insights on several of the key variables. In this paper, we focus on the most important and perhaps the least specific variable, "understanding of the market" and "user needs" which is believed to result in products with "high value."

One of the principal findings of our large sample survey was that "user needs" and "customer and market understanding" are of central importance in predicting new product success or failure, a result that parallels the findings of the pioneering SAPPHO pairwise comparison study [7]. This result, however, does little to illuminate how a firm goes about achieving such understanding. What's more, citing user needs ex post facto as a key explicatory variable in product success can be simply disregarded as tautological. Of course, it can be argued the company "understood" user needs if the product was successful. Expanding on such criticisms, Mowery and Rosenberg [8] have pointed out that the term "user need" is in any event vague and lacks the precision with which economists define related market variables such as demand. What seem to be important, however, is to determine whether there are identifiable ex post ante actions that organizations take that develop and refine the firm's understanding of the customer's needs.

In most of the instances in which interviewees indicated a product had succeeded because of "better understanding of customer needs," they were able to support this view by citing specific actions or events. Both the experiential background of the management and developing team as well as actions taken during the development and launch process were viewed as important.

One line of argument went thus: we understood customer needs because the managers, engineers and marketing people associated with the product were people with long-term experience in the technology and/or market. In such a situation, some executives argue, very little market research is required because the company's management has been close to the customer and to the dynamics of his changing requirements all along. As the group vice-president of a major instrument manufacturer explained, "We were able to set the right design objectives, particularly cost goals, because we knew the business, *we could manage by the gut* (authors' emphasis)."

This approach was evident in other firms also. When "Perfecto," a leading U.S. process equipment manufacturer, induced by a request from one of its European customers, commissioned a domestic market survey to assess potential demand for a new product that combined the functions of two of its existing products, the result

was almost unanimously negative. Because of a quirk in the process flow in U.S. plants (which differed from European plants), domestic customers did not immediately see significant value in the integrated product. Notwithstanding the market survey data, Perfecto executives continued to believe that the product would prove to be highly cost effective for their worldwide customers. Buoyed by enthusiasm in Europe and a feeling of deep understanding of his customers that was the result of 13 years of experience in the numerically controlled process equipment market, Perfecto's president gave the project the go ahead. His experience and self-confidence paid off. There was ultimately a significant demand for the new machine on both sides of the Atlantic.

These experience-based explanations, however, are only partially useful blueprints for action. The argument simply says that experienced people do better at new product development than the inexperienced, a hypothesis confirmed by our earlier research and that of others [9].

Most of our informants, however, characterized the capture of "user needs" in action-oriented terms. For the successful product in the dyad, they described the company as having more openly, frequently, carefully and continuously solicited and obtained customer reaction before, after and during the initiation of the development and launch process. In some cases, the attempt to get customer reaction went to an extreme. "Electrotest," a test equipment manufacturer conducted design reviews for a successful new product at their lead customers' plants. In general the successful products were the result of ideas which originated with the customers, filtered by experienced managers. In one case customers were reported to have "demanded" that an instrument manufacturer develop a new logic tester. As a rule, the development process for the successful products was characterized by frequent and in-depth customer interaction at all levels and throughout the development and launch process. While we did not find (and did not look for), what Von Hippel discovered in his careful research on electronic instruments, that users had in many cases already developed the company's next product, it was clear that, more so than any other constituency, they could point out the ideas that would result in future product successes [10].

But when listening to customers, it's not enough

to simply put in time. It is of paramount importance to listen to potential users without preconceptions or hidden agendas. Some companies become enamored with a new product concept and fail to test the idea against the reality of the marketplace. Not surprisingly, they find later that either the benefit to the customer was more obvious to the firm than to the customer himself or the product benefits were so specific that the market was limited to the original customer. For these reasons, the president of an automated test equipment manufacturer provided the following admonition, "When listening to customers, clear your mind of what you'd like to hear – Zen listening."  .

Unless this careful listening cascades throughout the company's organization and is continually "market"-checked, new products will not have the value to the customer that results in a significant commercial success. A predominant characteristic of the 20 successful industrial products that we examined in our case studies is that they resulted in almost immediate economic benefits to their users, not simply in terms of reduced direct manufacturing or operating costs. The successful products seemed to respond to the utility function of potential customers, which included such considerations as quality, service, reliability, ease of use and compatibility.

Low cost or extraordinary technical performance, per se, did not result in commercial success. Unsuccessful products were often technological marvels that received technical excellence awards and were written up in prestigious journals. But typically such extraordinary technical performance comes at a high price and is often not necessary. "Very high performance, at a very high price. This is the story behind virtually every one of our new product failures," is how a general manager at "International Instruments," an instrument manufacturer with a reputation for technical excellence, described the majority of his new product disappointments.

In contrast to this phenotype, new product successes tend to have a dramatic impact on the customer's profit-and-loss account directly or indirectly. "Miltec," an electronic systems manufacturer, reported that its successful electronic counter saved their users 70 percent in labor costs and down-time. "Informatics," a computer peripheral manufacturer, developed a very successful magnetic head that was not only IBM compatible but 20 percent cheaper and it offered a three times greater performance advantage. An integrated satellite navigation receiver developed by "Marine Technology," a communications firm, so drastically reduced on-board downtime in merchant marine ships in comparison to the older modular models that the company was overwhelmed by orders. The first 300 units paid for the $2.5 million R&D investment; overall 7000 units were sold. By comparison, the unsuccessful products provided little economic benefit. Not only were they usually high-priced but often they were plagued by quality and reliability problems, both of which translate into additional costs for the user.

## 4. How should product success be measured?

Our original surveys used a unidimensional success taxonomy. Success was defined along a simple financial axis. Successful products produced a high return while unsuccessful products resulted in less than break-even returns. Using this measure, our population of successes and failures combined to form a clearly bimodal distribution (fig. 2) that reinforced our assumption that we were dealing with two distinct classes of phenomena. While obtaining and plotting this type of data went beyond what most prior success-failure researchers had deemed necessary to provide, our detailed case studies lead us to conclude that this may not have been enough.

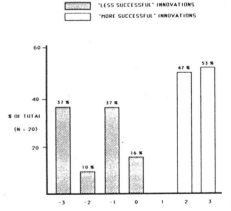

Figure 2. Distribution of successes and failures by degree of success/failure for case studies.

*M.A. Maidique and B.J. Zirger / New product learning cycle*                    305

Success is defined as the achievement of something desired, planned, or attempted. While financial return is one of the most easily quantifiable industrial performance yardsticks, it is far from the only important one. New product "failures" can result in other important byproducts: organizational, technological and market development. Some of the new product failures that we studied led to dead ends and resulted in very limited organizational growth. On the other hand, many others – the majority – were important milestones in the development of the innovating firm. Some were the clear basis for major successes that followed shortly thereafter.

International Instruments, a large electronics firm, developed a new instrument based on a new semiconductor technology (diode arrays) that the firm had not yet used in one of its commercial products. The instrument, though technically excellent, was developed for a new market where the company did not have its traditionally keen sense of what value meant to the customer. Few units were sold and the product was classified as a failure. On the other hand, the experience gained with the diode array technology became the basis for enhancement of other product families based on this newly gained technical knowledge. Secondly, the organization learned about the characteristics of the new market through the diode array product, and, armed with new insights, a redesigned product was developed which was a commercial success. Was the diode array product really a failure, its developers asked?

In this and other cases we observed, the failure contributed naturally to the subsequent successes by augmenting the organization's knowledge of new markets or technologies or by building the strength of the organization itself. An example from the public domain illustrates this point. After Apple Computer had been buffeted by the manufacturing and reliability problems that plagued the Apple III launch, which caused Apple to lose its lead in the personal computer market and to yield a large slice of the market to IBM. Apple's chairman summed up the experience thus [11], "There is no question that the Apple III was our most maturing experience. Luckily, it happened when we were years ahead of the competition. It was a perfect time to learn." As demonstrated by the manufacturing quality of the Apple IIe and IIc machines, Apple, that is the Apple II division,

learned a great deal from the Apple III mishaps. Indeed, Sahal has pointed out that success in the development of new technologies is a matter of learning [12]. "There are few innovations," he points out, "without a history of lost labor. What eventually makes most techniques possible is the object lesson learned from past failures." In his classic study of technological failures, Whyte argues that most advances in engineering have been accomplished by turning failure into success [13]. To Whyte engineering development is a process of learning from past failures.

Few would think of the Boeing Company and its suppliers as a good illustration of Sahal's and Whyte's arguments. Rosenberg, however, has pointed out that early 707s, for many years considered the safest of airplanes, went into unexplainable dives from high altitude flights. The fan-jet turbine blades used in the jumbo jet par excellence, Boeing's famed 747, failed frequently under stress in the 1969–1970 period [14]. Despite these object lessons, or perhaps because of them, Boeing makes more than half of the jet-powered commercial airliners sold outside of the Soviet block. According to the executive vice-president of the Boeing Commercial Airplane Company, himself a preeminent jet aircraft designer, "We are good partly because we build so many airplanes. We learn from our mistakes, and each of our airplanes absorbs everything we have learned from earlier models and from other airplanes." [15].

*Learning by doing, using and failing*

It has long been recognized that there is a strong learning curve associated with manufacturing activity. Arrow [16] characterized the learning that comes from developing increasing skill in manufacturing as "learning by doing." Learning by doing results in lower labor costs. The concept of improvement by learning from experience has been subsequently elaborated by the Boston Consulting Group and others to include improvements in production process, management systems, distribution, sales, advertising, worker training, and motivation. This enhanced learning process, which has been shown for many products to reduce full costs by a predictable percentage every time volume doubles, is called the experience curve [17].

Rosenberg, based on his study of the aircraft industry, has proposed a different kind of learning process, "learning by using" [16, pp.120–140]. Rosenberg distinguishes between learning that is "internal" and "external" to the production process. Internal learning results from experience with manufacturing the product, "learning by doing"; external learning is the result of what happens when users have the opportunity to use the product for extended periods of time. Under such circumstances, two types of useful knowledge may be derived by the developing organization. One kind of learning (embodied) results in design modifications that improve performance, usability, or reliability, a second kind of learning (disembodied) results in improved operation of the original or the subsequently modified product.

In our study we found another type of external learning, a "learning by failing," which resulted in the development of new market approaches, new product concepts, and new technological alternatives based on the failure of one or more earlier attempts (fig. 3). When a product succeeds, user experience acts as a feedback signal to the alert manufacturer that can be converted into design or operating improvements (learning by using). For products that generate negligible sales volume, little learning by using takes place. On the other hand, products that fail act as important probes into user space that can capture important information about what it would take to make a brand new effort successful, which sometimes makes them the catalyst for major reorientations. In this sense, a new product is the ultimate market study. For truly new products it may be the only effective means of sensing market attitudes. According to one of our respondents, a vice-president of engineering of "California Computer," a computer peripherals manufacturer, "No one really knows if a truly new product is worth anything until it has been in the market and its potential has been assessed."

Another dimension of "learning by failing" relates to organizational development. A failure helps to identify weak links in the organization and to inoculate strong parts of the organization against the same failure pattern. The aftermath of the Apple III resulted in numerous terminations at Apple Computer, from the president to the project manager of the Apple III project. Those remaining, aided by new personnel, accounted for the well-implemented Apple III redesign and reintroduction program and the highly successful Apple IIe follow-on product [11].

When the carryover of learning from one product to another is recognized, it becomes clear that the full measure of a product's impact can only be determined by viewing it in the context of both the products that preceded it and those that followed. While useful information can be obtained by focusing on individual products or pairs of products, *the product family is a far superior unit of analysis from which to derive prescriptions for practicing managers.* The product family incorporates the interrelationship between products, the learning from failures as well as from successes. Thus, it is to product families, including false starts, not to individual products, that financial measures of success should be more appropriately applied.

Consider a triplet of communications products developed over a 10-year period by an electronics system manufacturer. For several years Marine Technology had developed and marketed commercial and military navigation systems. These systems were composed of separate components manufactured by others, such as a receiver, teletype, and a minicomputer, none of which was specifically designed for the harsh marine environment. Additionally, this multicomponent ap-

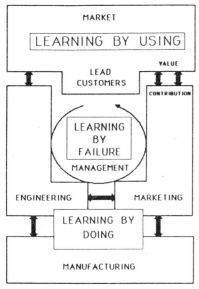

Figure 3. A model of internal and external learning.

proach, though technically satisfactory, took up a great deal of space, which is at a premium on the bridge of a ship. Each of Marine Technology's new product generations attempted to further reduce the number of components in the system. By 1975 a bulky HP minicomputer was the only outboard component.

The need for a compact, rugged, integrated navigation system had thus been abundantly clear to Marine Technology engineers and sales people. Therefore, when microprocessors became available in the early 1970s, it was not surprising that Marine Technology's general manager initiated a program to develop a new lightweight integrated navigation system specially designed for the marine environment. The product was developed by a closely knit design team that spent six to eight months working with potential customers, and later market testing prototypes. Two years later the company introduced the MT-1, the world's first microprocessor-based integrated navigation system. The product was an instant success. Over 7000 units were sold at a price of $25,000 per unit. At this price, margins exceeded 50 percent.

Shortly after the success of the MT-1 was established, engineering proposed a new product (the MT-2) to Marine Technology's newly appointed president. The MT-2 was to be about one-sixth the volume of the MT-1 and substantially cheaper in price. The president was so impressed with a model of the proposed product that he directed a team, staffed in part by the original MT-1 design team members, to proceed in a top secret effort to develop the MT-2. The team worked in isolation, only a handful of upper management and marketing people were aware of the project. Three and a half years and $3,5M later, the team had been able – by sacrificing some features – to shrink the product as promised to one-sixth the size of the MT-1 and to reduce the price to about $10,000. But almost simultaneously with the completion of the MT-2's development, a competitor had introduced an equivalent product for $6000. Furthermore, the product's small size was not considered a major advantage. Key customers indicated the previous product was "compact enough". The company attempted to eliminate some addition features to tailor the product to the consumer navigation market, but it found that it was far too expensive for this market, yet performance and quality were too low for its traditional commercial and military markets. The product was an abject economic failure. Most of the inventory had to be sold below the cost.

A third product in the line, the MT-3, however, capitalized on the lessons of the MT-2 failure. The new MT-3 was directed specifically at the consumer market. Price, not size, was the key goal. Within two years the MT-3 was introduced at a price of $3000. Like the MT-1, it was a major commercial success for the company. Over 1500 have been sold and the company had a backlog of 600 orders in 1982 when the case histories were completed.

At the outset of this abbreviated product family vignette, we said the family consisted of three products. In a strict sense, this is correct, but in reality there were four products, starting with what we will call the MT-0, the archaic modular system. The MT-0 was instrumental to the success of the MT-1. Through the experience with customers that it provided, it served to communicate to the company that size and reliability improvements would be highly valued by customer in the commercial and military markets in which the company operated. With the appearance of microprocessor technology, what remained was a technical challenge, usually a smaller barrier to success than deciphering how to tailor a new technology to the wants of the relevant set of customers, as the company found out through the MT-2.

The success of the MT-1 was misread by the company to mean, "the smaller, the more successful," rather than, "the better we understand what is important to the customer the more successful." The company had implicitly made an inappropriate trade-off between performance, size, and cost. They acted as if they had the secret to success – compact size – and by shutting off its design team from its new as well as its old customers ensured that they would not learn from them the real secrets to success in the continually evolving market environment. It remained for the failure of the MT-2 to bring home to management that, by virtue of its new design, the company was now appealing to a new customer group that had different values from its traditional commercial and military customer. Equipped with this new learning, the company was now able to develop the successful MT-3.

## 5. The new product learning cycle

There are several lessons to be learned from the history of Marine Technology's interrelated succession of products. First, their experience clearly illustrates the importance of precursors and follow-on products in assessing product success. To what extent, for instance, was the MT-2 truly a failure, or, alternatively, how necessary was such a product to pave the way for the successful MT-3? With hindsight one can always argue that the company should have been able to go directly to the MT-3, but wasn't to some extent the learning experience of the MT-2 necessary? Secondly, the story illustrates once again the importance of in-depth customer understanding as well as continuous interaction with potential customers throughout the development process even at the risk of revealing some proprietary information. Whatever learning might have been possible before entering the consumer market was shunted aside by the .company's secretive practices.

The product evolution pattern of "Computronics," a startup computer systems manufacturer, reinforces these findings. One of Computronics' founders had developed a new product idea for turnkey computer inventory control system for jobbers (small distributors) in one of the basic industries. From his experience as a jobber in this industry, he knew that it was virgin territory for a well-conceived and supported computerized system. During the development process, the company enlisted the support of the relevant industry association. Association members offered product suggestions, criticized product development, and ultimately the association endorsed the product for use by its members. The first Compu-100 system was shipped in 1973. Ten years later, largely on the strength of this product and its accessories, corporate sales had doubled several times and reached nearly $100 million, and the company dominated the jobber market.

As the company's market share increased, however, management recognized that new markets would have to be addressed if rapid growth was to continue. In early 1977, the company decided to take what seemed a very logical step to develop a system that would address the needs of the large wholesale distributors in the industry. Based on its earlier successes, the company planned to take this closely related market by storm. After a few visits

to warehousing distributors, the product specifications were established and development began under the leadership of a new division established to serve the high end of the business. Since no one at Computronics had first-hand experience with this higher level segment of the distribution system, a software package was purchased from a small software company, but it took a crash program and several programmers a year to rewrite the package so that it was compatible with Computronics hardware. After testing the Compu-200 at two sites, the company hired a team of additional sales representatives and prepared for a national roll-out. Ten million dollars of sales were projected for the first year.

First year revenues, however, were minimal. Even three years after the launch the product had yet to achieve the first year's target revenue. What had happened? The new market would appear at first glance to be a perfect fit with Computronics' skills and experience, yet a closer examination revealed considerable differences in the new customer environment which, nonetheless, were brushed away in a cavalier manner by Computronics' management, who were basking in the glow of the Compu-100's success.

As organizations in such a euphoric state often do, Computronics grossly underestimated the task at hand. The large market for warehousing distributor inventory systems was attractive to major competitors such as IBM and DEC. But only a cursory study of the new customers and their buying habits was carried out. The tacit assumption was that large warehousing distributors were simply grownup jobbers. Yet these new customers were now much more sophisticated, had used data processing equipment for other functions, and generally required and developed their own specialized software. Increased competition and radically greater customer sophistication combined to require that Computronics be represented by a highly experienced and competent sales force. But because of the hurry to launch the product, Computronics skipped the customary training for sales representatives and launched the field sales force into a new area for the firm: the complex long-term business of selling large items ($480,000 each) to a technically knowledgeable customer. By believing that repeating past practices would reproduce past successes, Computronics had turned success into failure.

"Every victory," Carl Jung [18] once wrote, "contains the germ of a future defeat." Starbuck and his colleagues [19] have observed that successful organizations accumulate surplus resources that allow them to loosen their connections to their environments and to achieve greater autonomy, but they explain, "this autonomy reduces the sensitivity of organizations to changing environmental conditions...organizations become less able to perceive what is happening so they fantasize about their environments and it may happen that reality intrudes only occasionally and marginally on these fantasies." Fantasies create a myth of invincibility, yet an old Chinese proverb [20] says, "There is no greater disaster than taking on an enemy lightly."

Marine Technology's management fantasized that they had the secret of success: smaller is better. Computronics had a fantasy that similarly extrapolated their past victories: new markets will be like old markets. This is a pattern that repeats itself over and over in business. We have already alluded to one of the best publicized contemporary examples of this phenomenon: Apple Computer's Apple III on the heels of its colossally successful Apple II precursor. Even IBM is not exempt from this cycle. After taking one-third of the market with its PC (personal computer) despite its late entry, a senior executive at the IBM PC Division stated, "We can do anything." [21]. "Anything" did not, as it happens, include the follow-on product to the PC, the PCjr, which – in contrast to the original PC – was not adequately test marketed to determine how consumers would react to its design features and ultimately had to be dropped from the IBM product line. IBM and Computronics, however, have both, at least temporarily, become more humble. Both are soliciting customer inputs so that they can redesign their disappointments.

The flow from success to failure, and back to success again, at Marine Technology illustrated a rhythm that we were to encounter repeatedly in our investigations. In the simplest terms, failure is the ultimate teacher. From its lessons the persistent build their successes. Success, on the other hand, often breeds complacency. Moreover, success seems to create a tendency to ignore the basics, to believe that heroics are a substitute for sound business practice. As the general manager of "Automatrix," a test equipment manufacturer, pointed out, "It's hard, very hard, to learn from your

successes." Ironically, success can breed failure for firms that continue to view the future through the prism of present victories, especially in a dynamic industry environment.

These observations have led us to propose a model of new product success and failure in which successes and failures alternate with an irregular rhythm. This is not to say that for every success there must be a complementing failure. Most industrial products – about three out of five – succeed despite popular myths to the contrary [22]. For some highly successful companies, as many as three out of four new products may be commercially successful. Most companies continuously learn by using, through their successful new products, and – as in the case of Marine Technology – they continuously develop improved designs. This is what most new product efforts are about – minor variations on existing themes.

But continued variations on a theme do not always lead to major successes. In time, further variations are no longer profitable, and the company usually decides to depart from the original theme by adopting a new technology – microprocessors, lasers, optics – or to attack a new market – consumer, industrial, government – or, alternatively, organizational changes, defections, or promotions destroy part of the memory of the organization so that the old now seems like the new. Changes in any of these three dimensions can result in an economic failure or, in our terms, new

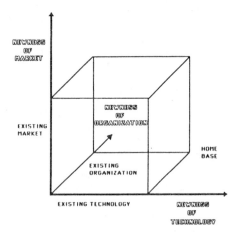

Figure 4. Learning by moving away from home base.

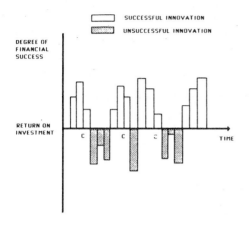

C = MARKET, TECHNOLOGICAL OR ORGANIZATIONAL
CHANGE

Figure 5. A typical new product evolution pattern.

learning about a technology, a market, or about the strengths and weaknesses of a newly formed group as shown in fig. 4, an extension of the familiar product–customer matrix originally proposed by Ansoff [23]. This recurrent cycle of success and failure is shown graphically in fig. 5.

In the model, a sequence of successes is followed by either a major organizational change, changes in product design, technology, or market directions that prompt an economic failure, which in turn spurs a new learning pattern. The model assumes a competitive marketplace, however, and is less likely to be applicable to a monopolistic situation in which a single firm dictates the relationship between customer and supplier. A second caveat is that while the pattern is roughly depicted as regular, in general it will be irregular, but the cycle of oscillation between economic success and failure, we believe, will still hold.

### 5.1. Success as a stochastic process

Success in new products is never assured. Too many uncontrolled external variables influence the outcome. Occasional or even frequent failure is a way of life for product innovations. As Addison reminds us in his Cato, "Tis not in mortals to command success." [24]. But while it is not possible to assure the outcome of any one product trial,

it is possible to increase the likelihood that a product or group of products will be successful. Addison goes on to add, "We'll do more, Sempronius, *we'll deserve it*." (authors' emphasis) The eight factors that we identified at the outset of this article, and the cyclic model we propose, are an attempt to help managers conceptualize the new product development process so as to improve the proportion of economic successes. But on the other hand, it would be a mistake to attempt to increase the number of successes by reducing new product risk to zero by cautions, deliberate management. In the process, rewards may be also reduced to the same level.

Failure, as we have tried to argue, is part and parcel of the learning process that ultimately results in success. Sahal [12] sums up the process thus, "What eventually makes the development of new techniques possible is the object lesson learned from past failures... profit by example". The important thing is to have a balance between successes and failures that results in attractive returns. Here a lesson from experienced venture capitalists, masters at the success forecasting game, is useful. As part of another research project, the authors have interviewed some of the nation's most successful and experienced venture capital investors whose portfolios have generally shown gains of 25–35 percent over the past 10 years. Given a large pot of opportunities, experienced venture capitalists believe they can select a group that will on the average yield an excellent return, yet few professionals are so sanguine that they believe that they can with certainty foretell any one success; they've seen too many of their dreams fail to meet expectations.

A new product developed by "Electrosystems," a military electronics company, seemed to fit a venture capitalist's dream. The company's new product, a phase-locked loop, had its origin with one of their key customers, the requisite technology was within their area of expertise, and a powerful executive championed the product throughout its development. A large market was anticipated. Thus far, a good bet, one might conclude. What's more, the resulting product was a high quality instrument. Yet the product brought little in the way of revenues to the firm for an alternative technology that solved the same problem in a cheaper way was simultaneously developed and introduced by a competitor.

Five years later, again spurred by a customer requirement, Electrosystems developed an electronic counter as part of a well-funded and visibly championed development program. This time, however, the product saved the customer 70 percent of his labor costs, considerably reduced his downtime, and there was no alternative technology on the horizon. This product was very successful. The point here is not that the product that ultimately produced a cost advantage to the customer was more successful. That much is self-evident. The point is that at the outset both products looked like they would provide important advantages to the customer. After all, they both originated with customers. Both projects were well-managed and funded and technologically successful. Yet one met with unpredictable external competition that blunted its potential contribution. The company did not simply fail and then succeed. It succeeded because it pursued both seemingly attractive opportunities. In other words, success generally requires not one but several, sometimes numerous, well-managed trials. This realization prompted one of our wisest interviewees, the Chief Engineer of "Metalex," an instrument manufacturer, to sit back and say, "I've found the more diligent you are, the more luck you have."

This is the way both venture capitalists and many experienced high-technology product developers view the new product process. Venture capitalists who have compiled statistics on the process have found that only 60 percent of new ventures result in commercial success, the rest are a partial or complete loss. (Not surprisingly, this is about the same batting average that Cooper found in his study of industrial products.) About 40–50 percent of new venture-capital backed ventures produce reasonable returns, and only 10–15 percent result in outstanding investments. But it can be easily computed that such a combination of investments can produce a 25–30 percent return or more as a portfolio.

### 5.2. New research directions

Our research on new product success and failure has led us to reconsider our unit of analysis. Choosing the new product as the basic unit of analysis has many advantages. New products are clearly identifiable entities. This facilitates gathering research data. New products have individualized sales forecasts and return on investment criteria, and managements generally know whether these criteria are satisfied. "Successes" can be culled from "failures."

Our results, however, indicate that if financial measures of success are to be applied as criteria, a more appropriate unit of analysis is the product family. Before an individual product is classified as a failure, its contribution to organizational growth, market development, or technological advance must be gauged. New products strongly influence the performance of their successors, and in turn are a function of the victories and defeats of their predecessors. Before the laurels are handed over to a winning team, an examination should be made of the market, technological, and organizational base from which the team launched its victory (fig. 4).

One of IBM's most notable product disasters was the Stretch computer. IBM set out to develop the world's most advanced computer, and, after spending $20 million in the 1960s for development, only a few units were sold.

On the heels of the Stretch fiasco came one of the most successful products of all time, the IBM 360 series. But when IBM set out to distribute kudos, it recognized that much of the technology in the IBM 360 was derived from work done on the Stretch computer by Stephen Dunwell, once the scapegoat for the Stretch "setback." Subsequently Mr. Dunwell was made an IBM fellow, a very prestigious position at IBM that carries many unique perks [25]. As Newton once said, "If I have seen far it is because I stood on the shoulders of giants." [26].

We were able to gain insight into this familial product interrelationship because our success-failure dyads were often members of the same product family. But even though they were interrelated, they represented only a truncated segment of a product family. Nonetheless, in some sites, for example Marine Technology, we were able to collect data on three or four members of a product family. On the other hand, our efforts, to date, fall far short of a systematic study of product families. This is the central task of the next stage of our research.

Our limited results, however, bring into question research that focuses on the product as the unit of analysis, including our own. Consider one of our principal research findings, which is also buttressed by the findings of several prior investigators: successful products benefit from existing strengths of the developing business unit. The implication of this finding is that organizations should be wary of exploring new territories. In contrast to this result, our observations would lead us to argue just the opposite, that firms should continuously explore new territories even if the risk of failure is magnified [27]. The payoff is the learning that will come from the "failures" which will pave the way for future successes.

Careful validation of the cyclic model of product development proposed here could have other important consequences for our understanding of technology-based firms. If indeed the pattern proposed in fig. 5 is generalizable to firms that are continuously attempting to adapt to new markets and technologies, then there are important implications for management practice.

First, the model implies that new product development success pivots on the effectiveness of intra and inter company learning. This conclusion puts a premium on devising a managerial style and structure that serves to catalyze internal and external communication. Second, by implicitly taking a long-term view of the product development process, the model emphasizes the importance of long-term relationships with employees, customers, and suppliers. Out of such a view comes a high level of understanding, and therefore of tolerance for failure to achieve commercial success at any one given point in the product line trajectory. Firms need to learn that product development is a journey, not a destination. These preliminary findings are compatible with an exploratory study of new product development in five large successful Japanese companies completed by Imai and his colleagues [28]. One of the principal findings of their research was that the firms studied were characterized by an almost "fanatical devotion towards learning – both within organizational membership (sic) and with outside members of the interorganizational network." This learning, according to the authors, played a key role in facilitating successful new product development. It appears that when successful at new product development, small and large U.S. companies operate in a very similar manner to the best-managed Japanese firms.

Many key questions, however, remain to be settled. Is there an optimal balance between successes and failures? Are Japanese firms susceptible to the same oscillating pattern between success and failure as American firms? How does this balance change across industries? How can tolerance for failure be communicated without distorting the ultimate need for economic success? How can a firm learn from the failures of others? Are there characteristic success-failure patterns for a group of firms competing in the same industry? These and other related questions will occupy us in the next phase of our research.

## References

[1] R.C. Cooper, A Process Model for Industrial New Product Development, *IEEE Transactions on Engineering Management* EM-30 (1) (1983) 2–11.

[2] M.A. Maidique and B.J. Zirger, A Study of Success and Failure in Product Innovation: The Case of the U.S. Electronics Industry, *IEEE Transactions on Engineering Management* EM-31 (4) (1984) 192–203.

[3] B.J. Zirger and M.A. Maidique, (forthcoming), Empirical Testing of a Conceptual Model of Successful New Product Development, to be submitted to *Management Science*.

[4] C.G. Jung, *The Undiscovered Self* (New American Library, 1957) p. 17.

[5] R.C. Cooper, The Dimensions of Industrial New Product Success and Failure. *Journal of Marketing* 43 (1979) 102.

[6] The authors wish to express their appreciation to the following graduate students and doctoral candidates, who assisted in preparation of the individual case studies: P. Achi, G. Ananthasubramanianium, R. Angangco, C. Badger, B. Billerbeck, R. Cannon, D. Chinn, L. Christian, B. Connor, A. Dahlen, S. Demetrescu, B. Drobenko, R. Farros, H. Finger, H. Jagadish, L. Girault-Cuevas, R. Guior, T. Hardison, Y. Honda, J. Jover, C. Koo, T. Kuneida, S. Kurasaki, M. Lacayo, D. Lampaya, D. Ledakis, L. Lei, R. Ling, S. Makmuri, P. Matlock, C. Mungale, R. Ortiz, B. Raschle, R. Reis, B. Russ, E. Saenger, J. Sanghani, V. Sanvido, F. Sasselli, R. Simon, P. Stamats, R. Stauffer, L. Taurel, B. Walsh, F. Zustak.

[7] R. Rothwell, C. Freeman, A. Horley, V.I.P. Jervis, Z.B. Robertson and J. Townsend, SAPPHO Updated-Project SAPPHO, Phase II, *Research Policy* 3 (1974) 258–291. See also C. Freeman, *The Economics of Industrial Innovation* (Penguin Books, Harmondsworth., 1974). pp. 161–197.

[8] D. Mowery and N. Rosenberg, The Influence of Market Demand Upon Innovation: A Critical Review of Some Recent Empirical Studies *Research Policy* 8 (1979) 101–153.

[9] A.C. Cooper and A.V. Bruno, Success Among High-Technology Firms *Business Horizons* 20 (2) (1977) 16–22.

[10] E.A. Von Hippel, Users as Innovators, *Technology Review* No. 5 (1976) 212–239.

[11] M.A. Maidique, J.S. Gable, and S. Tylka. *Apple Computer (A)&(B)*, Case #S-BP-229(B) (Stanford Business School

Central Services, Graduate School of Business, Rm. 1, Stanford, CA, 1983). See also M.A. Maidique and C.C. Swanger, *Apple Computer: The First 10 Years*, Case # PS-BP-245 (Stanford Business School Central Services, Graduate School of Business, Rm. 1, Stanford, CA, 1985).

[12] D. Sahal, *Patterns of Technological Innovation*, (Addison-Wesley, Reading MA., 1981)p. 306.

[13] R.R. Whyte, *Engineering Progress Through Trouble* (Institution of Mechanical Engineers, London, 1975).

[14] N. Rosenberg, *Inside the Black Box, Technology and Economics* (Cambridge University Press, Cambridge, 1982) pp. 124–126.

[15] J. Newhouse, *The Sporty Game* (Alfred A. Knopf, New York, 1982). p. 7.

[16] K. Arrow, The Economic Implications of Learning By Doing, *Review of Economic Studies* (June 1962).

[17] B. Henderson, *Perspectives on Experience* (Boston Consulting Group, 1968) (third printing, 1972).

[18] C.G. Jung, *Psychological Reflections* (Princeton University Press, New York, 1970). p. 188.

[19] W. Starbuck, A. Greve, and B.L. Hedberg, Responding to Crisis *Journal of Business Administration* No. 9 (1978) 111–137.

[20] Lao Tzu, *Tao Te Ching* (Penguin Books, New York, 1983). p. 131.

[21] D. Le Grande, as quoted in "How IBM Made Junior an Underachiever," *Business Week* June 25 (1984) 106.

[22] R.G. Cooper, Most Products *Do* Succeed, *Research Management*, (Nov.-Dec. 1983) 20–25.

[23] H.I. Ansoff, *Corporate Strategy* (McGraw-Hill, New York, 1965). pp. 131–133.

[24] J. Bartlett, *Bartlett's Familiar quotations, 14th edn., (Little, Brown and Company, New York, 1968). p. 393.*

[25] T. Wise, *IBM's $5B Gamble, Fortune* (September 1966); A Rocky Road to the Marketplace, *Fortune* (October 1966); Bob Evans, personal communication. (Mr. Evans was program manager for the IBM-360 system.)

[26] J. Bartlett, *Bartlett's Familiar Quotations*, 13th edn., (Little, Brown and Company, New York, 1968). p. 379.

[27] In an exploratory study of the relationship between the degree of "newness" of a firm's portfolio of products and its economic performance the authors concluded that some "newness" results in better economic performance than "no newness". M.H. Meyer and E.B. Roberts, *New Product Strategy in Small High Technology Firms*, WP # 1428-1-84 (Sloan School of Management, Massachusetts Institute of Technology, May 1984).

[28] K. Imai, I. Nonaka, and H. Takeuchi, *Managing the New Product Development Process: How Japanese Companies Learn and Unlearn*, Institute of Business Research, Hitotsubashi University, Kunitachi (Tokyo, Japan, 1982). pp. 1–60. See also P.R. Lawrence and D. Dyer, *Renewing American Industry* (The Free Press, New York, 1983). p. 8.

# [12]

# Sectoral patterns of technical change:
# Towards a taxonomy and a theory

Keith PAVITT *

*Science Policy Research Unit, University of Sussex, Brighton BN1 9RF, UK*

Final version received January 1984

The purpose of the paper is to describe and explain sectoral patterns of technical change as revealed by data on about 2000 significant innovations in Britain since 1945. Most technological knowledge turns out not to be "information" that is generally applicable and easily reproducible, but specific to firms and applications, cumulative in development and varied amongst sectors in source and direction. Innovating firms principally in electronics and chemicals, are relatively big, and they develop innovations over a wide range of specific product groups within their principal sector, but relatively few outside. Firms principally in mechanical and instrument engineering are relatively small and specialised, and they exist in symbiosis with large firms, in scale intensive sectors like metal manufacture and vehicles, who make a significant contribution to their own process technology. In textile firms, on the other hand, most process innovations come from suppliers.

These characteristics and variations can be classified in a three part taxonomy based on firms: (1) supplier dominated; (2) production intensive; (3) science based. They can be explained by sources of technology, requirements of users, and possibilities for appropriation. This explanation has implications for our understanding of the sources and directions of technical change, firms' diversification behaviour, the dynamic relationship between technology and industrial structure, and the formation of technological skills and advantages at the level of the firm, the region and the country.

* The following paper draws heavily on the SPRU data bank on British innovations, described in J. Townsend, F. Henwood, G. Thomas, K. Pavitt and S. Wyatt, *Innovations in Britain Since 1945*, SPRU Occasional Paper Series No. 16, 1981. The author is indebted to Graham Thomas and to Sally Wyatt who helped with the statistical work, to numerous colleagues inside and outside SPRU for their comments and criticisms, and to Richard Levin and two anonymous referees for their detailed and helpful comments on a longer and more rambling earlier draft. The research has been financed by the Leverhulme Trust, as part of the SPRU programme on innovation and competitiveness.

Research Policy 13 (1984) 343–373
North-Holland

## 1. Introduction

### 1.1. Purpose

The subject matter of this paper is sectoral patterns of technical change. We shall describe and try to explain similarities and differences amongst sectors in the sources, nature and impact of innovations, defined by the sources of knowledge inputs, by the size and principal lines of activity of innovating firms, and by the sectors of innovations' production and main use.

It is recognised by a wide range of scholars that the production, adoption and spread of technical innovations are essential factors in economic development and social change, and that technical innovation is a distinguishing feature of the products and industries where high wage countries compete successfully on world markets [55]. However, representations of the processes of technical change found in economics are in many respects unsatisfactory. According to Nelson:

> In the original neo-classical formulation, new technology instantly diffuses across total capital. In the later vintage formulation, technology is associated with the capital that embodies it and thus adoption of a new technique is limited by the rate of investment. [29]

Whilst such assumptions may be convenient or useful in macro-economic model building and analysis, they have – as Nelson [29] and Rosenberg [42] have pointed out – two important limitations. First, they make exogenous the production of technology and innovations. Second, they do not reflect the considerable variety in the sources, nature and uses of innovations that is revealed by empirical studies and through practical experience.

Such formulations of technical change are not

therefore very useful for analysts or policy makers concerned with either the nature and impact of technical change at the level of the firm or the sector, or with R&D policy at the level of the firm, the sector or the nation. Hence, the importance, we would argue, of building systematically a body of knowledge – both data and theory – that both encompasses the production of technology, and reflects sectoral diversity. The following paper is a contribution to this objective.

## 1.2. The data base

What makes is possible is data collected by Townsend et al. [60] on the characteristics of about 2000 significant innovations, and of innovating firms, in Britain from 1945 to 1979. The methodology, results and limitations are spelt out fully in the original publication. Suffice here to say that:

(1) Innovation is defined as a new or better product or production process successfully commercialised or used in the United Kingdom, whether first developed in the UK or in any other country.

(2) Significant innovations were identified by experts knowledgeable about, but independent from, the innovating firms; information about the characteristics of the innovations was collected directly from the innovating firms.

(3) The sample of innovations covers three and four digit product groups accounting for more than half the output of British manufacturing. At the two digit level, the sectoral distribution of innovations is similar to that measured by numbers of patents, but is not to that measured by expenditures on R&D activity. In concrete terms, this reflects a slight over-representation of innovations in mechanical engineering and metals; a considerable over-representation in instruments and textiles; a slight under-representation in chemicals and electronics; and a considerable under-representation in aerospace. [1]

(4) Experts in different sectors defined the threshold of significance at different levels, which means that our sample of innovations cannot be used to compare the volume of innovations amongst sectors. However, it can be used to compare patterns of innovative activity within sectors, where the results are consistent with other independent sources of data on innovative activities in the UK and elsewhere (see [36]).

(5) The data measure significant innovations introduced into the UK. They do not measure significant world innovations, nor do they capture the incremental and social innovations that often accompany significant technical innovations. We shall assume that the data on significant innovations are the visible manifestations of deeper processes, involving incremental and social, as well as significant, innovations. We shall also assume that, although the pattern of innovative activities in the UK does have some distinctive features [2], what we are measuring on the whole reflects patterns in most industrial countries, rather than the specific characteristics of the UK.

## 1.3. Approach and structure

Given the nature of the problem as posed in subsection 1.1, and of the large data base as described in subsection 1.2, the reader might legitimately expect a paper that is largely econometric in nature: an alternative model of technical change to neoclassical ones would be proposed and formalised, and a series of statistical tests would be carried out, that discriminate between the explanatory powers of the competing models. However, this will not be the approach followed, for reasons that go beyond the intellectual propensities and professional limitations of this particular author. Although the statistical data are more comprehensive and systematic than any others previously assembled on innovations, the sample still has a number of limitations. As we have seen, it covers just one half of manufacturing, so important gaps remain. For purposes of statistical analysis, it can be grouped into 11 sectoral categories at the two digit level, and into 26 categories at the three and four digit level. Statistical data on other sectoral properties often cannot be conveniently assembled into the same categories and for the same time periods. We were therefore faced with a choice between "creating" data to make any regressions econometrically more convincing, or making for-

---

[1] For the number of innovations produced in each two digit sector, see table 2, column 3. For the three to four digit sectors included in the sample, see table 1.

[2] See, for example [34;35].

mal statistical analysis a minor part of the paper. We chose the latter approach, although tentative econometric analysis is described in the Appendix to this paper, and discussed in section 4.

This approach has the advantage of allowing the patterns of the statistical data to be compared to the mind's eye with the rich range of sectoral and firm studies of technical change that have accumulated over the past 25 years. Given that no obvious model of sectoral patterns of technical change emerges from previous theoretical writings, such direct and visual comparisons turned out to be particularly useful.

We present and discuss the main features of the data in section 2, and compare them with some prevailing theoretical assumptions. In section 3, we suggest a taxonomy of sectoral patterns of innovative activity, and a theoretical explanation, that are consistent with the data. In section 4, we explore some of the analytical implications of such a theory, and in section 5 we suggest further research that should be done.

## 2. Sectoral patterns of innovation

### 2.1. Analysis of the data

The information contained in the data bank describes characteristics of significant innovations and of innovating firms. In this paper, we shall be using information on the institutional sources of the main knowledge inputs into the innovations, on the sectors of production and of use of the innovations, and on the size and the principal sectors (or product groups or lines) of activity of the innovating firms.

Sources of the main knowledge inputs into the innovations were identified by asking the sectoral experts and the innovating firms to identify the type of institution that provided up to the three most important knowledge inputs into each innovation. This information provides a basis for assessing the relative importance in providing such knowledge, of the innovating firms themselves, of other industrial firms, and of institutions providing public knowledge, such as universities and government laboratories. This is done in subsection 2.2.

Information on the sectors of production of innovations comes from the sectoral experts, and

on sectors of use from the innovating firms [3]. We define innovations that are used in the same sectors as those in which they are produced (e.g. direction reduction of steel) as *process* innovations, and those that are used in different sectors (e.g. the Sulzer Loom) as *product* innovations. Such information provides what can be considered as the technological equivalent of an input/output table. It shows how intersectoral patterns of production and sale of goods is reflected in intersectoral transfers of technology. It is strictly equivalent in purpose, if not in method, to the table compiled recently for the USA by Scherer [51]. It is discussed in subsection 2.3.

Information on the size and principal sector of activity of innovating firms was provided by the firms themselves, and sometimes checked through other sources. Size is measured in terms of total world employment, and (for the innovations in the period from 1969 to 1979) also of employment in the UK. Such information allows comparisons of the size distribution of innovating firms amongst sectors, over time, and in comparison to other indices of economic activity.

Information on the principal activity of innovating firms allows comparisons, amongst sectors and over time, of the degree to which firms produce innovations outside their principal sector of activity, and to which innovations in sectors are produced by firms with their principal activity elsewhere. Such comparisons can be seen as the equivalent for technology of comparisons of firms' diversification in output, employment or sales. Patterns of size and of "technological diversification" of innovating firms are analysed in subsection 2.4.

It is to be noted that each innovation in the data base is attributed three numbers in the Standard Industrial Classification, or Minimum List Heading, as it is called in the UK: (1) the sector of production of the innovation; (2) the sector of use of the innovation; (3) the sector of the innovating firm's principal activity. We are therefore able to construct an (as yet incomplete) three-dimensional matrix encompassing links amongst sectors in the production and use of innovations, and in the sectoral patterns of "technological diversification" of innovating firms. Such a construct enables us to

---

[3] When an innovation found a use in more than one sector, we defined the main user sector as the sector of use.

compare sectors in terms of:

(1) The sectoral *sources* of technology *used* in a sector: in particular, the degree to which it is generated within the sector, or comes from outside through the purchase of production equipment and materials.

(2) The institutional *sources* and *nature* of the technology *produced* in a sector: in particular, the relative importance of intramural and extramural knowledge sources, and of product and process innovations.

(3) The *characteristics* of *innovating firms*: in particular, their size and principal activity.

Such comparisons have been made systematically by the author, at the two and the three to four digit level, in the preparation of this paper. They were essential for an evaluation of the empirical validity of prevailing models of technical change, and *a fortiori* for working out the sectoral taxonomy and theory proposed in section 3. However, they will not be reproduced in comprehensive detail since they are long, tedious and sometimes potentially confusing. We shall instead present statistical material mainly at the two digit sectoral level, although we shall also refer to some patterns at the three to four digit level.

Suffice to say here that a central feature in our search for a taxonomy and an explanatory theory was the classification of innovations in each sector according to whether or not the sectors of production, of use, and the principal activity of the innovating firm, are the same. There are five possible combinations:

*Category 1*: sectors of production, use, and principal firm activity are all the same: e.g. a process innovation by a steel making firm. (MLH [4] 311)

*Category 2*: sectors of production and principal firm activity are the same, but different from sector of use: e.g. a specialised firm making textile machines (MLH 335), designing a new textile machine (MLH 335) for use in the textile industry (MLH 411).

*Category 3*: sectors of principal firm activity and of use of the innovation are the same, but different from the sector of production of the innovation: e.g. a shipbuilding firm (MLH 370) develops a special machine tool (MLH 332), for use in building ships (MLH 370).

*Category 4*: sectors of production and use of the innovation are the same, but different from that of the firm's principal activity: for example, a firm principally in general chemicals (MLH 271) develops a process innovation in textiles (MLH 411).

*Category 5*: sectors of production of the innovation, of its use, and of the firm's principal activity are all different: for example, a firm principally in electronic capital goods (MLH 367) develops and produces an innovation in instrumentation (MLH 354.2) for use in making motor vehicles (MLH 381).

In the particular examples given above, the categories are the same at the two digit as at the three to four digit level. But in some cases they are not. For example, a firm in general chemicals (MLH 271), producing an innovation in pharmaceuticals (MLH 272), for use in medical services (MLH 876) will fall into category 5 at the three digit level, and category 2 at the two digit level.

## 2.2. Institutional sources of main knowledge inputs

As we have already pointed out, experts could allocate up to three institutional sources of knowledge inputs for each innovation. All provided one such source, about 40 percent provided two sources, but only 3 percent provided three sources.

The results at the three to four digit level are summarised in table 1. Only about 7 percent of the knowledge inputs comes from the public technological infrastructure (higher education, government laboratories, and research associations). The highest proportion is reached in a number of electronics sectors, but even here it is never as much as 25 percent. On the other hand, 59 percent came from within the innovating firms themselves, and about a third from other industrial firms.

These data have a number of imperfections. Given that they were collected mainly from industrial experts, and that only about 1.5 sources were identified for each innovation, they underestimate the contribution made by the public technological infrastructure to person-embodied knowledge and to essential background knowledge for the innovations. [5] More generally, the distribu-

---

[4]  MLH = Minimum List Heading.
[5]  See Gibbons and Johnston [14] for an excellent analysis of these sources.

Table 1

Distribution of knowledge inputs into significant innovations, according to institutional source

| Sector [a] | Source of knowledge inputs (%) [b] | | | Number of observations |
|---|---|---|---|---|
| | Intra-firm | Other firm | Public Infrastructure | |
| Food (211-229) | 53.4 | 44.6 | 2.0 | 101 |
| Pharmaceuticals (272) | 62.8 | 37.2 | 0 | 129 |
| Soap and detergents (275) | 60.0 | 40.0 | 0 | 30 |
| Plastics (276) | 40.4 | 55.2 | 4.4 | 114 |
| Dyestuffs (277) | 68.1 | 30.5 | 1.4 | 69 |
| Iron and steel (311) | 47.7 | 44.9 | 7.4 | 149 |
| Aluminium (321) | 68.0 | 28.0 | 4.0 | 50 |
| Machine tools (332) | 64.1 | 29.8 | 6.1 | 231 |
| Textile machinery (335) | 61.2 | 36.6 | 2.2 | 278 |
| Coal-mining machinery (339.1) | 52.3 | 31.6 | 16.1 | 199 |
| Other machinery (339.4 + 339.9) | 59.1 | 36.6 | 4.3 | 115 |
| Industrial plant (341) | 51.6 | 41.9 | 6.5 | 31 |
| Instruments (354.2) | 61.6 | 25.2 | 13.2 | 440 |
| Electronic components (364) | 48.2 | 37.1 | 14.7 | 170 |
| Broadcasting equipment (365) | 64.4 | 33.9 | 1.7 | 59 |
| Electronic computers (366) | 50.6 | 33.3 | 16.1 | 81 |
| Electronic capital goods (367) | 67.2 | 9.7 | 23.0 | 113 |
| Other electrical goods (369) | 60.8 | 35.3 | 3.9 | 51 |
| Shipbuilding (370) | 47.9 | 43.8 | 8.2 | 73 |
| Tractors (380) | 78.7 | 21.3 | 0 | 47 |
| Motor vehicles (381) | 69.3 | 29.7 | 1.0 | 101 |
| Textiles (411-429) | 67.3 | 32.7 | 0 | 110 |
| Leather goods and footwear (431/450) | 44.4 | 48.1 | 7.4 | 54 |
| Glass (463) | 48.2 | 44.6 | 7.1 | 56 |
| Cement (464) | 62.5 | 33.3 | 4.2 | 24 |
| Paper and board (481) | 66.7 | 28.2 | 5.1 | 39 |
| Other plastics (496) | 55.8 | 41.9 | 2.3 | 43 |
| Other | – | – | – | 56 |
| Total | 58.6 | 34.0 | 7.4 | 3013 |

[a] Numbers in brackets refer to the appropriate Minimum List Heading.

[b] Each row adds up to 100 percent.

tion of knowledge sources in this kind of study depends heavily on the definitions and time perspectives of the data collected. [6] In spite of these imperfections, the distribution of knowledge

[6] See, for example, the classic US controversy at the end of the 1960s: the Hindsight and Traces studies arrived at very different conclusions about the contribution of basic research to industrial innovation. For a comparison, see Pavitt and Wald [39].

sources in table 1 is not dissimilar to that found in other studies. [7].

Given that innovating firms evaluate their own knowledge contributions at nearly 60 percent of the total, we cannot realistically assume that there exists a generally available and applicable stock or pool of knowledge, where each firm – being very

[7] See Langrish et al. [21], and Gibbons and Johnston [14].

K. Pavitt / Sectoral patterns of technical change

small in relation to the total stock or pool – can gain much more from drawing on the pool, rather than by adding to it. The concept of the general "pool" or "stock" of knowledge misses an essential feature of industrial technology, namely, the firm-specific and differentiated nature of most of the expenditures producing it. In Britain and elsewhere, about three-quarters of all expenditures on industrial R&D is on "D", and an equivalent sum is spent on testing and manufacturing start up. [8] The purpose of these expenditures is to mobilise skills, knowledge and procedures in the firm in order to commercialise specific products and production processes, with the characteristics of operation, reliability and cost that satisfy user needs. Specificity is an essential feature of innovations and innovative activity in capitalist firms – both in terms of functional applications, and of the ability of the innovating firm to appropriate the relevant knowledge for a period of time.

This feature is missed in any simple equation of "technology" with "information." Whilst it may be reasonable to describe *research* and *invention* as producing "information" that is quickly and easily transmitted, [9] it is grossly misleading to assume that *development* and *innovation* have similar properties. Given their specific characteristics, the costs of transmission from one firm to another can be high, even in the absence of legal protection or secrecy in the innovating firm [7;33;57]. As Nelson [30] has recently argued, technological knowledge has both proprietary and public aspects, although table 1 and other studies suggest that the former outweigh a latter.

These features are missed in some representations of technology in a production function. According to Salter:

...the production function concept ... could refer either to techniques which have been developed in detail, or to techniques which are feasible in principle but have not been developed because the necessary economic pressures are absent. [48, p.26]

Salter plumps for the latter and, in doing so, makes exogenous to his analysis most of the innovative (i.e. development and post-develop-

ment)' activities of industrial firms. As Rosenberg [42] has pointed out, most firms do not (and in the light of the above discussion cannot) have information on a full and complete range of alternative techniques. The assumption that most technological knowledge is or could be publicly available and generally applicable has little foundation in reality.

### 2.3. Sectoral patterns of production and use of innovations

As already described above, the innovation data base compiled by Townsend et al. [60] describes sectoral patterns of production and use of innovations in the UK. On the basis of a different method, Scherer [51] has compiled similar information for the USA. He obtained detailed data on the sectoral allocations of R&D resources in more than 400 large US firms in the 1970s. On the basis of examination of the patenting activity of these firms, he was also able to attribute the "output" of this R&D to sectors of use. Scherer's work covers more than 40 US sectors of production and use. The data collected by Townsend et al., on the other hand, cover small and medium sized, as well as large firms, but not all sectors. Most important for the purposes of this paper, both studies show comparable results in sectoral patterns of production and use of technology. [10]

Following Scherer, we define as product innovations those innovations that are used *outside* their sector of production, and *process* innovations as those that are used *inside* their sector. [11] Both studies confirm the prevalence of *product* innovations which accounted for 73.8 percent in the USA, according to Scherer, and 75.3 percent in the UK, when sectors are defined at the three to four digit level, and 69.6 percent when defined at the two digit level.

---

[8] For a recent review of empirical findings on the total costs of innovation, see Kamin et al. [19].
[9] See the classic paper by Arrow [3].

[10] See Pavitt [36].
[11] This definition is not strictly the same as product or process innovation at the level of the firm. Thus, what is a product innovation for the firm will be a process innovation for the sector, when the firm's innovation is purchased and used in the same sector; conversely, a process innovation in the firm will be a product innovation for the sector, when the firm produces and uses its capital goods. However, for the firm, as well as the sector, product innovation predominates. See Townsend et al. [60, tables 9.1 and 9.2].

Table 2
Innovations produced and used in two digit sectors

| Innovations used in sector | | Sector [a] | Innovations produced in sector | |
|---|---|---|---|---|
| Percentage produced in sector | Number | | Number | Percentage that are product innovations |
| (1) | (2) | (3) | (4) | (5) |
| 52.9 | 68 | III Food and drink | 65 | 44.7 |
| 60.5 | 71 | V Chemicals | 251 | 82.9 |
| 60.7 | 130 | VI Metal manufacture | 137 | 42.3 |
| 68.1 | 169 | VII Mechanical engineering | 662 | 82.7 |
| 38.4 | 60 | VIII Instrument engineering | 332 | 93.1 |
| 80.8 | 107 | IX Electrical and electronic engineering | 339 | 60.1 |
| 32.2 | 90 | X Shipbuilding | 52 | 44.1 |
| 37.6 | 221 | XI Vehicles | 128 | 35.2 |
| 16.2 | 377 | XIII Textiles | 91 | 32.9 |
| 60.0 | 45 | XIV&XV Leather and Footwear | 34 | 26.5 |
| 46.1 | 63 | XVI Bricks, Pottery, glass and cement | 72 | 85.0 |
| na | 823 | Other | 61 | na |
| 41.9 [b] | 2224 | Total | 2224 | 69.6 |

[a] Roman numerals refer to the appropriate Order Headings.
[b] For the 1401 innovations in the sample that are attributed a sector of use.

Scherer's more complete and comprehensive data for the USA show a clear difference in the production and use of innovations between manufacturing and the other sectors of the economy (i.e. agriculture, mining, service industries, private and public services). For manufacturing as a whole, the ratio of production to use of technology is about 5.3 to 1. Outside manufacturing it is about 0.1 to 1, and the proportion of all the technology used outside manufacturing that is generated there amounts to less than 7 percent. In other words, manufacturing produces most of the innovations that get used in other parts of the economy.

However, manufacturing itself is far from homogeneous in patterns of production and use of innovations. Table 2 shows at the two digit level, the relevant characteristics of those sectors of British manufacturing for which we have a satisfactory sample of innovations. Column 5 shows the percentage of all innovations produced in each sector that are purchased and used in other sectors: in other words, the percentage of product innovations. These are relatively most important in instruments, mechanical engineering, chemicals, building materials (mainly glass and cement) and electrical and electronic engineering, whilst process innovations predominate in leather and footwear, textiles, vehicles, metal manufacture, shipbuilding and food and drink. Data at the three to four digit

level show that all the mechanical engineering product groups covered in the survey are strongly orientated towards product innovations whilst, within the chemical and the electrical/electronic sectors, there are two product groups with high percentages of process innovations: soaps and detergents, and broadcasting equipment.

Column 1 in table 2 shows the percentage of innovations used in each sector that are produced in the same sector: in other words, the degree to which each sector generates its own process innovations. [12] They show that most two digit sectors of manufacturing in the sample make a significant contribution to developing their own process technologies. The main exception is textiles, which is heavily dependent on innovations from other sectors.

Finally, a comparison between columns 4 and 2 of table 2 shows the differences between production and use of innovations in each sector. Production is greater than use in chemicals, mechanical engineering and instruments, and electrical/electronic products. The two are roughly in balance in industries characterised by continuous process

---

[12] Column 2 shows 823 innovations produced in the identified sectors of manufacturing but used elsewhere. Unlike Scherer, we cannot in this context usefully allocate these innovations to user sectors, since we do not yet have a sample of innovations produced by these sectors of use.

technology (i.e. food and drink, metal manufacture, building materials), whilst more innovations are used than produced in sectors characterised by assembly operations (i.e. shipbuilding and vehicles). These assembly industries also draw on a wider range of sectors for their process technologies than do those characterised by continuous process technology.

How does this pattern of production and use of innovations compare with the "vintage" model of technical change, which assumes that all technology is capital-embodied and enters the economy through investment? In his original formulation of this model, Salter [48] was very well aware of its limitations. He recognised the importance of innovations in capital goods, and of product innovations, but made them exogenous. He also stated that other assumptions made it "highly simplified" (p. 64): for example, that technical change involves no cumulative effects from one generation of capital equipment to another, or that "best practice" performance is clearly defined and instantly reached.

Nonetheless, Salter's assumptions do reflect the reality of most of the economy, namely non-manufacturing, where technical change comes mainly through the purchase of equipment, materials and components from manufacturing. Within manufacturing, it also reflects accurately the sources of process innovations in the textile industry. However, his characterisation of the sources of technical change at the more modern end of manufacturing industry is less satisfactory, in three respects.

First, whilst it may be conceptually correct in certain economic models to assume – as Salter does – that improvements in the performance of capital goods (i.e. product innovations) are equivalent to the relative cheapening of capital goods (i.e. process innovations), such an assumption is misleading about the directions and sources of technical change in the capital goods sector. Innovative activities are in fact heavily concentrated on product innovation: no amount of process innovation in, for example, the production of mechanical calculators would have made them competitive with the product innovations resulting from the incorporation of the electronic chip.

Second, Salter's model assumes that process innovations come to user sectors already developed. However, we see in table 2 that a significant

proportion of the innovations used in modern manufacturing are developed and produced in the innovating sectors themselves. It is worth dwelling a bit on one of the possible reasons why. We know from the research of Gold [15], Sahal [47] and others that two of Salter's simplifying assumptions are false: in continuous process and assembly industries, there is in fact cumulative learning, and "best practice" performance is rarely easily defined or quickly reached. The same design, engineering and operating skills that enable rapid learning are also capable of making innovations, particularly in production equipment. In other words, sectors with complex and expensive process technologies devote considerable technical resources to ensuring that equipment is used efficiently and continuously improved.

Third, and more generally, the production of all innovations is made exogenous to Salter's model. Before suggesting in section 3 a framework that makes such production endogenous, we shall describe characteristics of innovating firms in different sectors.

*2.4. Characteristics of innovating firms: Size and technological diversification*

Table 3 summarises the main features of the size distribution of innovating firms in different sectors. Columns 7–9 classify them according to the principal sector of activity of the innovating firm. This classification shows a relatively big contribution by small firms (1–999 employees) in mechanical and instrument engineering, textiles, and leather and footwear; and by large firms (10,000 and more employees) in the other sectors. This sectorally differentiated pattern is very similar to that emerging from a study of significant innovations and innovating firms undertaken for the USA. [13]

Columns 1–3 of table 3 show the size distribution of innovating firms according to the sector of the innovations, rather than the principal sector of the innovating firms' activity. In sectors where large firms predominate, the two size distributions are very similar. However, in mechanical and instrument engineering and in textiles, both the number of innovations and the relative contribu-

---

[13] See [20]. A comparison between the two sets of results is made in [60, table 5.3].

Table 3
Distribution of Innovations by firm size [a] and by sector

| By sector of innovation | | | | Sector [b] | By sector of firm activity | | | |
|---|---|---|---|---|---|---|---|---|
| Percentage distribution [c] | | | Number of innovations | | Number of innovations | Percentage distribution [c] | | |
| 10,000 + | 1000–9999 | 1–999 | | | | 10,000 + | 1000–9999 | 1–999 |
| (1) | (2) | (3) | (4) | (5) | (6) | (7) | (8) | (9) |
| 72.3 | 10.8 | 17.0 | 65 | III Food and drink | 78 | 79.5 | 7.7 | 12.8 |
| 74.9 | 16.8 | 8.4 | 251 | V Chemicals | 290 | 82.4 | 7.9 | 9.6 |
| 63.5 | 31.4 | 5.1 | 137 | VI Metal manufacture | 143 | 62.9 | 32.8 | 4.2 |
| 35.2 | 30.5 | 34.3 | 662 | VII Mechanical engineering | 536 | 24.3 | 36.9 | 38.8 |
| 41.0 | 16.6 | 42.4 | 332 | VIII Instrument engineering | 187 | 24.6 | 21.4 | 54.0 |
| 66.4 | 15.9 | 17.7 | 339 | IX Electrical and electronic engineering | 343 | 65.9 | 12.2 | 22.0 |
| 57.7 | 38.5 | 3.8 | 52 | X Shipbuilding | 89 | 61.8 | 34.8 | 3.3 |
| 70.3 | 18.0 | 11.7 | 128 | XI Vehicles | 158 | 72.2 | 20.3 | 7.6 |
| 56.0 | 30.8 | 13.2 | 91 | XIII Textiles | 77 | 35.1 | 40.3 | 24.7 |
| 11.8 | 20.6 | 67.6 | 34 | XIV&XV Leather and footwear | 50 | 44.0 | 18.0 | 38.0 |
| 70.8 | 18.1 | 11.1 | 72 | XVI Bricks, pottery, glass and cement | 87 | 74.7 | 16.1 | 9.1 |
| – | – | – | 112 | Other | 227 | – | – | – |
| 53.2 | 21.9 | 24.9 | 2265 | Total | 2265 | 53.2 | 21.9 | 24.9 |

[a] Measured by number of employees.
[b] Roman numerals refer to the appropriate Order Headings.
[c] Rows add up to 100 percent.

tions of large firms are bigger when classified by sector of innovation, than when classified by the principal sector of activity of the innovating firm. In other words, a relatively large number of innovations are produced in these sectors by relatively large firms with their principal activities in other sectors.

Table 4 shows that for the sample as a whole,

Table 4
The distribution of innovations produced outside innovation firms' principal two-digit activities

| Innovations in other sectors by firms with principal activities in the sector | | Sector [a] | Innovations in the sector by firms with principal activities in other sectors | |
|---|---|---|---|---|
| % | Number | | Number | % |
| (1) | (2) | (3) | (4) | (5) |
| 30.8 | 78 | III Food and drink | 65 | 17.0 |
| 26.5 | 290 | V Chemicals | 251 | 15.2 |
| 34.3 | 143 | VI Metal manufacture [b] | 137 | 31.4 |
| (37.0) | (119) | | (93) | (19.4) |
| 16.0 | 536 | VII Mechanical engineering | 662 | 32.1 |
| 19.8 | 187 | VIII Instrument engineering | 332 | 54.6 |
| 23.8 | 343 | IX Electrical and electronic engineering | 339 | 23.0 |
| 58.4. | 89 | X Shipbuilding | 52 | 28.9 |
| 33.5 | 158 | XI Vehicles | 128 | 18.0 |
| 24.7 | 77 | XIII Textiles | 91 | 36.3 |
| 50.0 | 50 | XIV&XV Leather and footwear | 34 | 26.5 |
| 32.4 | 87 | XVI Bricks, pottery, glass and cement | 72 | 18.1 |
| – | 227 | Other | 102 | – |
| 31.5 | 2265 | Total | 2265 | 31.5 |

[a] Roman numerals refer to the appropriate Order Headings.
[b] Percentages between brackets refer to Iron and steel only.

31.5 percent of the innovations are produced by firms with their principal activities in other two digit sectors. Column 5 shows that a relatively large proportion of innovations in mechanical and instrument engineering and textiles are produced by firms with their principal activities elsewhere (32.1, 54.6 and 36.3 percent respectively), whilst column 1 shows that firms with their principal activities in mechanical and instrument engineering and in textiles produce a relatively small proportion of innovations in other sectors (16.0, 19.8 and 24.7 percent respectively).

Column 1 also shows the sectors where firms principally in them produce a proportion of innovations in other sectors that is above or round about the average: food and drink, metal manufacture, shipbuilding, vehicles, leather and footwear, and building materials. This is in contrast with firms principally in chemicals, or in electrical and electronic products, neither of which produce relatively high proportions of innovations beyond their two digit sector (26.5 and 23.8 percent respectively). Similarly, a relatively small proportion of innovations in these two sectors are produced by firms principally in other sectors (15.2 and 23.0 percent respectively).

This pattern suggests, amongst other things, that a relatively high proportion of innovations in mechanical and instrument engineering are produced by firms typified by continuous process and assembly production, such as metal manufacture, shipbuilding and vehicles. A more detailed examination of the data base confirms that this is the case. Innovations in two fundamentally important sectors of production technology – mechanical and instrument engineering – are therefore made both in relatively small specialised firms in these sectors, and in relatively large firms in continuous process and assembly industries.

One question springs to mind, when examining the data in tables 3 and 4: to what extent are the intersectoral differences in the size distribution of innovating firms, and in their patterns of technological diversification, similar to those found in the size distribution and patterns of sectoral diversification, in terms of sales, output and employment? Given the gaps in the data in the UK censuses of production, it is not possible to provide a straightforward answer to this question. Certainly, there are similarities: small firms makes a relatively greater contribution to net output and employment in mechanical and instrument engineering than in the other two digit sectors in our sample; and over time, both the increasing contribution to the production of innovations of firms with more than 10,000 employees and the constant share of firms with less than 200 employees, are reflected in trends in both output and employment.

The similarities are at first sight far less apparent in patterns of diversification. A comparison with Hassid's analysis [17], based on data from the UK census of production, shows that diversification at the two digit level is considerably less in net output than it is in the production of innovations: 14.0 percent in 1963 and 16.9 percent in 1968, compared to 31.5 percent for the whole period from 1945 to 1979. Neither is there any close relationship across sectors between the degree to which firms principally in them diversify into other sectors in net output, and in the production of innovations.

However, there is a similarity in the sectors into which firms diversify: a comparison of table 4 above with Hassid's data [17, table 3] shows that, in terms of both the production of innovations and the net output, mechanical and instrument engineering are sectors where relatively large contributions are made by firms principally in other sectors, whilst relatively small contributions are made in food, chemicals, electrical and electronic engineering, and vehicles by such firms.

Taking these comparisons further will need much more time and space, and will not be done in this paper. Our contribution here hopefully will be to enrich the ways in which such comparisons will be interpreted and explained. In particular, we intend to go beyond explanations of sectoral patterns of production of innovations simply in terms of sectoral industrial structures. Even if there turned out to be perfect statistical correlations across sectors between firm size and sectoral patterns of output, on the one hand, and firm size and sectoral patterns of production of innovations, on the other, it would be wrong to interpret the latter simply as causal consequences of the former. This would neglect the causal links running from the latter to the former: that is, from diversification in the production of innovations to diversification in output, and from the production of innovations to firms growth and firm size.

Most of the empirical studies of patterns of

diversification do in fact refer to the notion of "technological proximity" in explaining diversification in output [4;16;17;46;62]; our analysis and explanation will try to give some additional empirical and theoretical content to this notion. Similarly, a number of writers have recently stressed the causal links running from innovation to firm size [23,32]; we shall begin to explain, amongst other things, why high rates of innovation do not necessarily lead to heavily concentrated industries. Before doing this, however, we propose in section 3 how and why patterns of technological development and innovation differ amongst sectors.

## 3. Towards a taxonomy and a theory

### 3.1. The ingredients

Two central characteristics of innovations and innovating firms emerge from section 2. First, from subsection 2.2 it is clear that most of the knowledge applied by firms in innovations is not general purpose and easily transmitted and reproduced, but appropriate for specific applications and appropriated by specific firms. We are therefore justified in assuming, like Rosenberg [42], that, in making choices about which innovations to develop and produce, industrial firms cannot and do not identify and evaluate all innovation possibilities indifferently, but are constrained in their search by their existing range of knowledge and skills to closely related zones. In other words, technical change is largely a cumulative process specific to firms. What they can realistically try to do technically in future is strongly conditioned by what they have been able to do technically in the past.

The second characteristic is, of cource, variety. From subsections 2.3 and 2.4, it emerges that sectors vary in the relative importance of product and process innovations, in sources of process technology, and in the size and patterns of technological diversification of innovating firms. Nonetheless, some regularities do begin to emerge. In subsection 2.3, we can see a whole class of sectors where – as in vintage models – technical change comes mainly from suppliers of equipment: non-manufacturing and traditional sectors of manufacturing like textiles. We also ssee that the other manufacturing sectors make a significant contribu-

tion to their process technology. However, whilst firms in assembly and continuous process industries tend to concentrate relatively more of their innovative resources on process innovations, those in chemicals, electronic and electrical engineering, mechanical engineering, and instrument engineering devote most of these resources to product innovation.

In subsection 2.4, we see that sectors making mainly product innovations can be divided into two categories. First, firms principally in the chemicals and electronic and electrical sectors are relatively big, they diversify relatively little beyond their two digit category in producing innovations, and they produce a relatively high proportion of all the innovations in the two sectors. Second, firms principally in mechanical engineering and instrument engineering are relatively small, they diversify technologically relatively little beyond their two digit category, and they make a smaller contribution to all the innovations in the two sectors, given the important contribution made by relatively large user firms, particularly those in sectors typified by assembly and continuous process production.

In subsections 3.2–3.5 below, we shall try to categorise and explain these characteristics: in other words, to propose a taxonomy and a theory of sectoral patterns of technical change. Ideally, these should be consistent with the data so far presented. They should also be capable of further empirical refinement and test, given the inadequacies of the data at present available, and in particular of using what is mainly static, cross-sectional data as the basis for a theory that is essentially dynamic.

In our proposed taxonomy and theory, the basic unit of analysis is the innovating firm. Since patterns of innovation are cumulative, its technological trajectories will be largely determined by what is has done in the past in other words, by its principal activities. Different principal activities generate different technological trajectories. These can usefully be grouped into the three catogories, that we shall call supplier dominated, production intensive, and science-based. These different trajectories can in turn be explained by sectoral differences in three characteristics: sources of technology, users' needs, and means of appropriating benefits. The three categories, the differing technological trajectories, and their underlying causes are

Table 5
Sectoral technological trajectories: Determinants, directions and measured characteristics

| Category of firm | Typical core sectors | Determinants of technological trajectories | | | Technological trajectories | Measured characteristics | | | |
|---|---|---|---|---|---|---|---|---|---|
| | | Sources of technology | Type of user | Means of appropriation | | Source of process technology | Relative balance between product and process innovation | Relative size of innovating firms | Intensity and direction of technological diversification |
| (1) | (2) | (3) | (4) | (5) | (6) | (7) | (8) | (9) | (10) |
| Supplier dominated | Agriculture; housing; private services; traditional manufacture | Suppliers; Research extension services; big users | Price sensitive | Non-technical (e.g. trademarks, marketing, advertising, aesthetic design) | Cost-cutting | Suppliers | Process | Small | Low vertical |
| Production intensive — Scale intensive | Bulk materials (steel, glass); assembly (consumer durables & autos) | PE suppliers; R&D | Price sensitive | Process secrecy and know-how; technical lags; patents; dynamic learning economies | Cost-cutting (product design) | In-house; suppliers | Process | Large | High vertical |
| Production intensive — Specialised suppliers | Machinery; instruments | Design and development users | Performance sensitive | Product design know-how; knowledge of users; patents | Product design | In-house; customers | Product | Small | Low concentric |
| Science based | Electronics/electrical; chemicals | R&D; Public science; PE | Mixed | R&D know-how; patents; process secrecy and know-how; dynamic learning economies | Mixed | In-house; suppliers | Mixed | Large | Low vertical / High concentric |

* PE = Production Engineering Department.

summarised in table 5. Before discussing them in greater detail, we shall identify briefly the three traditions of analysis on which the taxonomy and the theory are based.

First, there are analysts who have deliberately explored the diversity of patterns of technical change. In particular, Woodward [69] has argued that appropriate organisational forms and mixes of skills for manufacturing firms are a function of their techniques of production, which she divided into three: small batch production and unit production, large batch and mass production, and continuous process production. Our proposal is in the same spirit but, whilst it has some common elements, its focus is different: encompassing product as well as process changes, and linkages with suppliers, customers and other sources of technology. Already in the 18th century, Adam Smith was aware of diversity in the sources of technical change, and of its dynamic nature; as we shall soon see, he identified many elements of our proposed taxonomy in Chapter One of *The Wealth of Nations* [54].

Second, there is the work of Penrose [41] on the nature of firms' diversification activities, and the importance of their technological base. Recent French writings, exploring the notion of *filière*, are in the same tradition [58], as is the work of Ansoff [2] and others on business strategy, and the recent contribution by Teubal [59] on the nature of technological learning.

Third, a number of analysts have explored the cumulative and dynamic nature of technical change: for example, Dosi [8], Freeman et al. [12], Gold [15] Nelson and Winter [31;32], Rosenberg [42;43] and Sahal [47]. From their research has emerged the notion of "technological trajectories," namely, directions of technical development that are cumulative and self-generating, without repeated reference to the economic environment external to the firm.

Nelson has gone further and suggested a framework for explaining technological trajectories [20]. He has argued that in any institutional framework, public or private, market or non-market, technical change requires mechanisms for generating technical alternatives; for screening, testing and evaluating them; and for diffusing them. In the Western market framework, the rate and direction of technical change in any sector depends on three features: first, the sources of technology; second, the

nature of users' needs; third, the possibilities for successful innovators to appropriate a sufficient proportion of the benefits of their innovative activities to justify expenditure on them.

For our purposes, there can be a number of possible sources of technology. Inside firms, there are R & D laboratories and production engineering departments. Outside firms, there are suppliers, users, and government financed research and advice. Similarly, users' needs can vary. For standard structural or mechanical materials, price is of major importance one certain performance requirements are met. For machinery and equipment used in modern and interdependent systems of production, performance and reliability will be given a higher premium relative to purchase price. In the consumer sector – as Rosenberg [41] and Gershuny [15] have pointed out – modern equipment is used extensively for "informal" household production. However, compared to their equivalents in the formal economy, purchase price will have a higher premium relative to performance, given that household systems of production are relatively small scale, with little technical interdependence, and with weak pressures of competition from alternative production systems.

The methods used by successful innovators to appropriate the benefits of their activities compared to their competitors will also vary. [14] For example, process innovations can be kept secret; some product innovations can be protected by natural and lengthy technical lags in imitation (e.g. aircraft), whilst others require parent protection (e.g. pharmaceuticals); and both product and process innovations may be difficult to imitate because of the uniqueness of the technological knowledge and skills in the innovating firm.

These ingredients are summarised in table 5, where column 1 defines the categories of firm, column 2 enumerates typical core sectors for such firms, columns 3–5 describe the determinants and the nature of the technological trajectories of the firms, and columns 7–10 identify some of the measured characteristics of these trajectories. We shall now go on to describe and discuss them in more detail.

---

[14] For more detailed discussion, see Taylor and Silberston [46], Scherer [50] and von Hippel [64–66].

### 3.2. Supplier dominated firms

Supplier dominated firms can be found mainly in traditional sectors of manufacturing, and in agriculture, housebuilding, informal household production, and many professional, financial and commercial services They are generally small, and their in-house R&D and engineering capabilities are weak. They appropriate less on the basis of a technological advantage, than of professional skills, aesthetic design, trademarks and advertising. Technological trajectories are therefore defined in terms of cutting costs.

Supplier dominated firms make only a minor contribution to their process or product technology. Most innovations come from suppliers of equipment and materials, although in some cases large customers and government-financed research and extension services also make a contribution. Technical choices resemble more closely those described in Salter's vintage model, the main criteria being the level of wages, and the price and performance of exogenously developed capital goods.

Thus, in sectors made up of supplier dominated firms, we would expect a relatively high proportion of the process innovations used in the sectors to be produced by other sectors, even though a relatively high proportion of innovative activities in the sectors are directed to process innovations. According to Scherer's data on the sectoral patterns of production and use of technology in the USA [51, table 2], the following sectors have such characteristics: textiles; lumber; wood and paper mill products; printing and publishing; and construction; in other words, precisely the types of sectors predicted by our taxonomy and theory. [15]

With our data on innovating firms in the UK, we are able to identify these and other characteristics of supplier dominated firms (as well as those of production intensive and science-based firms, described in subsections 3.3 and 3.4 below). Table 6 shows clearly the supplier dominated characteristics of textile firms. Before describing them, we shall define precisely the content of each of the columns of table 6, since tables 7, 8 and 9 present similar figures for the other categories of firms:

*Column 1* defines the principal two digit sector of activity of the innovating firms.

*Column 2* gives the percentage of innovations used in the sector that are produced by innovating firms principally in the sector. [16] It shows the degree to which firms in the sector develop their own process technology.

*Column 3* shows the percentage of innovations produced by firms principally in the sector that are used in other sectors: in other words, the percentage of product innovations. [17]

*Column 4* shows the size distribution of innovating firms principally in the sector. These figures are identical to those in columns 7, 8 and 9 of table 3.

*Column 5* gives more detail on the nature of innovating firms' innovations outside their principal sector of activity. It breaks down the figures of column 1, table 4 between "vertical" and "concentric/conglomerate" technological diversification. These terms are taken from the writings of Ansoff [2] on business strategy. The "vertical" figure is the percentage of the innovations produced by innovating firms, that are outside the innovating firms' principal sector of activity, but used within the innovating firms' sector: it reflects the relative importance of technological diversification into the equipment, materials and components for their own production. The "concentric/conglomerate" figure is the percentage of the innovations that are both produced and used outside the principal sector of the innovating firms' activities: it reflects the relative importance of technological diversification into related and unrelated product markets.

*Column 6* shows the origins of all the innovations in the sector, broken down between those produced by firms principally in the sector, those both produced and used by firms principally producing outside the sector (i.e. users of the output of the sector), and those from other sources. The figure in the first sub-column of column 6 adds up to 100 percent with the figure in column 5 of table 4.

---

[15] Scherer's data are incomplete for agriculture and for services, which we would predict to have similar characteristics.

[16] This percentage is not identical to the one in column 5 of table 2, since the former is based on the sector of the innovation, whilst the latter is based on the sector of principal activity of the innovating firm.

[17] This percentage is not identical to the one in column 1 of table 2, for the reasons given in footnote 16.

Table 6
Characteristics of innovations produced and used by firms producing principally textiles, and leather & footwear

| Principal sector of firm's activity (2-digit) (1) | Innovations used that are produced by firm | | Innovations produced by firms that are used in other sectors | | Size distribution of innovating firm (rows add up to 100%) | | | Innovations produced by firms in sector (No. produced) |
|---|---|---|---|---|---|---|---|---|
| | % | Number used | % | Number produced | 10,000+ | 1000–9999 | 1–999 | |
| | (2) | | (3) | | (4) | | | |
| XIII Textiles | 15.6 | 377 | 23.4 | 77 | 35.1 | 40.3 | 24.7 | 77 |
| XIV&XV Leather and Footwear | 48.9 | 45 | 56.0 | 50 | 44.0 | 18.0 | 38.0 | 50 |
| Total: All sectors in sample | 49.3 | 1401 [a] | 64.0 | 2265 | 53.1 | 21.9 | 24.9 | 2265 |

| Principal sector of firm's activity (2-digit) (1) | % [b] firms' innovations outside principal sector of activity are | | % of innovations in firms' sector of activity produced by | | | Innovations produced in sector (No.) |
|---|---|---|---|---|---|---|
| | Concentric/conglomerate | Vertical | Firms principally in the sector | Firms principally in other sectors that produce and use the innovation | Other | |
| | (5) | | | (6) | | |
| XIII Textiles | 3.9 | 20.8 | 63.8 | 2.2 | 34.0 | 91 |
| XIV&XV Leather and Footwear | 42.0 | 8.0 | 73.5 | – | 26.5 | 34 |
| Total: All sectors in sample | 20.3 | 11.2 | 68.6 | 11.2 | 20.3 | 2265 |

[a] Includes only those innovations used in sectors specified in table 2.
[b] The sum of the two percentages is equal to that in column 1 in table 4.

In the case of textile firms, table 6 shows a high degree of dependence on external sources for process technology (column 2), a relatively small proportion of innovative activity devoted to product innovations (column 3), a relatively small average size of innovating firm (column 4), technological diversification mainly vertically into production technology with very little movement into other product markets (column 5), and a relatively big contribution to innovations in the sector by firms with their principal activities elsewhere, but not from sectors using textiles (column 6). More detailed data show the considerable importance to textile firms of machinery firms in supplying process technology, and of chemical firms in supplying process technology and in making innovations in the textile sector itself.

Table 6 also shows that innovating firms principally producing in leather and footwear do not fall so neatly into the category of supplier dominated firms. Certainly they are relatively small (column 4), and their users make a relatively small contribution to innovation in their principal sector of activity (column 6). However, they also produce a sizeable proportion of product innovations (column 3), as well as making a strong contribution to their own process technology (column 2), and they have a high degree of concentric/conglomerate technological diversification (column 5).

Close examination shows that all this technological diversification is into textile machinery innovations that find their main use in the textile sector. This pattern reflects the coding practice used by Townsed and his colleagues in their survey [60]. However, it does not reflect the fact that there is no separate SIC category for leather working machinery, that innovations in textile machinery have applications in the manufacture of leather goods, and that – although the main uses of the identified innovations in textile machinery were in the textile sector – they also found uses in the manufacture of leather goods. In other words, firms principally in leather goods were in fact making a major contribution to the development of their own process technology. In this case, they begin to join the production intensive category, which we shall now describe.

### 3.3. Production intensive firms

Adam Smith described some of the mechanisms associated with the emergence of production intensive firms, namely, the increasing division of labour and simplification of production tasks, resulting from an increased size of market, and enabling a substitution of machines for labour and a consequent lowering of production costs. Improved transportation, increasing trade, higher living standards and greater industrial concentration have all contributed to this technological trajectory of increasing large-scale fabrication and assembly production. Similar opportunities for cost-cutting technical change exist in continuous processes producing standard materials, where the so-called two-thirds engineering law means that unit capacity costs can potentially be decreased by 1 percent by every 3 percent increase in plant capacity.

The technological skills to exploit these latent economies of scale have improved steadily over time. In fabrication and assembly, machines have been able to undertake progressively more complex and demanding tasks reliably, as a result of improvements in the quality of metals and the precision and complexity of metal forming and cutting, and in power sources and control systems. In continuous processes, increased scale and high temperatures and pressures have resulted from improvements in materials, control instrumentation and power sources. [13]

The economic pressure and incentives to exploit these scale economies are particularly strong in firms producing for two classes of price-sensitive users: first, those producing standard materials; second, those producing durable consumer goods and vehicles. In reality (if not in various models of technical change), it is difficult to make these scale-intensive processes work up to full capacity. Operating conditions are exacting, with regard to equipment performance, controlling physical interdependencies and flows, and the skills of operatives. In such complex and interdependent production systems, the external costs of failure in any one part are considerable. If only for purposes of "trouble-shooting," trained and specialist groups for "production engineering" and "process engineering" have been established. As Rosenberg [42] has shown, these groups develop the capacity to identify technical imbalances and bottlenecks which, once corrected, enable improvements in productivity. Eventually they are able either to specify or design new equipment that will improve

---

[13] See Levin [22] for well documented examples.

productivity still further. Thus, one important source of process technology in production-intensive firms are production engineering departments.

Adam Smith also pointed out that process innovations are also made "... by the ingenuity of the makers of machines when to make them became the business of a peculiar trade" [54]. The other important source of process innovations in production-intensive firms are the relative small and specialised firms that supply them with equipment and instrumentation, and with whom they have a close and complementary relationship. Large users provide operating experience, testing facilities and even design and development resources for specialised equipment suppliers. Such suppliers in turn provide their large customers with specialised knowledge and experience as a result of designing and building equipment for a variety of users, often spread across a number of industries. Rosenberg [42] describes this pattern as "vertical disintegration" and "technological convergence". He draws his examples from metal-forming machinery; the same process can be seen at work today in the functions of production monitoring and control performed by instruments. These specialised firms have a different technological trajectory from their users. Given the scale and interdependence of the production systems to which they contribute, the costs of poor operating performance can be considerable. The technological trajectories are therefore more strongly oriented towards performance-increasing product innovation, and less towards cost-reducing process innovation.

The way in which innovating firms appropriate technological advantage varies considerably between the large-scale producers, and the small-scale equipment and instrument suppliers. For the large-scale producers, particular inventions are not in general of great significance. Technological leads are reflected in the capacity to design, build and operate large-scale continuous processes, or to design and integrate large-scale assembly systems in order to produce a final product. Technological leads are maintained through know-how and secrecy around process innovations, and through inevitable technical lags in imitation, as well as through patent protection. For specialised suppliers, secrecy, process know-how and lengthy technical lags are not available to the same extent as a means of appropriating technology. Competi-

tive success depends to a considerable degree on firm-specific skills reflected in continuous improvements in product design and in product reliability, and in the ability to respond sensitively and quickly to users' needs.

The characteristics of large-scale producers and of specialised suppliers in the production intensive category are reflected in tables 7 and 8. Table 7 shows that, in our sample of innovations, firms with their principal activities in five of the two digit sectors in our sample have the characteristics of scale-intensive producers in the production intensive category: food products, metal manufacturing, shipbuilding, motor vehicles, and glass and cement. In these categories, innovative firms produce a relatively high proportion of their own process technology (column 2), to which they devote a relatively high proportion of their own innovative resources (column 3). Innovating firms are also relatively big (column 4), they have a relatively high level of vertical technological diversification into equipment related to their own process technology (column 5), and they make a relatively big contribution to all the innovations produced in their principal sectors of activity (column 6).

Table 8 shows the very different pattern in mechanical and instrument engineering firms. They also produce a relatively high proportion of their own process technology (column 2), but the main focus of their innovative activities is the production of product innovations for use in other sectors (column 3). Innovating firms are relatively small (column 4); they diversify technologically relatively little, either vertically or otherwise (column 5); and they do not make a relatively big contribution to all the innovations produced in their principal sector of activity, where users and other firms make significant contributions (column 6).

A more detailed examinations of the data at the three digit level shows that, within mechanical engineering, firms in all the product groups in the sample have a high proportion of their innovative resources devoted to product innovation, are technologically relatively specialised, and (with the exception of firms principally producing industrial plant) are relatively small. However, about 20 percent of the innovations are made by general engineering firms that produce in a range of mechanical engineering products, and the size distribu-

Table 7
Characteristics of innovations produced by firms producing principally in scale-intensive sectors

| Principal sector of firm's activity (2-digit) (1) | Innovations used that are produced by firm (2) | | Innovations produced by firms that are used in other sectors (3) | | Size distribution of innovating firm (rows add up to 100%) (4) | | | Innovations produced by firms in sector (No. produced) |
|---|---|---|---|---|---|---|---|---|
| | % | Number used | % | Number produced | 10,000+ | 1000–9999 | 1–999 | |
| III Food | 58.8 | 68 | 48.8 | 78 | 79.5 | 7.7 | 12.8 | 78 |
| VI Metal manufacturing | 62.3 | 130 | 43.4 | 143 | 62.9 | 32.8 | 4.2 | 143 |
| X Shipbuilding | 64.5 | 90 | 34.8 | 89 | 61.8 | 34.8 | 3.3 | 89 |
| XI Motor vehicles | 45.7 | 221 | 36.9 | 158 | 72.2 | 20.3 | 7.6 | 158 |
| XVI Glass and cement | 68.3 | 63 | 50.6 | 87 | 74.7 | 16.1 | 9.1 | 87 |
| Total: All sectors in sample | 49.3 | 1401 [a] | 64.0 | 2265 | 53.1 | 21.9 | 24.9 | 2265 |

| Principal sector of firm's activity (2-digit) (1) | % [b] firms' innovations outside principal sector of activity are (5) | | Innovations produced by firms in sector (No.) | % of innovations in firms' sector of activity produced by (6) | | | Innovations produced in sector (No.) |
|---|---|---|---|---|---|---|---|
| | Concentric/conglomerate | Vertical | | Firms principally in the sector | Firms principally in other sectors that produce and use the innovation | Other | |
| III Food | 16.7 | 14.1 | 78 | 83.1 | 3.1 | 13.9 | 65 |
| VI Metal manufacturing | 17.5 | 16.8 | 143 | 68.6 | 8.0 | 23.4 | 137 |
| X Shipbuilding | 21.3 | 37.1 | 89 | 71.2 | 13.5 | 15.4 | 52 |
| XI Motor vehicles | 12.6 | 20.9 | 158 | 82.0 | 1.6 | 16.4 | 128 |
| XVI Glass and cement | 13.8 | 18.4 | 87 | 81.9 | 5.6 | 12.5 | 72 |
| Total: All sectors in sample | 20.3 | 11.2 | 2265 | 68.6 | 11.2 | 20.3 | 2265 |

[a] Includes only those innovations used in sectors specified in table 2.
[b] The sum of the two percentages is equal to that in column 1 in table 4.

Table 8

Characteristics of innovations produced and used by firms producing production equipment

| Principal sector of firm's activity (2-digit) (1) | Innovations used that are produced by firm (2) | | Innovations produced by firms that are used in other sectors (3) | | Size distribution of innovating firm (rows add up to 100%) (4) | | | Innovations produced by firms in sector (No. produced) |
|---|---|---|---|---|---|---|---|---|
| | % | Number used | % | Number produced | 10,000+ | 1000–9999 | 1–999 | |
| VII Mechanical engineering | 55.1 | 169 | 82.6 | 536 | 24.3 | 36.9 | 38.8 | 536 |
| VIII Instrument engineering | 58.4 | 60 | 81.4 | 187 | 24.6 | 21.4 | 54.0 | 187 |
| Total: All sectors in sample | 49.3 | 1401[b] | 64.0 | 2265 | 53.1 | 21.9 | 24.9 | 2265 |

| Principal sector of firm's activity (2-digit) | %[b] firms' innovations outside principal sector of activity are (5) | | Innovations produced by firms in sector (No.) | % of innovations in firms' sector of activity produced by (6) | | | Innovations produced in sector (No.) |
|---|---|---|---|---|---|---|---|
| | Concentric/conglomerate | Vertical | | Firms principally in the sector | Firms principally in other sectors that produce and use the innovation | Other | |
| VII Mechanical engineering | 15.1 | 0.9 | 536 | 68.1 | 15.3 | 16.8 | 633 |
| VIII Instrument engineering | 9.7 | 10.2 | 187 | 45.2 | 19.3 | 35.5 | 332 |
| Total: All sectors in sample | 20.3 | 11.2 | 2265 | 68.6 | 11.2 | 20.3 | 2265 |

[a] Includes only those innovations used in sectors specified in table 2.
[b] The sum of the two percentages is equal to that in column 1 in table 4.

tion of which is bigger than other mechanical engineering, being close to the average for the sample of innovations as a whole. In instrument engineering, innovations are produced by firms in a wide range of user sectors, as well as by firms principally in mechanical engineering and in electronic capital goods.

### 3.4. Science-based firms

The third category, namely science-based firms, was also foreseen (if not observed) by Adam Smith who spoke of the contribution of technical of "... those who are called philosophers or men of speculation, whose trade it is not to do anything, but to observe everything; and who, upon that account, are often capable of combining together the powers of the most distant and dissimilar objects." From the data on innovations described above, science-based firms are to be found in the chemical and the electronic/electrical sectors. In both of them, the main sources of technology are the R&D activities of firms in the sectors, based on the rapid development of the underlying sciences in the universities and elsewhere.

As Freeman et al. [12] have shown, the development of successive waves of products has depended on *prior* development of the relevant basic science: in particular, of synthetic chemistry and biochemistry for the chemical industry; and of electromagnetism, radio waves and solid state physics for the electrical/electronic industry. Synthetic chemistry has enabled the development of a wide range of products, with useful structural, mechanical, electrical, chemical or biological characteristics, ranging from bulk materials replacing wood, steel and natural textiles, to specialised and expensive chemical and biological agents for medical or other uses. Post-war advances in the fundamentals of biochemistry are enabling the extension of these skills and techniques into biological products and processes.

Advances in electromagnetism, radio waves and solid state physics have enabled products and applications related to the availability of cheap, decentralised and reliable electricity, communications and (now) information processing, storage and retrieval. Applications in electricity vary from huge transformers to small motors within mechanical systems, in communications from expensive radar and satellite tracking systems to cheap transistor radios, and in information from huge computers to electronic wristwatches.

This pervasiveness has dictated the technological trajectories of firms in the science based sectors. The rich range of applications based on underlying science has meant that successful and innovative firms in them have grown rapidly, [19] and have had little incentive to look for innovative opportunities beyond their principal sector. Given the sophistication of the technologies and underlying sciences, it has been difficult for firms outside the sectors to enter them. The pervasive applications have also meant a wide variance in relative emphasis on production and process technology within each of the sectors, reflecting the different cost/performance trade-off for consumer goods, standard materials and specialised professional applications.

Firms appropriate their innovating leads through a mix of methods (i.e. patents, secrecy, natural technical lags, and firm-specific skills). Patent protection is particularly important in fine chemicals, with specific high grade applications, where the predominant product innovations can be quickly and cheaply imitated without it. [20] In addition, dynamic learning economies in production have been an important barrier to the entry of imitators in continuous process technology, large-scale assembly and – over the past 25 years – in the production of electronic components. According to Dosi [8], the particularly rapid rate and the form of technical change in electronic components involved a "paradigm shift." New firms have been able to enter the electronics industry, and to grow rapidly by aggressive product innovation coupled with the exploitation of steep dynamic economies of scale.

In the data on innovations in the UK collected by Townsend and his colleagues, characteristics of science-based firms emerge most clearly for those principally in chemicals, Table 9 shows that they produce a relatively high proportion of their own process technology (column 2), as well as a high proportion of product innovations that are used in other sectors (column 3). They are also relatively big (column 4), most of their technological diversification is concentric/conglomerate rather

[19] See, for example, the research of Rumelt [56] on the growth and diversification of US firms.

[20] See, in particular, the empirical studies of Taylor and Silberston [56].

Table 9

Characteristics of innovations produced and used by firms producing principally chemicals and electrical/electronic products

| Principal sector of firm's activity (2-digit) (1) | Innovations used by firm that are produced by firm | | Innovations produced by firms that are used in other sectors | | Size distribution of innovating firm (rows add up to 100%) | | | Innovations produced by firms in sector (No. produced) |
|---|---|---|---|---|---|---|---|---|
| | % (2) | Number used | % (3) | Number produced | 10,000+ | 1000–9999 | 1–999 (4) | |
| V Chemicals | 77.4 | 71 | 78.0 | 290 | 82.4 | 7.9 | 9.6 | 290 |
| IX Electrical and electronic engineering | 80.2 | 107 | 60.9 | 343 | 65.9 | 12.2 | 22.0 | 343 |
| Total: All sectors in sample | 49.3 | 1401 [a] | 64.0 | 2265 | 53.1 | 21.9 | 24.9 | 2265 |

| Principal sector of firm's activity (2-digit) (1) | % [b] firms' innovations outside principal sector of activity are | | Innovations produced by firms in sector (No.) | % of innovations in firms' sector of activity produced by | | | Innovations produced in sector (No.) |
|---|---|---|---|---|---|---|---|
| | Concentric/conglomerate | Vertical (5) | | Firms principally in the sector | Firms principally in other sectors that produce and use the innovation (6) | Other | |
| V Chemicals | 21.7 | 4.8 | 290 | 84.8 | 2.4 | 12.8 | 251 |
| IX Electrical and electronic engineering | 21.5 | 2.3 | 343 | 77.0 | 11.5 | 11.5 | 339 |
| Total: All sectors in sample | 20.3 | 11.2 | 2265 | 68.6 | 11.2 | 20.3 | 2265 |

[a] Includes only those innovations used in sectors specified in table 2.
[b] The sum of the two percentages is equal to that in column 1 in table 4.

270

*The Economics of Innovation*

364 *K. Pavitt / Sectoral patterns of technical change*

than vertical (column 5), and they produce a relatively high proportion of all the innovations made in their principal sector of activity (column 6). More detailed data also show that, within the two digit chemical sector, the detergent product group has a relatively high proportion of process innovations; and that the technological diversification of chemical firms outside their principal two digit sector is mainly into instruments, machinery and textiles. According to table 9, firms principally in electronic and electrical engineering also have most of the predicted characteristics of science-based firms: a relatively high contribution to own process technology (column 2), relatively big innovating firms (column 4), mainly concentric/conglomerate diversification [21] (column 5), and a relatively big contribution to all innovations in their principal sector of activity (column 6).

However, the proportion of product innovations, although absolutely large, is relatively small (column 3); more detailed data show that this cannot be explained simply by the preponderance of process innovations in broadcasting equipment, but also reflects a high proportion of innovations in electronic components that are produced and used by firms principally producing electronic capital goods. Furthermore, the relatively big contribution to the production of innovations made by firms with less than 1000 employees (table 9, column 4) reflects the increasing contribution made in the 1970s by such firms in the computer product group.

Finally, more detailed data suggest that large, diversified firms make a bigger contribution to innovations by science-based firms, than to those by specialised equipment supplies. As we saw in subsection 3.3, general engineering firms produced 20 percent of all the innovations in mechanical engineering. In chemicals, firms principally in general chemicals produced about 40 percent of the whole; and in electronics/electrical products, firms principally in electronics capital goods produced about 50 percent.

### 3.5. Technological linkages and changing trajectories

Linkages amongst the different categories of firm go beyond those described in the production

[21] More detailed data show that this is mainly into the mechanical engineering and scientific instruments sectors.

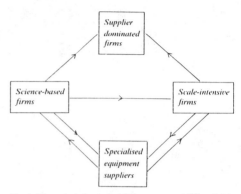

Fig. 1. The main technological linkages amongst different categories of firm.

intensive category (subsection 3.3. above). Figure 1 tries to represent the main technological flows emerging from our taxonomy and theory. Supplier dominated firms get most of their technology from production intensive and science-based firms (e.g power tools and transport equipment from the former; consumer electronics and plastics from the latter). Science-based firms also transfer technology to production intensive ones (e.g. the use of plastics, and of electronics, in the automobile industry). And, as we have seen, science-based and production intensive firms both receive and give technology to specialised suppliers of production equipment.

We have also argued that technological linkages amongst sectors can go beyond transactions involving the purchase and sale of goods embodying technology. They can include flows of information and skills, as well as technological diversification into the main product areas of suppliers and customers. Examples include the contribution of scale-intensive firms to the technology of their equipment suppliers and of chemical and electronics firms to innovations in textiles, scientific instruments and mechanical engineering.

Our data do not yet enable us to analyse if and how patterns of technical change in specific sectors change over time. We have hinted in subsection 3.3 that sectors can shift from the supplier dominated to the production-intensive pattern as a result of access to larger markets by individual firms, and of autonomous and induced improvements in capital goods: a contemporary example might be certain commercial and financial services, given producer concentration and rapid technical progress in information processing equipment. On the other hand, analysts like Utterback and Abernathy [70] would predict on the basis of their "product cycle" model that, where process technology has matured, sectors may shift from the production intensive to the supplier dominated pattern: for example, in bulk synthetic chemicals today, it is said that this focus has shifted from the chemical firms to their specialised suppliers of process equipment [6]. Whatever regularities in such change are eventually observed the above two examples suggest that trends in the *rate* of technological change will be an important explanatory variable. Of particular interest will be a systematic exploration of the effects of radical technological changes (e.g. solid state electronics) on prevailing paths and patterns of technical change. [22]

## 4. Some analytical implications

Our proposed taxonomy and theory have a number of implications for analysis of the nature, sources, determinants and economic effects of technical change. We shall now identify some of the most obvious ones, without pretending to be comprehensive in either breadth or depth of discussion.

### 4.1. Science and technology push versus demand pull

There is the continuing debate about the relative importance of "science and technology push" and "demand pull" in determining patterns of innovative activity, and in triggering innovative activity. As Mowery and Rosenberg [26] and others have pointed out, both technology push and demand pull are necessary for any successful innovation, and much of the debate about the relative importance of the two has been ill-conceived. Nonetheless, according to Schmookler [53], "demand-pull" has been a stronger influence than "science and technology push" on patterns of innovative activity, both across industry and over time. Across industry, he found a stronger statistical association between the volume of innovative

activity in capital goods (as measured by patents) and the volume of investment activity in user industries, than between the volume of innovative activity and of output in the supplier industries. Over time, he found that changes in the volume of innovative activity followed changes in the volume of investment activity. Using a more comprehensive data base, Scherer [52] has recently confirmed the former of Schmookler's findings, but could find no evidence of a lag between investment and innovative activities.

In our taxonomy, the close relationship between investment in user sectors and innovative activities in upstream capital goods comes as no surprise. Investment activities in supplier dominated and production intensive firms are likely to stimulate innovative activities in both the production engineering departments of user firms, and the upstream firms supplying capital goods. [22] To the extent that these investment activities are planned in advance, and co-ordinated with the activities of production engineering departments of investing firms and with firms supplying production equipment, we would also expect – as Scherer found – that the lag between investment and innovative activities would tend to disappear.

However, we would not expect in our science-based firms a similarly neat and lagged correspondence between the volume of investment in user sectors, and of innovative activities. Recent research by Walsh [68] has shown that the emergence of major new product families in the chemical industry in the twentieth century has been *preceded* by an upsurge of scientific and inventive activities. Furthermore, Scherer [52] found that in materials sectors, in contrasts to capital goods, the statistical relationship between the volume of innovative activities and of investment in user sectors is much weaker; given the role of the chemical industry in developing synthetic *substitute* materials, this should not surprise us. Finally, Scherer [52] found that the relationship between the volume of innovative activities and the output of the supply industry becomes much stronger when account is taken of difference amongst sectors in scientific and technological opportunity – the relationship between the two being particularly strong in the

---

[22] For further discussion on the automobile industry see Anderson et al. [1]. More generally see Ergas [9].

[23] User sectors covered in Schmookler's analysis included petroleum refining, synthetic fibres, glass, sugar, tobacco, railroads, textiles and apparel, and timber and paper.

organic chemicals and electronics sectors, where we would expect science-based technical opportunities to be particularly strong.

### 4.2. Product versus process innovation

Our proposed theory also offers an explanation of the balance in different sectors between product and process innovation. We would expect the relative importance of product innovation in a sector to be positively associated with its R & D and patent intensity; and negatively associated with proxy measures of the scale and complexity of its process technology, such as its capital/labour ratio, average size of production plant, or sales concentration ratios.

The reasoning behind such an expectation runs as follows. In product groups with a high proportion of science-based firms, we would expect a relatively high R & D intensity, and a high proportion of product/market opportunities generated outside the product groups. The relationship should be even stronger between patent intensity and product innovation, given that – in addition to R & D activities – patent statistics reflect the innovative activities in small firms, and the production engineering departments of large firms, both of which are particularly important sources of product innovation in mechanical and instrument engineering. On the other hand, in sectors with a relatively high proportion of production intensive firms, we would expect both a realtively high proportion of resources to be devoted to process innovations, on the one hand, and relatively high capital intensities, size of plant and industrial concentration on the other.

As can be seen in the Appendix to this paper, the regression based on our (very imperfect) statistics are consistent with our expectations (E1, E2, E3). [24] The signs are correctly predicted and, in some equations, explanatory variables are significant at the 1 percent and $2\frac{1}{2}$ percent level. Only the capital–labour ratio has a low explanatory power in all of the equations that we tried, which may say as much about the problems of measuring capital as about the predictive powers of our theory.

---

[24]  E1, E2 etc. refers to the relevant equations in the Appendix.

### 4.3. The locus of process innovation

Our taxonomy and theory also lead to expectations about the degree to which firms develop their own process innovations, or buy them from "upstream" suppliers of production equipment. In sectors with supplier-dominated firms, we would expect firms and production plant to be small in size, and innovations to come by definition from suppliers. In sectors with production intensive firms, we would expect firms and plant to be large in size, and a high proportion of process technology to be generated in-house. The same will be the case in science-based firms, especially in products involving continuous process and assembly technologies. In other words, we would expect a positive relationship between the proportion of a sector's process technology generated in-house, on the one hand, and the size of firms and of plant in the sector on the other.

Other writers have made related but somewhat different predictions, namely, that upstream equipment suppliers became relatively more important sources of process innovations as the absolute size of the market for the production process equipment grows. For Rosenberg [42], this reflects a greater division of labour in production resulting from a larger size of market. For Utterback and Abernathy [70], it reflects the large size and technological stability in firms at the later stages of the product cycle.

Von Hippel [67] and Buer [5] make predictions from a different basis, arguing that the balance between in-house development and recourse to upstream suppliers depends on the prospective benefits to be appropriated by the user of the production equipment. They argue that the benefits of appropriation by the user – compared to those of the supplier – increase with the degree of concentration in the user sector. The proportion of process technology developed in-house will therefore increase with the degree of user concentration. The data at present at our disposal does not enable an authoritative statistical test of these various hypotheses. Our measure of the proportion of process technology developed in-house is somewhat shaky, and we do not have comprehensive data on sources of process technology for sectors outside manufacturing. However, we can explore the relationship across sectors between the proportion of process technology developed in-house, on the one hand, and a range of variables reflecting the different hypotheses described above: average size of innovating firms, capital–labour ratio and average plant size (this writer's hypothesis); volume of investment in plant and equipment in equipment-using sectors (Rosenberg; Utterback and Abernathy); five firm concentration ratios in equipment using sectors (von Hippel; Buer).

This author's explanatory variables perform least well. Although the signs are all correctly predicted, none is statistically significant. However, the other hypotheses receive strong statistical confirmation (E4). The proportion of process technology developed by firms in the sector is negatively related to the absolute size of the market for process equipment, and positively to the degree of concentration of sales in the user sector.

### 4.4. Diversification

On the economic impact of technical change, our taxonomy and theory may also offer some insights into mechanisms of diversification, whether in terms of R&D and technology, or in terms of economic activity. Nelson [27] once suggested a positive relationship between the performance of basic research by firms and the diversity of their output, given that the uncertain results of basic research are more likely to find a use in a diversified firm than a specialised one. According to Scherer, however, the results of statistical analysis of the relationship between spending on basic research, and total R&D, on the one hand, and diversification, on the other "... have been mixed and to some extend contradictory" [49, p. 422].

According to our taxonomy, those related to total R&D are likely to be so, since we postulate a different causality, and predict an indeterminate and messy relationship between the variables. It is indeterminate (or, at least, non-linear), given that we predict relatively low levels of technology-based two digit diversification in sectors that are both R&D intensive (chemicals, instruments, and electrical/electronics), and low R&D spenders (supplier dominated). It is messy, given that the potential for technology-based diversification in science-based firms is much higher at the three digit than at the two digit level.

Furthermore, in both production intensive and supplier dominated firms the links between technology and production diversification may be

weak. This emerges from a comparison of Hassid's data on production diversification [17] in British firms with those for technology in table 4. Production intensive firms diversify less in production than in technology, possibly because they do not exploit themselves all the opportunities open to them for technology-based diversification upstream into equipment supply. Textile firms, on the other hand, diversify more in production than in technology, possibly because of non-technological complementarities with other sectors.

However, we can, on the basis of our taxonomy, make some predictions about the factors determining potential technological paths of diversification in innovating firms, as a function of their principal activity. The relative importance of upstream (i.e. vertical) technological diversification into sectors supplying equipment is likely to be negatively associated with R&D intensity (which tends to provide technological opportunities concentrically or downstream), and positively associated with the scale and complexity of production technology (which induces innovative activities on production techniques and upstream equipment). Using the capital–labour ratio, and average plant size as proxy measures for scale and complexity of production technology, we find none of the expected statistical relationships at the three digit level. However, at the two digit level, and using the 20 firm concentration ratio as a proxy for scale and complexity of process technology, the statistical relations are as expected, and significant at the 1 percent level (E5).

Our taxonomy and theory may also help us better understand the links at the level of the firm between firm strategy and R&D strategy. Although much study has been devoted to the "tactical" problems of the management of activities necessary for innovations, [25] relatively little attention has been devoted to the "strategic" question of the role of technology in determining the future activities of the firm, and in particular its future product lines.

We propose a model that identifies the "technological trajectories" of firms as a function of their principal activities, and that enables us to predict possible paths of technological diversification across product lines and sectors. Given the wealth and detail of statistical data now becoming availa-

---

[25] See the survey by Rothwell [45].

ble on individual firms' technological activities, it will be possible to put our predictions to the statistical test by answering two questions. First, do firms with the same principal activities have statistically similar distributions of technological activity across product groups and technical areas? Second, are the distributions those predicted from our taxonomy and theory? Whilst we should not claim to be able to predict the specific competitive strengths and weaknesses of particular firms, we would at least be able to identify and explain the technological opportunities and constraints that in part govern their behaviour and choice.

However, we can predict with greater certainty that, at the level of individual firms, the degree of technological diversification will be positively associated with its size. This will reflect three mechanisms in our taxonomy and theory: first, large-scale production intensive firms procuding innovations upstream, principally in mechanical engineering and instruments; second, the possibilities open to small and specialised firms producing production equipment to remain small, competitive and technologically dynamic; third, the possibilities open to science-based firms for technological diversification beyond their principal three digit (but within their principal two digit) sector. Given these patterns of technological diversification in science-based firms, we would expect this relationship to be stronger at the three digit than at the two digit level.

Our data on innovations confirm these predictions. The size distribution of firms producing innovations outside their principal three digit sector is more skewed than average innovating firms towards large size: 69.9 (53.2) percent with 10,000 and more employees; 14.0 (23.2) percent with between 1000 and 9999 employees; 16.1 (23.7) percent with fewer than 1000 employees. [26] Across three digit sectors, we find a positive and statistically significant relationship (at the 5 percent level) between the degree to which innovating firms diversify technologically outside their three digit sector, and their average size in each sector.

Finally, we would predict on the basis of our taxonomy that, amongst science-based firms, relatively high levels of basic research will allow more innovations, more diversification beyond three to

four digit sectors and more growth. In a recent study, Link and Long [24] found that the two most significant factors explaining differences amongst 250 US manufacturing firms in the proportion of sales spent on basic research were diversification at the four digit level, and having principal activities in science-based sectors. Although our proposed causality runs the other way, our results are consistent with those of Link and Long. Similarly, in a study of US firms in the petrochemicals industry, Mansfield [25] recently found a positive relationship between basic research as a percentage of value added, on the one hand, and the rate of growth of total factor productivity on the other hand. If one assumes further that growth of total factor productivitiy is positively associated with growth of output, then Mansfield's results are consistent with our taxonomy and theory.

### 4.5. Firm size and industrial structure

The causal links running from innovation to firm growth and to firm size are central to the recent research on the dynamics of Schumpeterian competition by Nelson and Winter [32]. They predict that, in industry with rapid rates of technical change, with uncertainty in the outcomes of investments in innovative activities, and with the strong possibilities for innovative firms to appropriate their innovative advantage, there are powerful tendencies over time towards the concentration of both production and innovative activities.

Our data and theory are consistent with these assumptions and outcomes for our science-based category of firms, but not for our supplier dominated or production intensive categories. In supplier dominated firms, any increase in firm size usually cannot be attributed to innovation, given that not much of it is generated in the sector, although increased size may enable (as described by Adam Smith) the introduction of more efficient process technology. In production intensive firms, innovation is associated with large and increasing size not, as Nelson and Winter [32] suggest, through the uneven exploitation amongst firms of a rich crop of new product/market opportunities, but through the search for increasing static scale economies in production. [27]

---

[26] Numbers in brackets refer to the percentage for all innovations: see table 4.

[27] See, for example, Levin [22].

The most important difference between Nelson and Winter's and our proposed model is the stable existence of small firms making innovations in production equipment and instrumentation. Rosenberg's description of textile machinery firms in the first half of 19th century [42] is not very different – apart from the state of the technological art – from Rothwell's description of textile machinery firms in the second half of the 20th century [44]. As we have been in subsection 2.4, small, specialised and technologically dynamic equipment suppliers in mechanical and instrument engineering continue to live in symbiosis with even larger production intensive and science-based firms, and to confound trends towards Schumpeterian concentration. This is puzzling given that, as Rosenberg [42] has pointed out, common skills, techniques and know-how underlie all mechanical engineering products, just as they do in chemical-based and electrical/electronic-based firms. Why, then, have firms in these science-based sectors typically diversified and grown big on the basis of their accumulated skills, whereas those in mechanical and instrument engineering typically have not?

No definite answer can be given in this paper. Suffice here to suggest that explanations probably lie in sectoral differences in technology sources, users' requirements and appropriability. [28] Compared to chemical and electronic firms, those in mechanical and instrument engineering depend more on their customers for information and skills related to the operating performance, and to the design, development and testing of their products; they therefore can afford to remain small, but do not accumulate the same range and depth of technological skills. They also sell in markets that do not have such pronounced product cycle characteristics, and therefore have less market pressure to diversify. Finally, they find it more difficult to appropriate the benefits of their innovations, given the overwhelming importance of produce innovation, and relatively low barriers to entry, resulting from relatively small scale expenditures on product development, and the existence of many independent sources of skills and know-how in the production engineering departments of large firms.

Innovative small firms are now to be found not only in instruments and mechanical engineering, but also in electronics: according to Townsend et al. the share of firms with up to 1000 employees increased in electronics in the 1970s. There has been one essential difference between innovative firms in instruments and mechanical engineering innovations, and those in electronics. Whilst the former have on the whole remained relatively small and specialised, a few of the latter became very large through precisely the mechanism of innovation and growth described by Nelson and Winter.

According to Dosi [8], new small firms can become big in a sector when there is a "paradigm shift" in technology, which alters radically the rate, direction and skills associated with a technological trajectory. However, whilst this might serve to explain the entry of new firms in the US electronics industry from 1950 to 1970, based on advances in solid state technology, it cannot explain the relative stability of structure of the world chemical industry over the past 60 years, in spite of successive waves of radical innovations – or "paradigm shifts" – growing out of synthetic chemistry.

The reasons for this difference must probably be sought once again in the nature of the scale barriers facing new entrants. In electronics (especially solid-state components and related equipment), static scale barriers are low, but there are very steep dynamic economies in production. This means that a small and successful innovator can quickly become very big, since imitators are chasing the innovator down steeply declined cost curves. In chemicals, on the other hand, there are high static scale barriers to new entrants: in bulk chemicals, there are big static economies of scale; in fine chemicals, there are systems of public regulation and control for new products that require heavy expenditures on testing and screening.

This discussion suggests that formal models of the dynamics of Schumpeterian competition, like those developed by Nelson and Winter, would more accurately reflect a varied reality in technological trajectories, if they were to explore a range of assumptions about new entrants and static and dynamic economies of scale; about pressures for market diversification; and about complementary relations between producers and users of capital goods.

---

[28]  For a more detailed exploration of this question, see Ergas [10].

## 5. Future perspectives

We began this paper with some dissatisfaction with existing conceptualisations of technical change. Based on systematic empirical data, we have tried to show why; and we have proposed another conceptualisation which, we hope, more accurately reflects the cumulative and varied nature of the technical change to be found in a modern economy. It is not necessary here to summarise the main conclusions of our analysis, since this is done at the beginning of the paper. Suffice to suggest some directions for the future.

First, our proposed taxonomy needs to be tested on the basis of complete sectoral coverage of the characteristics of innovations in Britain, of accumulated case studies, and of other data on innovative activities that become available. Our analysis suggests that R&D statistics do not measure two important sources of technical change: the production engineering departments of production intensive firms, and the design and development activities of small and specialised suppliers of production equipment. For reasons that are discussed elsewhere [37], it is probably that statistics on patenting activity capture innovative activity from these sources more effectively than do R&D statistics. The detailed information now becoming available on patenting activity by company should therefore enable a considerable step forward. As Rosenberg has observed [42], theoretical and practical advances have depended on good systems of measurement, and on accurate and comprehensive data. US patenting statistics could eventually enable the thorough econometric analysis that we considered and rejected at the beginning of this paper.

Second, our taxonomy itself needs to be modified and extended. Greater emphasis should be given to the exploitation of natural resources in the use of large-scale production equipment and instrumentation, [29] and therefore included in our production intensive category. And a fourth category should be added to cover purchases by government and utilities of expensive capital goods related to defence, energy, communications and transport.

Third, our taxonomy may have a variety of uses

for policy makers and analysts. At the very least it may help to avoid general and sterile debates about the relative contribution of large and small firms to innovation, and the relative importance of "science and technology push" compared to "demand pull." It may also increase the value and effectiveness of micro-studies and micro-policies for technical change, by suggesting questions to ask at the beginning, and by putting results in a broader perspective at the end.

Fourth, the taxonomy and the theory may turn out to have more powerful uses. As we have seen in section 4 of this paper, they cast a different and perhaps fresh light on a number of important aspects of technical change: for example, the sources and directions of innovative activities; their role in the diversification activities of industrial firms and in the evolution of industrial structures; and the accumulation of technological skills and advantages within industrial firms. They may also give us a firmer understanding of the determinants of the sectoral patterns of comparative technological advantage that have emerged in different countries. [30] Nelson and Winter [31] have rightly observed that analysis of technical change has been "balkanised"; perhaps the concepts in this paper will help towards re-unification.

Fifth, our taxonomy and theory contain one obvious and important warning for both practitioners of policies for technical change, and academic social scientists concerned with is conceptualisation. Given the variety in patterns of technical change that we have observed, most generalisations are likely to be wrong, if they are based on very specific practical experience, however deep, or on a simple analytical model, however elegant.

For policy makers – many of whom come from the hard sciences and engineering – this means accepting that personal experience and anecdotal evidence from colleagues are an insufficient basis for policies that cover a range of technical activities. It also implies a need for sympathy towards systematic data collection on scientific and technological activities. Such data may be flawed in precision, but they do have the advantage of being comprehensive.

For the academic social scientists, one implica-

---

[29]  See, for example, Townsend [61].

[30]  For further discussion, see [38;40].

Table 10
Definition and description of variables

| Symbol | Description | Source |
|--------|-------------|--------|
| Prop 3 | Proportion of innovations used outside their 3 digit sector of production | Data bank on innovations |
| Prop 2 | Proportion of innovations used outside 2-digit sector of production | Column 1, table 2 |
| Inhouse 3 | Proportion of innovations used in sector that are produced by sector/firms in the sector (3 digit) | Data bank on innovations |
| vertical | Proportion of innovations by firms principally in sector that are vertical diversification (2 digit) | Table 6–9, column 5 |
| R/Y | Total R&D in manufacturing firms as a percentage of net output in 1975 (2 and 3 digit) | Business monitor, M014, 1979, table 20, (HMSO) |
| PSU | Average plant size (3 digit) | Information supplied by Dept. of Industry; based on industrial census, 1977 |
| $C_5$ | Proportion of sales in first five firms in 1970 (3-digit) | Business monitor, PA1002, 1975, table 9 (HMSO) |
| T/Y | Patents granted in the UK as a percentage of net output in 1975 (2 digit) | Same as R/Y; Townsend et al., table 11.1 |
| $D_{20}$ | Proportion of sales in first 20 firms in (2 digit) | Same as PSU |
| I | Expenditure on plant and machinery, 1970 (3 digit) | Same as $C_5$ |

tion is that analytical models of technical change are likely to become more complex and more numerous [31] Salter's vintage model of technical change [48] may be an accurate reflection of what happens outside industry and in traditional manufacturing; but in mass assembly and continuous process industries, the emphasis placed on investment and production as sources of technical change by such writers as Schmookler [53], Gold [15], Sahal [47] and even Kaldor [18] and Verdoorn [63] may be more appropriate; whilst the Schumpeterian dynamics of innovation, growth and concentration in science-based sectors are better reflected in the models and analyses of writers like Freeman [41;42], Nelson and Winter [32] and Dosi [8]. As we have seen in this paper, the variety in sectoral patterns of technical change was recognised by Adam Smith. Perhaps his is a tradition to which we should return.

[31] This same point is made by Gold [15].

## Appendix

### Some exploratory statistical analysis

As we pointed out in section 3 of this paper, inadequacies in data are one set of reasons why this paper is not econometric in nature. Some of the main inadequacies are as follows:

● The data bank on UK innovations, together with the other available data on industrial characteristics, allow at the most 11 data points at the two-digit level, and 26 points at the three-digit level;

● Whilst the data bank on UK innovations covers the period from 1945 to 1980, other systematic and detailed data on UK industrial activity began to emerge only at the end of 1960s;

● Some industrial statistics are not readily available in the degree of detail that suit the purposes of our analysis: for example, the patent intensity measure (T/Y) is not readily available at the three-digit level.

Table 11
Results of selected regressions

| Equation | Dependent variable | Independent variables: sign and significance | | | | | $R^2$ | d.f. | $F$ statistic |
|----------|--------------------|----------------------------------------------|---|---|---|---|-------|------|---------------|
| E1 | Prop 3 | $+ R/Y$ [b] | $- PSU$ [a] | | | | 0.22 | 22 | 4.432 [b] |
| E2 | Prop 3 | $+ R/Y$ | | $- C_5$ [b] | | | 0.23 | 15 | 3.475 |
| E3 | Prop 2 | | | $- D_{20}$ | $+ T/Y$ [a] | | 0.54 | 8 | 6.872 [b] |
| E4 | Inhouse 3 | | | $+ C_5$ [a] | | $- 1$ [a] | 0.56 | 15 | 11.786 [a] |
| E5 | Vertical | $- R/Y$ [a] | | $+ D_{20}$ [a] | | $- K/L$ | 0.71 | 7 | 9.013 [a] |

[a] Significant at 1% level.
[b] Significant at $2\frac{1}{2}$% level.

Thus a proper statistical exercise, using the UK data base on innovations, will probably have to await the completion of sectoral coverage, and will require considerable statistical efforts to compile matching data from other sources. In the meantime, our statistical analysis can be only exploratory. The results discussed in section 4 of the paper are described in more detail in tables 10 and 11.

## References

[1] M. Anderson, D. Jones and J. Womack, Competition in the World Auto Industry: Implications for Production Location, in: *The Future of the Automobile: A Trilateral View* (forthcoming, 1984).

[2] H. Ansoff, *Corporate Strategy* (Penguin Books, Harmondsworth, 1968).

[3] K. Arrow, Economic Welfare and the Allocation of Resources for Invention, in: *The Rate and Direction of Inventive Activity* (Princeton University Press, 1962).

[4] C. Berry, *Corporate Growth and Diversification* (Princeton University Press, 1975).

[5] T. Buer, *Investigation of Consistent Make or Buy Patterns of Selected Process Machinery in Selected US Manufacturing Industries*, Ph.D. dissertation, Sloane School of Management, MIT, 1982.

[6] Bureau de d'Economie Theorique et Appliquée, *Les Perspectives de la Chimie en Europe* (Université Louis Pasteur, Strasbourg, 1982).

[7] D. De Melto et al., *Preliminary Report: Innovation and Technological Change in Five Canadian Industries* Economic Council of Canada, Discussion Paper No. 176 (1980).

[8] G. Dosi, Technological Paradigms and Technological Trajectories, *Research Policy* 11 (1982).

[9] H. Ergas, Corporate Strategies in Transition, in: A. Jacquemin (ed.), *Industrial Policy and International Trade* (Cambride University Press, 1983).

[10] H. Ergas, The Inter-Industry Flow of Technology: Some Explanatory Hypotheses (mimeo) (OECD, Paris, 1983).

[11] C. Freeman, *The Economics of Industrial Innovation*, 2nd edition (Francis Pinter, London, 1982).

[12] C. Freeman, J. Clark and L. Soete, *Unemployment and Technical Innovation: A study of Long Waves and Economic Development* (Francis Pinter, London, 1982).

[13] J. Gershuny, *After Industrial Society?* (Macmillan, London, 1978).

[14] M. Gibbons and R. Johnstone, The Roles of Science in Technological Innovation, *Research Policy* 3 (1974).

[15] B. Gold, *Productivity, Technology and Capital* (Lexington Books, Lexington, MA, 1979).

[16] M. Gort, *Diversification and Integration in American Industry* (Princeton University Press, 1962).

[17] J. Hassid, Recent Evidence on Conglomerate Diversification in UK Manufacturing Industry, *The Manchester School* 43 (1976).

[18] N. Kaldor, *The Causes of the Slow Rate of Economic Growth of the United Kingdom* (Cambridge University Press, 1966).

[19] J. Kamin et al., Some Determinants of Cost Distributions in the Process of Technological Innovation, *Research Policy* 11 (1982).

[20] H. Kleinman, *Indicators of the Output of New Technological Products from Industry*, Report to US Science Foundation (National Technical Information Service, US Department of Commerce, 1975).

[21] J. Langrish et al., *Wealth from Knowledge* (Macmillan, London, 1972).

[22] R. Levin, Technical Change and Optimal Scale: Some Evidence and Implications, *Southern Economic Journal* 44 (1977).

[23] R. Levin and P. Reiss, Tests of a Schumpeterian Model of R and D Market Structure, in: Z. Grilliches (eds.), *R and D, Patents and Productivity* (University of Chicago Press, 1984).

[24] A. Link and J. Long, The Simple Economies of Basic Scientific Research: A Test of Nelson's Diversification Hypothesis, *Journal of Industrial Economics* 30 (1981).

[25] E. Mansfield, Basic Research and Productivity Increase in Manufacturing, *American Economic Review* 20 (1980).

[26] D. Mowery and N. Rosenberg, The Influence of Market Demand upon Innovation: A Critical Review of Some Recent Empirical Studies, *Research Policy* 8 (1979).

[27] R. Nelson, The Simple Economics of Basic Scientific Research, *Journal of Political Economy* (1959).

[28] R. Nelson, *The Moon and the Ghetto* (Norton, New York, 1977).

[29] R. Nelson, Research on Productivity Growth and Productivity Differences: Dead Ends and New Departures, *Journal of Economic Literature* 19 (1981).

[30] R. Nelson, The Role of Knowledge in R and D Efficiency, *Quarterly Journal of Economics* (1982).

[31] R. Nelson and S. Winter, In Search of a Useful Theory of Innovation, *Research Policy* 5 (1977).

[32] R. Nelson and S. Winter, *An Evolutionary Theory of Economic Change* (Harvard University Press, Cambridge, MA, 1982).

[33] K. Oshima, in: B. Williams, *Science and Technology in Economic Growth* (Macmillan, London, 1973).

[34] K. Pavitt (ed.), *Technical Innovation and British Economic Performance* (Macmillan, London, 1980).

[35] K. Pavitt, Technology in British Industry: A Suitable Case for Improvement, in: C. Carter (ed.), *Industrial Policy and Innovation* (Heinemann, London, 1981).

[36] K. Pavitt, Some Characteristics of Innovative Activities in British Industry, *Omega* 11 (1983).

[37] K. Pavitt, R and D, Patenting and Innovative Activities: A Statistical Exploration, *Research Policy* 11 (1982).

[38] K. Pavitt, *Patterns of Technical Change: Evidence, Theory and Policy Implications*, Papers in Science, Technology and Public Policy, No. 3 (Imperial College/Science Policy Research Unit, 1983).

[39] K. Pavitt and S. Wald, *The Conditions for Success in Technological Innovation* (OECD, Paris, 1971).

[40] K. Pavitt and L. Soete, International Differences in Economic Growth and the International Location of Innovation, in: H. Giersch (ed.), *Emerging Technologies: Consequences for Economic Growth, Structural Change, and Employment* (JCB Mohr, 1981).

[41] E. Penrose, *The Theory of the Growth of the Firm* (Blackwell, Oxford, 1959).

[42] N. Rosenberg, *Perspectives on Technology* (Cambridge University Press, 1976).

[43] N. Rosenberg, *Inside the Black Box: Technology and Economics* (Cambridge University Press, 1982).

[44] R. Rothwell, *Innovation in Textile Machinery: Some Significant Factors in Success and Failure*, SPRU Occasional Paper No. 2 (University of Sussex, 1976).

[45] R. Rothwell, The Characteristics of Successful Innovators and Technically Progressive Firms, *R and D Management* 7 (1977).

[46] R. Rumelt, *Strategy, Structure and Economic Performance* (Graduate School of Business Administration, Harvard University, 1974).

[47] D. Sahel, *Patterns of Technological Innovation* (Addison-Wesley, New York, 1981).

[48] W. Salter, *Productivity and Technical Change*, 2nd Edition (Cambridge University Press, 1966).

[49] F. Scherer, *Industrial Market Structure and Economic Performance* (Rand McNally, 1981).

[50] F. Scherer, *The Economic Effects of Compulsory Patent Licensing* (New York University, 1977).

[51] F. Scherer, Inter-industry Technology Flows in the United States, *Research Policy* 11 (1982).

[52] F. Scherer, Demand Pull and Technological Invention: Schmookler Revisited, *Journal of Industrial Economics* XXX (1982).

[53] J. Schmookler, *Invention and Economic Growth* (Harvard University Press, Cambridge, MA, 1966).

[54] A. Smith, *An Inquiry into the Nature and Causes of the Wealth of Nations* (G. Routledge (1895 Edition)).

[55] L. Soete, A General Test of Technological Gap Trade Theory, *Review of World Economics* 117 (1981).

[56] C. Taylor and A. Silberston, *The Economic Impact of the Patent System* (Cambridge University Press, 1973).

[57] D. Teece, *The Multinational Corporation and the Resource Cost of International Technology Transfer* (Ballinger, New York, 1977).

[58] J. Toledano, A Propos des Filières Industrielles, *Revue d'Economie Industrielle* (1978).

[59] M. Teubal, *The Role of Technological Learning in the Exports of Manufactured Goods: The Case of Selected Capital Goods in Brazil and Argentina*, Discussion Paper No. 82.07 (Maurice Falk Institute for Economic Research in Israel, 1982).

[60] J. Townsend, F. Henwood, G. Thomas, K. Pavitt and S. Wyatt, *Innovations in Britain Since 1945*, Occasional Paper No. 16 (Science Policy Research Unit, University of Sussex, 1981).

[61] J. Townsend, Innovation in Coal-Mining Machinery, in K. Pavitt [34].

[62] M. Utton, *Diversification and Competition* (Cambridge University Press, 1979).

[63] P. Verdoorn, I Fattori che Regolaro lo Suiluppo della produttivita de lavoro, *L'Industrie* (1949).

[64] E. von Hippel, The Dominant Role of Users in the Scientific Instrument Innovation Process, *Research Policy* 5 (1976).

[65] E. von Hippel, A Customer-Active Paradigm for Industrial Product Idea Generation, *Research Policy* 7 (1978).

[66] E. von Hippel, The User's Role in Industrial Innovation, in: B. Dean and J. Goldhar (Eds.), *Management of Research and Innovation*, Studies in the Management Sciences, Vol. 15 (North-Holland, Amsterdam, 1980).

[67] E. von Hippel, Appropriability of Innovation Benefit as a Predictor of the Source of Innovation, *Research Policy* (1982).

[68] V. Walsh, Invention and Innovation in the Chemical Industry: Demand Pull or Discovery Push?, *Research Policy* (1984), forthcoming.

[69] J. Woodward, *Management and Technology* (HMSO, London, 1958).

[70] J. Utterback and W. Abernathy, A Dynamic Model of Process and Product Innovation, *Omega* 3 (1975).

# [13]

Science and Public Policy, volume 13, number 1, February 1986. Published by Beech Tree Publishing, 10 Watford Close, Guildford, Surrey GU1 2EP, England

# Inter-disciplinary research

## Japanese innovation in mechatronics technology

### Fumio Kodama studies technological fusion

Fumio Kodama is a Professor at the Graduate School for Policy Science, Saitama University, Urawa, Saitama 338, Japan.

He studied engineering at Tokyo University, and has worked for the Ministry of International Trade and Industry; the Studiengruppe für Systemforschung, Heidelberg, Germany; the Department of Social Engineering, Tokyo Institute of Technology; and the Department of Government, Hamilton College, New York, USA.

*Mechatronics is the combination of mechanics and electronics and is an example of technological fusion in which several different industries are involved. This has to be a two-way process, and each industry must research into products other than their principal ones. Technological fusion may well become a standard method of innovation in high technology. This will require good inter-company relations.*

*Although Japan's history has been mainly in the adaptation of foreign technology, she has been an innovator since the creation of mechatronics.*

JAPAN HAS CERTAINLY been successful in designing products and production systems based on foreign basic technologies. However, it is often said that Japan is still an adapter as much as an innovator.[1] The US National Science Foundation's study is often cited as proof for this view. It found that Japanese scientists developed only two of the 185 innovative technologies studied, from 1953 through to 1961.

However, more than 20 years have passed since then. Therefore, the argument that the Japanese are not innovators is based on outdated evidence. We should ask what has happened since 1961. Were there increases in innovations by the Japanese during the 60s and 70s? If there were, what were they and what were their characteristics? Are there differences in types of innovation between those from the West and those from Japan?

### Mechatronics revolution in Japan

In 1975, the Japanese created a new word, 'mechatronics', by combining mechanics and electronics. Essentially it implies the following two categories of products:

- The marriage of electronic technology to mechanical technology resulted in the birth of a more sophisticated range of technological products. Typical examples are Numerically Controlled (NC) machine tools and industrial robots.
- Products in which a part, or the whole, of a standard mechanical product was superseded by electronics. Typical examples are digital clocks and electronic calculators.

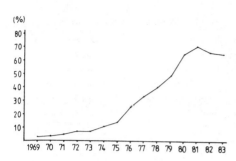

**Figure 1. Diffusion rate of NC machine tools**

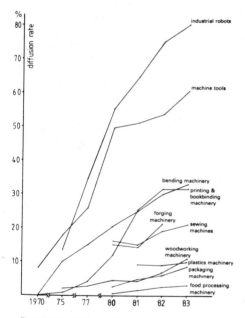

**Figure 2. Diffusion curves of mechatronics technology**

In order to measure the diffusion of mechatronics technology in the various types of machinery, some indicator should be developed. In the case of machine tools, the diffusion rate can be measured by the ratio of the numerically controlled machine tools to the total production of machine tools, as shown in Figure 1. A marked increase in the diffusion rate, in fact, occurred in 1975.

By the same token, a 'mechatronized machine' is defined as a machine with computer control. The diffusion rate can be measured by the ratio of the mechatronized machine to the total production of the machine. On the basis of this measure, the diffusion curves of mechatronics in various categories of machines are obtained as shown in Figure 2.

Those categories of machinery whose diffusion rate of

*Japanese innovations in mechatronics technology*

mechatronics is above 30% are industrial robots, machine tools, bending machinery, and printing and bookbinding machinery. Those categories of machines which are not yet widely mechatronized are woodworking machinery, plastics-processing machinery, packaging machines and food-processing machines.

We also observe a significant difference in the growth rate of production between these two groups. The group of machinery with higher than 30% in diffusion rate of mechatronics has higher growth rate. On the other hand, the group with less than 30 percent in the diffusion is lower in growth rate. Thus, there seems to be a positive correlation between the diffusion rate and the growth rate. This indicates the possibility that the group of machinery whose growth is stagnated can regain a growth momentum by the introduction of mechatronics technology.[2]

There is also a difference in the introduction of mechatronized machines between large enterprises and small and medium ones. While 71.9% of large enterprises introduced the mechatronized machines, only 25.8% of small and medium enterprise did. Therefore, the mechatronics technology which is appropriate for the needs of small and medium enterprises will be developed in the near future.

### Mechatronics as Japanese innovation

The Mechatronics revolution was generated by the fusing of mechanical and electronic technology. Therefore, I would argue that there are two types of innovations: one is 'technological breakthrough' and the other is 'technological fusion'. A typical example of the former is the transistor revolution, and of the latter the mechatronics revolution.

Breakthrough-type innovation is associated with strong leadership of a particular industry, and fusion-type becomes possible by a concerted effort of the several different industries involved. Developments in the Japanese machine tool industry are a case in point. The mechatronics revolution in this industry has become possible only with the co-operation of three other industries outside the machine tool itself.

First, FANUC developed a small and reliable controller which could be produced inexpensively. This made possible the wider use of the NC machine tool, which had previously been used only by special industries like the aeroplane industry. Secondly, the ball-screw was developed by NSK. This made possible control by servo-motor, which is low in torque, by substantial reduction in the friction coefficient. Thirdly, painting a new material (Teflon) on the sliding bed of the machine tool made low speed and uniform movement possible, an absolute necessity for the operation of a machine tool.

Fusion-type innovation contributes not to the radical growth of certain companies, but to the gradual growth of all companies of the relevant industries. The semiconductor revolution of the late 50s in the USA brought about a major

---

**The mechatronics revolution in the Japanese machine tool industry has become possible only with the co-operation of three other industries providing a small and reliable controller, a ball-screw and Teflon**

---

*Japanese innovations in mechatronics technology*

reshuffle to the relevant industries. Many of the existing vacuum-tube manufacturers went out of business, while some of the new entrants such as Texas Instruments, Motorola, and Fairchild, grew rapidly. In 1966, the market share of the new entrants was 65%, while that of the previous vacuum-tube manufacturers was only 26%.[3]

On the other hand, the Japanese production of machine tools has risen from fourth in the world after the USSR to first, in the last five years. However, there was no substantial change of market share of existing machine tool firms during this period.

Fusion-type innovation can be induced by industrial policy, while the breakthrough-type is associated with defense policy. Let us look into the development of industrial policy which induced the mechatronics revolution. Before 1971, the Law on Temporary Measures for the Development of Machinery Industry (enacted in 1956) and the Law on Temporary Measures on the Development of Electronics Industry (enacted in 1957) were enforced independently of each other. In 1971, these two laws were transformed into the Law on Temporary Measures for the Development of Specified Machinery and Electronics Industries.

The Mechatronics Revolution was intended in that law.[4] In the Diet (parliament), the Minister of MITI explained the objectives of the law as follows:

"In deciding upon an Intensification Plan, the competent minister shall take note of the increased inter-relationships among different industries, in particular, between the machinery and the electronic machinery and equipment, and shall pay due consideration to the direction of so-called 'consolidation of machinery and electronics into one' or 'systematization of them'."

**Data base for analysis of technological fusion**

The process of innovation of the technological fusion type begins with the industry's interests in product fields other than its principal ones. Therefore, the traditional dichotomy between product and process innovation is not helpful in analyzing technology fusion. More relevant is whether or not a sector's industrial R&D is done within or outside its principal product fields.

The industrial R&D by each sector within its principal product fields is supposed to be directed toward either improving existing products or seeking technological breakthroughs. The industrial R&D activity outside its own principal product fields is directed toward creating technology fusion.

The unusually rich Japanese R&D data source collected in the Survey of Research and Development by the Statistics Bureau of the Prime Minister's Office makes it possible for us to implement the conceptualization described above into an empirical study. For all the Japanese companies with a capital of 100 million yen or more (3 803 companies in 1982), intra-mural expenditure on R&D is disaggregated into 31 different product fields.

A company like, say, Hitachi is asked under survey instructions to break its R&D expenditure into such categories as chemical products, fabricated metal products, ordinary machines, household electric equipment, communication and electronic equipment, automobiles, precision instruments. This is an alternative to reporting expenditure in one lump assigned to Hitachi's primary industry – electrical machinery manufacturing. Expenses which are diffi-

**Table 1. Classification of principal product fields**

| Industrial sector | Principal product fields |
|---|---|
| Food manufacturing | Food products |
| Textile mill products | Textile products |
| Pulp and paper products | Pulp and paper products |
| Printing and publishing | Printing and publishing |
| Industrial chemicals | Chemical fertilizers and organic and inorganic chemical products Chemical fibers |
| Oil and paints | Oil and paints |
| Other chemical products | Other chemical products |
| Drugs and medicines | Drugs and medicines |
| Petroleum and coal products | Petroleum products |
| Rubber products | Rubber products |
| Ceramics | Ceramic products |
| Iron and steel | Iron and steel |
| Non-ferrous metals and products | Non-ferrous metals |
| Fabricated metal products | Fabricated metal products |
| Ordinary machinery | Ordinary machinery |
| Electrical machinery, equipment and supplies | Household electrical appliances Other electric equipment |
| Communication and electronic equipment | Communication and electronic equipment and electric gauges |
| Motor vehicles | Automobiles |
| Other transport equipment | Ships Aircraft Other transportation equipment |
| Precision equipment | Precision instruments |
| Other manufacturing | Other manufacturing products |

cult to classify by types of product, are divided proportionally on the basis of the number of researchers.[5]

Since an industrial sector's effort toward technological fusion is defined as the sector's R&D activity outside its principal product fields, we must first distinguish the two types of product fields for each sector: its principal product fields and those which are not principal. This distinction was made among manufacturing industries. In other words, every product field produced by manufacturing industries is to be classified into the principal product fields of one of the 21 manufacturing industrial sectors. The classification table is shown in Table 1.

Based on the data available for R&D expenses, we can formulate the technology fusion as follows:
Let

$E_{ijt}$ = *i*-th industry's R&D expense into *j*-th industry's principal product fields in *t*-th year,
$(i, j = 1, \ldots, N; t = 1, \ldots, T)$

46

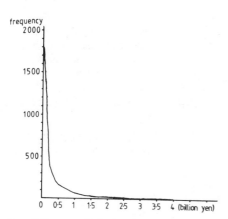

**Figure 3. Frequency distribution of R&D expenditure for technological fusion**

$D_t$ = research expenditure deflator of $t$-th year (the reference year is 1975),

then, the real R&D expenditure for technological fusion can be represented by

$$R_{ijt} = E_{ijt}/D_t.$$

Since the data is available every year from 1970 to 1982, we can pool a large amount of data and produce a frequency distribution of all the $R_{ijt}$'s. As is shown in Figure 3, the distribution is exponential. In 80% of all the non-zero $R_{ijt}$'s, the expense is less than one billion yen.

The exponential distribution implies that almost all the industry's R&D expenditure outside its principal product fields is for exploratory search and little for advanced development. It also reflects the dynamic process of R&D, where a heavy investment is realized only after many exploratory searches have been conducted for a long time and a good prospect is proven. Furthermore, it indicates the very nature of R&D, that almost all the exploratory research fails and very few projects survive for advanced development.

### Dynamics of technological fusion

To construct a dynamic model, we need a dynamic interpretation of the exponential distribution obtained in Figure 3. As time passes, an R&D program progresses from an exploratory phase through an advanced development phase. Thus, its annual investment increases with the passage of time, as long as its prospect continues to be favorable. However, at any time when its prospect is found to be

---

**A heavy investment in R&D is only realised after many exploratory searches have been conducted for a long time and a good prospect proven: few projects survive for advanced development**

---

unfavorable, it can be cancelled, so an increase in its investment is no longer expected. On this basis, we can think of a survival type model of an R&D program's investment as follows:

Let

$R(C)$ = the probability that an R&D program can survive until its annual investment reaches $C$,

then, the probability that an R&D program is cancelled before it reaches the investment level of $C$, can be represented by,

$$1 - R(C)$$

Let

$f(C)$ = the probability density function of $C$ (the probability that an R&D program is cancelled at the amount of $C$),

then, $f(C)$ can be represented by,

$$f(C) = d/dC[1 - R(C)] = - R'(C). \qquad (1)$$

Let

$r(C)$ = the cancelling probability of an R&D program whose investment level is $C$,

then, $r(C)$ can be formulated as the probability that an R&D program is cancelled, given that it can survive up to the investment level of $C$, therefore, the probability $r(C)$ can be represented by,

$$r(C) = f(C)/R(C) = - R'(C)/R(C). \qquad (2)$$

By assuming that an R&D program's cancelling probability $r(C)$ is independent of its investment level $C$, we can derive an exponential distribution of an R&D program's annual investment. However, it is not always appropriate to assume that an R&D program's cancelling probability is independent of its investment level. In other words, we have to concepualize the 'cancelling probability' as the probability function of $C$.

Firstly, exploratory research can be defined as that where the investment $C$ is smaller, and advanced development as that whose $C$ is larger. Secondly, the cancelling probability of an exploratory research can be supposed to be higher, and that of an advanced development to be lower, because the prospect of an R&D program in the advanced development phase is already proven through the exploratory research which preceeds it.

Therefore, generally speaking, we can assume that the cancelling probability function $r(C)$ is a decreasing function of $C$. On this basis, the cancelling probability function can be represented as an exponential curve as follows:

$$r(C) = a*\exp(-bC). \qquad (3)$$

Thus, by substituting (3) into (2), we can calculate the probability density function of $C$, as follows:

$$f(C) = a*\exp[(a/b)*\exp(-bC) - bC - a/b] \qquad (4)$$

For each of 21 industrial sectors, R&D expenses into 20 product fields outside its principal product field are available from 1970 through 1982. Therefore, for each industrial sector, we can use 260 data points for the curve fitting of $f(C)$ in the equation (4). A non-linear least square method, Marquard Method, was used.

The result of the curve fitting is shown in Table 2, with the coefficient of determination. In the sector termed other manufacturing, we cannot complete the estimation process because convergence conditions are not met.

*Japanese innovations in mechatronics technology*

**Table 2. Result of curve fitting**

| Industrial sector | a | b | Coefficient of determination |
|---|---|---|---|
| Food manufacturing | 0.4439 | 0.3955 | 0.9142 |
| Textile mill products | 0.3306 | 0.1889 | 0.9197 |
| Pulp and paper products | 0.5681 | 0.5737 | 0.9965 |
| Printing and publishing | 0.5309 | 0.3236 | 0.9204 |
| Industrial chemicals | 0.0844 | 0.0102 | 0.8864 |
| Oil and paints | 0.4513 | 0.3220 | 0.8967 |
| Drugs and medicines | 0.5376 | 0.6793 | 0.9889 |
| Other chemical products | 0.3840 | 0.2627 | 0.9683 |
| Petroleum and coal products | 0.4768 | 0.5200 | 0.9722 |
| Rubber products | 0.4507 | 0.2681 | 0.9153 |
| Ceramics | 0.2995 | 0.1478 | 0.9111 |
| Iron and steel | 0.2968 | 0.2261 | 0.9451 |
| Non-ferrous metals and products | 0.2772 | 0.1372 | 0.9388 |
| Fabricated metal products | 0.2991 | 0.1879 | 0.9571 |
| Ordinary machinery | 0.1753 | 0.1399 | 0.7894 |
| Electrical machinery | 0.3029 | 0.6336 | 0.9344 |
| Communication and electronics | 0.4460 | 0.5211 | 0.9885 |
| Motor vehicles | 0.2777 | 0.1454 | 0.9643 |
| Other transport equipment | 0.3998 | 0.2680 | 0.9755 |
| Precision equipment | 0.4153 | 0.4657 | 0.9813 |
| Other manufacturing | – | – | – |

## Realization of technological fusion

Considering the dynamics of R&D, we can assume that research reaches the development stage only if the expense exceeds a certain amount. What is important for this purpose is the demarcation between the exploratory phase and the development phase.

The demarcation can be done on the basis of the cancelling probability. We can define an R&D program in the development phase as one whose cancelling probability is smaller than a specified value $r^*$. Then, based on each industry's estimated relation between the cancelling probability ($r$) and the annual investment ($C$), we can identify the threshold value of annual investment, beyond which an R&D program can be supposed to enter the development phase. In other words, we can get the threshold value $C_i^*$ for each industry. These boundary values for each industry between exploratory search and advanced development are shown in Table 3.

The mechatronics revolution occurred as a result of the technological fusion between mechanical technology and electronics technology. Thus, the minimum unit of technology fusion is the pair of two different industrial sectors. However, one-way investment might only be diversification effort and not lead to innovation.

On the other hand, if the investment is done two-ways, it might lead to the creation of a new technological area, and possibly to innovation. For example, the ceramics industry had invested in product fields such as ordinary machinery, electrical machinery and electronics. However, 'new ceramics' was created only after the machinery and electronics industries began to invest in ceramics.

## The essence of technological fusion is its reciprocity: it is only realized when there is two–way investment thus becoming reciprocal between two industries

Therefore, the essence of technological fusion is its reciprocity. It is realized only when there is two-way investment thus becoming reciprocal between two industries. We can call this investment 'realized technology fusion' and formulate it as follows:

Let

$$F_{ijt} = \begin{cases} 1 \text{ if } R_{ijt} > C_i^* \text{ and } R_{jit} > C_j^*, \\ 0 \text{ otherwise,} \end{cases}$$

then, technological fusion is realized between the $i$-th and $j$-th industry, only if $F_{ijt} = 1$.

After constructing a model of the realization mechanism of technological fusion, our interest is directed to analysing the structure of technological fusion. It is best described using a graph. In the non-directed graph, each industry is represented by vertex, and the arc is represented by the $F_{ijt}$ so the arc exists if $F_{ijt} = 1$.

Such a graph can be constructed for each year; some of them are shown in Figures 4 to 7 (those of 1970, 1974, 1975, and 1982).

**Table 3. Identification of threshold values.**

| Industrial sector | threshold value (¥ million) |
|---|---|
| Food manufacturing | 467 |
| Textile mill products | 822 |
| Pulp and paper products | 365 |
| Printing and publishing | 626 |
| Industrial chemicals | 1 834 |
| Oil and paints | 579 |
| Drugs and medicines | 300 |
| Other chemical products | 648 |
| Petroleum and coal products | 369 |
| Rubber products | 695 |
| Ceramics | 984 |
| Iron and steel | 639 |
| Non-ferrous metals and products | 1 003 |
| Fabricated metal products | 773 |
| Ordinary machinery | 656 |
| Electrical machinery | 231 |
| Communication and electronics | 355 |
| Motor vehicles | 948 |
| Other transport equipment | 650 |
| Precision equipment | 382 |

*Japanese innovations in mechatronics technology*

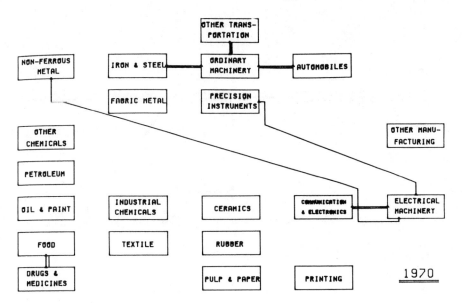

Figure 4. Technical fusion in Japan in 1970

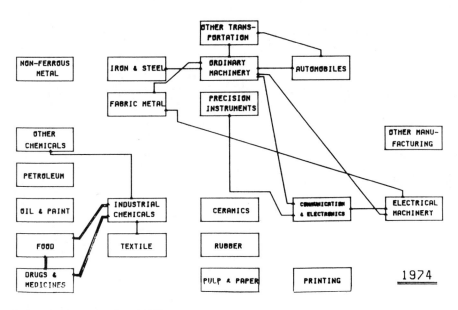

Figure 5. Technical fusion in Japan in 1974

*Japanese innovations in mechatronics technology*

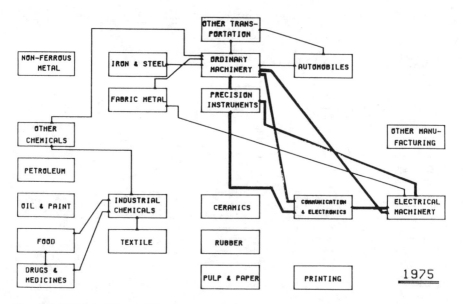

Figure 6. Technical fusion in Japan in 1975

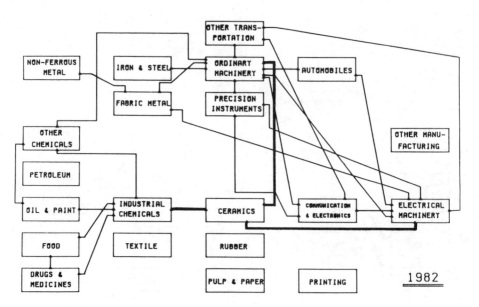

Figure 7. Technical fusion in Japan in 1982

## High technology and technological fusion

Let us describe how some of the so-called high technologies such as bio-technology, mechatronics and new ceramics were developed.

First of all, through the years studied, technological fusions are clustered around three major industries — ordinary machinery, electrical machinery, and industrial chemicals. The first two industries belong to the fabrication industry, while the last one belongs to the material industry. In 1970 (Figure 5) there is no technological fusion realized among these three clusters.

In 1974 (Figure 6), the triple connection emerges among food, drugs and medicines and industrial chemicals. This can be interpreted as the emergence of 'bio-technology'. The dual connection between food and drugs and medicines, which is supposed to represent fermentation technology, appeared since 1971. By joining of industrial chemicals to this connection, bio-technology was established as a high technology area.

As far as 'mechatronics' is concerned, technological fusion begins to foster between the ordinary machinery industry and the electrical machinery industry after 1971. However, it is not until 1975 that the quadruple connection begins to appear persistently among ordinary machinery, precision instruments, electrical machinery and communication and electronic equipment (Figure 7). Therefore, we can identify the realization of the mechatronics revolution by the persistent existence of this connection.

By 1982 (Figure 8), the technological fusion between ceramics and ordinary machinery and between ceramics and electrical machinery were formed. This connection represents the emergence of 'new ceramics'. The connection between ceramics and ordinary machinery, which represents fine ceramics, was established in 1980. Then, the connection between ceramics and industrial chemicals, which indicates the emergence of the new material, was established in 1981.

About the macro-trend of technological fusion from the 70s to the 80s, we can make the following observation. During the 1970s, there had been no fusion between the material industry and the fabrication one. The fusions occurred only within the fabrication industries such as mechatronics and within the material industries such as bio-technology. However, since 1980, fusions have appeared frequently between these two sets of industries.

Through the structural analysis, we can draw the conclusion that in the 1960s, there had been no major technological fusion. A first example of innovation of this type appeared in the 1970s. This was the 'Mechatronics Revolution' in the mid-70s. We have found that technological fusion between material technology and fabrication technology is expected to be realized in the 1980s.

## Some worldwide implications

We could identify almost all the high technologies, such as bio-technology, mechatronics and new ceramics, in terms of technological fusion concept and method. Therefore, we can say that technological fusion will become a standard mode of innovation.

Good company-to-company relations are a condition for success in technology fusion. Still more important is R&D diversification within the same organization. If it is true, then, Japan will take more responsibility as one of the world centers of innovation in the high technology area in future.

This might be one reason why an increasing number of big foreign multinationals, including Imperial Chemical Industries, the British chemical giant, Siemens of West Germany, and Texas Instruments of the US, are now thinking of building their own research laboratories on Japanese soil. Also, Du Pont Co has recently decided to build a research laboratory in Yokohama.

According to Du Pont, what is more important than the size and the growth potential of the Japanese market, is that their products should be accepted by Japanese manufacturers, who demand very high standards of the material supplier, so that their products are proven world wide.

The Japanese research laboratory will become one of the three focal points besides the research laboratories in Delaware and Geneva in the field of engineering plastics and be connected by an on-line information network. The technical information collected through the contacts with Japanese engineers mainly from the customer companies, are to be distributed world-wide through the one-line network.[6]

The mechatronics revolution in Japan might have a significant impact on the developing nations. Japan has, owing to its past history, not imported any foreign labor. This has played a role in accelerating automation to enable individual business to survive. Mechatronics development played a role equal to that of foreign labor in some other countries. In other words, Japan developed a non-human work force (such as robots) to the extent that the production plants scarcely need human labor regardless of its cost. This has created a new situation in which certain types of industry which were transplanted to developing countries have returned to developed countries.

## References

1. "Can the Japanese Create?", *Newsweek*, July 2 1984, page 27.
2. MITI, *Vision of Industrial Machinery* (Tsushou-Sangyou-Chousakai, 1984).
3. J E Tilton, *International Diffusion of Technology* (The Brookings Institution, 1971).
4. MITI, *Electronics & Machinery Industry in the Seventies* (Tsushou-Sangyou-Chousakai, 1971).
5. Statistical Bureau, Prime Minister's Office, the Government of Japan, *Report on the Survey of Research and Development*.
6. "Japan becomes a Battlefield", *Asahi Newspaper*, May 20 1985.

# Part IV
# The Selective Environment Confronting Innovative Firms

# [14]

European Economic Review 12 (1979) 319-340. ⓒ North-Holland Publishing Company

## FIRM SIZE AND INVENTIVE ACTIVITY

### The Evidence Reconsidered

### Luc L.G. SOETE*

*I.D.S., University of Sussex, Brighton, Sussex, BN1 9RE, England*

This paper analyses the relationship between firm size and inventive activity in the United States for the late 'seventies. It is argued that the inventive activity measure used, R&D expenditure, is a more 'neutral' measure in relation to firm size, than both R&D employment and the number of patents. Contrary to most empirical research in this field, the analyses carried out in the present paper indicate that inventive activity seems to increase more than proportionately with firm size.

## 1. Introduction

Empirical analyses of the relationship between inventive activity and size of firms have increased over the last 20 years at an impressive rate. The subject having nowadays acquired a 'reviewing' status [see, among others, Freeman (1974), Scherer (1970), and Kamien and Schwartz (1975)], the validity of the conclusions arrived at has been less and less challenged. It has to be admitted that the 'consensus' which has emerged out of practically all empirical studies, namely a strong rejection of the 'Schumpeterian'-hypothesis[1] that 'large-scale establishments or units of control' would be the most powerful engines of technological change has rendered any consistent challenge rather obscure. To quote the most authoritative study on the subject [Scherer (1965b, p. 1122)]:

> 'Perhaps a bevy of fact-mechanics can still rescue the Schumpeterian engine from disgrace, but at present the outlook seems pessimistic.'

However, this apparently final and general rejection of the Schumpeterian-hypothesis leaves several important questions unanswered.

*I am greatly indebted to C. Cooper, C. Freeman, J.M. McLean, K. Pavitt, M. Vandoorne and an anonymous referee of this journal for critical comment. Any errors are, of course, my own.

[1]The analysis presented here will be limited to an empirical verification of the size–inventive activity relationship. Subsequent references made to the 'Schumpeterian'-hypothesis should be understood within this limited scope. In so far as this implies a very crude simplification of the far richer 'Schumpeterian'-argument, the analysis presented here, just as the majority of previous empirical studies in the field, might actually be inadequate, as 'mere size is neither necessary nor sufficient' [Schumpeter (1950, p. 101)].

(1)   At the theoretical level, one may well wonder why large generally transnational firms, fully exploiting their technical, financial and marketing economies of scale advantages, would not do so in the field of technical progress,
and suffer from dis-economies of scale in coordinating and controlling R&D
activities. More precisely, what is the theoretical background of findings like
[Scherer (1970, p. 361)]:

> 'Most technically progressive American firms appear ... to be those with
> sales of less than $200 million at 1955 price levels'?

The identification of a specific bench-mark seems to be an empirical finding,
apparently based on no a priori theoretical justification, and consequently
very much subject to the methodology used by the author, the reliability of
the data, the choice of the variables analysed, and the statistical significance
of the results obtained.

(2)   At the empirical level, several fundamental questions can be raised on
each of these issues. Let us pick out two crucial areas. First, the reliability of
the data. As compared to the actual mid-70's world, the data generally used
is clearly obsolete. Scherer's (1965a, b) most influential analyses were based
on 1955 R&D employment and 1959 patent data. One of the most recent
empirical analyses [Shrieves (1978)] is based on 1965 data. The important
changes in the size of firms as well as inventive activity which have occurred
over the last 10–20 years have been fundamental. One might thus well
wonder if the majority of empirical studies bear any resemblance to the
present world.

   Second, the choice of the variables analysed. The two measures generally
used are R&D employment and the number of patents. The question raises
to what extent these proxies do not overestimate the inventive activity
contribution of small firms. R&D employment, as inventive activity proxy, is
indeed only one out of five possible identifiable groups of R&D input costs[2]
accounting for less than a third in total R&D expenditure cost. Evidence
published by the National Science Foundation suggests that the R&D cost
per scientist and engineer increases with size [NSF (1976)], from $35,100 for
the less than 1,000 employees size class to $72,300 for the more than 25,000
employees size class (1974), or in other words that the other R&D inputs,
such as materials and supplies and/or capital equipment, increase with size at
a far higher rate than the number of scientists and engineers.[3] Consequently

[2]R&D employment is considered here to cover only the number of scientists and engineers.
Other commonly considered R&D input costs are 'other supporting personnel', 'material and
supplies', 'durable equipment', 'land and buildings' and 'other R&D costs', such as energy, water,
maintenance, etc. For more detail, see Soete (1977).
[3]This might be due to an increase, with firm size, of R&D capital intensity, or higher R&D
costs, such as expensive and complex prototype or pilot plant costs, higher testing and Federal
Regulation costs, etc.

R&D employment data overestimates the technical inventive contribution of small firms. Data on the number of patents on the other hand will suffer from the intrinsic variation in economic significance of the patent concept, which might, as Scherer (1965b) himself has admitted, not be random as between firms of different size. Schmookler (1966), and Taylor and Silbertson (1973) have gathered patent information which suggests that big firms do indeed patent a smaller proportion of what they invent. Patent statistics will consequently 'tend to exaggerate the contribution of the smaller firms to inventive output' [Freeman (1974, p. 207)], and be biased against the Schumpeterian-hypothesis.

The evidence presented in this article is based on R&D expenditure data, considered to be more neutral in relation to firm size. The lack of reliable, individual firms' R&D expenditure data, covering a high proportion of total company financed R&D, explains the fact that R&D expenditure has seldom been used in empirical analyses. Since June 1976 Business Week publishes 'for the U.S. individual firms' R&D expenditure data collected on the basis of a new accounting standard definition of R&D, highly reliable and closely comparable to the NSF data. To exclude the possible depressive effects of 1975, evidence based on 1976 is also presented.

For both years, the Business Week Survey covers more than 95% of total company financed R&D expenditure in the United States. The methodology followed is similar to that worked out in previous empirical analyses, especially Scherer's (1965a, b) and Hamberg's (1964) most influential and accepted ones.

Section 2 presents evidence on size classes, and the results of the compilation of size and R&D concentration ratios. In section 3 the results of the non-linear regression analyses are presented.

## 2. Some simple tests

Most of the 1960-incentives for carrying out more detailed empirical analyses on the size-inventive activity relationship have actually been 'provoked' by the National Science Foundation's broad size classification, in which the biggest size class, i.e., firms with more than 5,000 employees also covered firms with more than 500,000 employees. This ill-defined size class became a sort of research obsession for most empirical analyses, resulting in the finding that [Scherer (1970, p. 360)]:

> 'Increases in size beyond an employment level of roughly 5,000 employees are not in general accompanied by a more than proportional rise in innovative inputs or outputs.'

Fortunately, since 1972 the NSF has further subclassified firms in this size class into three, more meaningful, size classes, namely firms with more than

25,000 employees, firms with between 10,000 and 24,999 employees and firms with between 5,000 and 9,999 employees.

Table 1, covering the years 1972 to 1974, contains the R&D sales ratios for different size classes, for total R&D expenditure, and company financed R&D only. The figures indicate that in both cases, total R&D or company financed R&D only, firms in the largest size class, i.e. firms with more than 25,000 employees, carry out twice as much R&D as related to sales than firms in the following size class. While the R&D sales ratios do differ less between the different size classes when one considers company financed R&D only, the R&D intensity of firms in the biggest size class is still higher than that of firms in any other size class.

Size is of course a relative concept, and might have changed over time. While in 1955 only 75 firms had more than 25,000 employees, in 1974 there were 126 R&D performing firms with more than 25,000 employees [NSF (1976)]. In addition the size class of firms with more than 25,000 employees is still a very ill-defined size class, with firms with more than 27 times the 25,000 threshold level.

On the basis of the Business Week data we have calculated some additional, more meaningful size classes. The result of these calculations are shown in table 2.

Once again, the figures do not conform to Scherer's findings. For 1975, as well as 1976, 'gigantic' firms with more than 250,000 employees had an R&D sales ratio which was twice as high as the following size class.[4]

An analysis of inventive activity and size through size groups remains, however, arbitrary, depending on the choice of specific size class thresholds. To avoid this arbitrariness, size and R&D concentration ratios were computed.

First, however, one is faced with the choice of a meaningful scale or size variable. As argued by Scherer (1965a), the sales measure will be the most neutral size variable. In 1975 or 1976, however, a ranking of firms by sales will be strongly influenced by the 1973 oil-crisis and the doubling in the price of oil.

In 1955, the year Scherer used for his analysis, there were only two oil companies, among the twelve biggest sales corporations (*Fortune*, June 1956).

---

[4]The reason for the firms in the third size class, i.e., firms with between 50,000 and 99,999 employees having a slightly higher R&D sales ratio than the firms in the bigger size class, i.e. firms with between 100,000 and 249,999 employees, can be explained by the fact that we are dealing with R&D performing firms only, covering the 'big' – up to 100,000 employees – manufacturing firms, but excluding 'smaller' manufacturing firms, which carried out less than $1 million R&D, and thus not reported in the Business Week Survey. Inclusion of those firms brings the R&D sales ratio of the third and fourth size classes down.
The following R&D sales ratios were obtained for the year 1975, taking into account the 157 *Fortune*-firms, with more than 25,000 employees: 5 firms with more than 250,000 employees – 3.8, 15 firms with between 100,000 and 249,999 employees '– 1.8, 43 firms with between 50,000 and 99,999 employees – 1.5, 94 firms with between 25,000 and 49,999 employees – 1.01.

Table 1

R&D funds as a percentage of net sales for different size classes.[a]

| Size classes | Total R&D funds | | | | | | Company financed R&D funds | | | | | |
|---|---|---|---|---|---|---|---|---|---|---|---|---|
| | as % of total | | | as % of net sales | | | as % of total | | | as % of net sales | | |
| | 1972 | 1973 | 1974 | 1972 | 1973 | 1974 | 1972 | 1973 | 1974 | 1972 | 1973 | 1974 |
| More then 25,000 employees | 72.47 | 73.67 | 73.56 | 4.7 | 4.5 | 3.9 | 66.22 | 67.41 | 67.90 | 2.5 | 2.4 | 2.3 |
| 24,999–10,000 employees | 11.05 | 10.53 | 10.34 | 2.0 | 1.8 | 1.5 | 13.43 | 13.33 | 13.21 | 1.4 | 1.3 | 1.2 |
| 9,999–5,000 employees | 5.50 | 5.50 | 5.61 | 1.9 | 1.8 | 1.6 | 7.76 | 7.57 | 7.60 | 1.5 | 1.5 | 1.4 |
| 4,999–1,000 employees | 6.22 | 5.88 | 6.00 | 1.7 | 1.6 | 1.6 | 7.34 | 6.84 | 6.68 | 1.3 | 1.3 | 1.2 |
| Less than 1,000 | 4.76 | 4.43 | 4.49 | 1.7 | 1.6 | 1.7 | 5.25 | 4.84 | 4.60 | 1.5 | 1.5 | 1.5 |
| Total (in $million) | 19,383 | 20,921 | 22,369 | 3.4 | 3.3 | 2.9 | 11,326 | 12,696 | 14,038 | 2.0 | 2.0 | 1.9 |

[a]*Source:* Calculated from National Science Foundation (1976).

Table 2

Company financed R&D funds as % of net sales for firms with more than 25,000 employees.[a]

| Size classes | 1975 | | | | 1976 | | | |
|---|---|---|---|---|---|---|---|---|
| | Number of firms | R&D funds (in $ million) | Sales (in $ million) | R&D/sales (in %) | Number of firms | R&D funds (in $ million) | Sales (in $ million) | R&D/sales (in %) |
| More than 250,000 employees | 6 | 4,003 | 118,210 | 3.39 | 6 | 4,496 | 152,602 | 2.95 |
| 249,999–100,000 employees | 15 | 2,226 | 127,487 | 1.75 | 14 | 2,379 | 136,507 | 1.74 |
| 99,999–50,000 employees | 38 | 2,755 | 146,366 | 1.88 | 41 | 3,160 | 170,956 | 1.85 |
| 49,999–25,000 employees | 74 | 2,253 | 180,421 | 1.25 | 79 | 8,706 | 209,652 | 1.29 |
| Total more than 25,000 employees | 133 | 11,236 | 572,484 | 1.96 | 140 | 12,740 | 669,716 | 1.90 |
| Total BWS | 730 | 14,516 | 786,430 | 1.85 | 598 | 16,225 | 867,174 | 1.87 |

[a]Source: Calculated from Business Week, June 28, 1976, and June 27, 1977.

In 1975, there were no less than nine oil companies among the seventeen biggest sales corporations (*Fortune*, May 1977). This overemphasis on oil companies, because of a sudden increase in the price of oil, appearing directly in the sales figure, renders the use of the sales measure as 'neutral' scale variable impossible.[5]

We consequently had to reject a simple computation of sales and R&D concentration ratios on the basis of a ranking of firms by sales. Two alternatives were worked out. They are presented in tables 3 and 4. In the first case, we have ranked firms by employment. While this ranking system

Table 3

Concentration of employment, sales and company financed R&D funds for all R&D performing firms.[a]

| Number of firms included, ranked by employment | 1975 % of total of all 730 firms | | | 1976 % of total of all 598 firms | | |
|---|---|---|---|---|---|---|
| | Empl. | Sales | R&D | Empl. | Sales | R&D |
| First 4 | 16.47 | 12.76 | 18.60 | 17.70 | 14.36 | 19.95 |
| First 8 | 23.78 | 18.55 | 29.59 | 25.53 | 20.17 | 30.09 |
| First 12 | 28.05 | 21.52 | 33.82 | 29.87 | 23.13 | 34.19 |
| First 16 | 31.57 | 29.40 | 39.79 | 33.44 | 30.93 | 40.20 |
| First 20 | 34.60 | 31.84 | 42.01 | 36.57 | 33.34 | 42.37 |
| First 30 | 36.36 | 40.70 | 49.25 | 42.71 | 37.71 | 49.20 |
| First 40 | 45.86 | 45.49 | 53.72 | 47.61 | 43.43 | 53.25 |
| First 50 | 49.42 | 46.03 | 57.33 | 51.73 | 47.15 | 57.76 |
| First 100 | 63.98 | 66.27 | 72.57 | 67.37 | 66.70 | 71.06 |
| All 598 | | | | 100.00 | 100.00 | 100.00 |
| All 730 | 100.00 | 100.00 | 100.00 | | | |

[a]*Source:* Calculated from *Business Week*, June 28, 1976, and June 27, 1977.

might favour somewhat the Schumpeterian-hypothesis, one should nevertheless bear in mind that the employment concept conforms best to the NSF size classification and more generally to the U.S. Census 'size of establishment' classifications. As such it is a perfectly correct size measure. In the second case, we have excluded the oil companies (together with servicing firms) from the analysis. Sales and R&D concentration ratios have then been computed on the basis of a ranking of firms by sales.[6]

[5]In addition, as the Business Week Survey itself acknowledges, the R&D expenditure data of the oil companies are somewhat 'deceptive. Big Oil's R&D expenses do not include the industry's expenditures for oil exploration. These costs are capitalized.' (*Business Week*, June 28, 1976, p. 82).

[6]The reasonableness of our method can be illustrated by computing sales and R&D concentration ratios on the basis of the 1972 sales order, i.e. before the oil crisis, using the actual 1975 sales and R&D values. The CR-4 sales ratio is 15.85, the CR-4 R&D ratio is 17.31, the CR-8 sales ratio is 24.02, the CR-8 R&D ratio is 27.49, etc. The R&D concentration ratios are clearly higher than the sales concentration ratios.

Table 4

Concentration of sales, employment and company financed R&D funds for all R&D performing firms, excluding oil and service firms.[a]

| Number of firms included, ranked by sales | 1975 % of total of all 644 firms | | | | 1976 % of total of all 543 firms | | | |
|---|---|---|---|---|---|---|---|---|
| | Sales | Empl. | R&D | R&D/sales (%) | Sales | Empl. | R&D | R&D/sales (%) |
| First 4 | 17.27 | 17.04 | 24.92 | 3.31 | 19.20 | 18.65 | 25.18 | 3.07 |
| First 8 | 24.72 | 25.41 | 30.86 | 2.87 | 27.12 | 27.67 | 31.68 | 2.73 |
| First 12 | 28.92 | 29.34 | 35.83 | 2.85 | 31.41 | 31.48 | 36.51 | 2.71 |
| First 16 | 32.50 | 32.80 | 38.78 | 2.74 | 34.95 | 35.06 | 40.33 | 2.70 |
| First 20 | 35.79 | 35.57 | 43.37 | 2.78 | 38.23 | 38.07 | 43.63 | 2.67 |
| First 30 | 42.50 | 41.46 | 51.25 | 2.77 | 45.19 | 44.10 | 52.12 | 2.70 |
| First 40 | 47.79 | 46.03 | 56.28 | 2.70 | 50.49 | 49.10 | 55.57 | 2.57 |
| First 50 | 52.18 | 50.58 | 59.64 | 2.62 | 55.03 | 53.34 | 59.26 | 2.52 |
| First 100 | 67.48 | 64.69 | 72.71 | 2.47 | 71.01 | 70.08 | 73.13 | 2.41 |
| All 543 | | | | | 100.00 | 100.00 | 100.00 | 2.34 |
| All 644 | 100.00 | 100.00 | 100.00 | 2.3 | | | | |

[a]*Source:* Calculated from *Business Week*, June 28, 1976, and June 27, 1977.

The evidence contained in tables 3 and 4 is diametrically opposed to the Scherer findings based on patents and R&D employment. R&D expenditure is consistently more concentrated among the largest firms, ranked either by employment or sales.

In addition, the R&D/sales ratios given in table 4 do also support the Schumpeterian-hypothesis. To conclude this second part, it can be argued that the information gathered on the basis of recent R&D expenditure data does not seem to support the Scherer assumption, that inventive *inputs* increase less than proportionately with size.

## 3. Results of the regressions

The relationship between size and inventive activity can be studied in a more rigorous way through regression methods. The analysis covers all R&D performing firms, reported in the Business Week Survey, with more than $100 million sales.[7]

It is necessary to introduce this arbitrarily chosen threshold level. The firms with less than $100 million sales reported in the Business Week Survey are indeed exceptional. To be included in the Business Week Survey, firms had to spend more than $1 million on R&D. The big majority of small R&D performing firms with less than $1 million R&D expenditure were con-

[7]I.e., 532 firms out of 730 in 1975 and 502 firms out of 598 in 1976.

sequently not reported in the survey. Inclusion of those small, highly specialized R&D firms in the analysis would consequently bias the results in favour of the smallness hypothesis.[8] Secondly, the Scherer argument is not so much linked with these very small firms. The controversial findings relate mainly to 'intermediate' size firms. To quote Kamien and Schwartz (1974, p. 24):

> 'Regardless of the measures of innovational activity employed, the findings on firm size have been rather consistent: with the possible exception of the chemical industry, there is hardly any support for the hypothesis that intensity of innovational activity increases with firm size. Intensity appears greatest for *intermediate* size firms.'

Even with the exclusion of these very small firms, the analysis for the years 1975 and 1976 covers still more than 98% of total company financed R&D expenditure reported in the Business Week Survey, or more than 94% for 1975 and 97% for 1976 as compared to the total NSF figure.

## 3.1. Logarithmic regression results

Simple linear regressions between individual firms' R&D expenditure and their corresponding employment, sales or assets, will only illustrate the obvious, i.e., that the amount spent on R&D increases with size. What has to be established is whether R&D expenditure increases more than proportionately with size.

Following Hamberg (1964) this can be done by regressing R&D expenditure to $aX_i^b\varepsilon_i$, where $X$ is the firm size variable.

In logarithmic form

$$\log RD_i = \log a + b \log X_i + \varepsilon_i,$$

where $b$ is the scale parameter indicating increasing returns when greater than unity, and decreasing returns when less than unity.

Scherer (1965a, pp. 257–258) criticized this specific procedure because of the problem of estimating the logarithm of non-R&D performing firms. Dealing with R&D performing firms only, one is not faced with this problem here. At the same time, however, it should be pointed out that in this case, we penalize 'the case for bigness most' [Scherer (1965a)].

---

[8]This is not to deny the existence of quite new, inventive entrepreneur based very small firms. It should be noted that generally speaking, in each industry the smallest firm had the highest R&D sales ratio. In 1976 however, a number of these very small firms were no longer reported in the Business Week Survey. It is difficult therefore to assess clearly the role of those very small R&D performing firms.

The following results were obtained:

(1) *For all R&D performing firms with sales of more than $100 million*

1975    $\log RD = 1.350 + 1.126^* \log Empl$,        $R^2 = 0.60$,    $N = 532$,
           (0.107) (0.039)

1976    $\log RD = 1.968 + 1.002 \log Empl$,         $R^2 = 0.66$,    $N = 502$,
           (0.090) (0.032)

(standard errors are given between brackets).

For both years the scale coefficient $b$ is greater than unity. At the 1% significance level, however, we can reject the null hypothesis *for b equal to one* only for the year 1975. The 1976 result is not significant.[9]

(2) *For all large R&D performing firms with more than 25,000 employees*

1975    $\log RD = -1.327 + 1.239^{**} \log Empl$,      $R^2 = 0.46$,    $N = 133$,
           (0.472) (0.116)

1976    $\log RD = -0.976 + 1.185^{***} \log Empl$,     $R^2 = 0.47$,    $N = 140$.
           (0.433) (0.107)

For both years the scale coefficient $b$ is greater than unity, but only significant at the 5% and 10% level respectively.

(3) *For R&D performing firms, with more than $100 million sales, grouped into 17 industries*[10]

When analysing the size-inventive activity link, industry by industry, one is no longer faced with the problem of an oil-biased sales figure. The 1973 oil price increase, having affected mainly the oil companies 'sales' size figure, is supposed to be random between oil-firms of different size.

By combining both the availability of 1975 and 1976 data, and the choice of the employment or sales size measures, one will obtain four separate regression results for each of the seventeen industries analysed. These results are presented in table 5.

---

[9]This seems to be mainly due to the above mentioned bias in favour of smallness. Indeed, while in 1975 the Business Week Survey covered 730 firms, and in 1976 only 598 firms, the 1976 survey covered more large firms than 1975 survey (in 1976, Continental Group: rank 46, Esmark: rank 75, Combustion Engineering: rank 88, and Emerson Electric: rank 100 were also included).

[10]The Business Week classification was followed. However, there are serious problems with any 'firm' industry classification. Highly diversified firms had to be classified under one specific industry. The Business Week industry classification was followed because it was believed the most 'objective' classification, insofar as it was 'given' by the R&D survey source. Excluded were non-manufacturing 'industries' such as lodging, leisure time, oil service, publishing service and telecommunications, meaningless industries such as conglomerates and appliances, and industries with less than 10 firms, i.e. containers. Grouped together were general and special machinery into machinery, metals and mining and steel into primary metals, food, beverages and tobacco into food.

No general conclusions can be drawn from table 5. For most industries, the results indicate that the coefficient is not significantly different from one, or in other words that R&D expenditure increases at a constant proportion of firm size. Only in the case of the automotive, instruments, office equipment, miscellaneous and textiles industries, clear more than proportionate (the first four industries) and less than proportionate (textiles) R&D-size patterns could be observed.

The logarithmic regression results obtained above suffer from the assumed monotonicity in the relationship between inventive activity and size. The importance of the small, intermediate and large firms in the general logarithmic result obtained might vary however considerably.

## 3.2. Cubic regression results

To identify possible inflection points revealing non-monotonicity in the relationship between inventive activity and size, Scherer estimated his measure of inventive activity – R&D employment (1965a) and the number of patents (1965b) – as a function of a simple, squared and cubic size variable (sales). On the basis of this non-linear regression equation, Scherer was able to identify inflection points, i.e. that amount of sales where the second derivative was set equal to nil. The following two general results were obtained:

$$RD \cdot Empl = -0.1 + 2.21S - 0.49S^2 + 0.032S^3, \qquad R^2 = 0.51, \quad N = 352, \qquad (1)$$
$$\phantom{RD \cdot Empl = } (11.05) \ (-7.00) \ (8.00)$$

$$Patents = -3.79 + 144.42S - 23.86S^2 + 1.457S^3, \qquad R^2 = 0.45, \quad N = 448, \qquad (2)$$
$$\phantom{Patents = } (10.00) \quad (-4.93) \ (4.61)$$

($t$-values between brackets).

Setting the first derivative equal to nil indicates a quadratic equation, the roots of which give the sales value of the maximum and minimum of the curve. As illustrated in fig. 1, for eq. (1) the maximum is at $3.36 billion sales, the minimum at $6.85 billion sales. For eq. (2), as fig. 1 indicates, the roots are complex, meaning that no maximum or minimum can be identified. The second derivatives, when set to nil give the following inflexion points: for eq. (1) $5.10 billion sales, for eq. (2) $5.5 billion sales. On the basis of this information, Scherer (1965b, p. 1106) concluded that:

> 'Since only three firms in the sample of 448 [GM, Standard Oil of New Jersey (nowadays Exxon) and Ford] had 1955 sales greater than $5.5 billion, and since the cubic (increasing returns) coefficient *is of doubtful statistical significance*, the indication is that patent outputs generally increase less than proportionately with increases in sales among corporations large enough to appear on Fortune's 1955 list.'

Table 5

Logarithmic regression results for seventeen manufacturing industries, 1975 and 1976 (standard errors between brackets).

| Industry groups | 1975 | | | | | 1976 | | | | |
|---|---|---|---|---|---|---|---|---|---|---|
| | No. of firms | With employment | | With sales | | No. of firms | With employment | | With sales | |
| | | Scale coeff. | $R^2$ | Scale coeff. | $R^2$ | | Scale coeff. | $R^2$ | Scale coeff. | $R^2$ |
| *Part 1. Significantly greater than 1* | | | | | | | | | | |
| Automotive | 28 | 1.21[a] (0.058) | 0.94 | 1.13[b] (0.049) | 0.95 | 25 | 1.20[a] (0.068) | 0.93 | 1.15[a] (0.050) | 0.96 |
| Office equip. | 19 | 1.23[c] (0.119) | 0.86 | 1.23[c] (0.121) | 0.86 | 23 | 1.19[c] (0.096) | 0.88 | 1.20[c] (0.096) | 0.88 |
| Instrument | 22 | 1.55[a] (0.182) | 0.78 | 1.64[a] (0.220) | 0.74 | 30 | 1.19[a] (0.211) | 0.53 | 1.35[c] (0.170) | 0.69 |
| Miscellaneous | 52 | 1.43[a] (0.134) | 0.70 | 1.36[b] (0.135) | 0.67 | 47 | 1.18[c] (0.103) | 0.75 | 1.22[b] (0.098) | 0.78 |
| *Part 2. Not-significantly different from 1* | | | | | | | | | | |
| Aircraft | 15 | 1.29 (0.197) | 0.77 | 1.26 (0.195) | 0.76 | 12 | 1.44[b] (0.158) | 0.89 | 1.31[a] (0.150) | 0.88 |
| Paper | 12 | 1.48[c] (0.248) | 0.78 | 1.45[c] (0.243) | 0.78 | 11 | 1.21 (0.303) | 0.64 | 1.13 (0.296) | 0.62 |
| Machinery | 47 | 1.09 (0.103) | 0.71 | 1.16 (0.104) | 0.74 | 47 | 1.10 (0.100) | 0.73 | 1.10 (0.095) | 0.75 |

| | | | | | | | | | |
|---|---|---|---|---|---|---|---|---|---|
| Fuel | 19 | 1.70ª (0.231) | 0.76 | 1.46ª (0.137) | 0.87 | 18 | 1.13 (0.180) | 0.71 | 0.86 (0.113) | 0.78 |
| Rubber | 13 | 1.06 (0.086) | 0.93 | 1.15 (0.085) | 0.94 | 13 | 0.98 (0.055) | 0.97 | 1.11 (0.077) | 0.95 |
| Drugs | 29 | 1.23 (0.147) | 0.72 | 1.25ᵇ (0.118) | 0.81 | 27 | 0.97 (0.109) | 0.76 | 1.07 (0.113) | 0.78 |
| Electrical, electronics | 39 | 0.72ª (0.064) | 0.78 | 0.54ª (0.129) | 0.32 | 40 | 1.13 (0.093) | 0.79 | 1.05 (0.100) | 0.74 |
| Chemicals | 39 | 1.05 (0.1p9) | 0.71 | 1.14 (0.109) | 0.75 | 36 | 0.87 (0.089) | 0.74 | 0.96 (0.084) | 0.79 |
| Building material | 29 | 0.74 (0.197) | 0.34 | 0.99 (0.237) | 0.39 | 21 | 0.58ᵇ (0.187) | 0.34 | 0.63ᶜ (0.196) | 0.35 |
| Metals | 25 | 0.76 (0.184) | 0.43 | 0.76 (0.171) | 0.46 | 23 | 0.77ᶜ (0.131) | 0.62 | 0.71ᵇ (0.131) | 0.58 |
| Personal care products | 14 | 0.95 (0.315) | 0.43 | 1.25 (0.219) | 0.73 | 14 | 0.94 (0.170) | 0.72 | 1.003 (0.151) | 0.79 |
| Food | 40 | 0.93 (0.119) | 0.62 | 1.05 (0.130) | 0.62 | 37 | 0.73ª (0.084) | 0.68 | 0.79ᵇ (0.101) | 0.64 |
| *Part 3. Significantly smaller than 1* | | | | | | | | | |
| Textiles | 15 | 0.52ª (0.138) | 0.52 | 0.68 (0.187) | 0.50 | 9 | 0.26ª (0.149) | 0.30 | 0.26ª (0.198) | 0.20 |

ªSignificant at the 1% level.
ᵇSignificant at the 5% level.
ᶜSignificant at the 10% level.

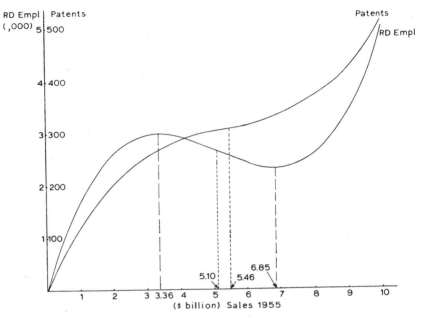

Fig. 1. Scherer's cubic regression results.

This interpretation of cubic regression results raises several important questions.

First, in relation to the patent cubic regression, one may well wonder what is the justification of introducing a cubic term ($S^3$) 'of doubtful significance' which, later on in the interpretation of the results, is actually ignored because its relevance is limited to three firms. Scherer's interpretation suggests that, in fact, a simple quadratic regression would be more relevant and fit better with the data. But, as shown in Scherer's appendix table, a simple quadratic equation reduces the variance residual as compared with the simple linear regression with only 0.6%, not significant at the 1% level. In other words, the 'of doubtful significance' cubic 'increasing returns'[11] sales term is absolutely crucial to the significant variance reduction of the non-linear cubic regression, in no way justifying its exclusion later on, when interpreting the results.

Second, and far more important, one may question the relevance of Scherer's cubic regression analysis. The explanatory power of both eqs. (1)

[11]The notions 'increasing' and 'decreasing' returns are used following Scherer. It should however be remembered that both notions are actually not related to 'increasing (decreasing) returns' to R&D, i.e. R&D (dis)economies of scale, measured as R&D output/input ratios for specific R&D size classes, but are a somewhat misused abreviation of a 'more than proportionate increase' and 'less than proportionate increase of R&D expenditure (or employment) with firm size'.

and (2) is actually rather low. The relevant area of a cubic fitting should consist mainly of the actual area between the maximum and minimum, or vice versa. While this fact might explain, to a certain extent, Scherer's ease in excluding the three largest U.S. firms, a closer look at the 1955 firms' sales data reveals some interesting facts.

In the case of the patent equation, no clear maximum or minimum could be identified, the roots of the first derivative being imaginary. For eq. (1), however, it can be established that, over the relevant range, i.e. between the maximum of \$3.36 billion sales and the minimum of \$6.85 billion sales, there are exactly four firms.[12] In other words, out of 352 firms, Scherer's cubic regression covers over its relevant range less than 1.5% of the whole sample of firms.

Similar cubic regressions were carried out using the 1975 and 1976 R&D expenditure data, referred to above. For reasons discussed earlier, the size variable chosen was the employment measure. To allow some close comparisons with Scherer's analysis, regressions using the sales measure were also worked out. The following results were obtained [*t*-statistic values in brackets, * significant at the 1% level, ** significant at the 5% level]:

*For 1975 with employment (in thousands) as size measure*

$$RD = 17.235 + 6.482*Empl + 0.0398*Empl^2 - 0.000042*Empl^3,$$
$$(0.7) \quad (6.65) \quad (9.58) \quad (-11.39)$$
$$R^2 = 0.77,$$
$$F(3,528) = 594.47*,$$

$$\text{min} = -73.04, \quad \text{max} = 704.31, \quad \text{inflex.p.} = 315.63,$$
$$SER_{cubic} = 408.61, \qquad\qquad SVRF(1,528) = 129.81*,^{13}$$
$$SER_{quadratic} = 455.63, \quad R^2 = 0.72, \quad SVRF(1,529) = 45.43*,$$
$$SER_{simple} = 474.36, \quad R^2 = 0.69, \qquad F(1,530) = 1185.191*.$$

*For 1976 with employment as size measure*

$$RD = 33.0361 + 6.5265*Empl + 0.04804*Empl^2 - 0.00005*Empl^3,$$
$$(1.18) \quad (5.88) \quad (10.00) \quad (-11.67)$$
$$R^2 = 0.69,$$
$$F(3,498) = 619.165*,$$

$$\text{min} = -61.90, \quad \text{max} = 697.71, \quad \text{inflex.p.} = 317.91,$$
$$SER_{cubic} = 451.06, \qquad\qquad SVRF(1,498 = 136.11*,$$
$$SER_{quadratic} = 508.47, \quad R^2 = 0.73, \quad SVRF(1,499) = 40.32*,$$
$$SER_{simple} = 528.08, \quad R^2 = 0.71, \qquad F(1,500) = 1218.48*.$$

---

[12]Ford, Standard Oil NJ with 'increasing returns', and U.S. Steel and Chrysler with 'decreasing returns'.

[13]$SER$ = standard error of the regression, $SVR$ = significance of the incremental variance reduction.

For both years the cubic regression is undoubtedly the best fit, as indicated by the increase in $R^2$ [a significant (at the 1% level) incremental variance reduction of 8%] and the decrease in the standard error of the regression. In addition, all regression coefficients are significant at the 1% level. As illustrated in fig. 2 and in contrast to Scherer, the cubic regression covers over the relevant range 531 firms out of 532 in 1975, and 500 firms out of 502 in 1976.[14]

For both years the results indicate exactly the opposite pattern to Scherer's findings, as a comparison between figs. 1 and 2 quite clearly illustrates. For all firms except five, for both years, 'increasing returns' were found up to a point of, respectively, 315,630 and 317,910 employees, from whereon 'decreasing returns' set in.[15]

When the sales measure is chosen as size variable, identical results are obtained.

*For 1975 with sales (in $ million) as size measure*[16]

$$RD = 53,150.074 + 94.148*S + 0.0132*S^2 - 0.000000302*S^3,$$
$$\quad (1.69) \qquad (3.85) \qquad (6.44) \qquad (-7.95)$$
$$R^2 = 0.58,$$
$$F(3,528) = 247.489*,$$

min = 3,220, max = 32,280, inflex.p. = 14,530,

$SER_{cubic} = 551.14,$ $\qquad\qquad$ $SVRF(1,528) = 63.21*,$
$SER_{quadratic} = 582.65,$ $R^2 = 0.53,$ $SVRF(1,529) = 28.33*,$
$SER_{simple} = 597.48,$ $R^2 = 0.51,$ $F(1,530) = 551.04*.$

[14]The exception in both years being ATT, essentially a non-manufacturing firm, not reported in the *Fortune* list. When ATT is excluded from the sample and replaced by its major manufacturing subsidiary, Western Electric (assuming an identical R&D sales ratio), the following result for 1975 is obtained:

$$RD = -16.586 + 9,432*Empl + 0.0149 \, Empl^2 - 0.00000723 \, Empl^3, \quad R^2 = 0.76,$$
$$\quad (-0.67) \quad (8.31) \qquad (2.28) \qquad\qquad (0.91) \qquad\qquad F(3,528) = 557.37*,$$
min = -264.88, max = 1640.61, inflex.p. = 687.87,

$SER = 399.996,$ $SVRF(1,528) = 0.825.$

In other words, we found increasing returns *for all firms*, General Motors with its 681 thousand employees falling just under the inflexion point, or in the 'increasing returns' area of the cubic regression. But as the result rather nicely suggests, the cubic regression is obviously not the best fit, the cubic term being actually not significant, just as the cubic incremental variance reduction. The best fit is the following quadratic regression:

$$RD = -26.701 + 10.244*Empl + 0.00914*Empl^2, \quad R^2 = 0.76,$$
$$\quad (-1.21) \quad (14.70) \qquad\quad (6.18) \qquad\qquad F(2,529) = 835.93*,$$
min = -560.36, $SER = 399.93,$ $SVRF(1,529) = 38.20*,$

which indicates continuous 'increasing returns' for all firms. This only illustrates the important underestimation of the generally observed 'increasing returns' pattern, not only because of the inclusion of R&D performing firms only, but also because of the inclusion of some large, essentially non-manufacturing, R&D performing firms in the firm sample.

[15]The five firms with 'decreasing returns' are ATT, General Motors, Ford, ITT, and General Electrics.

[16]For the sake of readability, all sales regressions are in $100 R&D.

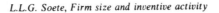

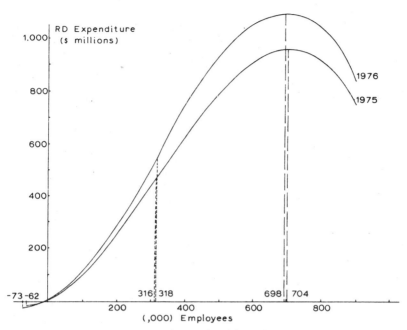

Fig. 2.  Cubic regression results with employment.

*For 1976 with sales as size measure*

$$RD = 36{,}727.505 + 142.710*S + 0.004787**S^2 - 0.000000099*S^3,$$
$$\quad (0.95) \qquad (5.28) \qquad (2.29) \qquad\qquad (-2.84)$$
$$R^2 = 0.56,$$
$$F(3{,}498) = 214.63*,$$

$$\text{min} = -11{,}090, \quad \text{max} = 43{,}330, \quad \text{inflex.p.} = 16{,}120,$$
$$SER_{cubic} = 647.84, \qquad\qquad SVRF(1{,}498) = 8.08*,$$
$$SER_{quadratic} = 652.42, \quad R^2 = 0.557, \quad SVRF(1{,}499) = 5.73**,$$
$$SER_{simple} = 655.50, \quad R^2 = 0.552, \qquad F(1{,}500) = 615.34*.$$

While the 1976 result is somewhat less significant, the cubic regression remains, however, clearly the best fit, in terms of significance of variance reduction or decrease in standard error of the regression. In addition, over the relevant range, the cubic regression covers, once again, 530 and 500 firms out of 532 and 502 firms respectively. As illustrated in fig. 3, for both years 'increasing returns' were found for all firms, except six, up to a point of $14.53 and $16.12 billion sales respectively.[17]

[17]Interestingly, apart from the non-manufacturing firm ATT, and Scherer's 'increasing returns' firms, General Motors and Ford, the three other firms which showed 'decreasing returns' were all oil companies. In view of what has been said above about oil-sales figures, this finding is not surprising.

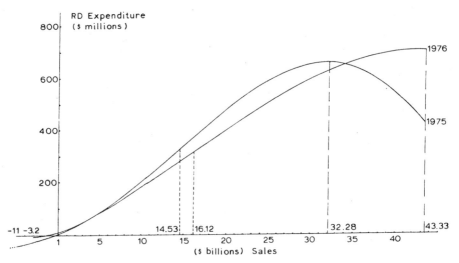

Fig. 3.   Cubic regression results with sales.

Similar non-linear regressions were carried out for each of the seventeen industries identified above.[18]

Table 6 summarizes the best fit for each of the seventeen industry-groups, obtained on the basis of a 5% significant incremental variance reduction. A cubic regression was clearly the best fit in the case of nine industries (part 1), a quadratic regression in the case of four industries (part 2), for the four remaining industries (part 3), the non-linear regression method did not give any significant result.

It is extremely difficult to try to generalise on the basis of these individual industry regressions. However, some general patterns can be observed.

(1)   For the office equipment, personal care products and chemical industries, *large* firms do clearly carry out proportionately more R&D than small firms. For the first two industries the more than proportionate increase seems to prevail over the whole range of firms. For the chemical industry, a clear turning point could be identified. By contrast in the case of the drugs, metals and food industries an opposite pattern emerges. Large firms carry out proportionately less R&D than small or medium-sized firms. In the case of the food industry a clear turning point could be identified.

(2)   As in the case of the 'global' inter-firm cubic regression analysis, 'increasing returns', with the exception of the largest firms prevail in the case of the automotive, machinery, instruments and miscellaneous industries. By

[18]Complete results can be obtained from the author.

contrast, and similarly to Scherer's (1965b) industry results, 'diminishing returns', with the exception of the largest firms, can be observed in the fuel, tyre and rubber and electrical and electronics industries.

(3) Finally, in the case of the aircraft, paper, textiles and building materials industries, the non-linear regression analyses do not pass the significance tests.

## 4. Conclusion

The statistical evidence presented in this paper casts doubts as to the validity of most empirical analyses and results in the field of firm size and inventive activity. At the global level, the computation of concentration ratios, the analysis of logarithmic regressions as well as cubic regressions, all indicated that innovational effort, as measured by company financed R&D expenditure, tends to increase more than proportionately with firm size.

These conclusions, as compared to previous empirical analyses, have been obtained on the basis of an inventive activity measure, which, although once again only a very limited proxy, might be considered as a more neutral measure in relation to size, than both R&D employment or the number of patents, generally used in previous empirical analyses. In addition, the actual data relates to the mid-70's and covers more than 95% of total company financed R&D, or in other words, is more reliable and relevant for the present U.S. situation, than most data used in previous empirical analyses. Finally, it should be pointed out that the conclusions are based on consistency over the years 1975 and 1976, and between the sales and employment size variable.

At the industry level, it is more difficult to draw a general picture from the results obtained. On the one hand, the logarithmic regression results indicated that for the large majority of industries, no distinct 'increasing' or 'decreasing' pattern could be discerned. The cubic regression results on the other hand indicated for only six industries, very distinct 'increasing' (3) or 'decreasing' (3) returns patterns for large firms. For the other industries, confirmation of a typical Scherer-pattern of 'diminishing returns except for a few giant firms' [Scherer (1965b, p. 1108)] was found for three industries. Confirmation of our global 'increasing returns except for the largest firms' for four industries. Consequently, no general and final conclusions can be drawn from the individual industry results.

Nevertheless, on the basis of the global as well as individual industry results obtained above, one can conclude *no* evidence exists in favour of the Scherer assumption that inventive activity increases less than proportionately with increases in firm size, or that 'bigness might...be a stifling factor' [Scherer (1965a, p. 265)], in relation to industrial research and development.

Table 6

Non-linear regression results for seventeen industry groups.[a]

| Industry group | Best fit | | Exceptions |
|---|---|---|---|
| *Part 1. Significant Cubic Regression Results* | | | |
| *(A) 'Diminishing returns', except for the industry leaders* | | | |
| 1. Fuel | $RD = 1180443.238{**} + 124.888{*}S - 0.0063{*}S^2 + 0.000000101{*}S^3$ <br> (−2.71) (6.34) (−4.93) (5.05) | $R^2 = 0.95$ <br> $F(3, 15) = 89.59{*}$ | Exxon, Texaco |
| 2. Tyre & rubber | $RD = -45.69 + 21.02{*}Empl - 0.302{*}Empl^2 + 0.00145{*}Empl^3$ <br> (−1.71) (6.90) (−5.00) (5.03) | $R^2 = 0.98$ <br> $F(3, 9) = 125.55{*}$ | Goodyear, Firestone |
| 3. Electrical, electronics | $RD = -41.43 + 14.86{*}Empl - 0.053{**}Empl^2 + 0.00012{**}Empl^3$ <br> (−1.15) (6.34) (−2.30) (2.43) | $R^2 = 0.97$ <br> $F(3, 35) = 369.18{*}$ | General Electrics, Westinghouse |
| *(B) 'Diminishing returns', except for the large firms* | | | |
| 4. Chemicals | $RD = -15531.933 + 273.36{**}S - 20.0443S^2 + 0.0000074{***}S^3$ <br> (−0.22) (2.53) (−1.26) (2.48) | $R^2 = 0.94$ <br> $F(3, 32) = 154.66{*}$ | 8 largest firms |
| *(C) 'Increasing returns', except for the industry leaders* | | | |
| 5. Automotive | $RD = 48255.72 + 87.65{**}S + 0.0141{*}S^2 - 0.000000218{*}S^3$ <br> (0.96) (2.30) (4.57) (−3.63) | $R^2 = 0.99$ <br> $F(3, 24) = 1406.1{*}$ | General Motors, Ford |
| 6. Machinery | $RD = 46193.03{**} - 38.27S + 0.165{*}S^2 - 0.000017{*}S^3$ <br> (2.24) (−0.58) (4.15) (−3.00) | $R^2 = 0.97$ <br> $F(3, 43) = 459.72{*}$ | Caterpillar |
| 7. Miscellaneous | $RD = 42.69{*} - 8.12{*}Empl + 0.686{*}Empl^2 - 0.00454{*}Empl^3$ <br> (2.85) (−2.71) (5.66) (−4.09) | $R^2 = 0.97$ <br> $F(3, 48) = 591.88{*}$ | Minnesota Mining & Mng. |
| 8. Instruments | $RD = 42949 - 146.145S + 1.221{*}S^2 - 0.000215{*}S^3$ <br> (0.90) (−0.54) (3.96) (−4.14) | $R^2 = 0.99$ <br> $F(3, 18) = 863.05{*}$ | Eastman Kodak |
| *(D) 'Increasing returns', except for the large firms* | | | |
| 9. Food | $RD = 25.23 - 1.13Empl + 0.218Empl^2 - 0.00255{**}Empl^3$ <br> (1.01) (−0.31) (1.86) (−2.53) | $R^2 = 0.63$ <br> $F(3, 36) = 19.11{*}$ | 15 largest firms |

*Part 2. Significant Quadratic Regression Results (cubic regression not-significant)*

*(A) 'Diminishing returns' for all firms*

10. Drugs

$RD = -114695.146 + 936.509*S - 0.241**S^2$
$(-1.29)$ $(4.49)$ $(-2.69)$
$R^2 = 0.69$
$F(2, 26) = 28.70*$

11. Metals

$RD = -2141.378 + 119.539*S - 0.006665**S^2$
$(-0.10)$ $(5.04)$ $(-2.28)$
$R^2 = 0.82$
$F(2,20) = 45.05*$

*(B) 'Increasing returns' for all firms*

12. Office equipment

$RD = -27838.014 + 478.445*S + 0.008829*S^2$
$(-1.01)$ $(20.96)$ $(6.21)$
$R^2 = 0.998$
$F(2, 20) = 5027.05*$

13. Personal care products

$RD = 26648.999 + 58.999S + 0.0226*S^2$
$(0.88)$ $(1.36)$ $(3.16)$
$R^2 = 0.96$
$F(2, 11) = 134.28*$

*Part 3. No Conclusive Evidence (cubic and quadratic regressions not-significant)*

14. Aircraft

$RD = -149.2 + 19.97*Empl$
$(-0.59)$ $(4.82)$
$R^2 = 0.70$
$F(1,10) = 23.22*$

15. Textiles

$RD = 6.59 + 0.532*Empl$
$(1.75)$ $(3.64)$
$R^2 = 0.51$
$F(1, 13) = 13.28*$

16. Building materials

$RD = 16677.73 + 79.21*S$
$(0.85)$ $(4.29)$
$R^2 = 0.49$
$F(1, 19) = 18.38*$

17. Paper

$RD = 14406 + 64**S$
$(0.49)$ $(2.81)$
$R^2 = 0.44$
$F(1, 10) = 7.89**$

[a]$RD$ is in $100, $S$ in $ million, when $S$ is the size measure, and $RD$ is in $100,000, $Empl$ in thousands, when $Empl$ is the size measure. One asterisk indicates significance at 1% level, and two asterisks denote significance at 5% level.

## References

Business Week, 1976, Where private industry puts its research money, June 28, 62–84.

Business Week, 1977, What 600 companies spend for research, June 27, 62–64.

Freeman, C., 1974, The economics of industrial innovation (Penguin Books Ltd., Harmondsworth).

Hamberg, D., 1964, Size of firm, oligopoly and research: The evidence, Canadian Journal of Economics and Political Science 30, no. 1, 62–75.

Kamien, M.I. and N.L. Schwartz, 1974, Market structure and innovation, in: H.R. Clauser, ed., Progress in assessing technological innovation (Technomic Publ. Co., Westport) 23–25.

Kamien, M.I. and N.L. Schwartz, 1975, Market structure and innovation: A survey, Journal of Economic Literature 23, no. 1, 1–37.

National Science Foundation, 1976, Research and development in industry 1974, NSF Report no. 76-322.

Scherer, F.M., 1965a, Size of firm, oligopoly, and research: A comment, Canadian Journal of Economics and Political Science 31, no. 2, 256–266.

Scherer, F.M., 1965b, Firm size, market structure, opportunity, and the output of patented inventions, American Economic Review 55, no. 5, 1097–1125.

Scherer, F.M., 1970, Industrial market structure and economic performance (Rand McNally, Chicago, IL).

Schmookler, J., 1966, Invention and economic growth (Harvard University Press, Cambridge, MA).

Schumpeter, J.A., 1950, Capitalism, socialism and democracy, 3rd ed. (Harper and Row, New York).

Shrieves, R.E., 1978, Market structure and innovation: A new perspective, Journal of Industrial Economics 26, no. 4, 329–347.

Soete, L., 1977, Deflating R&D expenditures: An application to U.S. R&D, OECD Report no. DSTI/SPR/77 22/17 (Paris).

Taylor, C.T. and Z.A. Silbertson, 1973, The economic impact of the patent system (Cambridge University Press, London).

# [15]

THE JOURNAL OF INDUSTRIAL ECONOMICS

Volume XXXII          September 1983          No. 1

## FIRM SIZE AND TECHNICAL CHANGE IN A
## DYNAMIC CONTEXT

### Raphael Kaplinsky

#### I. THE PROBLEM

THE relationship between firm size and technical change has long been a pre-occupation in the literature, preceding the flurry of macroeconomic studies which followed the discovery of the 'residual factor' by Solow, Dennison and others. Although this concern goes back at least to the writings of Marx, it was Schumpeter who first emphasized the relationship between firm size and technical change. Schumpeter [19], writing in 1942, pointed out that market imperfections—namely the ever-increasing trend towards oligopolistic market structures—did not necessarily result in sub-optimal levels of invention and innovation.

> "Thus it is not sufficient to argue that because perfect competition is impossible under modern industrial conditions—or because it always has been impossible—the large-scale establishment or unit of control must be accepted as a necessary evil inseparable from the economic progress which it is prevented from sabotaging by the forces inherent in its productive apparatus. What we have got to accept is that it has come to be the most powerful engine of that progress of the long-run expansion of total output not only in spite of, but to a considerable extent through, this strategy which looks so restrictive when viewed in the individual case and from the individual point of time. In this respect, perfect competition is not only impossible but inferior, and has no title to being set up as a model of ideal efficiency" (Schumpeter [19, p. 101]).

For some years this assertion of Schumpeter's was widely accepted. But then a number of detailed empirical studies were undertaken resting on 1950s data (Scherer [17] and [18] and 1960s data (Shrieves [20]). These began to suggest that beyond a certain size (roughly 5,000 employees, according to Scherer) inventive activity rose less than proportionately with bigness. Soete [22], in an important study, has questioned these conclusions, resting his argument on more recent 1970s data, with a different sample (i.e. excluding oil companies) and a different indicator of inventive activity (i.e. R and D as % of sales rather than numbers of R and D workers or patents registered). Soete's conclusions are unequivocal and, *at a macroeconomic level and within a restricted time period (1974–6)*, wholly believable—there is clearly a positive relationship between size and the effort expended in changing technology.

39

40                                RAPHAEL KAPLINSKY

By contrast, and more recently, Rothwell and Zegveld [16] assembled a variety of country studies, some of which suggest that small and medium sized firms (that is those employing less than 500 people) are relatively invention- and innovation-intensive in some sectors and in some countries.

We are faced therefore with contrasting sets of views on the relationship between firm size and technical change.[1] Although to some extent these con- flicting views arise as a consequence of using different indicators of technical change—i.e. input measures (number of employees or % of sales in R and D) versus output measures (patents)—there remains a residual set of views which directly conflict with each other. The purpose of this paper is to argue, by illustration with a single sector, *computer-aided design* (CAD), that the above- mentioned studies reach their varying conclusions in a largely static frame- work. Thus, whilst there is always a tendency towards concentration in capitalism, the relationship between firm size and technical change is a dynamic one, ensuring that static generalisations at any single point of time are not very helpful.

In the following section we describe the market structure in the CAD sector and analyse how this has changed over the past decade.[2] In section IV we analyse the nature of the barriers to entry in this sector and illustrate how these are typical of other emerging software-intensive microelectronic-based sectors. Finally in section V we return to the earlier discussion on the relation- ship between firm size and inventive activity.


### II. COMPUTER AIDED DESIGN TECHNOLOGY

CAD is a particularly good example of a software intensive industry. Building on a fairly standard set of microelectronic hardware (predominantly mini- computers) and peripheral components (television screens, computer memory, drawing devices and digitising boards[3]) systems are available to undertake a wide range of tasks to assist designers and draughtspersons in their work. This assistance is of two major sorts. The first involves *basic graphic software* which speeds up the process of drawing;[4] the second involves a wide variety of *applications programs* to meet particular design needs in all sectors of engineering (electrical, civil, mechanical, chemical), cartography, business analysis and animation.

The price of these systems starts from around $30,000 for a single termina system which is suitable only for drawing, to around $1.5 m for a 30 termina system which provides both a wide variety of analytical applications programs

---

[1] See also Kamien and Schwartz [12] for a survey of additional literature in this subject.
[2] Much of the detailed case-study material is drawn from Kaplinsky [14].
[3] These are flat surfaces which are used to convert drawing specifications to the digital format utilised by electronic systems.
[4] Or the reproduction of design information in other forms which may be relevant e.g. paper tape for CNC machine tools.

and a capability to undertake numerous, unrelated batch processing tasks such as payrolls and customer billing. Of these prices, around 30 percent is hardware; the rest comprises overheads and a considerable input of software.

The origins of this industry lay in the aerospace and defence sectors in the late 1950s and 1960s. By the early 1970s CAD began to be used in the electronic sector, diffusing to mechanical engineering and cartography over the past five years. The industry expects the civil engineering and architectural sectors to be the major growth point in the second half of the 1980s. The growth of this sector has been quite remarkable. Having reached around $80 m in 1976, the sector 'took off' with the value of output reaching around $1 b in 1980. Projections of sales value for 1984 are between $5 b and $8 b. By comparison, the projection for global sales of robots is only $2 b by 1990, and only $4 b for Colour TVs in the USA in 1984. As another indicator of the phenomenal growth of the CAD sector, if the industry had grown at the same rate as IBM between 1976 and 1980, its sales would have only been around $120 m in 1980, and if it had followed the same growth path as DEC (the most successful of the mini-computer firms, the 'success story' of the 1970s), its size in 1980 would only have been around $250 m.

### III. MARKET STRUCTURE

Potentially the market for CAD systems is segmented into three major divisions, namely:

(i) mainframe based systems which are partly used for graphics and partly for information processing and analytical tasks;

(ii) minicomputer based systems dedicated to graphics use, which can undertake a variety of different applications programs but with limited ability to perform complex analytical programs;

(iii) microcomputer based systems with a basic draughting software and dedicated to a few applications programs with a very limited analytical capability.

Each of these systems could be made available by turnkey suppliers, selling complete systems of hardware and software, or by specialised vendors which provide software alone. However the running so far over the past decade has been made almost entirely by the minicomputer-based turnkey systems, with the exception of IBM (whose presence[5] has hitherto largely been limited to very large companies each using a relatively large number of graphics terminals with the processing mainframe also being used on a batch-basis for additional heavy-analytic and data-processing activities) and the emerging

---

[5] However IBM markets only its mechanical software. Its electronic software is not marketed outside of affiliates since IBM are concerned that this would divulge proprietary information regarding component, integrated circuit and computer architecture.

42                                    RAPHAEL KAPLINSKY

TABLE I

MARKET SHARES (%) AND CONTROLLING SHAREHOLDINGS OF MAJOR US TURNKEY CAD
SUPPLIERS

| | Market Shares (%) | | | | |
|---|---|---|---|---|---|
| | *1976* | *1977* | *1978* | *1979* | *1980* |
| Applicon | 14.5 | 15.1 | 10.9 | 9 | 8.8 |
| Auto-trol | 10 | 11.4 | 13 | 10.6 | 8.9 |
| Calma | 14.3 | 15.5 | 16 | 13.6 | 13.8 |
| Computervision | 28.1 | 25.6 | 25.8 | 32.6 | 33.2 |
| Gerber | 3.6 | 1.3 | 2.6 | 3.2 | 4.1[*] |
| IBM | 21.4 | 18.2 | 13.6 | 12.7 | 12.2 |
| Intergraph | 8.2 | 8.3 | 12 | 9.3 | 9.8 |
| Unigraphics | | | 3.3 | 2.4 | 2.3 |
| Other | | | | | 6.9 |

[*] Excluding estimated sales of PC800 dedicated electronic systems sold by a different division, Gerber's share falls to 2.3% in 1980.

| | Shareholdings | |
|---|---|---|
| | *Control* | *Other significant* |
| Applicon | Original founders | General Electric owns 28%; will divest due to purchase of Calma |
| Auto-trol | Hillman Foundation (c75%) | 25% public + employees |
| Calma | General Electric (100%) | |
| Computervision | Founding president and vice president (22%) | Institutions |
| Gerber | Gerber Scientific (80%) | Public (20%) |
| IBM | Public 100% | |
| Intergraph | Eight directors and employee fund[b] (40.6%) | Public (13.2%) Employees (46.2%) |
| Unigraphics | McDonnel Douglas (100%) | |

[b] Voting rights of employees fund held by founder and his wife.

sales of software systems such as those of Cambridge Interactive Systems[6] and Compeda,[7] both of the UK.

Currently seven US firms dominate this turnkey market[8]—the shares of these individual firms are shown in Table I for the period 1976–80. The most significant factor which emerges from this tabulation is the growing dominance of the market by Computervision whose share grew from 28.1% in 1976 to 33.2% in 1980, at the expense of all of the other turnkey vendors except Inter-

[6] CIS markets, with increasing success, a 3D modelling capability and a basic draughting system. Annual sales are less than $10 m.
[7] Compeda, a UK government sponsored firm, markets a very successful 3D system (PDMS) to check interference between pipes in process plant design. Its annual turnover is less than $5 m.
[8] We refer, here, to the market for CAD systems in the engineering (electronic, mechanical, civil and structural) architecture, retailing and publishing sectors. Excluded are the fields of business graphics (which according to one source—the Harvard Newsletter on Computer Graphics [9]—was worth $200 m. in 1981) and animation.

graph. It is significant that the extraordinarily high growth rate of the industry means that despite a 78.4% annual growth in sales between 1979 and 1980 a firm like Auto-trol was faced with a declining market share, or that Gerber, with a 31.4% p.a. growth rate over the same period[9] must be seen as struggling for survival!

Given the paucity of data on the various firms operating in this sector it is not easy to be precise in describing the evolving market structure. Nevertheless it is possible to distinguish between four distinct periods in the industry's development.

### (a) *Pre 1969: Industry Origins*

In this initial period of industry development the running was made almost entirely by existing large firms in the defence, aerospace and aeronautical industries with the collaboration of mainframe computer manufacturers such as IBM. The first technical breakthrough (the light pen and screen, allowing for interactive use) occurred in the 1950s during the development of the SAGE early-warning radar system. By the 1960s the aerospace industry became the major user, pushed by the US Air Force which actively attempted to widen applications to other manufacturing industries in the late 1960s. During this latter period General Motors began the development of its DAC ('Design Augmented by Computers') programme.

In summary, therefore, during this early period there was hardly any 'market' for CAD, with most developments occurring to assist own-use by large, technologically advanced mechanical-engineering corporations in the US and (to a lesser extent) in the UK.[10]

### (b) *1969–74: Dynamic new firms*

In this short second period, the industry began to change its nature significantly by rapidly diffusing its product to the electronics sector. The primary impetus for this were new small firms begun by software writers spinning off from other industries. These comprised two groups. The first were those with specific experience in CAD software in the aerospace and automobile sectors—a particularly influential group moved west to Southern California and formed a company called Systems Science Software which over the years provided the basic software for many of the current turnkey vendors; another Huntsville Alabama firm was established by ex IBM employees feeding off displaced software manpower as the neighbouring Apollo moon-programme was wound down. The second source of software writers were those emerging

---

[9] Excluding estimated sales of $10 m for the dedicated electronics system produced by an affiliate.

[10] According to Radar and Wingert [15], the UK CAD industry was more advanced than the German industry in the 1960s due to the relative strength of the UK aircraft industry.

from the electronics sector itself (especially IBM) who were attracted by the low barriers to entry and the obvious future potential of the CAD sector.

The consequence was a variety of new firms, initially making digitising equipment and subsequently moving to the supply of complete turnkey systems. This group includes all of the current major US turnkey vendors except IBM and Gerber (whose origins lie in computerised plotters and cutters for the garments industry). By contrast in Europe (and especially the UK) the emergent CAD capability in this time period arose directly within established electronics firms (such as Racal, Plessey and ICL) who produced equipment for their own needs.

In summary, therefore, this second period of industry development saw the emergence of new, independent firms and the rapid diffusion of the technology out of the defence, aerospace and automobile sectors to the electronics industries.

### (c) *1974–80 The trend to concentration*

By around 1974 most of the major suppliers were established, protected (as we shall see in section IV) by a large investment of software in a suite of specialised applications programs. At this point CAD equipment began to penetrate manufacturing industry. The rate of diffusion proved to be so rapid in this sector that the aggregate industry growth rate increased from around 55% p.a. to around 80% p.a. All the vendors, despite different specialisations (e.g. Intergraph and Auto-trol in cartography, Calma in electronics; Computervision and Applicon in both electronics and mechanical engineering) adopted a similar strategy of expanding their range of applications programs to provide comprehensive cover to all industries. But this diversification, together with the cost of financing such heady rates of expansion, necessitated the raising of financial resources. In the case of Auto-trol and Applicon, this meant recourse to venture capital.[11] But all firms—including those owned by venture capital—were forced both to sell shares in the stock market and into long and short-term debt.

At the same time as these established CAD suppliers were raising funds, predators were emerging amongst established Corporations. First McDonnel Douglas took over United Computing in 1974 changing its name to Unigraphics. Then around 1975, Gerber, a major name in the garments sector, expanded its range of operations, buying in software from Systems Science Software. But most significant was the action of US-based General Electric (GE), one of the largest mechanical engineering corporations in the world. Initially GE had taken a 28% share of Applicon as a speculative investment. Then in the late 1970s GE changed its chairman—the new incumbent was

---

[11] Such was the growth rate of the industry, that the $50,000 (plus commercial loans of $3.6 m) invested by the Hillman Foundation (a family trust seeking 'explosive growth sectors') in Auto-trol in 1973 was worth over $100 m by 1981.

struck by the outdatedness of GE's technology and its vulnerability to Japanese and European competition. Already a joint venture of Fujitsu Fanuc and Siemens had made very heavy inroads into the US machine tool numerical control sector eroding GE's former dominance and achieving a 15% market share within five years. Consequently GE has begun radically to alter its structure moving up the technological stream towards the 'factory of the future'.[12] This involved the acquisition of a semiconductor firm (Intersil) for $235 m, the beefing up of its machine-tool NC capability (costing $31 m) and buying Calma.[13] GE paid around $170 m for Calma in 1981—its previous owners, United Telecom, had boughtout Calma for a mere $17 m two years earlier.

There are reasons to believe that GE will be setting a trend. Whilst the remaining independent vendors all profess to want to maintain their independence, this may not be possible. For example, because of fund raising issues in the stock market, the founding two shareholders of Computervision, the market leader, now control only 22% of its shares—the remainder being held by the public, predominantly institutions. Computervision is therefore now extremely vulnerable to a takeover bid. The remaining independent firms—Applicon and Intergraph are still controlled by their founders. It must be an open question whether they, too can withstand acquisition offers.[14]

Therefore one pressure towards concentration has already been described, namely vertical and horizontal integration by enterprises in other sectors. A second tendency towards concentration is the organic tendency within the CAD sector itself, namely the growing market presence of Computervision (and Intergraph) at the expense of industry minors. Computervision has not only increased its market share (from 28% to 33% between 1976 and 1980) but is in the process of becoming a TNC itself with the decision to set up a manufacturing subsidiary in Europe.

To summarise, therefore, this third phase of industry development was associated with the growing size of CAD firms, the growing organic trends towards concentration within the sector, and a tendency for formerly independent CAD firms to be swallowed by existing TNCs.

### (d) *Post 1980. Maturity*

In the most recent development which is only just emerging we can once again see the emergence of new, small firms spun-off from larger, older and established firms. To understand their significance we need to go a little deeper into the nature of CAD technology. CAD systems, as we have seen, are built around two sets of software, basic graphics and applications oriented. The

[12] See Business Week [3] and [5].
[13] Having done so GE is forced to divest itself of the holding in Applicon.
[14] Indeed Applicon was itself taken over by a French Transnational, Schlumberger, in early 1982.

46                         RAPHAEL KAPLINSKY

advantage of *mainframe* based systems is that they are not only able to cope with
the heaviest requirements of particular applications programs, but they are
also able to undertake complementary batch processing tasks such as payroll
and inventory controls. Their disadvantages are that they are costly (an entry
cost of over $500,000 with unit-terminal costs of around $60,000), that they are
vulnerable to breakdown of the centralised host computer and memory, and
that the mainframe suppliers have hitherto developed only a limited range of
applications programs. By contrast the *mini-computer based turnkey vendors* have
developed the most comprehensive range of applications software, most of
which can be used independently from mainframe computers. They have
lower entry costs (around $200,000) with lower unit terminal costs. The major
disadvantage is their weaker processing capability which limits their use for
heavy-analytical applications programs and hinders their response rate to
users.

But recently, as the CAD vendors have penetrated a wider user base, a
'space' has begun to emerge for dedicated systems. That is amongst users (e.g.
engineering firms using printed circuit boards and draughting firms) who have
no need for a comprehensive suite of applications programs and whose
engineering data processing requirements are not extensive. Their needs can
be met by microprocessor driven systems which provide basic graphics
software with a single (or small number of) applications programs. Such
systems, based upon already 'mature' applications programs developed by the
turnkey vendors are rapidly beginning to emerge, selling for around $30,000
each. The vendors are new firms begun by ex-employees of existing CAD
vendors. For example, Avera Inc., was set up by two ex-Applicon employees
(one had worked there for seven years) and one ex Intel employee. Set up
with $150,000 of capital the single-terminal systems are sold for $39,250. One
of the ex-Applicon founders described its origins in the following way:

> "While at Applicon, request-upon-request would come in for design
> automation equipment priced at $50,000 or less".
> (Harvard Newsletter on Computer Graphics, [10]).

To summarise, therefore, this most recent stage of industry development has
seen two divergent trends—a continued tendency to concentration and an
opposing tendency for the entry of new small firms selling limited capability
dedicated systems.


IV. BARRIERS TO ENTRY

The key to the discussion of firm size and technical change lies in the barriers
to new entrants. For, in the context of constrained market growth, the
expansionary momentum of existing enterprises provides a constant tendency
towards concentration of ownership and production. This momentum can be
undermined only if space exists for new entrants into the industry. We therefore

FIRM SIZE AND TECHNICAL CHANGE                  47

consider the problem of entry barriers in the CAD industry at some length, partly because we believe the discussion throws some light on the emerging software-intensive industries and partly because it illuminates the discussion of our central concern, namely the relationship between firm size and innovative activity.

Investment in the CAD sector is a relatively profitable activity, both in relation to potential income streams[15] and in appreciation of capital stock. Consequently the incentive to new entrants is substantial. Yet given the small number of firms which dominate the industry, it is evident that there must be barriers to entry.

The primary barrier to entry in the CAD industry is technology.[16] It is now widely accepted that technology is a "free" or "public" good, that is it is not used-up in consumption and is available for multiple and indefinite use. (Arrow [1]). Therefore unless some mechanisms can be found to protect proprietary rights over technology, there will be no incentive, under a market system, for the generation of new technology. In the case of embodied technology—for example, machinery—this function is partly performed by the patent system which gives exclusive power for exploitation to the owner of the patent or its licensees. But, as has recently emerged in a series of well publicised court-cases, software cannot be patented;[17] it can only be copyrighted which is easily circumventable. Yet for the CAD industry to have maintained such dramatic changes in technology, there must by necessity have been a process of *effective* appropriation, whatever the *legal* rights may have been.

The primary factor protecting existing producers from new entrants has been the scale of software inputs necessary to offer a competitive package of applications programs. In Table II we detail the extent of R and D inputs of those firms for which information exists; in Table III we detail (without mentioning the names of firms to avoid disclosing proprietary information) the current numbers of software writers they employ and, where available, the accumulated input of software person years in their system. It can be seen from Table II that compared to US industry in general, the CAD industry invests a very large proportion of sales in R and D. This proportion is high even relative to information processing in general where the 1979 average was only 6.1% of sales (Business Week [4]) and the 1980 average was 2%. From Table III it can be seen that most CAD suppliers currently employ over 100 software writers per year, expanding these numbers at well over 30% p.a. Some of the vendors

[15] Computervision and Intergraph, for example, have had significantly higher return on equity than either DEC or the Fortune 500 average (Kaplinsky, [14]).

[16] There are only insignificant economies of scale in production at the level of output of most of the relevant firms. Only IBM and Computervision make their own computers and even they buy-in the peripherals from external suppliers.

[17] However, a very recent ruling (May, 1981) of the US Supreme Court has determined that 'firmware' (a form of software written into particular pieces of hardware—see later), can be patented. This is almost certainly likely to have a profound impact upon the direction of technological change in the whole of the electronics sector.

TABLE II
R AND D AS % OF SALES

R and D as % of sales

| | 1969 | 1970 | 1971 | 1972 | 1973 | 1974 | 1975 | 1976 | 1977 | 1978 | 1979 | 1980 |
|---|---|---|---|---|---|---|---|---|---|---|---|---|
| Applicon | | | | | | | | 11 | 8.4 | 12.8 | 8.9 | 11.2 |
| Auto-trol[a] | | | | | | 22.8 | 13 | 14.6 | 12.6 | 15.7 | 14 | 12 |
| Computervision | 671 | 28 | 4.4 | 6.4 | 9.7 | 11.8 | 12.3 | 8.9 | 9.6 | 8.3 | 8.8 | 11 |
| Intergraph | | | | | | | | 6.5 | 5.7 | 7.6 | 10.1 | 15.9 |
| Gerber | | | | | | | | | | | | |
| All US industry | 2.2 | 2.2 | 2.1 | 2 | 2 | 1.9 | 1.9 | 1.9 | 1.9 | 1.9 | 1.9 | 2 |

Source: Interviews, annual reports, Soete [21], Soete [22] and Business Week, June editions.
[a] In 1980, Auto-trols ratio of R and D expenditure to sales (which at 12% of sales, was the lowest ratio for the firm since 1974) was the fourth highest ratio of the 744 US Corporations surveyed by Business Week; its R and D expenditure per employee was the third highest of the sample.

TABLE III
1980 SOFTWARE STAFF AND ACCUMULATED PERSON YEARS OF SOFTWARE[a]

| Firm code | Numbers employed | Accumulated years of software in system |
|---|---|---|
| a | 40 | 130 person years post bought-in package in 1974 |
| b | 150–200 | 1000 person years |
| c | 103 | NI |
| d | 345 | NI |
| e | 125 | NI |
| f | 120 | NI |
| g | 110 | 600 person years in 2D draughting package plus 400 person years in bought-in mechanical outline |
| h | 88 | 500 person years of software; 7 million lines of software. |

*Source:* Interviews.

[a] Excludes personnel on hardware development, but includes those working on operating systems of minicomputers.

*Note:* firm code is not in the same order as in previous tables.

were able to detail their stock of software—over 1,000 person years in some cases and over 7 m lines of code in others.

These absolute sunken R and D expenditures are in themselves not a sufficient deterrent to entry. After all in 1980 prices, even Computervision had accumulated less than $80 m of R and D, and some of that was in the development of their own minicomputer; compare this with the $1.5 b profits earned by General Electric in 1980 alone. The critical protective factors are that this software development occurs in a relatively specialised sector in the context of a general shortage of software writers. But more importantly, much of the necessary software development is sequential—as one of the founders of Computervision describes it, "One can't make a baby in one month with nine women".[18]

Although these accumulated R and D expenditures are a significant form of appropriation and consequently an effective barrier to the entry of new firms, some CAD firms nevertheless take additional steps to avoid the disclosure of proprietary software information to competitors;[19] this involves control over the software itself and over the movement of personnel.

(a) *Control over software*

Software programs can basically be divided into two segments—object code (usually referred to as machine code), which is made up of a string of 0's and 1's (i.e. binary code) and sourcecode which is a higher level of

[18] A similar example can be drawn from the automobile industry. When Agnelli, the head of Fiat, was asked whether selling the Fiat 124 design to the Russians would not provide fatal competition to his firm, he answered "If we are still producing the Fiat 124 in 5 years time, we will go bankrupt anyhow"!

[19] These observations are based on visits made to 13 vendors and 24 users in the UK and the US in early 1981. For a full description see Kaplinsky [14].

programming language, which assembles the object code into less cumbersome bundles of instructions. None of the CAD firms objected to the release of object code to users (since it is an essential requirement for the functioning of their hardware) except for IBM which does not market its electronic CAD software. But significant differences were displayed in the attitude of firms towards the release of sourcecodes. Four of the CAD supplying firms had no objection to its release, although one observed that the sourcecode itself would be inoperable without a particular item of hardware over which it maintained tight and exclusive control; a second of these firms had merged with a parent which had developed its own software, and observed that even though it had unfettered access to this software with the full cooperation of its affiliate, it took years to unravel; a third firm only released sourcecode if the user entered a "Proprietary Software Agreement".

The remaining firms retained tight physical control over the sourcecode, despite their general observations that they would not feel unduly threatened if their competitors obtained access to it. In one of these companies, which employs over 100 software programmers, only 4 people have access to the full store of sourcecode; in another case a user reported that the CAD suppliers applications engineers came and physically removed the sourcecode which they had "inadvertently obtained".

(b) *Control over personnel*

The flow of manpower, holding firm-specific rather than individual-specific knowledge is an important concern for all CAD firms, although of diminishing importance as the stock of software grows and individual specific knowledge becomes increasingly differentiated from firm specific knowledge.[20] There are a number of notable examples of the gains and losses flowing from such mobility. In the mid-1970s, a team of West Coast software writers prepared the basic mechanical applications package for Computervision having earlier performed a similar task for Gerber. When the 1975 recession forced economies on Computervision, the head-office in the Boston-area tried to regain control over these programmers and wanted them to return to the East Coast. With few exceptions they refused and the recalcitrants formed their own company, Systems Science Software, later taken over by Calma. Computervision responded with a law-suit alleging (i) unfair competition, (ii) breach of contract not to compete (iii) Contractual interference and (iv) "conspiracy". Calma counter-sued for $127.5 m punitive damages (under the Sherman anti-trust act), but both claims were eventually dismissed without damages.

---

[20] A major method through which CAD suppliers appropriate the individual knowledge of programmers is by insisting on the use of structured programming techniques. These involve the use of standard procedures for software writing which are easily intelligible and assimilable by other software writers.

However the upshot was a damaging delay (until 1978) in the development of Calma's own mechanical applications package since Calma had to ensure that it would not lay itself open to further litigation. A second example is that of the recent move by the ex-head of Computervisions European marketing division to Intergraph.[21] And a third example is that of Gerber, anxious to establish a strong package of mechanical applications software, which has recently 'poached' 12–15 software writers from Unigraphics which has developed over the years a strong suite of relatively bug-free mechanical applications programmes.

Reflecting the importance, albeit declining, of this transfer of personnel is a repeated tendency to increase the costs to individuals of leaving the company. Intergraph requires its newly appointed European marketing manager to resell his stock to the company if he leaves their employment; the same company specifically sees its employee stock option and bonus plans as a way of reducing employee turnover. In another case of a CAD bureau control was kept over one key software writer by the granting of a concessionary mortgage for the purchase of a house. But these safeguards are not always wholly effective: one user pointed out that whole sections of the software manuals of two different suppliers were almost identical, reflecting the mobility of manpower between these firms.

(c) *Firmware*

It is an increasingly common occurrence in the electronics industry for software-intensive firms to wire-in particular sets of software into hardware. In part this reduces the input of programming, which both saves costs and speeds-up processing time. But more importantly it 'hides' software from potential competitors, and following a recent US Supreme Court ruling, unlike software, firmware is patentable. For example Intergraph has a major competitive advantage over its competitors in being able to insert and withdraw information rapidly from its storage discs; the substance of this advantage is wired-in to a separate set of hardware called a "scanner-processor" which Intergraph makes itself under carefully protected conditions. The move to increasing firmware is a major area of effort by all of the CAD vendors.

In conclusion therefore it is clear that whilst legal proprietary rights over CAD technology are of little effect, CAD suppliers are nevertheless increasingly able to maintain proprietary control over their software. Applicon, which has two US patents for hardware, recognises the limited utility of these and of patents in general.

---

[21] As an incentive to change firms this individual was given the opportunity to purchase 45,000 shares at $4.17 each prior to public flotation. Two weeks after the public issues these shares were worth $30, giving him a stock appreciation of $1.16 m. (See Dean Witter Reynolds Inc [7, p. 2].).

52                                RAPHAEL KAPLINSKY

"The company does not consider that its success will depend upon its ability to obtain and defend patents, but rather on its ability to offer its customers high-performance products at competitive prices" (Blyth Eastman Paine Webber [2, p. 19]).

Auto-trol comes to an identical conclusion:

"The company does not hold any patents or licenses covering its graphics systems. It may be possible for competitors of the company to copy aspects of its systems even though the company regards such aspects as proprietary. However the Company believes that, because of the rapid pace of technological change in the electronics industry, patent protection is of lesser significance than factors such as the knowledge and experience of the Company's management and personnel and their ability to develop and market its products".
(Hambrecht and Quist [9, p. 20]).

In the face of this effective appropriation of technology, of the sequential imperative in software development and the minimum scale in input required to develop a wide-ranging set of applications programs, the barriers to entry are high (but not insurmountable). A number of examples illustrate this:

(a) *General Electric*

General Electric is one of the largest industrial corporations in the world with a 1980 turnover of $25 b, and is considered to be the largest user of CAD systems in the world. Its various divisions currently use over 100 systems,[22] and plan to purchase an additional 25 systems per annum. In the face of increasing technology-based competition in all of its markets, the company has made a major decision to upgrade its own technology and in particular, through association between its new semiconductor division, its machine-tool division and the CAD affiliate (now all grouped in its Industrial Controls Group), to develop the "factory of the future". An essential ingredient of this was a CAD/CAM capability—instead of starting afresh GE tried to increase its 28% speculative holding in Applicon, which had a particularly strong capability in mechanical engineering CAD software. When this failed it switched its attention to Calma which was a less attractive proposition since its historic strength lay in electronics applications.

(b) *IBM*

In the mid-1970s IBM made a decision to expand its mechanical applications CAD capabilities for two major reasons. The first was the need to extend sales growth in the face of declining hardware prices; the second

---

[22] In the order of Computervision and Applicon, with Calma a poor third, being used predominantly for electronic systems.

was its own need for CAD/CAM applications as it struggled to keep abreast of competition within its own sector. Despite having around 150 person years of software in their system, they preferred to buy-in Lockheeds software package since it had a track-record of successful main-frame based users. Lockheed are currently reputed to have around 120 people upgrading and maintaining this package.

(c) *Gerber*

As we have seen, Gerber was an early entrant to the CAD/CAM market, having bought in the basic mechanical software from Systems Science Software in 1973, and investing over 70 person years of software to upgrade it by 1979. However their effort languished for some years and it was only when a new president was recruited from United Technologies in 1978 that their CAD activities began to expand significantly. This was followed by the separation of Gerber Systems Technology (now the CAD division) from Gerber Scientific in 1979, and the sale of 20% of its equity to the public in March 1981. Since 1979 Gerber has been struggling to increase its market share through, by its own admission, extensive price-discounting and the widening of software applications programs. But the costs of this have been substantial:[23] just prior to the sale of 20% of its stock to the public in March 1981, GST had

— accumulated losses (by 31/12/80) of $1.453 m and expected these to increase until at least May 1981.
— GS had written-off $4 m of debt by GST in exchange for 320,000 shares.
— $2.081 m of the expected stock issue of $7.1 m would go to repay additional debt to GS.
— Additional long term debt of $4.5 m.
— these losses were incurred despite the sale of a technology licence to a Japanese firm which netted $1 m in advance, plus an annual minimum royalty on sales, plus a share of its licensee's pre-tax profits.

These barriers to entry are most substantial in relation to the comprehensive application program systems offered by the existing turnkey suppliers using mini and mainframe computers. There is, however, an emerging space for microprocessor driven systems which has been made possible by two factors. The first, and obvious, precondition, is the development of increasingly powerful microprocessors. The second is the maturity of specific applications programs which significantly lower the barriers to entry in these limited areas.

---

[23] See Hambrecht and Quist [9].

54                          RAPHAEL KAPLINSKY

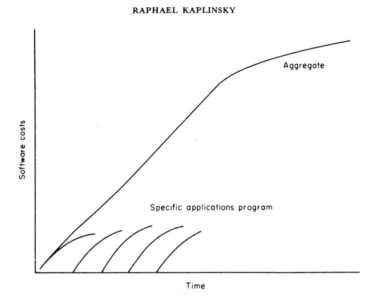

FIGURE 1

Software development—Aggregate and applications curves

In order to grasp the significance of this latter point it is necessary to understand that in the CAD industry there is a distinction between the *average* and
*marginal* cost of systems. This distinction partly arises from the imperative to all
CAD suppliers to employ a large overhead of software writers. These software
writers are in general divided into three groups. The first is committed to the
development of operating systems, the second into a small number who upgrade and maintain existing applications programs and the larger number who
are involved in developing the new applications programs which are necessary
to keep an all-round presence in the industry. From each supplier's point of
view, therefore, the software development process takes the form as represented
by Figure 1: a constant overhead investment in software, made up of a
family of matured packages and an increasing family of new packages.
Evidence of the existence of this type of mature packages is provided in Figure
2 for three specific applications, sculptured surfaces and view independent
construction developed by one particular supplier, and orthographic piping
developed by another.

Microprocessor driven CAD systems are aimed at this market of matured
applications programs, of which basic graphics capabilities (that is, the ability
to draw lines, arcs and so on which are necessary for computer-aided draughting) is the most obvious. From the vendor's point of view the software needs
little attention and the system can be sold at a price which is close to its
marginal cost, that is the cost of the hardware input.

FIRM SIZE AND TECHNICAL CHANGE                    55

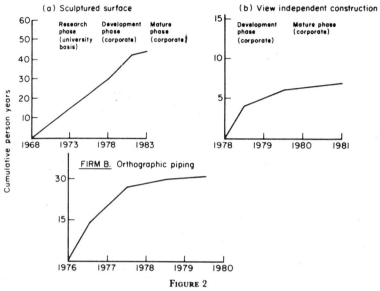

FIGURE 2

Examples of matured applications programmes

*Source:* Interviews with CAD Supplying Firms

There are a great number of such small firms springing up in North America[24] and Europe. Many of them offer basic graphics capabilities with perhaps one applications program, often an auto-routing electronics program. Many of these firms are started by former employees of established turnkey suppliers who recognised that these turnkey firms were overstretched and unable to satisfy the limited needs of small-scale users.

## V. FIRM SIZE AND TECHNICAL CHANGE IN RELATION TO INDUSTRY GROWTH CURVES

We have gone into some detail in describing the genesis and growing maturity of the CAD industry. This has been done because we believe that it throws light on the relationship between firm size and technical change. In Figure 3 we attempt to chart the nature of this industry growth curve,[25] which we believe to be representative of other software intensive microelectronic sectors. In general the radical nature of the technology has meant that the origin of these industries is to be found in larger user-firms who innovate to meet their own

[24] Where according to one estimate there are at least 60 different suppliers.
[25] This pattern is particularly evident for the US electronics sector, only in recent years has it begun to emerge in Europe and Japan.

56                          RAPHAEL KAPLINSKY

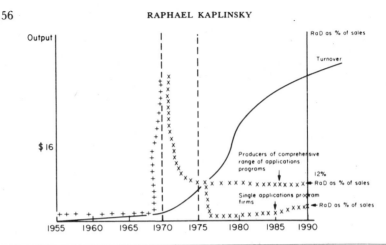

| | Industry origins | Dynamic new firms | Trend to concentration | Maturity |
|---|---|---|---|---|
| Diffusion of product | Defence, aerospace | Electronics | Mechanical engineering | Mechanical engineering Civil engineering Business graphics |
| Source of innovation | For own use | External sales Own use | External sales Own use | External sales Own use |
| Innovative firms | Very large firms | New small firms | Medium firms | Large and very large firms New small firms |

FIGURE 3

Industry Growth Curve for Software Intensive Industries Based on Actual and Projected Growth of CAD Industry

product needs. Thereafter, in the second phase, key individuals spin-off from the pioneers to establish new small firms dedicated to the development of the product. During the third phase these firms grow and become less vulnerable to new entrants as accumulated software protects them from new entrants. At the same time their strong growth potential and their key strategic value attracts large predators from other sectors. In the final phase new small entrants begun by people spinning off from existing CAD suppliers, find a role within particular mature applications programs.

It is believed that this growth pattern is largely representative of other software-intensive industries. For example in the word-processing sector the industry appears to be rapidly moving into the third phase (trend to concentration), with new entrants from outside the subsector (e.g. Exxon) and organic growth from within (e.g. Wang). By contrast the automatic testing equipment has already passed through the stage of concentration and the industry is now seeing the emergence of small firms producing dedicated sets of equipment. A third example is that of microcomputers where the entrance of IBM, Zerox and the Japanese firms appears to signal the transition between the second and third phases.[26]

In many ways this notional growth curve of software intensive industries proximates that of the pre-microelectronic era. There is one crucial difference, however. In the earlier pre-microelectronic period, the mature phase was not characterised to the same extent by the emergence of new small firms. This was because concentration was underpinned by economies of scale in production (e.g. automobiles). The industries under discussion are distinctive because their relatively high input of software, with its associated variation between average and marginal costs of production, allows for economies of scale only in relation to new products. The manufacture of existing products (e.g. mature applications programs) is therefore open to new entrants if they can gain access to the technology itself. And in many cases, as we have seen in the CAD and automatic testing equipment industries, there are bits of the technology (e.g. particular applications programs) which are often individual, rather than firm, specific, thereby providing the opportunity for new entrants.

### V. TECHNICAL CHANGE AND FIRM SIZE RECONSIDERED

In the above discussion we have deliberately characterised the problem loosely as being one of 'technical change' or more loosely innovation, rather than R and D or patents. With respect to patents, we have observed that there is little scope for patenting in these types of industries. In relation to R and D, this measure is not a very useful indicator of innovation. Historically R and D levels in the CAD industry (as we can see from Figure 3) have varied and show no constant relation to industry growth or the introduction of new products—they more clearly reflect the changes in the phase on the industry growth cycle.

This observation enables us to return to the debate on firm size and technical change. Our argument is that the existing studies in this area are largely static—they observe a particular relationship at one point of time (perhaps a period of 2–3 years) and then project this as characterising a trend. The 'truth' is rather more complicated—it is not possible to determine whether large or small firms are inherently more innovative since it depends so largely on which period of industry life-cycle one is measuring. For example in the CAD sector in the 1950s large firms were relatively innovative; in the late 1960s and early 1980s new small firms played an important role, whereas in the mid-1970s medium-sized firms were most prominent.

It might well be argued that however valid these observations are at a sectoral level, when observations are aggregated across a large number of sectors we might nevertheless expect a trend to emerge. In answering this we

[26] G de Jonquieres [11].

58                                    RAPHAEL KAPLINSKY

are drawn to the debate on long-wave cycles where Freeman [8] and Clark
*et al.* [6] argue (convincingly, in our view) that we can distinguish long-wave
cycles associated with major heartland technologies which provide big-wave
effects to overwhelm the average of a large number of observations (Kaplinsky
[13]). Each of these has an expansionary upswing of new product development
and a rationalising downswing of cost-reduction, product improvement and
reduction of lead-time. Thus in the same way that we can expect the relationship between firm size and technical change to vary between the different
phases of an industry growth cycle, so we can expect it to vary between
different phases of the long-wave cycle. For example the upswing is likely to be
dominated by new firms expanding organically, and later to be taken over by
existing firms or to grow themselves into very large firms (e.g. IBM) as the
cycle moves into the downswing.

RAPHAEL KAPLINSKY,                                          ACCEPTED APRIL 1982
*The Institute of Development Studies,*
*University of Sussex,*
*Brighton, Sussex BN1 9RE*

## REFERENCES

[1] ARROW, K. J., Economic Welfare and the Allocation of Resources for Invention,
    in the *Rate and Diffusion of Inventive Activity: Economic and Social Factors*, National
    Bureau of Economic Research, Princeton University Press, 1962.
[2] BLYTH, EASTMAN PAINE WEBBER INC., and ALEX BROWN AND SONS, 20 July 1980,
    Prospectus for Issue of 1,000,000 Shares of Common Stock of Applicon.
[3] *Business Week*, 'GE's New Input for "Factories of the Future"' 22nd December,
    1980.
[4] *Business Week*, Survey of R and D, June 30th, 1980.
[5] *Business Week*, 'Attacking GE's Grip on Controls', 16th March, 1981.
[6] CLARK, J., FREEMAN, C. and SOETE, L., 'Long Waves and Technological
    Developments in the 20th Century', mimeo, Brighton, 1980.
[7] DEAN WITTER REYNOLDS INC, and THE ROBINSON-HUMPHREY COMPANY INC.,
    Preliminary Prospectus for Issue of 1,500,000 Shares of Common Stock of
    Intergraph Corporation, 25th February, 1981.
[8] FREEMAN, C., 'The Kondratiev Long Wave, Technical Change and Unemploy-
    ment', *Proceedings of OECD Meeting of Experts on Structural Determinants of
    Employment and Unemployment*, (OECD, Paris, 1977).
[9] HAMBRECHT and QUIST, Prospectus for Issue of 500,000 Shares of Common Stock
    of Auto-trol Technology Corporation, San Francisco, 24th January, 1979.
[10] *Harvard Newletter on Computer Graphics*, Vol 3 No 4, 1981, and Vol 3 No 9, 1981.
[11] G. DE JONQUIERES, 'Personal Computers Come of Age', *Financial Times*, 21st
    Auguest, 1981.
[12] KAMIEN, MORTON I. and SCHWARTZ, NANCY L., 'Market Structure and
    Innovation: A Survey', *Journal of Economic Literature*, 3, No 1 (March 1975),
    pp. 1–37.
[13] KAPLINSKY, R., 'Radical Technical Change and Export-Orientated Industri-
    alisation: The Impact of Micro-electronics, *Vierteljahresberichte*, Probleme der
    Entwicklungslander, No 83, (March 1981), pp. 81–99.

FIRM SIZE AND TECHNICAL CHANGE                    59

[14] KAPLINSKY, R., *Computer Aided Design—Electronics, Comparative Advantage and Development*, (Frances Pinter, London, 1982).

[15] RADER, M., and WINGERT, B., *Computer Aided Design in Great Britain and the Federal Republic of Germany—Current Trends and Impacts*, (Karlsruhe, Kernforschungszentrum, 1981).

[16] ROTHWELL, R. and ZEGVELD, W., *Industrial Innovation and Public Policy: Preparing for the 1980s and the 1990s*, (Frances Pinter, London, 1982).

[17] SCHERER, F. M., 'Size of Firm, Oligopoly and Research: A Comment', *Canadian Journal of Economics and Political Science*, Vol 31 No 2 (May, 1965) pp. 256–66.

[18] SCHERER, F. M., 'Firm Size, Market Structure, Opportunity and the Output of Patented Inventions', *American Economic Review*, Vol 55 No 5, (December 1965), pp. 1097–25.

[19] SCHUMPETER, J. A., *Capitalism, Socialism and Democracy*, (Harper and Bros, New York, 1942).

[20] SHRIEVES, R. E., 1978, 'Market Structure and Innovation: A New Perspective' *Journal of Industrial Economics*, Vol 26, No 4, (June 1978), pp. 329–47.

[21] SOETE, L. L. G., 'Size of Firm, Oligopoly and Research: A Reappraisal', *Extrait de Reseaux*, Nos 35–36, 1977.

[22] SOETE, L. L. G., 'Firm Size and Inventive Activity', *European Economic Review*, Vol 12, (August, 1979), pp. 319–40.

# [16]

*The Economic Journal*, **91** (*December* 1981), 907-918

*Printed in Great Britain*

## IMITATION COSTS AND PATENTS:
## AN EMPIRICAL STUDY*

*Edwin Mansfield, Mark Schwartz and Samuel Wagner*

It has long been recognised that the costs of imitating new products have an important effect on the incentives for innovation in a market economy.[1] As Arrow (1962) and others have pointed out, if firms can imitate an innovation at a cost that is substantially below the cost to the innovator of developing the innovation, there may be little or no incentive for the innovator to carry out the innovation. In their discussions of the innovation process, economists frequently have called attention to the major role played by the costs of imitation, but there has been little or no attempt to measure these costs, to test various hypotheses concerning the factors influencing them, or to estimate their effects. In this paper, we report some findings of what seems to be the first study of this topic. In addition, we present data regarding the effects of patents on imitation costs and on the rate of innovation.

### I. IMITATION COSTS AND TIMES

Many economists, including Scherer (1977) and Mansfield *et al.* (1977*b*), have cited the need for empirical studies of imitation costs and imitation times. To carry out such a study, we obtained data from firms in the chemical, drug, electronics, and machinery industries concerning the cost and time of imitating (legally) 48 product innovations. By imitation cost we mean all costs of developing and introducing the imitative product, including applied research, product specification, pilot plant or prototype construction, investment in plant and equipment, and manufacturing and marketing startup.[2] (If there was a patent on the innovation, the cost of inventing around it is included.) By imitation time we mean the length of time elapsing from the beginning of the imitator's applied research (if there was any) on the imitative product to the date of its commercial introduction.[3]

The firms were chosen more or less at random from among the major firms in these four industries in the Northeast of the United States, and the new pro-

* The research on which this paper is based was supported by grants to Mansfield by the National Science Foundation which, of course, is not responsible for the views expressed here. We appreciate this support, as well as the cooperation of the firms that provided data, without which this study could not have been done. A preliminary version of this paper was presented by Mansfield at the 1980 meetings of the American Economic Association. Parts of this paper were contained in the 1981 Andersen Lectures that he presented at the University of Brussels, and in invited lectures he gave at Middlebury College and at the International Institute of Management in Berlin.

[1] For example, see Arrow (1962) and Freeman (1974).
[2] For definitions of these terms, see Mansfield *et al.* (1971) and Mansfield (1980).
[3] For many products, the estimate of imitation cost (and of imitation time) was an average of two estimates provided by the firms, each reflecting a somewhat different set of assumptions.

Table 1

*Imitation Cost (Divided by Innovation Cost) of 48 New Products, by Industry and Cost of Innovation*

| Imitation cost (divided by innovation cost) | Innovations costing more than $1 million | | | Innovations costing less than $1 million | | |
|---|---|---|---|---|---|---|
| | Chemicals | Drugs | Electronics and machinery | Chemicals | Drugs | Electronics and machinery |
| (A) Number of new products | | | | | | |
| Less than 0·20 | 1 | 1 | 1 | 1 | 0 | 0 |
| 0·20 and under 0·40 | 0 | 3 | 0 | 0 | 0 | 2 |
| 0·40 and under 0·60 | 1 | 1 | 2 | 5 | 0 | 0 |
| 0·60 and under 0·80 | 2 | 5 | 0 | 2 | 0 | 4 |
| 0·80 and under 1·00 | 2 | 3 | 1 | 2 | 1 | 1 |
| 1·00 and over | 2 | 2 | 1 | 1 | 0 | 1 |
| Total | 8 | 15 | 5 | 11 | 1 | 8 |
| (B) New products weighted by innovation cost* (%) | | | | | | |
| Less than 0·20 | 3 | 3 | 17 | 15 | 0 | 0 |
| 0·20 and under 0·40 | 0 | 11 | 0 | 0 | 0 | 34 |
| 0·40 and under 0·60 | ‡ | 1 | 53 | 46 | 0 | 0 |
| 0·60 and under 0·80 | 44 | 54 | 0 | 13 | 0 | 36 |
| 0·80 and under 1·00 | 15 | 21 | 9 | 22 | 100 | 18 |
| 1·00 and over | 38 | 9 | 22 | 4 | 0 | 11 |
| Total† | 100 | 100 | 100 | 100 | 100 | 100 |

\* The weighted number of new products is expressed as a percentage of the column total.
† Because of rounding errors, items may not sum to column total.
‡ Less than 0·5.

ducts were chosen more or less at random from among those introduced recently by these firms.[1] In 34 of the cases, the new product had already been imitated, so the data are based on actual experience. In the remaining 14 cases, no imitator had appeared as yet, but the innovating firm provided us with detailed estimates that were regarded as being reliable.[2] Also, in all 48 cases,

[1] We say that the firms and innovations were chosen 'more or less' at random because a table of random numbers really was not used. In some cases, the sample was a systematic sample from a list; in other cases, there were so few innovations in the time frame we selected that the choice was automatic. Both successful and unsuccessful new products were included in the sample. About half of the innovations turned out to be successful (in the sense that they were relatively profitable to the innovator). A high percentage of the firms we approached agreed to co-operate so there was little problem of nonresponse. A considerable number of in-depth interviews were held with major officials of each firm to insure that the data were as accurate as possible. Nineteen of the innovations occurred in the chemical industry (including petroleum refining); sixteen occurred in the drug industry; ten occurred in the electronics industry; and three occurred in the machinery industry. Five of the new products were first introduced before 1960; fifteen were first introduced during the 1960s; and 28 were first introduced during 1970–6.

[2] In each such case, the innovating firm provided an estimate of how much money and time it would have cost the most likely (and most efficient) imitator to have imitated the product. In some cases, it was assumed that the time-cost combination that would have been chosen by the imitator was midway between the least-cost combination and the least-time combination. According to the firms, these estimates are unlikely to be very wide of the mark. If we had dropped these cases from the sample, we would have risked the introduction of a serious bias. Thus, this seemed to be the best feasible procedure. This procedure also was used in other cases, and seemed accurate enough for present purposes.

Table 2

*Imitation Time (Divided by Innovation Time) of 48 New Products, by Industry and Cost of Innovation*

| Imitation time (divided by innovation time) | Innovations costing more than $1 million | | | Innovations costing less than $1 million | | |
|---|---|---|---|---|---|---|
| | Chemicals | Drugs | Electronics and machinery | Chemicals | Drugs | Electronics and machinery |
| (A) Number of new products | | | | | | |
| Less than 0·30 | 1 | 2 | 1 | 2 | 0 | 0 |
| 0·30 and under 0·50 | 1 | 5 | 1 | 2 | 0 | 2 |
| 0·50 and under 0·70 | 1 | 3 | 1 | 4 | 1 | 2 |
| 0·70 and under 0·90 | 3 | 0 | 0 | 1 | 0 | 1 |
| 0·90 and under 1·10 | 1 | 3 | 1 | 1 | 0 | 1 |
| 1·10 and over | 1 | 2 | 1 | 1 | 0 | 2 |
| Total | 8 | 15 | 5 | 11 | 1 | 8 |
| (B) New products weighted by innovation cost* (%) | | | | | | |
| Less than 0·30 | 3 | 10 | 35 | 16 | 0 | 0 |
| 0·30 and under 0·50 | 2 | 28 | 17 | 36 | 0 | 16 |
| 0·50 and under 0·70 | 35 | 24 | 19 | 27 | 100 | 23 |
| 0·70 and under 0·90 | 22 | 0 | 0 | 16 | 0 | 14 |
| 0·90 and under 1·10 | 18 | 16 | 22 | 4 | 0 | 18 |
| 1·10 and over | 19 | 23 | 9 | 2 | 0 | 30 |
| Total† | 100 | 100 | 100 | 100 | 100 | 100 |

\* The weighted number of new products is expressed as a percentage of the column total.
† Because of rounding errors, items may not sum to column total.

data were obtained from the innovating firm concerning the costs of the innovation, as well as the time it took to bring the innovation to market (from the beginning of applied research to the date of its commercial introduction).

The innovations included in the sample vary widely in importance, but practically all are major new products that are central to the innovators' activities, not peripheral to their main business. For 30 of the 48 products, the innovation cost exceeded $1 million; for 12 products, it exceeded $5 million. About 70% of the innovations were patented. In only one case did the innovator license the imitating firm. In all other cases, the imitator received no help from the innovator. In general, these firms did not appear to be very interested in licensing these innovations, at least in the relevant time period, often because they did not feel it was in their interest to encourage potential rivals.

On the average, the ratio of the imitation cost to the innovation cost was about 0·65, and the ratio of the imitation time to the innovation time was about 0·70. As shown in Tables 1 and 2, there is considerable variation about these averages. In about half of the cases, the ratio of imitation cost to innovation cost was either less than 0·40 or more than 0·90. In about half of the cases, the ratio of imitation time to innovation time was either less than 0·40 or more than 1·00. Products with a relatively high (low) ratio of imitation cost to innovation cost tended to have a relatively high (low) ratio of imitation time to innovation time.[1]

It may come as a surprise that imitation cost was no smaller than innovation cost in about one seventh of the cases. This was not due to any superiority of the imitative product over the innovation. Instead, in a substantial percentage of these cases, it was due to the innovator's having a technological edge over its rivals in the relevant field. Often this edge was due to superior 'know-how' – that is, better and more extensive technical information based on highly specialised experience with the development and production of related products and processes. Such know-how is not divulged in patents and is relatively inaccessible (at least for a period of time) to potential imitators.

Based on these results, it appears that innovators routinely introduce new products despite the fact that other firms can imitate these products at about two thirds (often less) of the cost and time expended by the innovator.[2] In some cases, this is because, although other firms could imitate these products in this way, there are other barriers to entry (for example, lack of a well-known brand name) that discourage potential imitators. But to a greater extent (at least in this sample), it seems to be due to a feeling on the part of the innovators that, even if imitators do begin to appear in a relatively few years, the innovation still will be profitable.

## II. THE IMITATOR'S TIME-COST TRADEOFF FUNCTION

Clearly, the time it takes a firm to imitate a new product can generally be reduced by spending more money. Each product's imitator was confronted by a time-cost tradeoff function, which is the relationship between the amount spent by the imitator and the length of time it would take to imitate this new product.[3] The time-cost combination chosen by the imitator is one point on this tradeoff function. In most cases, we obtained an estimate of the minimum time that the imitator could have taken to carry out the project, and the corresponding cost, as well as an estimate of the minimum cost and the corresponding time. Together with other information, this enabled us to determine the approximate position of the imitator's time-cost tradeoff function for most products. If imitation cost is measured as a percentage of innovation cost and if imitation time is measured as a percentage of innovation time, all of these time-cost tradeoff functions can be plotted on the same graph. When this is done, we find that a product's ratio of imitation cost to innovation cost is a good indicator of how high and how far to the right the product's time-cost tradeoff function is located.

---

[1] The correlation coefficient between a product's ratio of imitation cost to innovation cost and its ratio of imitation time to innovation time is about 0·8.

[2] The available data pertain only to innovations that were introduced, not to those where the incentives were insufficient for their introduction. Although they cannot measure the effects of imitation cost on how many innovations were introduced, they provide valuable evidence concerning the characteristics of those that were introduced.

[3] For further discussion of time-cost tradeoff functions, see Scherer (1967, 1980), Mansfield *et al.* (1971, forthcoming), and Baldwin and Childs (1969).

Using the time-cost tradeoff function for each product, we computed the arc elasticity of cost with respect to time. The median value of this elasticity is about 0·7, which means that a 1 % reduction in time results in about a 0·7 increase in cost, on the average.[1] These elasticities pertain to the imitation time that is midway between the minimum time and the time corresponding to minimum cost. Since the time-cost tradeoff function is convex, this elasticity increases as imitation time falls (and approaches its minimum value), and decreases as imitation time rises (and approaches the time corresponding to minimum cost). For most products, the minimum-time imitation cost is less than 50 % greater than the minimum imitation cost, but in some cases the difference is 100 % or more. Ordinarily, the minimum-cost imitation time is less than 75 % greater than the minimum imitation time, but in over one-fourth of the cases the difference is 100 % or more (Table 3).

Table 3

*Ratio of Minimum-Time Imitation Cost to Minimum Imitation Cost, and Ratio of Minimum-Cost Imitation Time to Minimum Imitation Time, Percentage Distribution of New Products in the Sample*

| Value of ratio | Minimum-time imitation cost ÷ minimum imitation cost | Minimum-cost imitation time ÷ minimum imitation time |
|---|---|---|
| | (% of new products) | |
| 1·00 and under 1·25 | 36 | 18 |
| 1·25 and under 1·50 | 33 | 24 |
| 1·50 and under 1·75 | 6 | 24 |
| 1·75 and under 2·00 | 6 | 3 |
| 2·00 and under 2·25 | 12 | 15 |
| 2·25 and under 2·50 | 6 | 6 |
| 2·50 and over | 0 | 9 |
| Total | 100* | 100* |

* Because of rounding errors, the percentages do not sum to the column total.

### III. DETERMINANTS OF IMITATION COSTS

The following hypotheses help to explain the substantial variation among products in the ratio of imitation cost to innovation cost.[2]   First, we would

[1] Estimates of the elasticity of cost with respect to time could be obtained for 39 products. In 5 cases, it was less than 0·25; in 10 cases, it was 0·25 and under 0·50; in 12 cases, it was 0·50 and under 1·00; in 10 cases, it was 1·00 and under 2·00; and in 2 cases, it was 2·00 and over.

[2] These hypotheses also help to explain the variation among products in the ratio of imitation time to innovation time, since (as pointed out in note 1 on p. 910) a product's ratio of imitation time to innovation time is positively correlated with its ratio of imitation to innovation cost.

For some purposes, one might want to explain the variation among products in the ratio of imitation cost to innovation cost when the ratio of imitation time to innovation time is held constant (at its mean value). Based on our estimates of the time-cost tradeoff functions, we were able to make rough estimates of most products' ratio of imitation cost to innovation cost under these circumstances. When these estimates are used (in place of $C_i$) in equation (2), the results are relatively unchanged. Thus, the hypotheses discussed in this section can explain the variation among products in both the unadjusted ratio of imitation cost to innovation cost and the ratio of imitation cost to innovation cost when the ratio of imitation time to innovation time is held constant.

expect the $i$th product's ratio of imitation cost to innovation cost (denoted by $C_i$) to be inversely related to the proportion of the $i$th product's innovation cost that goes for research (rather than product specification, pilot plant or prototype, plant and equipment, or manufacturing or marketing startup). An imitator frequently can spend much less time and money on research than the innovator because the product's existence and characteristics provide the imitator with a great deal of information that the innovator had to obtain through its own research. On the other hand, an imitator often has to go through many of the same steps as the innovator with respect to pilot plant or prototype construction, investment in plant and equipment, and manufacturing and marketing startup.

Second, we would expect $C_i$ to be relatively large if the $i$th product is a new drug where the Food and Drug Administration requires that an imitative product must be tested in much the same way as the innovative product with which it competes. As Kitch (1973) and others have pointed out, this requirement increases the money and time that an imitator must spend. (How much it increases them is a matter of some debate; results on this score are given below.) Third, we would expect $C_i$ to be relatively small if the $i$th product consists of a new use for an existing material and if some firm other than the innovator has patents on this material. In such cases, the patent holder often can imitate the innovation relatively cheaply and quickly.[1]

To test these hypotheses, we assume that

$$C_i = \alpha_0 + \alpha_1 R_i + \alpha_2 D_i + \alpha_3 G_i + z_i, \qquad (1)$$

where $R_i$ is the percentage of the innovation cost that went for applied research in the case of the $i$th product, $D_i$ is a dummy variable that equals 1 if the $i$th innovation was an ethical drug (subject to regulation of the sort described above) and 0 otherwise, $G_i$ is a dummy variable that equals 1 if the $i$th product was a new use for an existing material on which a firm other than the innovator holds patents and 0 otherwise, and $z_i$ is a random error term. Data were collected regarding $R_i$, $D_i$, and $G_i$ for 28 of the products in our sample,[2] and we computed least-squares estimates of the $\alpha$'s. The results are

$$C_i = 0.838 - 0.00684 R_i + 0.310 D_i - 0.536 G_i. \quad (\bar{R}^2 = 0.49) \qquad (2)$$
$$(11.8) \quad (3.80) \qquad (2.31) \qquad (2.41)$$

The $t$-ratios are given in parentheses.

[1] In one case in our sample, an agricultural chemical firm found a new use for a particular chemical. This firm's supplier held a patent on the broad group of chemicals of which this chemical was part, but was unaware of this new use. When the innovator marketed the chemical for this new use, the supplier could (and did) imitate the innovation quickly and at a low cost.

Another factor we would like to include in equation (1) is the extent of the imitator's technological capabilities and know-how, relative to those of the innovator, but we could find no way to measure this factor adequately.

[2] The sample was composed of two subsamples, each of which was collected quite independently from the other. In the subsample for which Schwartz was particularly responsible, we obtained the data needed to test these hypotheses. In the other sub-sample, for which Wagner was particularly responsible, we did not obtain these data, but focused attention on other questions instead. Equation (4) is also based only on the former subsample. One product was not included in equation (2) because the imitator received a license from the innovator, but if this product is included, the results do not change in any significant way. Interaction terms were also included in equation (2), but were not significant.

Each of the regression coefficients in equation (2) has the expected sign, is statistically significant, and is large enough so that the effect of each independent variable is substantial. If $R_i$ increases by 20 percentage points, $C_i$ decreases by about 0·14. If the $i$th product is a new drug, $C_i$ is about 0·31 larger than would otherwise be the case. If the $i$th product is a new use for an existing material on which a firm other than the innovator holds the patents, $C_i$ is about 0·54 smaller than would otherwise be the case. These three independent variables can explain about half of the variation in $C_i$.

### IV. PATENTS AND IMITATION COSTS

Still another factor that affects the ratio of imitation cost to innovation cost is whether or not the innovator has patents on the new product. Contrary to popular opinion, patent protection does not make entry impossible, or even unlikely. Within 4 years of their introduction, 60% of the patented successful innovations in our sample were imitated. Nonetheless, patent protection generally increases imitation costs. To obtain information concerning the size of this increase, the firms in our sample were asked to estimate how much the value of $C_i$ for each patented product increased because it was patented. The median estimated increase in $C_i$ was 11%. They also were asked to estimate how much the value of $C_i$ for each unpatented product would have increased if it had been patented. The median estimated increase in $C_i$ was only about 6%. (Indeed, for 2 of these products, patent protection would have reduced the money and time required for imitation because in these cases the innovator could keep secret the essential information underlying the product, whereas if it patented it, some of the information would have been disclosed.) The fact that a patent resulted in a larger increase in the imitation costs of the patented products than of the unpatented products was, of course, a major reason why some products were patented and others were not.[1]

In the ethical drug industry, patents had a bigger impact on imitation costs than in the other industries, which helps to account for survey results[2] indicating that patents are regarded as more important in ethical drugs than elsewhere. The median estimated increase in $C_i$ due to patent protection was about 30% in ethical drugs, in contrast to about 10% in chemicals and about 7% in electronics and machinery. Without patent protection, it frequently would have been relatively cheap (and quick) for an imitator to determine the composition of a new drug and to begin producing it. However, for many of these electronics and machinery innovations, it would have been quite difficult for imitators to determine from the new product how it is produced, and patents would not add a great deal to imitation cost (or time).[3] These results are in accord with Taylor

---

[1] Since some of the products in the sample were inherently unpatentable, they had to be omitted, so the results reported in this paragraph are based on 43 products. Using the Wilcoxon test, the difference between the median increase in $C_i$ for patented and unpatented products is significant at the 0·05 probability level. In the entire sample of 48 products, the percentage that was patented was 81 (drugs), 63 (chemicals), and 69 (electronics and machinery).

[2] For a description of these surveys and their results, see Taylor and Silberston (1973) and Scherer (1977).

[3] Taylor and Silberston (1973) point out that a high proportion of patents in electronics are thought to be of doubtful validity, and that, even if an electronics patent is valid, it may afford little

and Silbertson's (1973) conclusion that the lack of patent protection would reduce the rate of expenditure on innovative activity to a greater extent in drugs than in other industries.

## V. IMITATION COSTS, ENTRY, AND CONCENTRATION

We turn now from the determinants of imitation costs to their effects on entry and concentration. Holding constant the discounted profit (gross of the imitation cost) that the imitator expects to earn by imitating a new product, the new product is more likely to be imitated if the imitation cost is small. To discourage entry, the innovator may adopt pricing (and other) policies to reduce the imitator's expected discounted gross profit if the imitation cost is low. Taking this into account, is it still true that the probability of entry is inversely related to the size of the imitation cost? To find out, we determined whether each product in the sample was imitated within 4 years[1] after it was first introduced. (Innovations that had been on the market less than 4 years and unsuccessful innovations clearly had to be omitted.) Then we carried out a logit analysis to determine whether $C$ – the ratio of imitation cost to innovation cost – influences the probability that entry of this sort occurred within 4 years. Letting $P$ be the probability that such entry did *not* occur, we found that

$$\ln\left(\frac{P}{1-P}\right) = -3 \cdot 10 + 3 \cdot 92 C. \qquad (3)$$
$$(2 \cdot 04)\ (1 \cdot 97)$$

Thus, imitation cost seems to be related in the expected way to whether or not entry occurs.[2]

Imitation cost may also affect an industry's level of concentration. We would expect an industry's concentration level to be relatively low if its members' products and processes can be imitated easily and cheaply.[3] For each of the 16 detailed industries included in the sample, we calculated the mean value of $C_i$, the mean for the $j$th industry being denoted by $\bar{C}_j$. Then to estimate the relationship between the mean imitation cost and the concentration level, we

---

protection. See Taylor and Silberston (1973), chapter 12. For some ways (other than patents) in which electronics firms protect their products from imitation, see *Science*, 202, November 24, 1978, pp. 848–9. Also see Scherer (1977).

Although the median increase in imitation cost due to patents (outside the drug industry) is rather small, the increase in some cases is very substantial. Outside drugs, patents increased imitation cost by 100% or more in about one-quarter of the cases. This helps to explain our findings in Section VI below.

[1] In the bulk of the cases, the new product could have been imitated in 2 years or less even if the imitator carried out the project at the most leisurely pace. In practically all cases it could be imitated in 3 years or less. Thus, 4 years was plenty of time for an imitator to enter.

[2] Note that a one-tailed test is appropriate here. The methods used to estimate this equation are described in Berkson (1953). For an analysis of entry rates in the chemical industry that estimates the effects of certain kinds of imitation costs, see Mansfield *et al.* (1977 b), pp. 119–22. For some evidence that imitation costs influence the gap between social and private rates of return from innovations, see Mansfield *et al.* (1977 a).

[3] In their simulation model, Nelson and Winter (1978) use a hypothetical 'ease of imitation factor' which is defined differently from our $C_i$, but it seems clear that this factor is closely related to what our $C_i$ measures.

regressed each industry's 4-firm concentration ratio, $K_j$, on $\bar{C}_j$, the result being[1]

$$K_j = 6 \cdot 22 + 61 \cdot 5 \bar{C}_j. \qquad (4)$$
$$(8 \cdot 80) \ (12 \cdot 8)$$

This finding, which seems to be the first empirical evidence regarding the relationship between the ease of imitation and the level of concentration, is entirely consistent with this hypothesis. Given the large number of factors influencing an industry's concentration level, it is interesting that this relationship is relatively close ($r^2 = 0 \cdot 60$). Differences among industries in the technology transfer process (including transfers that are both voluntary and involuntary from the point of view of the innovator) may be able to explain much more of the interindustry variation in concentration levels than is generally recognised.

## VI. PATENTS AND THE RATE OF INNOVATION

Finally, we turn to one of the most important and controversial questions concerning the patent system: what proportion of innovations would be delayed or not introduced at all if they could not be patented? To shed light on this question, we asked each innovating firm whether it would have introduced each of its patented innovations in our sample if patent protection had not been available. Although answers to such questions have obvious limitations and must be treated with caution, they should shed some light on this topic, about which so little is known.[2]   According to the firms, about one-half of the patented innovations in our sample would not have been introduced without patent protection. The bulk of these innovations occurred in the drug industry. Excluding drug innovations, the lack of patent protection would have affected less than one-fourth of the patented innovations in our sample.

Taylor and Silberston (1973) have provided estimates of the proportion of R and D expenditures in various U.K. industries that would not have been carried out without patent protection. Applying the industry weights in our sample to their data, one would expect that about 36 % of the R and D expenditures of the firms in our sample would not have been carried out under these circumstances, if U.S. and British firms are alike in this regard. This is somewhat less[3] than the proportion of innovations that, according to the firms, would not have been introduced without patent protection.[4]

---

[1] To prevent confusion, note that each concentration ratio refers to all the detailed industry's products, not just the new products in our sample. In effect, we treat the products in our sample in each detailed industry as a sample of all the detailed industry's products, and use $\bar{C}_j$ as a measure of the ease with which all the latter products can be imitated.

[2] These data could be obtained for 31 innovations. Some innovations could not be included because they were unpatentable or because no reliable information could be obtained from the firm. For a good discussion of what currently is known about this topic, see Scherer (1977 and 1980) and Taylor and Silberston (1973).

[3] This difference is statistically significant at the 0·05 probability level.

[4] There is no reason to expect the proportion of R and D expenditures that would not be carried out without patent protection to equal the proportion of innovations that would not be carried out under these circumstances. If the innovations that would not be carried out tend to be less R and D-intensive than those that would be carried out under these circumstances, the former proportion would be less

One important reason why patents frequently are not regarded as crucial is that they often have only a limited effect on the rate of entry. For about half of the innovations, the firms felt that patents had delayed the entry of imitators by less than a few months.[1] Although patents generally increased the imitation costs, they did not increase the costs enough in these cases to have an appreciable effect on the rate of entry. But although patent protection seems to have only a limited effect on entry in about half of the cases, it seems to have a very important effect in a minority of them. For about 15 % of the innovations, patent protection was estimated to have delayed the time when the first imitator entered the market by 4 years or more.

According to many economists, patent protection tends to be more important to smaller firms than to larger ones. However, although this proposition seems reasonable, the existing evidence on this score is weak and sometimes contradictory.[2] To test this proposition, we carried out a logit analysis to see whether $\pi$, the probability that an innovation would have been introduced without patent protection, is related to $S$, the 1976 sales of the firm that carried out the innovation. Since practically none of the drug innovations would have been introduced without patent protection, such innovations were excluded.[3] The results are:

$$\ln\left(\frac{\pi}{1-\pi}\right) = 0.878 + 0.00012S.$$
$$\qquad\qquad (1.03)\ \ (0.030)$$
(5)

Since the coefficient of $S$ is far from statistically significant, there is no evidence that patent protection was more likely to be deemed essential for innovations carried out by smaller firms than for those carried out by larger ones.[4]

## VII. CONCLUSION

At a purely theoretical level, imitation costs have long played a major role in economic models of innovation and technological change, but systematic empirical investigations have been lacking. While the present study is only a relatively small-scale undertaking with obvious limitations, we believe that it

---

than the latter. Also, there is no reason to expect that American and British firms would behave in exactly the same way. Thus, if patents are regarded as more important in the United States than in the United Kingdom, this would result in the sort of difference we observe. In addition, there are sampling errors in both our estimates and those of Taylor and Silberston.

[1] Each innovating firm was asked to estimate how much sooner the first imitating firm would have entered the market if the new product had not had patent protection. The resulting estimates are rough, but, according to the firms, they are reasonably accurate. They seem consistent with the findings in the first paragraph of this section. Outside drugs, patents were estimated to delay the entry of imitators by 2 years or more in 25 % of the cases.

[2] See Scherer (1977).

[3] Had the drug innovations been included, a bias might have resulted, since, as noted above, patents are regarded as particularly important in the drug industry. Thus, since the drug firms were larger than the average in the sample, this might have resulted in a spurious inverse relationship between $\pi$ and $S$. $S$ is measured in billions of dollars.

[4] These results may be due in part to the fact that practically all of the innovating firms in the sample are quite large. If a larger number of very small firms were included, the results might be more in line with the proposition in the text.

demonstrates both that empirical investigations of this topic can be carried out and that, unless such investigations are carried out, we are unlikely to understand many fundamental aspects of the economics of technological change. In our view, there is a considerable need for more studies of the size, determinants, and effects of imitation costs.

Our findings should help to promote the search for more realistic and useful models of the innovative process. In recent years, there has been a tendency for such models to assume that the innovator receives all of the benefits from an innovation and that imitation can be ignored. (For example, see Dasgupta and Stiglitz (1980) and Loury (1979).) And in studies of optimal patent life, it is often assumed that the patent holder is free from imitation for the life of the patent. Although we understand how convenient such assumptions may be, our results suggest how considerably they depart from reality. (Recall, for example, that about 60 % of the patented innovations in our sample were imitated within 4 years.) We hope that the excellent theorists who are working in this area will soon be able to relax these assumptions.[1]

This study also sheds new light on the effects of the patent system. Contrary to the assumption of many economic models, a patent frequently does not result in a 17-year monopoly over the relevant innovation. Patents do tend to increase imitation costs, particularly in the drug industry, but excluding drugs, patent protection did not seem essential for the development and introduction of at least three-fourths of the patented innovations studied here. From the point of view of public policy, this obviously is an interesting finding.

*University of Pennsylvania*

*Date of receipt of final typescript: May 1981*

### REFERENCES

Arrow, K. (1962). 'Economic welfare and the allocation of resources for invention.' In *The Rate and Direction of Inventive Activity*. New York: National Bureau of Economic Research.
Baldwin, W. and Childs, G. (1969). 'The fast second and rivalry in research and development.' *Southern Economic Journal*, July, pp. 18–24.
Berkson, J. (1953). 'A statistically precise and relatively simple method of estimating the bioassay with quantal response, based on the logistic function.' *Journal of the American Statistical Association*, pp. 565–99.
Dasgupta, P. and Stiglitz, J. (1980). 'Industrial structure and the nature of innovative activity.' ECONOMIC JOURNAL, June, pp. 266–93.
Freeman, C. (1974). *The Economics of Industrial Innovation*. Middlesex: Penguin.
Kitch, E. (1973). 'The patent system and new drug application.' In *Regulating New Drugs* (ed. R. Landau), pp. 81–108. Chicago: University of Chicago.
Loury, G. (1979). 'Market structure and innovation.' *Quarterly Journal of Economics*, (August), pp. 395–410.

[1] The innovator may receive far less than other firms that subsequently introduce the innovation in a somewhat different way or at a more propitious time. Even if the innovator is very successful, imitators may gain a substantial share of the benefits. Models that ignore considerations of this sort should be viewed with caution, since (among other reasons) they omit factors that are important impediments to firms' appropriation of the benefits from their innovations. By doing so, they may exaggerate the incentive for firms to invest in R and D and other innovative activities.

Mansfield, E. (1980). 'Basic research and productivity increase in manufacturing.' *American Economic Review*, (December).
——, Rapoport, J., Schnee, J., Wagner. S. and Hamburger, M. (1971). *Research and Innovation in the Modern Corporation*. New York: W. W. Norton.
——, Rapoport, J., Romeo, A., Wagner, S. and Beardsley, G. (1977a). 'Social and private rates of return from industrial innovations.' *Quarterly Journal of Economics*, vol. 16, May, pp. 221–40.
——, Rapoport, J., Romeo, A., Villani, E., Wagner, S. and Husic, F. (1977b). *The Production and Application of New Industrial Technology*. New York: W. W. Norton.
——, Romeo, A., Schwartz, M., Teece, D., Wagner, S. and Brach, P. (forthcoming). *Technology Transfer, Productivity and Economic Policy*. New York: W. W. Norton.
Nelson, R. and Winter, S. (1978). 'Forces generating and limiting concentration under Schumpeterian competition.' *Bell Journal of Economics*, vol. 9, (Autumn), pp. 524–48.
Scherer, F. M. (1967). 'Research and development resource allocation under rivalry.' *Quarterly Journal of Economics*, vol. 81, August, pp. 359–94.
——, (1977). *The Economic Effects of Compulsory Patent Licensing*. New York: New York University Monograph 1977–2 in Finance and Economics.
——, (1980). *Industrial Market Structure and Economic Performance*, 2nd ed. Chicago: Rand McNally.
Taylor, C. and Silberston, Z. (1973). *The Economic Impact of the Patent System*. Cambridge University Press.

# [17]

# Appropriability of innovation benefit as a predictor of the source of innovation *

ERIC VON HIPPEL

*Alfred P. Sloan School of Management, MIT, Cambridge, MA 02139, USA*

Final version received October 1981

It has been empirically observed that, in some industries product users are the most frequent sources of product innovations while, in other industries, product manufacturers are. I hypothesize that such differences are caused by differences in the ability of these two "functional" categories of innovators to appropriate innovation benefit. I explore this hypothesis by examining the real-world effectiveness of mechanisms (such as patents and lead time) used for the appropriation of innovation benefit and the dependence of this effectiveness on the functional relationship between innovator and innovation.

## 1. Introduction

Empirical studies of the functional locus of innovation, the variable modeled in this paper and first studied by Peck [1] categorize innovators in terms of the *functional* relationship via which they derive benefit from the innovations they create. Thus, if one is studying a sample of process machinery innovators, those who use the innovative machinery in production would be grouped in terms of that functional relationship into a "user" category, innovators who benefit economically from manufacturing the process machinery innovations grouped into a "manufacturer" category, etc.

The functional locus of innovation has proven very useful in innovation research because it is reliably measurable and because it often displays very strong differences between samples examined. Thus, we see from table 1 that Berger [5] and

Boyden [6] find that 100% of their samples of, respectively, engineering polymer innovations and polymer additive innovations were developed by manufacturers of these. In sharp contrast, Lionetta [7] and von Hippel [9] find users to be the developers of 85% and 68% respectively of the samples of process machinery innovations whose antecedents they investigated.

The striking differences empirically observed in the functional locus of innovation are doubtless a function of several variables. In this paper, however, I explore the hypothesis that such differences can be effectively modeled in terms of one variable only: the different abilities of would-be innovators holding different functional relationships to a given innovation to appropriate benefit from that innovation. [1] More specifically, I hypothesize that the functional locus of innovation can be effectively modeled in terms of appropriability of innovation benefit if and as three conditions hold in the real world, namely, would-be innovators: (1) *are not* able to capture benefit from non-embodied knowledge characterizing their innovations: (2) *are* able to capture benefit from output-embodied knowledge relating to their innovations; and (3) differ significantly in their *ability* to capture benefit from output-embodied innovation knowledge. In the following sections of this paper I identify and explore the real-world effectiveness of mechanisms available to innovators for the appropriation of innovation benefit, and provide an initial empirical test of the proposed model.

* The research reported on in this paper was supported by the National Science Foundation under Grant no. PRA 77-07830.

[1] Readers interested in a more general discussion of appropriability of innovation benefit may wish to refer to key papers by Arrow [10], Nelson [11], and Pakes and Schankerman [12], in addition to the pioneering paper by Peck [1].

Table 1
Empirical data on the functional source of commercialized industrial innovations

| Study | Nature of innovations and sample selection criteria | | Innovation developed [a] by | | |
|---|---|---|---|---|---|
| | | *n* | User (%) | Mfr (%) | Other (%) |
| Knight [2] | Computer innovations 1944–1962: | | | | |
| | – system reaching new performance high | 143 | 25 | 75 | |
| | – systems with radical structural innovations (level 1) | 18 | 33 | 67 | |
| Enos [3] | Major petroleum processing innovations | 7 | 43 | 14 | 43 [b] |
| Freeman [4] | Chemical processes and process equipment available for license, 1967 | 810 | 70 | 30 | |
| Berger [5] | All engineering polymers developed in US after 1955 with >10 mm pounds produced in 1975 | 6 | 0 | 100 | |
| Boyden [6] | Chemical additives for plastics: all plasticizers and UV stabilizers developed post World War II for use with four major polymers | 16 | 0 | 100 | |
| Lionetta [7] | All pultrusion processing machinery innovations first introduced commercially 1940–1976 which offered users a major increment in functional utility | 9 | 89 | 11 | |
| von Hippel [8] | Scientific instrument innovations: | | | | |
| | – first of type (e.g. first NMR) | 4 | 100 | 0 | |
| | – major functional improvements | 44 | 82 | 18 | |
| | – minor functional improvements | 63 | 70 | 30 | |
| von Hippel [9] | Semiconductor and electronic subassembly manufacturing equipment: | | | | |
| | – first of type used in commercial production | 7 | 100 | 0 | |
| | – major functional improvements | 22 | 63 | 21 | 16 [c] |
| | – minor functional improvements | 20 | 59 | 29 | 12 [c] |

[a] Attribution of an innovation to a user or manufacturer "developer" is determined by which of these first builds and utilizes the innovation in conformance with his economic function. Thus, attribution to a user source is made if a user builds and *uses* an innovation before a manufacturer builds and sells a commercial version. And conversely, attribution to a manufacturer source is made if a manufacturer builds and *sells* a commercial version of an innovation before a user builds and uses a home-made version; NA data excluded from percentage.
[b] Attributed to independent inventors/invention development companies.
[c] Attributed to joint user–manufacturer innovation projects.

## 2. The ability to predict the functional locus of innovation as a function of the appropriability of innovation-related benefit

The economic benefits which an innovator might obtain from his innovation can be segregated into two mutually exclusive and jointly exhaustive categories: (1) benefit from "output-embodied" knowledge and (2) benefit from non-embodied knowledge. Benefit from output-embodied knowledge is obtained by an innovator via in-house use of his innovation in his product and/or process and the consequent embodiment of its value in the output of his firm. Benefit from non-embodied knowledge is obtained by an innovator from the sale or licensing of non-embodied knowledge regarding his innovation to others. Let us consider whether we would logically expect to be able to predict the functional locus of innovation – i.e. the functional relationship of innovator to innovation – under each of two extreme cases regarding the ability of an innovator to capture benefit from his innovation:

Case 1 Total ability to capture benefit from output-embodied knowledge and total ability to capture benefit from non-embodied knowledge.
Case 2 Total ability to capture benefit from output-embodied knowledge but *no* or only an

imperfect ability to capture benefit from non-embodied knowledge.

## 2.1. Predictions regarding the functional locus of innovation under case 1 conditions

If we assume that an innovator has "perfect", costlessly enforceable property rights to his innovation, i.e. if, without cost to himself, he can totally control its diffusion and capture benefit from innovation users, manufacturers, and others to the point where adoption becomes a matter of indifference to them, then the benefits capturable by an innovator would be the same no matter what his own functional relationship to the innovation at issue. Thus, under case 1 conditions we can make no prediction regarding the functional locus of innovation on the basis of appropriability of benefit considerations.

The reasoning behind the above conclusion is that costless [2] enforcement of property rights would allow any innovator to set the fees charged to each innovation beneficiary, and each class of beneficiaries, so as to attain the maximum return. The role which the innovator himself happens to play with regard to the innovation – user, manufacturer, etc. – does not influence his fee-setting decision because he is equally able to capture innovation returns from his own company and other companies. This being so, he has no incentive to concentrate benefits in his own company even if the direct return from the particular innovation can be "leveraged" [3] by its user to create larger "other returns" over time.

---

[2] If the above-described inability to predict the locus of innovation under case 1 conditions is to hold, costless enforcement of property rights is required for the following reason: since marketing of an innovation and enforcement of payment can be reasonably assumed to be costless for an innovating firm when it captures output-embodied benefit by utilizing the innovation knowledge in its own processes and/or products, *non*-costless marketing of an enforcement of payments for use of innovation knowledge by other firms would create a differential between benefit attainable from in-house and external use of the innovation and generate a preference for the former. This in turn would allow an incremental benefit from the same innovation to accrue to those innovators with a larger in-house use for it – and create a differential incentive to innovate as a function of locus of innovation.

[3] Suppose, for example, that a minor cost-reducing process innovation were made available to one of several manufac-

## 2.2. Predictions regarding the functional locus of innovation under case 2 conditions

Under case 2 conditions we assume that: (1) the innovator has temporary monopoly power over the innovation information embodied in his output and thus is able to capture significant benefit from embodying that knowledge in the output of his firm; and (2) the innovator has *no* or only a very imperfect ability to capture benefit from diffusing non-embodied information regarding his innovation to others. Faced with this situation, the economically rational firm, seeking to maximize its joint return from output-embodied knowledge and non-embodied knowledge, would wish to move to a greater reliance on embodying its knowledge in output. *If* firms differ in their *ability* to embody innovation knowledge in their output, they will also clearly differ in their ability to benefit from a given innovation and therefore in their economically rational willingness to invest the resources required to innovate. This, in turn, will allow us to predict the functional locus of innovation when and if the differences in ability to appropriate benefit from output-embodied innovation knowledge are large enough to be observable under real-world conditions.

Whether or not and to what degree each of these conditions does in fact accurately describe the real world is an empirical matter which I will take up in the following sections of this paper. A simple example of the predictive power regarding the locus of innovation which we will acquire where these conditions do hold, however, can be seen in the following: Given case 2 conditions an independent inventor is much less likely to invent than are would-be innovators with other functional relationships to the innovation opportunity,

---

turers of a commodity with previously equal manufacturing costs, financial resources, etc. If further innovations or other changes did not intervene, the commodity producer benefitting from the innovation could in principle increase his market share as a consequence of innovation and thus "leverage" the direct benefits of the innovation, perhaps manyfold. But note that, even under such a set of circumstances, the innovator has no incentive to prefer to increase or decrease the market share of his own company relative to that of his competitors because he can, given perfect information, also charge the benefiting company for such second (and *n* th) order benefits arising from the innovation up to the point of indifference.

because an independent inventor has *only* non-embodied knowledge to sell.

### 3. Real-world ability of innovators to appropriate benefit from non-embodied innovation knowledge

In section 2 it was concluded that, if we were to be able to model the functional locus of innovation as a function of the appropriability of innovation benefit, innovators should *not* be able to effectively capture benefit from the licensing or sale of non-embodied knowledge regarding their innovation to others. Only two benefit capture mechanisms currently exist in the United States which allow innovators the possibility of capturing benefit from non-embodied innovation knowledge: (1) patent legislation (federal) allows an innovator to charge others for using freely available information published in his patent; and (2) trade secret legislation (state) allows an innovator to license knowledge to a user(s) and put the recipient under the legal duty of maintaining the secrecy of that information so that it will not become a free good on the marketplace. (Both of these mechanisms can also be used to capture benefit from output-embodied innovation knowledge, and we explore their effectiveness in this regard in section 4.2 below.)

*3.1. Patent legislation as a mechanism for capturing benefit from non-embodied innovation knowledge*

A patent grants an inventor the right to exclude others from the use of his invention for a limited period. In return for the right to exclude not only those who copy the invention but also those who independently discover the same thing, the inventor must disclose the invention to the public at the time of the patent's issue. This disclosure, contained in the patent itself, must be sufficiently detailed so that those "ordinarily skilled in the art" may copy and utilize the invention after the patent's expiration. While considerable information exists on the number of patents acquired by various firms and industries over time and on the various correlations between such "patent rates", firm size, R&D expenditures, and similar variables, very little information exists on the real-world effect of a patent grant on an inventor's ability to gain benefit from the non-embodied

knowledge characterizing his invention [13]. I review the available empirical data below.

Evidence of a patent system's effectiveness as a mechanism for allowing the capture of benefit from non-embodied innovation knowledge and/or benefit from output-embodied innovation knowledge can be seen in its influence on an innovator's willingness to invest in research and development, while evidence of its effectiveness in allowing benefit capture from non-embodied knowledge *only* can be seen via data on license agreements and related payments. A recent study by Taylor and Silbertson [14] provides both types of evidence.[4] Evidence regarding the effect of patent protection on an innovator's willingness to invest in R&D was obtained via a questionnaire ("Form B") which asked: "Approximately what proportion of your R&D in recent years would not have been carried out if you had not been able to patent any resulting discoveries?" [16]. The data derived from this question are shown in table 2. Note that 24 of the 32 returns indicate that only 5% or less of recent R&D expenditures would not have been undertaken if patent protection had not been available [17].

A direct measure of the ability to capture benefit from non-embodied innovation knowledge afforded to innovators by patents may be obtained

[4] Taylor and Silberston examined the impact of British and foreign patents on a sample of 44 British and multinational firms involved in five broad "classes" of industrial activity: chemicals (including pharmaceuticals and petrochemicals); oil refining; electrical engineering (including electronics); mechanical engineering; and man-made fibers. Approximately 150 firms were invited to join the study. Coded as being in one of the five specified classes, they were selected from a "comprehensive list of U.K. quoted companies" on the basis of their net assets in 1960: In each class all companies showing net assests in excess of 10 million pounds in 1960 were selected, and every seventh company of the remainder was selected from a list tabulated in ascending order of net assets in 1960. Finally, "some additions were made to take account of mergers and acquisitions and to include unquoted companies". Eventually "just over 100" firms responded to the letter of invitation. Sixty-five expressed interest, but "some twenty of these indicated that patents were a very minor aspect of their operations and were firmly believed to have no significance on the business... this left 44 firms which agreed to participate in the inquiry" [15]. Of these, 30 ultimately agreed to participate fully and fill out the detailed questionnaires provided by the authors, while the remaining 14 agreed to provide more limited information and to be interviewed.

Table 2
Estimated proportions of R&D expenditure dependent on patent protection: twenty-seven responding companies [a]

| Industry | Estimate of R&D affected [b] | | | | |
|---|---|---|---|---|---|
| | None or negligible | Very little (less than 5%) | Some (5–20%) | Substantial (over 20%) | Total returns |
| | Number of returns | | | | |
| Chemicals: | | | | | |
| – Finished and speciality | 1 | 2 | 1 | 4 | 8 |
| – Basic | 1 | 2 | 1 | 0 | 4 |
| Total chemicals | 2 | 4 | 2 | 4 | 12 |
| Mechanical engineering | 7 | 1 | 0 | 2 | 10 |
| Man-made fibers | 1 | 1 | 0 | 0 | 2 |
| Electrical engineering | 7 | 1 | 0 | 0 | 8 |
| Total | 17 | 7 | 2 | 6 | 32 [c] |
| Percentage of returns | 53% | 22% | 6% | 19% | 100% |

[a] Table redrawn from Taylor and Silberston [22, table 9.1, p. 107].
[b] Percentages refer to the estimated reduction in annual R&D expenditure in recent years that would have been experienced, had patent monopolies not been available.
[c] Some companies made returns for more than one activity.

by looking at licensing cost and benefit data. To the extent that an effective patent monopoly is provided to an innovator, he might choose to exercise it by a policy: (1) excluding all competitors; (2) selectively licensing some applicants; or (3) licensing all applicants for a royalty and/or other consideration. If the innovator chooses to reap benefit from non-embodied innovation knowledge via his patent monopoly by use of policy option (3), licensing all comers, diffusion of the innovation may be assumed freely to occur and the maximum value of benefit from non-embodied knowledge capturable by the innovator via the patent mechanism can be approximately represented by licensing fees and/or other considerations received minus patenting and licensing costs incurred by the innovating firm. In the event, most firms studied by Taylor and Silberston claimed to be following policy option (3), a policy of licensing all "responsible" applicants, rather than options (1) or (2). Indeed, the authors note, "we were repeatedly assured that the main problem for the licensing department is to interest reputable firms in taking licenses rather than dissuading them from doing so, and many licensing specialists to whom we talked were plainly puzzled that their task might be seen in the latter rather than the former light" [18]. Patent-related cost and benefit

data provided by Taylor and Silberston's "main sample" of 30 firms will be found summarized in table 3.

Taken together, tables 2 and 3 suggest that, except in the pharmaceutical field (for particular reasons noted in footnote 9 below), firms do not find the patent grant to be of significant benefit. [5]

[5] A study performed by a group of candidates for the Master's Degree at Harvard Business School [19] also contains some information on the value of patents to firms which hold them. A questionnaire was pilot tested, modified, and then sent out to a sample of 266 firms known to hold a relatively large number of patents [20]. Sixty-nine of the questionnaires (26%) were completed and returned in time to be included in the study's analysis phase. All but four of these respondents held more than 100 patents and collectively they "held approximately 45,500 patents, or about 13.5% of all the unexpired U.S. patents held by domestic corporations at the end of 1956" [21]. One of the questions attempted to determine the importance of patents to firms by asking the "executive responsible for technical change" to "please state briefly the importance of patents to the company". Thirty-seven responded in a manner which the students felt they would clearly categorize as follows: "very important", 8; "some importance", 14; "not very important", 15 [22]. While, unfortunately, neither the question nor the coding categories used are clear on what interviewers or interviewees meant by "important", we find the results suggestive in light of the Taylor and Silberston data: 40% of a sample of interviewees from companies selected because they patent a great deal felt that patents are "not very important to their companies".

Table 3

Relationship of 1968 patent expenditures to 1968 patent-related receipts in Taylor and Silberston "main sample" of thirty companies [14]

| Industry | 1<br>1968 UK license and royalty receipts [a]<br>£ (million) | 2<br>1968 UK patenting and licensing expenditures [b]<br>£ (million) | 3<br>1968 R&D expenditures in UK [c]<br>£ (million) | 4<br>1968 license receipts as % of R&D expenditures plus patenting and licensing expenditures (cols. 1−[2+3]) | 5<br>1968 license receipts as % of 1968 UK sales<br>col. 1<br>note d |
|---|---|---|---|---|---|
| Chemicals | | | | | |
| – Pharmaceuticals | 3.7 | NA | 7.1 | NA | 6 |
| – Other finished and speciality | 0.2 | NA | 10.1 | | 0.04 |
| – Basic | 2.4 | NA | 3.3 | NA | 1 |
| Total chemicals | 6.3 | 0.99 | 20.5 | 29 | 1.1 |
| Mechanical engineering | 1.4 | | 7.3 | 18 | 0.4 |
| Man-made fibers | 0.7 | 0.37 | 7.6 | 9 | 0.2 |
| Electrical engineering | 2.3 | 0.65 | 50.5 | 4 | 0.3 |

Except as noted in a–d below, data in all columns were derived from the same set of companies. N.B. that Taylor and Silberston have *not* logged patent and R&D expenditures data relative to receipt data on licensing, royalty, and sales. *All* table 2 data are for 1968.

[a] *Source:* Taylor and Silberston, table 8.7, p. 164. (T&S note that data from oil companies in sample and "one large electrical" group are excluded from table 8.7.)

[b] *Source:* Taylor and Silberston, table 6.4, p. 109. (T&S note that data from oil companies are excluded from table 6.4.)

[c] *Source:* Taylor and Silberston, table 8.1, col. 2, p. 109. I have excluded oil company data from basic chemical category to make this data base more compatible with table 6.4. T&S offer more aggregated R&D expenditure data in table 6.4, whose magnitudes deviate from those shown in table 8.1 by 20–40%. These discrepancies are unexplained, but our uses of that data are not sensitive to corrections of this magnitude.

[d] *Source:* Taylor and Silberston, table 8.1, col. 4, p. 145.

This finding has emerged in the face of three study elements which would tend to raise the level of benefit shown: (1) the authors noted in their discussion of sample selection (see footnote 4 outlining the study methodology) that firms which did not feel that patents significantly affected them tended to decline to join the study sample; (2) the authors noted that, "to avoid understating the impacts of patents", they chose to "err on the high side" [18] in their acquisition of data for table 1; (3) the authors also noted that the license agreements which resulted in the costs and benefits shown in table 2 involved the transfer of and payment for valuable unpatented "know-how" in addition to the transfer of information protected by patents and that "this may result in some overstatement of the true payment for patent licenses themselves". Note, however, that some understatement of real benefits may also be present because remissions of any *non*-monetary benefits (e.g.

cross-licensing) are omitted from table 2 [23].

Another study whose data can be used to assess the possible benefits from non-embodied knowledge that corporations reap through licensing of their patents was conducted by Wilson [24] who reports data on royalty payments submitted by some U.S. corporations to the U.S. Securities and Exchange Commission in 1971 on Form 10K. [6]

[6] In 1971 firms wre required to report royalty payments if they were "material" with the precise interpretation of that term being left up to individual firms. Focusing on the *Fortune* listing of the 1000 largest manufacturing corporations in 1971; Wilson found that 518 had considered their royalty receipts "material" enough to report to the SEC. Since he was interested only in royalty payments for "technology licenses", he used various means to detect and winnow from the sample firms which reported royalty payments for such things as trademarks, copyrights, and mineral rights [25]. The end result of this process was a sample of 350 royalty figures for 1971 which Wilson felt were largely or entirely payments

Table 4
Wilson and Taylor–Silberston royalty payment data compared

| Industry | Wilson [24] (1971 US data) | | Taylor and Silberston [14] (1968 UK data) | |
|---|---|---|---|---|
| | % of US sales by firms in sample [a] | Royalties paid as % of firm 1971 sales [a] | Royalties paid as % of firm 1968 sales [b] | "Industrial activity" |
| Chemicals | | | | Chemicals |
| – Industrial | 76.4 | 0.244 | 0.042 | – Basic |
| – Drug | 72.8 | 0.745 | 0.635 | – Pharmaceuticals |
| – Other | 51.4 | 0.034 | 0.044 | – Other finished and speciality |
| Machinery | 40.2 | 0.051 | 0.255 | Mechanical engineering |
| Electrical | 40.5 | 0.13 | 0.182 | Electrical engineering |

[a] *Source*: Wilson [24, table 12, p. 169]. Note that the data presented here are computed from Wilson's sample of 350 royalty reports, *not* his larger sample comprised of these reports plus estimated data.
[b] *Source*: Royalty and license fee expenditures data from Taylor and Silberston [14], table 8.7, col. 3, p. 164, sales data from table 8.1, col. 4, p. 145. (Petrochemicals have been removed from the basic chemicals category of table 8.1 to make this category compatble with the equivalent category of table 8.7.)

The reader will find Wilson's data for the SIC categories apparently most similar to the "industrial activity classes" examined by Taylor and Silberston compared in table 4.

Even though derived from a different source and country, the Wilson data have magnitudes quite similar to the Taylor and Silberston data. While unfortunately the table 4 data are for royalty payments rather than receipts (the Wilson data providing information on payments only), it is likely that the bulk of technical agreements would be between firms in the same industry.[7] If so, it would follow that the low magnitude of royalty payments in the Wilson data implies that royalty

receipts would also be found low in the industries sampled. This would be in line with the Taylor and Silberston data indicating that the benefit captured by innovators from the sale of non-embodied knowledge is indeed low in most industries.

The slim data base I have just reviewed indicates that, in industry aggregate terms, innovators do not capture much benefit from the sale of non-embodied innovation knowledge via the patent mechanism. Are these data congruent with "tests of reason" which one can apply to the matter? Let us explore. First, does it make economic sense that firms would take out patents if these do not, on average, yield much economic benefit? The answer is yes – because the cost of applying for patents is also low. The cost of the average patent application prosecuted by a corporation is on the order of $5,000 today.[8] (Even this small cost is often not very visible to corporate personnel deciding on a patent application "purchase" because it is typically subsumed within the overall cost of operating a corporate patent department.)

___

for "technical agreements", a term he does not define, but which presumably includes both patent and technical know-how-related payments. The responses of these 350 firms were then aggregated under appropriate "2 and 3 digit SIC codes" (not given) and displayed in tabular form. (Wilson used the 350 reports of corporate royalty payments to develop estimates of royalty payments to all members of the industries he studied, and then compared these estimates with industry-level data on corporate R&D expenditures collected by the National Science Foundation. As I find Wilson's estimating procedures inappropriate for our purposes here, I use only the direct company report data he provides.)

[7] This point is never explicitly examined, but is apparently assumed in Taylor and Silberston [14]. See especially the in-depth studies of Pharmaceuticals, Basic Chemicals, and Electronics in that source.

[8] In 1961 the Commissioner of Patents reported the cost of an average patent application prosecuted by a corporation to be $1,000 to $2,500, and the cost of a single application prosecuted by an attorney for an individual to be $680 [26]. My own recent conversations with several corporate patent attorneys yielded an estimate that the "average patent application prosecuted by a corporation" currently costs on the order of $5,000.

Second, what do we know about the nature of the patent grant and of the real-world workings of the patent office and the courts? And, is it reasonable in the light of what is known to conclude that the patent grant is likely to offer little benefit to its holder? Consider the following three points.

(1) It is important to note that a patent, if valid, gives a patentee the right to exclude others from using his invention, but it does *not* give him the right to use it himself if such a use would infringe the patents of others. For example, Fairchild has a patent on the so-called planar process, an important process invention used in the manufacture of integrated circuits. If firm B invents and patents an improvement on that process, it may not use its improvement invention without licensing the planar process from Fairchild and Fairchild may not use the improvement either without licensing it from firm B. Thus, in rapidly developing technologies where many patents have been issued and have not yet expired, it is likely that any new patent cannot be exercised without infringing the claims of numerous other extant patents. Given this eventuality, the benefit of a particular patent to an inventor would very probably be diminished because he might be prevented from using his own invention or he might be forced to cross-license competitors holding related patents in order to practice his invention.

(2) The patent system places the burden on the patentee of detecting an infringer and suing for redress. Such suits are notoriously long and expensive and both defendants and plaintiffs tend to avoid them assiduously. For the defendant the best outcome in recompense for all his time and expense is judicial sanction to continue this alleged infringement, while the worst outcome would involve the payment of possibly considerable penalties. For the plaintiff the likelihood that a court will hold a patent valid and infringed – as opposed to invalid and/or not infringed – is on the order of one to three [27]. If a patentee has licensees already signed up for a patent at issue, he has a high incentive to avoid litigation: If he loses, and the odds are that he will, he loses payments from all licensees, not just the potential payments from the particular infringer sued.

(3) The patent grant covers a particular means of achieving a given end but not the end itself, even if the end and perhaps the market it identifies are also novel. A would-be imitator can "invent around" a patent if he can invent a means not specified in the original inventor's patent. In the instance of the Polaroid and Xerography processes and a few other notable cases, determined competitors could not, in fact, invent around the means patented by the inventor. In most instances and in most fields, however, inventing around is relatively easy because there are many known means by which one might achieve an effect equivalent to the patented one, given the incentive to do so. Where inventing around is possible, the practical effect is to make the *upper* bound value of an inventor's patent grant equal to the estimated cost to a potential licensee of such inventing around.

Taken in combination, the observations made above may be applied to provide a very reasonable explanation for the relatively low benefit from non-embodied knowledge which we have found innovators in most fields obtaining via the patent grant. [9] Thus, in sum, we see via both data and test

---

[9] As an example, consider the application of these observations to the value of patents obtained in the field of semiconductor electronics.

The semiconductor field is currently a very fast-moving one in which many unexpired patents exist which address closely related subject matter. The possible consequence – confirmed as actual by corporate patent attorneys for several US semiconductor firms whom I interviewed – is that many patentees are unable to use their own inventions without the likelihood of infringing the patents of others. Since patents challenged in court are unlikely to be held valid, the result of the high likelihood of infringement accompanying use of one's own patented –' or unpatented – technology is not paralysis of the field. Rather, firms will in most instances simply ignore the possibility that their activities might be infringing the patents of others. The result is what Taylor and Silberston's interviewees in the electronic components field termed "a jungle", and what one of my interviewees termed a "Mexican Standoff". Firm A's corporate patent department will wait to be notified by attorneys from firm B that it is suspected that A's activities are infringing B's patents. Since possibly germane patents and their associated claims are so numerous, it is in practice usually impossible for firm A – or firm B – to evaluate firm B's claims on their merits. Firm A therefore responds – and this is the true defensive value of patents in the industry – by sending firm B copies of "a pound or two" of its possible germane patents with the suggestion that, while it is quite sure it is not infringing B, its examination shows that B is in fact probably infringing A. The usual result is cross-licensing with a modest fee possibly being paid by one side or the other. Who pays, it is important to note, is determined at least as much by the contenders' relative willingness to pay to avoid the expense and bother of a court fight as it is by the merits of the particular case.

of reason that the patent grant does not effectively enable innovators to capture benefit from non-embodied innovation knowledge in most fields.

### 3.2. Trade secret legislation as a mechanism for capturing benefit from non-embodied innovation knowledge

Trade secrets, like patents, can be used to capture benefit from non-embodied innovation

---

Thus, in the semiconductor field, except for a very few patent packages which have been litigated, which have been held valid, and which most firms license without protest – notably the Bell transistor patents and the Fairchild planar process patents – the patent grant is worth very little to inventors who obtain it. Indeed, the one value suggested to us – defense against the infringement suits of others – suggests that perhaps the true net value of the patent system to firms in the semiconductor industry is negative because it requires all to assume the overhead burden of defensive patenting.

In sharp contrast to the situation pertaining in most other industries and the electronics field in particular, the patent grant seems to confer significant benefit to innovators in the pharmaceutical field, as indicated by the Taylor–Silberston and Wilson data discussed in tables 3 and 4. My own discussions with corporate patent attorneys working for pharmaceutical firms brought out two likely reasons: (1) unusually "strong" patents are obtainable in the chemical field, of which pharmaceuticals is a part, and (2) it is often difficult to "invent around" a pharmaceutical patent. Pharmaceutical patents can be unusually strong because one may patent an actual molecule found to have useful medical properties and its analogs (in contrast to only the *particular* means to a given end in other fields). One need not make each analog claimed, but can simply refer to lists of recognized functional equivalents for each component of the molecule at issue. For example, if a molecule has ten important component parts, one patent application might claim $X$ plus 10 recognized functional equivalents of $X$ for each part. Obviously, by this means an inventor may claim millions of specific molecules without actually having to synthesize more than a few. Furthermore, demonstration that any of the analogs so claimed does not display the medical properties claimed does not invalidate the patent.

Pharmaceutical patents are difficult to "invent around" because the mechanisms by which pharmaceuticals achieve their medical effects are usually not well understood. Thus, would-be imitators do not gain much insight by examining a competitor's patented molecule proven to produce a desired medical effort. Eloquent testimony to this fact is provided by the pharmaceutical industry's research practice of synthesizing great numbers of molecules and "screening" these for possible medical activity rather than synthesizing only a few molecules predicted to have a given activity. The knowledge required for such prediction is seldom available today.

---

knowledge. (As noted earlier, their effectiveness in capturing benefit from output-embodied innovation knowledge will be explored in section 4.2 below.) Trade secrets, also sometimes termed "know-how", typically refer to inventions and/or knowledge which can be kept secret even *after* development is completed and commercial exploitation begun. The possessor of a trade secret has an indefinite period of exclusive use of his invention or discovery. Trade secret legislation allows him to keep the information entirely secret or to make legally binding contracts with others in which the secret is revealed in exchange for a fee or other consideration and a commitment to keep the information secret. A trade secret possessor may take legal steps to prevent its use by others *if* they can be shown to have discovered the secret through unfair and dishonest means such as theft or breach of a contract promising to keep it secret.

A legally protectable monopoly of indefinite duration would appear to make trade secrecy a very attractive mechanism for capturing innovation benefit. It is, however, an option only for innovations which can in fact be kept secret since the holder of a trade secret cannot exclude anyone who independently discovers it or who legally acquires the secret by such means as accidental disclosure or "reverse engineering". In practice, trade secrets have proven to be effective only with regard to product innovations incorporating various technological barriers to analysis, or with regard to process innovations which can be hidden from public view.

There are, in the first instance, certain innovations embodied in products which, while sold in the open market and thus available for detailed inspection by would-be imitators, manage nevertheless to defy analysis for some technological reason and which cannot therefore be reverse engineered. Complex chemical formulations sometimes fall into this category, the classic case being the formula for Coca-Cola. Such barriers to analysis need not be inherent in the product – they can sometimes be added on by design. Thus, some electronic products gain some protection from analysis via use of a packaging method ("potting") and packaging materials which cannot easily be removed without destroying the proprietary circuit contained within [28]. Methods for protecting trade secrets embodied in products accessible to competitors need not be foolproof to be effective – they simply have to raise enough of a barrier in a given case to create an unattractive cost benefit equation for would-be imitators in that case.

In the second instance, process innovations such as novel catalysts or process equipment can be protected effectively as trade secrets, whether or not they could be "reverse engineered" by a would-be imitator allowed to examine them, simply because they can be exploited commercially while shielded from such examination behind factory walls.

Few empirical data exist on the information protected as trade secrets: There is no central registry for such material analogous to the U.S. Patent Office, and even those trade secrets which are revealed to others to obtain benefits from non-embodied innovation knowledge, the subset of interest to us here, are contained in private contracts which do not usually appear on any public record unless litigated [29]. While some examples exist of major benefits from non-embodied knowledge being reaped by innovators via licensing of trade secrets [30], I argue that the typical effectiveness of this mechanism is severely limited for two reasons. First, the mechanism is clearly not applicable to product or process innovations which are not commercially exploitable while concealed behind factory walls and which are amenable to reverse engineering if accessible to inspection by imitators – and these considerations apply to many industries and many innovations. Second, a trade secret licensor can only gain redress under trade secret legislation if he can document the *specific* illegal act which diffused his innovation to unlicensed parties. A licensor finds such specificity difficult to achieve if he seeks to license non-embodied knowledge to many licensees.

## 4. Real-world appropriability of benefit from output-embodied innovation knowledge

In the previous section we found that an innovator's ability to appropriate benefit from non-embodied knowledge is low in most industries. If this is so, then significant economic reward, if any, must come primarily from the innovator's ability to appropriate benefit from output-embodied knowledge. The logical necessity of this conclusion is clear – the two categories of economic benefit are mutually exclusive and jointly exhaustive.

The ability of an innovator or innovating firm to capture benefit from output-embodied innovation knowledge derives from its ability to establish a quasi-monopoly position with respect to that innovation. I propose that two "levels" of quasi-monopoly are germane: (1) quasi-monopoly which an innovation affords to the entire industry of which the innovator is a member, and a portion of which the innovator derives in accordance to his "size"; and (2) quasi-monopoly which an innovation affords to the single innovating firm relative to other members of his industry. The ability to capture benefit from output-embodied innovation knowledge which these two levels of quasi-monopoly afford to firms is additive. I examine each, and the mechanisms by which each is achieved. While related empirical data are also explored in this section, I have found it to be so sparse on the issues addressed that the findings can best be seen as suggestive. Research approaches discussed, on the other hand, offer useful models for the additional empirical work required.

*4.1. Benefit from output-embodied knowledge appropriable by an innovating firm via creation of an industrywide quasi-monopoly*

I define an industry as made up of all firms making products which are close substitutes (i.e. have high cross-elasticity of demand). Firms in an industry may share in an industrywide quasi-monopoly if significant barriers exist which deter free entry to the industry by additional firms. Examples of such barriers to industry entry are specialized facilities, specialized production skills, and specialized sales forces, which are required for functioning effectively in an industry, which are possessed by firms already in that industry, but which must be acquired by potential new entrants.

Barriers to industry entry by new firms are common but difficult to measure. Consider, as an example, the barriers which face a firm which is a member of an industry characterized by a given functional relationship to an innovation (e.g. an industry which uses semiconductor process equipment to make semiconductors) and which wishes to join an industry characterized by another functional relationship to that innovation (e.g. the industry which manufactures semiconductor process equipment).[10] These two types of firms are really in very different businesses. Each has a great deal of know-how, organizational arrangements, and capital equipment which is quite specialized to build its existing products and to serve its existing customer base. Thus, the semiconductor manufacturer has a sales force which specializes in serving semiconductor buyers. This force would be entirely inappropriate for selling semiconductor process equipment: the customers are different, the sales techniques are different (samples of semiconductor devices can be given out as a selling technique, but not samples of semiconductor process equipment), and the specialized knowledge which the salesman must have is completely different (a salesman with an electrical engineering background can help customers with problems in selecting and using semiconductor devices; a background in solid state physics would be considerably more appropriate for a salesman trying to sell the semiconductor process equipment used to grow the ultrapure single silicon crystals used in semiconductor device manufacture).

If the sales, organizational, and production infrastructure which a company uses to serve one functional role relationship to a given innovation cannot effectively be used in the service of a different functional relationship, then it follows that a firm wishing to change such relationships must also set up a new infrastructure appropriate to this new role. Further, since the costs of the infrastructures of competitors already having the role relationships the innovator wishes to acquire are typically allocated across many products (e.g. a "line" of process equipment or a "line" of semiconductor devices), the would-be new entrant must develop/adopt/buy a similar line of product to sell if he wishes to be economically competitive.

All these requirements, I suggest, represent significant barriers to industry entry.[11]

Where significant barriers to industry entry do exist, an innovation made by one member of the industry can establish an industry-level quasi-monopoly with respect to that innovation which in turn can allow the industry as a whole to increase its rate of profit and/or volume of sales and thus reap benefit from output-embodied innovation knowledge. As an example, consider an innovation in plastics molding machinery made by a producer of a commodity plastic such as polyethylene. Assume the innovation allows molders of plastic items to significantly decrease their production costs. Further assume, as is realistic, that machinery innovation itself cannot be protected effectively via patent or other means by the innovator and that the machine works equally well using polyethylene manufactured by any supplier of such. Under these circumstances adoption of the innovation by molders might well increase demand for polyethylene more rapidly than supply could respond (it takes many years to build a new polyethylene plant) and the profits of all polyethylene producers – molding innovation developer and other producers alike – would then rise in proportion to their market share for polyethylene.

The assumptions embedded in the above machine innovation example – that the innovator has no ability to control or benefit from the diffusion of non-embodied knowledge regarding his innovation, and that the innovation benefit is instantly distributed to all competitors currently in the industry (i.e. increased profits on polyethylene are afforded to the innovating and non-innovating polyethylene producers simultaneously) – are equivalent to assuming the innovation to be a privately financed collective good. This being the case, the argument developed by Mancur Olson in his *The Logic of Collective Action* [31] can be applied to predict that the firm with the most to gain from the innovation is the one most likely to

---

[10] Note that firms holding different functional relationships to a given innovation are indeed in different industries according to the definition of "industry" cited previously, and that it is important to our model that barriers to entry exist between these industries. This is so because if it were easy, for example, for an innovation product manufacturer to become a product user at a moment's notice should such a course of action seem to promise an increased ability to capture benefit from the innovation, we would only be able to predict the functional locus of innovation in a weak sense, i.e. "the developer of $X$ innovation will *become* a user" rather than able to make the stronger statement that "the developer of $x$ innovation will be a firm and/or individual which currently is a member of the user community".

[11] It is important to note, however, that barriers to entry to a new industry (barriers to adding a new functional role with respect to a given innovation) may be considerably reduced if a firm does *not* want to make a full-scale entry into a new industry but simply wants to vertically integrate and *only* supply its own needs. Thus, if a semiconductor process machine user wishes to build a few units of an innovative process machine for in-house use, it does not need a sales force, an external field service force, nor a full line of equipment in order to spread the cost of these.

provide it to the group. (Firms holding any functional relationship to a given innovation are group members in Olson's sense if their relationship allows them the possibility of deriving output-embodied benefit from the innovation. The qualitative nature of the output in which the innovation benefit is embodied will differ, of course, in accordance with the functional role relationship of group member to innovation. For example, if the process equipment at issue is a plastics molding machine capable of making parts more cheaply, an equipment manufacturer's benefit is embodied in sales of the innovative molding machine; a plastic supplier's benefit is embodied in increased sales of plastic molding material.)

When and if industry-level quasi-monopolies do indeed provide significant benefits to would-be innovators, we should be able to observe empirically a concentration of innovations among what Olson terms the "larger" group members (quasi-monopoly participants). At the moment the only study I am aware of which offers an empirical research model that could test this hypothesis is by von Hippel [32].[12] The study focuses on semicon-

ductor process machinery innovations developed by firms that use such machinery in the manufacture of silicon-based semiconductors and contains data on the market share ranking of innovating user firms[13] in the year in which their sampled process machinery innovations were first used for commercial production of silicon-based semiconductors. This market share data can serve as an approximate measure of the relative amount of benefit from output-embodied innovation knowledge potentially appropriable by members of the sampled group of innovating user firms if we assume, as previously noted, that an innovation, once made by any one group member, becomes a collective good instantly provided to all members of that group. (Given this assumption, it is reasonable to conclude that the pre-innovation market shares of all group members whose outputs embody the innovation benefit will remain constant post-innovation. And if this is so, we may usefully approximate group member size by a group member's market share of silicon-based semiconductors at the time of the innovation's first commercial use.)

Note from table 5 that, four out of the five innovating user firms identified are ranked among the largest eight firms in terms of share of market in the year of first commercial use of their innovation(s).[14] This is the result we would expect if a significant industry-level quasi-monopoly existed and Olson's hypothesis were correct. I emphasize, however, that the results of this single study can only be seen as suggestive as it does not address reasonable alternative explanations for the finding (for example, it offers no information on the direction of causality involved in the observed correla-

---

[12] The method by which market share data were acquired in the study is fairly straightforward and is summarized in the notes to table 5. The method by which the sample of process machinery innovations was selected involved, first, selecting a subset of all process steps involved in each type of manufacture of silicon-based semiconductors. (Process steps and innovations studied are explicitly identified in von Hippel [33], table 1.) For each process step selected, the process machinery (if any) used in the initial commercial practice of that step was identified and included in the sample. Next, all subsequent improvements to process machinery for each step which offered a major improvement in functional utility to the user of such machinery (judged relative to previous best practice used in commercial manufacture) were identified and added to the sample. Finally an exhaustive list of process machinery innovations which offered any increment in functional utility to the user was collected for one randomly selected process step and these made up a sample of minor improvement innovations. All process equipment innovations in the sample were successful in the sense of receiving widespread use in their respective industries and becoming a commercially viable industrial good manufactured for commercial sale by at least one (and usually several) process equipment firms.

The "source" of each sampled innovation was determined via literature searches and interviews with user and manufacturer personnel. An innovation "source" was the firm which developed and built the first unit of equipment embodying the innovation which was used to produce commercially sold semiconductors. Innovations found to have a user source were coded as shown in table 5.

---

[13] Only firms with a use relationship to the sampled innovations are included in this study. Would-be innovators bearing other functional relationships to those innovations such as semiconductor machinery manufacturers, while also clearly in a position to gain benefit from output-embodied innovation knowledge and thus group members in Olson's sense, are excluded. This exclusion has no practical consequence here since, for reasons analogous to those spelled out in section 5 for the pultrusion industry study, it is quite certain that the "largest" group members with respect to this innovation sample are innovation users.

[14] Firm coded NA in table 5 were *not* smaller firms than those specifically identified: rather, in these instances, several major firms moved on the innovation so rapidly that I was unable accurately to determine retrospectively which of these had priority.

Table 5
Market rank of innovating vs. non-innovating user firms

| First innovating user firm | 1 Number of process equipment innovations [a] | | | 2 Date of first commercial use of process equipment innovation [a] | In year of first commercial use of process innovation | | | |
|---|---|---|---|---|---|---|---|---|
| | | | | | 3a 3b Innovative firm's semiconductor shipments [c] | | 4 Number of US semiconductor firms extant [d] | 5 Sales of parent firm [e] (total) $ (million) |
| | Initial | major | minor | | $ (million) | Industry rank | | |
| Fairchild | 1 | 1 | 3 | 1959 | 20 | 6 | 34 | 43 |
| | | | | 1960 | 27 | 6 | 47 | 68 |
| | | | | 1966 (3) | 146 | 2 | 50 | 207 |
| IBM | | 2 | 1 | 1965 | | 5 [c] | 50 | 3,700 |
| | | | | 1965 | | 5 [c] | 50 | 3,700 |
| | | | | 1967 | | 5 [c] | 53 | 5,300 |
| Western Electric | 1 | 1 | | 1956 | 4.5 | 6 | 26 | |
| | | | | 1960 | 27 | 6 | 47 | 7,900 |
| Hughes | 1 | | | 1970 | | NA | NA | NA |
| Motorola | | 1 | | 1961 | 28 | 6 | 53 | 298 |
| NA | 2 | 5 | 1 | | | | | |

[a] Data from von Hippel [33] and see text.

[b] Share of market rankings are derived by conversion of Tilton [34] data (p. 66, table 4–5) on percent of semiconductor shipments attributable to major firms into rankings (shipments data include in-house and government sales). Firms with the same shipment percent in given year are all given the same rank. Tilton's share of market data only covers the years 1957, 1960, 1963, and 1966. For innovations whose date of first commercial use (col. 1) falls between these years, data on the nearest of the years examined by Tilton are used. Conversion of SOM rankings into $ shipments was effected via use of Tilton's data on total semiconductor shipments (p. 90, table 4–7).

[c] IBM has, since 1962, been a major producer of silicon semiconductors for in-house use only, and thus "shipments" data are not available to determine IBM's market share rankings. Industry "guesstimates" of IBM's ranking in 1965 and 1967 place that firm conservatively among the top five producers for those years .

[d] Tilton, p. 52, table 4–1.

[e] Data from annual reports of parent companies. Fairchild was acquired by Fairchild Camera and Instrument in 1954, and therefore sales figures of the parent company are shown.

tion between innovation rates and market share). More empirical work will clearly be required on the issue.

*4.2. Benefit from output-embodied innovation knowledge appropriable by an innovating firm via creation of a firm-level quasi-monopoly*

I now move to a consideration of the mechanisms by which an innovating firm might hope to establish a quasi-monopoly with respect to all other firms, both current competitors and those currently outside the industry, and thus be in a position to capture benefit from output-embodied innovation knowledge via increases in profit rates and/or sales volume. I suggest that there are only three such mechanisms extant – patents, trade secrets (also termed know-how) and "response time" – when we exclude from consideration those comparative advantages one firm may have over another which, while they may aid an innovator, are really innovation-independent and may equally serve an imitator (e.g. a relatively favorable position with regard to finances, mineral rights, marketing channels, firm reputation, etc.). We will discuss each of these three extant mechanisms below.

As noted in section 3.1, a patent grants an inventor the right to exclude others from using his invention for a limited period in exchange for public disclosure of that invention. Patent legislation requires that this public disclosure be made at the time of the patent's issue and be in sufficient detail so that others "ordinarily skilled in the art" may readily imitate the invention, presumably upon the patent's expiration. The result of the public disclosure is that interested imitators have access to the invention and must be constrained by law, rather than by lack of knowledge, from using it – *if* the inventor is to be able to use the patent grant as a mechanism for maintaining a quasi-monopoly and garnering benefit from output-embodied innovation knowledge via his own exploitation of the invention. But, as we have seen previously, the law offers little effective protection to patent holders. The burden of finding any infringement is on the patentee – no mean task, particularly if the infringement does not involve a product sold on the open market but rather a process or machinery invention which an infringer may exploit and benefit from in the privacy of his factory. Moreover, the burden of prosecuting the infringer also falls on the patentee. Such prosecutions are notoriously long and expensive and studies of court records [27] have shown that the likelihood of a patent being held valid and infringed are on the order of three to one against the patent holder. Thus, the same evidence that led me to conclude earlier that the patent grant was not an effective mechanism for the capture of benefit from non-embodied innovation knowledge also leads me to conclude that the patent grant is not an effective mechanism for the capture of benefit from output-embodied innovation knowlege.

Trade secrets, a second possible means for the establishment of innovation-based quasi-monopolies at the level of the firm, refer to innovations which can be kept secret *after* development is completed and commercial exploitation begun. As was explained in section 3.2, secrecy can be maintained during commercial exploitation either because (1) the innovation cannot be "reverse engineered" and imitated even though available to inspection by would-be imitators skilled in the relevant analytical tools (the formula for Coca-Cola is the classic example of such) or (2) the innovation, while susceptible to reverse engineering if opened to the inspection of would-be imitators, can be hidden from such inspection by some means (e.g. process equipment developed by users and shielded within their own firms). As was noted earlier, essentially no hard data exist on the effectiveness with which innovations kept as trade secrets allow firms to establish firm-level quasi-monopolies and capture benefit from output-em-

bodied innovation knowledge. I am aware of two types of anecdotal data, however, which suggest that trade secrets can sometimes be a very effective benefit capture mechanism. First, many whom I have interviewed in corporations feel that the mechanism is very effective for innovations which can in fact be kept secret. (Logically, it is likely that the trade secret mechanism will be more effective in allowing the capture of benefit from output-embodied innovation knowledge than in allowing the capture of benefit from non-embodied innovation knowledge, as the latter use requires diffusion of the secret beyond the confines of the innovator's factory while the former does not.) Second, in some industries one can observe that firms incur significant expense to insure that outsiders do not get the chance to inspect their production equipment and/or techniques – implying that these firms do regard the knowledge protected as having significant economic value. [15] Clearly, more research into the effectiveness of trade secrets would be valuable.

The third mechanism noted above is one I term "response time". I define it as the period an imitator requires to bring an imitative product to market or to bring an imitative process to commercial usefulness when he has full and free access to any germane trade secrets or patented knowledge in the possession of the innovator. Response time exists simply because many barriers in addition to lack of knowledge must be overcome in order to bring any product or process – even an imitative one – to commercial reality. Engineering tooling must be designed, materials and components ordered, manufacturing plants made ready, marketing plans developed, etc. During the response time period an innovator by definition has a monopoly and is in a position to capture benefit from output-embodied innovation knowledge by increasing his rate of profit and/or his market share.

---

[15] Interestingly, there is a wide variation in the amount of effort firms exert to prevent inspection of their process trade secrets. In some firms and industries access is denied even to repairmen wishing to repair standard equipment located near proprietary equipment. In other firms and industries I have observed a willingness to allow free inspection of proprietary equipment and even a willingness to encourage its commercial manufacture and sale by others [30]. Such objectively codable differences in behavior may prove useful as one research measure of the economic value of trade secrets.

E. von Hippel / Innovation benefit                    109

In principle, if an imitator became aware of an innovator's protected knowledge at the moment he developed it there would be no response time protection for the innovator: both innovator and imitator could proceed with commercialization activities in tandem. Response time is an important innovation benefit capture mechanism in reality, however, because would-be imitators seldom become aware of an innovator's knowledge at the moment he develops it. Typically, in fact, an imitator only becomes aware of a promising new product when that product is introduced to the marketplace. Until that point the innovator has been able to protect his product from the eyes of interested competitors inside his factory. After that point, if the product is easily reverse engineered and has no patent protection only the response time mechanism can provide him with some quasi-monopoly protection from imitators.

The real world value of response time to innovators is suggested by the elaborate lengths to which innovators sometimes go to hide their new product plans prior to marketplace introduction – and the sometimes equally elaborate affects of would-be imitators to ferret these plans out. As in the case of trade secrets, however, little formal research exists on the value of response time – and what there is of it addresses "lead time" rather than response time.[16] Data from the one study I am aware of which touches on the correlation between the commercial success of a sample of industrial products and lead time, Project Sappho [36], indicate that the effect of lead time – and its response time component – may sometimes be easily discernible, however. If so, these could be empirically studied via retrospective measures such as relative commercial success of samples of "first-to-market" and "second-to-market" functionally equivalent product pairs (the measure used by Sappho).

[16] "Lead time" is commonly defined as the period starting when an innovator introduces a new product to the market and ending when the first "me-too" product is introduced by a competitor. Lead time may be caused by any of the three innovation benefit capture mechanisms presented in this paper or by numerous other factors. Thus, an innovator may seek to prolong his lead time beyond the period afforded by response time by denying would-be imitators access to relevant know-how or patents and/or by various other means such as adopting pricing strategies designed to forestall imitation [35].

The value of response (and lead time) to would-be innovators can be reasoned to be a function of various situation-specific factors. One such factor is the length of response time divided by length of customer purchase decision cycle. A high value of this factor favors the innovator over imitators. Consider one extreme example: a consumer "fad" item (very short purchase decision time) which sells in high volume for six months only. Assume that the item can be readily imitated – but can only be produced economically by mass-production tooling requiring six months to build. Obviously, response time here allows the innovator to monopolize the entire market if he can supply it with his initial tooling. At another extreme is an expensive capital equipment innovation which customers typically take two years to decide to buy, budget for, etc. – and which competitors can imitate in one year. Obviously, response time in this instance affords an innovator little protection. A second situation-specific factor involves the learning curve: the more units produced during the response time period and the steeper the learning curve, the greater the production cost advantage an innovator can accrue relative to potential imitators. A third factor is the size and "indivisibility" of production plant investment an innovation requires relative to market size. For example, if DuPont uses response time to invest in a special-purpose plant for the production of Teflon which is large enough to supply any foreseeable market expansion for several years ahead, incentives to imitate are considerably reduced.

## 5. Differences in the ability of would-be innovators to appropriate benefit from innovation-related knowledge

In section 2 I concluded that it would be possible in theory to model the functional locus of innovation in terms of the appropriability of innovation benefit if would-be innovators: (1) *are not* able to capture benefit from non-embodied knowledge; (2) *are* able to capture benefit from output-embodied knowledge arising from their output-embodied innovations; and (3) differ significantly in their ability to capture benefit from their output-embodied innovation knowledge. In section 3 I concluded that the two mechanisms which an innovator might use to capture benefit from non-embodied knowledge (namely, patents and trade secret legislation) are relatively ineffective, that would-be innovators in most industries are therefore *not* able to capture benefit from non-embodied knowledge and that model condition 1 was thus satisfied. In section 4 I concluded that model condition 2 was satisfied on logical grounds: since would-be innovators can only appropriate economic benefit from their innovations by selling non-embodied knowledge and/or output-embodied knowledge, and since the former cannot be done effectively in most industries, most innovators *must* appropriate economic benefit from output-embodied knowledge if they appropriate such benefit at all. In this section I proceed to a consideration of the third condition which must be met if the functional locus of innovation is to be predicted in terms of the appropriability of innovation benefit – presence of a significant difference in the *ability* of would-be innovators having different functional relationships to a given category of innovation to capture benefit from output-embodied innovation knowledge.

Clearly, a difference in the ability of would-be innovators to capture benefit from output-embodied innovation knowledge must be substantial if one is to be able to predict the functional locus of innovation in terms of this single variable. I will begin this section by describing a study which "proves-by-example" – that the differences of the required magnitude can exist in the real world and then will offer some tentative generalizations regarding characteristics of industries likely to be associated with the presence of such major differences.

*5.1. Differences in the ability to capture benefit from output-embodied innovation knowledge: the example*

The proof-by-example that innovators holding different functional relationships to the same set of innovations can differ substantially in their ability to capture innovation benefit draws heavily on a 1977 study by Lionetta [38] of innovation in a plastics fabrication technology called "pultrusion". [17]

In the portion of the study of interest here, [18] Lionetta studied the machinery used in the pultrusion process from the invention of that process in the early 1950s to 1977. He identified all successful process machine innovations which offered the machine user "a major increment in functional utility at the time of its introduction when judged relative to best practice extant at that time". Lionetta next sought to determine the "source" of each such innovation via a careful search of contemporary literature and by interviews with user and manufacturer personnel who were involved in or found to have knowledge of the innovation work. In some instances he found the innovation involved the development of equipment unique to pultrusion. In other instances the innovation involved a first application of equipment used in other industrial processes to the pultrusion process. If we define the innovating firm as the firm which built the first unit of equipment embodying the (original or adopted) process machinery innovation which was used in commercial pultrusion production, we find that eight of the nine major process machinery improvement innovations samples identified were developed by machinery users and only one by a machinery manufacturer [40]. [19]

---

pultrusion process involves pulling reinforcing material, usually fiberglass, simultaneously from a number of supply rolls into a tank containing a liquid thermoset resin such as polyester. The strands of reinforcement material emerge from the tank thoroughly wetted with resin and then pass through "preforming tooling" which aligns and compacts them into the desired cross-section. The compacted bundle of glass and liquid resin is then pulled through a heated die where the resin is cured and finally to a saw which cuts the continuously formed product into sections of the desired length. The entire pultrusion process is performed from start to finish on a single integrated machine. While the economic importance of this plastic fabrication process is still relatively small (only $60 million worth of "pultrusions" were produced in 1976), its use has grown at a real annual rate of 15–20% from 1967 to 1977, and some experts rank it second only to injection molding in terms of ultimate economic importance in the production of fiber-reinforced plastics [37].

[18] When a portion of Lionetta's study results were seen to be germane to the issues addressed in this paper, Lionetta was kind enough to join with the author in carefully cross-checking and updating the relevant subset. As a result, data presented here sometimes differ from the data presented in the 1977 study.

[19] This innovative machinery manufacturer, Goldsworthy Engineering, Inc., Torrence, Calif., was affiliated with a user of pultrusion machinery at Glastrusions, Inc., Torrence, Calif.,

---

[17] Currently limited to the manufacture of fiber-reinforced products of constant cross-section, the pultrusion process is used to fabricate such products as the fiberglass-reinforced rod used by makers of fiberglass fishing rods. In essence, the

In addition to determining the locus of process machinery innovation in pultrusion Lionetta examined the economics and structure of the US pultrusion machine user and pultrusion machine builder communities. He found approximately 40 firms using pultruders in 1976, producing an aggregate of $60 million worth of pultruded product, at an average price of $1.70 per pound and an average before tax profit of 12%. This product was produced on approximately 150 pultrusion machines, [20] each producing on the order of 200,000 pounds of pultrusions annually. Approximately 120 of these machines were found to have been "home-built" by the firms using them and only 30 to have been built by the only commercial builder, Goldsworthy Engineering, Inc. Pultrusion machine user firms were not able to supply useful data on the actual costs of the machines they had built over the years since they had often been built and rebuilt *ad hoc* by production engineers. However, Lionetta was able to estimate on the basis of data available on some recently built machines of "average" capacity (a machine capable of pultruding product with a cross-section of 6 by 7 inches) that a "home-built" machine of this capacity would have had a direct cost of $50,000–60,000 in 1977, while company price lists show that an equivalent machine from the sole commercial builder would have had a purchase price of approximately $95,000 at that time. Actual sales of commercially built pultruders were reported by the manufacturer to total four machines at an average price of $35,000 in the years prior to 1967 and 26 machines at approximately $105,000 [21] each in the period from 1967 to 1977. Sales, therefore, of commercially produced pultrusion equipment in the 1967–77 period were on the order of $270,000 per year.

The manufacturer reported sales during this period to be relatively flat despite the annual real increase in annual output of pultruded product averaging 15–20%.

Lionetta's data can be used to construct a test of reason which strongly supports the proposition that one functional category of would-be innovators (in this instance, the users of process machinery in the pultrusion industry) have a much greater ability to appropriate benefit from output-embodied innovation knowledge related to their innovations than do those having other functional relationships to the innovation (in this instance, process machinery manufacturers).

Recalling the mechanisms for the capture of benefit from output-embodied innovation knowledge discussed previously, consider first the relative ability of pultrusion machinery manufacturers and users to capture benefit from such knowledge via the establishment of firm-level quasi-monopolies. The two mechanisms which we found likely to be effective in the establishment of such monopolies were response time and trade secrets (know-how). In the instance of pultrusion machinery process innovations it is clear that only user innovators can hope to retain control of their innovation related know-how much beyond the point at which commercial use begins. This is so because pultrusion process machinery innovations can be reverse engineered if inspected by would-be imitators skilled in the art. And, while an innovating machine user can exploit the innovation commercially while keeping it hidden from such inspection behind his factory walls, an innovating machine builder must make the innovative equipment available to the inspection of potential purchasers if he is to reap output-embodied benefit from it. This in turn opens the way to imitation delayed only by the response time of would-be imitators.

Two categories of trade secret are germane to the process machinery innovations being considered here – trade secrets bearing on the use of innovative equipment and trade secrets bearing on its manufacture. For reasons analogous to those spelled out in the previous paragraph, I conclude that only users are in a position to benefit from trade secrets regarding the use of innovative equipment, because only users can exploit these commercially while keeping them secret from would-be imitators. In contrast and again for analogous reasons, I conclude that both machine builder and

---

at the time of the innovation work. As part of a conservative stance toward the "user as innovator" hypothesis being tested, however, this firm's innovations were coded as machine builder developed.

[20] Lionetta obtained estimates from experts which ranged from 87 to 200 extant pultrusion machines. Through computations based on average machine capacities he developed an estimate of 176 machines.

[21] The difference between the $95,000 list price for a commercial *equivalent* of an average home-built machine just noted in the text and Goldsworthy's average sales price is the inclusion of an optional RF curing unit costing on the order of $25,000 in many of the units sold by Goldsworthy but not present on home-built machines.

machine user have a similar capacity to keep trade secrets regarding the manufacture of innovative equipment, and that both the single extant pultrusion equipment manufacturer and the larger users have similar incentive to develop such, as both build pultrusion equipment on approximately the same scale.

Consider next the relative ability of pultrusion machinery manufacturers and users to capture benefit from output-embodied innovation knowledge via the establishment of industry-level quasi-monopolies. Barriers to entry, the mechanism which allows the establishment of an industry-level quasi-monopoly, presumably provide some protection against new entrants to both machine builders and machine users in the pultrusion field. Lionetta's data show, however, that the machine builder apparently is unable to appropriate benefit from output-embodied innovation knowledge as a result of these barriers because as noted earlier, users, although they do not enter the commercial machine business, have proven themselves capable of building machines to satisfy their in-house needs at a cost at or below a machine builder's sales price for similar machines – presumably because the user does not incur selling expenses as the machine builder must. And in the pultrusion industry the machine manufacturer does not make significantly more machines than the largest users – and thus cannot offset these extra costs via economy of scale savings.

In contrast, it is very likely that machine users can appropriate benefit from output-embodied innovation knowledge via increased profits and/or sales as a consequence of an innovation-related industry-level quasi-monopoly. This is so because process machinery innovations in pultrusion typically allow the pultrusion industry to enter new markets at the expense of competing materials such as aluminum by making it possible to manufacture new shapes via this method. Thus, hollow product tooling, one of the innovations whose antecedents were examined by Lionetta, enabled pultrusion to be used to manufacture shapes of hollow as well as solid cross-section. Similarly, the development of improved "pulling" mechanisms, also examined by Lionetta, made it possible to pultrude shapes of larger cross-sectional area than had been possible previously.

Accordingly we may conclude that process machinery users in the pultrusion industry have a much greater ability than machinery manufacturers to appropriate benefit from output-embodied innovation knowledge derived from firm- and industry-level quasi-monopolies. One can illustrate this discrepancy quantitatively via Lionetta's data which show that an additional pultrusion machine employed by a machines user will allow the manufacture of 200,000 pounds of additional pultrusions annually. At the 1976 annual sales price of $1.70 per pound and pre-tax profit of 12% we can see that such an additional volume will yield the machine user $41,000 additional pre-tax profit *annually*.

In contrast, each extra machine sold by a machine builder as a result of the innovations is worth only a one-time profit of $10,000 to that firm at the prevailing machine price of about $100,000 and pre-tax profit rate of 10%. Thus, the machine builder would have to sell approximately four additional units annually as a direct consequence of his innovation in order to obtain benefit from his output-embodied innovation knowledge equal to that obtained by an innovating user who has embodied the innovation in only one machine and sold an extra 200,000 pounds of product thereby. Such an incremental volume on the part of the machine builder seems implausibly high given the sales rate of 2.6 machines annually which that firm has recorded during the 1967–77 period. On the other hand, embodiment of the innovation in only one machine seems an implausibly conservative estimate for the larger user firms since, as I have determined via telephone survey, the top three firms in the field had more than 15 pultrusion machines each in 1978.

In sum, then, I propose that condition 3 holds in this instance. That is, I have shown a strongly discrepant ability of firms holding different functional relationships (user, manufacturer) to the same class of innovations to capture benefit from output-embodied innovation knowledge regarding these. Further, data on the locus of innovation in pultrusion are in accordance with what I would predict if conditions 1, 2, and 3 of the single factor model are met.

## 5.2. Toward generalization

In the pultrusion industry I found that process machinery users and process machinery manufacturers had sharply discrepant abilities to appropriate benefit from output-embodied innovation knowledge regarding process machinery innovations. I found, further, that the cause of this difference could be logically attributed to mechanisms for the appropriation of benefit from output-embodied innovation knowledge identified and discussed earlier in this paper. Specifically, I found that the pultrusion process machinery manufacturer was not in a position to establish and benefit from an industry-level quasi-monopoly with respect to process machinery innovations because users could – and did – construct machines embodying the innovations at a cost competitive with the manufacturer's price when that price incorporated only a "normal" level of profit. In contrast, I reasoned that users might well establish an industry-level quasi-monopoly and that this mechanism of benefit capture was therefore either ineffective for both users and manufacturers or effective for users only. Next, I found that pultrusion process machinery innovations could be reverse engineered if inspected by persons "skilled in the art". Since only user-innovators are in a position to appropriate benefit from output-embodied innovation knowledge characterizing their innovations while secreting them from inspection within their factory walls, I concluded that user-innovators were more favorably positioned than manufacturer-innovators with respect to establishing and maintaining firm-level quasi-monopolies based on response time and trade secrets related to the use of a process machinery innovation. In contrast, both users and manufacturers were found equally favorably positioned with respect to establishing and maintaining firm-level quasi-monopolies based on trade secrets related to the construction of innovative process machinery.

Since most process machinery innovations can be reverse engineered if inspected by someone skilled in the art – and since most process machinery can be constructed on ordinary metalworking machinery available to would-be innovators in all functional categories alike – I propose that our pultrusion industry findings are generalizable to most process machinery innovations. That is, we may generally expect that all but one mechanism for the capture of benefit from output-embodied innovation knowledge will favor the user – because only users can appropriate such benefit from innovative process machinery while shielding the

innovation from inspection by would-be imitators.[22] The sole mechanism *not* biased in favor of the user is, as was noted earlier, firm-level quasi-monopoly derived from trade secrets related to the construction of the process machinery innovation. Experience curve data indicate that the relative "amount" of this type of secret firms will acquire is a function of the relative number of machines they build.

On this basis one may venture the following economy-of-scale-related generalizations for all situations where users and manufacturers are the functional groups most favorably positioned to capture benefit from output-embodied innovation knowlege. When manufacturers of a given category of process machinery can reasonably expect to sell "many more" of a given process machinery innovation than any single large user can utilize, then process machinery manufacturers will be found to be the source of innovation in that category of process machines. Otherwise users will be found to develop – or pay for the development of – these. In a simple test of robustness of this generalization I interviewed process engineers at a razor blade manufacturer and a lamp manufacturer. In each instance the machine user firm was found to have developed and built the highly specialized equipment they required in-house. (An example of such equipment in the instance of the razor blade manufacturer was high-speed razor blade sharpening machinery and, in the instance of the lamp manufacturer, high-speed lamp assembly machinery). Both firms, however, were found to have purchased packaging machinery, used by many industries, from packaging machinery manufacturing firms.

The above generalization can be extended to explain why the locus of process machinery innovation might shift with time for some categories of process machinery, but not display such shift in others. Thus, the shift observed by Knight [42] from development of innovative computer hardware by users in the early days of that field to a later computer manufacturer locus of innovation is congruent with the single factor model. In contrast, I would not expect the locus of innovation to

---

[22] Note that there are exceptions to this user capability. For example, users of construction machinery used in the open clearly cannot shield innovations related to it "behind factory walls".

114                                    *E. von Hippel / Innovation benefit*

shift from user to manufacturer over time in the instance of razor blade sharpening machinery since the market for such specialized machines has been small in the past and will presumably remain so.

Although my own research to date on this variable has focused on the costs and benefits of certain categories of process machinery innovation, other categories of innovation look equally promising, and I would encourage investigation into many such. As noted earlier, Berger [5] and Boyden [6] have, for example, sampled plastics and plastics additive innovations respectively and have found all of these to have been developed by product manufacturers rather than product users. I suspect that further research would show this locus explicable in terms of the ability of users and manufacturers to appropriate benefit from output-embodied innovation knowledge in these categories of innovations. A particular plastic or additive is typically not essential to users since other materials exist which can do the job at a (usually minor) cost premium. To the manufacturer, however, a plastics and additive innovation which provides such a slight cost advantage may mean that major users of other materials (steel, aluminum, other plastics, etc.) replace these with the innovative material and quickly become major customers, thus allowing the innovator to capture significant benefit from output-embodied innovation knowledge.

In sum, I propose that the appropriability of benefit from output-embodied innovation knowledge is a variable which can usefully be incorporated in a model of the locus of innovation. I also propose that in some categories of innovation, not yet clearly delineated, the role of this variable in determining the locus of innovation is a strong one.

## References

[1] M.J. Peck, Inventions in the Postwar American Aluminum Industry, in: The Rate and Direction of Inventive Activity: Economic and Social Factors, A Report of the National Bureau of Economic Research (Princeton University Press, Princeton, NJ, 1962), pp. 279–298.

[2] K.E. Knight, A Study of Technological Innovation: The Evolution of Digital Computers, unpublished Ph. D. Dissertation, Carnegie Institute of Technology, 1963. Data shown in table 1 of this paper obtained from Knight's Appendix B, parts 2 and 3.

[3] J. Enos, Petroleum Progress and Profits (M.I.T. Press, Cambridge, MA, 1962).

[4] C. Freeman, Chemical Process Plant: Innovations and the World Market, National Institute Economic Review.

[5] A. Berger, Factors Influencing the Locus of Innovation Activity Leading to Scientific Instrument and Plastics Innovation, unpublished S.M. Thesis, M.I.T. Sloan School of Management, June, 1975.

[6] J. Boyden, A Study of the Innovation Process in the Plastics Additives Industry, unpublished S.M. Thesis, M.I.T. Sloan School of Management, January, 1976.

[7] W.G. Lionetta, Jr., Sources of Innovation Within the Pultrusion Industry, unpublished S.M. Thesis, M.I.T. Sloan School of Management, June, 1977. When a portion of Lionetta's study results were seen to be germane to the issues addressed in this paper, Lionetta was kind enough to join with the author in carefully cross-checking and updating the relevant subset. As a result, data presented in the present paper sometimes differ from the data presented in the 1977 study.

[8] E. von Hippel, The Dominant Role of Users in the Scientific Instrument Innovation Process, Research Policy, 5 (1976) 212–239.

[9] E. von Hippel, The Dominant Role of the User in Semiconductor and Electronic Subassembly Process Innovation, IEEE Transactions on Engineering Mangement, May, 1977.

[10] K.J. Arrow, Economic Welfare and the Allocation of Resources of Invention in: The Rate and Direction of Inventive Activity: Economic and Social Factors, A Report of the National Bureau of Economic Research (Princeton University Press, Princeton, NJ, 1962), pp. 609–626.

[11] R. Nelson, The Simple Economics of Basic Scientific Research, Journal of Political Economy, 67 (June 1959) 297–306.

[12] A. Pakes and M. Schankerman, The Rate of Obsolescence of Knowledge, Research Gestation Lags, and the Private Rate of Return to Research Resources, Discussion Paper Number 659, Harvard Institute of Economic Research, Harvard University, October, 1978.

[13] For a recent and extensive annotated bibliography of extant theoretical and empirical writings on this topic, see Institute for Defense Analyses, The Effects of Patent and Antitrust Laws, Regulations, and Practices on Innovation, 3 vols. National Technical Information Service (Arlington, VA, February, 1976).

[14] C.T. Taylor and Z.A. Silberston, The Economic Impact of the Patent System (Cambridge University Press, Cambridge, 1973).

[15] Ibid., p. 371.

[16] Ibid., see question 6 of section 6 of questionnaire, p. 396.

[17] Ibid., p. 30.

[18] Ibid., p. 196.

[19] F.M. Scherer et al., Patents and the Corporation, 2nd edition (Patents and The Corporation, J. Galvin, General Manager, Bedford, MA, 1959).

[20] The source of information in selecting the mail survey respondents was the list of corporate assignees in P.J. Federico, Distribution of Patents issued to Corporations

(1939–44), Study No. 3 of the Subcommittee on Patents, Trademarks, and Copyrights (Washington, DC, 1957), pp. 19–34.

[21] Scherer, op. cit., p. 107. A detailed breakdown of patent holdings of respondents is provided on pp. 108–109.

[22] Ibid., p. 117.

[23] Taylor and Silbertson, op cit., provides data in tables 8.4 (p. 153), 8.5 (p. 157), and 8.6 (p. 159) showing that only approximately half of the sampled license agreements in force in 1968 provided monetary return to the licensing firm in 1968. The distribution and amount of nonmonetary return possibly derived from these licenses in 1968 is not provided.

[24] R.W. Wilson, The Sale of Technology Through Licensing, unpublished Ph.D. Dissertation, Yale University, May, 1975.

[25] Ibid., Appendix, p. 152 ff., provides a detailed description of Wilson's data collection methods.

[26] Statement of Hon. David Ladd, Commissioner of Patents, before the Patents Trademarks and Copyrights Subcommittee of the Judiciary Committee, U.S. Senate, September 4, 1962, re: S.2225, as quoted in Elmer J. Gorn, Economic Value of Patents Practice and Invention Management (Reinhold, New York, 1964).

[27] See Carole Kitte. Patent Invalidity Studies: A Survey (National Science Foundation, Division of Policy Research and Analysis, January 1976), for references to and discussion of several such studies.

[28] D. Shapley, Electronics Industry Takes to Potting Its Products for Market, Science, 202 (November 24, 1978) 848–849. The practice of reverse engineering the IC designs of competitors is also discussed in How "Silicon Spies" get away with copying, Business Week, April 21 (1980) 178.

[29] Those interested in examining the literature which does exist on trade secrets will find the following two articles a useful starting point: J. Mahon, Trade Secrets and Patents Compared, Journal of the Patent Office Society, 50:8 (August 1968) 536; L. Orenbuch, Trade Secrets and the Patent Laws, Journal of the Patent Office Society, 52 (October 1979) 659.

[30] See, for example, Enos, op. cit., for a detailed examination of the licensing of patents and know-how and the related revenue streams in one industry.

[31] M. Olson, The Logic of Collective Action: Public Goods and the Theory of Groups (Harvard University Press, Cambridge, MA, 1965).

[32] E. von Hippel, Transferring Process Equipment Innovations from User-Innovators to Equipment Manufacturing Firms, R&D Management, 8 (October 1977) 13–22.

[33] E. von Hippel, The Dominant Role of the User, op. cit., p. 14.

[34] J.E. Tilton, International Diffusion of Technology: The Case of Semiconductors (The Brookings Institution, Washington, DC, 1971).

[35] D. Gaskins, Jr., Dynamics Limit Pricing: Optimal Pricing Under Threat of Entry, Journal of Economic Theory, 3 (September 1971) 306–322.

[36] B. Achilladelis et al., Report on Project Sappho to SRC: A Study of Success and Failure in Industrial Innovation (Science Policy Research Unit, University of Sussex, Brighton, August 1971), 2 vols. Table 3.8, vol. 1, p. 92. (Instrument data on that table are incorrect; numbers have been transposed. See Appendix C. Complete Data Matrix, code 1, vol. 2, p. 58, correct data.)

[37] S.H. Pickens, Pultrusion – The Accent on the Long Pull, Plastics Engineering, July (1975).

[38] Lionetta, op. cit.

[39] Ibid., table 9, pp. 50–51.

[40] Ibid., table 10, p. 57.

[41] Ibid., p. 25.

[42] Knight, op. cit.

# [18]

THE JOURNAL OF INDUSTRIAL ECONOMICS          0022-1821 $2.00
Volume XXXIV                December 1985                No. 2

## HOW RAPIDLY DOES NEW INDUSTRIAL TECHNOLOGY LEAK OUT?*

EDWIN MANSFIELD

There have been no systematic empirical studies of the speed at which various kinds of technological information leak out to rival firms. To help fill this gap, data were obtained from 100 American firms. According to the results, information concerning development decisions is generally in the hands of rivals within about 12 to 18 months, on the average, and information concerning the detailed nature and operation of a new product or process generally leaks out within about a year. These results have important implications both for incentives for innovation and for public policies aimed at stemming the outflow of technology.

### I. INTRODUCTION

To UNDERSTAND the process of industrial innovation and how rapidly innovations are imitated, it is obvious that economists should study the nature and extent of the information that firms have about their rivals' technology and R & D programs. Yet there have been no systematic empirical studies of the speed at which various kinds of technological information leak out to rival firms. In this paper, I summarize briefly the results of an investigation of this sort based on data obtained from 100 American firms. These results are some of the first that are available concerning this important topic.

### II. LEAKAGE OF INFORMATION CONCERNING DEVELOPMENT DECISIONS

How quickly is a firm's decision to develop a major new product or process known to its rivals? To obtain information on this score, a random sample of 100 firms was chosen from a list of firms in thirteen major manufacturing industries (chemicals, pharmaceuticals, petroleum, primary metals, electrical equipment, machinery, transportation equipment, instruments, stone, clay, and glass, fabricated metal products, food, rubber, and paper).[1] Each firm's chief executive officer was asked to provide an estimate of the average length

---

* The research on which this paper is based was supported by a grant from the National Science Foundation, which, of course, is not responsible for the views expressed here. I am indebted to the very large number of firms that provided the basic data without which this study could not have been carried out. Also, thanks go to Lawrence J. White of New York University for useful suggestions in revising the manuscript.

[1] This sample was chosen at random from a list of all firms in these industries spending over $1 million (or 1 percent of sales, if sales were at least $35 million) on R & D in 1981.

218

TABLE I

PERCENTAGE DISTRIBUTION OF FIRMS, BY AVERAGE NUMBER OF MONTHS BEFORE THE FIRM'S DECISION TO DEVELOP A MAJOR NEW PRODUCT OR PROCESS IS REPORTED TO BE KNOWN TO ITS RIVALS, 10 INDUSTRIES, UNITED STATES

| Industry | Products (Average Number of Months) | | | | | Processes (Average Number of Months) | | | | |
|---|---|---|---|---|---|---|---|---|---|---|
| | Less than 6 | 6 to 12 | 12 to 18 | 18 and more | Total[a] | Less than 6 | 6 to 12 | 12 to 18 | 18 and more | Total[a] |
| | (Percentage of Firms) | | | | | | | | | |
| Chemicals | 10 | 20 | 40 | 30 | 100 | 0 | 11 | 11 | 78 | 100 |
| Pharmaceuticals | 29 | 14 | 14 | 43 | 100 | 0 | 0 | 33 | 67 | 100 |
| Petroleum | 0 | 44 | 44 | 11 | 100 | 10 | 40 | 10 | 40 | 100 |
| Primary Metals | 40 | 20 | 20 | 20 | 100 | 20 | 60 | 20 | 0 | 100 |
| Electrical Equipment | 22 | 33 | 33 | 11 | 100 | 0 | 43 | 0 | 57 | 100 |
| Machinery | 0 | 43 | 21 | 36 | 100 | 0 | 25 | 25 | 50 | 100 |
| Transportation Equipment | 25 | 25 | 25 | 25 | 100 | 0 | 33 | 33 | 33 | 100 |
| Instruments | 18 | 27 | 36 | 18 | 100 | 20 | 20 | 20 | 40 | 100 |
| Stone, Clay, and Glass | 20 | 0 | 20 | 60 | 100 | 0 | 0 | 20 | 80 | 100 |
| Other[b] | 33 | 17 | 25 | 25 | 100 | 20 | 30 | 20 | 30 | 100 |
| Average | 20 | 24 | 28 | 28 | | 7 | 26 | 19 | 48 | |

Source: see section II.
[a] Because of rounding errors, figures sometimes do not sum to total.
[b] Fabricated products, food, rubber, and paper are included in the "other" category.

of time before such information is in the hands of at least some of its rivals. Of course, it is not easy to pinpoint exactly when the decision is made to develop a product or process, because for each product or process there generally is a series of such decisions, not one. Thus, we asked each firm to base its estimate on the first such decision it made concerning a particular product or process. For obvious reasons, this should result in a conservative estimate of the speed at which such information leaks out.

According to the firms in our sample, information concerning development decisions of this sort is generally in the hands of at least some of their rivals within about 12 to 18 months, on the average, after the decision is made (Table I).[2] For about one-fifth of the firms, information leaks out within 6 months, on the average, in the case of new product development. (In chemicals and glass, leakage of this sort occurs somewhat more slowly than in other industries.) Although firms ordinarily cannot tell precisely when such information is in the hands of their rivals, the firms in our sample seemed to feel that the averages they presented were accurate enough for present purposes. Nonetheless, it is obvious that the data in Table I (as well as Table II) are rough approximations.

Because new processes can be developed with less communication and interaction with other firms than can new products, process development decisions tend to leak out more slowly than product development decisions in practically all industries.[3] However, the difference, on the average (measured by the median), is less than 6 months. Thus, for both processes and products, the odds are better than 50-50 that a development decision will leak out in less than 18 months. If it takes about three years or more before a major new product or process is developed and commercialized (which is fairly typical in many industries), this means that there is a better-than-even chance that the decision will leak out before the innovation project is half completed.

## III. LEAKAGE OF INFORMATION CONCERNING A NEW PRODUCT OR PROCESS

Although rival firms are interested in a firm's development decisions, they generally are even more interested in the detailed nature and operation of the new product or process developed by the firm. That is, they would like to know how it functions and is made. According to the firms in our sample, this information is in the hands of at least some of their rivals within about a year,

---

[2] Although there are 13 industries, four (fabricated metal products, food, rubber, and paper) are lumped together as "other" in Table I because the sample contains relatively few firms in each of these industries. There was little or no problem of nonresponse. Only one firm provided no information. Besides the firms in the sample, other firms were contacted to obtain related types of information and to test the questionnaire. Practically all of the data were obtained through mail questionnaires and correspondence.

[3] For further discussion of the differences between products and processes in the ease of imitation, see Mansfield, Rapoport, Romeo, Villani, Wagner, and Husic [1977].

220

TABLE II

PERCENTAGE DISTRIBUTION OF FIRMS, BY AVERAGE NUMBER OF MONTHS (AFTER DEVELOPMENT) BEFORE THE NATURE AND OPERATION OF A NEW PRODUCT OR PROCESS ARE REPORTED TO BE KNOWN TO THE FIRM'S RIVALS, 10 INDUSTRIES, UNITED STATES.

| Industry | Products (Average Number of Months) | | | | | Processes (Average Number of Months) | | | | |
|---|---|---|---|---|---|---|---|---|---|---|
| | Less than 6 | 6 to 12 | 12 to 18 | 18 and more | Total[a] | Less than 6 | 6 to 12 | 12 to 18 | 18 and more | Total[a] |
| | (Percentage of Firms) | | | | | | | | | |
| Chemicals | 18 | 36 | 9 | 36 | 100 | 0 | 0 | 10 | 90 | 100 |
| Pharmaceuticals | 57 | 14 | 29 | 0 | 100 | 0 | 33 | 0 | 67 | 100 |
| Petroleum | 22 | 33 | 22 | 22 | 100 | 10 | 50 | 10 | 30 | 100 |
| Primary Metals | 40 | 20 | 0 | 40 | 100 | 40 | 40 | 0 | 20 | 100 |
| Electrical Equipment | 38 | 50 | 12 | 0 | 100 | 14 | 14 | 57 | 14 | 100 |
| Machinery | 31 | 31 | 31 | 8 | 100 | 10 | 20 | 0 | 40 | 100 |
| Transportation Equipment | 25 | 50 | 0 | 25 | 100 | 0 | 67 | 0 | 33 | 100 |
| Instruments | 50 | 38 | 12 | 0 | 100 | 33 | 33 | 33 | 0 | 100 |
| Stone, Clay, and Glass | 40 | 60 | 0 | 0 | 100 | 0 | 20 | 20 | 60 | 100 |
| Other[b] | 31 | 15 | 15 | 38 | 100 | 27 | 0 | 36 | 36 | 100 |
| Average | 35 | 35 | 13 | 17 | | 13 | 28 | 20 | 39 | |

Source: see section II.
[a] See note a, Table I.
[b] See note b, Table I.

on the average, after a new product is developed (Table II).[4] Indeed, for over one-third of the firms, it is in their hands within 6 months. For processes, this information leaks out more slowly, for reasons cited above. But even in this case, it generally leaks out in less than about 15 months. The major exception is chemical processes which frequently can be kept secret for a number of years.

There are many channels through which this information spreads. In some industries there is considerable movement of personnel from one firm to another, and there are informal communications networks among engineers and scientists working at various firms, as well as professional meetings at which information is exchanged. In other industries, input suppliers and customers are important channels (since they pass on a great deal of relevant information), patent applications are scrutinized very carefully, and reverse engineering is carried out. In still other industries, the diffusion process is accelerated by the fact that firms do not go to great lengths to keep such information secret, partly because they believe that it would be futile in any event. Thus, the intelligence-gathering process varies considerably from industry to industry (and from case to case).[5] In view of this diversity, it is remarkable that, with the exception of processes in a few industries like chemicals, there seems to be so little difference among industries in the rate of diffusion of such information. In practically all industries in Table II, the median time lag for products is between 6 and 12 months, and the median for processes (other than chemicals and drugs) is 6 to 18 months.

Of course, the fact that information of this sort leaks out relatively quickly does not mean that imitation will occur equally fast. It often takes considerable time to invent around patents (if they exist), to develop prototypes, to alter or build plant and equipment, and to engage in the manufacturing and marketing start-up activities required to introduce an imitative product or process. (The factors determining the cost and length of time taken by these activities are taken up in Mansfield, Schwartz, and Wagner [1981].) Nonetheless, the basic information concerning the nature and operation of the innovation, even if it is not sufficient in many cases to permit the immediate introduction of an imitative product or process, is of great importance to the innovator's rivals. And if it is true (as Table II indicates) that information of this sort is very likely to find its way into the hands of rivals within a year or two, this has obvious and important implications for both the incentives for innovation and for public policies aimed at stemming the outflow of technology to other countries.

---

[4] As in the case of Table I, the data in Table II should be viewed as rough approximations. See section II.

[5] For some relevant discussion concerning the electronics industry, see Rogers [1982]. Based on interviews I carried out with a sample of European and Canadian firms, there is a widespread feeling that information of this sort spreads more rapidly in the United States than in Europe, but the evidence is fragmentary.

222                    EDWIN MANSFIELD

### IV. IMPLICATIONS AND CONCLUSIONS

Specifically, the above findings seem to have at least three major implications. First, they help to explain why industrial innovations so often are imitated relatively soon after first introduction. Mansfield, Schwartz, and Wagner [1981] found that about 60 percent of the patented innovations in their sample were imitated within four years. Given that development decisions and new technology leak out so quickly (and that it is so often possible to invent around patents), it is easy to understand why this was the case. Moreover, these results provide new insight into the problems involved in providing proper incentives for innovation in a free-enterprise economy. The fact that information concerning new industrial technology spreads so rapidly helps to explain why many firms have great difficulty in appropriating much of the social benefits from their innovations.[6]

Second, the results suggest that differences in the rate of diffusion of technological information do not play a major role in explaining inter-industry differences in the ease with which innovations can be imitated. The interindustry differences in Table II seem too small to be of major importance in this regard.[7] In a previous paper,[8] we estimated the average cost of imitation in a variety of industries, studied the determinants of this cost, and showed that this cost was directly related to an industry's concentration level. Although one might suppose that there are considerable differences in the rate of diffusion of technological information, and that these differences are responsible for substantial differences in imitation costs (and thus for differences in concentration levels), this does not seem to be the case.

Third, turning to issues of public policy, the results help to indicate the magnitude of the difficulties faced by recent (and not so recent) attempts by the US government to prevent the outflow to other countries of new American technology. As is well known, the United States has tried in a variety of ways to stem the flow of defense-related industrial technology to various Communist countries.[9] Also, both government agencies and firms (like IBM) have been concerned about improper leaks of industrial technology

---

[6] Of course, it should be stressed once again that Tables I and II reflect firms' perceptions of how quickly technological information leaks out to their rivals, and that these perceptions undoubtedly contain errors. However, the fact that Tables I and II are so consistent with the data in Mansfield, Schwartz, and Wagner (1981) suggests that these tables, while only rough approximations, provide a reasonably adequate general picture. Moreover, for many important purposes, the firms' perceptions are what matter most. For example, firms' perceptions of how rapidly their new technology will leak out to their rivals determines how much of the social benefits of a prospective innovation they believe they can appropriate, and thus whether or not they are willing to develop and introduce such an innovation.

[7] Also, there is no direct relationship between an industry's average four-firm concentration ratio and its median in Table II. However, evidence of this sort is obviously very crude.

[8] See Mansfield, Schwartz, and Wagner [1981].

[9] For example, see 'Technology Transfer: A Policy Nightmare', *Business Week*, April 4, 1983. Also, Stobaugh and Wells [1984] and US Department of Commerce [1983] contain relevant material.

HOW RAPIDLY DOES NEW INDUSTRIAL TECHNOLOGY LEAK OUT?    223

to foreign firms. If the leakages typically are as quick and as great as our results seem to indicate, such efforts clearly face enormous problems.[10]

EDWIN MANSFIELD,                                                    ACCEPTED APRIL 1985
*Department of Economics,*
*University of Pennsylvania,*
*Philadelphia,*
*Pennsylvania 19104,*
*USA.*

### REFERENCES

MANSFIELD, E., SCHWARTZ, M. and WAGNER, S., 1981, 'Imitation Costs and Patents: An Empirical Study', *Economic Journal*, 91 (December), pp. 907–918.

MANSFIELD, E., ROMEO, A., SCHWARTZ, M., TEECE, D., WAGNER, S. and BRACH, P., 1982, *Technology Transfer, Productivity, and Economic Policy* (W. W. Norton, New York).

MANSFIELD, E., RAPOPORT, J., ROMEO, A., VILLANI, E., WAGNER, S. and HUSIC, F., 1977, *The Production and Application of New Industrial Technology* (W. W. Norton, New York).

ROGERS, E., 1982, 'Information Exchange and Technological Information', in D. Sahal (ed.), *The Transfer and Utilization of Technical Knowledge* (Lexington Books, Lexington).

STOBAUGH, R. and WELLS, L. (eds.), 1984, *Technology Crossing Borders* (Harvard Business School, Boston).

US DEPARTMENT OF COMMERCE, 1983, *An Assessment of US Competitiveness in High Technology Industries* (Government Printing Office, Washington, DC).

[10] In this connection, it is worth noting that the technologies transferred by US-based multinational firms to their overseas subsidiaries seem to leak out to non-US firms more slowly than is indicated by Table II. See Mansfield, Romeo, Schwartz, Teece, Wagner, and Brach [1982], pp. 38–40. Where possible, these firms may tend to avoid transferring overseas those technologies that are likely to leak out relatively quickly. (There is evidence that these firms are more hesitant to send overseas their process technology than their product technology, because they feel that the diffusion of process technology, once it goes abroad, is harder to control. See *ibid.*, p. 54.) Also, holding other factors constant, one would expect that American technology would leak out more rapidly, on the average, to US firms than to non-US firms.

# [19]

## COMPETING TECHNOLOGIES, INCREASING RETURNS, AND LOCK-IN BY HISTORICAL EVENTS*

*W. Brian Arthur*

This paper explores the dynamics of allocation under increasing returns in a context where increasing returns arise naturally: agents choosing between technologies competing for adoption.

Modern, complex technologies often display increasing returns to adoption in that the more they are adopted, the more experience is gained with them, and the more they are improved.[1] When two or more increasing-return technologies 'compete' then, for a 'market' of potential adopters, insignificant events may by chance give one of them an initial advantage in adoptions. This technology may then improve more than the others, so it may appeal to a wider proportion of potential adopters. It may therefore become further adopted and further improved. Thus a technology that by chance gains an early lead in adoption may eventually 'corner the market' of potential adopters, with the other technologies becoming locked out. Of course, under different 'insignificant events' – unexpected successes in the performance of prototypes, whims of early developers, political circumstances – a different technology might achieve sufficient adoption and improvement to come to dominate. Competitions between technologies may have multiple potential outcomes.

It is well known that allocation problems with increasing returns tend to exhibit multiple equilibria, and so it is not surprising that multiple outcomes should appear here. Static analysis can typically locate these multiple equilibria, but usually it cannot tell us *which* one will be 'selected'. A dynamic approach might be able to say more. By allowing the possibility of 'random events' occurring during adoption, it might examine how these influence 'selection' of the outcome – how some sets of random 'historical events' might cumulate to drive the process towards one market-share outcome, others to drive it towards another. It might also reveal how the two familiar increasing-returns properties of *non-predictability* and *potential inefficiency* come about: how increasing returns act to magnify chance events as adoptions take place, so that *ex-ante* knowledge of adopters' preferences and the technologies' possibilities may not suffice to predict the 'market outcome'; and how increasing returns

* I thank Robin Cowan, Paul David, Joseph Farrell, Ward Hanson, Charles Kindleberger, Richard Nelson, Nathan Rosenberg, Paul Samuelson, Martin Shubik, and Gavin Wright for useful suggestions and criticisms. An earlier version of part of this paper appeared in 1983 as Working Paper 83–90 at the International Institute for Applied Systems Analysis, Laxenburg, Austria. Support from the Centre for Economic Policy Research, Stanford, and from the Guggenheim Foundation is acknowledged.

[1] Rosenberg (1982) calls this 'Learning by Using' (see also Atkinson and Stiglitz, 1969). Jet aircraft designs like the Boeing 727, for example, undergo constant modification and they improve significantly in structural soundness, wing design, payload capacity and engine efficiency as they accumulate actual airline adoption and use.

might drive the adoption process into developing a technology that has inferior long-run potential. A dynamic approach might also point up two new properties: *inflexibility* in that once an outcome (a dominant technology) begins to emerge it becomes progressively more 'locked in'; and *non-ergodicity* in that historical 'small events' are not averaged away and 'forgotten' by the dynamics – they may decide the outcome.

This paper contrasts the dynamics of technologies' 'market shares' under conditions of increasing, diminishing and constant returns. It pays special attention to how returns affect predictability, efficiency, flexibility, and ergodicity; and to the circumstances under which the economy might become locked-in by 'historical events' to the monopoly of an inferior technology.

## I. A SIMPLE MODEL

Nuclear power can be generated by light-water, or gas-cooled, or heavy-water, or sodium-cooled reactors. Solar energy can be generated by crystalline-silicon or amorphous-silicon technologies. I abstract from cases like this and assume in an initial, simple model that two new technologies, $A$ and $B$, 'compete' for adoption by a large number of economic agents. The technologies are not *sponsored*[2] or strategically manipulated by any firm; they are open to all. Agents are simple consumers of the technologies who act directly or indirectly as developers of them.

Agent $i$ comes into the market at time $t_i$; at this time he chooses the latest version of either technology $A$ or technology $B$; and he uses this version thereafter.[3] Agents are of two types, $R$ and $S$, with equal numbers in each, the two types independent of the times of choice but differing in their preferences, perhaps because of the use to which they will put their choice. The version of $A$ or $B$ each agent chooses is fixed or frozen in design at his time of choice, so that his payoff is affected only by past adoptions of his chosen technology. (Later I examine the expectations case where payoffs are also affected by future adoptions.)

Not all technologies enjoy increasing returns with adoption. Sometimes factor inputs are bid upward in price so that diminishing returns accompany adoption. Hydro-electric power, for example, becomes more costly as dam sites become scarcer and less suitable. And some technologies are unaffected by adoption – their returns are constant. I include these cases by assuming that the returns to choosing $A$ or $B$ realised by any agent (the net present value of the version of the technology available to him) depend upon the number of previous adopters, $n_A$ and $n_B$, at the time of his choice (as in Table 1[4]) with

---

[2] Following terminology introduced in Arthur (1983), *sponsored* technologies are proprietary and capable of being priced and strategically manipulated; *unsponsored* technologies are generic and not open to manipulation or pricing.

[3] Where technologies are improving, it may pay adopters under certain conditions to wait; so that no adoptions take place (Balcer and Lippman, 1984; Mamer and McCardle, 1987). We can avoid this problem by assuming adopters need to replace an obsolete technology that breaks down at times $\{t_i\}$.

[4] More realistically, where the technologies have uncertain monetary returns we can assume von Neumann-Morgenstern agents, with Table 1 interpreted as the resulting determinate expected-utility payoffs.

Table 1

*Returns to Choosing A or B given Previous Adoptions*

|            | Technology $A$ | Technology $B$ |
|------------|----------------|----------------|
| $R$-agent  | $a_R + rn_A$   | $b_R + rn_B$   |
| $S$-agent  | $a_S + sn_A$   | $b_S + sn_B$   |

increasing, diminishing, or constant returns to adoption given by $r$ and $s$ simultaneously positive, negative, or zero. I also assume $a_R > b_R$ and $a_S < b_S$ so that $R$-agents have a natural preference for $A$, and $S$-agents have a natural preference for $B$.

To complete this model, I want to define carefully what I mean by 'chance' or 'historical events'. Were we to have infinitely detailed prior knowledge of events and circumstances that might affect technology choices – political interests, the prior experience of developers, timing of contracts, decisions at key meetings – the outcome or adoption market-share gained by each technology would presumably be determinable in advance. We can conclude that our limited discerning power, or more precisely the limited discerning power of an implicit *observer*, may cause indeterminacy of outcome. I therefore define 'historical small events' to be those events or conditions that are outside the *ex-ante* knowledge of the observer – beyond the resolving power of his 'model' or abstraction of the situation.

To return to *our* model, let us assume an observer who has full knowledge of all the conditions and returns functions, except the set of events that determines the times of entry and choice $\{t_i\}$ of the agents. The observer thus 'sees' the choice order as a binary sequence of $R$ and $S$ types with the property that an $R$ or an $S$ comes $n$th in the adoption line with equal likelihood, that is, with probability one half.

We now have a simple neoclassical allocation model where two types of agents choose between $A$ and $B$, each agent choosing his preferred alternative when his time comes. The supply (or returns) functions are known, as is the demand (each agent demands one unit inelastically). Only one small element is left open, and that is the set of historical events that determine the sequence in which the agents make their choice. Of interest is the adoption-share outcome in the different cases of constant, diminishing, and increasing returns, and whether the fluctuations in the order of choices these small events introduce make a difference to adoption shares.

We will need some properties. I will say that the process is: *predictable* if the small degree of uncertainty built in 'averages away' so that the observer has enough information to pre-determine market shares accurately in the long-run; *flexible* if a subsidy or tax adjustment to one of the technologies' returns can always influence future market choices; *ergodic* (not path-dependent) if different sequences of historical events lead to the same market outcome with probability one. In this allocation problem choices define a 'path' or sequence of $A$- and $B$-technology versions that become adopted or 'developed', with early adopters possibly steering the process onto a development path that is right for them, but one that may be regretted by later adopters. Accordingly, and in line with other sequential-choice problems, I will adopt a 'no-regret' criterion and say that the process is *path-efficient* if at all times equal development (equal adoption) of the technology that is behind in adoption would not have paid off better.[5] (These informal definitions are made precise in the Appendix.)

*Allocation in the Three Regimes*

Before examining the outcome of choices in our $R$ and $S$ agent model, it is instructive to look at how the dynamics would run in a trivial example with increasing-returns where agents are of one type only (Table 2). Here choice order does not matter; agents are all the same; and unknown events can make no difference so that ergodicity is not an issue. The first agent chooses the more favourable technology, $A$ say. This enhances the returns to adopting $A$. The next agent *a-fortiori* chooses $A$ too. This continues, with $A$ chosen each time, and $B$ incapable of 'getting started'. The end result is that $A$ 'corners the market' and $B$ is excluded. This outcome is trivially predictable, and path-efficient if returns rise at the same rate. Notice though that if returns increase at different rates, the adoption process may easily become path-inefficient, as Table 2

Table 2

*An Example: Adoption Payoffs for Homogeneous Agents*

| Number of previous adoptions | 0 | 10 | 20 | 30 | 40 | 50 | 60 | 70 | 80 | 90 | 100 |
|---|---|---|---|---|---|---|---|---|---|---|---|
| Technology $A$ | 10 | 11 | 12 | 13 | 14 | 15 | 16 | 17 | 18 | 19 | 20 |
| Technology $B$ | 4 | 7 | 10 | 13 | 16 | 19 | 22 | 25 | 28 | 31 | 34 |

shows. In this case after thirty choices in the adoption process, all of which are $A$, equivalent adoption of $B$ would have delivered higher returns. But if the process has gone far enough, a given subsidy-adjustment $g$ to $B$ can no longer close the gap between the returns to $A$ and the returns to $B$ at the starting point. Flexibility is not present here; the market becomes increasingly 'locked-in' to an inferior choice.

    Now let us return to the case of interest, where the unknown choice-sequence of two types of agents allows us to include some notion of historical 'small events'. Begin with the constant-returns case, and let $n_A(n)$ and $n_B(n)$ be the number of choices of $A$ and $B$ respectively, when $n$ choices in total have been made. We can describe the process by $x_n$, the market share of $A$ at stage $n$, when

---

[5] An alternative efficiency criterion might be total or aggregate payoff (after $n$ choices). But in this problem we have two agent types with different preferences operating under the 'greedy algorithm' of each agent taking the best choice at hand for himself; it is easy to show that under any returns regime maximisation of total payoffs is never guaranteed.

$n$ choices in total have been made. We will write the difference in adoption, $n_A(n) - n_B(n)$ as $d_n$. The market share of $A$ is then expressible as

$$x_n = 0{\cdot}5 + d_n/2n. \qquad (1)$$

Note that through the variables $d_n$ and $n$ – the difference and total – we can fully describe the dynamics of adoption of $A$ versus $B$. In this constant-returns situation $R$-agents always choose $A$ and $S$-agents always choose $B$, regardless of the number of adopters of either technology. Thus the way in which adoption of $A$ and $B$ cumulates is determined simply by the sequence in which $R$- and $S$-agents 'line up' to make their choice, $n_A(n)$ increasing by one unit if the next agent in line is an $R$, with $n_B(n)$ increasing by one unit if the next agent in line is an $S$, and with the difference in adoption, $d_n$, moving upward by one unit or downward one unit accordingly. To our observer, the choice-order is random, with agent types equally likely. Hence to him, the state $d_n$ appears to perform a simple coin-toss gambler's random walk with each 'move' having equal probability $0{\cdot}5$.

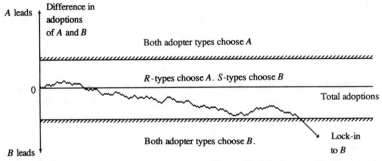

Fig. 1. Increasing returns adoption: a random walk with absorbing barriers

In the increasing-returns case, these simple dynamics are modified. New $R$-agents, who have a natural preference for $A$, will switch allegiance if by chance adoption pushes $B$ far enough *ahead* of $A$ in numbers and in payoff. That is, new $R$-agents will 'switch' if

$$d_n = n_A(n) - n_B(n) < \Delta_R = \frac{(b_R - a_R)}{r}. \qquad (2)$$

Similarly new $S$-agents will switch preference to $A$ if numbers adopting $A$ become sufficiently ahead of the numbers adopting $B$, that is, if

$$d_n = n_A(n) - n_B(n) > \Delta_S = \frac{(b_S - a_S)}{s}. \qquad (3)$$

Regions of choice now appear in the $d_n$, $n$ plane (see Fig. 1), with boundaries between them given by (2) and (3). Once one of the outer regions is entered, both agent types choose the same technology, with the result that this technology further increases its lead. Thus in the $d_n$, $n$ plane (2) and (3) describe barriers that 'absorb' the process. Once either is reached by random movement of $d_n$, the process ceases to involve both technologies – it is 'locked-in' to one technology only. Under increasing returns then, the adoption process becomes a random walk with absorbing barriers. I leave it to the reader to show that the allocation process with diminishing returns appears to our observer as a random walk with *reflecting* barriers given by expressions similar to (2) and (3).

### Properties of the Three Regimes

We can now use the elementary theory of random walks to derive the properties of this choice process under the different linear returns regimes. For convenient reference the results are summarised in Table 3. To prove these properties, we

Table 3

*Properties of the Three Regimes*

|  | Predictable | Flexible | Ergodic | Necessarily path-efficient |
|---|---|---|---|---|
| Constant returns | Yes | No | Yes | Yes |
| Diminishing returns | Yes | Yes | Yes | Yes |
| Increasing returns | No | No | No | No |

need first to examine long-term adoption shares. Under constant returns, the market is shared. In this case the random walk ranges free, but we know from random walk theory that the standard deviation of $d_n$ increases with $\sqrt{n}$. It follows that the $d_n/2n$ term in equation (1) disappears and that $x_n$ tends to 0·5 (with probability one), so that the market is split 50-50. In the diminishing returns case, again the adoption market is shared. The difference-in-adoption, $d_n$, is trapped between finite constants; hence $d_n/2n$ tends to zero as $n$ goes to infinity, and $x_n$ must approach 0·5. (Here the 50-50 market split results from the returns falling at the same rate.) In the increasing-returns-absorbing-barrier case, by contrast, the adoption share of $A$ *must* eventually become zero or one. This is because in an absorbing random walk $d_n$ eventually crosses a barrier with probability one. Therefore the two technologies cannot coexist indefinitely: one *must* exclude the other.

Predictability is therefore guaranteed where the returns are constant, or diminishing: in both cases a forecast that the market will settle to 50-50 will be correct, with probability one. In the increasing returns case, however, for accuracy the observer must predict $A$'s eventual share either as 0 or 100%. But either choice will be wrong with probability one-half. Predictability is lost. Notice though that the observer *can* predict that one technology will take the market; theoretically he can also predict that it will be $A$ with probability $s(a_R-b_R)/[s(a_R-b_R)+r(b_S-a_S)]$; but he cannot predict the actual market-share outcome with any accuracy – in spite of his knowledge of supply and demand conditions.

Flexibility in the constant-returns case is at best partial. Policy adjustments to the returns can affect choices at all times, but only if they are large enough to bridge the gap in preferences between technologies. In the two other regimes adjustments corespond to a shift of one or both of the barriers. In the diminishing-returns case, an adjustment $g$ can always affect future choices (in absolute numbers, if not in market shares), because reflecting barriers continue to influence the process (with probability one) at times in the future. Therefore diminishing returns are flexible. Under increasing returns however, once the process is absorbed into $A$ and $B$, the subsidy or tax adjustment necessary to shift the barriers enough to influence choices (a precise index of the degree to which the system is 'locked-in') increases without bound. Flexibility does not hold.

Ergodicity can be shown easily in the constant and diminishing returns cases. With constant returns only extraordinary line-ups (for example, twice as many $R$-agents as $S$-agents appearing indefinitely) with associated probability zero can cause deviation from fifty-fifty. With diminishing returns, any sequence of historical events – any line-up of the agents – must still cause the process to remain between the reflecting barriers and drive the market to fifty-fifty. Both cases forget their small-event history. In the increasing returns case the situation is quite different. Some proportion of agent sequences causes the market outcome to 'tip' towards $A$, the remaining proportion causes it to 'tip' towards $B$. (Extraordinary line-ups – say $S$ followed by $R$ followed by $S$ followed by $R$ and so on indefinitely – that could cause market sharing, have probability or measure zero.) Thus, the small events that determine $\{t_i\}$ *decide* the path of market shares; the process is non-ergodic or path-dependent – it is determined by its small-event history.

Path-efficiency is easy to prove in the constant- and diminishing-returns cases. Under constant-returns, previous adoptions do not affect pay-off. Each agent-type chooses its preferred technology and there is no gain foregone by the failure of the lagging technology to receive further development (further adoption). Under diminishing returns, if an agent chooses the technology that is ahead, he must prefer it to the available version of the lagging one. But further adoption of the lagging technology by definition lowers its payoff. Therefore there is no possibility of choices leading the adoption process down an inferior development path. Under increasing returns, by contrast, development of an inferior option can result. Suppose the market locks in to technology $A$. $R$-agents do not lose; but $S$-agents would each gain $(b_S - a_S)$ if their favoured technology $B$ had been equally developed and available for choice. There is regret, at least for one agent type. Inefficiency can be exacerbated if the technologies improve at different rates. An early run of agent-types who prefer an initially attractive but slow-to-improve technology can lock the market in to this inferior option; equal development of the excluded technology in the long run would pay off better to both types.

*Extensions, and the Rational Expectations Case*

It is not difficult to extend this basic model in various directions. The same qualitative results hold for $M$ technologies in competition, and for agent types in unequal proportions (here the random walk 'drifts'). And if the technologies arrive in the market at different times, once again the dynamics go through as before, with the process now starting with initial $n_A$ or $n_B$ not at zero. Thus in practice an early-start technology may already be locked in, so that a new potentially-superior arrival cannot gain a footing.

Where agent numbers are finite, and not expanding indefinitely, absorption or reflection and the properties that depend on them still assert themeselves providing agent numbers are large relative to the numerical width of the gap between switching barriers.

For technologies *sponsored* by firms, would the possibility of strategic action alter the outcomes just described? A complete answer is not yet known. Hanson (1985) shows in a model based on the one above that again market exclusion goes through: firms engage in penetration pricing, taking losses early on in exchange for potential monopoly profits later, and all but one firm exit with probability one. Under strong discounting, however, firms may be more interested in immediate sales than in shutting rivals out, and market sharing can reappear.[6]

Perhaps the most interesting extension is the expectations case where agents' returns are affected by the choices of future agents. This happens for example with *standards*, where it is matters greatly whether later users fall in with one's own choice. Katz and Shapiro (1985, 1986) have shown, in a two-period case with strategic interaction, that agents' expectations about these future choices act to destabilise the market. We can extend their findings to our stochastic-dynamic model. Assume agents form expectations in the shape of beliefs about the type of stochastic process they find themselves in. When the *actual* stochastic process that results from these beliefs is identical with the *believed* stochastic process, we have a rational-expectations fulfilled-equilibrium process. In the Appendix, I show that under increasing returns, rational expectations also yield an absorbing random walk, but one where expectations of lock-in hasten lock-in, narrowing the absorption barriers and worsening the fundamental market instability.

## II. A GENERAL FRAMEWORK

It would be useful to have an analytical framework that could accommodate sequential-choice problems with more general assumptions and returns mechanisms than the basic model above. In particular it would be useful to know under what circumstances a competing-technologies adoption market must end up dominated by a single technology.

In designing a general framework it seems important to preserve two properties: (*i*) That choices between alternative technologies may be affected by the numbers of each adopted at the time of choice; (*ii*) That small events 'outside the model' may influence adoptions, so that randomness must be allowed for. Thus adoption market shares may determine not the next

[6] For similar findings see the literature on the dynamics of commodity competition under increasing returns (e.g. Spence, 1981; Fudenberg and Tirole, 1983).

technology chosen directly but rather the *probability* of each technology's being chosen.

Consider then a dynamical system where one of $K$ technologies is adopted each time an adoption choice is made, with probabilities $p_1(\mathbf{x}), p_2(\mathbf{x}), \ldots, p_K(\mathbf{x})$, respectively. This vector of probabilities $\mathbf{p}$ is a function of the vector $\mathbf{x}$, the adoption-shares of technologies $1$ to $K$, out of the total number $n$ of adoptions so far. The initial vector of proportions is given as $\mathbf{x}_0$. I will call $\mathbf{p}(\mathbf{x})$ the *adoption function*.

We may now ask what happens to the long run proportions or adoption shares in such a dynamical system. Consider the two different adoption functions in Fig. 2, where $K = 2$. Now, where the probability of adoption of $A$ is higher than its market share, in the adoption process $A$ tends to increase in proportion; and where it is lower, $A$ tends to decrease. If the proportions or adoption-shares settle down as total adoptions increase, we would conjecture that they settle down at a fixed point of the adoption function.

In 1983 Arthur, Ermoliev, and Kaniovski proved that under certain

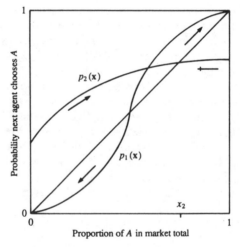

Fig. 2. Two illustrative adoption functions.

technical conditions (see the Appendix) this conjecture is true. A stochastic process of this type converges with probability one to one of the fixed points of the mapping from proportions (adoption shares) to the probability of adoption. Not all fixed points are eligible. Only 'attracting' or stable fixed points (ones that expected motions of the process lead towards) can emerge as the long run outcomes. And where the adoption function varies with time $n$, but tends to a limiting function $\mathbf{p}$, the process converges to an attracting fixed point of $\mathbf{p}$.

Thus in Fig. 2 the possible long-run shares are $0$ and $1$ for the function $p_1$ and $x_2$ for the function $p_2$.) Of course, where there are multiple fixed points, *which* one is chosen depends on the path taken by the process: it depends on the cumulation of random events that occur as the process unfolds.

We now have a general framework that immediately yields two useful theorems on path-dependence and single-technology dominance.

THEOREM I. *An adoption process is non-ergodic and non-predictable if and only if its adoption function* **p** *possesses multiple stable fixed points.*

THEOREM II. *An adoption process converges with probability one to the dominance of a single technology if and only if its adoption function* **p** *possesses stable fixed points only where* **x** *is a unit vector.*

These theorems follow as simple corollaries of the basic theorem above. Thus where two technologies compete, the adoption process will be path-dependent (multiple fixed points must exist) as long as there exists at least one unstable 'watershed' point in adoption shares, above which adoption of the technology with this share becomes self-reinforcing in that it tends to increase its share, below which it is self-negating in that it tends to lose its share. It is therefore not sufficient that a technology gain advantage with adoption; the advantage must (at some market share) be self-reinforcing (see Arthur, 1988).

### Non-Linear Increasing Returns with a Continuum of Adopter Types

Consider, as an example, a more general version of the basic model above, with a continuum of adopter types rather than just two, choosing between $K$ technologies, with possibly non-linear improvements in payoffs. Assume that if $n_j$ previous adopters have chosen technology $j$ previously, the next agent's payoff to adopting $j$ is $\Pi_j(n_j) = a_j + r(n_j)$ where $a_j$ represents the agent's 'natural preference' for technology $j$ and the monotonically increasing function $r$ represents the technological improvement that comes with previous adoptions. Each adopter has a vector of natural preferences $\mathbf{a} = (a_1, a_2, ..., a_K)$ for the $K$ alternatives, and we can think of the continuum of agents as a distribution of points $\mathbf{a}$ (with bounded support) on the positive orthant. We assume an adopter is drawn at random from this probability distribution each time a choice occurs. Dominance of a single technology $j$ corresponds to positive probability of the distribution of payoffs $\Pi$ being driven by adoptions to a point where $\Pi_j$ exceeds $\Pi_i$ for all $i \neq j$.

The Arthur-Ermoliev-Kaniovski theorem above allows us to derive:

THEOREM III. *If the improvement function $r$ increases at least at rate $\epsilon$ as $n_j$ increases, the adoption process converges to the dominance of a single technology, with probability one.*

*Proof.* In this case, the adoption function varies with total adoptions $n$. (We do not need to derive it explicitly however.) It is not difficult to establish that as $n$ becomes large: (i) At any point in the neighbourhood of any unit vector of adoption shares, unbounded increasing returns cause the corresponding technology to dominate *all* choices; therefore the unit-vector shares are stable fixed points. (ii) The equal-share point is also a fixed point, but unstable. (iii) No other point is a fixed point. Therefore, by the general theorem, since the limiting adoption function has stable fixed points only at unit vectors the process converges to one of these with probability one. Long-run dominance by a single technology is assured. ■

Dominance by a single technology is no longer inevitable, however, if the improvement function $r$ is bounded, as when learning effects become exhausted. This is because certain sequences of adopter types could bid improvements for two or more technologies upward more or less in concert. These technologies could then reach the upper bound of $r$ together, so that none of these would dominate and the market would remain shared from then on. Under other adopter sequences, by contrast, one of the technologies may reach the upper bound sufficiently fast to shut the others out. Thus, in the bounded case, some event histories dynamically lead to a shared market; other event histories lead to dominance. Increasing returns, if they are bounded, are in general *not* sufficient to guarantee eventual monopoly by a single technology.

### III. REMARKS

(1) To what degree might the actual economy be locked-in to inferior technology paths? As yet we do not know. Certainly it is easy to find cases where an early-established technology becomes dominant, so that later, superior alternatives cannot gain a footing.[7] Two important studies of historical events leading to lock-ins have now been carried out: on the QWERTY typewriter keyboard (David, 1985); and on alternating current (David and Bunn, 1987). (In both cases increasing returns arise mainly from coordination externalities.)

Promising empirical cases that may reflect lock-in through learning are the nuclear-reactor technology competition of the 1950s and 1960s and the US steam-versus-petrol car competition in the 1890s. The US nuclear industry is practically 100% dominated by light-water reactors. These reactors were originally adapted from a highly compact unit designed to propel the first nuclear submarine, the U.S.S. *Nautilus*, launched in 1954. A series of circumstances – among them the Navy's role in early construction contracts, political expediency, the Euratom programme, and the behaviour of key personages – acted to favour light water. Learning and construction experience gained early on appear to have locked the industry in to dominance of light water and shut other reactor types out (Bupp and Darian, 1978; Cowan, 1987). Yet much of the engineering literature contends that, given equal development, the gas-cooled reactor would have been superior (see Agnew, 1981). In the petrol-versus-steam car case, two different developer types with predilections toward steam or petrol depending on their previous mechanical experience, entered the industry at varying times and built upon on the best available versions of each technology. Initially petrol was held to be the less

---

[7] Examples might be the narrow gauge of British railways (Kindleberger, 1983); the US colour television system; the 1950s programming language FORTRAN; and of course the QWERTY keyboard (Arthur, 1984; David, 1985; Hartwick, 1985). In these particular cases the source of increasing returns is network externalities however rather than learning effects. Breaking out of locked-in technological standards has been investigated by Farrell and Saloner (1985, 1986).

promising option: it was explosive, noisy, hard to obtain in the right grade, and it required complicated new parts.[8] But in the United States a series of trivial circumstances (McLaughlin, 1954; Arthur, 1984) pushed several key developers into petrol just before the turn of the century and by 1920 had acted to shut steam out. Whether steam might have been superior given equal development is still in dispute among engineers (see Burton, 1976; Strack, 1970).

(2) The argument of this paper suggests that the interpretation of economic history should be different in different returns regimes. Under constant and diminishing returns, the evolution of the market reflects only *a-priori* endowments, preferences, and transformation possibilities; small events cannot sway the outcome. But while this is comforting, it reduces history to the status of mere carrier – the deliverer of the inevitable. Under increasing returns, by contrast many outcomes are possible. Insignificant circumstances become magnified by positive feedbacks to 'tip' the system into the actual outcome 'selected'. The small events of history become important.[9] Where we observe the predominance of one technology or one economic outcome over its competitors we should thus be cautious of any exercise that seeks the means by which the winner's innate 'superiority' came to be translated into adoption.

(3) The usual policy of letting the superior technology reveal itself in the outcome that dominates is appropriate in the constant and diminishing-returns cases. But in the increasing returns case laissez-faire gives no guarantee that the 'superior' technology (in the long-run sense) will be the one that survives. Effective policy in the (unsponsored) increasing-returns case would be predicated on the nature of the market breakdown: in our model early adopters impose externalities on later ones by rationally choosing technologies to suit only themselves; missing is an inter-agent market to induce them to explore promising but costly infant technologies that might pay off handsomely to later adopters.[10] The standard remedy of assigning to early developers (patent) rights of compensation by later users would be effective here only to the degree that early developers can appropriate later payoffs. As an alternative, a central authority could underwrite adoption and exploration along promising but less popular technological paths. But where eventual returns to a technology are hard to ascertain – as in the U.S. Strategic Defence Initiative case for example – the authority then faces a classic multi-arm bandit problem of choosing which technologies to bet on. An early run of disappointing results (low 'jackpots') from a potentially superior technology may cause it

---

[8] Amusingly, Fletcher (1904) writes: '...unless the objectionable features of the petrol carriage can be removed, it is bound to be driven from the road by its less objectionable rival, the steam-driven vehicle of the day.'

[9] For earlier recognition of the significance of both non-convexity and path-dependence for economic history see David (1975).

[10] Competition between *sponsored* technologies suffers less from this missing market. Sponsoring firms can more easily appropriate later payoffs, so they have an incentive to develop initially costly, but promising technologies. And financial markets for sponsoring investors together with insurance markets for adopters who may make the 'wrong' choice, mitigate losses for the risk-averse. Of course, if a product succeeds and locks-in the market, monopoly-pricing problems may arise. For further remarks on policy see David (1987).

perfectly rationally to abandon this technology in favour of other possibilities. The fundamental problem of possibly locking-in a regrettable course of development remains (Cowan, 1987).

### IV. CONCLUSION

This paper has attempted to go beyond the usual static analysis of increasing-returns problems by examining the dynamical process that 'selects' an equilibrium from multiple candidates, by the interaction of economic forces and random 'historical events'. It shows how dynamically, increasing returns can cause the economy gradually to lock itself in to an outcome not necessarily superior to alternatives, not easily altered, and not entirely predictable in advance.

Under increasing returns, competition between economic objects – in this case technologies – takes on an evolutionary character, with a 'founder effect' mechanism akin to that in genetics.[11] 'History' becomes important. To the degree that the technological development of the economy depends upon small events beneath the resolution of an observer's model, it may become impossible to predict market shares with any degree of certainty. This suggests that there may be theoretical limits, as well as practical ones, to the predictability of the economic future.

*Stanford University*

*Date of receipt of final typescript: May 1988*

### APPENDIX

*A. Definitions of the Properties*

Here I define precisely the properties used above. Denote the market share of $A$ after $n$ choices as $x_n$. The allocation process is:

(i) *predictable* if the observer can *ex-ante* construct a forecasting sequence $\{x_n^*\}$ with the property that $|x_n - x_n^*| \to 0$, with probability one, as $n \to \infty$;

(ii) *flexible* if a given marginal adjustment $g$ to the technologies' returns can alter future choices;

(iii) *ergodic* if, given two samples from the observer's set of possible historical events, $\{t_i\}$ and $\{t_i'\}$, with corresponding time-paths $\{x_n\}$ and $\{x_n'\}$, then $|x_n' - x_n| \to 0$, with probability one, as $n \to \infty$;

(iv) *path-efficient* if, whenever an agent chooses the more-adopted technology $\alpha$, versions of the lagging technology $\beta$ would not have delivered more had they been developed and available for adoption. That is, path-efficiency holds if returns $\Pi$ remain such that $\Pi_\alpha(m) \geqslant \text{Max}_j \{\Pi_\beta(j)\}$ for $k \leqslant j \leqslant m$, where there have been $m$ previous choices of the leading technology and $k$ of the lagging one.

---

[11] For other selection mechanisms affecting technologies see Dosi (1988), Dosi *et al.* (1988), and Metcalfe (1985).

## B. The Expectations Case

Consider here the competing standards case where adopters are affected by *future* choices as well as past choices. Assume in our earlier model that $R$-agents receive additional net benefits of $\Pi_A^R$, $\Pi_B^R$, if the process locks-in to their choice, $A$ or $B$ respectively; similarly $S$-agents receive $\Pi_A^S$, $\Pi_B^S$. (Technologies improve with adoption as before.) Assume that agents know the state of the market $(n_A, n_B)$ when choosing and that they have expectations or beliefs that adoptions follow a stochastic process $\Omega$. They choose rationally under these expectations, so that actual adoptions follow the process $\Gamma(\Omega)$. This actual process is a *rational expectations equilibrium process* when it bears out the expected process, that is, when $\Gamma(\Omega) \equiv \Omega$.

We can distinguish two cases, corresponding to the degree of heterogeneity of preferences in the market.

*Case* (i). Suppose initially that $a_R - b_R > \Pi_B^R$ and $b_S - a_S > \Pi_A^S$ and that $R$ and $S$-types have beliefs that the adoption process is a random walk $\Omega$ with absorption barriers at $\Delta_R'$, $\Delta_S'$, with associated probabilities of lock-in to $A$, $P(n_A, n_B)$ and lock-in to $B$, $1 - P(n_A, n_B)$. Under these beliefs, $R$-type expected payoffs for choosing $A$ or $B$ are, respectively:

$$a_R + rn_A + P(n_A, n_B)\Pi_A^R \tag{4}$$

$$b_R + rn_B + [1 - P(n_A, n_B)]\Pi_B^R. \tag{5}$$

$S$-type payoffs may be written similarly. In the actual process $R$-types will switch to $B$ when $n_A$ and $n_B$ are such that these two expressions become equal. Both types choose $B$ from then on. The actual probability of lock-in to $A$ is zero here; so that if the expected process is fulfilled, $P$ is also zero here and we have $n_A$ and $n_B$ such that

$$a_R + rn_A = b_R + rn_B + \Pi_B^R$$

with associated barrier given by

$$\Delta_R = n_A - n_B = -(a_R - b_R - \Pi_B^R)/r. \tag{6}$$

Similarly $S$-types switch to $A$ at boundary position given by

$$\Delta_S = n_A - n_B = (b_S - a_S - \Pi_A^S)/s. \tag{7}$$

It is easy to confirm that beyond these barriers the actual process is indeed locked in to $A$ or to $B$ and that within them $R$-agents prefer $A$, and $S$-agents prefer $B$. Thus if agents believe the adoption process is a random walk with absorbing barriers $\Delta_R'$, $\Delta_S'$ given by (6) and (7), these beliefs will be fulfilled, and this random walk will be a rational expectations equilibrium.

*Case* (ii). Suppose now that $a_R - b_R < \Pi_B^R$ and $b_S - a_S < \Pi_A^S$. Then (4) and (5) show that switching will occur immediately if agents hold expectations that the system will definitely lock-in to $A$ or to $B$. These expectations become self-fulfilling and the absorbing barriers narrow to zero. Similarly, when non-improving standards compete, so that $r$ and $s$ are zero, in this case again beliefs that $A$ or $B$ will definitely lock-in become self-fulfilling.

Taking cases (i) and (ii) together, expectations either narrow or collapse the switching boundaries. They exacerbate the fundamental market instability.

## C. The Path-Dependent Strong-Law Theorem

Consider a dependent-increment stochastic process that starts with an initial vector of units $\mathbf{b_0}$, in the $K$ categories, 1 through $K$. At each event-time a unit is added to one of the categories 1 through $K$, with probabilities $\mathbf{p} = [p_1(x), p_2(x), ..., p_K(x)]$, respectively. (The Borel function $\mathbf{p}$ maps the unit simplex of proportions $S^K$ into the unit simplex of probabilities $S^K$.) The process is iterated to yield the vectors of proportions $\mathbf{X_1}, \mathbf{X_2}, \mathbf{X_3}, ....$

THEOREM. *Arthur, Ermoliev, and Kaniovski* (1983, 1986)

(i) Suppose $p\colon S^K \to S^K$ is continuous, and suppose the function $p(x) - x$ possesses a Lyapunov function (that is, a positive, twice-differentiable function $V$ with inner product $\{[p(x) - x], V_x\}$ negative). Suppose also that the set of fixed points of $p$, $B = \{x\colon p(x) = x\}$ has a finite number of connected components. Then the vector of proportions $\{X_n\}$ converges, with probability one, to a point $z$ in the set of fixed points $B$, or to the border of a connected component.

(ii) Suppose $p$ maps the interior of the unit simplex into itself, and that $z$ is a stable point (as defined in the conventional way). Then the process has limit point $z$ with positive probability.

(iii) Suppose $z$ is a non-vertex unstable point of $p$. Then the process cannot converge to $z$ with positive probability.

(iv) Suppose probabilities of addition vary with time $n$, and the sequence $\{p_n\}$ converges to a limiting function $p$ faster than $1/n$ converges to zero. Then the above statements hold for the limiting function $p$. That is, if the above conditions are fulfilled, the process converges with probability one to one of the stable fixed points of the limiting function $p$.

The theorem is extended to non-continuous functions $p$ and to non-unit and random increments in Arthur, Ermoliev and Kaniovski (1987 b). For the case $K = 2$ with $p$ stationary see the elegant analysis of Hill *et al.* (1980).

### REFERENCES

Agnew, H. (1981). 'Gas-cooled nuclear power reactors.' *Scientific American*, vol. 244, pp. 55–63.
Arthur, W. B. (1983). 'Competing technologies and lock-in by historical small events: the dynamics of allocation under increasing returns.' International Institute for Applied Systems Analysis Paper WP-83-92, Laxenburg, Austria. (Center for Economic Policy Research, Paper 43, Stanford).
—— (1984). 'Competing technologies and economic prediction.' *Options*, International Institute for Applied Systems Analysis, Laxenburg, Austria. No. 1984/2, pp. 10–3.
Arthur, W. B., Ermoliev, Yu. and Kaniovski, Yu. (1983). 'On generalized urn schemes of the polya kind.' *Kibernetika*, vol. 19, pp. 49–56. English translation in *Cybernetics*, vol. 19, pp. 61–71.
—— —— and —— (1986). 'Strong laws for a class of path-dependent urn processes.' In *Proceedings of the International Conference on Stochastic Optimization, Kiev 1984*, Springer Lecture Notes Control and Information Sciences, vol. 81, pp. 187–300.
—— —— and —— (1987 a). 'Path-dependent processes and the emergence of macro-structure.' *European Journal of Operational Research*, vol. 30, pp. 294–303.
—— —— and —— (1987 b). 'Non-linear urn processes: asymptotic behavior and applications.' International Institute for Applied Systems Analysis. Paper WP-87-85, Laxenburg, Austria.
—— (1988). 'Self-reinforcing mechanisms in economics.' In *The Economy as an Evolving Complex System* (P. Anderson, K. Arrow and D. Pines (eds)), Reading, Massachusetts: Addison–Wesley.

Atkinson, A. and Stiglitz, J. (1969). 'A new view of technical change.' ECONOMIC JOURNAL, vol. 79, pp. 573–80.

Balcer, Y. and Lippman, S. (1984). 'Technological expectations and the adoption of improved technology,' *Journal of Economic Theory*, vol. 34, pp. 292–318.

Bupp, I. and Derian, J. (1978). *Light Water: How The Nuclear Dream Dissolved*. New York: Basic.

Burton, R. (1976). 'Recent advances in vehicular steam engine efficiency.' Society of Automotive Engineers, Preprint 760340.

Cowan, R. (1987). 'Backing the wrong horse: sequential choice among technologies of unknown merit.' Ph.D. Dissertation. Stanford.

David, P. (1975). *Technical Choice, Innovation, and Economic Growth*. Cambridge: Cambridge University Press.

—— (1985). 'Clio and the economics of QWERTY.' *American Economic Review Proceedings*, vol. 75, pp. 332–7.

—— (1987). 'Some new standards for the economics of standardization in the information age.' In *Economic Policy and Technological Performance*, (P. Dasgupta and P. Stoneman, eds.) Cambridge: Cambridge University Press.

—— and Bunn, J. (1987). 'The economics of gateway technologies and network evolution: lessons from electricity supply history.' Centre for Economic Policy Research, Paper 119, Stanford.

Dosi, G. (1988). 'Sources, procedures and microeconomic effects of innovation.' *Journal of Economic Literature* vol. 26, pp. 1120–71.

——, Freeman, C., Nelson, R., Silverberg, G. and Soete, L. (eds.) (1988). *Technical Change and Economic Theory*, London: Pinter.

Farrell, J. and Saloner, G. (1985). 'Standardization, compatibility, and innovation.' *Rand Journal of Economics*, vol. 16, pp. 70–83.

—— (1986). 'Installed base and compatibility: innovation, product preannouncements and predation.' *American Economic Review*, vol. 76. pp. 940–55.

Fletcher, W. (1904). *English and American Steam Carriages and Traction Engines* (reprinted 1973). Newton Abbot: David and Charles.

Fudenberg, D. and Tirole, J. (1983). 'Learning by doing and market performance.' *Bell Journal of Economics*, vol. 14, pp. 522–30.

Hanson, W. (1985). 'Bandwagons and orphans: dynamic pricing of competing systems subject to decreasing costs.' Ph.D. Dissertation, Stanford.

Hartwick, J. (1985). 'The persistence of QWERTY and analogous suboptimal standards.' Mimeo, Queen's University, Kingston, Ontario.

Hill, B., Lane, D. and Sudderth, W. (1980). 'A strong law for some generalized urn processes.' *Annals of Probability*, vol. 8, pp. 214–26.

Katz, M. and Shapiro, C. (1985). 'Network externalities, competition, and compatibility.' *American Economic Review*, vol. 75, pp. 424–40.

——, and —— (1986). 'Technology adoption in the presence of network externalities.' *Journal of Political Economy*, vol. 94, pp. 822–41.

Kindleberger, C. (1983). 'Standards as public, collective and private goods.' *Kyklos*, vol. 36, pp. 377–96.

Mamer, J. and McCardle, K. (1987). 'Uncertainty, competition and the adoption of new technology.' *Management Science*, vol. 33, pp. 161–77.

McLaughlin, C. (1954). 'The Stanley Steamer: a study in unsuccessful innovation.' *Explorations in Entrepreneurial History*, vol. 7, pp. 37–47.

Metcalfe, J. S. (1985). 'On technological competition.' Mimeo, University of Manchester.

Rosenberg, N. (1982). *Inside the Black Box: Technology and Economics*. Cambridge: Cambridge University Press.

Strack, W. (1970). '*Condensers and Boilers for Steam-powered Cars*.' NASA Technical Note, TN D-5813, Washington, D.C.

Spence, A. M. (1981). 'The learning curve and competition.' *Bell Journal of Economics*, vol. 12, pp. 49–70.

# [20]

## Clio and the Economics of QWERTY

By Paul A. David[*]

Cicero demands of historians, first, that we tell true stories. I intend fully to perform my duty on this occasion, by giving you a homely piece of narrative economic history in which "one damn thing follows another." The main point of the story will become plain enough: it is sometimes not possible to uncover the logic (or illogic) of the world around us except by understanding how it got that way. A *path-dependent* sequence of economic changes is one of which important influences upon the eventual outcome can be exerted by temporally remote events, including happenings dominated by chance elements rather than systematic forces. Stochastic processes like that do not converge automatically to a fixed-point distribution of outcomes, and are called *non-ergodic*. In such circumstances "historical accidents" can neither be ignored, nor neatly quarantined for the purpose of economic analysis; the dynamic process itself takes on an *essentially historical* character. Standing alone, my story will be simply illustrative and does not establish how much of the world works this way. That is an open empirical issue and I would be presumptuous to claim to have settled it, or to instruct you in what to do about it. Let us just hope the tale proves mildly diverting for those waiting to be told if and why the study of economic history is a necessity in the making of economists.

*Department of Economics, Encina Hall, Stanford University, Stanford, CA 94305. Support provided for this research, under a grant to the Technological Innovation Program of the Center for Economic Policy Research, Stanford University, is gratefully acknowledged. Douglas Puffert supplied able research assistance. Some, but not the whole, of my indebtedness to Brian Arthur's views on QWERTY and QWERTY-like subjects is recorded in the References. I bear full responsibility for errors of fact and interpretation, as well as for the peculiar opinions abbreviated herein. A fuller version with complete references, entitled "Understanding the Economics of QWERTY or Is History Necessary?," is available on request.

### I. The Story of QWERTY

Why does the topmost row of letters on your personal computer keyboard spell out QWERTYUIOP, rather than something else? We know that nothing in the engineering of computer terminals requires the awkward keyboard layout known today as "QWERTY," and we all are old enough to remember that QWERTY somehow has been handed down to us from the Age of Typewriters. Clearly nobody has been persuaded by the exhortations to discard QWERTY, which apostles of DSK (the Dvorak Simplified Keyboard) were issuing in trade publications such as *Computers and Automation* during the early 1970's. Why not? Devotees of the keyboard arrangement patented in 1932 by August Dvorak and W. L. Dealey have long held most of the world's records for speed typing. Moreover, during the 1940's U.S. Navy experiments had shown that the increased efficiency obtained with DSK would amortize the cost of retraining a group of typists within the first ten days of their subsequent full-time employment. Dvorak's death in 1975 released him from forty years of frustration with the world's stubborn rejection of his contribution; it came too soon for him to be solaced by the Apple IIC computer's built-in switch, which instantly converts its keyboard from QWERTY to virtual DSK, or to be further aggravated by doubts that the switch would not often be flicked.

If as Apple advertising copy now says, DSK "lets you type 20–40% faster," why did this superior design meet essentially the same rejection as the previous seven improvements on the QWERTY typewriter keyboard that were patented in the United States and Britain during the years 1909–24? Was it the result of customary, nonrational behavior by countless individuals socialized to carry on an antiquated technological tradition? Or, as Dvorak himself once suggested, had there

*VOL. 75 NO. 2*　　　*ECONOMIC HISTORY*　　　*333*

been a conspiracy among the members of the typewriter oligopoly to suppress an invention which they feared would so increase typewriter efficiency as ultimately to curtail the demand for their products? Or perhaps we should turn instead to the other popular "Devil Theory," and ask if political regulation and interference with the workings of a "free market" has been the cause of inefficient keyboard regimentation? Maybe it's all to be blamed on the public school system, like everything else that's awry?

You can already sense that these will not be the most promising lines along which to search for an economic understanding of QWERTY's present dominance. The agents engaged in production and purchase decisions in today's keyboard market are not the prisoners of custom, conspiracy, or state control. But while they are, as we now say, perfectly "free to choose," their behavior, nevertheless, is held fast in the grip of events long forgotten and shaped by circumstances in which neither they nor their interests figured. Like the great men of whom Tolstoy wrote in *War and Peace*, "(e) very action of theirs, that seems to them an act of their own free will, is in an historical sense not free at all, but in bondage to the whole course of previous history..." (Bk. IX, ch. 1).

This is a short story, however. So it begins only little more than a century ago, with the fifty-second man to invent the typewriter. Christopher Latham Sholes was a Milwaukee, Wisconsin printer by trade, and a mechanical tinkerer by inclination. Helped by his friends, Carlos Glidden and Samuel W. Soule, he had built a primitive writing machine for which a patent application was led in October 1867. Many defects in the working of Sholes' "Type Writer" stood in the way of its immediate commercial introduction. Because the printing point was located underneath the paper carriage, it was quite invisible to the operator. "Non-visibility" remained an unfortunate feature of this and other up-stroke machines long after the flat paper carriage of the original design had been supplanted by arrangements closely resembling the modern continuous roller-platen. Consequently, the tendency of the typebars to clash and jam if struck in rapid

succession was a particularly serious defect. When a typebar stuck at or near the printing point, every succeeding stroke merely hammered the same impression onto the paper, resulting in a string of repeated letters that would be discovered only when the typist bothered to raise the carriage to inspect what had been printed.

Urged onward by the bullying optimism of James Densmore, the promoter-venture capitalist whom he had taken into the partnership in 1867, Sholes struggled for the next six years to perfect "the machine." From the inventor's trial-and-error rearrangements of the original model's alphabetical key ordering, in an effort to reduce the frequency of typebar clashes, there emerged a four-row, upper case keyboard approaching the modern QWERTY standard. In March 1873, Densmore succeeded in placing the manufacturing rights for the substantially transformed Sholes-Glidden "Type Writer" with E. Remington and Sons, the famous arms makers. Within the next few months QWERTY's evolution was virtually completed by Remington's mechanics. Their many modifications included some fine-tuning of the keyboard design in the course of which the "*R*" wound up in the place previously allotted to the period mark ".". Thus were assembled into one row all the letters which a salesman would need to impress customers, by rapidly pecking out the brand name: TYPE WRITER

Despite this sales gimmick, the early commercial fortunes of the machine, with which chance had linked QWERTY's destiny remained terrifyingly precarious. The economic downturn of the 1870's was not the best of times in which to launch a novel piece of office equipment costing $125, and by 1878, when Remington brought out its Improved Model Two (equipped with carriage shift key), the whole enterprise was teetering on the edge of bankruptcy. Consequently, even though sales began to pick up pace with the lifting of the depression and annual typewriter production climbed to 1200 units in 1881, the market position which QWERTY had acquired during the course of its early career was far from deeply entrenched; the entire stock of QWERTY-embodying machines in the United States could not have much exceeded 5000 when the decade of the 1880's opened.

Nor was its future much protected by any compelling technological necessities. For, there were ways to make a typewriter without the up-stroke typebar mechanism that had called forth the QWERTY adaptation, and rival designs were appearing on the American scene. Not only were there typebar machines with "down-stroke" and "front-stroke" actions that afforded a visible printing point; the problem of typebar clashes could be circumvented by dispensing with typebars entirely, as young Thomas Edison had done in his 1872 patent for an electric print-wheel device which later became the basis for teletype machines. Lucien Stephen Crandall, the inventor of the second typewriter to reach the American market (in 1879) arranged the type on a cylindrical sleeve: the sleeve was made to revolve to the required letter and come down onto the printing-point, locking in place for correct alignment. (So much for the "revolutionary" character of the IBM 72/82's "golf ball" design.) Freed from the legacy of typebars, commercially successful typewriters such as the Hammond and the Blickensderfer first sported a keyboard arrangement which was more sensible than QWERTY. Then so-called "Ideal" keyboard placed the sequence DHIATENSOR in the home row, these being ten letters with which one may compose over 70 percent of the words in the English language.

The typewriter boom beginning in the 1880's thus witnessed a rapid proliferation of competitive designs, manufacturing companies, and keyboard arrangements rivalling the Sholes-Remington QWERTY. Yet, by the middle of the next decade, just when it had become evident that any micro-technological rationale for QWERTY's dominance was being removed by the progress of typewriter engineering, the U.S. industry was rapidly moving towards the standard of an upright front-stroke machine with a four-row QWERTY keyboard that was referred to as "the Universal." During the period 1895–1905, the main producers of non-typebar machines fell into line by offering "the Universal" as an option in place of the Ideal keyboard.

## II. Basic QWERTY-Nomics

To understand what had happened in the fateful interval of the 1890's, the economist must attend to the fact that typewriters were beginning to take their place as an element of a larger, rather complex system of production that was technically interrelated. In addition to the manufacturers and buyers of typewriting machines, this system involved typewriter operators and the variety of organizations (both private and public) that undertook to train people in such skills. Still more critical to the outcome was the fact that, in contrast to the hardware subsystems of which QWERTY or other keyboards were a part, the larger system of production was nobody's design. Rather like the proverbial Topsy, and much else in the history of economies besides, it "jes' growed."

The advent of "touch" typing, a distinct advance over the four-finger hunt-and-peck method, came late in the 1880's and was critical, because this innovation was from its inception adapted to the Remington's QWERTY keyboard. Touch typing gave rise to three features of the evolving production system which were crucially important in causing QWERTY to become "locked in" as the dominant keyboard arrangement. These features were *technical interrelatedness, economies of scale*, and *quasi-irreversibility* of investment. They constitute the basic ingredients of what might be called QWERTY-nomics.

Technical interrelatedness, or the need for system compatibility between keyboard "hardware" and the "software" represented by the touch typist's memory of a particular arrangement of the keys, meant that the expected present value of a typewriter as an instrument of production was dependent upon the availability of compatible software created by typists' decisions as to the kind of keyboard they should learn. Prior to the growth of the personal market for typewriters, the purchasers of the hardware typically were business firms and therefore distinct from the owners of typing skills. Few incentives existed at the time, or later, for any one business to invest in providing its employees with a form of general human capital which so readily could be taken

VOL. 75 NO. 2          ECONOMIC HISTORY          335

elsewhere. (Notice that it was the wartime U.S. Navy, not your typical employer, that undertook the experiment of retraining typists on the Dvorak keyboard.) Nevertheless the purchase by a potential employer of a QWERTY keyboard conveyed a positive pecuniary externality to compatibly trained touch typists. To the degree to which this increased the likelihood that subsequent typists would choose to learn QWERTY, in preference to another method for which the stock of compatible hardware would not be so large, the overall user costs of a typewriting system based upon QWERTY (or any specific keyboard) would tend to *decrease* as it gained in acceptance relative to other systems. Essentially symmetrical conditions obtained in the market for instruction in touch typing.

These decreasing cost conditions—or *system scale economies*—had a number of consequences, among which undoubtedly the most important was the tendency for the process of intersystem competition to lead towards de facto standardization through the predominance of a single keyboard design. For analytical purposes, the matter can be simplified in the following way: suppose that buyers of typewriters uniformly were without inherent preferences concerning keyboards, and cared only about how the stock of touch typists was distributed among alternative specific keyboard styles. Suppose typists, on the other hand, were heterogeneous in their preferences for learning QWERTY-based "touch," as opposed to other methods, but attentive also to the way the stock of machines was distributed according to keyboard styles. Then imagine the members of this heterogenous population deciding in random order what kind of typing training to acquire. It may be seen that, with unbounded decreasing costs of selection, each stochastic decision in favor of QWERTY would raise the probability (but not guarantee) that the next selector would favor QWERTY. From the viewpoint of the formal theory of stochastic processes, what we are looking at now is equivalent to a generalized "Polya urn scheme." In a simple scheme of that kind, an urn containing balls of various colors is sampled with replacement, and every drawing of a ball of a specified color results

in a second ball of the same color being returned to the urn; the probabilities that balls of specified colors will be added are therefore increasing (linear) functions of the proportions in which the respective colors are represented within the urn. A recent theorem due to W. Brian Arthur et al. (1983; 1985) allows us to say that when a generalized form of such a process (characterized by unbounded increasing returns) is extended indefinitely, the proportional share of one of the colors will, with probability one, converge to unity.

There may be many eligible candidates for supremacy, and from an *ex ante* vantage point we cannot say with corresponding certainty which among the contending colors —or rival keyboard arrangements—will be the one to gain eventual dominance. That part of the story is likely to be governed by "historical accidents," which is to say, by the particular sequencing of choices made close to the beginning of the process. It is there that essentially random, transient factors are most likely to exert great leverage, as has been shown neatly by Arthur's (1983) model of the dynamics of technological competition under increasing returns. Intuition suggests that if choices were made in a forward-looking way, rather than myopically on the basis of comparisons among the currently prevailing costs of different systems, the final outcome could be influenced strongly by expectations. A particular system could triumph over rivals merely because the purchasers of the software (and/or the hardware) expected that it would do so. This intuition seems to be supported by recent formal analyses by Michael Katz and Carl Shapiro (1983), and Ward Hanson (1984), of markets where purchasers of rival products benefit from externalities conditional upon the size of the compatible system or "network" with which they thereby become joined. Although the initial lead acquired by QWERTY through its association with the Remington was quantitatively very slender, when magnified by expectations it may well have been quite sufficient to guarantee that the industry eventually would lock in to a de facto QWERTY standard.

The occurrence of this "lock in" as early as the mid-1890's does appear to have owed something also to the high costs of software "conversion" and the resulting *quasi-irreversibility of investments* in specific touch-typing skills. Thus, as far as keyboard conversion costs were concerned, an important asymmetry had appeared between the software and the hardware components of the evolving system: the costs of typewriter software conversion were going up, whereas the costs of typewriter hardware conversion were coming down. While the novel, non-typebar technologies developed during the 1880's were freeing the keyboard from technical bondage to QWERTY, typewriter makers were by the same token freed from fixed-cost bondage to any particular keyboard arrangement. Non-QWERTY typewriter manufacturers seeking to expand market share could cheaply switch to achieve compatibility with the already existing stock of QWERTY-programmed typists, who could not. This, then, was a situation in which the precise details of timing in the developmental sequence had made it privately profitable in the short run to adapt machines to the habits of men (or to women, as was increasingly the case) rather than the other way around. And things have been that way ever since.

### III. Message

In place of a moral, I want to leave you with a message of faith and qualified hope. The story of QWERTY is a rather intriguing one for economists. Despite the presence of the sort of externalities that standard static analysis tells us would interfere with the achievement of the socially optimal degree of system compatibility, competition in the absence of perfect futures markets drove the industry prematurely into standardization *on the wrong system*—where decentralized decision making subsequently has sufficed to hold it. Outcomes of this kind are not so exotic. For such things to happen seems only too possible in the presence of strong technical interrelatedness, scale economies, and irreversibilities due to learning and habituation. They come as no surprise to readers prepared by Thorstein Veblen's classic passages in *Germany and the Industrial Revolution*

(1915), on the problem of Britain's undersized railway wagons and "the penalties of taking the lead" (see pp. 126–27); they may be painfully familiar to students who have been obliged to assimilate the details of deservedly less-renowned scribblings (see my 1971, 1975 studies) about the obstacles which ridge-and-furrow placed in the path of British farm mechanization, and the influence of remote events in nineteenth-century U.S. factor price history upon the subsequently emerging bias towards Hicks' labor-saving improvements in the production technology of certain branches of manufacturing.

I believe there are many more QWERTY worlds lying out there in the past, on the very edges of the modern economic analyst's tidy universe; worlds we do not yet fully perceive or understand, but whose influence, like that of dark stars, extends nonetheless to shape the visible orbits of our contemporary economic affairs. Most of the time I feel sure that the absorbing delights and quiet terrors of exploring QWERTY worlds will suffice to draw adventurous economists into the systematic study of essentially historical dynamic processes, and so will seduce them into the ways of economic history, and a better grasp of their subject.

### REFERENCES

Arthur, W. Brian, "On Competing Technologies and Historical Small Events: The Dynamics of Choice Under Increasing Returns," Technological Innovation Program Workshop Paper, Department of Economics, Stanford University, November 1983.

Arthur, W. Brian, Ermoliev, Yuri M. and Kaniovski, Yuri M., "On Generalized Urn Schemes of the Polya Kind," *Kibernetika*, No. 1, 1983, *19*, 49–56 (translated from the Russian in *Cybernetics*, 1983, *19*, 61–71).

____, ____, and ____, "Strong Laws for a Class of Path-Dependent Urn Processes," in *Proceedings of the International Conference on Stochastic Optimization, Kiev*, Munich: Springer-Verlag, 1985.

David, Paul A., "The Landscape and the Machine: Technical Interrelatedness, Land Tenure and the Mechanization of the Corn Harvest in Victorian Britain," in D. N.

McCloskey, ed., *Essays on a Mature Economy: Britain after 1840*, London: Methuen, 1971, ch. 5.

_____, *Technical Choice, Innovation and Economic Growth: Essays on American and British Experience in the Nineteenth Century*, New York: Cambridge University Press, 1975.

Hanson, Ward A., "Bandwagons and Orphans: Dynamic Pricing of Competing Technological Systems Subject to Decreasing Costs," Technological Innovation Program Workshop Paper, Department of Economics, Stanford University, January, 1984.

Katz, Michael L. and Shapiro, Carl, "Network Externalities, Competition, and Compatibility," Woodrow Wilson School Discussion Paper in Economics No. 54, Princeton University, September, 1983.

Veblen, Thorstein, *Imperial Germany and the Industrial Revolution*, New York: MacMillan, 1915.

# [21]

# IMPULSE AND DIFFUSION IN THE STUDY OF TECHNICAL CHANGE

J.S. Metcalfe

A common model of innovation diffusion is extended to incorporate the interaction of demand growth and capacity growth, building in part on work by Kuznets and Burns on industrial growth and retardation. It is shown how price and production cost evolve during a diffusion process, and how Schumpeter's theory of the transient nature of innovator's profits has a natural place within the analysis of diffusion. The framework is intended to assist future analysis of the links between the diffusion and the evolution of a given technology, taking account of, eg, learning by doing, production bottlenecks and the inducement to innovation, and producer/adopter interaction to improve technological performance.

IT WILL not be doubted that some of the more reliable facts concerning technical change relate to the diffusion of innovation, the process by which new technologies displace, or substitute for, existing technologies. A wealth of evidence has accumulated to indicate substantial differences in the rates at which the same innovation is diffused in different industries, and in the rates at which different innovations are diffused in the same industry. Important contributions have been made[1] which successfully link observed diffusion patterns to the few key variables which economic theory predicts are relevant to the process of technology displacement. Despite this undoubted success, an air of unease pervades much recent writing on diffusion,[2] manifesting itself in the dilemma over whether diffusion curves are best viewed as sequences of moving equilibrium, or as a disequilibrium adjustment to a given long-run position.

I shall argue that this is related to the narrow focus of past diffusion research, and that advances are now to be made by recognizing a broader scope to, and relevance of, diffusion phenomena. Diffusion of innovation is one dimension of that vitally important but not well understood problem of the transition between different economic equilibria. It represents the study in the small of disequilibrium situations, of Schumpeter's process of creative destruction. From this perspective, compelling links can be made between the micro-study

J.S. Metcalfe is professor of economics at the Department of Economics, University of Manchester, M13 9PL, UK. Thanks are due to R. Coombs and P. Saviotti for helpful comments on a previous version of this paper.

FUTURES October 1981        0016-3287/81/050347-13$02.00 © 1981, IPC Business Press

of diffusion phenomena and the general process of modern industrial growth, in which the impulses associated with technological innovations are absorbed into the economic structure. [1]

As one explores these links, it becomes clear that current diffusion theory is dominated by a concern with demand-related phenomena. The role of supply factors is almost entirely neglected [1] and, consequently, important interactions between the growth of demand and the growth of productive potential are ignored. I shall suggest that these interactions are vital to a proper understanding of diffusion phenomena, and that they should play an important part in the relation between diffusion and induced innovation. The third part of this paper will develop a simple framework for analysing the interaction of demand and supply during diffusion. This is preceded by a general discussion of the theme of impulse and transition in industrial growth, notably drawn from the writings of Burns, Kuznets, and Hicks. We start with a brief outline of the standard diffusion model and its more important defects.

## The standard diffusion model

Though economists have brought a variety of different approaches to the analysis of diffusion, this section concentrates upon the summary statements of diffusion provided by measures of diffusion speed. If, for example, we focus on inter-firm diffusion, measures of diffusion speed are provided by the parameters of the best-fitting time trend to observations on the number of firms utilizing an innovation. Often this best-fitting trend turns out to be a sigmoid (eg logistic) curve, and this is associated with the following rationalization of the diffusion process.

Imagine that, at a particular point in time, an innovation is 'introduced'; say, a new production process embodied in durable capital equipment. This innovation offers some economic advantage over prevailing methods, and so disturbs the constellation of forces defining the existing equilibrium. The innovation creates a potential for change, and we wish to know how quickly this impulse will be exhausted by a process of diffusion. Part of the answer is provided by an analysis of the speed at which firms in the relevant industry decide to adopt the innovation. [3] We know that firms will not adopt the innovation immediately, even when it appears to be economically rational so to do. Why not? The standard diffusion model argues as follows.

An analogy is drawn between the process of inter-firm diffusion and the spread of an epidemic in a homogeneous, randomly mixing population of fixed size. The spreading of the epidemic is akin to the spreading of information about the innovation among a population of potential adopters, each being uncertain of the precise relevance of the innovation to its own operations. When information is costly to acquire and the innovation typically has several technical attributes, firms can resort to an indirect form of 'learning by doing'—learning by observing the experience of existing adopters. At any point in time, firms view differently the advantages offered by the innovation to their own operations but, over time, the process of adoption involves a gradual convergence of viewpoint as all adopting firms acquire a common perception of the innovation's worth.

Simple though this analogy is, it is a useful starting point. Information imperfections and uncertainty are highlighted and it suggests, for example, that the technical complexity or novelty of an innovation may be an important factor in its diffusion. Most important of all, the epidemic analogy provides an underpinning for the logistic curves which often provide an adequate summary of diffusion trends. Denoting the number of adopters at time $t$ by $x(t)$, the epidemic model leads to the following differential equation to govern the diffusion process

$$\dot{x}(t) = \beta \, x(t) \, [n{-}x(t)] \qquad\qquad\qquad\qquad (1)$$
$$x(0) = z$$

where, $n$ is the equilibrium number of potential adopters, $z$ is the initial, unexplained number of 'innovating' adopters, and $\beta$ is the adoption coefficient. The magnitude of $\beta$ reflects the speed at which information is spread between firms and the amount of information required to make a positive adoption decision. The properties of this logistic process are well known, and we simply list the more relevant ones as follows:[6]

- The impulse provided by the innovation creates a potential for future adoption measured by $n{-}z$. From the initial level $z$, adoption approaches its equilibrium level $n$, monotonically along a logistic curve, with inflexion point at $n/2$.[7]
- There is a continuous retardation in the proportionate growth rate of adoption, which approaches zero as diffusion approaches its equilibrium level.
- The time taken for the number of adopting firms to pass between two arbitrary values is inversely proportional to the product $n\beta$. We call this product the diffusion coefficient, and for any given innovation it is usually estimated as one of the parameters of the logistic time trend fitted to the adoption data.[8]

The attraction of this standard model is that it is possible to relate estimated values of the diffusion coefficient to predictable economic characteristics of the innovation and the adoption environment. The diffusion coefficient is found to be greater, the greater the profitability of the innovation and the smaller the capital investment required to adopt it.[9] There is also evidence that adoption proceeds more quickly in science based, R and D performing industries, and that such factors as the age and qualifications of senior management, and the size distribution of adopting firms, are important in explaining the pace of diffusion.[10]

Despite the obvious success of this approach, there are powerful reasons for believing it diverts attention away from important aspects of the diffusion process. There are two objections I wish to emphasize. The first relates to the static nature of the standard diffusion model—a given innovation is diffused within an unchanging adoption environment, although there are well documented reasons for expecting both innovation and environment to change as diffusion proceeds. Improvements to the innovation, general economic growth, changes in relative commodity and input prices, and other complementary or competing innovations, can all be expected to occur during diffusion. Instead of a single diffusion curve, we have an envelope of successive diffusion curves, each appropriate to a given set of innovation and adoption environment characteristics, each with its own values of $n$ and $\beta$. While any given set of characteristics generates a logistic process, the envelope need not conform to the logistic pattern, and its exact shape will depend on the temporal incidence of the changes in characteristics.[11] Gold[12] and Davies[13], for example, have argued that observed diffusion paths primarily reflect changes in the innovation and adoption environment, rather than a process of learning within a static situation. As Gold observes, the standard diffusion model

rests on the implicit static assumption that the diffusion levels reached in later years also represent active adoption prospects during earlier years.[14]

In his important study, which skilfully blends the learning aspects of the standard model with changes in the equilibrium adoption level, Davies has shown how non-logistic, but sigmoid, diffusion curves can be generated, the shape of which depends on the pattern of post-innovation improvement in the new technology.[15]

This brings us to the second main objection. We have so far treated changes in the innovation and adoption environment as exogenous to the diffusion process. However, an important category of changes will be endogenous and foremost among these, it seems, will be the profitability of adoption. As soon as profitability is considered, several awkward questions surface. The emphasis in diffusion research is upon the profitability of using an innovation as seen by potential adopters, but what of profitability as perceived by the producers of the innovation? Surely this is of equal importance, since the innovation can only be diffused if it is produced. Moreover, high profitability for the producers would seem to imply low profitability for the adopters. This suggests a crucial weakness in the standard diffusion model: it focuses attention entirely on the demand for an innovation by potential adopters. The supply side is ignored,[16] and with it the question of how the profitability of adopting and producing the innovation is determined. Profitability influences the pace of diffusion but, equally, the pace of diffusion will influence profitability. On this crucial matter, the standard model is silent.

Before we turn to a more detailed treatment of profitability and diffusion, we briefly examine three studies of industrial growth by Burns, Kuznets, and Hicks which implicitly treat demand and supply aspects of diffusion.[17] These studies provide useful perspectives on the diffusion process.

## Laws of industrial growth

Their central theme is the close connection between economic growth and qualitative, structural change induced by technological innovation. The following quotations, one from Schumpeter[18] and the other from Kuznets,[19] provide a clear statement of this theme.

industrial change is never harmonious advance with all elements of the system actually moving, or tending to move in step. At any given time, some industries move on and others stay behind; and the discrepancies arising from this are an essential element in the situations that develop.

As we observe the various industries within a given national system, we see that the lead in development shifts from one branch to another. The main reason for this shift seems to be that a rapidly developing industry does not continue its vigorous growth indefinitely, but slackens its pace after a time, and is overtaken by industries whose period of rapid development comes later.

Replace 'industries' by 'innovations', and we see perfect examples of the theme of impulse and diffusion in the study of technical change. The connections with diffusion are further reinforced when we find that both Kuznets and Burns were concerned to explain the retardation of industrial growth.[20] As noted above this is a corollary of a sigmoid diffusion process.

Leaving aside differences of detail and the general factors of population growth and international competition, the retardation-generating elements which they emphasize are three-fold: inter-commodity competition, inelasticity in supplies of productive inputs, and post-innovation patterns of technical progress.

On the first, innovations may stand in a competitive or complementary relation with existing lines of production, restricting the growth of the former and accelerating the growth of the latter. For each innovation, limits exist on the growth of its market demand. The equilibrium market is constrained by a demand curve, but this equilibrium constraint is only binding after a period of transition to overcome market resistance.[21]

The second set of retarding forces relate to the supply side of industrial growth. Inelasticities in the supply of labour, materials, and machinery imply that as the production of an innovation grows they can raise the supply price of inputs and, *ceteris paribus*, reduce profitability in production. In turn, we can expect that the level of profitability will influence the supply of finance available to invest in the innovation, and thus the pace of transition to the new equilibrium. Of course, finance and machines can only provide a temporary bottleneck, but inelasticities in primary input supplies of labour and materials can permanently constrain the equilibrium utilization of the innovation.[22]

Hicks has recently incorporated similar considerations in his more macro-economic discussions of the connection between economic growth and science-based technical progress embodied in durable capital equipment.[23] He discusses the path of transition following an innovation-related impulse to growth, and argues that the bottlenecks experienced during the transition will depend on the characteristics of the innovation and the diffusion environment, though there is no explicit treatment of relevant technical dimensions or their relation to various bottlenecks.

The final factor considered by all three authors is the pattern of post-innovation improvement in a technology. A major growth impulse is provided by any innovation which can generate scope for a sequence of secondary improvement innovations, extending the market, lowering production costs, and overcoming specific bottlenecks. Moreover, the pattern of secondary improvement is not arbitrary but, according to Kuznets and Burns, will evolve according to Wolff's Law.[24] The scope for improvement in any technology is bounded, and approach to this limit is slowed down by the increasing difficulty in generating successive incremental improvements. As corollaries to this, the more significant improvements tend to cluster close to the original time of innovation; many of these will not be foreseen at the time of innovation; and the cumulative impact of the secondary improvements will often exceed the impact of the initial innovation. Retardation in the rate of secondary innovation is thus a dominant factor in the overall tendency to retardation in the growth of a new industry.

## Impulse, diffusion and profitability

We shall now relate this more general perspective on industrial growth to the standard model of the diffusion of innovation. Our discussion is meant to be suggestive, not exhaustive.

Imagine that the innovation in question is a new industrial material, eg rayon, which has certain advantages relative to existing competing materials. These advantages determine the equilibrium market for the innovation, and will depend on its technical properties and price relative to those of competing materials. Given an equilibrium market, we shall assume that the process of inter- and intra-firm adoption of the new material generates a logistic pattern of physical demand growth, thus

$$g_d(t) = b[m(p) - y(t)], \text{ and } y(0) = z \tag{2}$$

where $g_d(t)$ is the proportionate rate of growth of demand at $t$, $y(t)$ is the rate of demand at $t$, $b$ is the 'adoption' coefficient, $z$ is the initial rate of demand, and $m(p)$ is the equilibrium market demand which, for pedagogic convenience, we assume depends upon $p$ as follows

$$m(p) = c - a\, p(t) \tag{3}$$

A lower price for the new material extends the equilibrium market, making it profitable to adopt in an increasing range of production processes. The parameters of Equation (3) will depend on several factors, including the price of competing materials and the comparative performance characteristics of the new and competing materials. We shall call Equation (3) the equilibrium demand curve for the innovation with adjustment to equilibrium determined by Equation (2). It is clear that the adjustment path depends upon the behaviour of the innovation's price, for as $p(t)$ changes, so the profitability of adopting the new material also changes.[25]

But how is $p(t)$ to be determined? Is the price path arbitrary, an exogenous component of the diffusion story, or is it (as a Schumpeterian perspective would suggest) determined by the process of diffusion? To answer this question we must turn to the supply side, the growth of capacity to produce the new material.

The crux of our argument is that the rate of increase in capacity depends on the profitability of producing the new material, in that the supply of capital to finance capacity expansion, from ploughed back funds and external funds, increases as the rate of return on investment increases. Under capitalism, profit is both the inducement and the means to effect the transition between different equilibria. The profitability of this new activity depends upon three elements: the price of the innovation (as yet undetermined), the technology of its production, and the price of the necessary material and labour inputs. Let the technology be described by a capital:output ratio $v$ and a unit input requirements coefficient $\ell$—inputs of labour and raw materials here being treated as a composite, for expositional convenience alone. Let $w$ be the price paid for this composite input, and let $d$ denote the capital replacement or depreciation ratio. The rate of profits $r$, the ratio of profits to capital invested, is then defined by:

$$r = \frac{p(t) - w(t)\ell - dv}{v} \tag{4}$$

Following Burns and Kuznets,[26] we shall assume that as the output of the new activity expands, so the price which has to be paid for the composite input increases, and we assume, again for simplicity, that this relation is linear:

$$w(t) = w_0 + w_1 x(t) \tag{5}$$

Combining Equations (4) and (5), we see that the rate of return is smaller the larger the scale of production, $x(t)$. Note that we have assumed constant returns to scale, though the extensions to decreasing and increasing returns are obvious.

One final element is needed, the relation between profit and capacity growth. Let $\pi$ be the fraction of the internally generated profits ploughed back in capacity expansion, and let $\mu$ be the ratio of external to internal funds invested at any time. It follows that the growth rate of capacity $g_S$ is linked to the rate of profits by:

$$g_S(t) = \pi(1+\mu)r(t) \tag{6}$$

The values of $\pi$ and $\mu$ will reflect alternative uses of corporate resources and barriers to entry into the new industry. Combining Equations (4), (5) and (6), we have:[27]

$$g_S(t) = \frac{p(t) - h_0 - h_1 x(t)}{k} \tag{7}$$

One implication of Equation (7) is immediate. Given technology and the price of the new material, the growth of capacity will follow a logistic curve, reaching a saturation level when prime cost is driven into equality with the given price.[28] From both the capacity growth and the demand growth perspectives, we therefore find a logistic process to govern diffusion, in which the price of the innovation plays a key role. Price not only determines the equilibrium market, it also determines the rate of growth of capacity to supply that market.

In our closed economy, the growth of demand and the growth of capacity cannot stray out of step for long. Profit-conscious producers will not want to forgo profitable investments or to build up permanent excess capacity. This immediately suggests a function for price, to balance the growth of demand with the growth of productive capacity, not necessarily at each point in time but certainly on a secular basis.[29] We shall call such a transition path a balanced diffusion path.

If we hold constant the fundamental parameters of the diffusion process, relating the the supply of finance, the innovation's technology, the equilibrium demand curve, and the supply conditions of the composite non-capital input, we can trace out the balanced diffusion paths for output, prices, costs, and profits as follows. Along the balanced path, we have $g_d(t) = g_S(t) = g(t)$, and $y(t) = x(t)$.

Substituting Equation (7) into (3), and the outcome into (2), we have:

$$g(t) = b[c - a(kg(t) + h_0 + h_1 x(t)) - x(t)]$$

or

$$g(t) = B[C - x(t)]$$

$$x(0) = z$$

(8)

with

$$B = \frac{b(1+ah_1)}{1 + abk} \text{ and } C = \frac{c - ah_0}{1 + ah_1}$$

The balanced diffusion process is a logistic diffusion process with parameters which reflect the joint dynamics of demand growth and capacity growth. The saturation output level $C$ depends on technology and the parameters of the equilibrium demand and input supply schedules in Equations (3) and (5).

The balanced adoption coefficient $B$ depends on technology and the co-efficients $b$ and $k$, which govern the dynamics of demand and capacity growth. Figure 1 illustrates the main implications to be drawn from this simple framework. The innovation of the new material acts as an impulse in the economy creating a potential for growth equal to $C$ with a post-innovation adjustment gap of $C$-$z$. This adjustment gap is eliminated by a diffusion process in which the demand for the innovation and the capacity to produce it grow in step. Figure 1a shows the logistic path followed by the output of the new material. The balanced diffusion coefficient is given by the product $BC$, and this is independent of $h_1$, and thus of the elasticity of supply of the composite input. By contrast, the standard diffusion model is one in which the price of the new material is constant over time, with a perfectly elastic supply of materials, labour, and external capital finance to the industry so that capacity growth adjusts passively to the growth of demand. In our more general framework, we find that as diffusion proceeds, the price changes and, with it, the profitability of adopting and producing the new material.

Figure 1b shows the path for the growth rate of output, that familiar curve of retardation with growth dropping asymptotically to zero as diffusion proceeds. Retardation occurs even with a fixed technology. Because the growth rate declines continuously, it follows from Equation (6) that the rate of profits on capital invested in the industry also declines continuously, and here we can see the relevance of Schumpeter's viewpoint on profits and innovation. Profits are the reward for entrepreneurial activity, accruing to those who innovate and disturb the pre-existing economic structure. But the innovator's reward is temporary, destined to be eliminated during the diffusion process. Profit[30]

attaches to the creation of new things, to the realization of the new value system. It is at the same time the child and victim of development.

The harmony between Schumpeter's view of profits and retardation is closely connected with the role of competition in the diffusion process. Figure 1c shows the effect of the balanced diffusion process upon unit prime cost, price and profit margins—the excess of price over unit prime cost. As the industry expands, the increasing price of the composite input pulls up unit prime cost along the path $h(0) - h(t)$, tending toward the stationary level $h_0 + h_1 C$. The price of the new

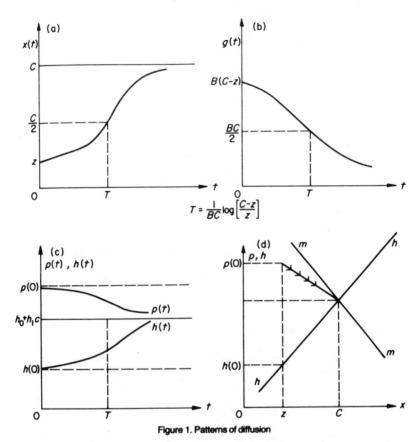

Figure 1. Patterns of diffusion

material, however, is shown falling along the path $p(0) - p(t)$ toward the same stationary level so that, over time, profit margins are progressively squeezed.[31] For adopters, the reductions in price imply an increase in the profit to be gained by switching to the new material, and provide scope for competitive pressure to be put on the remaining firms to hasten their adoption decisions. From this we see how ambiguous is the relation of diffusion speed to measures of profitability. Profitability is perceived differently by the producers and the adopters of the innovation, and for both it varies systematically, and in opposite directions, over time. To relate a hybrid measure of diffusion speed to a single measure of adopting profitability hides more than it illuminates.[32] The pace of diffusion depends on supply-side constraints just as much as it does on constraints to adoption.

Finally, Figure 1d plots the implied relations between price and output. The curves $m$–$m$ and $h$–$h$ are the adopters equilibrium demand curve and the producers equilibrium supply curve, respectively, and they intersect at output level $C$. From the initial price $p(0)$ and output level $z$, price and output follow the arrowed path until $C$ is reached and the new material is part of the stationary economic routine.

To summarize. Given the fundamental data, the balanced diffusion path is governed by two factors, the adjustment gap $C-z$, and the dynamic elements in demand and capacity growth, as summarized by $B$. This potential for growth can be eliminated only because it is profitable to make the transition to $C$—profitable, that is, to adopt the new material *and* to build up the capacity to produce it.[33]

The purpose of this framework is to serve as a starting point from which further questions can be asked. A great many of these will already have occurred to the reader, but I confine myself to the following observations. For example, this framework allows us to investigate the effect of differences in fundamental data on the paths of balanced diffusion. In practice, changes in fundamental data are likely to occur throughout the diffusion process, continually shifting $m-m$ and $h-h$ in Figure 1d, redefining $B$ and $C$, and producing new balanced growth curves. Only by fluke is the outcome likely to be capable of summary by a logistic trend. Economic growth, for example, will normally shift the curve $m-m$ upwards so that the saturation level $C$ rises steadily over time. If general growth is fast enough, we might even experience acceleration in the diffusion rate rather than retardation.[34]

In a modern industrial economy, $C$ may also change because of other complementary and competing innovations which stimulate or contract the market for the new material. In the latter case, growth may be cut short, and turned into decadence, long before the full adjustment potential of the innovation is exploited. Diffusion is always relative; it reflects the comparative merits of competing technologies so that one must always look beyond the specific innovation to gain a full understanding of its diffusion. Notice also that the process of diffusion extends the market as price falls. The often made observation that perceptions of the market at the time of innovation understate the final market, then falls into place. The diffusion environment is not static; it changes as a very consequence of diffusion.

Turning now to the important dimension of post-innovation improvements in technology, we can see how our framework helps sift relevant research questions. One may first distinguish improvements in the utilization technology from improvements in the production technology. Improvements in the former shift the equilibrium demand curve, and thus $C$, while improvements in the latter shift the unit prime cost schedule, changing $C$ and, to the extent that improvements influence the capital:output ratio, $B$. A question which is immediately raised is how the relative balance of these different types of improvements changes during the diffusion process. May it not be that the nature of improvements and the rate at which they occur are a function of the diffusion environment and thus of the pace of diffusion?[35]

There is a further important aspect to this. The pace of diffusion will influence the rate at which plant designs can exploit economies of scale, and the rate at which producers and adopters can mutually improve technology by way of learning by doing. The pace of diffusion will also determine the incidence of supply bottlenecks, and thus the direction of secondary innovative activity; different diffusion speeds may generate different sequences and types of improvement. In other words, the innovation which is being diffused is itself changing as a consequence of the diffusion process. Further considerations will be the position of the innovation in the input–output structure, and the maturity of the technologies to which it is related. These will influence the types of bottlenecks faced, and the possibility of induced technical changes in related sectors.

We have seen how profit margins will be highest in the early stages of a new activity, and this will provide the incentive to seek improvements and reinforce the likelihood that they will be clustered early in the innovation's life. The slackening of technical progress may then reflect not only the operation of Wolff's Law, but also the exhaustion of the profit potential of the new industry as it approaches its equilibrium size.[36] As technology changes during the diffusion process a further factor may be expectations of future technical change. As Rosenberg has argued,[37] such expectations may depress the growth of demand or reduce propensities to invest in the new productive technology and on either count the effect will be to reduce the balanced adoption co-efficient, $B$, and slow diffusion. Finally, the 'steamship effect' cannot be ignored. The displacement of old technologies by an innovation may stimulate competing improvements in the former, with impacts on the diffusion of the innovation which should now be clear.

On each of the points raised above, there is scope for linking together analysis of the diffusion of innovation with analysis of the inducement to innovation. But this is simply another way of pointing out the limitations of the static diffusion model.

## Conclusion

We have attempted to provide a more complete perspective on the diffusion process by integrating the growth of productive capacity with the more traditional focus upon the diffusion of demand. We have shown how this wider perspective links diffusion research with important contributions to the study of industrial growth, and fits in neatly with Schumpeter's emphasis on the transient nature of the profits to be gained from innovation. The impulses generated by technical change give rise to adjustment potentials. How these are determined and eliminated is central to an understanding of diffusion. We have also suggested that the pace and direction of technical change is a function of the diffusion process

It cannot be stressed too strongly how tentative this framework of analysis is. Restrictions on space make it impossible to incorporate some of the important insights of Nelson and Winter,[38] to allow for technology differences among producers of the innovation, to incorporate barriers to entry such as patent restrictions, or to allow for foreign trade and investment. Such developments are properly subjects of separate papers.

### Notes and references

1. For the most recent studies of diffusion see, for example, E. Mansfield *et al*, *The Production and Application of New Industrial Technology* (New York, W.W. Norton, 1977), chapters 6 and 7; S.

358 *Impulse and diffusion in the study of technical change*

Davies, *The Diffusion of Process Innovations* (Cambridge University Press, 1979); L. Nabseth, "The diffusion of innovations in Swedish industry", in B.R. Williams, ed, *Science and Technology in Economic Growth* (Macmillan, 1973); A.A. Romeo, "The rate of limitation of a capital-embodied process innovation", *Economica*, February 1977, *44*, 1, pages 63–70; A.A. Romeo, "Inter-industry and inter-firm differences in the rate of diffusion of an innovation", *Review of Economics and Statistics*, August 1975, *57*, 3, pages 311–319; G. Rosseger, "Diffusion and technological specificity", *Journal of Industrial Economics*, September 1979, *28*, 1, pages 39–53; S. Globerman, "Technological diffusion in the Canadian tool and die industry", *Review of Economics and Statistics*, November 1975, *42*, 4, pages 428–434; and papers by Baker, Gold, and Hayward in M.J. Baker, *Industrial Innovation* (Macmillan, 1979).

2. See L. Nabseth and G. Ray, *The Diffusion of New Industrial Processes*, (Cambridge University Press, 1974); B. Gold, "Technological diffusion in industry: research needs and shortcomings", *Journal of Industrial Economics*, March 1981, *24*, 3, pages 247–269; and Gold in Baker (ed), reference 1.

3. I shall not be directly concerned with the links between impulse, transition, and long waves, though their interconnection will be obvious to the reader of J.J. van Duijn, "The long wave in economic life", *De Economist*, 1977, *125*, 4, pages 544–576.

4. An important exception is N. Rosenberg, *Perspectives on Technology* (Cambridge University Press, 1976), Chapter 11.

5. It is only part of the answer because the outcome also depends on the rapidity of intra-firm diffusion of the innovation.

6. See Davies, reference 1, chapter 2, for a full treatment.

7. If $z > n/2$, we would only observe the upper branch of this curve.

8. Let $y(t) = (x(t)-n)/x(t)$; then in a regression of the form $\log y(t) = a + bt$, we find that $a = \log[(n-z)/z]$ and $-b = n\beta$, the diffusion coefficient.

9. Papers by Mansfield and Griliches pioneered the role of profitability and capital cost variables in explaining diffusion speed; see E. Mansfield, "Technical change and the rate of imitation", *Econometrica*, October 1961, *29*, 4, pages 741–766, and Z. Griliches, "Hybrid corn: an exploration in the economics of technical change", *Econometrica*, October 1957, *25*, 4, pages 501–522.

10. See Mansfield, reference 1, chapter 7; Romeo, reference 1 (both articles); and Davies, reference 1, chapter 8. The latter provides the most exhaustive treatment to date of the effect of industrial concentration on the pace of diffusion. The central hypothesis appears to be that information spreads more quickly in a concentrated industry.

11. Absence of a logistic curve should not therefore be equated with irrelevance of the logistic information/epidemic process.

12. See Gold, reference 2, first item.

13. See Davies, reference 1.

14. See Gold, reference 2, page 250.

15. See Rosenberg, reference 4.

16. See Rosenberg, reference 4.

17. See S. Kuznets, *Secular Movements in Production and Prices* (Boston, Houghton Miflin, 1930); the summary in chapter 9 of S. Kuznets, *Economic Change*, (London, Heinemann, 1954); A.F. Burns, *Production Trends in the United States since 1870* (New York, National Bureau of Economic Research, 1934); J.R. Hicks, *Capital and Time*, (Oxford, Clarendon Press, 1973); and J.R. Hicks, "Industrialism" in *Economic Perspectives* (Oxford, Clarendon Press, 1977).

18. J. Schumpeter, *Business Cycles, Volume 1* (McGraw Hill, 1939), pages 101–102.

19. See Kuznets, reference 17, first item, pages 4–5.

20. Burns went as far as to call retardation a "law of industrial growth"; reference 17, pages 169–173.

21. Burns, reference 17, pages 127–128; see also J. Schumpeter, *The Theory of Economic Development* (Oxford University Press, 1961 – first published 1934), page 87; and Kuznets, reference 17, first item, pages 258 and 266.

22. Kuznets presents a detailed discussion of how the influence of supply bottlenecks depends on the position of the innovating industry in the input–output structure of the economy. Kuznets, reference 17, first item, pages 41–49.

23. See, in particular, Hicks, reference 17—his first item, and the earlier version in Chapter 10 of his second item.

24. Kuznets, reference 17, first item, pages 11–41; and Burns, reference 17, pages 141–143.
25. See, for example, G. Chow, "Technical change and the demand for computers", *American Economic Review*, December 1967, *57*, pages 1110–1130.
26. See also Schumpeter, reference 18, page 100.
27. The coefficients in Equation (7) are to be interpreted as follows: $h_0 = w_0 \ell + dv$ is prime cost at a zero level of industry output, including in $w_0$ the appropriate element for a normal rate of return on invested capital. $h_1 = w_1 \ell$ is marginal prime cost. $k^{-1} = \pi(1+\mu)/v$ is the amount of profit required to expand capacity by one unit, given that capital funds come from internal and external sources.
28. This saturation level equals $(\bar{p}-h_0)/h_1$, for price $\bar{p}$.
29. The importance of the closed economy assumption will here be obvious.
30. Schumpeter, reference 21, pages 153–154, and reference 18, pages 104–105.
31. Note that $p(t)$ need not follow a falling path, the outcome depending on the relative dynamics of demand and capacity growth. However, the excess of $p(t)$ over $h(t)$ always declines with diffusion.
32. See Gold, reference 2, on the general inadequacy of profit measures.
33. The total profit earned by the producers of the innovation, the area between the curves $p(t)$ and $h(t)$ in Figure 1c, is proportional to the adjustment gap. Note that total profit is independent of the path of adjustment.
34. Considerations of this nature go some way to explaining Gold's negative comments on the Kuznets–Burns retardation thesis; B. Gold, "Industry growth patterns: theory and empirical results", *Journal of Industrial Economics*, November 1964, *8*, 1, pages 53–73.
35. See Utterback for related discussion of the pattern of innovation over a product's life cycle; J.M. Utterback, "The dynamics of product and process innovation in industry", in C.T. Hill and J.M. Utterback (eds), *Technological Innovation for a Dynamic Economy* (Pergamon, 1979).
36. This point is raised in J. Schmookler, *Invention and Economic Growth* (Harvard University Press, 1966).
37. N. Rosenberg, "On technological expectations", *Economic Journal*, September 1976, *86*, 3, pages 523–535.
38. See R.R. Nelson and S. Winter, "Towards useful theory of innovation", *Research Policy*, January 1977, *6*, 1, pages 36–76.

# Part V
# Patterns of Innovation, Trajectories, Cycles and Paradigms

# [22]

*The Economic Journal*, **86** (*September* 1976), 523–535
Printed in Great Britain

## ON TECHNOLOGICAL EXPECTATIONS[1]

I

One of the most important unresolved issues in the theory of the firm and in the understanding of productivity growth is the rate at which new and improved technologies are adopted.[2] I will argue that expectations concerning the future course of technological innovation are a significant and neglected component of these issues, inasmuch as they are an important determinant of entrepreneurial decisions with respect to the adoption of innovations.

Recent work in various aspects of economic theory and measurement has pointed, once again, to the important role played by expectations of future change in influencing the behaviour of economic agents. In a number of instances the expectation of future changes has led to quite different patterns of behaviour than might have been expected to have taken place if it had been anticipated that no changes in level and/or trend would occur. What would appear to be aberrational or irrational behaviour on the basis of such expectations of no changes is often fully explained once allowance is made for a different set of expectations about the future.

In this paper I should like to draw a similar analogy for the study of the diffusion of technological innovations. The timing and nature of the adoption decision on the part of individual business firms is a key question with major implications for both the micro and macro levels of analysis. I will suggest that there are expectational elements in the adoption decision which have not been given the attention and explored as systematically as could be done to illuminate the diffusion process. Often the explanation of specific rates and patterns of technique adoption seems difficult to comprehend under the implicit conditions assumed, i.e. of no future changes in the technological and economic spheres. Yet, as in other parts of economic analysis, the introduction of attention paid to various types of expectations, not only of prices but, more interestingly, of expectations concerning the future rate of technological change itself, will provide some important insights. Since the technological future is, inevitably, shrouded in uncertainty, it is not surprising both that different entrepreneurs will hold different expectations, and also that entrepreneurial behaviour will further differ due to varying degrees of risk aversion on the part of decision-makers.

[1] I am heavily indebted to Stanley Engerman for his encouragement and frequent counsel in developing the central argument of this paper and in exploring some of its implications. The paper has also benefited greatly from Paul David's searching criticism of an earlier draft, and from valuable comments and suggestions by David Mowery, W. B. Reddaway, Ed Steinmuller, George Stigler and an anonymous referee. I am also grateful to the National Science Foundation for financial support during the time this paper was being written.

[2] Ed Mansfield's work has forcefully called attention both to the general overall slowness as well as to the wide differentials in adoption rates among different innovations. See, for example, Ed Mansfield, *Industrial Research and Technological Innovation* (W. W. Norton and Co., New York, 1968), chapter 7.

In terms of historical issues there are two patterns of expectations with quite different implications which need to be examined. One, which has been implicit in the comparisons of nineteenth century technological change in the United States and the United Kingdom, is the impact of steady but differing rates of technological change in the two economies. As pointed out by Habakkuk, and more formally by Williamson, the effect of the expectation of higher rates of technological change in the United States should have led to a shorter optimal life for American machinery – i.e. in some sense a more rapid introduction of new techniques.[1] More interesting, perhaps, are other patterns of expectations which may be more important in studying the diffusion process. Specifically, at certain times it may be more plausible to anticipate an acceleration of the rate of technological change. Similarly, there may be situations where large-scale improvements are confidently expected *after* the introduction of some major innovation.[2] In such cases these expectations may lead to a surprising result of making rational a delay in the widespread diffusion of the innovation. Therefore, in analysing any historical decision with respect to diffusion, one must be sensitive to the specific nature of the expectations held by entrepreneurs with respect to the future course of technology.

II

If, as Alfred North Whitehead once asserted, the history of western philosophy may be adequately described as a series of footnotes upon Plato, it may equally be said of the study of technological innovation that it still consists of a series of footnotes upon Schumpeter. Although the footnotes may be getting longer, more critical and, happily, richer in the recognition of empirical complexities, we still occupy the conceptual edifice which Schumpeter built for the subject. Inevitably, therefore, Schumpeter's concepts constitute our point of departure.

Schumpeter's theory of capitalist development, it will be recalled, starts out from the circular flow of economic life where producers and consumers are all in equilibrium, and where all adjustments and adaptations have been made. Schumpeter then introduces an innovation – a shift in the production function – into this circular flow. The entrepreneurial response to this new profit prospect in turn generates a sequence of alterations in the behaviour of economic actors, beginning with an expansion of bank credit and including, eventually, a secondary wave of investment activity imposed on top of the primary wave as the expectations of the larger business community are affected by the evidence and by the consequences of business expansion.[3]

---

[1] H. J. Habakkuk, *American and British Technology in the Nineteenth Century* (Cambridge University Press, 1962), and Jeffrey Williamson, "Optimal Replacement of Capital Goods: The Early New England and British Textile Firm", *Journal of Political Economy*, Nov./Dec. 1971.

[2] For earlier empirical studies dealing with the life-cycle of specific technological innovations, see Simon Kuznets, *Secular Movements in Production and Prices* (Houghton Mifflin, 1930), chapter 1, and Arthur F. Burns, *Production Trends in the United States Since 1870* (National Bureau of Economic Research, 1934), especially chapter 4.

[3] J. A. Schumpeter, *The Theory of Economic Development* (Harvard University Press, 1934), chapters 1 and 2.

Schumpeter himself was so much persuaded of the large elements of risk and uncertainty inherent in the innovation decision that he down-played the role of rational calculation itself in the decision-making process. The Schumpeterian entrepreneur is a distinctly heroic figure, prepared (unlike most mortals) to venture forth boldly into the unknown. His decisions are not the outcome of precise and careful calculation and, Schumpeter emphasised, cannot be reduced to such terms.

The point to be made here is that there is a further dimension of uncertainty in the innovation decision of a sort not emphasised by Schumpeter in his stress on the *discontinuous* nature of technological innovation. This is, quite simply, the uncertainty generated not only by technological innovations elsewhere in the economy, but *by further improvement in the technology whose introduction is now being considered.* Schumpeter's argument creates a presumption that the first innovator reaps the large rewards. Nevertheless, the decision to undertake innovation $X$ today may be decisively affected by the expectation that significant improvements will be introduced into $X$ tomorrow (or by the firmly held expectation that a new substitute technology, $Y$, will be introduced the day after). The possible wisdom of waiting is reinforced by observations, abundantly available to all would-be entrepreneurs, concerning the sad financial fate of innumerable earlier entrepreneurs who ended up in the bankruptcy courts because of their premature entrepreneurial activities.[1] As soon as we accept the perspective of the ongoing nature of much technological change, the optimal timing of an innovation becomes heavily influenced by expectations concerning the timing and the significance of *future* improvements. Even when a new process innovation passes the stringent test of reducing new average total costs below old average variable costs, it may not be adopted. The reason for this is that the entrepreneur's views about the pace of technological improvements may reflect expectations of a higher rate of technological obsolescence than that allowed for by conventional accounting procedures in valuing the investment. Moreover, accounting formulae may not give adequate recognition to the "disruption costs" involved in introducing new methods, especially when such disruptions are frequent. Thus, a firm may be unwilling to introduce the new technology if it seems highly probable that further technological improvements will shortly be forthcoming.[2] This problem

[1] Marx long ago called attention to "the far greater cost of operating an establishment based on a new invention as compared to later establishments arising *ex suis ossibus*. This is so very true that the trail-blazers generally go bankrupt, and only those who later buy the buildings, machinery, etc., at a cheaper price, make money out of it" (Karl Marx, *Capital* (Foreign Languages Publishing House, Moscow, 1959), vol. III, p. 103). He also called attention to the rapid improvements in the productivity of machinery in its early stages as well as the sharp reduction in the cost of its production. "When machinery is first introduced into an industry, new methods of reproducing it more cheaply follow blow by blow, and so do improvements, that not only affect individual parts and details on the machine, but its entire build" (Karl Marx, *Capital* (Modern Library Edition, New York, no date), vol. I, p. 442). In a footnote on that page, Marx cites approvingly Babbage's statement: "It has been estimated, roughly, that the first individual of a newly invented machine will cost about five times as much as the construction of the second." For a discussion of related problems with respect to the growth of nations, see Ed Ames and Nathan Rosenberg, "Changing Technological Leadership and Economic Growth", ECONOMIC JOURNAL, March 1963.

[2] Fellner's discussion of what he calls "anticipatory retardation" is relevant here. See William Fellner, "The Influence of Market Structure on Technological Progress", *Quarterly Journal of Economics*

of how the optimal timing of innovation is affected by expectations of discontinuous technological change is an extremely significant one which has
received relatively little attention in the theoretical literature.[1] Nor have
there been systematic empirical studies of the phenomenon.

In their earliest stages, innovations are often highly imperfect and are
known to be so. Innumerable "bugs" may need to be worked out.[2] If one
anticipates significant improvements, it may be foolish to undertake the
innovation now – the more so the greater the size of the financial commitment
and the greater the durability of the equipment involved. Whereas the
Schumpeterian innovator experiences abnormally high profits until the
"imitators" catch up with him, the impetuous innovator may go broke as
a result of investing in a premature model of an invention. This apparent
distinction follows from the earlier-stated difficulties of Schumpeter's concept
of innovation with its emphasis on discontinuity and its implication that all
problems in the introduction of a new product or process have already been
completely solved. Moreover, as Mansfield points out: "In cases where the
invention is a new piece of equipment, both the firm that is first to sell the
equipment and the firm that is first to use it may be regarded as innovators.
The first user is important because he, as well as the supplier, often takes
considerable risk."[3]

---

(1951), pp. 556–77, as reprinted in R. Heflebower and G. Stocking (eds.), *Readings in Industrial
Organization and Public Policy* (Richard D. Irwin, 1958). The discussion of "anticipatory retardation"
appears on pages 287–8 of that volume.

[1] Of course attention has been paid to the optimal timing of the introduction (and scrapping) of
machinery, but these models generally do not deal with problems of expected future changes in
technology. Rather, they are more often concerned with issues relating to relative factor prices, future
product demands, or the relation between machine use and deterioration. While the expectations
relating to technology can no doubt be easily incorporated into such models, the specific problem is
virtually unexplored. For a brief discussion, see Vernon L. Smith, *Investment and Production* (Harvard
University Press, 1961), pp. 143–5. The relationship between expectations concerning the rate of
technological progress and the rate of return on investment in the context of a model of embodied
technological change is discussed by Robert Solow in *Capital Theory and the Rate of Return* (North
Holland Publishing Co., 1963, pp. 61–4). For an interesting treatment of a somewhat related problem,
how the introduction of a new technology will be affected by expected future growth in demand
under different forms of market structure, externalities and property rights, see Yoram Barzel,
"Optimal Timing of Innovations", *Review of Economics and Statistics*, August 1968.

[2] This term should be taken to include a great many production problems involving the use of
new equipment which it is almost impossible to anticipate and which become apparent only as a
result of extensive use – e.g. metal fatigue in aeroplanes. William Hughes has made this point well
with respect to exploration of the scale frontier in electric power generation: "Even under the most
favorable conditions for advancing the scale frontier the cost side of the equation imposes fairly strict
upper limits on the economical pace of advance, and trying to force the pace could mean sharply
rising cost of development. The experience required for pushing out the scale frontier is related to
time and cannot be acquired by increasing the number of similar new units. Perhaps the greatest
uncertainties connected with units arise from problems that may not show up until the units have
been in operation a few years. For the industry as a whole, the socially optimal number of pioneering
units during the first two or three years of any major advance in scale, design, or steam conditions
is probably rather small, most often ranging from perhaps two or three or half a dozen" (William
Hughes, "Scale Frontiers in Electric Power," in William Capron (ed.), *Technological Change in
Regulated Industries* (The Brookings Institution, Washington, D.C., 1971), p. 52). One of the other
virtues of the Hughes article is its forceful reminder of the intimate link which often exists between
technological progress and economies of scale. "The realization of latent scale economies is an
especially important form of technological progress in the utility industries" (*ibid.*, p. 45).

[3] Edwin Mansfield, *Industrial Research and Technological Innovation, op. cit.*, p. 83.

De Tocqueville long ago pointed out a distinctive characteristic of the American scene: "...I accost an American sailor, and I inquire why the ships of his country are built so as to last but for a short time; he answers without hesitation that the art of navigation is every day making such rapid progress that the finest vessel would become almost useless if it lasted beyond a certain number of years. In these words, which fall accidentally and on a particular subject from a man of rude attainments, I recognize the general and systematic idea upon which a great people directs all its concerns."[1] Similarly, expectations of future changes may have the effect, not of delaying innovation, but of determining some of the specific characteristics of the innovation chosen. An adaptation to these expectations might be deliberately to construct cheaper and flimsier capital equipment. Thus, for example, as between two economies with different expected rates of future technical change, it would be anticipated that optimal life would be shorter where expected changes are largest.[2] And, correspondingly, an anticipated acceleration in the course of technological improvement could lead to the selection of equipment with expected optimal life shorter than would otherwise be chosen.

Central to the analysis of the problem of expectations with respect to further improvements in technology, is the question of the specific source of subsequent improvements. It may be that these improvements can only be brought about by the process which we have come to call "learning by doing", in which case the pace of improvement is itself determined by either the producers' accumulated experience over time or by their cumulative output.[3] Alternatively, improvements may be rigidly linked to the passage of time necessary to acquire information about the results of earlier experience.[4] Consider the problems associated with the introduction of commercial jet aeroplanes. Britain introduced the Comet I two years before the Americans began the development of a jet airliner. Yet the Americans eventually won out. In retrospect, it is apparent that the American delay was salutary rather than costly to them, and that Boeing and Douglas chose the moment to proceed better than did de Havilland. "Their delay allowed them to offer airplanes that could carry

[1] Alexis De Tocqueville (trans. Henry Reeve), *Democracy in America*, 2 vols. (D. Appleton and Company, New York, 1901), vol. i, p. 516.

[2] For a discussion of optimal replacement in the *ante bellum* textile industries of the United States and the United Kingdom, see Williamson, *op. cit.* For a criticism of the Williamson article which does not alter the relationship between expected rates of technical change and optimal life, see David Denslow, Jr., and David Schulze, "Optimal Replacement of Capital Goods in Early New England and British Textile Firms: A Comment", *Journal of Political Economy*, May/June 1974.

[3] See Paul David, "Learning by Doing and Tariff Protection: A Reconsideration of the Case of the Ante-Bellum United States Cotton Textile Industry", *Journal of Economic History*, September 1970, and Tsuneo Ishikawa, "Conceptualization of Learning by Doing: A Note on Paul David's 'Learning by Doing and...The Ante-Bellum United States Cotton Textile Industry'", *ibid.*, December 1973. Note the importance of this distinction as well as that between learning which can be freely captured by others and that which accrues solely to the learner. This latter distinction will have important implications for the number of firms in an industry as well as the optimal entry date for any one firm. See Barzel, *op. cit.*

[4] This is not really "learning by doing" in the usual sense, which is restricted to learning by participation in the production process, even though it does involve the passage of time and the accumulation of experience. However, the distinctions above concerning the "appropriability" of the information generated by the experience remain important for examining entry decisions.

up to 180 passengers when the Comet IV carries up to 100, and a cruising speed of 550 m.p.h. instead of 480 m.p.h. – hard commercial advantages that they could offer because they were designing for later and more powerful engines. But they were also aided by the delay of four years in making the Comet safe after its accidents from metal fatigue."[1] More generally, information concerning the useful life of metal components could only be derived from prolonged periods of use and experience. Which forms of improvements may be expected to dominate, and the conditions under which they may become available to other firms, will have important implications not only for entrepreneurs making entry or adoption decisions, but also for public policy concerning efficient growth.

There are many possible reasons why waiting may be the most sensible decision. Indeed, often there may be no real choice. On the purely technological level, innovations in their early stages are usually exceedingly ill-adapted to the wide range of more specialised uses to which they are eventually put. Potential buyers may postpone purchase to await the elimination of "bugs" or the inevitable flow of improvements in product performance or characteristics. On the other hand, they may have to wait through the lengthy process of product redesign and modification before a product has been created which is suitable to specific sets of final users. Thus, widely used products such as machine tools, electric motors and steam engines have experienced a proliferation of time-consuming changes as they were adapted to the varying range of needs of ultimate users. In the case of machine tools, for example, there was a successful search for the application of specific machine tool innovations across a wide variety of industrial uses.[2] In the case of final consumer goods, the redesigning is likely to be primarily concerned with the development of product varieties suitable to the financial resources of different income groups. What is observed over their life cycles is a gradual expansion of their quality range to accommodate these final users.[3] Today's academics are keenly aware of this problem when deciding whether to purchase today or to defer the purchase of pocket calculators, given their expectations of ongoing improvement in their capacities and characteristics. Similar problems have characterised the selection decision with respect to the last few

[1] Ronald Miller and David Sawers, *The Technical Development of Modern Aviation* (Praeger Publishers, New York, 1970), p. 27. For an American failure in the attempted development of the "Demon" fighter plane under the pressures of the Korean War, see Eighth Report of the Preparedness Investigating Sub-committee of the Committee on Armed Services, United States Senate (84th Congress, 2d Session), *Navy Aircraft Procurement Program: Final Report on F3H Development and Procurement* (United States Government Printing Office, Washington, 1956). The specific failure here was that numerous airframes became available years before it was possible to develop a jet engine with the required performance characteristics. In the lugubrious tone of the congressional investigating committee which was appointed to account for the resulting loss of several hundred million dollars: "What has somehow been overlooked is that the essential procurement practice employed with respect to the Demon fighter would inevitably result in some wastage of airframes if the engine were not forthcoming" (*ibid.*, pp. 9–10).
[2] Nathan Rosenberg, "Technological Change in the Machine Tool Industry, 1840–1910", *Journal of Economic History*, December 1963.
[3] For historical evidence in support of these assertions, see Dorothy Brady, "Relative Prices in the Nineteenth Century", *Journal of Economic History*, June 1964, pp. 145–203.

generations of computers, and may also have influenced the choice between purchase and rental on the part of users.[1]

There are some areas, of course, where the pressures militate very heavily against delay – as in weapons acquisition. Nevertheless, even when the costs of being late may be regarded as uniquely high, considerations of technological expectations cannot be ignored. Peck and Scherer, in their very careful study of weapons procurement, rephrase two of the key questions. First, "Should we begin developing this newly feasible weapon system immediately to ensure early availability, or should we wait a year or so until the state of the art is better defined so that fewer costly mistakes will be made during the development?" Secondly, "...should funds be committed to long lead time production items early in the development program so that full-scale production can start as soon as the development is completed?"[2]

A recent important instance in which the combination of long lead time and rapid technological change led to an apparent large misallocation of resources is the case of automobile emission controls. Under pressure from the federal government, American automakers, with production lead times of four or five years, were required to specify which anti-pollution technology would be incorporated into the 1975 automobiles. The catalytic converter seemed at that time to be a proven and more certain solution to the problem than did alternative technologies, such as the still-unproven stratified-charge engine. However, the subsequent development of this latter technology produced a solution to automobile emissions which was superior to the catalytic converter. Foreign automakers, such as Honda, with shorter production lead times than the Americans, were able to adopt the stratified-charge technology, thus avoiding what now appears to be the costly and premature commitment of American auto firms. (It is important to note, however, that some of the difficulty in this particular case is due to uncertainty concerning the future of the emission standards themselves as well as technological uncertainty.)

Problems such as these have, of course, a long history. In his book on the early history of electrical equipment manufacturing, Harold Passer extensively documents the marketing difficulties which confronted makers before 1900. During this period, expectations of rapid technical improvement were firmly entrenched in the minds of potential buyers, and such expectations served to reduce present demand. "The manufacturer has to convince the prospective buyer that no major improvements are in the offing. At the same time, the manufacturer must continue to improve his product to maintain his com-

---

[1] See William F. Sharpe, *The Economics of Computers* (Columbia University Press, New York, 1969), particularly chapter 7.

[2] Merton J. Peck and Frederic M. Scherer, *The Weapons Acquisition Process: An Economic Analysis* (Division of Research, Graduate School of Business Administration, Harvard University, Cambridge, 1962), pp. 283, 318. The authors also observe: "The risks of early investment in production are impressive – in some programs enormous quantities of special tools and manufactured material became worthless due to unexpected technical changes. On the other hand, the gamble has been successful and valuable time savings have been achieved in other programs (such as in the prewar British radar effort and in the first U.S. ballistic missile programs) by preparing for production concurrently with development" (*ibid.*, pp. 318–19).

petitive position and to force existing products into obsolescence."[1] Passer's statement neatly identifies the horns of the dilemma which threaten to impale the entrepreneur in the early stages of product innovation. One must attempt to persuade potential buyers of product stability at the same time as one commits resources to the search for product improvement so as not to fall behind the pace of such improvement which is set by one's competitors.

The implications of such considerations may be very great for the innovation process. When these intertemporal considerations loom very large, a rapid rate of technological progress need by no means result in as rapid a rate of introduction of new technological innovation. As Sayers has pointed out for Great Britain:

> There were times, between the wars, when marine engineering was changing in such a rapid yet uncertain way that firms in the highly competitive shipping industry delayed investment in the replacement of old high-cost engines by the new low-cost engines. In the middle 'twenties progress was rapid in all three propulsion methods – the reciprocating steam-engine, the geared steam-turbine and the diesel motor. Minor variations are said to have brought the number of possible combination types up to nearly a hundred. For some classes of ships there was momentarily very little to choose between several of these combinations, and shipowners were inclined to postpone placing orders until a little more experience and perhaps further invention had shown which types would be holding the field over the next ten years. Put in economic terms, the shipowners' position was that, though total costs of new engines might already be less than running costs of old engines, the profit on engines of 1923 build might be wiped out by the appearance in 1924 of even lower-cost engines, the purchase of which would allow a competitor (who had postponed the decision) to cut freights further. Also there was uncertainty as to which of two types of 1923 engine would prove to work at lower cost. If shipowner $A$ installed engine $X$, and shipowner $B$ installed engine $Y$, whose costs in 1923 appeared to equal those of $X$, a year's experience might show that in fact $Y$ costs were much lower than $X$ costs, in which event shipowner $A$ would have done better to wait until 1924 before installing new engines.[2]

[1] Harold Passer, *The Electrical Manufacturers, 1875–1900* (Cambridge, Harvard University Press, 1953), p. 45. The 1880s and the 1890s were, in fact, a period of continuous product improvement in incandescent lighting, and it was only with the advent of metallic filaments in the early years of the twentieth century that the incandescent lamp established its decisive superiority over gas lighting and arc lighting. Even so, the record from 1880 to 1896 is one of startling improvements in product efficiency and reductions in cost. Bright has stated: "The following figures show the approximate course of list prices per lamp for standard 16-candlepower lamps from 1880 to 1896: 1880–6, $1.00; 1888, 80 cents; 1891, 50 cents; 1892, 44 cents; 1893, 50 cents; 1894, 25 cents; 1895, 18–25 cents; 1896, 12–18 cents...In 1896 a dollar could buy approximately six standard carbon-filament lamps which would give more than twelve times as many lumen-hours of light as a single lamp of the same candlepower costing a dollar in 1880" (Arthur A. Bright, Jr., *The Electric-Lamp Industry* (New York, Macmillan, 1949), pp. 93 and 134).

[2] R. S. Sayers, "The Springs of Technical Progress in Britain, 1919–39", ECONOMIC JOURNAL, June 1950, pp. 289–90. These circumstances might also be described as a case of "technological uncertainty" as to which specific methods would yield the greatest long-run effect, but the impact

For a much more recent period, Walter Adams and Joel Dirlam call attention to the U.S. Steel Corporation's concern over the imminence of future improvements as an explanation for their delay in introducing the oxygen steel-making process.

> U.S. Steel conceded that "some form of oxygen steel-making will undoubtedly become an important feature in steelmaking in this country", but it declined to say when or to commit itself to introducing this innovation. Indeed, three years later, *Fortune* still pictured the Corporation as confronted by "painfully difficult choices between competing alternatives – for example, whether to spend large sums for cost reduction *now* [1960], in effect committing the company to *present* technology, or to stall for time in order to capitalise on a new and perhaps far superior technology that may be available in a few years".[1]

Expectations of continued improvement in a new technology may therefore lead to postponement of an innovation, to a slowing down in the rate of its diffusion, or to an adoption in a modified form to permit greater future flexibility. Moreover, one must consider expectations relating not only to possible improvements in the technology being considered, but also the possibility of improvement in both substitute and complementary technologies. Further improvements in an existing product may be held up because of the expectation that a superior *new* product will soon be developed.[2] At the same time expectations of continued improvement in the *old* technology, which the new technology is designed to displace, will exercise a similar effect. There is much evidence to suggest that historically, the *actual* improvement in old technologies after the introduction of the new were often substantial and played a significant role in slowing the pace of the diffusion process, so that this provides a quite reasonable basis for such a set of expectations. The water wheel continued to experience major improvements for at least a century after the introduction of Watt's steam engine; and the wooden sailing ship was subjected to many major and imaginative improvements long after the introduction of the iron-hull steamship.[3] During the 1920s the competition of the internal combustion engine is said to have been responsible for much technological improvement in steam engines, while in the same period the competition from the radio stimulated experiments which led to the new

---

upon diffusion is the same. Habakkuk has called attention to a similar experience in shipbuilding immediately after the opening of the Suez Canal: "It accelerated the technical perfection of the steamer; the rate of technical progress was so rapid that the steamers built in the early 'seventies were unable to compete with those completed in the middle of the decade..." (H. J. Habakkuk, "Free Trade and Commercial Expansion, 1853–1870", in *The Cambridge History of the British Empire*, vol. 2, p. 762).

[1] Walter Adams and Joel Dirlam, "Big Steel, Invention, and Innovation", *Quarterly Journal of Economics*, May 1966, pp. 181–2. Emphasis by Adams and Dirlam.

[2] Jewkes *et al.* have pointed out that "...improvements in the more traditional methods of producing insulin were held up by the widespread belief that a synthesized product would soon be found". See John Jewkes, David Sawers and Richard Stillerman, *The Sources of Invention* (Macmillan and Co., London, 1958), p. 232.

[3] See Nathan Rosenberg, "Factors Affecting the Diffusion of Technology", *Explorations in Economic History*, Fall 1972, for a more extended discussion.

and improved type of cable which was introduced in 1924.[1] The Welsbach mantle, perhaps the single most important improvement in gas lighting, was introduced after the electric utilities had begun to challenge the gas utilities over the respective merits of their lighting systems. The Welsbach gas mantle brought about a dramatic increase in the amount of illumination produced by a standard gas jet.[2] Not only the diffusion of technologies but also the effort devoted to the development of new technologies may be decisively shaped by expectations as to future improvements and the continued superiority of existing technologies. One explanation for the limited attention devoted to the development of the electric motor for many years was the belief that the economic superiority of the steam engine was overwhelming and beyond serious challenge.[3] The decision to neglect research on the electrically powered car in the early history of the automobile industry reflected the belief, justified at the time, in the total superiority of the internal combustion engine (this neglect may soon be repaired!). Similarly, the limited shift to nuclear sources of power over the past quarter century has been influenced by continued improvements in thermal efficiency based upon the "old-fashioned" but still apparently superior fossil fuel technologies. It seems equally clear that the recent growing pessimism about future fossil fuel supplies is likely to accelerate the concern with nuclear technologies, and lead to a more rapid rate of technical improvements there as experience accumulates. This will first require, however, a careful sorting out and distinction between short-term and long-term phenomena. Large-scale commitment of private resources to nuclear energy (or shale processing) is unlikely so long as investors in energy-supplying industries anticipate that the price of oil is likely to fall sharply from its post-October 1973 levels.[4]

[1] Sayers, *op. cit.*, pp. 284–5.

[2] "The Welsbach mantle was a lacy asbestos hood which became incandescent when attached over a burning gas jet. It increased the candlepower six-fold with a white light far superior to the yellowish flame of the bare jet...The Welsbach mantle, improved by many changes in the original design, extended the life of gas lighting nearly half a century. It sustained the gas utilities while they were discovering other productive uses for gas which would permit them to give up the struggle against electric lighting" (Charles M. Coleman, *P.G. and E. of California*, the Centennial Story of Pacific Gas and Electric Company, 1852–1952), p. 81.

Even the old arc-lamp technology experienced substantial improvements in response to the competition of new forms of lighting. See Bright, *op. cit.*, pp. 213–18.

It is interesting to note that, even though the gas industry could not indefinitely meet the competition of electricity in lighting, the gas industry as a whole continued to find new uses for its product and experienced no long-term decline. "Despite the declining importance of gas in lighting, the manufactured-gas industry as a whole has grown continually. The competition of the carbon lamp and the old open arc during the 1880s had encouraged the gas industry to spread its field to heating, and it was that use which permitted the industry to continue expanding when its lighting market was destroyed. Cooking, space heating, water heating, and later refrigeration resulted in a steady growth in the value of products of the industry from $56,987,290 in 1889 to $512,652,595 in 1929" (Bright, *op. cit.*, p. 213).

[3] Kendall Birr, "Science in American Industry", in David Van Tassel and Michael Hall (eds.), *Science and Society in the United States* (The Dorsey Press, Homewood, Illinois, 1966), p. 50.

[4] Dependence upon price expectations has, of course, been extensively discussed elsewhere. The purpose of the present article is confined to calling attention to the significance of expectations with respect to technological change itself. Expectations about future changes in technology might themselves be produced by projecting the anticipated influence of relative price changes on the innovation process. The willingness to explore for new techniques which involve factor combinations drastically

The recent efforts by oil firms to gain control of competing technologies – coal and uranium – may be seen as attempts to assure long-term market control by minimising the potential threats arising from technological breakthroughs in the provision of substitute products.[1] The earlier experience of gas companies in meeting the competition of electricity is also highly instructive in this regard. The ubiquitousness of "Gas and Electric" utility companies in the United States today suggests something of their past success in making the transition from the old to the new technology.

Expected profitability will not only be affected negatively by expected improvements in substitute technologies; it will also be affected positively by expected technological improvements in complementary technologies. Since innovation in steel-making will be affected not only by innovations in aluminum or pre-stressed concrete which provide potential substitutes for steel, but also by technological changes in petroleum refining which increase the size of the automobile-producing sector, the entrepreneur must consider expected developments in these other sectors. The profitability of technological changes in electric power generation will be favourably affected by metallurgical improvements which provide power plant components with increased capacity to tolerate higher pressures and temperatures in the form of high-strength, heat-resistant alloys. On the other hand, improvements in power generation would have a limited impact upon the delivered cost of electricity without improvements in the transmission network which reduce the cost of transporting electricity over long distances. The point is that the *need* for and expected availability of complementary innovations will often affect the profitability and therefore the diffusion of an innovation.[2] Therefore single technological breakthroughs hardly ever constitute a complete innovation.[3] It is for this reason – the expected as well as realised changes in other sectors – that decisions to adopt an innovation are often postponed in situations which might otherwise appear to constitute irrationality, excessive caution, or over-attachment to traditional practices in the eyes of uninformed observers.

---

different from those which currently prevail, will in turn depend upon the magnitude of expected price shifts.

[1] Such attempts, by providing a limited diversification for these firms, reduce the risks they face, and this may conceivably have some role in encouraging research activity.

[2] See Fishlow's discussion of the importance of expectations with respect to transport improvements and their impact upon American land settlement patterns. Albert Fishlow, *American Railroads and the Transformation of the Ante-Bellum Economy* (Harvard University Press, 1965). Fishlow explains why mid-western railroads were profitable immediately after their construction as a result of the process of anticipatory settlement. More broadly, it would be of interest to examine the impact of the expectations generated by transport improvements upon agricultural practices in the older areas of the northeast.

Parker and Klein have argued that the mechanisation of American agriculture which so increased its productivity would not have occurred in the absence of those transport improvements which made it possible to introduce its products into world markets. See William Parker and Judith Klein, "Productivity Growth in Grain Production in the United States, 1840–60 and 1900–10", in Studies in Income and Wealth No. 30, *Output, Employment and Productivity in the United States after 1800* (Columbia University Press, 1966).

[3] Rosenberg, "Factors Affecting the Diffusion of Technology", *op. cit.*

### III

Some significant (and superficially paradoxical) implications can be drawn from this discussion. Specifically, the relationship between the rate of technological change and the rate of technological innovation and diffusion is by no means a simple one, and may well be the opposite of intuitive expectations. A rapid rate of technological change may lead to a seemingly slow rate of adoption and diffusion, or to the introduction of machinery which fails to incorporate the most "advanced" technology, so long as it leads potential buyers to anticipate, by extrapolation, a continued or accelerating rate of future improvements. A decision to buy now may be, in effect, a decision to saddle oneself with a soon-to-be-obsolete technology.[1] Conversely, when the rate of technological change slows down and the product stabilises, the pace of adoptions may increase owing to the much greater confidence on the part of potential buyers that the product will *not* be superseded by a better one in a relatively short period of time. Thus the lag behind the "best available" methods might appear less when technological change is at a slower rate or is decelerating than when it is more rapid. In this sense, our argument may explain the failure of firms to function at the "best practice" frontier – such failure may owe a great deal to differences in entrepreneurial expectations about the future pace of technological improvement.[2]

There are two distinct issues involved here. One is the rate of improvement of best practice technology. The second is the rate of adoption of those best practice methods. If the two were independent, any lag in adoption would seem to impose social costs. However, as seems clear from historical experience, an important explanation of lagged adoption is the environment created by the high rate of improvement of best practice technology. Thus, a lagged rate of adoption is the "price" paid by technologically dynamic economies for their technological dynamism.

Clearly, a further examination of the adoption of technological innovations must be conducted within an enlarged framework which includes expectations not only of own-improvements but of improvements in the range of closely-linked substitutes and complements as well. Further research along such lines may considerably improve our understanding of the diffusion process. For the present, I would suggest that decisions to postpone the adoption of an innovation are often based upon well-founded and insufficiently-appreciated expectations concerning the future time-flow of further improvements. Even the most widely accepted justification for postponement, the elimination of conspicuous but not overwhelmingly serious technical difficulties, or "bugs",

---

[1] As discussed, the effect might also be to lead to the initial adoption of a more flexible set of techniques which more readily permits the adoption of future improvements. For an analogous argument with respect to the benefits of flexibility in the design of plant and equipment, see George Stigler, "Production and Distribution in the Short Run", *Journal of Political Economy*, June 1939. Reprinted in American Economic Association, *Readings in the Theory of Income Distribution* (Philadelphia, 1946).

[2] For a discussion of other reasons for the failure to operate at the "best practice" frontier, see W. E. G. Salter, *Productivity and Technical Change* (Cambridge University Press, 1960), chapter 4.

can reasonably be interpreted as merely a special case of expectations of future technological improvement. In this case, the expectations approach complete certainty that the technical difficulties can shortly be eliminated by recourse to the application of ordinary engineering skills. I suggest, finally, that entrepreneurs may be making appraisals of the future payoff to innovations of greater objective validity than are made by social scientists who invoke all sorts of extra-rational factors to account for the delay or "lag" in the adoption and diffusion of innovation. Practical businessmen tend to remember what social scientists often forget: that the very rapidity of the overall pace of technological improvement may make a postponed adoption decision privately (and perhaps even socially) optimal.

NATHAN ROSENBERG

*Stanford University*

*Date of receipt of final typescript: February 1976*

# [23]

*OMEGA*, The Int. Jl of Mgmt Sci., Vol. 3, No. 6, 1975. Pergamon Press. Printed in Great Britain

# A Dynamic Model of Process and Product Innovation

## JAMES M UTTERBACK

Massachusetts Institute of Technology Center for Policy Alternatives

## WILLIAM J ABERNATHY

Harvard University Graduate School of Business Administration

*(Received December 1974; in revised form May 1975)*

This article reports results from empirical tests of relationships between the pattern of innovation within a firm and certain of the firm's characteristics: the stage of development of its production process and its chosen basis of competition. The hypothesized relationships posed for the present investigation are a synthesis of prior research by the present authors on two distinct but complementary conceptual models of innovation, concerning respectively: the relationship between competitive strategy and innovation, and the relationship between production process characteristics and innovation. The empirical investigation is carried out with data available from the Myers and Marquis study of successful technological innovation in five different industry segments.

The essential aspects of the hypothesized relationships are that the characteristics of the innovative process will systematically correspond with the stage of development exhibited by the firm's production process technology and with its strategy for competition and growth. As a more specific example these relationships predict that there will be coherent patterns in the stimuli for innovation (market, production or new technology); in the types of innovation (product or process, original or adopted, etc.) and in barriers to innovation.

The presently reported statistical evidence is decidedly favorable to the hypothesized relationships, even though the adaptations needed to implement tests with existing data introduce dependencies that limit conclusions which would otherwise be warranted. The broad implication is that strong and important relationships exist among the capability of a firm to innovate, its competitive strategy and the posture of its production resources.

MOST studies of new product and process technology to date have been descriptive and have attempted to identify consistent patterns in the sources of ideas and problem solutions used, communication processes, and characteristics of successful innovations [12]. Past work does suggest central tendencies and systematic variations in the innovative process, but offers no higher level explanation, or theory, of why these tendencies and variations are observed [9].

*Utterback, Abernathy—Dynamic Model of Process and Product Innovation*

Our purpose is to suggest some ideas for an integrative theory which will predict differences in the innovative process and in the types of innovations attempted between firms and between different industrial segments.

# IDEAS FOR AN INTEGRATIVE THEORY OF THE INNOVATIVE PROCESS

The essence of our argument is that characteristics of the innovative process and of a firm's innovation attempts will vary systematically with differences in the firm's environment and its strategy for competition and growth, and with the state of development of process technology used by a firm and by its competitors.[1] We assume that a firm can affect its environment only in minor ways. Therefore we argue there will be a strong mutual relationship between a firm's choice of a strategy and its environment[2] and given its strategy, between the types of product and process innovations that a firm undertakes and the way its productive resources will be deployed, particularly the state of development achieved in its production processes.

The conceptual basis for a model that encompasses these mutual relationships between innovation, competitive strategy and state of process development originates in the integration of two separate but complementary lines of inquiry that have been pursued independently by the present authors. One such line of inquiry has concerned the relationship between a firm's competitive environment and the objectives underlying the pattern of innovation it undertakes, whether performance maximizing, sales maximizing, or cost minimizing (addressed in [12, 13] and in research in progress). The other line of inquiry has considered the relationship between the development of a firm's production process characteristics and the type of innovative activity it undertakes, e.g. the type, source and stimuli of innovation (addressed in [1, 2] and research currently underway). Subsequent paragraphs integrate these separate approaches into a common conceptual model that relates innovation to product and process evolution; develop hypotheses; present some preliminary tests of these hypotheses using previously collected data on successful industrial innovation [7],[3] and discuss implications with respect to corporate strategy, production technology and environment.

---

[1] Lawrence and Lorsch (1967) in developing a similar argument with respect to variations in firms' organization structure and integrative mechanisms consider the production technology used by the firm and its competitors to be a part of the firm's environment [6].

[2] Only one or a few alternative competitive strategies will be appropriate for a given environment and set of resources. However, a firm may choose to change both its strategy and its environment.

[3] One of the authors, James Utterback, was privileged to be involved in the original study with the late Professor Donald G Marquis who kindly provided the basic data for further analysis which could not be undertaken at the time.

*Omega, Vol. 3, No. 6*

# A MODEL OF PROCESS DEVELOPMENT

A production process is the system of process equipment, work force, task specifications, material inputs, work and information flows, etc. that are employed to produce a product or service. The basic idea underlying the proposed model of process development is that as a production process develops over time toward levels of improved output productivity, it does so with a characteristic evolutionary pattern: it becomes more capital intensive, direct labor productivity improves through greater division of labor and specialization, the flow of materials within the process takes on more of a straight line flow quality (that is flows are rationalized), the product design becomes more standardized, and the process scale becomes larger. Productivity gains result from concurrent and often incremental changes in these several variables, some of which are stimulated by changes in the market, external to the firm (i.e. volume and product standardization) and some of which arise from within the firm.

As a process continues to develop toward states of higher productivity through incremental changes in these factors, a cumulative effect is achieved that significantly alters the overall nature of the process. Definite stages of development that are similar in different industries and economic sectors can be identified in the characteristics of the productivity factors of various processes. The pattern of changes from one stage to another in the process are pervasive in character going beyond the physical attributes to the productivity factors themselves. As a process develops there may also be changes in the internal organizational structure, the development of a supplier industry for special materials, and technology based capital goods. We will describe three different stages of process development which are referred to here as uncoordinated, segmental and systemic.

*Uncoordinated.* Early in the life of process and product, market expansion and redefinition result in frequent competitive improvements. The rates of product and process changes are high and there is great product diversity among competitors. Typically the process itself is composed largely of unstandardized and manual operations, or operations that rely upon general purpose equipment. During this state, the process is fluid, with loose and unsettled relationships between process elements. Such a system is "organic" and responds easily to environmental change, but necessarily has "slack" and is "inefficient".[4]

*Segmental.* As an industry and its product group mature, price competition becomes more intense. Production systems, designed increasingly for efficiency, become mechanistic and rigid. Tasks become more specialized and are subjected to more formal operating controls. In terms of process, the production system

---

[4] The term "organic" and the contrasting term "mechanistic" are used to describe the nature of organizational relationships within a company or department, as developed earlier by Burns and Stalker (1961).

*Utterback, Abernathy—Dynamic Model of Process and Product Innovation*

tends to become elaborated and tightly integrated through automation and process control. Some subprocesses may be highly automated with process specific technology while others may still be essentially manual or rely upon general purpose equipment. As a result, production processes in this state will have a segmented quality. Such extensive development cannot occur however until a product group is mature enough to have sufficient sales volume and at least a few stable product designs.

*Systemic.* As a process becomes more highly developed and integrated and as investment in it becomes large, selective improvement of process elements becomes increasingly more difficult. The process becomes so well integrated that changes become very costly, because even a minor change may require changes in other elements of the process and in the product design. Process redesign typically comes more slowly at this stage, but it may be spurred either by the development of new technology or by a sudden or cumulative shift in the requirements of the market. If changes are resisted as process technology and the market continue to evolve, then the stage is set for either economic decay or a revolutionary as opposed to evolutionary change.

The unit of analysis used here is not necessarily the firm, but rather the overall production process which is employed to create a product (or service). The term *process segment* will be used to describe the elements which would typically be managed by the senior operating executive in an organization. In the simplest case of a firm with a small set of related products, this will be the operations of the firm itself. However, in the case of a conglomerate, or a firm with a high degree of vertical integration, it will be more appropriate to consider each division as a segment. In the case of highly fragmented industries a process segment might reasonably be defined to include the activities of several firms.

The essential idea here is that a process, or productive segment, tends to evolve and change over time in a consistent and identifiable manner as described above.[5]

# THE MODEL OF PRODUCT DEVELOPMENT

A product innovation is a new technology or combination of technologies introduced commercially to meet a user or a market need. As was the case with process development a basic idea underlying the proposed model of product innovation is that products will be developed over time in a predictable manner with initial emphasis on product performance, then emphasis on product variety and later emphasis on product standardization and costs.

This idea has the advantage that it allows one to distinguish both among the innovative patterns of firms in an industry at a given time and among those of a given firm at different times based on dominant competitive strategy. Thus, a

[5] For a more complete discussion of this model see Abernathy and Townsend (1975) [1].

firm at one time may attempt to be the first to introduce technically advanced products (performance-maximizing), or to watch others innovate but be prepared to quickly adapt and introduce new product variations and features (sales-maximizing), or to enter the market later in the product life cycle with simpler and less expensive versions (cost-minimizing) [3, 10]. Similarly, the strategies of a firm or segment may evolve from one dominant strategy to another with time. Research on the product life cycle has started from the perspective of treating product characteristics as the unit of analysis, and several studies have shown a relationship with changing process characteristics.[6] Studies of major products (petrochemicals, automotive, electronics) in international trade have demonstrated a consistent pattern [15].

*Performance-maximizing.* In the early phases of the product life cycle the rate of product change is expected to be rapid and margins to be large. A firm with a performance-maximizing strategy might be expected to emphasize unique products and product performance, often in the anticipation that a new capability will expand customer requirements.

A majority of innovations produced by performance-maximizing firms would be expected to be market-stimulated with a high degree of uncertainty about their ultimate market potential. Technology to meet market needs may come from many sources. Innovation may often arise from unexpected sources or directions of inquiry. Performance-maximizing firms would be expected to rely more heavily on external sources of information, and on more diverse sources of information than would others.

The industry will probably be composed of relatively few firms, and these will be either small new firms or older firms entering a completely new market based on their existing technological strengths. Production capacity will be flexible permitting easy variation in production input, and will tend to be located near affluent markets and where a variety of production inputs are available.

In the beginning stages of both the product and process segment's development, corresponding to the uncoordinated state, product markets are ill defined, products are nonstandard and the production process is inchoate. Product innovation tends to be driven or stimulated by new market needs and opportunities. The critical insight for innovation is often obtained by identifying the relevant product requirements rather than in new scientific results or advanced technology. The locus for innovation is in the individual or organization that is intimately familiar with needs. Here if advanced technology is critical, it is predominantly so in applications to product rather than process innovation. Technological innovations which may have market application, lie fallow until markets can be identified or created.

*Sales-maximizing.* As experience is gained by both producers and users of a product, market uncertainty will be correspondingly reduced. We might expect a greater degree of competition based on product differentiation with

---

[6] See for example Stobaugh (1972) [11] and Vernon (1966) [14].

*Utterback, Abernathy—Dynamic Model of Process and Product Innovation*

some product designs beginning to dominate. Sales-maximizing firms would tend to define needs based on their visibility to the customer. Innovations leading to better product performance might be expected to be less likely, unless performance improvement is easy for the customer to evaluate and compare.

The reduction in market need uncertainty, with greater diffusion of product use enables increased application of advanced technology as a source of further product innovation. The result will more often be product variation, or new components. More fundamental changes might occur with the intent of replacing an existing product rather than creating an entirely new product application. Economic impact can be almost immediate. At the same time forces that reduce the rate of product change and innovation are beginning to build up. As obvious improvements are introduced it becomes increasingly difficult to better past performance, users develop loyalties and preferences and the practicalities of marketing, distribution, maintenance, advertising, etc. demand greater standardization. Advanced technology plays an increasingly important role here in stimulating product innovation and process innovation.

This stage of product innovation roughly corresponds to the segmental stage of process evolution. Process changes will largely be stimulated by the demand for increased output and these may tend to be discontinuous (or major) process innovations that involve new methods of organization and product design as well as production.

*Cost-minimizing.* As the product life cycle evolves product variety tends to be reduced and the product becomes standardized. Then as a progression the basis of competition begins to shift to product price, margins are reduced, the industry often becomes an oligopoly, and efficiency and economies of scale are emphasized in production. As price competition increases production processes become more capital intensive and may be relocated to achieve lower costs of factor inputs. Relocation may shift capacity overseas.[7]

In the cost-minimizing stage significant change frequently involves both product and process modifications and must be dealt with as a system. Because investment in process equipment in place is high and product and process change are interdependent, innovations in both product and process may be expected to be principally incremental. The prospects for high rates of market and organizational growth from radical innovation, either product feature improvement or cost reduction, is not appreciable. Under these conditions, however, both product and process features are well articulated and easily analyzed. The conditions necessary for the application of scientific results and systems techniques are present. Unfortunately the pay-off required to justify the cost of change is large while potential benefits are often marginal. Innovations

[7] This model has been used very successfully in explaining international trade. In terms of the present purposes it is particularly interesting because of the relationship hypothesized between product characteristics and process characteristics.

*Omega, Vol. 3, No. 6*

will typically be developed by equipment suppliers for whom the incentives are relatively greater and adopted by the larger user firms [5].

## INNOVATION AND STAGE OF DEVELOPMENT

The pattern of relationships between a segment's stage of development and innovation can be conceptualized as shown in Fig. 1. Changes in frequency of innovation are shown on the vertical axis and related to the stage of process and product development on the horizontal axis. Presenting the ideas discussed above in this manner implies an orderly and even progression of product and process development, standardization and increase in sales volume. Process segments which exhibit the highest rates of improvement in productivity do indeed seem to progress rapidly through the stages indicated. But this is not necessarily the case for all process segments [1].

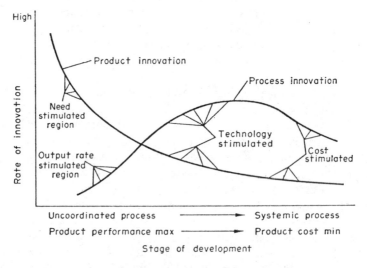

FIG. 1. *Innovation and stage of development.*

There is reason to believe that in many cases the progression may stop for long periods, or even reverse. A firm which does pursue the evolution of its process segment to the extreme however may find that it has achieved the benefits of high productivity only at the cost of decreased flexibility and innovative capacity. It must face competition from: innovative products that are produced by other more flexible segments that are more capable of substituting products, foreign imports, competing products from other industries with high cross-elasticity of demand, or process changes by customers to eliminate the product directly [2].

*Utterback, Abernathy—Dynamic Model of Process and Product Innovation*

In other cases it may not be possible to achieve progression because of certain barriers or from a strategic point of view the firm may find it advantageous to inhibit progression by maintaining a high rate of product or model change. Any of these considerations may alter the path of progression for a particular segment without necessarily changing the relationship among the characteristics of strategy, innovation and process development, exhibited at a given stage for a given process segment. It may also be that computer aided manufacturing will ultimately reduce some of the interdependence between product and process change and deflect the pattern represented in Fig. 1, but until this happens it does not obviate the general proposition presented by Fig. 1 and descriptive model—that for a usefully large class of process segments, important internal consistency will be present among strategy, innovation and process characteristics.

Several important issues in managing technological innovation are addressed by the model: the natural locus of innovation (or the most potentially fruitful source); the most appropriate type of innovation; and the array of barriers to innovation [1].

1. The locus of innovation shifts with the stage of development. During the unconnected stage in the development of a process, innovative insight comes from those individuals or organizations that are intimately familiar with the recipient process, rather than those intimately familiar with new technologies. The critical input is not state-of-the-art technology but new insights about the need. Later, in the systemic stage, needs are well defined, "system like", and easily articulated. These needs lend themselves to complex technological solutions and the innovator will frequently be one that brings new technological insights to the problem. This may be a formal engineering or R & D group, an equipment company, or some other external source. In undertaking action to stimulate innovation, it is important to appreciate these distinctions so that the most likely sources of innovation can be identified, nurtured, and supported.

2. The type of innovation that is likely to succeed, whether technologically complex or simple, and whether applied to product or process, also depends upon the stage of development. During the unconnected state most technological applications are to the products that the productive segment will produce. Few are to process improvement and those that do occur tend to be simple in application and to address single needs. Complex technological systems of process equipment do not "take" well when the recipient process is ill defined, uncertain and unstructured. Systems technology has not been very successfully applied to solve ill defined process needs. The converse is true in the systemic stage. Isolated radical innovations, of even major significance, seldom gain ready acceptance when the recipient productive

segment is in the systemic stage. The seemingly isolated innovation must in reality be incorporated as change throughout the systemic productive segment. A realistic assessment of the type of innovations that will be successful, and how they should be introduced, depends upon an understanding of the productive process that will receive them.

3. The total array of barriers to an innovation, like the appropriate type of innovation, changes composition with the stage of development. In the unconnected stage, resistance centers around perceptions of irrelevance. Will the innovation work and meet a need? In the systemic stage resistance stems from the disruptive nature of innovation. Will it displace vested interest and disrupt current practice? The model begins to help to clarify the changing nature of these barriers.

# A TEST OF THE FEASIBILITY OF THE MODEL WITH DATA FROM MYERS AND MARQUIS' STUDY

Myers and Marquis' [1969] study of 567 commercially successful innovations (from five industries and 120 firms) provides data on such questions as whether each innovation was a product, component or process, on its cost and impact on the production process and other details which should be helpful in performing at least an initial feasibility test of many aspects of the model outlined above.

To carry out an initial feasibility test of the model using this data the following steps were taken. First, the firms included in the Myers and Marquis study were classified by stage of development (Stage I, II or III) corresponding to three categorical intervals along the ordinate of Fig. 1. Since the identity of firms included in the original study remains confidential this classification was performed by the first author of the present paper based on data reflecting patterns in source of information for the reported innovations. As noted in (1) above the model predicts that the sources of information of most frequent importance will depend upon the stages of development. Second, a set of hypotheses were developed that would be tested using the data. These were formulated by the second author who had not previously had access to the data or results from its analysis. Finally characteristics of innovative behavior were analyzed by firms' stage of development to test the hypotheses.

This procedure assumes a certain equivalence between a process segment and a firm that should be recognized. The model as developed above relates to the characteristics of a process segment or single product line, while analysis has been carried out by firm. In general it would not be anticipated that the innovative characteristics of a multidivisional firm would correspond to the characteristics of one of the process segments included in its portfolio of segments, unless all or most were in approximately the same stage of development, or of

*Utterback, Abernathy—Dynamic Model of Process and Product Innovation*

course unless the firm were essentially a single product firm. To abridge limitations in the data which result because the original study focused on the characteristics of firms rather than those of subsidiary product lines or divisions and because of confidentiality agreements which prohibit further efforts to enrich available data, the present method of analysis relies upon reported characteristics of the firm as surrogates for the characteristics of the process segment. While this assumption is not ideal it does not severely distort the conceptual basis of the hypotheses because of the special characteristics of the data set and precautions taken in the classification methodology. First, the majority of the firms included are small, and therefore likely to have the characteristics of a single product firm. Second, it is our understanding that with large firms the original data collection effort typically focused on one division so that the reported data is much more likely to reflect the desired characteristics of the responsible division or business group rather than the corporate shell. Finally, firms which failed to exhibit a coherent pattern of innovation, as would be anticipated for multidivisional firms which provided data about segments in different stages of development, have been excluded from the subset of firms presently analysed. An analysis of the set of firms excluded on this basis shows that on average they reported more innovations per firm than other groups, which tends to support the idea that they would be large multidivisional firms. Taken collectively these conditions provide sufficient equivalency so that the so called characteristics of the firms can be used as surrogates for process segment characteristics.

To implement a classification methodology, the stimulus to which a majority of a firm's innovations responded seemed the most reasonable way to classify firms into stages. The resulting partitions will represent differences in the nature of uncertainties and the competitive environment the firm may face. Thus the predominant stimuli, as shown in Fig. 1, are the point of departure for our predictions. Two variables in the Myers and Marquis study, "primary initiating factor for the innovation" and "nature of the information used", provide operational measures for the predominant stimuli. For example, if a majority of the firm's innovations were initiated by production related factors such as "quality failure or deterioration" or "attention drawn to high cost" *and* if the nature of information used in these cases was "information relating to the availability of capital equipment or materials" or "data concerning equipment or materials utilization" then that firm was classified in the systemic-production cost-minimizing stage. Similar definitions and classification criteria are applied to these two variables (primary initiating factor and the nature of information used) to assign each firm to a stage, as described in the Appendix. In brief these are:

*Stage I*    Uncoordinated process
           Product performance-maximizing strategy

Omega, *Vol.* 3, *No.* 6

Classified on the basis that most innovations
are market need stimulated.

*Stage II* Segmental process
Sales-maximizing strategy
Classified on the basis that most innovations
are stimulated by technological opportunities.

*Stage III* Systemic process
Cost-minimizing strategy
Classified on the basis that most innovations
are stimulated by production related factors.

In fact most of the firms (77 of 120) do show a dominant pattern as expected.
These firms also contributed a majority (330 of 567) of the innovations in the
sample. While data on firms would have allowed us to use the entire sample, the
present method does provide a usefully large subset (of 77 firms and 330
innovations).

The measured characteristics of innovations in the Myers and Marquis data
support quantitative tests of six specified hypotheses that arise from the general
model. These were either selected from the set of several hypotheses that had
been developed as described above or from the present conceptual model and
previously referenced work. Tests of the hypotheses are reported and discussed
below and are considered a source of strong, if preliminary, evidence supporting
the validity of the model.

*Hypothesis* 1. The proportion of product innovations undertaken by firms
will be largest in Stage I and will be less for firms in Stages II and III. Conversely, the proportion of process innovations will be expected to be small in
Stage I, but process innovations are expected to be predominant in Stage III
(as shown graphically in Fig. 1).

TABLE 1. NATURE OF THE INNOVATION AND STAGE OF DEVELOPMENT

| Nature of the innovation | Firms' stage of product and process development | | | |
| --- | --- | --- | --- | --- |
| | Stage I | Stage II | Stage III | Row total |
| Product | 114 | 46 | 13 | 173 |
| | 65·5 | 49·5 | 20·6 | 52·4 |
| Component | 39 | 8 | 6 | 53 |
| | 22·4 | 8·6 | 9·5 | 16·1 |
| Process | 21 | 39 | 44 | 104 |
| | 12·1 | 41·9 | 69·8 | 31·5 |

$\chi^2 = 80\cdot70634$, $P < 0\cdot0001$.

*Utterback, Abernathy—Dynamic Model of Proces nd Product Innovation*

A breakdown of frequencies of product, component, and process innovations in Myers and Marquis' sample with firms classified into Stages I–III is shown in Table 1. The results support the hypothesis ($P < 0.0001$), with 65·5% of the innovations introduced by firms in Stage I being new products and only 12·1% processes followed by a complete reversal, 20·6% products and 69·8% processes in Stage III. We did expect a larger degree of component innovation in Stage II than is in fact the case.

The data in Table 1 cannot be plotted directly to derive the curves in Fig. 1, because the data can only be expressed accurately as percentages, while Fig. 1 shows both expected frequencies and rates of change (the slope of the curves) of product and process innovation. The proportions of product and process innovations shown in Table 1 are consistent with those which could be derived from frequency data plotted as in Fig. 1. We recognize that the qualifying basis for a Stage III classification (stimulated by production related factors), bears a natural relationship to the hypothesized high frequency of process innovations for this category. To argue that this dependency detracts from the validity of the test would miss the point of the model. The strength of the model derives from the fact that it is an integrative framework encompassing a broad range of independently logical relationships. The intuitive plausibility of such results are therefore taken as support rather than detracting considerations.

*Hypothesis* 2. The emphasis and priority given by the firm to innovation as a competitive strategy will be greatest in Stage I and will be less for firms in Stages II and III.

TABLE 2. PRIOR ACTIVITY OF FIRM AND STAGE OF DEVELOPMENT

| Prior activity of the firm* | Firms' stage of product and process development | | | |
| --- | --- | --- | --- | --- |
| | Stage I | Stage II | Stage III | Row total |
| High priority | 74 | 29 | 14 | 117 |
| | 42·5 | 31·2 | 22·2 | 35·5 |
| Low priority | 58 | 26 | 30 | 114 |
| | 33·3 | 28·0 | 47·6 | 34·5 |
| Related problem | 19 | 14 | 11 | 44 |
| | 10·9 | 15·1 | 17·5 | 13·3 |
| Not working on the problem | 23 | 24 | 8 | 55 |
| | 13·2 | 25·9 | 12·7 | 16·6 |

$\chi^2 = 21.06704$, $P < 0.01$.
* The question asked was whether the firm or the innovator was actively working on the problem.

This hypothesis follows directly from our argument about frequency of innovation and the changing nature of firms' strategies for competition and growth as a segment matures. It can be tested directly using Myers and Marquis' data as in Table 2 by looking at the percentage of successful innovations intro-

*Omega, Vol. 3, No. 6*

duced which were given high priority during their development by firms in each stage. This figure is highest (42·5%) in Stage I, and steadily declines in Stages II (31·2%) and III (22·2%). The data support the hypothesis ($P < 0·01$).

*Hypothesis* 3. A larger proportion of innovations introduced by firms in Stage I will incorporate new technology as opposed to existing technology transferred from other applications.

TABLE 3. DEGREE OF INVENTION AND STAGE OF DEVELOPMENT

| Degree of invention required | Firms' stage of product and process development | | | |
| --- | --- | --- | --- | --- |
| | Stage I | Stage II | Stage III | Row total |
| Little | 25 | 18 | 21 | 64 |
| | 14·4 | 19·4 | 33·3 | 19·4 |
| Considerable | 71 | 46 | 30 | 147 |
| | 40·8 | 49·5 | 47·6 | 44·5 |
| Invention needed | 78 | 29 | 12 | 119 |
| | 44·8 | 31·2 | 19·0 | 36·1 |

$\chi^2 = 19·14243$, $P < 0·001$.

Innovations introduced by firms in Stage I are expected to be relatively more original, not necessarily more complex or sophisticated technologically. They may frequently involve synthesis of existing (though not widely known) technical information into a new concept or invention. Myers and Marquis asked for each case whether "a high degree of inventiveness was called for, so that it may be said that 'invention' was required" [7, p. 78]. Table 3 shows that 44·8% of the innovations sampled for firms in Stage I were considered to have required invention, while this was true for fewer (31·2%) in Stage II and in Stage III (19·0%). Fully one third of the innovations by firms in Stage III required little or no change in existing technology to accomplish. These data strongly ($P < 0·001$) support the hypothesis.

*Hypothesis* 4. Most innovations introduced by firms in Stage I will be original, while in Stage III most will be adopted (from material suppliers, equipment suppliers, by license, imitation, etc.)

Three-quarters (74·2%) of the innovations introduced by firms in Stage I were original products and components while half (50·8%) of all innovations introduced in Stage III were wholly adopted from other firms. While there were few process innovations in Stage I (21 cases, 12·1% as shown in Table 1), as large a proportion of process as product innovations were original (18 of the 21). These data strongly support the hypothesis ($P < 0·0001$) as shown in Table 4.

*Hypothesis* 5. Innovations introduced in Stage I will require little perceived change in process technology. Innovations introduced in Stage II will require the greatest degree of perceived change in process technology, while those in Stage III will result in only incremental and/or adopted process changes.

*Utterback, Abernathy—Dynamic Model of Proces  ⁿd Product Innovation*

TABLE 4. ORIGINAL OR ADOPTED INNOVATION AND STAGE OF DEVELOPMENT

| Original or adopted innovations | Firms' stage of product and process development | | | |
| --- | --- | --- | --- | --- |
| | Stage I | Stage II | Stage III | Row total |
| Original products and | 129 | 44 | 12 | 185 |
| components | 74·2 | 47·3 | 19·1 | 56·1 |
| Original processes | 18 | 34 | 19 | 71 |
| | 10·3 | 36·6 | 30·2 | 21·5 |
| Adopted products, | 27 | 15 | 32 | 74 |
| components, and processes | 15·5 | 16·1 | 50·8 | 22·4 |

$\chi^2 = 72\cdot826, P < 0\cdot0001.$

The basis for the hypothesis originates from the proposition that production processes are more fluid or adaptable in early stages of development. Change is normal and even though considerable change may be involved *vis à vis* later stage segments, it is not expected that it will be perceived or reported as significant. Myers and Marquis were implicitly following a concept similar to that in Fig. 1 when they asked in each case about the impact of the innovation on the production process. They comment that "relatively small product changes may be of great significance to the firm if they result in large changes in the manufacturing process" (as in Stage III). And, "even a fairly large product innovation may have relatively little significance to the production process" (as in Stage I) [7, p.78]. Looking at their data again classified by firms' stage in product development in Table 5 one can see that fully half (50·0%) of the innovations introduced by firms in Stage I required no change whatever in the production process. On the other hand nearly half (43·0%) of the innovations in Stage II required a wholly new process for their production or use, and half (49·2%) of the Stage III innovations were adopted (new for the firm only). These data support the hypothesis ($P < 0\cdot0001$).

TABLE 5. IMPACT ON PRODUCTION PROCESS AND STAGE OF DEVELOPMENT

| Impact of the innovation on the production process | Firms' stage of product and process development | | | |
| --- | --- | --- | --- | --- |
| | Stage I | Stage II | Stage III | Row total |
| New process | 39 | 40 | 17 | 96 |
| | 22·4 | 43·0 | 27·0 | 29·1 |
| New for the firm only | 48 | 20 | 31 | 99 |
| | 27·6 | 21·5 | 49·2 | 30·0 |
| No change | 87 | 33 | 15 | 135 |
| | 50·0 | 35·5 | 23·8 | 40·9 |

$\chi^2 = 27\cdot96568, P < 0\cdot0001.$

*Omega, Vol.* 3, *No.* 6

*Hypothesis* 6. Costs of innovations introduced by firms in Stage I will be relatively greater than those for Stage II and will be lowest for firms in Stage III.

*Hypothesis* 7. Most firms in Stage I will be relatively small while most firms in Stages II and III will be relatively large.

The last two hypotheses will be discussed together, because they are the net result of counter balancing forces and because at first glance they appear contradictory. Hypothesis 6 follows logically from the fact that we expected innovations in Stage I to be given high priority, to be original and to require inventiveness, while those in Stage III were expected to be given lower priority and to be largely adopted from other firms (suppliers or competitors). While the cost of introducing innovations of an equivalent degree of novelty is expected to be much higher for Stage III firms, they are not expected to introduce innovations of such a radical nature. Rather it is hypothesized that priorities here will be placed on less expensive incremental change that will not be disruptive, and on balance the cost per innovation will be lower. At the same time we argued that firms in Stage I would tend to be small, that more firms would enter in Stage II, that some would grow rapidly and others merge or drop out so that Stage III would be characterized by a few large firms competing on the basis of scale economies and low costs. Can a small firm succeed with high cost innovations?

Project SAPPHO [8] which compared paired cases of commercially successful and unsuccessful innovations found that this was indeed the case. The greater the amount of resources devoted to a project the more likely it was to be a success. But resources devoted bore no relationship to firm size. Small firms concentrating their resources on a few large projects tended to succeed, while larger firms which devoted fewer resources to more projects tended to fail when trying to introduce the same innovation. Thus the hypotheses are not necessarily contradictory.

Table 6 shows that Stage I innovations are expensive, with 21·3% costing

TABLE 6. COST OF INNOVATION IN THOUSANDS AND STAGE OF DEVELOPMENT

| Cost of the firms' innovations (thousands) | Firms' stage of product and process development | | | |
|---|---|---|---|---|
| | Stage I | Stage II | Stage III | Row total |
| Less than $25 | 44 | 22 | 36 | 102 |
| | 25·3 | 23·7 | 57·1 | 30·9 |
| $25–$100 | 51 | 41 | 8 | 100 |
| | 29·3 | 44·1 | 12·7 | 30·3 |
| $100–$1000 | 42 | 21 | 13 | 76 |
| | 24·1 | 22·6 | 20·6 | 23·0 |
| More than $1000 | 37 | 9 | 6 | 52 |
| | 21·3 | 9·7 | 9·5 | 15·8 |

$\chi^2 = 37 \cdot 06130$, $P < 0 \cdot 0001$.

more than one million dollars as opposed to 9·7 and 9·5% in Stages II and III respectively. More than half (57·1%) of the Stage III innovations were incremental (cost less than $25,000) as opposed to one-quarter (25·3%) in Stage I. These data support ($P < 0·0001$) hypothesis 6.

Data on firm size were not available for the entire sample. However, those firms for which size (sales volume) data are lacking are most likely to be smaller than average and privately owned. Table 7 displays data on size and dominant type of innovations introduced for those cases where data are available.

TABLE 7. FIRM SIZE AND STAGE OF DEVELOPMENT

| Sales in $000,000 | Firms' stage of product and process development | |
|---|---|---|
| | Stage I | Stages II and III |
| Less than 100 | 24 | 2 |
| More than 100 | 16 | 15 |

$\chi^2 = 11·1887, P < 0·01.$

Twenty-four of the firms classified as being in Stage I were relatively small having sales of less than one hundred million dollars, while 16 had sales of more than this amount. Moreover, 18 of the 24 small firms had sales of less than ten million dollars. Conversely only two firms in Stages II and III combined were small while 15 were large. These data support ($P < 0·01$) hypothesis 7.

# DISCUSSION

We believe that the conceptual model outlined above represents several important and original conbutritions.

It is a serious attempt to formulate a multivariate hypothesis about the process of innovation in firms and to explain variations noted in past descriptive studies. The model suggests a consistent pattern of variables which will change systematically with changes in firms' product and process development. Further, it suggests ways to integrate concepts of the innovative process from different disciplines and perspectives including: economics (firm size and market structure, product costs and price elasticity, trade flows) management and engineering (type of innovation, cost impact on production process, degree of technical change required) and organization theory and behavior (organization structure, formality, planning process, communication).

The model facilitates predictive statements about differences between firms in different competitive environments and with varying resources and constraints. It suggests some ideas of the dynamics of the innovative process as the firm and

*Omega, Vol. 3, No. 6*

its environment change. It provides some ideas of possible and plausible cause and effect relationships—explanations about why systematic variations in the innovation process may occur as a firm grows and changes.

An initial feasibility test using Myers and Marquis data provides compelling support for each one of the hypotheses derived from the model. The idea of looking at differences between firms rather than looking for differences in the characteristics of individual successful innovations provides significant insights not gained in the original analysis of the same data.

The model has operational relevance. That is it suggests the sources and types of innovations a given firm might expect to undertake successfully, critical resources required and potential problems or constraints. Special attention is called to the interrelated nature of decisions within the firm. The capabilities of a firm to innovate, to achieve efficient operations, etc. cannot be divorced from one another, but are a matter of overall strategy.

Many problems remain before these claims can be fully investigated or supported. Each of the hypotheses implied by our argument should be formally stated and examined in the light of existing literature and cases. Further feasibility testing using existing sets of data can be easily accomplished. Hypotheses about innovation process dynamics will typically have to be tested by using retrospective data for process segments for time periods on the order of decades. An investment in sustained longitudinal study of cases where product and process evolution is occurring rapidly would be useful.

Careful descriptive studies of product and process innovation have contributed much to our understanding. But we believe further efforts along established directions for empirical research, attempting to draw and refine general propositions, will have little marginal benefit. A synthesis and integration along lines similar to those suggested above is required in our opinion if we are to achieve a more comprehensive and useful understanding of technological change as it involves the firm.

# REFERENCES

1. ABERNATHY WJ and TOWNSEND PL (1975) Technology, productivity and process change. *Technol. Forecasting & Soc. Change* 7 (4), 379–396.
2. ABERNATHY WJ and WAYNE K (1974) Limits of the learning curve. *Harv. Bus. Rev.* 52 (5), 109–119.
3. ANSOFF H and STEWART JM (1967) Strategies for a technology-based business. *Harv. Bus. Rev.* 45 (6), 71–83.
4. BURNS T and STALKER GM (1961) *The Management of Innovation*. Tavistock, London.
5. FREEMAN C (1968) Chemical process plant: innovation and the world market. *Nat. Inst. Econ. Rev.* (45), 29–51.
6. LAWRENCE R and LORSCH JW (1967) *Organization and Environment*. Division of Research, Harvard Business School, Boston.
7. MYERS S and MARQUIS DG (1969) *Successful Industrial Innovations*. National Science Foundation, NSF 69–17, Washington, D.C.

*Utterback, Abernathy—Dynamic Model of Process and Product Innovation*

8. Robertson AB, Achilladelis B and Jervis P (1972) *Success and Failure in Industrial Innovation: Report on Project SAPPHO*. Center for the Study of Industrial Innovation, London.
9. Rosenbloom RS (1974) *Technological Innovation in Firms and Industries: An Assessment of the State of the Art*. Working Paper, HBS 74–8, Harvard Business School, Boston.
10. Simmonds WHC (1973) Toward an analytical industry classification. *Technol. Forecasting & Soc. Change* 4 (1), 375 385.
11. Stobaugh RD (1972) How investment abroad creates jobs at home. *Harv. Bus. Rev.* 50 (5), 118–126.
12. Utterback JM (1974) Innovation in industry and the diffusion of technology. *Science* 183, 620–626.
13. Utterback JM (1975) Successful industrial innovation: a multivariate analysis. *Decision Sci.* January.
14. Vernon R (1966) International investment and international trade in the product cycle. *Q. J. Econ.* 80 (2), 190–207.
15. Wells LT (1972) *The Product Life Cycle and International Trade*. Division of Research, Harvard Business School, Boston.

# APPENDIX

*Details of the classification of firms into stages I–III*

*Stage I: uncoordinated process, product performance-maximizing strategy*
Classified on the basis that the primary initiating factor was market related *and* that the information used was about design or performance characteristics or state of the art for the largest group of the firm's innovations. Includes 52 firms of which 10 reported a single innovation meeting the criteria, and 174 innovations; a mean of 3·35 innovations per firm.

*Stage II: segmental process, sales-maximizing strategy*
Classified on the basis that the primary initiating factor was the perception of a technical opportunity to create or improve a product or the production process *and* that the information used was (as above) about design or performance characteristics or state of the art for the largest group of the firm's innovations. Includes 14 firms of which 2 reported a single innovation meeting the criteria, and 93 innovations; a mean of 6·65 innovations per firm.

*Stage III: systemic process, cost-minimizing strategy*
Classified on the basis that the primary initiating factor was production related or administrative *and* that the information used was about capital equipment or materials or the use of equipment or materials for the largest group of the firm's innovations. Includes 11 firms of which 2 reported a single innovation meeting the criteria, and 63 innovations; a mean of 5·72 innovations per firm.

*Unclassified*
Firms having no significant group of innovations meeting one of the sets of critieria stated above. Includes 43 firms of which 10 reported a single commercially successful innovation, and 33 firms reported 227 innovations with a mean of 6·87 per firm (a mean of 5·50 per firm overall).

Thirteen ties (usually cases having 2 or 4 innovations divided evenly between two sets of criteria) were broken by comparing the firm's distribution of cases with the marginal distribution for the industry. The firm was then classified on the basis of the greatest difference between its pattern and the marginal distribution. That is if most housing supplier firms were cost-minimizing, and if the firm in question had an equal number of sales-maximizing and cost-minimizing innovations it would be classified as sales-maximizing. Five doubtful cases, where two categories had roughly the same number of innovations with the unclassified category usually being slightly larger were classified using the same procedure for ties.

# [24]

# Technological guideposts and innovation avenues

Devendra SAHAL

*Graduate School of Business Administration, New York University, New York, NY 10003, USA*

Final version received October 1983

This paper presents an integrative view of innovation processes based on a theory of systems developed by the author over the past few years. In its essence, one of the most important clues to the origin of innovations is to be found in the fact that the performance of every technology depends upon its size and structure. Specifically, as a technology is continuously made to become larger or smaller, the relationship between its size and structural requirements changes, which in turn, severely limits the scope of its further evolution. Thus the origin of a wide variety of innovations lies in *learning* to overcome the constraints that arise from the process of *scaling* the technology under consideration. In short, technical progress is best characterized as a process of learning by scaling.

These considerations in turn point to a trilogy of innovations corresponding to three main types of technological constraints: *structural innovations* that arise from a process of differential growth whereby the parts and the whole of a system do not grow at the same rate; *material innovations* involving a change in the construction stuff; and *systems innovations* that arise from the integration of two or more *symbiotic technologies* in an attempt to simplify the outline of the overall structure. The proposed trilogy is shown to account for the emergence of various techniques including the so-called revolutionary innovations in a variety of fields.

The theory is developed and illustrated through three case studies of technical progress in the aircraft, farm tractor, and computer industries. The results of our investigation further reveal that the process of innovation is best conceived in terms of a certain topography of technological evolution. Specifically, we find that technical progress is invariably characterized by the existence of what may be called technological guideposts and innovation avenues that lay out certain definite paths of development. Chance determines which amongst many technological guideposts will be chosen in the course of development. Once the development is well along a certain innovation avenue, necessity prevails until another point connecting other technological guideposts and innovation avenues is reached. This brings chance back to the fore and the process continues. In sum, the process of technological evolution is determined by the interplay of chance and necessity rather than one at the exclusion of the other.

Research Policy 14 (1985) 61–82
North-Holland

## 1. Toward an integrative view of technology

Traditionally, studies of technical change processes have varied between two extreme views. One of the earliest views used to be that technology dictates the mode of socio-economic evolution. The clearest exposition of this view is provided by Karl Marx [6, p. 92]:

> The Landmill gives you society with the feudal lord; the steam mill, society with the industrial capitalist.

Marx of course knew a great deal more about technological change than his remarks above would seem to indicate. Evidently, he was making his point by exaggeration. It was nevertheless an exaggeration that many took to their heart – including some of the most prominent social scientists of our times. William Ogburn, who laid the foundations of a whole school of sociology, confidently asserted that it is the changes in "material culture" that cause changes in "nonmaterial culture". In his own words [10, p. 85]:

> It should be no surprise to sociologists that various forms and shapes which our social institutions take and the many shifts in their function are the result of adjustments – not to a changing natural environment, not to a changing biological heritage – but adaptations to a changing technology.

In a similar vein, Joseph Schumpeter, whose work inspired a whole generation of economists, held that technical progress was an autonomous force with profound implications of an economic nature. He even foresaw the decay of capitalism resulting from the rise of monopoly power as a consequence of technological innovation [20, p. 84]:

... In capitalist reality as distinguished from its textbook picture, it is not (price) competition which counts but the competition from the new commodity, the new technology, the new source of supply, the new type of organization (the largest scale of unit of control for instance) – competition which commands a decisive cost or quality advantage and which strikes not at the margins of the profits and the outputs of the existing firms but at their foundations and their very lives.

By the 1950s, however, the above view of technical progress as *deus ex machina* had come under increasing criticism. It was evident that technical progress played a central role in the long term economic growth. Yet, there was no real explanation of how or why technical progress occurred in the first place. Following the result of a number of studies, it soon became apparent that the chain of causation had to be reversed. As Jacob Schmookler put it in his well-known study of the subject [19, [. 209]:

While our ignorance may dictate the continued treatment of technological change as an exogenous variable *in our economic models*, it is plain that *in the economic system* it is primarily an endogenous variable.

It was now held that the socioeconomic evolution was a precondition rather than a result of technological progress. Thus, the intellectual history of the subject had come to a full circle.

In recent years, it has been increasingly recognized that neither of the above two extreme views of the subject is wholly justified. We need greater eclecticism in place of earlier extremism in our conception of technical change processes.

This paper presents an integrative view of technology based on a theory of evolutionary systems developed by the author over the last several years [13–17]. In its essence, technology occupies a distinct niche of its own which is best understood from within rather than exclusively from without. Viewed from the proposed standpoint, technology both shapes its socioeconomic environment and is in turn shaped by it. Neither is a sole determinant of the other; rather, the two codetermine each other.

## 2. The origin of innovations in morphogenesis

The point of departure of the theory advanced in this paper is the well-known observation that change in the size of an object beyond a certain point requires change in its form and structure as well [13;22]. If geometric proportions of an object are kept unchanged with change in its size, its area increases as the square and the volume as the cube of its length. Thus if the length of an object is doubled, its area is increased by four times and its volume by eight times. From a functional point of view, however, no system can endure for long if its volume is greatly in excess of its area. The reason is simple. Some of the essential properties of the system such as capacity for heat generation and weight depend upon its volume whereas other properties such as capacity for heat dissipation and strength depend upon its area. Thus a system cannot remain unchanged both geometrically and functionally with change in its size; rather, it must seek to offset the excess of its volume by selectively increasing the linear and a real dimension of its parts. In consequence, the parts and the whole of a system do not grow at the same rate. The growth of a system is generally accompanied by change in its form.

We therefore find that the basins of large rivers tend to be proportionately longer as compared to those of small streams. This is because the length of the river's main channel disproportionately increases with increase in its drainage area. Likewise, large ships are characterized by proportionately smaller beam length. In an essentially similar way, small plants tend to be more slender compared with large trees. Moreover, large trees branch proportionately more as compared with small plants so as to maintain a certain parity between their surface area and the volume. So, also, large bridges cannot hold without the support of exceptionally heavy girders. Similarly, large wheels require proportionately fatter tires as is particularly evident in some sports cars. Often a system cannot survive if its size is continuously changed without a concomitant change in its shape.

We are therefore assured that contrary to the narrative of Jack the Giant Killer, Jack had no reason to be afraid of the giant [22]. If the giant were ten times as large as an average man, and had similar proportions, he would indeed be a weakling at best. This is because his weight would be a thousand times that of the average man. However, the cross-sections of his bones would be only a hundred times those of the average man so that every square inch of his bone had to support ten times the weight withstood by a square inch of the average man's bone. Chances were that the giant could not walk one step without fracturing his thighs. Jack had every reason to feel perfectly safe and sound.

More generally, the form of a system must be appropriate to its size. In consequence, we find that the observed variety of forms is often more apparent than real. To take one among many examples, Gothic architecture characterized by flying buttresses along with ribbed vaulting and the pointed arch is easily distinguishable from the classical and renaissance architecture characterized by the solid wall exhibiting regular windows. We are told that the origin of Gothic form lay in the mystical spirit whereas the origin of the classical and renaissance form lay in the materialistic spirit of the day. It is equally true, however, that the characteristic elements of both architectural forms are attributable to the necessity of transferring the weight of the structure to the ground while attempting to increase its overall size.

Frequently, change in the size of an object also necessitates change in the material employed in its construction. Thus it is often necessary to use special heat-resistant alloys in constructing the blades of large turbines. The current R&D effort to develop single crystals of the nickel chromium super alloys in making new blades for jet engine turbines is a case in point. So, also, it is essential to insert steel rods in casting the large concrete beams. Such provisions are unnecessary for small objects. One other way to overcome the adverse effect of change in the size of an object is to eliminate unnecessary material in its construction. Thus it is commonplace to use large steel beams in the "I" form so as to conserve their strength for supporting the weight of the structure under consideration.

Finally, change in the size of an object often introduces various complications in its structure. Thus large organisms cannot survive without increased differentiation of functions leading to the development of a respiratory mechanism because the quantity of respiratory tissues varies as the cube, whereas the surface of gas exchange varies as the square, of linear dimensions. Small organisms,

on the other hand, can do without gills or lungs, because gas exchange can occur fast enough for metabolism by means of diffusion alone. Similarly, large turbogenerators need specialized insulation devices because the volts per turn on each coil quadruples, whereas the thickness of the turn-to-turn insulation only doubles with the doubling of linear dimensions. Larger transformers also require complicated methods of cooling in the form of additional fins, coolant pumps and fans because heat generation varies as the cube, whereas heat dissipation varies as the square, of linear dimensions. Such complications are unnecessary for small devices.

Thus, change in the size of a system is generally accompanied by differential growth of its components in relation to the whole, change in the materials of construction and increase in the complexity of its structure. However, these processes cannot continue indefinitely without degenerating into absurdities. In consequence, there is a limit to the growth of every system of a given form. The story has it that the tower of Babel was never completed because divinity, concerned by the prospects of intrusion, put words in the mouths of builders that no one could understand. A more likely reason for the apparent failure of the mission would seem to lie in the vast dimensions of the proposed structure. Similarly, in modern times, we find that the height of the fractionation towers for petroleum refining is limited by the exceptionally heavy supports required for the distillation tray. So, also, the miniaturization of electronic devices is limited by the complexity of interconnections between the components. In essence, the very processes that initiate the evolution of a system eventually limit its future evolution. It is therefore to be expected that for any given form of the system, the range of appropriate sizes is limited.

The thesis is advanced here that one of the most important clues to understanding the process of innovation is to be found in the web of links between the functional performance of a technology and its size and structure. Thus, it is conceivable that the origin of innovations lies in *learning* to overcome the constraints that arise from the process of *scaling* the technology under consideration.[1] In short, technological evolution is best

---

[1] A consideration of some of the related issues will be found in earlier works of the author [13–16].

characterized as a process of learning by scaling.

Specifically, three major types of innovations may be identified on the basis of technological constraints noted above. First, we have what may be called *structural innovations* that arise out of the process of differential growth whereby the parts and the whole of a system do not grow at the same rate. Second, we have what may be called the *material innovations* that are necessitated in an attempt to meet the requisite changes in the criteria of technological construction as a consequence of changes in the scale of the object. Finally, we have what may be called the *systems innovations* that arise from integration of two or more *symbiotic technologies* in an attempt to simplify the outline of the overall structure. The distinction between the three categories of innovations is relative rather than absolute. As discussed below, their origin can be invariably traced to the simple fact that a technology can properly function only for a particular combination of size and structure.

## 3. A metaevolutionary explanation of revolutionary innovations

Two features of technological progress stand out above all others. First, economies of scale have played a prominent role in the innovative activity across a wide variety of fields. We find therefore that aircraft have become progressively larger whereas electronic devices have become progressively smaller in size over the course of time. [2] Second, however, a close examination of the evidence reveals that the basic form of the key technique within any given field has remained unchanged over long periods of time. Thus, *a priori*, according to the theory advanced here, it may be inferred that the origin of a wide variety of innovations lies in certain natural limitations to the evolution of technology discussed above. The point seems to be one of great generality. John Locke once remarked that it is of great use to the sailor to know the length of his line, though he cannot with it fathom all the depths of the ocean. This is

likewise true of technical explorations: the knowledge of constraints is of paramount importance. We find therefore that innovations depend upon the coexistence of certain developing as well as limiting processes. [3] The following case studies of technical progress may help make this clear.

### 3.1. Technical progress in the aircraft industry

It is often claimed that the introduction of DC-3 aircraft in 1936 marked the beginning of a new era in the development of technology. This is certainly borne out by the evidence. The DC-3 was a product of a great deal of prior development effort. In turn, it became a focal point of significant further development of technology. Thus it is noteworthy that the essential features of the DC-6 introduced in 1951 were identical with those of DC-3. The difference between the two lay in the degree of refinement rather than in the kind of design. Individually, these refinements were of a minor nature. Collectively, however, they had a major impact on the capability of technology. As Miller and Sawers put it [7, p. 128]:

> What did not happen to airliner design is more interesting than what did in the quarter-century between the introduction of the DC-2 and that of the big jets in 1958. Airliners changed from the DC-2 mostly in size, number of engines and power; and these alterations sufficed to increase their cruising speed from 170 m.p.h. to 310–330 m.p.h. and their range with capacity payload from 600 miles to 4760 miles ... The enormous growth in air travel between the 1930's and 1950's was not the result of any great improvement in the design of the airliner, though it was helped by its higher speed and longer range which made international air travel practical. All the efficiency that made the airliner a cheap enough means of travel to attract passengers in a significant number depended on the innovations of the early 1930's.

Thus, while the essential form of the aircraft design remained unchanged, the sale of technology significantly increased during the time period from 1936 to 1948 (see fig. 1). As a consequence, the

---

[2] As Nelson and Winter note [8], the phenomenon of continual changes in the scale of technology is sufficiently general to warrant the status of a natural trajectory. See also an excellent paper by Dosi [3] which presents a somewhat similar viewpoint.

[3] As discussed elsewhere by the author [14], this is true not only in technological but in organizational and social innovations as well.

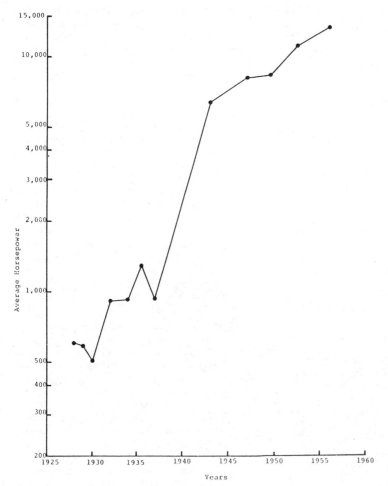

Fig. 1. Growth in the size of aircraft technology.

combination of piston engine and propeller had reached the limit of its performance by the late 1940s. One main constraint to technical progress lay in the fact that propellers became increasingly noisy and inefficient as their tips approached the speed of sound which in turn restricted the maximum speed of the aircraft. Further advances in technology were also limited by metal fatigue resulting from high vibrations as a consequence of increase in the engine power over the course of time. Thus, both the speed and power-to-weight ratio of the piston engine aircraft had peaked out at levels that were much too low for supersonic flight. It was essential to try out the hitherto dormant jet engine to find a way out of the impasse.

The jet aircraft was first successfully flown as early as 1939. However, the use of the jet engine in aircraft was beset by a number of problems. Its range was limited by its high fuel consumption. Its reliability was uncertain because of the use of new alloys and high temperatures at which it operated.

Its capability to develop thrust at low speed was restricted. The jet engine did have one basic merit: it was relatively light and compact. The fuel consumption of jet aircraft was gradually reduced with the development of axial flow compressors from 1948 to 1957. Its power and efficiency were further improved by the installation of a fan type engine in the early 1960s and then by gradually raising the bypass ratio (the proportion of air that passes through only the fan). Together these developments ensured the dominance of the jet powered airliner as the most economical means of transportation for flights of more than 200 miles carrying 50 or more passengers. The jet engine was of course a truly pathbreaking innovation. What is significant for the purpose of the present study is that its importance lay in the fact that it was a systems innovation: it simplified the form of aircraft design – inasmuch as it was based on a rotating rather than a reciprocating mechanism – thereby circumventing the constraint to further development of technology.

A number of other important advances in aircraft technology are demonstrably attributable to material innovations. Thus, a great deal of progress in the airframe technology has been made possible by development of new materials such as duralumin and various other aluminium alloys that are as light as possible and yet strong enough to withstand various stresses in the course of flight. Similarly, advances in engine technology have come not only through development of improved fuels but also through continuous search of metals that are both light and can withstand high temperatures and pressure. Thus the development of the jet aircraft was in no small measure made possible by the development of titanium-based alloys that could withstand higher temperatures than aluminium. Likewise, the installation of a fan type of engine in the jet aircraft was largely made possible by improved alloys. Moreover, major technical advances in the future are expected to come from substitution of composite materials for aluminium alloys in airframe construction and from the development of heat resistant turbine blades. Two alternative approaches are being pursued towards the development of these new blades. The first approach seeks to make the blades from a single crystal of an alloy so as to avoid the boundaries between grains of metal which often cause fatigue. The second approach attempts to

orient the grains in a common direction during the production process. Further advances in the performance of jet aircraft hinge upon the outcome of these efforts.

Finally, yet other advances in aircraft technology have been made possible by various structural innovations. As a prime example of this we find that the transition from the space frame to monocoque or single shell construction in 1930s was dictated by the sheer increase in the aircraft load and speed resulting from increase in the scale of technology. The swept wings were likewise an outcome of the attempts to circumvent the constraint posed by increase in the fatigue as a result of increase in the engine power.

## 3.2. Technical progress in the farm tractor industry

It is generally agreed that the introduction of the Fordson and Farmall models during 1917–1926 touched off a whole series of technical advances in the farm tractor industry. The Fordson was a product of the assembly line while inaugurating the frameless type of design. Its low cost of production was an important spur to widespread diffusion of technology. The Farmall was the first general purpose tractor rather than just a plowing machine. Its adaptability made it possible to utilize the tractor for a wide variety of farm operations including harvesting. Together, these two models marked the emergence of a basic pattern of tractor design that has remained intact to this day except for numerous refinements. As Reece put it [12, p. 125]:

> Tractor production throughout the world has settled down into a small number of distinct tractor forms, skid-steered track layers, toolframe tractors, and the conventional two-wheel (2 W.D.) machine and its four wheel drive (4 W.D.) variants ... production is ... totally dominated by the rigid frame, 2 W.D. tractors with a small proportion of 4 W.D. adaptations. This form of tractor was first introduced by Ford in 1917 .... Since then great progress has been made in detailed design and the machine has become much more complex, but no further really significant changes have occurred.

Similarly, in the view of one industry spokesman [4, p. 9]:

The Farmall has undergone many changes in power and utility since it was introduced. Though each year has seen important refinements, the essential features have remained the same.

It is noteworthy that the basic pattern of tractor design was a culminating point of a series of development efforts ranging well over a decade. Its very consolidation also made it a starting point for a great many further technical changes via a process of incremental changes and increases in the scale of technology (see fig. 2). However, the phenomenal increase in tractor power along with endless modifications of an essentially one and the same pattern of design also made the technology so complicated that by late 1930s it was no longer possible to further improve its performance. Clearly, a limit to technological development had been reached. This necessitated the development

of three point linkage for control of integrated implements so as to overcome the constraint to further evolution of technology.

An integral tractor plow supported by a three point hitch was originally developed as early as 1917. This was perfected into a combined system of linkage and hydraulic control in 1935. The Ferguson system, as it came to be called, was undoubtedly an outstanding innovation. Its importance lay in the fact that it was a systems innovation: it simplified the pattern of tractor design in its entirety by streamlining the combined tractor implement system, thereby circumventing the constraint to further development of the technology.

The origin of a number of other important advances in tractor technology clearly lies in material innovations. The reliability of the tractor in the infant stage of its development was much improved by the development of hardened alloy-steel bevel gears. The success of the Fordson trac-

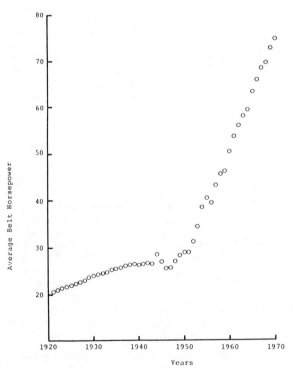

Fig. 2. Growth in the scale of farm tractor technology.

tor was in no small part made possible by the substitution of cast iron for boiler plate steel. One important source of improvement in the modern day tractor engine is to be found in the substitution of aluminium for cast iron in the construction of pistons. A wide variety of other technical advances are demonstrably attributable to various advances in metallurgical techniques such as alloy and deep drawing forging, heat treating practices, and gear manufacturing and testing devices.

Finally, structural innovations have played a significant role in enhancing the capability of the technology. The substitution of rubber tires for steel wheels in farm tractors is an important case in point. It was largely made possible by the differential reduction in the size of the drive wheels in relation to the overall tractor size over several years. The introduction of dual rear wheels and the adoption of the four-wheel drive were similarly an outcome of the attempts to increase drawbar pull under adverse soil conditions with increase in tractor size over the course of time.

### 3.3. Technical change in the computer industry

It is commonly recognized that the notion of a mechanical device capable of performing arithmetic operations in a digital manner dates back to the time of Pascal and Leibniz in the seventeenth century. It is also widely agreed that one milestone in technical progress was the "analytical engine" (a general purpose machine) conceived and designed by Charles Babbage during 1823–1871. However, what is often overlooked is that the analytic engine marked the emergence of a certain basic form of computer design that has persisted to this day except for numerous refinements. According to one careful account of the genesis of modern day computer technology [18, p. 1042]:

> Babbage's design had all the elements of a modern general-purpose digital computer; namely: memory, control, arithmetic unit, and input/output. The memory was to hold 1,000 words of 50 digits each, all in counting wheels. Control was to be by means of sequences of Jacquard punched cards. The very important ability to modify the course of a calculation according to the intermediate results obtained – now called conditional branching – was to be incorporated in the form of a procedure for

skipping forward or backward a specified number of cards. As in modern computer practice, the branch was to be performed or not depending upon the algebraic sign of a designated number. The arithmetic unit, Babbage supposed, would perform addition or subtraction in one second while a $50 \times 50$ multiplication would take about one minute. Babbage spent many years developing a mechanical method of achieving simultaneous propagation of carries during addition to eliminate the need for fifty successive carry cycles. Input to the machine was to be by individual punched cards and manual setting of the memory counters; output was to be punched cards, printed copy, or stereotype molds. When random access to a table of functions – stored on cards – was required, the machine would ring a bell and display the identity of the card needed.

The major headway in the construction of computers of course had to wait until 1944 when an electromechanical computing machine called Mark I was successfully made operational. Even so, Babbage's design had left a lasting imprint on the shape of the technology to come. As Howard Aiken, the leader of the team that built Mark I, reportedly put it: "If Babbage had lived 75 years later, I would have been out of a job." A number of successful electronic digital computers soon followed.

By the late 1940s the technology had reached the limit of its performance. One main obstacle to further technical progress lay in the fact that vacuum tubes generated prodigious amounts of heat which in turn limited their reliability and operating life. The constraint was of course particularly severe in the case of large systems. For example, the first electronic computer ENIAC developed in 1945 contained nearly 18,000 tubes. It represented something of the state of the art. Larger systems were infeasible because of the prohibitive amount of time required to detect and replace the defective tubes. Moreover, the design of vacuum tubes prohibited reductions in size and cost.

By the same token it was apparent that the capability of computers could be significantly improved if the constituent elements of technology could be made smaller. Obviously, electric pulses would have to traverse shorter distances, thereby making it possible to increase the number of oper-

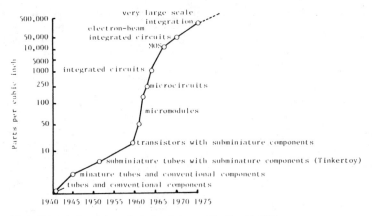

Fig. 3. Miniaturization of electronic devices (Braun and MacDonald, 1978).

ations per unit of time. Thus a series of efforts got underway to substitute the transistor for vacuum tubes in computers. These attempts also marked the emergence of a trend toward miniaturization of electronic devices that was to continue to this day (see fig. 3).

The transistor was invented in 1948 but its initial capability was distinctly inferior to that of the valve. Not only that the frequency performance of the transistor was more restricted, it was far less reliable in comparison with the vacuum tube. It was not any easy task to design a transistor to provide the requisite characteristics. Moreover, it was especially difficult to produce transistors of uniform characteristics. These obstacles could only be gradually overcome.

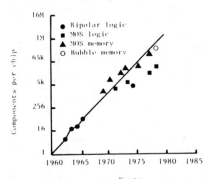

Fig. 4. Growth in the complexity of semiconductor devices (Noyce, 1977).

In 1950 Western Electric developed the technique of single crystal growing consisting of a new method of growing and doping germanium crystals. This made it possible to increase the yield in the production of transistors while increasing their resistance to shock. Two years later, General Electric developed the so-called alloy process which in turn made it possible to significantly improve the switching capabilities of the transistor. In 1953 Philco devised the technique of jet etching leading to the development of surface barrier transistors in the following year. Together these developments paved the way to increase the frequency range and switching speeds of the transistor. Soon thereafter, transistors had virtually displaced vacuum tubes in nearly all types of computers.

By the early 1960s the discrete semiconductor devices had reached the limit of their performance just as the vacuum tubes had reached the peak of their capability a decade earlier. One main obstacle to technical progress lay in the fact that the chances of system failure greatly increased with the increase in the number of interconnections between components. In essence, the problem was one of a tyranny of numbers. Clearly, the trend toward increasing complexity of technology had acquired a firm hold (see fig. 4). Thus reliability became a significant obstacle – a systematic hurdle that could not be overcome merely through improving the reliability of individual components. One way to surmount this "tyranny of numbers" lay in the application of the integrated circuit invented by Texas Instruments in 1958.

The integrated circuit was clearly an outcome of much prior research and development effort spanning over a decade. Even so, it was beset by a number of problems. In particular, it lacked a suitable means of production. This limitation was overcome with the development of planar process by Fairchild in 1960, itself an outgrowth of the older process of oxide masking and diffusion devised by Western Electric in 1955. The prospects for the integrated circuits nevertheless remained limited by the problem of poor production yields up to mid-1960s. One solution to this problem lay in the discovery by Motorola that yields could be improved by a factor of as much as four by reducing wafer area to one fourth of its earlier size because wafer defects were not distributed in a random fashion. By 1970 it became possible to devise an MOS (Metal Oxide Semiconductor) integrated circuit. This made it possible to put an even greater number of circuits on a single piece of silicon because it required much less power than the earlier bipolar integrated circuit. In the following year it became possible to place the entire central processing unit of a computer on a single chip of silicon leading to the successful development of the microprocessor. The age of very large scale integration had begun.

In retrospect, it is widely agreed that the transistor, integrated circuit and microprocessor were momentous innovations. What is noteworthy for the purpose of the present study is that they were systems innovations: their importance lay in the fact that they made it possible to progressively streamline the structure of technology, thereby paving the way for the truly phenomenal advances in the capability of computer (and other) technologies. Moreover, it is evident that the advances in computer technology have been intimately linked with the advances in the material sciences.

In the future, systems and material innovations are likely to play an even more important role in technical progress. One indication is provided by the very high speed integrated circuit (VHIC) program undertaken by the U.S. Department of Defense [5]. Briefly, the program seeks to reduce the size of semiconductor devices by a factor of 4:1 from 5 $\mu$m feature size to 1.25 $\mu$m feature size (i.e. circuit line width drawn on a single piece of silicon chip) in its initial phase. However, there are a number of constraints to meeting the proposed

objective. Note that both the device density and resistance of interconnection between components increase, whereas device current and voltage decrease, as the square of the scale reduction factor. Thus, if the goal is met, it should be possible to construct devices that consume only 1/16th as much power as current devices but are nearly 16 times as complex as the current technology. The resulting increase in current density raises numerous problems of its own such as electromigration of motion of atoms induced by current in metallic wires and difficulty of heat removal. Both systems and material innovations will be needed to overcome the spending constraints. Thus it may be necessary to develop new circuit forms such as the Josephson junction (to circumvent the cooling problem) as well as new compound materials such as gallium arsenide (to overcome the electromigration problem).

Three conclusions emerge from the above case analyses. First, the theory accounts for a wide variety of technical advances in terms of the proposed trilogy of structural, material, and systems innovations.

Second, it is commonly said that certain innovations such as the jet engine, the three point hitch and control system, and the modern electronic computer constitute revolutionary breakthroughs. While this viewpoint is obviously correct as far as it goes, it is both vacuous and a mere *petito principi*. Both from a theoretical and policy point of view, the crucial question is: what determines the occurrence of revolutionary breakthroughs? If the considerations advanced here are any guide, the origin of *revolutionary innovations* lies in certain *metaevolutionary processes* involving a combination of two or more *symbiotic technologies* whereby the structure of the integrated system is drastically simplified. Thus the advent of the jet engine lay in the combination of jet propulsion and gas turbine. The three point hitch and control system originated in an attempt to integrate the farm tractor and implement technology. The electronic computer resulted from a marriage of the programmable calculating machine and solid state technology. This is likewise true of the radical process innovation. Thus the development of the planar process was made possible by blending the techniques of diffusion and chemical etching, and photolithography originally developed for printing purposes.

Third, it is apparent that the innovation process in a wide variety of fields is governed by a common system of evolution. Typically, the process of technological development within any given field leads to the formation of a certain pattern of design. The pattern in turn guides the subsequent steps in the process of technological development. Thus innovations generally depend upon bit-by-bit modification of an essentially invariant pattern of design. This basic design is in the nature of a *technological guidepost* charting the course of innovative activity. [4]

There is an important corollary to the above proposition. It is that technical advances do not take place in a haphazard fashion. Rather, they are expected to occur in a systematic manner on what may be called *innovation avenues* that designate various distinct pathways of evolution. We may say that the technological guideposts point to the innovation avenues just as the innovation avenues lead to technological guideposts. In what follows, we will attempt to determine if the process of innovation is in fact canalized as indicated by the theory.

## 4. Invariant factors in innovation processes

In order to test the hypothesis of innovation avenues, two issues must be addressed. First, it needs to be ascertained whether there in fact exists a stable relationship between the performance and the scale of any given technology over the course of time. Second, and more importantly, it is imperative to determine whether these relationships in turn imply the existence of some invariant factors in the evolution of technology. [5]

The notion of an invariant factor may be formalized as follows. Consider the flow of a viscous fluid through the tube governed by the well-known Poiseuille law $J = (\pi/8)(Pr^4/\eta)$, where $J$ is the volume flow rate of the fluid, $P$ the pressure gradient, $r$ the radius and $\eta$ the viscosity. The dimensions of $J$, $P$, $r$, and $\eta$ are $L^3T^{-1}$, $ML^{-2}T^{-2}$, $L$, and $ML^{-1}T^{-1}$, respectively, where

$M$, $L$, and $T$ denote the dimensions of mass, length, and time, respectively. The parameter $\eta$ is illustrative of a *dimensional constant* that appears in many physical laws. Specifically, it is a *system dependent constant* whose value uniquely characterizes any given system. By the same token, its value systematically differs for different systems even under a fixed set of scales of measurement. A more general type of a dimensional constant is a *universal constant* such as the speed of light whose value is always observed to be the same for a fixed set of scales of measurement. Note, moreover, that the dimensions of the both sides of Poiseuille's equation are exactly the same, i.e., $L^3T^{-1}$. The equation is therefore dimensionally homogeneous, i.e. it is invariant under the scale change transformation $x' = Kx$ where $x$ is a general variable and $K$ an arbitrary constant.

It is well known that a dimensionally homogeneous equation can always be reformulated in terms of dimensionless products. Thus Poiseuille's law can be equally well expressed in terms of the following dimensionless product:

$$\Pi = J\eta P^{-1}r^{-4}$$

It can be readily verified that $\Pi$ is dimensionless because it is given by $M^0L^0T^0$. In essence, it is a criterion of similarity in comparing the flows of two or more viscous fluids.

The example as a whole points to a very general proposition: the existence of a law necessarily implies the existence of certain dimensional constants and dimensionless numbers which together constitute the invariant properties of the system.

In the light of the above considerations, the essence of our theoretical investigation can be very simply put forth. It is an attempt to determine what, if any, dimensional constants and dimensionless numbers can be found to characterize the evolution of technology. Clearly, if any dimensional constants and dimensionless numbers can be found, and if the data prove that they in fact remain relatively constant or vary within a limited range despite changes in the scale of technology, it can be justifiably concluded that technical progress is governed by an *inner* logic or law of its own. [6]

---

[4] A further discussion of the concept of a technological guidepost can be found in earlier works of the author [13].

[5] The following exposition of an invariant factor is deliberately made as simple as possible. The specific methodology employed here was originally developed by Stahl [21]. A rigorous treatment of the concept of an invariant factor in evolution will be found in an earlier work of the author [13].

[6] In a fundamental sense, such a law of technical progress is illustrative of a very general principle of self-resemblance proposed elsewhere by the author [13]. It is well described by the ancient adage that the more an object changes the more it remains the same.

Table 1
The process of learning by scaling in the evolution of aircraft technology, 1928–1957 [a]

| Dependent variable (Y) | Independent variable (W) | Estimated relationships | $R^2$ | $S$ |
|---|---|---|---|---|
| 1. Average horsepower | Average gross take-off weight (lb) | $\log Y = -2.78 + 1.039 \log W$ <br> $(0.17)\ (0.016)$ | 0.99 | 0.07 |
| 2. Average wing-loading (pounds per square foot) | Average gross take-off weight (lb) | $\log Y = -2.05 + 0.542 \log W$ <br> $(0.31)\ (0.03)$ | 0.97 | 0.13 |
| 3. Cruise speed (miles per hour) | Average gross take-off weight (lb) | $\log Y = 2.37 + 0.293 \log W$ <br> $(0.35)\ (0.03)$ | 0.88 | 0.14 |
| 4. Service ceiling ($\times 1000$ miles) | Average gross take-off weight (lb) | $\log Y = 1.74 + 0.133 \log W$ <br> $(0.22)\ (0.02)$ | 0.79 | 0.09 |
| 5. Normal full load cruise range (miles) | Average gross take-off weight (lb) | $\log Y = 1.351 + 0.564 \log W$ <br> $(0.50)\ (0.04)$ | 0.93 | 0.21 |
| 6. No. of engines | Average gross take-off weight (lb) | $\log Y = -2.32 - 0.314 \log W$ <br> $(0.31)\ (0.03)$ | 0.91 | 0.13 |
| 7. Initial climb rate | Average gross take-off weight (lb) | $\log Y = 6.61 + 0.04 \log W$ <br> $(0.29)\ (0.02)$ | 0.19 | 0.12 |
| 8. Passenger capacity | Average gross take-off weight (lb) | $\log Y = -5.35 + 0.822 \log W$ <br> $(0.19)\ (0.02)$ | 0.99 | 0.07 |
| 9. Empty weight in (lb) | Average gross take-off weight (lb) | $\log Y = -0.17 + 0.968 \log W$ <br> $(0.15)\ (0.01)$ | 0.99 | 0.06 |

[a] *Definitions:* $R^2$ is the coefficient of determination and $S$ is the standard error of the estimate. Standard errors of the coefficients are indicated in parentheses.
*Source of data:* Sahal [17].

The first case examined here is the evolution of aircraft technology during the time period 1928–1957. Several measures of technical progress are considered including changes in both performance variables (e.g. horsepower, cruise speed, and passenger capacity) as well as design variables (e.g. wing loading and number of engines). The scale of technology is measured in terms of gross take-off weight of the aircraft in pounds. The parametric estimates of the relationships between chosen measures of technology and its scale are presented here in table 1. The explanatory power of these relationships is generally excellent as indicted by coefficients of determination. This is further illustrated here in figs. 5–10. It can be seen that there exist highly stable patterns of technological evolution. The results also indicate that the evolution of aircraft technology is accompanied by a process of *differential growth* of its various dimensions. We find therefore that the increase in the passenger capacity has been proportionately smaller than the increase in the overall scale of technology (eq. 8, table 1). In turn, this had made it possible for complexity of technology measured

in terms of number of engines to increase at an even pace in relation to increase in the linear dimensions of the system [eq. 6, table 1]. In conclusion, it may be said that a wide variety of advances in aircraft technology are demonstrably attributable to the process of learning by scaling.

A number of dimensionless products and dimensional constants based on the variables under consideration are presented in table 2. The data in table 1 confirm that they are virtually independent of the scale of the technology. The conclusion to be drawn is that the evolution of aircraft technology has, in fact, been characterized by the existence of certain invariant factors. This may be further illustrated by means of the following examples.

The first invariant factor ($I_1$) listed in table 2 is the ratio of cruise range to wing loading with a numerical value of 29.98. For the 10,130 lb Ford Trimotor model 4-AT-E introduced in 1929 we obtain a value of $I_1 = 43.41$; for the 100,000 lb DC-6B introduced in 1951 we obtain a value of $I_1 = 40.93$, notwithstanding the gross take-off weight ratio of nearly 10:1. Thus the invariant

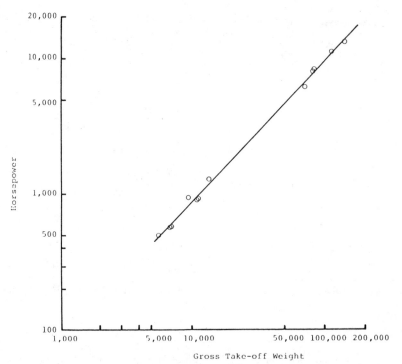

Fig. 5. Relationship between horsepower and size of aircraft, 1928–1957.

factor $I_1$ is practically constant across a wide variety of aircraft models; the small variation in its value is attributable to the weak scale effect as indicted by its associated residual scale exponent value of 0.02. Interestingly, Boeing 707-120 with a weight of 258,000 1b at the time of its introduction in 1958 turns out to have a value of $I_1 = 28.30$ which is remarkably close to the representative

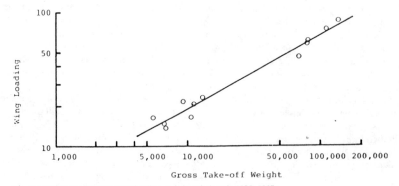

Fig. 6. Relationship between wing loading and size of aircraft, 1928–1957.

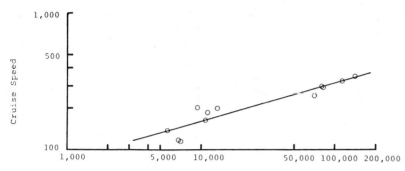

Fig. 7. Relationship between cruise speed and size of aircraft, 1928–1957.

numerical value of $I_1 = 29.98$ given in table 2 even though it was not included in our original sample. In essence, it would be possible to predict the advent of jet aircraft by means of the proposed theoretical concepts.

As a second example consider the invariant factor ($I_5$) listed in table 2, specified as (wing loading × cruise range)/(passenger capacity × cruise speed). For the Ford Trimotor, $I_5 = 5.47$; for the DC-6B, $I_5 = 9.18$; and for the Boeing 707, $I_5 = 4.08$, despite the tremendous differences in the scale of technology. The remaining invariant

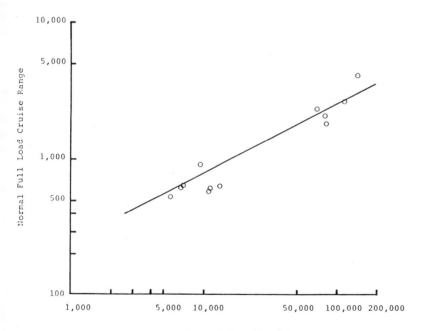

Fig. 8. Relationship between range and size of aircraft, 1928–1957.

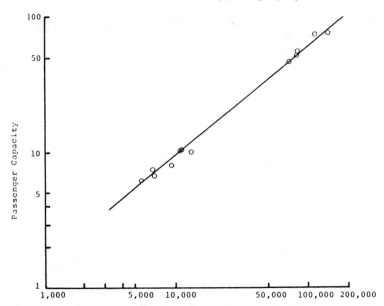

Gross Take-off Weight

Fig. 9. Relationship between passenger capacity and weight of aircraft, 1928–1957.

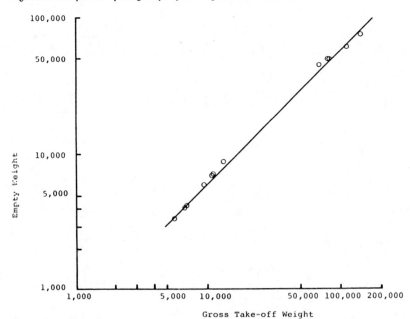

Gross Take-off Weight

Fig. 10. Relationship between empty weight and gross take-off weight of aircraft, 1928–1957.

Table 2

Invariant factors in the evolution of aircraft technology

| Invariant | Composition | Scaling laws | Resulting parameter | Residual scale exponent |
|---|---|---|---|---|
| $I_1$ | $\dfrac{\text{Cruise range}}{\text{Wing loading}}$ | $\dfrac{3.86(W)^{0.564}}{0.128(W)^{0.542}}$ | 29.98 | 0.02 |
| $I_2$ | $\dfrac{\text{Climb rate} \times \text{empty weight}}{\text{Horsepower}}$ | $\dfrac{742.48(W)^{0.04} \times 0.84(W)^{0.968}}{0.06(W)^{1.039}}$ | 10,394.72 | $-0.03$ |
| $I_3$ | $\dfrac{\text{Passenger capacity} \times \text{service ceiling}}{\text{Empty weight}}$ | $\dfrac{4.75 \times 10^{-3}(W)^{0.822} \times 5.697(W)^{0.133}}{0.84(W)^{0.968}}$ | 0.032 | $-0.01$ |
| $I_4$ | $\dfrac{\text{Horsepower} \times \text{climb rate}}{\text{Passenger capacity} \times \text{cruise speed}}$ | $\dfrac{0.06(W)^{1.039} \times 742.48(W)^{0.04}}{4.75 \times 10^{-3}(W)^{0.822} \times 10.6(W)^{0.293}}$ | 884.78 | $-0.03$ |
| $I_5$ | $\dfrac{\text{Wing loading} \times \text{cruise range}}{\text{Passenger capacity} \times \text{cruise speed}}$ | $\dfrac{0.128(W)^{0.542} \times 3.86(W)^{0.564}}{4.75 \times 10^{-3}(W)^{0.822} \times 10.6(W)^{0.293}}$ | 9.81 | $-0.009$ |
| $I_6$ | $\dfrac{\text{Wing loading} \times \text{cruise speed}}{\text{Passenger capacity}}$ | $\dfrac{0.128(W)^{0.542} \times 10.6(W)^{0.293}}{4.75 \times 10^{-3}(W)^{0.822}}$ | 285.6 | 0.013 |

Table 3

The process of learning by scaling in the evolution of tractor technology, 1920–1968 [a]

| Case | Dependent variable ($Y$) | Independent variable ($W$) | Estimated relationship | $R^2$ | $s$ |
|---|---|---|---|---|---|
| 1. | Average belt horsepower | Average ballasted weight (lb) | $\log Y = -1.685 + 0.844 \log W$ (0.09) | 0.68 | 0.06 |
| 2. | Average drawbar horsepower | Average ballasted weight (lb) | $\log Y = -2.637 + 1.039 \log W$ (0.14) | 0.57 | 0.09 |
| 3. | Average fuel consumption (gal/h) | Average ballasted weight (lb) | $\log Y = -2.038 + 0.653 \log W$ (0.112) | 0.44 | 0.07 |
| 4. | Average drawbar pull (lb) | Average ballasted weight (lb) | $\log Y = -0.36 + 0.978 \log W$ (0.07) | 0.81 | 0.04 |
| 5. | Average number of cylinders | Average ballasted weight (lb) | $\log Y = -0.727 + 0.339 \log W$ (0.08) | 0.28 | 0.05 |
| 6. | Average speed (miles per hour) | Average ballasted weight (lb) | $\log Y = -0.014 + 0.147 \log W$ (0.147) | 0.02 | 0.09 |
| 7. | Crankshaft speed (r.p.m.) | Average ballasted weight (lb) | $\log Y = 1.787 + 0.349 \log W$ (0.21) | 0.06 | 0.13 |
| 8. | Slip of drivers (%) | Average ballasted weight (lb) | $\log Y = 3.107 - 0.625 \log W$ (0.22) | 0.15 | 0.14 |
| 9. | Average bore (in) | Average stroke (in) | $\log Y = 0.10 + 0.74 \log W$ (0.04) | 0.89 | 0.02 |

[a] *Definitions:* $R^2$ is the coefficient of determination and $S$ is the standard error of the estimate. Standard errors of the coefficients are indicated in parentheses.

*Source of data:* Sahal [17].

factors provided in table 2 can be interpreted in a similar way.

The second case examined here is the evolution of farm tractor technology during the time period 1920–1968. As before, several measures of technical progress are considered, including, changes in both performance variables (e.g. drawbar horsepower, fuel consumption and field speed) as well as design variables (e.g. average number of cylinders and bore dimension). The scale of technology is measured in terms of ballasted tractor weight in pounds. The parametric estimates of the relationship between chosen measures of technology and its scale are presented here in table 3. The explanatory power of these relationships is fairly good in most instances as indicated by the coefficients of determination. Thus, it is evident that there exist certain systematic patterns of technical progress. The results further indicate that the evolution of tractor technology is accompanied by a process of differential growth in its various dimensions. We find therefore that the increase in the bore has been proportionately smaller in comparison with increase in the stroke length (eq. 9, table 3). In consequence, the complexity of the tractor engine measured in terms of the number of cylinders has increased at an even pace in relation to its linear dimensions (eq. 5, table 3). The conclusion to be drawn is that a wide variety of innovations in arm tractor technology have also resulted from the process of learning by scaling.

A number of dimensionless products and dimensional constants based on the variables under

consideration are presented in table 4. An application of the data in table 3 verifies that they are largely independent of scale of technology. Thus they may be justifiably regarded as invariant factors in the innovation process. The following examples may help make this clear.

The first invariant factor ($I_1$) listed in table 4 is the product of fuel consumption and slip of drivers. For the 6460 1b kerosene-powered tractor, Case 15–27, introduced by the J.1. Case Thrashing Co. in 1920 we obtain a value of $I_1 = 35.4$; for the 18,900 1b diesel-powered tractor, Massey-Ferguson 1135, introduced in 1973 we obtain a value of 30.55, despite the weight ratio of nearly 3:1. Interestingly enough, the latter model was not included in our sample. Yet we are able to predict its characteristics fairly well.

As a second example, consider the invariant factor ($I_2$) listed in table 4 which is specified as (drawbar pull × speed)/(drawbar horsepower). For the Case 15–27 the value of $I_2 = 375.19$; for the Massey-Ferguson 1135, $I_2 = 374.80$. The relative constancy or limited variation of these invariant factors convincingly demonstrates the existence of innovation avenues in the course of technical progress.

The final case examined here is the evolution of electronic computer technology over the time period 1951–1980. The specific measure of technical progress chosen for the purpose of analysis is a composite index of operations performed per second that incorporates several elements of speed: the speed of executing a particular arithmetic op-

Table 4

invariant factors in the evolution of tractor technology

| Invariant | Composition | Scaling laws | Resulting parameter | Residual scale exponent |
|---|---|---|---|---|
| $I_1$ | Slip of drivers × fuel | $1279.38(W)^{-0.625} \times 9.33 \times 10^{-3}(W)^{0.653}$ | 11.94 | 0.03 |
| $I_2$ | $\dfrac{\text{Drawbar pull} \times \text{speed}}{\text{Drawbar horsepower}}$ | $\dfrac{0.44(W)^{0.978} \times 0.97(W)^{0.147}}{2.31 \times 10^{-3}(W)^{1.039}}$ | 184.76 | 0.08 |
| $I_3$ | $\dfrac{\text{Drawbar pull}}{\text{Fuel consumption} \times \text{no. of cylinders}}$ | $\dfrac{0.44(W)^{0.978}}{9.33 \times 10^{-3}(W)^{0.653} \times 0.19(W)^{0.339}}$ | 248.21 | −0.014 |
| $I_4$ | $\dfrac{\text{Drawbar pull} \times \text{slip}}{\text{Crankshaft speed}}$ | $\dfrac{0.44(W)^{0.978} \times 1279.38(W)^{-0.625}}{61.23(W)^{0.349}}$ | 9.19 | 0.004 |
| $I_5$ | $\dfrac{\text{Crankshaft speed} \times \text{no. of cylinders}}{\text{Fuel consumption}}$ | $\dfrac{61.23(W)^{0.349} \times 0.19(W)^{0.339}}{9.33 \times 10^{-3}(W)^{0.653}}$ | 1246.91 | 0.03 |

78                               D. Sahal / Technological guideposts

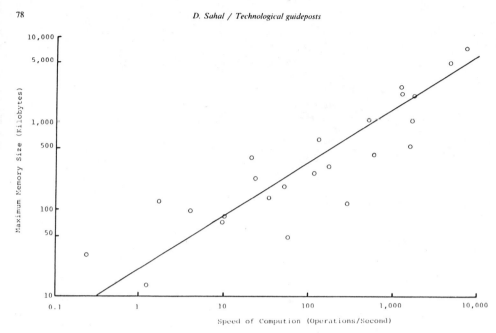

Fig. 11. Relationship between speed and capacity of digital computers, 1951–1980.

eration, the speed of solving a standard problem such as inversion of a matrix of any given size, the speed of reading the data into and out of memory, and speed of performing certain input/output functions. The scale of technology is measured in terms of maximum memory size in kilobytes.

The relationship between the chosen index of computational speed and capacity is depicted here in fig. 11. It can be seen that the agreement between the theory and the data is fairly good. Thus the proposed relationship explains more than 82 percent variance in the data. The slope of the speed capacity relationship is estimated to be 1.62. Finally, a close examination of the data reveals that the observed deviations from the estimated relationship are attributable to differences in the best practice and general practice technology.

## 5. The topography of technological evolution

In an important work in theoretical biology, C.H. Waddington has put forth the concept of "cherods" or necessary paths of development which bears several interesting parallels to the

concept of "innovation avenues" presented in this study. Waddington was concerned with the study of embryonic development [23]. However, his terminology and pictorial representation of development is equally well suited to bringing out certain implications of the viewpoint proposed here. [7]

Our point of departure is a topographical representation of technological evolution depicted in fig. 12. A developing object such as an infant technology is shown here as a ball. Starting in a low basin, the ball may roll along any one of the two valleys. It is chance that determines the specific valley chosen. Once a specific valley has been opted for, the ball can keep rolling on its own momentum until the next branch point is encountered at which stage chance once again predominates over necessity. Such a representation of technological evolution is consistent with a point noted earlier: beyond a certain stage, quantitative changes in the scale of an object are invariably transformed into certain qualitative changes with profound implications for its morphological, func-

[7] See also Prigogine for a somewhat similar view from a different premise [11].

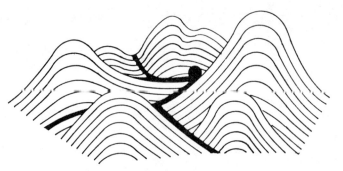

Fig. 12. The topography of technological evolution.

tional, and structural properties. Thus technical progress is neither wholly systematic nor wholly chaotic.

It should also be noted that the developing object can only ascend through various slopes if its form is progressively modified. Eventually, it may reach one of the several hilltops if its form is perfected through a process of constant refinement. The higher the peak, the greater the perfection. Relatedly, the lower the valley, the greater the difficulty of improvement and of leaving a given pathway. The overall topography itself can be altered by a wide variety of socio-economic forces. In consequence, the developing object may end up either remaining at a peak or climbing up successively higher peaks.

The proposed topographical representation of technological evolution helps clarify several points of interest. It is very generally the case that a technology, during the initial stages of its development, branches off in multiple directions. The development of the computer in the digital and analog form is an example of this, as is the development of the farm tractor along the track type and the wheel type. We find, moreover, that each of these multiple forms of technology evolves along a path of its own which in turn may split into separate paths from time to time. As an obvious example of this we find that the evolution of the digitial computer occurred along two paths: towards large computers and maxicomputers; and towards the minicomputer, microcomputer and the computer-on-a-chip in the offing. In essence, development of every technology is characterized by the existence of a unique evolutionary path or an innovation avenue. Occasionally, these avenues may also fuse together in what was earlier described as a process of integration symbiotic technologies.

Furthermore, the process of technological evolution is characterized not only by *specific innovation avenues* that concern individual industries as discussed above, but *generic innovation avenues* as well, that cut across several industries. As an example of the latter, the evolution of microelectronics is an important case in point. We find therefore that technology in both telecommunications and computer industries is evolving on a common generic innovation avenue.

Finally, it is apparent that the emergence of a new innovation avenue through *fusion* of two or more avenues or through *fission* of an existing avenue can give rise to sudden changes in the mode and tempo of technical progress. The conclusion to be drawn is that we should be prepared to expect surprises in the course of technological evolution because of – not in spite of – the existence of innovation avenues.

## 6. Conclusions and policy implications

This study has presented a general theoretical view of innovation processes. In its essence, one of the most important keys to understanding the origin of innovations is to be found in the simplest of facts: that the performance of every technology depends upon its size and structure. The proposed viewpoint markedly differs from the traditional, neoclassical economic theory viewpoint according to which the origin of innovation is to be found in the capital and labor intensity of the technology. Nevertheless, the two theoretical views are broadly complementary. Our view pertains to the *origin* of new techniques; the neoclassical view is relevant to the *resulting impact* on the activity of firms and industries concerned.

The proposed viewpoint also sheds new light on the controversy as to the relative importance of demand versus supply side factors in technical progress. According to the results of our investigation, the considerations of demand and supply are of little significance in and of themselves. Rather, their importance depends on their bearing on the internal structure of technology. it is the process of morphogenesis rather than demand or supply as such that is central to the process of innovation. What counts is not only the advances in scientific knowledge and the industry's sales *per se*. Above all, what matters is the fine structure of interaction between a multiplicity of factors including variables of both an economic as well as a physical nature.

In recent years, a certain ecological view of technology has gained increasing prominence among people from various fields and walks of life. The basic premise of "eco-philosophy" is to be greatly commended: the choice of a particular scale of technology has profound *socio-economic* repercusions. The viewpoint advanced here adds an altogether new and hithertofore overlooked rationale to this movement. It is that the size of technology has equally far-reaching implications for the possibilities of *innovation* as well. The proponents of eco-philosophy do of course have a valid claim, namely, that extreme in size is to be avoided for the sake of *humanity*. It needs to be added, however, that extreme in size is to be avoided for the sake of *creativity* as well.

The crux of the matter is that as technology is continuously made to become larger or smaller, the relationship between its size and structural requirements changes which, in turn, severely limits the scope of its further evolution. We find therefore that the origin of a wide variety of innovations lies in attempts to overcome certain natural limitations to a technology's betterment as a consequence of change in its scale.

These considerations in turn point to a trilogy of material, structural, and systems innovations corresponding to three main types of technological

constraints. It is interesting to note that a number of input–output analyses indicate that innovations in the development of new materials have played a central role in the growth of industrial productivity [2]. According to the theory advanced here, this is to be expected.

The structural innovations concerning the nature of product design also play a vital role in technical progress, a role that is so obvious that it is often ignored. For example, consider the controversy surrounding the lack of technical progress in the automobile industry. Expert opinion would have us believe that the problem lies in certain institutional aspects of the industry such as its vertically integrated structure. Yet, such a viewpoint fails to explain why no such problem exists in the case of the telecommunications industry with a similar vertically integrated structure. If the considerations advanced here are any guide, it is conceivable that one root cause of the automobile industry's stagnation lies in the stagnation of its product design. This is evidenced by the industry's early decisions to discard certain potentially outstanding forms of design against the background of changes in consumer tastes – e.g. Ford's Model T car and Chrysler's airflow car –. which may be likened to throwing away good money after bad. it goes without saying that the structure of an industry plays an important role in its innovative performance. it needs to be added however, that the structure of its technology may well be an equally important determinant of its performance.

Finally, the systems innovations that originate in an integration of two or more symbiotic technologies constitute the most important types of innovations. We have already discussed their significance at length. Suffice it here to add that their importance is likely to grow in the future. It has been observed that the thrust of national policy during the remainder of the twentieth century ought to be to promote the *diffusion* and transfer of certain key technologies such as microelectronics across broad areas of industrial application [15]. Equally important, it seems that the focus of the policy must shift once this objective has been achieved. Beginning from the twenty-first century, we may expect an accelerating trend towards what may be called the *fusion* of certain important technologies based on intermingling of knowledge from a wide variety of fields. In this respect, Kodak's new camera, an outcome of the joint effort of photochemists and electronics experts, seems a good pointer to the shape of things to come. Whatever the case may be, it seems imperative that management of R&D activity must show greater willingness and preparation to undertake essentially *trans-disciplinary* projects in the future.

The proposed trilogy of innovations is illustrative of another important point. It is that the constraining factors play an even more significant role in comparison with the facilitating factors in technological evolution. There is obviously a parallel here to a well known Biblical dictum: "Except a corn of wheat fall into the ground and die, it abideth alone; but if it die, it bringeth forth much fruit." This may be disconcerting to many policy planners. However, as the considerations advanced here make it plain, a major constraint is always a major catalyst to technical progress provided the management is willing to ensure adequate experimentalism in the conduct of R&D activity.

The results of our investigation further reveal that the process of innovation is best conceived in terms of a certain topography of technological evolution. Specifically, we find that in a wide variety of cases technical progress is characterized by innovation avenues that lay out various distinct paths of development. There are a number of important policy implications in this. To begin with, it is apparent in the light of our earlier research findings [13], that some innovation avenues are fairly broad whereas others are relatively narrow. Some may also be flat whereas others may be bumpy. Thus the direction and tempo of the innovation process may well be easier to adjust in some fields than in others. Accordingly, the appropriate technology strategy must differ from one industry to another.

Second, public support of R&D activity ought to be based on careful consideration of the relevant innovation avenues. In particular, the timing of support is crucial. Very generally, the development of a technology is best promoted when the underlying innovation avenue is approaching either a point of branching off or merging into several distinct but related innovation avenues. In most other circumstances, efforts to change the course of technical progress from without may not only be ineffective but wasteful as well.

Third, the process of technological evolution is determined by the interplay of chance and necess-

ity rather than one at the exclusion of the other. Chance determines which amongst many innovation avenues will be chosen in the course of development. Once the development is well along a certain innovation avenue, necessity prevails until another point connecting other innovation avenues is reached. This brings chance back to the fore and the process continues. The implication is that there can never be one single optimal approach to the management of technology. Rather, an appropriate policy must be based on a judicious mixture of gradualism in the face of necessity and experimentalism in the face of chance.

Last, but not least, while technological evolution follows a logic of its own, its topographical make up depends upon a host of socio-economic forces at work. The conclusion to be drawn is that technology has a dual character: it is both an object and an instrument of socioeconomic evolution. In this respect, the proposed theory is admirably expressed by the maxim that "a hen is merely an egg's way of making another hen."

### References

[1] E. Braun and S. MacDonald, *Revolution in Miniature* (Cambridge University Press, Cambridge, 1978).

[2] A.P. Carter, *Structural Changes in the American Economy* (Harvard University Press, Cambridge, Mass., 1970).

[3] G. Dosi. Technological paradigms and technological trajectories, *Research Policy* 11 (1982) 147–162.

[4] International Harvester Spokesman, Fifty Years of Farmall, *Implement & Tractor* May 21 (1972) 9–10.

[5] P.J. Klan and B.M. Elson, Technical Survey: Very High Speed Integrated Circuits, *Aviation Week & Space Technology* Feb. 16 (1981) 48–85.

[6] K. Marx, *The Poverty of Philosophy* (Cooperative Publishing Society, Moscow, 1935).

[7] R. Miller and D. Sawers, *The Technical Development of Modern Aviation* (Routledge & Kegan Paul, London, 1969)

[8] R.R. Nelson and S.G. Winter, In Search of a Useful Theory of Innovation, *Research Policy* 6 (1977) 36–76.

[9] R.N. Noyce, Large-Scale Integration: What is Yet to Come?, *Science* 195 (1977) 1102–06.

[10] W. Ogburn, *On Culture and Social Change* (University of Chicago Press, Chicago, 1964).

[11] I. Prigogine, Time, Structure, and Fluctuations, *Science* 201 (1978) 777–785.

[12] A.R. Reece, The Shape of the Farm Tractor, *Proceedings of the Institution of Mechanical Engineers* 184 (1969–1970) (3Q) 125–131.

[13] D. Sahal, *Patterns of Technological Innovation* (Addison Wesley, Reading, Mass., 1981).

[14] D. Sahal, Structure and Self-Organization, *Behavioral Science* 27 (1982) 249–258.

[15] D. Sahal, Invention, Innovation and Economic Evolution, *Journal of Technological Forecasting and Social Change*, 1983.

[16] D. Sahal, Metaprogress Functions, *Journal of Technological Forecasting and Social Change*, 1983.

[17] D. Sahal, *Technological Yardsticks and Policies* (New York University Press, New York, 1983.

[18] R. Serrell, M.M. Astrahan, G.W. Patterson and I.B. Pyne, The Evolution of Computing Machines and Systems, *Proc. IRE* 50 (1962) 1039–1058.

[19] J. Schmookler, *Invention and Economic Growth* (Harvard University Press, Cambridge, Mass., 1966).

[20] J. Schumpeter, *Capitalism, Socialism, and Democracy*, 2nd edition (Harper, New York, 1947).

[21] W.R. Stahl, Dimensional Methods in Biology, *Science* 137 (1962) 205–211.

[22] D'Arcy W. Thompson, *On Growth and Form* (Cambridge University Press, Cambridge, 1917). [Abridged edition, J.T. Bonner (ed.) 1961].

[23] C.H. Waddington, *The Strategy of the Genes* (Allen & Unwin, London, 1957).

# [25]

World Development, Vol. 13, No. 3, pp. 441–463, 1985.
Printed in Great Britain.

0305–750X/85 $3.00 + 0.00
© 1985 Pergamon Press Ltd.

# Microelectronics, Long Waves and World Structural Change: New Perspectives for Developing Countries

CARLOTA PEREZ*
*Science Policy Research Unit,
University of Sussex, Brighton, UK*

**Summary.** — This article assesses the way in which emerging new technologies could enhance development prospects. To do this, it first presents a long-term view of the relationship between the techno-economic sphere and the socio-institutional framework, defining the present period as one of transition and structural change. It then outlines the main characteristics of the technological revolution based on microelectronics. It finally argues that these characteristics will offer a completely new range of opportunities for reshaping development strategies.

## 1. INTRODUCTION

At present, the prospects for developing countries seem bleaker than ever. As general stagnation continues, with short-lived spurts of growth in the industrialized world, export opportunities for the Third World are significantly reduced. This, combined with the rising cost of imports and a reduction in investment flows, is putting unbearable pressures on weak debt-ridden economies. At the same time, the electronics revolution seems to have widened the technological gap to unbreachable proportions.

This article will present an alternative view. It will argue that the world is experiencing a structural crisis, during which, in spite of the obvious difficulties, there would be greater — rather than lesser — scope for a major positive change in development prospects.

The argument is based on a somewhat Schumpeterian[1] interpretation of the so-called Kondratiev long waves.[2] The explanation proposed here for the recurrence of cycles of about 50 years' duration in economic growth, attributes a central role to the diffusion of successive technological revolutions, representing a quantum jump in potential productivity for all or most of the economy. The reason for the long wave pattern would be that, to yield its full growth potential, each of these 'techno-economic paradigms' — as we shall call them — requires a fundamental restructuring of the socio-

institutional framework, on the national and international levels. The resulting social and institutional transformations then determine the general shape of economic development, or the 'mode of growth' of the next long wave. A Kondratiev wave is thus defined here as the rise and fall of a mode of growth and each crisis as the painful transition from one mode of growth to the next.

The present period is seen as one such transition. The mode of growth that led to the boom of the 1950s and 1960s has run its course. The world must now make the transition from a set of social and institutional arrangements, shaped by the characteristics — and fostering the full deployment — of a constellation of mass production technologies based on low-cost oil, to another capable of fruitful and appropriate interaction with a new system of flexible technologies, based on low-cost electronics.

This means that extrapolations from the past or from the turbulent present are misleading. If and when a new upswing is unleashed in the world economy, it is likely to be framed by a set of national and international institutions, which will differ as much from those of the 1950s and 1960s as these differed from the prevailing conditions in the 'Belle Epoque' at the turn of the century. It also means that the present is precise-

---

*Former Director of Technological Development at the Ministry of Industry of Venezuela.

ly the period of creation of those future conditions and that all social actors, including the developing countries, can and should take an active part in that complex — and obviously conflict ridden — trial-and-error process.

To undertake this task successfully however, it is essential to identify the new range of the possible. The deeper the understanding of the potentialities and limitations of the new 'techno-economic paradigm,' the greater the scope for shaping it imaginatively and effectively through innovative action in the social and institutional spheres.

Section 2 of this paper will introduce the concept of 'techno-economic paradigms' and present an outline of the long wave argument.[3] This theoretical framework is a necessary prerequisite for understanding the relevance of the discussions that follow. Section 3 undertakes the analysis of the defining features of the presently diffusing microelectronics paradigm, touching upon some of the questions it raises for development strategies. Section 4 is a brief exploration into the challenges and opportunities facing the developing countries in the present transition.

As a whole, the article is intended as food for thought. The reader will find no statistics; references will be sparse, though hundreds could be given; examples will be provided only when they seem indispensable to illustrate an idea rather than to prove it. This is fully intentional. The paper is conceived mainly as a contribution for opening new paths in development thinking. As the argument evolves, it will become increasingly clear that we are making a case for defining the present period as a time for informed speculation and bold experimentation.

## 2. TECHNOLOGY AND LONG WAVES

Conventional wisdom tends to see technology as a matter for scientists and engineers, and its evolution as a series of individual inventions resulting in continuous cumulative advance; furthermore, most people find it easier to think of technologies in the plural, in view of their tremendous variety. Yet, since technology is the 'how' and the 'what' of production, it is in fact very much a social and economic matter. The process of technological advance in terms of knowledge and inventions is a relatively autonomous process, but innovation — i.e. application and diffusion of specific techniques in the productive sphere — is very much determined by social conditions and economic profit decisions. Thus technical change can be accelerated or held back by social and economic factors.[4]

Even the autonomy of the research process is only relative, and economic criteria are implicitly present in the minds of scientists and engineers. The object has always been to turn base metals into gold and not the reverse. So, although a great proportion of basic science is endogenously guided, applications and development efforts, while still keeping a certain amount of autonomy, are much more directly engaged in the interplay of 'supply push' and 'demand pull' with the users of innovations in the economic sphere.[5]

The readiness to absorb or demand new technology varies greatly under different economic conditions, even in the same firm; and the sorts of technical solutions sought in the economic sphere can change in nature depending on a variety of internal and external factors affecting productivity, profitability and markets. In recent decades, much social science research has focused on the nature of this techno-economic interaction. On a general level, innovations have been classified by their impact on productivity, as to whether they are mainly labor saving or capital saving;[6] by their relative importance, distinguishing radical from incremental innovations[7] and by their object, either process or product.[8] Other efforts have focused on the pattern of evolution of each particular innovation leading to the notion of technological trajectories.[9] This concept is used to describe the path from birth to maturity of any particular technology, from the generally awkward first introduction, followed by the identification of one bottleneck after another bringing forth complementary innovations, through successive incremental improvements, leading to the final optimization and relative standardization of the process or product, after which further efforts bring diminishing returns.[10]

Plotted against time, the level of productivity achieved by a particular technological process, as it is subjected to successive improvements through additional investment, would then present the 'S' shape of many biological growth processes.

This growing body of literature has made it increasingly clear that technical change does not occur at an even rhythm, but neither is it merely a random process. Further still, the analysis of the patterns of propagation of new technologies across the economy tends to confirm Schumpeter's view about the bunching of innovations and their diffusion in bandwagon fashion. It has been found, for example, that during certain periods, process innovations tend to outstrip product innovations in most industries.[11] This suggests that innovations in equipment goods occur in clusters.

Here we are interested in the relationship between these waves of technical change and long cycles in economic growth. In this context, Christopher Freeman[12] has introduced the notion of 'new technological systems,' to describe clusters of interrelated product and process, technical and organizational innovations, affecting many branches of the economy. Taking the accent away from the first introduction of single innovations and focusing on their rate of diffusion as interconnected systems of technical change, Freeman points to patterns of structural change in the economy which, through their widespread social consequences, could underlie the Kondratiev long waves.

Here we would like to fuse the concepts of technological trajectories and technological systems and take them one step further. We suggest that these notions are applicable to the analysis of the whole body of technology during relatively long periods. We propose that it is possible to identify each successive Kondratiev wave with the deployment of a specific, all-pervasive, technological revolution. In other words, that behind the apparently infinite variety of technologies of each long-wave upswing, there is a distinct set of accepted 'common-sense' principles, which define a broad technological trajectory towards a general 'best practice' frontier. These principles are applied in the generation of innovations and in the organization of production in one firm after another, in one branch after another, within and across countries. As this process of propagation evolves, there is a prolonged period of economic growth, based on relatively high profits and increasing productivity. But, gradually, as the range of applications is more or less fully covered and when, through successive incremental improvements, the best practice frontier is actually approached, the forces underlying that wave of prosperity dwindle. As this occurs, limits to growth are encountered by more and more sectors of the economy, profits decrease, and productivity growth slows down.

Yet, well before the downswing is visible as a general phenomenon, diminishing returns are experienced by some of the most dynamic firms and sectors. Among them, there ensues a complex trial-and-error process spurred by the profit motive. It results in waves of mergers and acquisitions, various forms of speculation, efforts to 'stretch' the technologies by containing labor costs or relocating. But it also involves a persistent search in the pool of the technologically feasible for what would potentially be economically profitable. This intensified feedback interaction between the technological and economic spheres, eventually leads — through discovery and rediscovery — to the gradual emergence and

subsequent rapid development of new technical elements. As these prove capable of overcoming the specific bottlenecks encountered within the mature technologies, imitation and further innovation along those lines, gradually converge in synergistic fashion to define a general model to follow. Each new model is based on a different set of 'common-sense' principles, indicating a higher best practice frontier, destined once again to transform the whole techno-economic system.

The downswing of each long wave sets in as the process of abandonment of the exhausted model and the initial propagation of the new.

### (a) A techno-economic paradigm as a set of common sense guidelines for technological and investment decisions

Technological decisions are taken in a specific socio-economic context and in turn influence that context. Economic theory would have us believe that managers take into account the relative prices not just of labor and capital, in general, but of each possible combination of different types of labor, of different types of equipment and of different sorts of inputs, for a range of possible products. But, how does this work in practice?

We suggest that the behavior of the relative cost structure of all inputs to production follows more or less predictable trends for relatively long periods. This predictability becomes the basis for the construction of an 'ideal type' of productive organization, which defines the contours of the most efficient and 'least cost' combinations for a given period. It thus serves as a general 'rule-of-thumb' guide for investment and technological decisions. That general guiding model is the 'techno-economic paradigm.' As it generalizes, it introduces a strong bias in both technical and organizational innovation. Eventually, the range of choice in technique is itself contained within a relatively narrow spectrum, as the supply of capital equipment increasingly embodies the new principles. Furthermore, for each type of product, expected productivity levels, optimal scales and relative prices become gradually established, together with the forms of competition in each market.

The process can be seen as analogous to the appearance of a new genetic pool, which contains the blueprint for a great variety of organisms (products and processes) and their forms of interrelation. It diffuses through hybridization, cross-breeding, evolution and new entrants. Its increasingly obvious advantages inevitably destine it to transform most and substitute many of the old 'species' and create a new 'eco-system.'

The focusing device or main organizing principle of this selective mechanism would be a particular input or set of inputs, capable of strongly influencing the behavior of the relative cost structure. Such an input, which we shall call the 'key factor,' is capable of playing a steering role because it fulfills the following conditions:

(1) clearly perceived low — and descending — relative cost,

(2) apparently unlimited supply (for all practical purposes),

(3) obvious potential for all-pervasive influence in the productive sphere, and

(4) a generally recognized capacity, based on a set of interwoven technical and organizational innovations, to reduce the costs and change the quality of capital equipment, labor and products.

This conjunction of characteristics holds today for microelectronics. For this reason, it is increasingly steering both engineering and managerial common sense towards its intensive use and gradually shaping the new 'best practice' frontier for old and new industries. It held until recently for oil, together with petrochemicals and other energy-intensive materials, which underlay the now exhausted mass production paradigm of the post-war upswing. In the previous long wave, at the turn of the century, the role of 'key factor' was played by low-cost steel, shaping the growth of the heavy mechanical, electrical and chemical engineering industries. The Victorian boom in the mid-19th century (the 'railway age') had low-cost coal and steam-powered transportation at its core. And, it could be argued that in the Industrial Revolution the role of 'key factor' fell upon low cost machine-tending and cotton-growing labor.

Of course, none of these inputs are really 'new' in a technical sense. Each had a previous history of development within the previous paradigm and even further into the past. The truly new aspect in each case is the drastic reduction in relative cost, which is generally associated with a technical or organizational breakthrough.[13] And, these breakthroughs are more likely to occur — or to be fully noticed, exploited and widely applied — when the set of technologies based on the prevailing key factor has exhausted its potential for further increasing productivity.

But, a full-fledged techno-economic paradigm grows in complexity and coherence, going far beyond technical change and affecting almost every aspect of the productive system. The full constellation — once crystallized — involves:

(1) New concepts of efficiency for the organization of production at the plant level.

(2) A new model for the management and organization of the firm.

(3) A distinctly lower labor input per unit of output, with a different skill profile of employment.[14]

(4) A strong bias in technological innovation, favoring key factor use.

(5) A new pattern of investment, favoring key factor related sectors, propelling and propelled by investment in a new infrastructural network.

(6) A consequent bias in the composition of production, with faster rates of growth in key factor related products.

(7) A redefinition of optimal scales leading to a redistribution of production between large and small firms.

(8) A new pattern in the geographic location of investment, based on the shift in comparative advantages (and disadvantages!).

(9) A restructuring of interbranch relationships, where those branches that produce or intensively use the key factor, become the new engines of growth and generate a new range of 'induced' activities, which generally proliferate in bandwagon fashion, once the upswing begins.

To give a rough illustration of these various elements, let us look at the now exhausted techno-economic paradigm. It came together in the 1920s and 1930s and underlay the present mode of growth established after World War II. It was based on low-cost oil and energy-intensive materials, especially petrochemicals. The model for efficient productive organization at the plant level was the continuous flow process or assembly-line for the mass production of identical products. The ideal type of firm was the 'corporation,' run by a separate, professional, managerial and administrative hierarchy; it included in-house R&D and operated in oligopolistic markets. Growth was led by giant oil, chemicals, automobile and other mass producers of durable goods for the defense or consumer markets. The growth and interplay of these core branches, induced the proliferation of the service sector (from gasoline stations and supermarkets to the advertising industry and the diversified financial sector), as well as the growth of the construction industry. It demanded increasing amounts of middle range specialization in both blue- and white-collar skills. It benefited from economies of agglomeration and required an ever-expanding highway network, together with oil and electricity distribution systems for energy-intensive production, transportation and life-styles.

Today, with cheap microelectronics widely

available (together with the consequent low-cost of information handling), a new techno-economic paradigm is coming together and diffusing. It is no longer 'common sense' to continue along the now expensive! path of energy and materials intensity. The 'ideal' productive organization, which has been evolving since the early seventies, brings together management, production and marketing into one single integrated system (a process we might call 'systemation'), for turning out a flexible output of preferably information-intensive, rapidly changing, products and services. Growth would presumably be led by the electronics and information sectors, propelling and propelled by an all-encompassing telecommunications infrastructure, which would bring down to negligible levels the cost of access for producers and consumers alike. The skill profile tends to change from mainly middle range to increasingly high and low range qualifications, and from narrow specialization to broader and multipurpose basic skills for information handling. Diversity and flexibility at all levels substitute uniformity and repetitiveness as 'common-sense' best practice.

But why the crisis? Why can the productive system not make a smooth transition from one paradigm to the other?

### (b) Long wave recessions as the manifestation of a 'mismatch' between the socio-institutional framework and the techno-economic sphere

The transition to a new techno-economic regime cannot proceed smoothly, not only because it implies massive transformation and much destruction of existing plant, but mainly because the prevailing pattern of social behavior and the existing institutional structure were shaped around the requirements and possibilities created by the previous paradigm. That is why, as the potential of the old paradigm is exhausted, previously successful regulating or stimulating policies do not work. In turn, the relative inertia of the socio-institutional framework becomes an insurmountable obstacle for the full deployment of the new paradigm. Worse still, the very diffusion of the new technologies, as far as conditions allow, is itself an aggravating factor because the new investment pattern disrupts the social fabric and creates unexpected cross-currents and counter-trends in all markets. Under these conditions, long wave recessions and depressions can be seen as the syndrome of a serious 'mismatch' between the socio-institutional framework and the new dynamics in the techno-economic sphere. The crisis is the emergency signal calling for a redefinition of the general mode of growth.

At the micro level, when numerical control or computer technology is introduced in a firm previously working with electromechanical technology, it is not possible to reap all the potential productivity increase without transforming the whole organization both at the plant and the office levels, including extensive retraining and redefinition of the forms of interaction. In a similar manner, when the full constellation of a new techno-economic paradigm tends to take over the bulk of production within a society, it will not yield its full growth potential until the socio-institutional framework is transformed to adapt to its requirements.

This would indicate that our 'ecosystem' analogy has a fundamental limitation. While in nature, it is the external environment that forces the adaptation of the living species; in economic development, it would be the environment that is reshaped to suit the potential of the new genetic pool. Yet it must be emphasized that, in spite of appearances, we are not making an argument for mere technological determinism. The variety of suitable environments is quite large, and whatever specific form is arrived at, from the wide range of viable options, will in turn determine the preferred ways in which the latent techno-economic potential develops through strong 'feedback' selective action and gradual mutual adjustment.

So, when the downswing of a long wave occurs, the new techno-economic paradigm to which institutions must respond is already diffusing. Ironically, it is precisely when the seeds of change are being sown around peak prosperity that institutions become more attached to practices that seem to have achieved the result of unrelenting growth. This is why it is particularly difficult to bring about the required profound transformations. Much more so in view of the fact that this inertia is also upheld by powerful vested interests.

Historically, when the required structural transformations have finally been brought about, creating the framework for a new mode of growth and unleashing the upswing, they have generally affected the following, among many other, aspects of society:

(1) The specific forms of operation and regulation of the various markets (product, labor, capital, money) on the national and international levels.

(2) The organization of the banking and credit systems.

(3) The relative proportions and character of public and private responsibility in genera-

tion, distribution and redistribution of income, as well as the corresponding social arrangements.

(4) The forms of organization of workers and major interest groups, together with the legal framework within which they operate.

(5) The provision of education and training in its quality, volume and the type of institutions in charge of it.

(6) The conditions under which inventions are generated, protected and traded.

(7) The international division of production as well as the means for regulating inter-country trade and investment.

(8) The international relative power balance and the arrangements for maintaining it.

To unleash the previous upswing, a change as profound and unprecedented as massive state intervention in the economy, along Keynesian principles, was necessary to foster the full deployment of the oil-based mass production paradigm. A complex set of demand management mechanisms was established, from the most direct, such as central control of the money supply and of the level of government spending, to the more indirect such as the expanding system of consumer credit and the public provision of national statistics for marketing and production planning. Trade unions became institutionalized, the working week and working year were shortened and unemployment and retirement benefits were generalized. This was made possible by the income tax system, which also sustained the 'public service' and 'government spending' mechanisms for redistribution of income. On the international level, these national arrangements were complemented by the UN organization, the leading role of the United States, Bretton Woods, the IMF, the GATT, the provisional Marshall Plan and the increasingly accelerated demise of colonial empires. All these developments created an adequate framework for growth based on mass production, as well as the means for regulating and fostering the fluid expansion of international investment and trade.[15]

### (c) *The construction of a new mode of growth as the outcome of an intensive process of social confrontation, creativity and compromise*

Clearly, such widely ranging changes do not occur all at once. They emerge gradually, converging into a more or less coherent framework. Nor do they come about easily. They require an enormous amount of inventiveness and experimentation as well as compromise. And, since any particular set of arrangements favors some groups to the detriment of others, its establishment does not occur without social and international confrontation. So, the construction of a new mode of growth is paced by the level of understanding, the weight of inertia and the opposition of those who fear it for real or imagined reasons. The time it takes to create the new framework and the specific form of the ultimate outcome depend on the relative strength of the various social forces and on their capacity to develop and implement viable innovative responses. Nothing, of course, can guarantee success nor that collapse or devastating war can be avoided.

During the last structural crisis in the 1930s, the present Third World was not among the players. Most countries were under colonial rule; and those that were not were marginal participants in the world economy, with no international institutions in which to make their voice heard. This time, as a result of the previous mode of growth, there are real possibilities of influencing the course of events for the next upswing. Some of the reasons for this relate to the world political scene, but others stem from the specific market expansion requirements of the new technologies.

However, the general direction of change required to accommodate a particular technological potential is more analogous to crossing an ocean than to following a railroad track. It is a wide space for innovation in social organization and national and international institutions. The proposed solutions can vary quite widely and very different political frameworks can achieve high rates of growth. That they can be as different as fascism and Keynesian democracy, was clearly seen in the last Kondratiev trough. Further still, as far as following a particular technological model for growth, the present socialist system can be seen as another of the alternatives that proved viable. We would suggest that, although with somewhat different manifestations, those countries have also encountered limits to growth and face the need to transform the socio-institutional framework. But this is not the place to discuss that issue.

The important idea to bear in mind is that what happens in the transition period has enormous bearing on the nature of the next upswing. Once an adequate mode of growth is established, it molds, regulates and determines the preferred ways in which the new technological potential is exploited. Because a quantum jump in productivity implies a quantum jump in wealth creating capacity, it contains, among the possible outcomes, widespread improvements in living standards.

Each transition, then, by implying a radical restructuring, reopens the question of the development perspectives of the various countries, as well as that of the better or worse distribution of the benefits of future growth, among social groups, regions and countries.

Thus, in spite of the crisis and because of the crisis, it is essential to open new spaces for development thinking in terms of the future. Yet, from what has been argued, social institutional and economic planning innovations are more likely to be viable if based on a deep understanding of both the demands and the potential, both the scope and the limitations of the new techno-economic paradigm. And this understanding is possible because, on the one hand, the paradigm has already diffused to a sufficient degree for recognition and, on the other, we now possess better analytical tools and more historical experience.

In this context, a basic task would be to detect the main features of the new pattern of techno-economic behavior based on the potential of the new technology, distinguishing what are merely survival tactics of those tied to the old paradigm from the more coherent initiatives pointing towards the future. It is upon these new trends that the appropriate institutional configuration must be constructed in this transition period.

In the following section, we attempt the analysis of the main features of the new paradigm which is gradually becoming more and more visible and more and more coherent, as organizational innovations within firms join the technical cluster growing around microelectronics.[16]

## 3. THE CHARACTERISTICS OF THE TECHNO-ECONOMIC PARADIGM BASED ON MICROELECTRONICS

In considering the specific features of the techno-economic paradigm which is taking shape around microelectronics, we shall try to make as clear a contrast as possible with those which have characterized the mass-production, oil-based paradigm. For the sake of brevity, the analysis will be limited to some of the essential features, albeit with a substantial amount of oversimplification.

The first part will analyze how the trend towards 'information intensity' would tend to modify input mix and investment patterns in terms of relative cost advantages. The second part will focus on the trend towards 'flexibility' in plant, in product mix and in product change over time. The third and last part of this section, will explore the new trends in firm organization: on the one hand, the concept of 'systemation,' and

on the other the potential for decentralization. In the course of the discussion, attention will be given to some of the issues raised for development strategies, always in a tentative spirit to stimulate thinking and experimentation.

### (a) *Information intensity vs energy and materials intensity*

The overriding feature of the new paradigm, and the one that is likely to have the most profound consequences, is the trend towards information intensity rather than energy and materials intensity in production. This stems directly from the very visible change in the general relative cost structure towards ever cheaper information handling potential through microelectronics and digital telecommunications.

It should be clear that this is a relative cost argument. It does not imply that energy or raw materials prices are expected to take an upward course in absolute terms, but that the decreasing cost and growing potential of microelectronics results in an increasing relative gap in the future.

In product engineering, there would be a tendency to redesign existing goods to make them smaller, less energy-consuming, with less moving parts, more electronics and more software. This has already been the case for a variety of products such as watches and clocks, calculators, cash registers, sewing machines and computers themselves, but the possibilities are far from being fully exploited. In addition, many needs that are today fulfilled with durable goods, due to the characteristics of the previous paradigm, might tend to be met with information-intensive services instead.

In plant engineering, not only would energy-saving techniques based on electronics be applied as a matter of good process design, but also materials saving techniques. The possibilities generated by both computer-aided design and computer-controlled manufacturing greatly increase precision and allow production to narrower tolerances. Furthermore, tighter inventory controls and on-line quality control would allow a reduction in waste and rejects. Both these trends, together with the reduction in size and parts already mentioned, would tend to reduce even further the amount of materials required per unit of product or, as Smith puts it, would greatly increase the 'productivity of resources'.[17]

*New products and services:* The most promising trend in sheer growth terms is the flourishing of innovations and entrepreneurial activity stemming directly from low cost electronics and data processing. This would be analogous to the flurry of consumer durables of the presently waning paradigm, which began to gather momentum in the 1920s with automobiles, radios and refrigerators, acquired full force through the 1950s, and peaked in the late 1960s with such products as electric can openers and electric carving knives. In that case, it was a question of identifying home activities that required the use of energy and designing a product to fulfill them and open a new market. In the present case, it would be a question of detecting home or, and especially, producer activities that require information handling or decision-making and designing an electronic product or a software package or setting up an information intensive service to open a new market. The important thing to note is that these new products or services are in fact relatively simple applications of already well-known principles so that there would be no doubt as to technical feasibility. Success would depend (as it did with consumer durables) on an adequate perception of market acceptance and the diminishing costs of inputs.

*Old and new giants*: This general advantage of information intensity is clearly revealed in the fact that, at present, in the midst of recession and strong inflationary pressures, the firms most closely related to the production or intensive use of microelectronics are showing generally high growth rates and their products are the only ones decreasing in price, even in absolute terms! As in previous paradigm shifts, this advantage, which translates into unusually high profit rates for some, selects the firms that, by growth or diversification, will become the largest and most dynamic of the next upswing. Consequently, some of the new firms in these sectors might join the ranks of the giants. But, also, some of the old giants in the mature industries are already showing — with more or less successful results — an increasing tendency, not just to transform their products and processes, but also to diversify into the new and more dynamic, information-intensive areas of the new paradigm: microelectronic components, equipment for the 'factory of the future' or the 'office of the future;' data processing, financial, technological and other producer services; telecommunications, satellites, fiber optics and other aspects of data transmission; and obviously, the 'starwars' military sector.[18]

*Impact on raw material producers*: The trends we have been discussing must be seen dynamically. The reduction in the energy and raw materials content of individual products, and the possibly faster growth of services, is a powerful force in reversing the Fourth Kondratiev trends that threatened to result in natural resource depletion. It does not, however, mean that producers of these basic inputs will face ever-dwindling markets. The initial reductions are likely to be the most drastic; but once a higher productivity of resources becomes the norm, the sheer expansion of production, especially when — or rather, if — the upswing gets underway, would allow a resumption of raw materials market growth, with probably lower, but certainly not negative, elasticity in relation to output.[19]

Thus, the new technologies based on low cost electronics could lead to a new pattern in inter-branch relationships and in the evolution of the general product mix. Not only would most production technologies undergo important changes, but also the goods they produce would become information intensive. The same would occur in most existing service industries, while there would be increasing growth in services of a totally new character. Under these circumstances, national and world gross product and trade can be expected to contain an increasing proportion of information and service related value added.

### (i) *New issues for developing countries*

Although this is only one of the features of the new paradigm, it can already serve as a guide for rethinking certain aspects of development strategies. In so far as trends in the developed world affect the various developing countries, significant changes can be expected in foreign investment patterns and in the composition of world trade. The first because there is a fundamental reshuffling of comparative advantages at the same time as there is an internal restructuring of transnational corporations. The second, because the faster rate of growth of information-intensive services in international trade would affect the evolution of export markets for raw materials and other Third World goods, as well as the composition of imports.

Already, the transmission and sale of processed information itself is reaching considerable proportions in international markets. In recent years, trade in patents and 'know-how' and other technological information has been growing faster than commodity trade. The increasingly transnational character of banking and financial services has been further expanded by computer technology and digital transmission. Consultancy firms both in traditional engineering and in the new 'systems' engineering areas are coming to the fore. Software services, standard, semi-custom and custom, are set for rapid growth.[20] And telecommunications itself, which is the main means of 'transportation' of most of the above services and many more, could grow at a much faster rate than the established means of physical transport.

These trends certainly require innovative responses. It is now essential to examine closely the service side of the balance of payments but, more than that, the concepts of 'industrialization' and 'import substitution' as well as 'export promotion' have to be redefined. All are now profoundly transformed to include the elusive 'software and information' areas which, in the form of technological policy, would have to be institutionally addressed and placed at the core, not at the side, of development thinking.

Depending upon how far advanced the country is along the previous path of industrialization, strategic decisions are in order regarding the telecommunications network, the electronics industry, the service sector, in its new much wider sense, and in particular the means to develop and protect local technical and consultancy capabilities. The latter will be crucial, not only to make a direct contribution, but also to help avoid a flood of misdirected technological services leading to a drain on economic resources.

The greatest challenge, however, lies in identifying the new opportunities. A more long-term view could bring forth new types of advantages. For raw materials producers, for instance, the fact that in the long run there would be a clear advantage in transportation costs for 'teletransmitted' services or for small-sized goods with high information value added, might lead to a rather unexpected development: it could generate a comparative advantage for local production of energy or materials intensive goods in resource-rich countries. That many OPEC countries have been investing heavily in such energy-intensive industries as aluminium, steel and petrochemicals could be interpreted as early manifestations of such a trend. The question is whether, in the case of certain products, further vertical integration will prove to be the most cost-effective arrangement to avoid the increasing share of multiple transportation costs in the final price.[21]

### (b) *Flexible vs mass production*

After information intensity, 'flexibility' is probably the most important key-word within the new paradigm. It challenges the old best practice concept of mass production in three central aspects. High-volume output of identical products is no longer the main route to high productivity, which can now be achieved for a diversified set of low-volume products. The 'minimum change' strategy in product development might no longer be necessary for cost-effectiveness, as rapid technical change becomes much less costly and less risky. Market growth on the basis of 'homogenous' demand is no longer essential, as the new technologies permit high profitability in catering to segmented markets and provide ample space for adapting production systems and output to specific local conditions and needs. Let us briefly discuss each of these features.

### (i) *Economies of scope or of specialization based on flexibility vs economies of scale based on homogeneity*

As regards the new potential for diversity in production, the new paradigm affects the accepted concepts of optimal scale of plant and market. When production, as well as productivity, depended on the repetitive movements of motors and workers and every change of model or tooling was down-time, optimal production costs were closely related to achieving high-volume production of identical units. With electronic controls and the relatively low cost of programming rapid changes in production schedules, such limitations disappear to a great extent.

It is, of course, still possible to apply the new technologies for mass production of certain components or products at a scale that could be a multiple of the previously established optimal size. However, the most significant change, rich in eventual combinations, is a quantum jump in potential productivity for small- and medium-batch production. It could be said that, with the new technologies, plant scale becomes relatively independent of market size. Thus, the question of 'barriers to entry' is redefined for most industries.

Flexible manufacturing technologies allow plant size to relate to a changing mix of a range of products submitted to similar transformation processes. On the one hand, one very large plant can produce for several relatively small markets, applying what is now being referred to as 'economies of scope'.[22] On the other hand, since individual pieces of equipment can be provided with 'intelligence,' they can display similar flexibility in performance. This opens a range of new opportunities for relatively small plants serving one or a set of small local markets or specific market 'niches.' These can achieve high productivity levels with 'economies of specialization,' not necessarily dependent on large scale.[23]

This potential for flexibility and adaptability has varying impact across industries and across activities within each industry. In general, the quantum jump in productivity allowed by microelectronics seems to be greatest precisely in those industries or activities that were least amenable to mass production techniques under the previous paradigm. Therefore, the activities most easily transformed are the most decision-intensive, such as office work, product design, stock control, quality control and others that were peripheral to the production process proper and, in the past, often constituted cost and time bottlenecks.

Equally, it is in the industries previously characterized by high rates of product change, high craft intensity and small or medium production runs, that the impact is greatest. This has already been the case in printing, which might in the future go through a further revolution, beyond ink and paper, using an array of new computer-related means of recording and disseminating information.[24] Mechanical engineering (and therefore a substantial portion of the capital goods industry), while continuing to be multi-process, multi-product, is being transformed by computer-aided design and manufacturing (CAD-CAM), flexible manufacturing systems (FMS) and computer-integrated manufacturing (CIM) into a continuous flow industry.[25] To a certain degree, the potential exists for a similar transformation in such areas as clothing and furniture.[26] These are sectors in which there has traditionally been a great number of small firms. This might change in the future as large firms introduce computerized flexible systems and tend to cover greater portions of a diversified market. The smaller firms could be successful on the basis of locational advantages or in skillfully selected market niches.

By contrast, assembly, a high-productivity area in mass production techniques, might become the bottleneck of flexible production facilities. Robots are clearly advantageous for ultra-high precision tasks such as electronic chip production; for the assembly of certain electronics products where quality is central and for hazardous or unpleasant activities such as spraying or welding. Their economics are very doubtful and controversial as regards medium or small-batch assembly, involving frequent changes in product range or in product design. The fact is that, whereas it is very easy for a computer to control the cutting of the most complex of shapes in a very small fraction of the time taken by a highly skilled operator, it is much more difficult for it and it requires much more sophisticated equipment and software to perform the apparently simple task of correctly picking up a part and inserting it in the right place. For this reason, in achieving economies of scope, the new low-cost flexibility available for design and the

other transformation processes could stumble against the high cost of batch assembly robotics.

Solutions are being sought in radical redesign of parts and products to make them more amenable to robot manipulation (in some cases even to the point of bypassing assembly altogether). Another route, which has already been put in practice, is subcontracting the assembly tasks with specialized local firms. Both trends will probably develop, depending on specific conditions. Overcoming the bottleneck, though, depends on whether the cost of robots and sensors as well as of their operation, can be substantially reduced. This might hinge on how quickly radical breakthroughs are made in 'artificial intelligence,' for low cost programming and reprogramming, as well as on the experience gained in the diffusion of robotics in certain manipulation tasks where they are bound to generalize, such as those involving high hazards, high skills, high precision or activities that could simply not be done by humans, such as deep sea mining or work in outer space.[27]

In the process industries, such as chemicals, paper, electricity, metallurgy, food processing, etc., the main impact might be in plant design. For continuous flow processes, which had applied electronic controls very early on, there might be a certain degree of reversal of the trend towards fixed output giant plants as a means for minimizing unit costs. The new potential for cost reduction by means of precise control of quantity and quality of inputs, throughputs and outputs as well as of process parameters might lead to smaller and/or more flexible design of plant, with greater adaptability to market and input variations, perhaps including closed-loop, no-waste systems.[28]

On the other hand, some batch processes, common in the pharmaceutical and food industries, might be transformed into continuous flow, while achieving economies of scope. Such new elements as flexible automatic feeding, electronic process controls, self-cleaning systems and automatic measuring and packaging, are being incorporated in 'piecemeal' fashion, but they could tend to come together as a total system and become the norm for many groups of products.

In service area, for information intensive activities, the flexibility potential, regarding both size and capacity to adapt product mix to changing market patterns, seems particularly great. In the case of software and information services, however, it will take a long time before the rules of the game are laid down both on the supply and on the demand side, since they are in the process of creating new markets, whose size is unknown and often depends on the rate of diffusion of other equipment or of infrastructure networks. Even the activity classes themselves await definitions in practice, before optimal product mix or scales are established. This trial-and-error process of boundary definition seems typical of the new industries in each paradigm shift: the 'model' Ford plant in the 1930s was vertically integrated even to include glass-making.

As regards the more traditional service activities, though, the change towards 'economies of scope' for the giants and 'economies of specialization' for the smaller firms seems to be under way. An article in the *Financial Times*[29] described the 'fundamental restructuring' of financial services, identifying 'three basic roles for successful participants:' (1) broad-based competitors, which would be the merged and reorganized giants with state-of-the-art information systems and very broad market coverage, product innovation, brand franchises and image advertising; (2) low-cost producers, which would be smaller firms with an emphasis on minimum cost in 'simple product lines targeted at the price-sensitive, commodity segment of the market;' and (3) speciality firms, also small, but geared at specific, highly demanding, semi-custom market niches.

This example of reorganization is a particularly clear illustration of what could tend to be the pattern of distribution of markets by firm sizes in many industries as they restructure. The largest firms would tend to widen their market coverage across a wide range of technologically dynamic products. This would leave spaces for small or medium firms, both in the more routine mass production areas of the market and in the exploitation of skillfully segmented, specialized market niches.

Outside industry and information intensive services, all other productive activities, from mining and agriculture[38] to distribution and most areas of the service sector are being more or less radically transformed by information technology in the direction of computer-controlled, input-adaptable, market-adaptable flexible systems.

Beyond traditional industry divisions a paradigm shift, as it sweeps across the productive sphere, not only transforms existing industries and creates new ones; it can also change established industry boundaries. The present shift may blur the distinction between manufacturing and services and, within each industry, it can modify the traditional patterns of horizontal or vertical integration. This aspect of the transition makes it difficult to assess what is really happening, when analyzing industry using the established classification system.

For developing countries, the changes brought about by the new flexible technologies mean, as they do for developed countries, that, on the whole, the bulk of existing plant is obsolete by international standards. Every single sector needs to be re-examined afresh to assess its prospects in national and international markets under the new conditions. The reasons that led firms or countries to concentrate resources in some industries, as opposed to others, might no longer be valid. Certain export-oriented sectors may face new difficulties; in others, previously adequate protection policies could prove incapable of stemming import competition.

Both national planning and individual project evaluation, by national or international agencies, would have to recognize a totally new set of conditions governing the choice of technique and scale. Assessing adequacy or competitiveness on the basis of past or even present average costs, without bearing in mind the dynamics of technical change, could be highly misleading and bring disastrous results. This would apply to any sector or project, for the changes tend to affect the whole spectrum. It is particularly crucial, however, in the case of the capital goods industry which, apart from its obvious impact in determining the productivity of the user industries, is in the midst of a profound transformation worldwide in both products and processes.

(ii) *Rapid technical change vs 'minimum change' strategy*

The new flexibility potential stretches beyond changes in optimal scale and variable output mix. It expands the capacity to make successive changes in products, both in appearance and in technical performance without great loss in efficiency.

The coupling of computer-aided design with computer-aided manufacturing (CAD-CAM),[31] together with on-going developments in computer-aided software, can reduce the relative cost of innovation and the time span of learning curves. This feature opens the way for rapid product change in time; and, although its impact could vary widely depending on the industry, it is likely to have a profound impact on business behavior. It could reshape the forms of competition and hence of oligopolistic practices in many areas; it may change the distribution of production between large and small firms, and it is likely to give a key role to the in-house research and development departments.

*Change in the forms of competition*: From past experience, it could be said that it is generally in the interest of highly concentrated oligopolies to administer technical change, by pacing the rhythm of innovations to take best advantage of each product cycle in yielding optimum overall profitability. We would argue that such a 'minimum change' strategy was indeed appropriate under the previous paradigm, based on mass production of identical units, within which product change implied high costs in dedicated equipment and tooling, as well as high risks. However, as the relatively low cost of flexibility and dynamism under the new conditions is realized, the struggle for market share could, in certain industries, increasingly take the form of fast innovation and imitation. This is already happening in the areas of software and electronics products where protection based on patenting seems extremely difficult to uphold.

*Opportunities for small and medium firms*: This capacity for quick technical change might have consequences in the long-run distribution of production between large and small or medium firms, because it is related to the question of 'barriers to entry'. Whereas the electronic components sector is already becoming concentrated and the level of investment at the present stage of development has reached prohibitive proportions,[32] wide areas of product applications and software are quite far from reaching that situation. It can be argued indeed that, with the powerful capabilities and low and decreasing cost of both components and development systems (i.e. equipment with which to design microprocessor based applications), there will, for a relatively long time, be ample space for new small firms with new products. And the same can be said about innovation in services, more so if telecommunications do become all-pervasive and cost-decreasing. Whether these firms become mere risk-takers, to be taken over by the giants if successful, or whether they will proliferate in bandwagon fashion and become typical of the next upswing, cannot be foreseen. Yet, the second course, which would guarantee continued market expansion for the components, the equipment, the services and the telecommunications produced by the giants, seems much more promising for overall growth.

*The role of research and development departments*: In the previous paradigm, the existence of an in-house R&D department was a 'best practice' feature indispensable in most large corporations. Its role, however, and the tightness of its relationship with management, marketing or the production process, varied widely across branches, depending on how science-based the products were. Already though, and perhaps even more in the future, the R&D department, or departments, are becoming a core management tool in most large firms. Furthermore, dynamic

R&D might increasingly be the key to the existence and survival of small and medium firms, especially in the electronics and information sectors.

In developing countries, most of the R&D is done in more or less academic institutes and (putting aside the question of the local relevance of some of the problems tackled) great difficulty is encountered in trying to transfer the results for application in the productive sphere. With the new paradigm, there would be greater need for in-house R&D efforts, directly linked to production, and for explicit technological strategies on the part of management, especially — though not only — in export oriented sectors.

(iii) *User-defined systems vs producer-defined products*

The conjunction of flexible production capabilities and greater information intensity of equipment and products generates another trend with far-reaching consequences: the diversity of applications available to the user.

The typical products of the previous Kondratiev were conceived to perform a single task or set of tasks that were more or less strictly defined by the manufacturer. Products based on microelectronics are, at least potentially, multipurpose. Not only are individual pieces of equipment increasingly versatile, but they can be linked together into diverse combinations, depending on user needs. This has become common in office equipment, where the market offers a range of basic core products and a range of optional peripheral elements. As the necessary drive towards standardization and compatibility advances in both hardware and software, the generalization of the trend towards modularity on the supply side for manufacturing equipment is also likely to advance. Final systems in use are thus, potentially, user defined, and can grow in complexity at a rhythm also dependent on the user.

This organic type of system growth creates scope for adaptability in process design on the part of producers. It can mean, for developing countries, that efforts at matching technical choice to specific local conditions have a better chance of success. Moreover, this adaptability also applies to the products made with those techniques. Under the mass production paradigm, the drive towards uniformity in consumption patterns encompassed the privileged minorities of all developing countries. The question of adapting either capital or consumer goods to diversity in climate or culture was not on the agenda, as long as productivity and profitability depended mainly on growing mass markets for identical products. The new technologies open the path — though nothing can guarantee it will be trodden — for adapting to diversity in conditions.

Taking advantage of this new potential is no easy matter. It requires overcoming decades of imitation; it implies a willingness to recognize local needs and building confidence in the real possibility of addressing them successfully. And, this applies both to the public and to the private sectors. The general point is that once the mass production constraint is eliminated as the only means of high productivity achievement, diversity in demand can become a source of investment opportunities. It can even create naturally protected markets and regional export advantages. Yet, fulfilling this potential requires vast amounts of individual, social and institutional creativity, based on adequate information and education, appropriate stimulating policies and, hopefully, a genuine interest in the welfare of the national population.

### (c) *New concepts for organizational efficiency*

When speaking about information intensity and flexibility, we seemed to assume that engineers and managers would immediately respond to the new dynamics in the relative cost structure and to the potential offered by the new technologies. The process, of course, is neither simple nor automatic. Yet the changes in the optimal organization of the firm are even more difficult as they require overcoming deeply rooted behavior patterns. In fact, the diffusion of a new technological style is also a conflict ridden process of creation through trial and error of a new organizational model as regards the management of the firm. This process is extremely uneven and tends to spread through 'sink or swim' imitation under competitive pressures. It is profoundly linked to the characteristics of the new technologies, especially to the features that contribute to the quantum jump in productivity in relation to previous practices. Here we shall discuss some of the elements already visible in the process of diffusion of the new organizational model.

Obviously, there is never one and only one form of organization of the firm at any one period. There are differences stemming from type of branch, national conditions, and particularly size and scope of firm. Yet, certain general principles can be widely accepted as constituting 'best practice' guidelines and will, therefore, tend to shape the organizational goals of most firms (and in the longer run even of most institutions).

It is in the sphere of these general principles that the following discussion will be placed.

Nevertheless, it should be kept in mind that the innovative process in this area is taking place now, and there is still much ground for creativity. Ford's first assembly line, which became the prototype for plant-level efficiency in the mass production paradigm, was established at the beginning of this century. However, Sloan's professional management model,[33] which became the 'ideal type' of corporate organization, was actually developed in General Motors some fifteen years later. Furthermore, it was only during World War II that organic links between industry, science and government were established as a feature of the Keynesian mode of growth.

### (i) *The internal organization of the firm: systemation vs automation*

The Fourth Kondratiev model of organization implied a sharp separation of plant management from economic management and, within each, a clear differentiation of activities to identify all forms of repetitiveness for subsequent automation. It was mainly an analytical model. It demanded focusing attention on parts or elements of processes; it led to detailed definition of tasks, posts, departments, sections, responsibilities and to complex hierarchies. The new paradigm is intrinsically synthetic. It focuses on links and systems of interrelations for holistic techno-economic coordination.

Although many applications of electronic equipment are generally referred to as 'automation,' we suggest the use of the term 'systemation' to describe the new trend towards merging all activities — managerial and productive, white and blue collar, design and marketing, economic and technical — into one single interactive system.[34] This term has the advantage of de-emphasizing mere 'hardware,' and emphasizing the systemic, feedback nature of the organizational 'software.' We believe this is an essential distinguishing feature between the new and the old model of firm organization.

In fact, many unsuccessful attempts at introducing electronic equipment may stem from thinking they are mere pieces of hardware, which can be incorporated into the previous plant or office with some retraining, for 'business as usual but hopefully better.' In reality, reaping the fruits of the new technology requires a profound transformation in the internal organization of the firm and in its interconnections with markets and suppliers.

In a sense, it could be said that information technology does for the firm what the assembly line did for the plant. The firm, as a whole, becomes a continuous flow system of activities, information, evaluations and decisions. But there is a crucial difference: whereas the assembly line was based on the constant repetition of the same sequence of movements, information technology is based on a system of feedback loops for the optimization of the most diverse — and changing — activities.

We have already seen that, in plant organiz-ation, the new technology not only changes the core transformation processes, but also the erst-while peripheral tasks such as design, stock control, quality control, maintenance, etc. Thus, the potential exists for the complete fusion of all production activities into one single, flexible, optimized system from the input to the output end. A similar integration can occur in the office through computerization and communications systems both internal and external.

Yet, although such trends in plant and office could already be considered enormous trans-formations, they are not the crucial part of the story. It is the possibility of merging both into a single system that constitutes the truly radical change at the organizational level. This stems from the potential provided by the equipment itself, which, at the same time as it controls the physical volumes and qualities of inputs, throughputs and outputs, can yield both the technical data and the economic information for constant monitoring of techno-economic peform-ance.

This does not mean, of course, that all firm activities would be physically on a unified space. Much to the contrary, telecommunications capa-bilities actually increase the degrees of freedom concerning location (including even that of indi-vidual people). In fact, they might lead to a much wider geographical dispersion, as urban agglom-erations lose their capacity to provide external economies. Nor does it imply that they would constitute a single unit. If the old corporate structure managed multi-plant, multi-country op-erations, the new technological infrastructure would allow the efficient management of world-wide, giant, complex and rapidly changing conglomerate structures. (And this is indeed the direction in which transnational corporations have been moving since the late 1960s).

(ii) *Relationship between production and markets: dynamic 'on-line' monitoring vs periodic planning*

But systemation goes beyond the internal organization of the firm and allows the establish-ment of relatively low-cost feedback loops with the market, for acquiring information in real time. This interconnection gives full meaning to the potential for flexibility in output previously discussed. The quickest way to convey the idea is probably through an example. Let us then look at a case in the highly volatile area of fashion.

Benneton, an Italian family firm described as 'one of the most successful clothing companies in Europe,'[35] is organized in a flexible network of production and distribution. At the market end it has 2500 national and international outlets, furnished with specially designed electronic cash registers that transmit on-line full data about which articles are being sold, their sizes and color. This information is centrally received and processed for decision-making at the design and production end. There, the output mix flexibility of the main production facilities is complemented by a network of 200 small firms in a sort of 'putting out' system that provides additional flexibility regarding volume, although possibly at the expense of these indirect workers. Allegedly the response time to market changes is reduced to 10 days.

This potential for reliable feedback loops with the market could have a profound impact on management practices. It can transform produc-tion planning from a periodic hit-or-miss activity into a more reliable day-to-day adaptive system, coupled with flexible production facilities. Pre-viously, production planning relied on the flow of orders, tempered by past experience, intuition and the availability of national statistics indica-tors; but this introduces an inevitable time lag resulting in wide inventory fluctuations. With electronic equipment and systemation, given the appropriate software, every aspect of the busi-ness can be monitored in detail and in 'real time.' Not only can the possible (model-simulated) or actual effects of any decision be known much faster than before, but also fine tuning and decision changing are much more rapidly per-formed. Short-term profit maximizing or profit flow optimizing through adjustments in costs, prices and volumes, as well as very tight inven-tory controls and dynamic production schedul-ing, can now be information-based.[36]

It is, of course, probable that the larger firms will be the ones to adopt the systemation model more fully. Nevertheless, the general concepts also apply to smaller firms.[37] In particular, the on-line market information systems could diffuse quite widely, as both producers and distributors adopt computerized equipment and telecom-munications become truly all-pervasive and low-cost.

(iii) *A new management style: information-based vs intuition-based skills*

These developments also tend to change the required management skills. Much of the experience of successful managers involved having the type of intuition that would lead to the right decisions in the face of scant information. That might be why the first reaction of traditional managers to the masses of data that could now be available is a certain sense of intoxication. In the future, coordination and information management skills are likely to become essential for daily operations. Creative, intuitive skills might be increasingly required for human relations and for the more strategic questions, such as investment or technological decisions as well as for the design of the information systems themselves.

As a matter of fact, since firm growth might often depend on market scope and technological dynamism, it could prove very ineffective for top management to ignore or delegate the technical questions. Both strategic and short-term decisions are likely to involve a tightly woven techno-economic package. Thus, the new conditions imply a substantial transformation in the required management skills, right through to the topmost levels.

(iv) *A new system of control: decentralized networks vs hierarchical bureaucracies*

Thus far, the analysis of the new organizational model, might have led the reader to believe that all forces within the new technology favored giant firms and centralized control. Nevertheless, there are very essential complementary characteristics that greatly widen the space for local autonomy and decentralization.

To begin with, the typical pyramidal organization is radically questioned. Until recently, the more complex the organization the greater the proliferation of intermediate control levels. The various layers of 'middle' management served as a sort of relay system collecting and processing information from below, taking minor decisions or suggesting major ones to top management or top government officials and then transmitting the final decisions downwards. Today, provided the adequate software, those relay and processing tasks can be done by computers, and the present function of middle managers made redundant.

This, in itself, already flattens the control system bringing decisions and actions closer together. But, if this were to lead to hyper-centralization of decision-making, the main flexibility potential of the new system would be hopelessly lost. The core feature of low cost microprocessors is the capacity for providing 'distributed intelligence,' which, in organizational terms, means distributed decision-making. An illustration from a hardware system, might clarify the implications. Let us look, for example, at the evolution of traffic control systems.

In electromechanical times, traffic light relay mechanisms were individually hand-set to change at prescribed intervals according to control plans drawn up at the central office, on the basis of sample 'counts' taken by hand or instrument. By the end of the first stage of computerized traffic control, all the information was being fed into a giant computer with very complex and expensive software, provided with a giant display of the city's traffic control system, where the hyper-centralized decisions were made. Today, infinitely more flexible systems have been developed with microprocessor intelligence at each traffic light. Information on traffic flows at each intersection is collected on-line, on the spot, so each set of lights can react to demand. Further intercommunications links are provided among intersections in an area or along a main route for collective coordination, and even wider systems of information sharing between areas can be established for further interactive optimization. In this new context, the central control unit acquires a monitoring and coordinating role in charge of designing and evaluating the distributed intelligence network. This type of system, apart from being infinitely less costly and amenable to modular installation, is far more effective and reliable than the totally centralized one.[38]

Bearing in mind the obvious limits to the analogy, it serves to make the organizational point quite clearly. A centralized decision-making system would have to be able to simulate every single possible combination of events with every single possible combination of elements, and this is indeed a cumbersome and nearly impossible task. If organizations are to be diversified and flexible, to take full advantage of the new potential, they will probably tend to be based on flexible, interactive, relatively autonomous units, linked in adaptive on-line systems of coordination under dynamic strategic management.

But, the analogy can be taken further. Because 'intelligence' can be provided for single pieces of equipment, central coordination is not indispensable for efficiency in every case, and many local and niche markets, for products or services, can be covered by independent small firms or cooperative networks. And, going still further, greater worker participation, already experimented with more widely in Japan but also in some Western firms, could give better results in both human and productivity terms. All the more so, because of the need for teamwork, multi-task posts and multi-purpose skills. This aspect, much to our regret, can not be discussed here.

Thus, in organizational terms, the new paradigm combines trends towards centralization and decentralization, towards more control and more autonomy, so the variety of combinations is likely to be quite wide, not only in the present transitional period, but probably into the future upswing.

Moreover, this applies not only to firms. The new organizational model, as in previous Kondratievs, overflows into all sorts of other social activities from the educational system to the functioning of government. 'Bureaucracy' in Weber's time was an innovation that led to the division of labor in the control sphere, increasing the efficiency of organizations during the Third Kondratiev. In the Fourth, it was taken to its utmost limits and has now become a cumbersome and costly bottleneck. Yet, both those who cry against government bureaucracies and those who defend them seem to be trapped in the same mental block: confusing the form of the organization with its purpose. The same social goals could now be achieved with a different and more efficient organization; and, rather than reduce the number of people at work, the object could often be to expand and enrich the goals.

*(v) Decentralization: a key feature for developing countries*

It would seem that an emphasis on taking advantage of the decentralizing potential of the new paradigm could open fruitful paths for the Third World. To begin with, the planning system itself might warrant radical rethinking. Central coordination of regional, local or sectorial units with a high degree of autonomy, especially economic, could prove more effective than either true centralized control or so-called 'indicative planning.' It should also be remembered that a model of organization is mainly a set of principles. It can, therefore, be applied with the 'least hardware' solution. There is indeed a danger of massive overinvestment and wrong technological choice. So, original solutions to real local needs, taking into account local conditions and limitations, are possible.[39]

But these solutions should be sought now, before technical choice becomes more rigid. If groups of developing countries are able to set and put into practice standards more appropriate to their specific conditions and a more adequate mode of growth, it is not unlikely that these could become powerful indicators for developed

country producers seeking export opportunities in the Third World.

It seems that the first locomotive was designed with horse-like legs; but, if it had been conceived in a world without horses, it might never have gone through that 'hybrid' stage. It is true that technology is not socially neutral, but perhaps its scope is greater than the limits imposed by those who have molded it.

To take just one current example: the typical pattern for electricity generation and distribution was established, in the Third Kondratiev, as a centralized network based on the use of low-cost steel for large engineering equipment. It was further pushed in this direction by mass-production concepts and the availability of low-cost oil, which closed-off the route of most other possible sources. Today, this same centralizing model sees nuclear power as the only real alternative. Existing infrastructure makes it difficult to conceive a truly diversified semi-decentralized system. Even in the introduction of solar technology, experimental stations have covered acres of land with solar collectors for central redistribution. This rather awkward form of application has been used in spite of the widespread agreement that it is more natural for a technology that collects an all-pervasive source of energy to install the generating equipment at the points of use.

Individual, national or regional initiatives, involving non-imitative behavior in these types of issues, could develop and gear the new potential towards more appropriate solutions for Third World conditions.[40]

In the following section, we shall explore the more general perspectives in the context of the changes in the international framework that can occur in long wave transitions.

## 4. CHALLENGES AND PERSPECTIVES FOR DEVELOPING COUNTRIES IN THE PRESENT LONG WAVE TRANSITION

If our long wave hypotheses are correct, the uppermost idea that should guide development strategy today is that planning must address the problems and opportunities of tomorrow and not those of yesterday. As we suggested at the beginning, this is a time for speculation and innovation. Although the future is built upon the past, in transition periods mere extrapolation from the past is useless and even counterproductive.

Obviously, the problem of arriving at successful responses in developing countries is tremendously complex. It requires not only an understanding of the new techno-economic paradigm, but also foreseeing the possible responses of the core industrialized countries, to prefigure the general climate of the future international framework; and, this has to be done in most cases in the face of scant financial resources and tremendous human hardship. Nevertheless, an adequate response is more likely with higher information and understanding. As we have seen, certain features of the new paradigm and of this specific transition could be used to advantage in opening new avenues for development.

### (a) *A new space for development thinking*

From what has been argued, the first point to keep in mind is that the transformation in the relative cost structure changes both comparative advantages and comparative disadvantages. For each country, this implies a fundamental rethinking of its relative advantage position within the new techno-economic paradigm to identify the new possibilities. This should not be misunderstood as going back on the discussion of static and dynamic comparative advantages, nor as a negation of the role of the state in creating or enhancing such advantages or using protective measures to overcome disadvantages. It merely means that the world of the past is dying and, with it, the opportunities it opened or closed. Only a reassessment of real possibilities can lead to adequate and innovative development policies.

This basic rethinking involves the question of specific resource endowment, location, size, cultural or environmental factors and previous areas of relative development. However, it also involves a reassessment of the technology gap. Since the new overarching technology is now at its relatively early stages, it is possible to attempt a direct entry without going through the technological stages it leaves behind. As Luc Soete[41] has pointed out in his analysis of the international diffusion of technology, each crisis in a long wave results in a restructuring of the relative positions of countries. This is partly because the new technologies allow 'leapfrogging' for some of the countries that do not carry the inertia of the previous industrial structure. In the particular area of microelectronics applications and software, Morris Teubal[42] has noted that technical knowledge of the type acquired in universities is the essential initial skill required. This is in contrast to the need for productive experience in traditional mechanical engineering or investment experience needed for success in the process industries. (Of course, this situation is tempor-

ary; as the new areas develop and standardize their practices, experience will once again become necessary for success).

These general comments apart, the route to development does not hinge on whether countries can or cannot enter the microelectronics or information race. Even industrialized countries might be wrong in believing that, with enough government funds to support the growth of information technology, they can unleash the recovery. We have already seen that the process of diffusion of the new technology, without changes in the socio-institutional framework, actually aggravates the crisis. The real question for developed countries is how to manage the transition. This does involve an effort to reorient economic activity by enhancing the conditions that stimulate a successful restructuring but also to avoid a collapse; and, this requires both temporary innovations to deal with the major ills brought about by the transition — especially unemployment — as well as more permanent ones to shape the future.

For developing countries, it is a question of taking advantage of the transitional phase to leap forward. This also requires socio-institutional transformations. However, since this is not the place to address the wider social issues, the discussion will be limited to an overview of the new degrees of freedom for achieving economic growth. Although increasing wealth can be unevenly distributed, better distribution and greater welfare are more likely with increasing wealth.

Because electronics and information technology, and especially its flexible organizational paradigm, can transform any activity, from mining and agriculture through health care and education to biotechnology and satellites, the real question is which activities to emphasize as the core of a development policy. The how, as was discussed in Section 3, seems to involve a much more integrated systems approach, requiring the development of design capacity for process, products, general organization and marketing systems. Thus, there might be higher chances of success by focusing on one or very few integrated complexes or flexible decentralized clusters of activities, centered around local resources or local conditions.

This approach could imply a revision of the traditional concept of 'industrialization,' substituting it with a much wider concept of integrated development. A more adequate approach to planning would reevaluate all wealth-creating activities, from agriculture and mining to information services, and all the elements of each process, from design through organization to national and world marketing. This means that no particular sector is intrinsically 'better' for development but that creating adaptive integrated systems and interactive links is better for the development of any sector.

### (b) Some old obstacles reduced

Traditionally, underdeveloped countries have suffered from the insufficient size of local markets, lack of an experienced and skilled workforce and a shortage of managers. Under the new conditions, these might no longer be such acute obstacles.

As we have seen, with good process and organizational design (and provided the goal is well chosen), it should now be possible to achieve high productivity levels on the basis of a small market for one product or a combination of them. These opportunities are further enhanced by the new potential for catering to specific local needs and conditions. So, developing countries could now play a more active role in segmented demand and product creation, for local markets as well as for international niches.

As regards the typical skill profile, the new technology can be applied with a combination of technical and professional personnel and relatively low-skilled, rapidly trained labor. Thus while the more industrialized countries must face the challenge of recycling the bulk of the redundant skills, developing countries could by-pass that previous bottleneck when entering new sectors of production.

As far as managers are concerned, the problem remains, but it now has a different character. Again, the need for the old skills can be more or less by-passed and the new skills, based on a capacity to design and coordinate information-intensive systems, can be acquired and developed. In this area, the innovation process is taking place now all over the world, so there is likely to be time for educational and trial-and-error learning. In this context, it might be worthwhile to reassess present efforts in professional education or training (including those to be acquired abroad). Also, since many previously trained engineers are often under-utilized in the passive operation of the old technologies, they can be turned into a valuable asset if they are well directed and given a more creative role.

### (c) Transnationals and autonomous development

It could be argued that the relatively autonomous industrialization of Third World countries is generally not in the interest of transnational corporations. For a long time, these countries have been said to be a source of cheap raw materials and labor, as well as a profitable market for mass-produced goods, either finished or assembled in local subsidiaries. However, if our long wave model is sound, this need no longer be the case.

In the first place, an energy and materials saving technology does not hinge upon the decreasing relative cost of oil or raw materials for increasing productivity, profitability and growth. In the particular case of oil, the transnationals in the field have accepted, and sometimes fostered, fully compensated nationalization and now derive profit from selling technological and marketing services to their erstwhile subsidiaries. A similar phenomenon is occurring in some of the metallurgical industries, where rather than setting up subsidiaries, transnationals have often entered either minority share agreements or design, construction and technology service contracts with developing countries. These events could be seen as analogous to the mixed blessing of political independence without economic autonomy. Yet, it is shortsighted to deny that they create better conditions for increased autonomy.

Secondly, there is reason to believe that transnationals may no longer seek the 'final assembly subsidiary' route. This practice originally served market expansion objectives and later, at the peak of the prosperity phase, became a stretching solution to the limits on productivity growth under the old paradigm, by reducing labor costs. While the new technologies are at their early stages, initial market expansion comes from product change and cost reductions, and there is much scope for cost reduction in process and organizational change in the main plants. Thus, although the question of robotized assembly is not yet clear, the trend towards off-shore migration, might be over, at least for some time.

By contrast, it can be argued that under the new conditions, a certain level of autonomous development in the Third World could be very important for the new transnationals as they restructure. High local investment levels would actually increase the world market for the core products of the new paradigm: electronic components, computerized office or production equipment and telecommunications, as well as engineering consultancy, plant design and construction and all other information intensive services, from financial to technological.

A certain historical parallel can be drawn with the Third Kondratiev 'Belle Epoque' upswing.

Then, the giant firms concentrated in steel (which we have suggested was the low cost 'key factor' of the period), electrical equipment, heavy chemicals, shipbuilding, engines and machinery, great engineering works and, in general, products destined for producers or governments. At that time, the spread of electricity led to a proliferation of small and medium firms serving local consumer markets (much of the food processing, ready-made clothing and of the early consumer durables industries were born under these conditions). It was a wave of small-scale industrialization with a vast geographical range following the electrical network, as opposed to the previous model of highly concentrated steam-powered industrial complexes in railroad centres and ports. Yet, without this wave of small industry and commerce, purchasing equipment and electricity and transforming the agricultural world, the giants would not have found the appropriate market growth.

Because this need for market expansion of the appropriate sort seems to have appeared at each transition, we would go as far as to argue that it is very unlikely that a new upswing can be unleashed without the development of at least a considerable group of Third World countries. To allow the achievement of the quantum jump in productivity promised by this new technology, the present internal markets of the developed countries plus the fringe high income groups of the Third World are clearly insufficient.

However, achieving this is no simple matter. In view of the present shortage of investment funds and the enormous levels of debt, moves to facilitate market expansion based on Third World development might require new transitional or permanent institutional arrangements for international income redistribution. Some of these might take the form of agreements on better prices for raw materials (which is what OPEC achieved in a unilateral way), but others might be oriented towards some form of international Keynesianism as was suggested in the Brandt Report.

Before all this is dismissed as utopian, we would like to invite the reader to imagine how it might have sounded in the early 1930s to say that, to bring forth the necessary market growth for economic revival, developed countries would have to raise the wages of the majority of manufacturing workers, organized in officially recognized labor unions, to a level where they could own a car and a house full of electrical appliances; that governments would have to directly employ a significant and growing proportion of the population, as well as to generalize

social security benefits, and that much of the labor shed by higher productivity manufacturing and mechanized agriculture would be taken up by a fast growing service sector, while the working week would be reduced to forty hours for all. Further still, let us try to imagine how the world looked to those living in the 'Belle Epoque' prosperity, when almost every industrialized country had or aspired to a colonial empire. It surely must have been very difficult to foresee the generalization of political independence in Africa and Asia. Neither of these series of developments occurred without conflict, of course, but both became central features of the general mode of growth.

### (d) *The risk of 'missing the boat'*

Of course, the so-called Third World does not exist as such. It is a concept based on real, and doubtless essential similarities, but it necessarily overlooks significant differences between countries. United Nations literature already distinguishes the 'newly industrializing countries' (NICs), at the upper end, and the poorest 'less developed countries,' at the lower. Other groups based on cultural or regional similarities or on resource endowment are also singled out for various purposes. In the transition, however, the recognition of the specific conditions of each country or group of countries is crucial. Yet, whatever their origins, these conditions must now be seen as starting points for the future, rather than as static obstacles.

Historically, long wave transitions have involved radical changes in the rules of the game. And, in spite of the obvious weight of relative power factors, the new rules are created by all the players. Thus, in the present transition, developing countries, both individually and through international organizations, can and should work constructively towards understanding the new conditions and in creating the new appropriate socio-institutional framework, on national and world levels.

Just as government institutions in developed countries can fruitlessly apply old policies because of the inertia created by past successes, developing country governments might miss the opportunities opened by the transition under the weight of inertia resulting from past frustration. Even the social and political groups who did benefit under recent conditions might find themselves on the losing end if they rely on the continuation of past practices.

In a sense, one could visualize long wave transitions as a sort of thawing out of the system, allowing fluidity of movement and a more or less wide spectrum of choice. Once the upswing gets underway, though, industries, social groups and countries are caught, as it were, in a certain growth path within the generally established new mode of growth. The opportunities and development perspectives of each are then high or limited, depending on the relative positions attained in the system. Leapfrogging then becomes very difficult indeed until the system reaches limits to growth again at the next peak of the long wave.

Even in the transition, there are tremendous restrictions, and there is a certain limit to just how far any particular country can advance. But, whatever the possibilities, the chances are much higher of taking advantage of them through a bold and fundamental rethinking of the development process, than if thwarted by the obstacles of the recent past.

Granted, this is particularly difficult for developing countries while the industrialized world persists in trying to overcome the crisis with the old practices. This, as was the case in the previous downswing, has resulted in fierce international competition, which in turn has led to a stiffening of nationalistic policies. Worse still, some see signs of a gradual growth in militaristic tendencies vaguely reminiscent of what happened in the thirties. Yet, this time, a world war would simply be the end.

Assuming the gravity of that danger precludes the war route, it might be that, as the various attempts at recovery result in short spurts of growth and the underlying crisis continues or even deepens, more creative and constructive solutions on a wider level will be sought. Under those circumstances, it is likely to become increasingly clear that to achieve a sustained recovery, industrialized countries, for their own sake, have to find solutions to the debt crisis and, in fact, have a stake in the development of the Third World.

The question remains whether the developing countries are preparing themselves to face the challenge and take best advantage of the new opportunities. There are, of course, no recipes.

## NOTES

1. See Schumpeter (1939).

2. Kondratiev (1935).

3. See also Perez (1983).

4. For an analysis of the various ways in which technological change occurs in interaction with economic and social factors, see Rosenberg, (1982).

5. Dosi (1982).

6. See Heertje (1977), pp. 161–167.

7. For a discussion of the concept of 'radical' innovations (as well as a different interpretation of long wave phenomena), see Mensch (1979). For a discussion of 'incremental' innovations as well as a good empirical example, see Hollander (1965). For a summary of the distinctions between incremental, radical and revolutionary innovations, see Freeman (1984).

8. See J. J. Van Duijn (1981) and (1983).

9. For a discussion of the concept of 'natural trajectories' in technical innovation, see Nelson and Winter (1977). For 'technological trajectories', see Dosi (1982).

10. The process of identifying and overcoming bottlenecks as a focusing device in steering technological advance both within a technology and across interrelated families is discussed by Rosenberg (1976) esp.

Part 2. The notion of diminishing returns to technical improvement is known as Wolff's Law. The original source is: *Die Volkswirtschaft der Gegenwart und Zukunft* (Leipzig: 1912).

11. J. J. Van Duijn (1981, 1983); Abernathy and Utterback (1978).

12. C. Freeman (1982); and Freeman *et al.* (1982), Chapter 4.

13. Steel existed subservient to iron, until the Bessemer and Siemens Martin processes slashed its cost to a tenth. Oil had been used for limited purposes until the internal combustion engine made it central for all sorts of transportation. And this use, together with oil-fueled generation of electricity, became cheap when low cost free-flowing oil, especially from the Middle East came on stream. Electronics began with tubes, then transistors and, for a long time developed within — and submitted to the 'logic' of — the mass production, energy intensive paradigm. It only became an all pervasive key factor when its original control functions fused in synergetic fashion with data processing. Subsequently, 'large scale integration' resulted in increasingly powerful, ever-cheaper microprocessors and other electronic 'chips.' Into the future, one could perhaps speculate that biotechnology might follow an analogous path as it grows and expands as an increasingly important industry, within the microelectronics-led paradigm. It may well make successive fundamental and incremental advances and gradually expand its sphere of influence beyond

pharmaceutical and food production. It is already affecting such apparently unrelated areas as mining and pollution control and experiments are under way for the production of microelectronic 'bio-chips.' Yet much ground might have to be covered before radical cost-cutting breakthroughs with all-pervasive influence are made.

14. This translates into new trends in the pattern of income distribution and in the evolution of consumer demand. For a brief discussion of these interactions, see Perez (1983), pp. 366–368.

15. For a similar approach to the relationship betwen the socio-institutional structure and the underlying technology, based on the concept of 'Regulation,' as well as a very comprehensive analysis of what he terms 'Fordist' modes of production and consumption, see Aglietta (1979).

16. Although the impact on employment is probably the most important single issue in the process of paradigm change, it will not be discussed here. Due to its complexity, it will be analyzed in a separate article. The reader is invited to keep the issue in mind in the course of the present discussion and to consult the growing bibliography on the subject. See, for example, Rada (1980); Lupton (1984); Freeman et al. (1984).

17. Smith (1983).

18. It should by now be clear that the general trend towards information intensity is not to be misconstrued as leading to a purely 'service economy.' Much to the contrary, most service applications of electronics are rendered by using manufactured equipment and the main market for many of the new services is the manufacturing industry.

19. Nevertheless, attention should also be paid to the wave of change in materials themselves. The diffusion of recycling techniques, fiber optics, ceramics and similar developments could substantially change the prospects for specific materials and influence energy consumption indirectly.

20. See *Business Week* (February 1984), pp. 54–71.

21. In the past, somewhat analogous conditions, created a 'natural' protective barrier for the growth of local construction materials and civil engineering industries.

22. Bylinsky (1983), pp. 50–51.

23. In a sense, one could suggest that for certain types of products or services the flexibility of electronic equipment could eventually change the idea that 'custom made' is equivalent to 'luxury.' The possibility of refined market segmentation in many areas together with an increase in the 'on-line' linkages between markets and suppliers could gradually allow the 'craft' potential of the new technologies to flourish. And this can occur both under factory type conditions and as a

home craft. For an example discussing both types of conditions in the case of weaving, see: 'Microelectronics in textile production: A family firm and cottage industry with AVL looms,' in Bhalla et al. (1984).

24. Hills (1984).

25. Kaplinsky (1984); S. Jacobsson (1982); Bessant (1984). See also other articles in this issue.

26. Hoffman and Rush (1984); and Guy (1984).

27. For further discussion on the issue of robotics, Ayres and Miller; and Jacobsson (1982).

28. For an example about the limits to economies of scale in the electrical industry and the trend towards flexible sourcing in the United States, see *Business Week* (1984b), pp. 68–71.

29. Allen et al. (1984).

30. Information intensity and flexibility in agriculture might be based not only on microelectronics, but also on biotechnology. Increasing research efforts are being made to develop natural pest-control systems and soil-enriching bateria, which could in time expand the agricultural frontier while reducing the need for petrochemical pesticides and fertilizers.

31. For a thorough discussion of the implications of CAD, see Kaplinsky (1982).

32. Dosi (1984).

33. See Drucker (1972).

34. A detailed analysis of 'intra-sphere and inter-sphere' automation and the concept of 'systemofacture,' can be found in Kaplinsky (1984). See also article in this issue.

35. Buxton (1983).

36. The generalization of on-line market monitoring implies the likelihood of dampening the short business cycles due to inventory fluctuations. An analogy can be made with the role played during the Fourth Kondratiev upswing (late 1940s to late 1960s) by the elaborate system of statistics established by national governments. This constituted a significant step upwards in the amount of information available for business planning and contributed, together with other measures, to reduce the intensity of short cycles, when compared with previous Kondratievs.

37. In Japan, no-inventory systems, called 'just-in-time' have been developed, which are less based on up-to-date equipment than on new management practices and greater worker involvement and participation. See Schonberger (1982).

38. I owe this example to Dr. R. Suarez, President of

EYT C.A., an electronics company in Caracas, Venezuela, where one such system was developed.

39. Peter Dempsey, managing director of Ingersoll Engineers, the firm responsible for the installation of over 50% of UK FMS systems, estimates that close to 70% of the benefits are achieved from organizational changes without any hardware; see Proceedings of FMS-2 (1984).

40. For a set of case studies involving imaginative applications of new technologies to Third World conditions, see Bhalla *et al.* (1984).

41. Soete (1983); see also article in this issue.

42. Teubal (1982).

# REFERENCES

Abernathy, J. and J. M. Utterback, 'Patterns of industrial innovation,' *Technology Review*, No. 88 (June–July 1978).

Aglietta, M., *A Theory of Capitalist Regulation: The U.S. Experience* (London: NLB, 1979).

Allen, R., J. Bleeke and A. Morgan, 'Pitfalls of converging financial services,' *Financial Times* (18 January 1984).

Ayers, R.U. and S. Miller, 'Robotics, CAM and industrial productivity,' *National Productivity Review*, Vol. 1, No. 1 (1982), pp. 452–468.

Bessant, J., 'Competition, technical change and employment in the UK foundry industry,' (Brighton, UK: Brighton Polytechnic, Innovative Research Group, 1984) (mimeo).

Bhalla, A., D. James and Y. Stevens (eds.), in *Blending of New and Traditional Technologies* (Dublin: ILO, Tycooly International, 1984).

*Business Week*, 'Software: the new driving force' (February 1984a).

*Business Week*, 'Are utilities obsolete: a troubled system faces radical change' (21 May 1984b).

Buxton, T., 'The man who fashioned a clothing empire,' *Financial Times* (29 October 1983).

Bylinsky, G., 'The race to the automatic factory,' *Fortune* (21 February 1983).

Dosi, G., 'Technological paradigms and technological trajectories,' *Research Policy*, Vol. 11, No. 3 (June 1982).

Dosi, G., *Technical Changes and Industrial Transformation: The Theory and an Application to the Semiconductor Industry* (London: Macmillan, 1984).

Drucker, P., *The Concept of the Corporation* (New York: Mentor, 1972).

Freeman, C., 'Science, technology and unemployment,' papers in Science, Technology and Public Policy, No. 1 (London: Imperial College of Technology and Science Policy Research Unit, 1982).

Freeman, C., 'Prometheus unbound', *Futures*, Vol. 16, No. 5 (October 1984), pp. 494–507.

Freeman, C., J. Clark, and L. Soete, *Unemployment and Technical Innovation: A Study of Long Waves and Economic Development* (London: Frances Pinter, 1982).

Freeman, C., J. Clark, K. Guy and L. Soete (eds.), *Technological Trends and Employment*, 4 vols. (Aldershot: Gower, 1984).

Guy, K. (ed.), *Technological Trends and Employment, Vol. 1, Basic Consumer Goods (Footwear; Food,*

*Drink and Tobacco; Textiles; Clothing)* (Aldershot: Gower, 1984).

Heertje, A., *Economic and Technical Change* (London: Weidenfeld and Nicolson, 1977).

Hills, P. (ed.), *The Future of the Printed Word* (London: Frances Pinter, 1984).

Hoffman, K., and H. Rush, *Microelectronics and Clothing: The Impact of Technical Change on a Global Industry* (Geneva: International Labour Office, 1984).

Hollander, S., *The Sources of Increased Efficiency: A Study of DuPont Rayon Plants* (Cambridge: MIT Press, 1965).

Jacobsson, S., 'Trends and implications of automation in the engineering sector' (Lund, Sweden: Research Policy Institute, 1982) (mimeo).

Kaplinsky, R., *Automation: The Technology and Society* (London: Longman, 1984).

Kaplinsky, R., *Computer-Aided Design: Electronics, Comparative Advantages and Development* (UNIDO; London: Frances Pinter, 1982).

Kondratiev, N. D., 'The long waves in economic life,' *Review of Economic Statistics*, Vol. 17 (November 1935), pp. 105–115.

Lupton, T. (ed.), *Proceedings of the International Conference on Human Factors in Manufacturing* (IFS and North Holland, 1984).

Mensch, F., *Stalemate in Technology Innovations Overcome Depression* (New York: Ballinger, 1979).

Nelson, R., and S. G. Winter, 'In search of a useful theory of innovation,' *Research Policy*, No. 6 (1977).

Perez, C., 'Structural change and assimilation of new technologies in the economic and social systems,' *Futures*, Vol. 15, No. 5 (October 1983), pp. 357–375.

*Proceedings of FMS-2* (Bedford: IFS Publications, 1984).

Rada, J., *The Impact of Microelectronics, A Tentative Appraisal of Information Technology* (Geneva: International Labour Office, 1980).

Rosenberg, N., *Perspectives on Technology* (Cambridge: Cambridge University Press, 1976).

Rosenberg, N., *Inside the Black Box: Technology and Economics* (Cambridge: Cambridge University Press, 1982).

Schonberger, *Japanese Manufacturing Techniques: Nine Hidden Lessons in Simplicity* (New York: Free Press, Macmillan, 1982).

Schumpeter, J. S., *A Theoretical, Historical and Statistical Analysis of the Capitalist Process* (New York: McGraw-Hill, 1939).

Smith, S. L., 'Address to the Joint CRMA-ADRIQ Conference on R&D and Canadian Industrial Policy' (Ottawa: Science Council of Canada, October 1983) (mimeo).

Soete, L., 'Long cycles and the international diffusion of technology,' paper presented at the International Seminar on Innovation, Design and Long Waves in Economic Development, Royal College of Art (London: 1983).

Teubal, M., 'The science and technology system of Israel,' paper presented at the Seminario Internacional Sobre Politicas Technologicas Instituto Torcuato di Tella (Buenos Aires: 1982).

Van Duijn, J. J., 'Fluctuations in innovations over time,' *Futures* (August 1981).

Van Duijn, J. J., *The Long Wave in Economic LIfe* (London: Allen and Unwin, 1983).

# [26]

# PROMETHEUS UNBOUND

Christopher Freeman

Professor Nicholas Onuf argued in the February 1984 issue of
*Futures* that those participating in the revival of interest in long
waves of economic activity had generally failed to relate their
analyses to the debate on growth spawned by *Limits to Growth*.
The challenge is taken up in this article, which relates the two
debates in terms of the role of technology in long-term growth
and cycles; changes in 'technological paradigm' are seen as a
major feature of each successive growth cycle. The article
finally discusses the effects of paradigm change on employment and investment, and confronts the central issue of
Onuf's paper—the social and political effects of the microelectronics revolution.

*Keywords*: economic growth; technological change; microelectronics

A RECENT ARTICLE by Nicholas Greenwood Onuf,[1] entitled "Prometheus
prostrate", relates the contemporary debate on long waves (Kondratiev cycles)
to the earlier one on *Limits to Growth*[2] in the world economy. Both these debates
represented a serious effort to understand and interpret long-term trends in
global economic development, and both preoccupied many of those interested in
problems of long-term forecasting and 'futurology' more generally.

But Onuf points out that "the long waves literature fails generally to place
itself in the decade long debate on growth", and comments: "This is all the
more surprising because some of the principals figured in the [*Limits to Growth*]
debate's early days". This article is an attempt to take up this challenge by one
of those named by Onuf, and who did indeed take part in both these debates.[3]

In particular, the article attempts to relate the two debates in terms of the role
of *technology* in long-term growth and cycles. It starts by discussing the explicit
and implicit assumptions about technology in the Massachusetts Institute of
Technology (MIT) models and some of their shortcomings. It then takes up the
question of the influence of technology on long waves of development and
argues that changes in 'technological paradigm' are a major feature of each

Professor Freeman is Deputy Director, Science Policy Research Unit, University of Sussex, Mantell
Building, Falmer, Brighton BN1 9RF, UK. This article is based on a lecture given at the Conservatoire
National des Arts et Métiers, Paris, 14 May 1984.

0016-3287/84/050494-14$03.00 © 1984 Butterworth & Co (Publishers) Ltd   **FUTURES October 1984**

successive growth cycle. The MIT models made no allowance for such changes in paradigm and consequently made unrealistic assumptions about the future consumption of materials and energy. Finally, the article discusses the effects of paradigm change on employment and investment, and attempts to take up the central issue of Onuf's[4] paper—the social and political aspects of the micro-electronic revolution.

### Technology and 'Limits to Growth'

Onuf[5] also himself regards technology as a crucial issue in both debates and defines the differences between the participants in terms of their theories, explicit or implicit, about the framework within which technological advances lead to economic growth. From this standpoint he identifies an important point of resemblance in form between the proponents of *Limits to Growth* and the much earlier Marxist literature emphasizing the 'limits to growth' imposed by a particular social and institutional framework.

However, this superficial point of resemblance disguises a much more fundamental difference. The MIT modellers were mainly concerned with what they believed to be the *absolute* limits to growth imposed by the finite environment of this planet, rather than the limitations of any particular social system. The Marxists, on the other hand, were primarily concerned with what they believed to be the relative and transitory limitations of a particular institutional framework—capitalism—and were boundlessly optimistic about the potentialities of technical change and future growth—once these constraints were lifted. Many economists criticized Malthus for his neglect of technical change in agriculture, as well as for his demographic theories, but Marx[6] was probably his most thorough-going and devastating critic. Thus 'room to grow' means something quite different in an environmentalist context than in a Marxist context.

The basic environmentalist argument that there are physical limits on this planet to the growth of population and of social artefacts is irrefutable. So too is the argument that *if* growth were to continue indefinitely on· a particular materials-intensive, energy-intensive, and capital-intensive path, physical limits of resource availability would sooner or later be encountered. The ecological movement of the 1970s and its reflection in the computer-based doom models of that period served a valuable purpose in drawing public attention to these ultimate limits. It was also valuable in highlighting the long-term global consequences of air and water pollution, associated with the reckless disregard of the social costs of a particular form of industrialization. Although energy did not figure as such in the early MIT models, much the same points can be made with respect to nuclear power.

The critique of the MIT models, however, related not to these fundamental limitations of the 'room to grow', nor to the gravity of the environmental hazards associated with a particular pattern of growth, nor yet to the global nature of the problems. It related to the possibilities open to human societies to make intelligent use of technical change over the next century and so to modify the pattern of growth, that living standards could still be vastly improved throughout the world whilst the gravest environmental hazards were averted.

By and large the MIT modellers were pessimistic about the possibilities of technical change of this type. They were also pessimistic about the responsiveness of social systems to pollution hazards and to demographic problems. This led them to advocate an immediate transition to slower growth and ideally to zero growth for the world economy. They disregarded almost completely the issue of labour-displacing technical change and the employment implications of their analysis.

Moreover, Onuf[7] is only half right when he says:

> In *Limits to Growth* and the debate it inspired, growth is taken for granted. Prometheus bounds. Everyone seems to agree that technological gains cause material growth . . .

It is true that the MIT modellers *did* allow for some possibilities of technical change. But in their formal modelling and in their presentation of the results of that modelling, they constrained the scope for technical change in many different ways. Prometheus bounds but only in certain limited directions and with a ball and chain around his ankles. These assumptions about technical change are often *implicit* in the specification of the equations, rather than explicit, which means that they are often disregarded in the debate.

Thus, for example, it is often overlooked that there are quite different assumptions about the long-term productivity of capital in the various subsectors of the MIT model.[8] In the industrial sector a constant capital–output ratio is assumed, whereas in the agricultural sector and in the materials sector a constant long-term decline in the productivity of capital is assumed. The effect of these differing assumptions is that in the heartland of manufacturing industry rapid growth continues unconstrained by capital shortages, whereas in the other primary sectors it fairly soon becomes severely constrained by capital shortage.

The combined effect of these differing assumptions about the rate and direction of technical change is to make the early collapse of the economy absolutely inevitable, *either* through the effects of capital shortage in the primary sectors working their way through the system, *or* through the devastating effects of worldwide pollution.

The transition to slower growth occurred perhaps rather sooner than the MIT modellers had expected; but it occurred not so much because *physical* limits were encountered even earlier than anticipated, as because of social, political and economic changes. Hence Onuf's point about the link between the long wave debate and the 'limits to growth' debate is important. It *was* true that many participants in the 1970s' debate tended to ignore the cyclical aspects of economic growth and in particular to disregard the possibility that economic stagnation or even deep depression might occur for long periods, for reasons which had little or nothing to do with physical limits or environmental hazards. The Marxists did indeed emphasize this possibility (or even inevitability), much more than most other social theorists. Onuf's point about the Marxist contribution to the debate, and Mandel's contribution in particular, is therefore a perfectly valid one—Mandel[9] was entitled to observe that he stood on somewhat lonely ground in 1968.

## Technology and long waves

When he turns to discuss the connection between technology and long waves ("regular substantial fluctuations in the growth curve of capitalism"), Onuf[10] appears to accept a Schumpeterian type of explanation. Indeed he criticizes Mandel for his mis-specification of the technology which might make a major contribution to a new upswing in the world economy, arguing that the electronics revolution can fulfil this role, whereas nuclear power cannot. When there is some choice among competing technologies, Onuf argues that "pressure will develop in favour of the cheapest among the candidates", and further comments: "Nuclear and electronic revolutions initially competed, but the former quickly and conclusively showed itself to be uncompetitive".

The available evidence appears to support Onuf in his contention, even though nuclear power is already an important source of electricity supply in some countries. A very substantial straw in the wind was the strategic decision of General Electric to shift the emphasis of its long-term strategy away from nuclear power and into the 'Factory of the Future'. However, it is not just a question of 'cheapness' and it would be a fair criticism that neither Schumpeter nor the Schumpeterians have really done enough to define their terms, so that the distinction between the Snark (a genuine technological revolution) and the Boojum (a false dawn) has not been clear.

The problem has become a little more complicated because one of the pioneers of the long wave revival, Mensch,[11] initially placed great emphasis on the appearance of many radical innovations during deep depressions. I and my colleagues[12] have argued elsewhere that such innovations could not form the basis of a major economic upswing since it takes one or more decades for the diffusion of innovations to have perceptible effects on investment and employment. Onuf also points out that for microelectronic technology to generate a worldwide economic upswing it must have been around for some time to become such a powerful engine of growth.

But whereas he appears to regard this as a departure 'from the norm', we would regard this as 'the norm', since our view of the successive technological revolutions is that they are clusters of economically and technologically related innovations amounting to 'new technological systems'[13] which are already established in the *previous* cycle of growth. It is therefore essential to distinguish between the following.

(1) *Incremental innovations.* These occur more or less continuously, although at differing rates in different industries, but they are concerned only with improvements in the existing array of products and processes of production. They are reflected in the official measures of economic growth simply by changes in the coefficients in the existing input—output matrix. Although their combined effect is extremely important in the growth of productivity, no single one has dramatic effects.

(2) *Radical innovations.* Although Mensch[14] has suggested that most of these are concentrated in deep depressions, we[15] have maintained that they are more randomly distributed. They are discontinuous events and their *diffusion* (as opposed to their first introduction) may often take a cyclical form and may be associated with long cycles of the economy as a whole. A new material, such as nylon or polyethylene, is an example of such innovations.

(3) *Technological revolutions.* These are the 'creative gales of destruction' which are at the heart of Schumpeter's long wave theory. The introduction of

electric power or railways are examples of such deep-going transformations. A change of this kind would of course carry with it many clusters of radical and incremental innovations, with a tendency for *process* innovations to be concentrated rather more in the later stages of diffusion. A vital characteristic of this third type of technical change is that it must have *pervasive* effects throughout the economy, ie it must not only lead to the emergence of a new range of products and services in its own right, it must also affect every other branch of the economy by changing the input cost structure and conditions of production and distribution throughout the system. It is the extension of the effects of a new technological system beyond the confines of a few branches to the economy as a whole, which constitutes the basis for the major upswings of the Kondratiev cycles, and which justifies the expression 'change of paradigm' or 'change of technological regime'.

*Defining a technological revolution*

We may thus define the characteristics of a genuine technological revolution as:

(1) *A drastic reduction in costs of many products and services.* In some areas this will be an order of magnitude reduction; in others, much less. But it provides the essential condition for Schumpeterian 'swarming', ie widespread perceived opportunities for new profitable investment.

(2) *A dramatic improvement in the technical characteristics of many products and processes*, in terms of improved reliability, accuracy, speed and other performance characteristics.

(3) *Social and political acceptability.* Although economists and technologists tend to think narrowly in terms of the first two characteristics, this third criterion is extremely important. Whereas the first two advantages are fairly quickly perceived, there may be long delays in *social* acceptance of revolutionary new technologies, especially in areas of application far removed from the initial introduction. Legislative, educational and regulatory changes may be involved, as well as fundamental changes in management and labour attitudes and procedures. For this reason too, the expression 'change of paradigm' best conveys the full flavour of this type of technical change. The interplay between techno-economic characteristics and the socio-institutional framework is the main theme of the final part of this article.

(4) *Environmental acceptability.* This may be regarded as a subset of (3) above, but, especially in recent times, it has become important in its own right. It is of particular significance in relation to the *Limits to Growth* debate and the distinction between nuclear power and microelectronics. It finds expression in the development of a regulatory framework of safety legislation, and procedural norms which accompany the diffusion of any major technology. Particularly hazardous technologies or those which are extremely expensive to control are severely handicapped, even if they do have some economic and technical advantages.

(5) *Pervasive effects throughout the economic system.* Some new technologies, as for example the float-glass process, have revolutionary effects and are socially acceptable, but are confined in their range of applications to one or a very few branches of the economy. For a new technology to be capable of

affecting the behaviour of the entire system, it must clearly have effects on investment decisions almost everywhere.

Using these five criteria it is relatively easy to see why nuclear power does not qualify as a technological revolution, since it fails on almost every one of them. The microelectronic, computer-based information revolution, by contrast, satisfies all five criteria.

A technological revolution therefore represents a major change of paradigm, affecting almost all major managerial decisions in many branches of the economy. Several authors have used the expression 'technological trajectory' or 'technological paradigm', but probably the most thorough and systematic exposition of the idea is in the work of Carlota Perez.[16] She defines a 'techno-economic paradigm' as a new set of guiding principles, which become the managerial and engineering 'common-sense' for each major phase of development.

Perez suggests that depressions represent periods of 'mismatch' between the emerging new techno-economic paradigm (already quite well advanced in a few branches of the economy during the previous long wave), and the institutional framework. The widespread profitable generalization of the new technological paradigm throughout the system is possible only after a period of change and adaptation of many social institutions to the potentialities of the new technology. The big boom periods of economic expansion occur when such a good 'match' between the new 'techno-economic paradigm' or 'style' of a long wave and the socio-institutional framework has been made.

This perspective enables us to identify some of the most critical weaknesses in the *Limits to Growth* models. They are based essentially on the extrapolation of the characteristics of one phase of growth and do not allow for the possibility of paradigm changes in the mode of growth. The characteristics of the MIT models are those of the 'fourth Kondratiev' upswing—a techno-economic paradigm based on cheap oil universally available as the foundation for energy-intensive, mass and flow production of standardized homogeneous commodities such as consumer durables, and the associated capital goods, components and services.

This techno-economic paradigm permitted the massive expansion of the world economy during and after World War II, following its successful development in the US automobile industry in the previous three decades and during the war itself. Although it enabled very big productivity increases in many branches of manufacturing and in agriculture, and an enormous associated proliferation of public and private service employment, it ultimately began to encounter 'limits' to further growth in the late 1960s and 1970s. This was not *just*, or even *mainly*, a question of the oil price increases, but of a combination of factors including the exhaustion of economies of scale, diminishing returns to further technical advance along existing trajectories (Wolf's Law), market saturation factors, pressures on input prices, declining capital productivity and the erosion of profit margins arising from all these factors, as well as the culmination of the competitive pressures from the Schumpeterian 'swarming' process.

The mistake of the MIT modellers (and of some Marxists) was to confuse the 'limits' of one particular development paradigm with the 'limits to growth' of the system in general. In the case of the MIT modellers, the limits were

perceived as absolute limits to further economic growth. In the case of the
Marxists, both in the 1930s and the 1980s, there was some tendency to see the
depression as the 'final crisis' of the capitalist social system. Thus, probably not
many Marxists (and not many other economists either) foresaw that the 1950s
and 1960s would witness the most rapid growth and the lowest levels of
unemployment in the industrialized countries in the history of capitalism.

Just because of the unexpected strength of the revival, during periods of
recovery there appears to be a tendency to 'revisionism' within the Marxist
stream of thought, critical of that element in Marx's analysis which points to the
fundamental limitations of the capitalist system. Revisionists explain the change
of paradigm as a more fundamental social adaptation of the system. From
Bernstein in the 1890s to Burnham in the 1940s, they emphasize the concentration of control in the hands of efficiently managed large firms, and the ability of
the state to manage the behaviour of the system as a whole. During periods of
deep depression, on the other hand, the opposite tendency comes to the fore with
an emphasis on the 'collapse' of the system and a permanent state of 'general
crisis'.

Similarly today, with the downswing of the fourth Kondratiev long wave,
there has been a pronounced increase in pessimism about the prospects for a
future return to high rates of growth, and a strong tendency to view the postwar
boom in retrospect as an exceptional spurt of growth, unlikely ever to be
repeated. This tendency is by no means confined to Marxists. In particular
there is widespread pessimism about the future prospects for employment and
much discussion about the 'collapse of work'. A great deal therefore depends on
the characteristics of a new technological paradigm which might conceivably lift
the system into a renewed phase of prosperous growth, and the institutional
changes which might be needed to make this possible. This article does not
assume that such a development is inevitable, only that it is a possibility. Despite
the pessimism, the social pressures for a renewal of growth are very strong
throughout the world and there are indeed some revolutionary advances in
technology, which should in principle make recovery possible.

## New technological paradigms and capital investment

Onuf[17] remarks that "Economists and technologists operating within the
dominant Keynesian tradition are disposed to see the curve of *technological*
growth as relatively smooth and the *rate* of such growth rather *constant*".
Although this may be true of the 'dominant Keynesian tradition', this was not
always true of Keynes himself.

In his *Treatise on Money* in 1930, Keynes[18] actually *did* acknowledge the role of
Schumpeterian revolutions in technology:

In the case of fixed capital, it is easy to understand why fluctuations should occur in the
rate of investment. Entrepreneurs are induced to embark on the production of fixed
capital or deterred from doing so by their expectation of the profits to be made. Apart
from the many minor reasons why these should fluctuate in a changing world, Professor
Schumpeter's explanation of the major movements may be unreservedly accepted.

This passage is remarkable for its unequivocal recognition of the role of new
technology in generating new surges of investment and growth in capitalist

societies. The tragedy of the Keynesian tradition was that it regressed from this standpoint to a purely abstract approach to the role of new technologies, and a one-sided emphasis on the role of demand in relation to the short-term business cycle. For the Keynesians it became a matter of relative indifference *which* were the new technologies and fast-growing sectors of the economy and the associated problems of structural change. They also ignored the problem of long-term swings in the *direction* of technical change, and of cyclical changes in the capital—output ratio. By a kind of imperceptible process the idea of a constant capital—output ratio shifted from the status of a convenient modelling assumption to the status of a generalization about growth.

Keynes *did*, however, concern himself with the long-term tendency to a decline in the marginal efficiency of capital (productivity of capital). His pessimism about this long-term tendency led him, like Marx and other classical economists, to envisage an ultimate slow-down in the whole growth process, through a loss of incentive to new investment. Although, as we have seen, he certainly did have glimpses of the regenerative impetus provided by new waves of technical innovation, he apparently did not see such waves as counteracting more than temporarily the long-term tendency to decline in capital productivity.

From an entirely different starting point and by a different chain of argument, Marx also came to the conclusion that the capitalist system suffered from a tendency to stagnation. In the Marxist framework, while the new technologies did indeed provide a temporary escape route from the otherwise inexorable competitive pressures on the rate of profit, they did so only by exacerbating the fundamental long-term problem of the rising 'organic composition of capital'.

However, within the Marxist tradition, a number of economists, including Kondratiev himself, Kalecki, the Cambridge economist Maurice Dobb, and Mandel, did recognize clearly the long-term cyclical aspects of this growth process. Maurice Dobb[19] in particular pointed out that the tendency to a falling rate of profit, which Marx and many other economists had identified, could be offset in several distinct ways for prolonged periods.

First, it could be offset in the way which most orthodox Marxist literature has emphasized—by a reduction in the level of real wages and by increasing work intensity. If this process were not offset by other stronger tendencies, then indeed there would have been the 'absolute immiseration' of the proletariat of which Marx spoke. That this tendency was not a purely imaginary one can be checked by many accounts of the conditions of the English working class in the first part of the 19th century.[20] Even though debate on this topic continues among economic historians, it is clear that pressure for a reduction of living standards was a serious phenomenon in many areas. The career of Robert Owen may be viewed as a sustained attempt to demonstrate, both in theory and in practice, that there was a real alternative to such downward pressures, in the form of better work organization, social reforms and superior technology. But he failed to make much impression on his fellow employers at the time, although he met with a better response from the Chartists and trade unionists.

However, the Owenite ideas of an alternative to the crude pressures on wages and work intensity were vindicated over the next century and a half. One of the reasons for the success of this alternative vision was clearly the existence of a real lower limit to the 'immiseration' tendency with its loss of working efficiency through physical exhaustion and loss of effective work incentives. The threat of serious social conflict, such as occurred in Britain in the 1830s, was clearly also an incentive to search for more constructive social alternatives to 'immiseration'.

The basis for a sustained (although cyclical) movement away from these lower limits of human misery and degradation was provided, outside the Third World countries, by successive technological revolutions. Each of these involved both a *widening* and a *deepening* of the capital stock in the system as a whole. It seems that each technological revolution ultimately led to a rise in capital intensity and to a fall in capital productivity as the limits of each paradigm were approached. But in the phase of recovery and high growth after the initial teething problems were overcome and infrastructural investment was in place, each major new technology greatly augmented the productivity of both capital and labour. Rosenberg[21] has pointed out that Marx was one of the economists who most clearly recognized these changes in capital productivity over time. Technical innovation cheapened in real terms the cost of the commodities needed to sustain the physical work capacity of the labour force and at the same time broadened the range of goods and services, customarily regarded as a necessary part of the standard of living, as well as reducing working hours.

The role of successive new techno-economic paradigms in offsetting the otherwise persistent pressures towards a declining marginal efficiency of capital was thus of the greatest historic importance. One of the most interesting results of Soete's[22] research in this context has been his finding that whereas capital productivity has been falling persistently in almost all sectors of the UK manufacturing industry since the 1960s, it has apparently been rising in the electronic computer industry and electronic components industry. It will take time before such benefits occur in other sectors, as the initial effect in the diffusion of new types of capital goods is often to make capital costs even higher. Only when the 'islands' of automation are linked together do the benefits of rising capital productivity accrue.

It is not without interest that Japan alone, among the leading industrial countries, shows small, positive gains in capital productivity in manufacturing through the 1960s and 1970s.[23] The rise in capital productivity in Japan appears to be only partly due to the more rapid diffusion of more advanced types of electronic capital goods and new information technologies, such as computer numeric control (CNC), robotics, computer-aided design (CAD) and so forth. At least in some industries it is also due to a parallel and even antecedent change in management attitudes and practices in relation to work organization—the 'just-in-time' system of assembly and component-supply networks and its concomitant reduction of stocks and work-in-progress, and the far greater responsibility for quality, repairs and maintenance devolved to much lower levels of the workforce than has been customary in the USA and Western Europe.[24]

Further infrastructural investment and a wider availability of the requisite skills may be necessary before any widespread and sustained rise in capital productivity can be realized in Western Europe. But in the absence of such an improvement in the productivity of capital it would be much more difficult to achieve high levels of employment, since any sustained expansion would run into problems of capital shortage. Although parts of the Japanese management style are transferable, they are not necessarily the most desirable way to exploit the new technologies. Greater responsibility and involvement at shop-floor level is certainly desirable for many reasons, but there is a range of possibilities, rather than one single model, for achieving this objective. Whether it can be achieved at all will depend, as Onuf rightly emphasizes, on wider social and political developments over the next decade, as well as on management and union attitudes and policies.

## New technological paradigms and labour

In the upswing phase of each long wave much new employment is associated with the expansion of the capital goods sector and the associated producer services. These services are likely to be particularly important in connection with the present technological revolution and are already one of the few growth areas for employment, even in general conditions of depression. Once an upswing gets under way, a wave of new investment induces employment growth in many other areas, to replace the old obsolescent capital stock and produce a new range of goods and services.

Historically, this has led in the past to periods of very strong demand for labour with new jobs far outstripping the loss of employment through labour-saving technical change. It has been estimated that unemployment fell as low as 1% in Britain before the crash of 1873.[25] The demand for labour in the indus-trializing countries—including the USA and Germany, which took over world technological leadership from Britain towards the end of the 19th century—was even stronger. Millions of immigrant workers were drawn into the labour force in both countries, both in the boom before 1914 and in the upswing of the 1950s and 1960s.

In such periods of high boom, even though the growth of labour productivity may be high, output growth tends to be even higher. Contrary to what is commonly assumed, the higher levels of unemployment are usually associated with relatively low growth of labour productivity. But as limits to further growth within an established paradigm are increasingly encountered, capital produc-tivity tends to fall and it becomes increasingly difficult to generate new employment.

If these tendencies could be offset by the timely growth of other new branches of the economy and/or by capital-saving technical advances on a sufficient scale, then the downswing phase of the long wave might be mitigated or averted (as to some extent in Japan). But it has been argued that inertia in the institutional and social framework, reinforced by the pressure of interest groups, conspires to frustrate such a favourable course of development.

The 'good match' between technology and social institutions, which had been such a favourable feature of the earlier recovery and boom, now becomes a hindrance to further change and development (or in Marx's terminology becomes a 'fetter' on the forces of production).

In these circumstances, the rate of profit tends to decline in all but a few branches of the economy. The balance in the pattern of investment now tends to shift increasingly from the simple expansion of capacity—to the rationalization of established plants. This shift carries with it a change in the balance-of-employment effects associated with this new investment. Because of the pressure on costs, labour-saving investment becomes of paramount importance and job displacement tends to outstrip new job creation.

Thus the predominant reaction to the appearance of limits to growth within an established paradigm is not one of rapid adoption of revolutionary new technologies and the introduction of new products. It is rather a tendency to seek protection and continuation for the established industries, products and methods, and to squeeze more out of them. This may involve using some elements of the newer technologies, but within the shell and overall framework of the old paradigm. The Kiel Institute research[26] has shown that protectionist tendencies emerged in each deep depression in response to, but not as the origin of, a slowdown in economic growth. Tendencies to seek sheltered markets in defence production, in colonies (in the 1880s and 1930s) or in areas subject to special influence (tied loans etc) also became stronger. Xenophobic and nationalistic tendencies are a characteristic response and are clearly evident in relation to immigrants throughout Europe, as they were in comparable periods in the 1880s and 1930s.

The renewed expansion of the system on the basis of the *old* paradigm, however, runs into enormous problems—capital shortage and inflationary problems based on the declining productivity of capital and the slowdown in labour productivity growth; and institutional problems, both national and international, based on the breakdown of the 'good match' between institutions and technology which characterized the high boom period. The breakdown of the 'good match' and the emergence of an increasing degree of mismatch is especially evident in two spheres—in the relationships with the peripheral Third World countries, and in the sphere of industrial relations *within* the leading industrial countries.

The issue of Third World indebtedness is beyond the scope of this paper, and it is clearly associated with the failure to sustain the expansionary impetus in the world economy as a whole. Attempts to maintain debt and interest payments at very high rates of interest must inevitably lead, and indeed have already led to an acute exacerbation of social and international conflicts.

So far as the labour market is concerned, the slowdown in productivity growth, increased cost-pressures and intensified competition, all lead to attempts to change the balance of bargaining power and the procedures of industrial relations in favour of capital and to the detriment of labour. This can be seen clearly at present in the UK, where the pressure on profit margins has been most intense and where the new industrial relations legislation of 1980 and 1982 is explicitly designed to weaken the power of the trade unions in industrial disputes.

The danger of this approach, which is characteristic of the first phase of the long wave downswing, is that it may gather momentum and be pressed to extreme limits, as in the 1930s. As in the analogous case of the Third World debtor countries, 'immiseration' through reductions in real wages and living standards may generate such social tensions that it can only be enforced by repressive political changes.

It is in this context that Onuf's comments on the use of information technologies as 'control' technologies are highly relevant. We hardly need to be reminded in 1984 that the manipulation of public opinion through centralized control of the media, and the detailed control and regulation of the behaviour of the labour force through 'Big Brother' systems of computerized supervision, are both real possibilities. Onuf speaks of 'friendly fascism' but it need not necessarily be 'friendly'.

Even without the benefits of computerized information and control systems, German fascism was successful in the 1930s, both in the suppression of the trade unions and in systems of 'thought control'. It was also successful in bringing about economic recovery. After Japan, which had already embarked on the invasion of Manchuria in 1931 and continued on the path of military expansion, Germany was the first major industrial country to recover from the 1930s' depression and to restore full employment. Schacht was the first effective Keynesian, albeit for rearmament and war. By contrast, Roosevelt's well intentioned programme of New Deal reforms in the 1930s failed to resolve the problem of mass unemployment before the outbreak of World War II.

The notion that the deep crisis of the 1930s heralded the end of the capitalist system was quite widespread at the time, and the alternatives were sometimes posed as either authoritarian military-type systems or socialism. The search for social and political solutions to the crisis actually included many other possibilities, but in the early stages the experience of Germany and the USSR seemed to dominate the stage.

### Socialism or barbarism

In circumstances which are in some ways comparable today Mandel and other Marxist economists have argued that the alternatives are *either* socialism *or* barbarism and war. But as in the 1930s this is to narrow too much the social and political alternatives and the complexity of the search process. Moreover, the socialist countries of Eastern Europe are themselves experiencing problems of structural adjustment and adaptation to the potential of the new technological paradigm. Both in the capitalist countries and in the countries of Eastern Europe, it is essential to take into account the specific peculiarities of the new paradigm, in order to understand the peculiar problems of finding viable economic and social solutions.

The 'multiplier' with the new paradigm, which could generate very positive benefits in terms of employment growth, depends on access to new information at all levels of society. As Schmookler[27] has pointed out, the effectiveness of any innovation depends on the number of people who use it and their capacity to improve on it. The full capital-saving and employment-generating potential of the new technologies can best be realized through a high level of participation in the design and implementation of new systems, whether they are flexible manufacturing systems (FMS) in industry, new office systems or new social services.

Consequently, the need for decentralization and devolution of responsibility and control are likely to become paramount issues, whether in predominantly capitalist or predominantly socialist systems. The search for viable combinations of central coordination of the level of investment and employment with maximum local involvement and participation in the design and development of new products and systems, is a fundamental challenge to social innovation. The problems of international coordination of worldwide economic expansion are even more daunting, since they also involve arrangements for more rapid and effective international transfer of technology.

Nevertheless, the new technologies do offer exceptionally favourable possibilities for hitherto undreamt of access to information at all levels of society, and enormous scope for active and creative involvement at work. The 'control' systems which dominate the future need not be those of Big Brother. They could be those which go some way towards realizing the humanistic and Promethean ideals of both liberals and socialists, for a combination of civil liberty and industrial democracy.

**Notes and references**

1. N. G. Onuf, "Prometheus prostrate", *Futures, 16* (1), February 1984, pages 47–59.
2. D. Meadows *et al, Limits to Growth* (New York, Universe Books, 1972).
3. H. S. D. Cole, C. Freeman, M. Jahoda and K. L. R. Pavitt, *Thinking about the Future* (London, Chatto and Windus, 1973, first published as two special issues of *Futures, 5* (1) and (2), February and April 1973); C. Freeman (ed), "Technical innovation and long waves in world economic development", Special issue of *Futures, 13* (4) and (5), August and October 1981.
4. Onuf, *op cit*, reference 1, pages 53–57.
5. *Ibid*, pages 49–50.
6. R. L. Meek (ed), *Marx and Engels on Malthus* (London, Lawrence, 1954).
7. Onuf, *op cit*, reference 1, page 49.
8. See chapter 6 in Cole *et al, op cit*, reference 3.
9. E. Mandel, "Explaining long waves of capitalist development", *Futures, 13* (4), August 1981, pages 332–338.
10. Onuf, *op cit*, reference 1, page 52.
11. G. Mensch, *Stalemate in Technology: Innovations Overcome the Depression* (New York, Ballinger, 1979).
12. C. Freeman, J. A. Clark and L. L. G. Soete, *Unemployment and Technical Innovation: A Study of Long Waves and Economic Development* (London, Frances Pinter, 1982), chapter 3.
13. *Ibid*, chapter 4.
14. Mensch, *op cit*, reference 10.
15. J. A. Clark, C. Freeman and L. L. G. Soete, "Long waves, inventions and innovations", *Futures, 13* (4), August 1981, pages 308–322.
16. C. Perez, "Structural change and the assimilation of new technologies in the economic and social system", *Futures, 15* (4), October 1983, pages 357–375; C. Perez, "Micro-electronics, long waves and world structural change: new perspectives for developing countries", *World Development*, 1984 (forthcoming); G. Dosi, "Technological paradigms and technological trajectories: the determinants and directions of technical change and the transformation of the economy", in C. Freeman (ed), *Long Waves in the World Economy*, (2nd edition, London, Frances Pinter, 1984).
17. Onuf, *op cit*, reference 1, page 51.
18. J. M. Keynes, *Treatise on Money*, Volume 2 (London, Macmillan, 1930), page 86.
19. M. Dobb, *Studies in the Development of Capitalism* (London, Routledge and Kegan Paul, 1946, 2nd edition, 1963).
20. See for example, G. N. von Tunzelmann, "The standard of living, investment and economic growth in England and Wales, 1760–1850", in L. Jörberg and N. Rosenberg (eds), *Technical Change, Employment and Investment* (Lund, Lund University Press, 1982).

21. N. Rosenberg, *Inside the Black Box: Technology and Economics* (Cambridge, Cambridge University Press, 1983), chapter 2.
22. L. L. G. Soete and G. Dosi, *Technology and Employment in the Electronics Industry* (London, Frances Pinter, 1983).
23. L. Soete and C. Freeman, "New technologies, investment and employment growth" (to be published by the OECD in the conference proceedings of Inter-Governmental Conference on Employment Growth in the Context of Structural Change, Paris, OECD, forthcoming).
24. R. J. Schonberger, *Japanese Manufacturing Technique: Nine Hidden Lessons in Simplicity* (New York, Free Press, 1982).
25. Dobb, *op cit*, reference 19, page 302.
26. H. H. Glismann, H. Rodemer and F. Wolter, *Lange Wellen Wirtschaftlichen Wachstums* (Kiel Discussion Paper No 74, 1980).
27. J. Schmookler, *Invention and Economic Growth* (Harvard University Press, 1966).

# Name Index

Abernathy, W. 112, 187, 271–3
Abramowitz, M. 55–6
Adams, W. 419
Agnew, H. 384
Aiken, H. 449
Altshuler, A. 137, 145
Ansoff, H.I. 245, 261–2
Arcangeli, F. 72, 142
Arena, R. 134
Arrow, K.J. 47–8, 51, 112, 117, 126, 133, 240, 321, 334
Arthur, W.B. 71, 91, 130–31, 133–5, 382, 385, 388, 393
Ashton, P. 122, 145
Atkinson, A.B. 71, 130
Avineri, S. 42

Babbage, C. 449
Balinky, A. 27
Barca, F. 141
Batallio, R.C. 51
Baumol, W.J. 11
Beer, J. 123
Berger, A. 346, 365
Bernal, J. 123
Blaug, M. 47
Boehm, G.A.W. 175
Bound, J. 139
Boyden, J. 346, 365
Braun, E. 123
Buer, T.C. 137, 272–3
Bunn, J. 384
Bupp, I. 384
Burns, A. 124, 396–7, 399–400
Burton, R. 385

Cainarca, G. 142
Carter, C. 144
Carty, J J. 163
Caves, R. 143
Chandler, A.D. 161
Chesnais, F. 113, 124, 126, 145
Cimoli, M. 143
Clark, J. 332
Clarke, K.B. 188
Cohen, W. 138, 145
Cohendet, P. 134
Colombo, M. 142

Constant, E.W. 112, 128
Contini, B. 143
Cooper, R.C. 118, 237, 246
Coriat, B. 131, 140
Cornwall, J. 55–6, 60
Cowan, R. 384, 386
Crandall, L.S. 392

Darian, J. 384
Dasgupta, P. 117, 145, 344
David, P. 71, 74, 87, 91, 112, 117–18, 128, 130–31, 133, 135, 148, 384
Davies, S. 74, 399
de Solla Price, D. 123
De Tocqueville, A. 415
de Tournemine, R.L. 134
Dealey, W.L. 390
Denison, E.F. 55, 313
Densmore, J. 391
Dirlam, J. 419
Dobb, M. 494
Dosi, G. 70–71, 73, 112–16, 118, 120–23, 128, 130–32, 136–7, 142–6, 149, 151, 187, 261, 268, 275, 277
Dulude, L. 125
Dvorak, A. 390

Ebeling, W. 77
Edison, T. 392
Egan, P.T. 122, 145
Egidi, M. 113, 121
Eigen, M. 75, 77
Eliasson, G. 145
Elliott, J.E. 24, 31–2
Enos, J. 118, 137
Ergas, H. 132, 136
Ermoliev, Y. 382, 388

Feistel, R. 77
Fisher, J.C. 88
Fisher, R.A. 77
Frankel, M. 134
Freeman, C. 112–13, 121–3, 128, 131, 143–4, 261, 268, 277, 291, 293, 332, 466
Friedman, M. 47–8
Fuller, J.K. 143